SECOND EDITION

COMPUTER NETWORKS

A Systems Approach

The Morgan Kaufmann Series in Networking
Series Editor, David Clark

For a list of forthcoming titles, please visit our Web site at
http://www.mkp.com/publish/mann/networking.htm

SECOND EDITION

Larry L. Peterson & Bruce S. Davie

COMPUTER NETWORKS

A Systems Approach

Morgan Kaufmann Publishers
San Francisco, California

Senior Editor Jennifer Mann
Director of Production and Manufacturing Yonie Overton
Production Editor Cheri Palmer
Editorial Assistant Karyn Johnson
Cover and Text Design Ross Carron Design
Cover Image Alain Choisnet / ImageBank
　　　　　　Normandy Bridge at Night, Normandy, France
Composition/Illustration Windfall Software, using ZzTEX
Copyeditor Ken DellaPenta
Proofreader Jennifer McClain
Indexer Steve Rath
Printer Courier Corporation

Designations used by companies to distinguish their products are often claimed as trademarks or registered trademarks. In all instances where Morgan Kaufmann Publishers is aware of a claim, the product names appear in initial capital or all capital letters. Readers, however, should contact the appropriate companies for more complete information regarding trademarks and registration.

Morgan Kaufmann Publishers
Editorial and Sales Office
340 Pine Street, Sixth Floor
San Francisco, CA 94104-3205
USA
Telephone 415 / 392-2665
Facsimile 415 / 982-2665
Email mkp@mkp.com
WWW http://www.mkp.com
Order toll free 800 / 745-7323

04 03 02 01 00 5 4 3 2 1

Library of Congress Cataloging-in-Publication Data

Peterson, Larry L.
　　Computer networks : a systems approach / Larry L. Peterson & Bruce
　S. Davie. — 2nd ed.
　　　　p. cm.
　　Includes bibliographical references.
　　ISBN 1-55860-514-2 (cloth). — ISBN 1-55860-577-0 (paper)
　　1. Computer networks. I. Davie, Bruce S. II. Title.
TK5105.5.P479 2000
004.6′5—dc21　　　　　　　　　　　　　　　　99-36400
　　　　　　　　　　　　　　　　　　　　　　CIP

To Lynn and Jody

FOREWORD

David Clark
Massachusetts Institute of Technology

I am pleased to report that this great book has gotten better. The philosophy of the book remains unchanged: to be timely but timeless in the material it presents. The timeless component is still there, better than ever. The book is an excellent introduction to the core concepts and fundamental principles that will remain useful even when the standards change and the technology evolves. If you want to understand how networks work, not just how the packet headers are formatted, this is the book to read.

To keep a book on the Internet timely takes a lot of work because the Internet evolves so rapidly. It is hard to remember that much less than a decade ago, nobody had heard of a URL, and only a few years ago, Internet telephony and Internet radio were idle speculations of the research community. The authors have put a lot of effort into updating the material to make it as current as possible—there are new sections on a number of important topics, ranging from quality of service to security—so the book can be used as a reference volume as well as a textbook for learning basic principles.

Other changes have the goal of making the examples easier to follow. The code fragments are no longer based on a specific operating system, but have been rewritten to assume a more generic execution environment. The objective is to reduce the effort that the student must put in before getting to the meat of the material, so that learning can proceed as rapidly as possible.

Networking is a fast-moving field. Everything, including a book, has to run fast just to keep up. And the book will help you keep up.

David Clark
Massachusetts Institute of Technology

The term *spaghetti code* is universally understood as an insult. All good computer scientists worship the god of modularity, since modularity brings many benefits, including the all-powerful benefit of not having to understand all parts of a problem at the same time in order to solve it. Modularity thus plays a role in presenting ideas in a book, as well as in writing code. If a book's material is organized effectively—modularly—the reader can start at the beginning and actually make it to the end.

The field of network protocols is perhaps unique in that the "proper" modularity has been handed down to us in the form of an international standard: the seven-layer reference model of network protocols from the ISO. This model, which reflects a layered approach to modularity, is almost universally used as a starting point for discussions of protocol organization, whether the design in question conforms to the model or deviates from it.

It seems obvious to organize a networking book around this layered model. However, there is a peril to doing so, because the OSI model is not really successful at organizing the core concepts of networking. Such basic requirements as reliability, flow control, or security can be addressed at most, if not all, of the OSI layers. This fact has led to great confusion in trying to understand the reference model. At times it even requires a suspension of disbelief. Indeed, a book organized strictly according to a layered model has some of the attributes of spaghetti code.

Which brings us to this book. Peterson and Davie follow the traditional layered model, but they do not pretend that this model actually helps in the understanding of the big issues in networking. Instead, the authors organize discussion of fundamental concepts in a way that is independent of layering. Thus, after reading the book, readers will understand flow control, congestion control, reliability enhancement, data representation, and synchronization, and will separately understand the implications of addressing these issues in one or another of the traditional layers.

This is a timely book. It looks at the important protocols in use today—especially the Internet protocols. Peterson and Davie have a long involvement in and much experience with the Internet. Thus their book reflects not just the theoretical issues in protocol design, but the real factors that matter in practice. The book looks at some of the protocols that are just emerging now, so the reader can be assured of an up-to-date perspective. But most importantly, the discussion of basic issues is presented in a way that derives from the fundamental nature of the problem, not the constraints of the layered reference model or the details of today's protocols. In this regard, what this book presents is both timely and timeless. The combination of real-world relevance, current examples, and careful explanation of fundamentals makes this book unique.

CONTENTS

When the first edition of this book was published in 1996 (nearly a hundred years ago in Internet time), it was a novelty to be able to order merchandise on the Internet, and a company that advertised its domain name was considered cutting edge. Today, Internet commerce is a fact of life, and it's not uncommon to hear of companies that include ".com" in their name—their legal corporate name, not their Internet name. Stockbrokers refer to "the .com stocks," and the valuation of a coffee retailer soars when it announces plans to develop an "Internet strategy." To point out that things change quickly on the Internet is a bit like pointing out that the sky is blue.

Despite these changes the question we asked in the first edition is just as valid today: What are the underlying concepts and technologies that make the Internet work? The answer is that much of the TCP/IP architecture continues to function just as was envisioned by its creators nearly 30 years ago. This isn't to say that the Internet architecture is uninteresting; quite the contrary. Understanding the design principles that underly an architecture that has not only survived but fostered the kind of growth and change that the Internet has seen over the past three decades is precisely the right place to start. Like the first edition, the second edition makes the "why" of the Internet architecture its cornerstone.

Audience

Our intent is that the book should serve as the text for a comprehensive networking class, at either the graduate or upper-division undergraduate level. We also believe that the book's focus on core concepts should be appealing to industry professionals who are retraining for network-related assignments, as well as current network practitioners who want to understand the "whys" behind the protocols they work with every day and to see the big picture of networking.

It is our experience that both students and professionals learning about networks for the first time often have the impression that network protocols are some sort of edict handed down from on high, and that their job is to learn as many TLAs (Three-Letter Acronyms) as possible. In fact, protocols are the building blocks of a complex system developed through the application of engineering design principles.

Moreover, they are constantly being refined, extended, and replaced based on real-world experience. With this in mind, our goal with this book is to do more than survey the protocols in use today. Instead, we explain the underlying principles of sound network design. We feel that this grasp of underlying principles is the best tool for handling the rate of change in the networking field.

Changes in the Second Edition

Our focus on the underlying principles of networking might sound like an excuse for not making changes in the second edition. On the contrary, the second edition tracks many of the most important recent advances in networking with the addition of a significant amount of new material. We have also deleted, reorganized, and changed the focus of existing material to reflect changes that have taken place over the past four years. In addition, we have responded to extensive feedback received from those who used the first edition, and even from some who did not use it. Changes in this edition include

- a new chapter on network security, including coverage of PGP, IPSEC, secure sockets, and firewalls

- a new chapter on network applications, which includes sections on SMTP, HTTP, SNMP, and DNS, as well as the RTP protocol used to build real-time multimedia applications

- comprehensively updated material on quality of service and congestion control, including the latest on Differentiated Services and RSVP

- expanded discussion of routing protocols, including OSPF and BGP

- a new section on wireless technology, including spread spectrum techniques and the emerging 802.11 standard

- expanded discussion of audio and video compression, including MPEG and MP3

- increased coverage of ATM, including LAN emulation (LANE)

- new material on building virtual private networks (VPNs) on top of the public Internet

- coverage of high-speed networking throughout the book rather than confining it to a single chapter

Two other significant changes affect the book as a whole. First, in response to feedback from instructors, we have removed the *x*-kernel as a pedagogical tool for understanding protocol implementations and replaced it with operating-system-independent C code. The details of this change are discussed below.

We have also significantly increased the number and quality of exercises at the end of each chapter. This work was spearheaded by a dedicated instructor who has taught from the first edition of our book since its inception.

Approach

For an area that's as dynamic and changing as computer networks, the most important thing a textbook can offer is perspective—to distinguish between what's important and what's not, and between what's lasting and what's superficial. Based on our experience over the past 20 years doing research that has led to new networking technology, teaching undergraduate and graduate students about the latest trends in networking, and delivering advanced networking products to market, we have developed a perspective—which we call the *systems approach*—that forms the soul of this book. The systems approach has several implications:

- Rather than accept existing artifacts as gospel, we start with first principles and walk you through the thought process that led to today's networks. This allows us to explain *why* networks look like they do. It is our experience that once you understand the underlying concepts, any new protocol that you are confronted with will be relatively easy to digest.

- Although the material is loosely organized around the traditional network layers, starting at the bottom and moving up the protocol stack, we do not adopt a rigidly layerist approach. Many topics—congestion control and security are good examples—have implications up and down the hierarchy, and so we discuss them outside the traditional layered model. In short, we believe layering makes a good servant but a poor master; it's more often useful to take an end-to-end perspective.

- Rather than explain how protocols work in the abstract, we use the most important protocols in use today—many of them from the TCP/IP Internet—to illustrate how networks work in practice. This allows us to include real-world experiences in the discussion.

- Although at the lowest levels networks are constructed from commodity hardware that can be bought from computer vendors and communication services that can be leased from the phone company, it is the software that allows networks to provide new services and adapt quickly to changing circumstances. It is for this reason that we emphasize how network software is implemented, rather than stopping with a description of the abstract algorithms involved.

■ Networks are constructed from many building-block pieces, and while it is necessary to be able to abstract away uninteresting elements when solving a particular problem, it is essential to understand how all the pieces fit together to form a functioning network. We therefore spend considerable time explaining the overall end-to-end behavior of networks, not just the individual components, so that it is possible to understand how a complete network operates, all the way from the application to the hardware.

■ The systems approach implies doing experimental performance studies, and then using the data you gather both to quantitatively analyze various design options and to guide you in optimizing the implementation. This emphasis on empirical analysis pervades the book.

■ Networks are like other computer systems—for example, operating systems, processor architectures, distributed and parallel systems, and so on. They are all large and complex. To help manage this complexity, system builders often draw on a collection of design principles. We highlight these design principles as they are introduced throughout the book, illustrated, of course, with examples from computer networks.

Software

As noted above, software and its implementation play an important role in a systems approach to understanding computer networks. The first edition used the *x*-kernel—a software framework for implementing network protocols—as a pedagogical tool, but since there was a startup cost in using the *x*-kernel, many people elected to not use it. For this reason, we have removed the *x*-kernel from the second edition. Code segments are still used throughout the book to illustrate how you might implement certain protocols and algorithms—in fact, we have added additional code—but these segments are given as operating-system-independent C code rather than *x*-kernel protocols. For users who want to continue using the *x*-kernel, the material removed from the book is still available online at http://www.cs.princeton.edu/xkernel.

Because we view network software as an essential component of networking, the second edition now includes an example of a simple application socket program in Chapter 1. Programming assignments based on Unix sockets are available online (see below).

Pedagogy and Features

The second edition retains several features that we encourage you to take advantage of:

■ *Problem statements.* At the start of each chapter, we describe a problem that identifies the next set of issues that must be addressed in the design of a network. This statement introduces and motivates the issues to be explored in the chapter.

■ *Shaded sidebars.* Throughout the text, shaded sidebars elaborate on the topic being discussed or introduce a related advanced topic. In many cases, these sidebars relate real-world anecdotes about networking.

■ *Highlighted paragraphs.* These paragraphs summarize an important nugget of information that we want you to take away from the discussion, such as a widely applicable system design principle.

■ *Real protocols.* Even though the book's focus is on core concepts rather than existing protocol specifications, real protocols are used to illustrate most of the important ideas. As a result, the book can be used as a source of reference for many protocols. To help you find the descriptions of the protocols, each applicable section heading parenthetically identifies the protocols described in that section. For example, Section 5.2, which describes the principles of reliable end-to-end protocols, provides a detailed description of TCP, the canonical example of such a protocol.

■ *Open issues.* We conclude the main body of each chapter with an important issue that is currently being debated in the research community, the commercial world, or society as a whole. We have found that discussing these issues helps to make the subject of networking more relevant and exciting.

■ *Recommended reading.* These highly selective lists appear at the end of each chapter. Each list generally contains the seminal papers on the topics just discussed. We strongly recommend that advanced readers (e.g., graduate students) study the papers in this reading list to supplement the material covered in the chapter.

Road Map and Course Use

The book is organized as follows:

■ Chapter 1 introduces the set of core ideas that are used throughout the rest of the text. In particular, it discusses what goes into a network architecture, and it defines the quantitative performance metrics that often drive network design.

■ Chapter 2 surveys a wide range of low-level network technologies, ranging from Ethernet to token ring to wireless. It also describes many of the issues that all data link protocols must address, including encoding, framing, and error detection.

■ Chapter 3 introduces the basic models of switched networks (datagrams versus virtual circuits) and describes one prevalent switching technology (ATM) in some detail. It also discusses the design of hardware-based switches.

■ Chapter 4 introduces internetworking and describes the key elements of the Internet Protocol (IP). A central question addressed in this chapter is how networks that scale to the size of the Internet are able to route packets.

■ Chapter 5 moves up to the transport level, describing both the Internet's Transmission Control Protocol (TCP) and Remote Procedure Call (RPC) used to build client-server applications in detail.

■ Chapter 6 discusses congestion control and resource allocation. The issues in this chapter cut across both the network level (Chapters 3 and 4) and the transport level (Chapter 5). Of particular note, this chapter describes how congestion control works in TCP, and it introduces the mechanisms used by both the Internet and ATM to provide quality of service.

■ Chapter 7 considers the data sent through a network. This includes both the problems of presentation formatting and data compression. The discussion of compression includes explanations of how MPEG video compression and MP3 audio compression work.

■ Chapter 8 discusses network security, ranging from an overview of cryptography protocols (DES, RSA, MD5), to protocols for security services (authentication, digital signature, message integrity), to complete security systems (privacy enchanced email, IPSEC). The chapter also discusses pragmatic issues like firewalls.

■ Chapter 9 describes a representative sample of network applications, including both traditional applications like email and the Web, and multimedia applications that use the Real-time Transport Protocol (RTP).

For an undergraduate course, extra class time will most likely be needed to help students digest the introductory material in the first chapter, probably at the expense of the more advanced topics covered in Chapters 6 through 8. Chapter 9 then returns to the popular topic of network applications. In contrast, the instructor for a graduate course should be able to cover the first chapter in only a lecture or two—with students studying the material more carefully on their own—thereby freeing up additional class time to cover the last four chapters in depth. Both graduate and undergraduate classes will want to cover the core material contained in the middle four chapters (Chapters 2–5), although an undergraduate class might choose to skim the more advanced sections (e.g., Sections 2.2, 2.9, 3.4, and 4.4).

For those of you using the book in self-study, we believe that the topics we have selected cover the core of computer networking, and so we recommend that the book be read sequentially, from front to back. In addition, we have included a liberal supply of references to help you locate supplementary material that is relevant to your specific areas of interest.

The book takes a unique approach to the topic of congestion control by pulling all topics related to congestion control and resource allocation together in a single place—Chapter 6. We do this because the problem of congestion control cannot be solved at any one level, and we want you to consider the various design options at the same time. (This is consistent with our view that strict layering often obscures important design trade-offs.) A more traditional treatment of congestion control is possible, however, by studying Section 6.2 in the context of Chapter 3 and Section 6.3 in the context of Chapter 5.

Exercises

Significant effort has gone into improving the exercises in the second edition. Specifically, we have enlisted Peter Dordal, who teaches the networking class at Loyola University of Chicago, to revamp the exercises. Peter has greatly increased the number of problems (from 196 to 362) and, based on class testing, dramatically improved their quality. The current set of exercises are of several different styles:

■ Analytical exercises that ask the student to do simple algebraic calculations that demonstrate their understanding of fundamental relationships

■ Design questions that ask the student to propose and evaluate protocols for various circumstances

■ Hands-on questions that ask the student to write a few lines of code to test an idea or to experiment with an existing network utility

■ Library research questions that ask the student to learn more about a particular topic

Also, as described in more detail below, *x*-kernel and socket-based programming assignments are available online.

Supplemental Materials and Online Resources

To assist instructors, we have prepared an instructor's manual that contains solutions to selected exercises. The manual is available from the publisher. Additional support materials, including lecture slides, figures from the text, socket-based programming assignments, and sample exams are available through the Morgan Kaufmann Web site at http://www.mkp.com. We suggest that you visit the page for this book every few weeks, as we will be adding support materials and establishing links to networking-related sites on a regular basis.

Acknowledgments

This book would not have been possible without the help of many people. We would like to thank them for their efforts in improving the end result. Before we do so, however, we should mention that we have done our best to correct the mistakes that the reviewers have pointed out and to accurately describe the protocols and mechanisms that our colleagues have explained to us. We alone are responsible for any remaining errors. If you should find any of these, please send email to our publisher, Morgan Kaufmann, at netbugs@mkp.com, and we will endeavor to correct them in future printings of this book.

First, we would like to thank the many people who reviewed drafts of various chapters. The list is long and includes Ken Calvert of the University of Kentucky, Douglas Jacobson of Iowa State University, Michel Barbeau of the University of Sherbrooke, Ken Klingenstein of the University of Colorado–Boulder, Robert Strader of Stephen F. Austin State University, Lee Hollaar of the University of Utah, James Ten-Eyck of Marist College, Walt Will of Luther College, David Hutchison of Lancaster University, Ivan Marsic of Rutgers University, Lee Leitner of Infocus and Nova Southeastern University, consultant Michael Cochran, Edward Balassanian of BeComm Corporation, Matt Bishop of UC–Davis, and Steve Casner of Cisco.

Second, several members of the Network Systems Group at Princeton and the University of Arizona contributed ideas, examples, corrections, data, and code to this book. In addition to those mentioned in the first edition, George Tzanetakis explained MP3 to us, and Chad Mynhier helped update the bibliography. As before, we want to thank the Defense Advanced Research Projects Agency and the National Science Foundation for supporting our networking research over the past several years.

Third, we would like to thank our series editor, David Clark, as well as all the people at Morgan Kaufmann who helped shepherd us through the book-writing process. A special thanks is due to our sponsoring editor, Jennifer Mann; her assistant, Karyn Johnson; and our production editor, Cheri Palmer. The whole crew at MKP has been a delight to work with.

Finally, we wish to thank our wives, Lynn Peterson and Jody Davie, who continue to support us in our obsession to explain how networks really work.

S uppose you want to build a computer network, one that has the potential to grow to global proportions and to support applications as diverse as teleconferencing, video-on-demand, electronic commerce, distributed computing, and digital libraries. What available technologies would serve as the underlying building blocks, and what kind of software architecture would you design to integrate these building blocks into an effective communication service? Answering this question is the overriding goal of this book—to describe the available building materials and then to show how they can be used to construct a network from the ground up.

PROBLEM

Building a Network

I must Create a System, or be enslav'd by another Man's; I will not Reason and Compare: my business is to Create.

—William Blake

Before we can understand how to design a computer network, we should first agree on exactly what a computer network is. At one time, the term *network* meant the set of serial lines used to attach dumb terminals to mainframe computers. To some, the term implies the voice telephone network. To others, the only interesting network is the cable network used to disseminate video signals. The main thing these networks have in common is that they are specialized to handle one particular kind of data (keystrokes, voice, or video) and they typically connect to special-purpose devices (terminals, hand receivers, and television sets).

What distinguishes a computer network from these other types of networks? Probably the most important characteristic of a computer network is its generality. Computer networks are built primarily from general-purpose programmable hardware, and they are not optimized for a particular application like making phone calls or delivering television signals. Instead, they are able to carry many different types of data, and they support a wide, and ever growing, range of applications. This chapter looks at some typical applications of computer networks and discusses the requirements that a network designer who wishes to support such applications must be aware of.

Once we understand the requirements, how do we proceed? Fortunately, we will not be building the first network. Others, most notably the community of researchers responsible for the Internet, have gone before us. We will use the wealth of experience generated from the Internet to guide our design. This experience is embodied in a *network architecture* that identifies the available hardware and software components and shows how they can be arranged to form a complete network system.

To start us on the road toward understanding how to build a network, this chapter does three things. First, it explores the requirements that different applications and different communities of people (such as network users and network operators) place on the network. Second, it introduces the idea of a network architecture, which lays the foundation for the rest of the book. Finally, it introduces some of the key elements in the implementation of computer networks.

Foundation

1.1   Requirements

We have just established an ambitious goal for ourselves: to understand how to build a computer network from the ground up. Our approach to accomplishing this goal will be to start from first principles, and then ask the kinds of questions we would naturally ask if building an actual network. At each step, we will use today's protocols to illustrate various design choices available to us, but we will not accept these existing artifacts as gospel. Instead, we will be asking (and answering) the question of *why* networks are designed the way they are. While it is tempting to settle for just understanding the way it's done today, it is important to recognize the underlying concepts because networks are constantly changing as the technology evolves and new applications are invented. It is our experience that once you understand the fundamental ideas, any new protocol that you are confronted with will be relatively easy to digest.

The first step is to identify the set of constraints and requirements that influence network design. Before getting started, however, it is important to understand that the expectations you have of a network depend on your perspective:

- An *application programmer* would list the services that his or her application needs, for example, a guarantee that each message the application sends will be delivered without error within a certain amount of time.

- A *network designer* would list the properties of a cost-effective design, for example, that network resources are efficiently utilized and fairly allocated to different users.

- A *network provider* would list the characteristics of a system that is easy to administer and manage, for example, in which faults can be easily isolated and where it is easy to account for usage.

This section attempts to distill these different perspectives into a high-level introduction to the major considerations that drive network design, and in doing so, identifies the challenges addressed throughout the rest of this book.

1.1.1   Connectivity

Starting with the obvious, a network must provide connectivity among a set of computers. Sometimes it is enough to build a limited network that connects only a few select machines. In fact, for reasons of privacy and security, many private (corporate) networks have the explicit goal of limiting the set of machines that are connected. In contrast, other networks (of which the Internet is the prime example) are designed to grow in a way that allows them the potential to connect all the computers in the world. A system that is designed to support growth to an arbitrarily large size is said to *scale*. Using the Internet as a model, this book addresses the challenge of scalability.

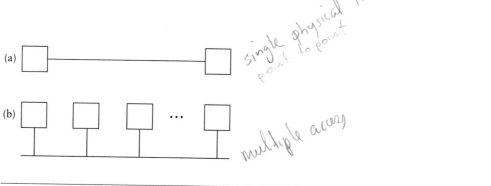

single physical link
point to point

multiple access

Figure 1.1   Direct links: (a) point-to-point; (b) multiple-access.

Links, Nodes, and Clouds

Network connectivity occurs at many different levels. At the lowest level, a network
can consist of two or more computers directly connected by some physical medium,
such as a coaxial cable or an optical fiber. We call such a physical medium a *link*, and
we often refer to the computers it connects as *nodes*. (Sometimes a node is a more
specialized piece of hardware rather than a computer, but we overlook that distinction
for the purposes of this discussion.) As illustrated in Figure 1.1, physical links are
sometimes limited to a pair of nodes (such a link is said to be *point-to-point*), while
in other cases, more than two nodes may share a single physical link (such a link is
said to be *multiple-access*). Whether a given link supports point-to-point or multiple-
access connectivity depends on how the node is attached to the link. It is also the case
that multiple-access links are often limited in size, in terms of both the geographical
distance they can cover and the number of nodes they can connect. The exception is a
satellite link, which can cover a wide geographic area.

If computer networks were limited to situations in which all nodes are directly
connected to each other over a common physical medium, then networks would either
be very limited in the number of computers they could connect, or the number of wires
coming out of the back of each node would quickly become both unmanageable and
very expensive. Fortunately, connectivity between two nodes does not necessarily imply a direct physical connection between them—indirect connectivity may be achieved
among a set of cooperating nodes. Consider the following two examples of how a
collection of computers can be indirectly connected.

Figure 1.2 shows a set of nodes, each of which is attached to one or more
point-to-point links. Those nodes that are attached to at least two links run software
that forwards data received on one link out on another. If organized in a systematic
way, these forwarding nodes form a *switched network*. There are numerous types of
switched networks, of which the two most common are *circuit-switched* and *packet-
switched*. The former is most notably employed by the telephone system, while the

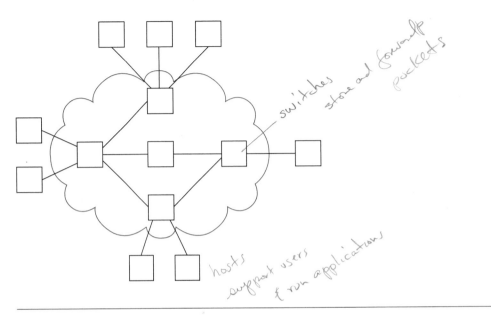

switches
store and forward
packets

hosts
support users
& run applications

Figure 1.2 Switched network.

latter is used for the overwhelming majority of computer networks and will be the focus of this book. The important feature of packet-switched networks is that the nodes in such a network send discrete blocks of data to each other. Think of these blocks of data as corresponding to some piece of application data such as a file, a piece of email, or an image. We call each block of data either a *packet* or a *message*, and for now we use these terms interchangeably; we discuss the reason they are not always the same in Section 1.1.2.

Packet-switched networks typically use a strategy called *store-and-forward*. As the name suggests, each node in a store-and-forward network first receives a complete packet over some link, stores the packet in its internal memory, and then forwards the complete packet to the next node. In contrast, a circuit-switched network first establishes a dedicated circuit across a sequence of links and then allows the source node to send a stream of bits across this circuit to a destination node. The major reason for using packet switching rather than circuit switching in a computer network is efficiency, discussed in the next subsection.

The cloud in Figure 1.2 distinguishes between the nodes on the inside that *implement* the network (they are commonly called *switches*, and their sole function is to store and forward packets) and the nodes on the outside of the cloud that *use* the network (they are commonly called *hosts*, and they support users and run application programs). Also note that the cloud in Figure 1.2 is one of the most important icons

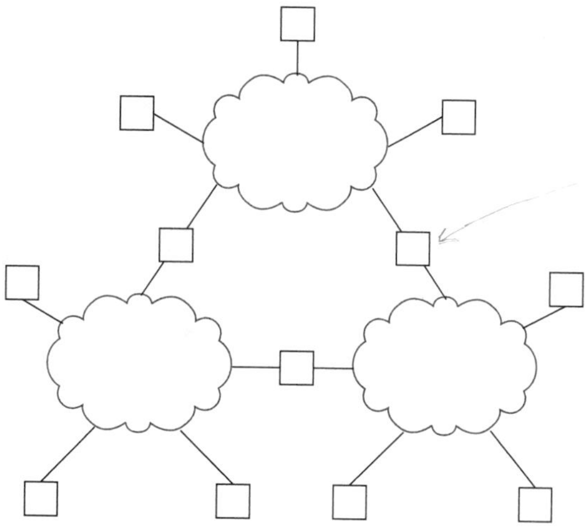

Figure 1.3 Interconnection of networks.

of computer networking. In general, we use a cloud to denote any type of network, whether it is a single point-to-point link, a multiple-access link, or a switched network. Thus, whenever you see a cloud used in a figure, you can think of it as a placeholder for any of the networking technologies covered in this book.

A second way in which a set of computers can be indirectly connected is shown in Figure 1.3. In this situation, a set of independent networks (clouds) are interconnected to form an *internetwork*, or internet for short. We adopt the Internet's convention of referring to a generic internetwork of networks as a lowercase *i* internet, and the currently operational TCP/IP Internet as the capital *I* Internet. A node that is connected to two or more networks is commonly called a *router* or *gateway*, and it plays much the same role as a switch—it forwards messages from one network to another. Note that an internet can itself be viewed as another kind of network, which means that an internet can be built from an interconnection of internets. Thus, we can recursively build arbitrarily large networks by interconnecting clouds to form larger clouds.

Just because a set of hosts are directly or indirectly connected to each other does not mean that we have succeeded in providing host-to-host connectivity. The final requirement is that each node must be able to say which of the other nodes on the network it wants to communicate with. This is done by assigning an *address* to each node. An address is a byte string that identifies a node; that is, the network can use a node's address to distinguish it from the other nodes connected to the network. When a source node wants the network to deliver a message to a certain destination node, it specifies the address of the destination node. If the sending and receiving nodes are not directly connected, then the switches and routers of the network use this address to decide how to forward the message toward the destination. The process of determining systematically how to forward messages toward the destination node based on its address is called *routing*.

This brief introduction to addressing and routing has presumed that the source node wants to send a message to a single destination node (*unicast*). While this is the most common scenario, it is also possible that the source node might want to *broadcast* a message to all the nodes on the network. Or a source node might want to send a message to some subset of the other nodes, but not all of them, a situation called *multicast*. Thus, in addition to node-specific addresses, another requirement of a network is that it support multicast and broadcast addresses.

The main idea to take away from this discussion is that we can define a *network* recursively as consisting of two or more nodes connected by a physical link, or as two or more networks connected by one or more nodes. In other words, a network can be constructed from a nesting of networks, where at the bottom level, the network is implemented by some physical medium. One of the key challenges in providing network connectivity is to define an address for each node that is reachable on the network (including support for broadcast and multicast connectivity), and to be able to use this address to route messages toward the appropriate destination node(s).

1.1.2 Cost-Effective Resource Sharing

As stated above, this book focuses on packet-switched networks. This section explains the key requirement of computer networks—efficiency—that leads us to packet switching as the strategy of choice.

Given a collection of nodes indirectly connected by a nesting of networks, it is possible for any pair of hosts to send messages to each other across a sequence of links and nodes. Of course, we want to do more than support just one pair of communicating hosts—we want to provide all pairs of hosts with the ability to exchange messages. The question, then, is how do all the hosts that want to communicate share the network, especially if they want to use it at the same time? And, as if that problem isn't hard enough, how do several hosts share the same *link* when they all want to use it at the same time?

To understand how hosts share a network, we need to introduce a fundamental concept, *multiplexing*, which means that a system resource is shared among multiple users. At an intuitive level, multiplexing can be explained by analogy to a timesharing computer system, where a single physical CPU is shared (multiplexed) among multiple jobs, each of which believes it has its own private processor. Similarly, data being sent by multiple users can be multiplexed over the physical links that make up a network.

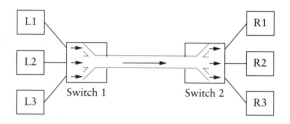

Figure 1.4 Multiplexing multiple logical flows over a single physical link.

To see how this might work, consider the simple network illustrated in Figure 1.4, where the three hosts on the left side of the network (L1–L3) are sending data to the three hosts on the right (R1–R3) by sharing a switched network that contains only one physical link. (For simplicity, assume that host L1 is communicating with host R1, and so on.) In this situation, three flows of data—corresponding to the three pairs of hosts—are multiplexed onto a single physical link by switch 1 and then *demultiplexed* back into separate flows by switch 2. Note that we are being intentionally vague about exactly what a "flow of data" corresponds to. For the purposes of this discussion, assume that each host on the left has a large supply of data that it wants to send to its counterpart on the right.

There are several different methods for multiplexing multiple flows onto one physical link. One common method is *synchronous time-division multiplexing* (STDM). The idea of STDM is to divide time into equal-sized quanta and, in a round-robin fashion, give each flow a chance to send its data over the physical link. In other words, during time quantum 1, data from the first flow is transmitted; during time quantum 2, data from the second flow is transmitted; and so on. This process continues until all the flows have had a turn, at which time the first flow gets to go again, and the process repeats. Another method is *frequency-division multiplexing* (FDM). The idea of FDM is to transmit each flow over the physical link at a different frequency, much the same way that the signals for different TV stations are transmitted at a different frequency on a physical cable TV link.

Although simple to understand, both STDM and FDM are limited in two ways. First, if one of the flows (host pairs) does not have any data to send, its share of the physical link—that is, its time quantum or its frequency—remains idle, even if one of the other flows has data to transmit. For computer communication, the amount of time that a link is idle can be very large—for example, consider the amount of time you spend reading a Web page (leaving the link idle) compared to the time you spend fetching the page. Second, both STDM and FDM are limited to situations in which the maximum number of flows is fixed and known ahead of time. It is not practical to resize the quantum or to add additional quanta in the case of STDM or to add new frequencies in the case of FDM.

The form of multiplexing that we make most use of in this book is called *statistical multiplexing*. Although the name is not all that helpful for understanding the concept, statistical multiplexing is really quite simple, with two key ideas. First, it is like STDM in that the physical link is shared over time—first data from one flow is transmitted over the physical link, then data from another flow is transmitted, and so on. Unlike STDM, however, data is transmitted from each flow on demand rather than during a predetermined time slot. Thus, if only one flow has data to send, it gets to transmit that data without waiting for its quantum to come around and thus without having to watch the quanta assigned to the other flows go by unused. It is this avoidance of idle time that gives packet switching its efficiency.

As defined so far, however, statistical multiplexing has no mechanism to ensure that all the flows eventually get their turn to transmit over the physical link. That is, once a flow begins sending data, we need some way to limit the transmission, so that the other flows can have a turn. To account for this need, statistical multiplexing defines an upper bound on the size of the block of data that each flow is permitted to transmit at a given time. This limited-size block of data is typically referred to as a *packet*, to distinguish it from the arbitrarily large *message* that an application program might want to transmit. Because a packet-switched network limits the maximum size of pack-

SANs, LANs, MANs, and WANs

One way to characterize networks is according to their size. Two well-known examples are LANs (local area networks) and WANs (wide area networks); the former typically extend less than 1 km, while the latter can be worldwide. Other networks are classified as MANs (metropolitan area networks), which usually span tens of kilometers. The reason such classifications are interesting is that the size of a network often has implications for the underlying technology that can be used, with a key factor being the amount of time it takes for data to propagate from one end of the network to the other; we discuss this issue more in later chapters.

An interesting historical note is that the term "wide area network" was not applied to the first WANs because there was no other sort of network to differentiate them from. When computers were incredibly rare and expensive, there was no point in thinking about how to connect all the computers in the local area—there was only one computer in that area. Only as

ets, a host may not be able to send a complete message in one packet. The source may need to fragment the message into several packets, with the receiver reassembling the packets back into the original message.

computers began to proliferate did LANs become necessary, and the term "WAN" was then introduced to describe the larger networks that interconnected geographically distant computers.

Another kind of network that we need to be aware of is SANs (system area networks). SANs are usually confined to a single room and connect the various components of a large computing system. For example, HiPPI (High Performance Parallel Interface) and Fiber Channel are two common SAN technologies used to connect massively parallel processors to scalable storage servers and data vaults. (Because they often connect computers to storage servers, SANs are sometimes defined as *storage* area networks.) Although this book does not describe such networks in detail, they are worth knowing about because they are often at the leading edge in terms of performance, and because it is increasingly common to connect such networks into LANs and WANs.

In other words, each flow sends a sequence of packets over the physical link, with a decision made on a packet-by-packet basis as to which flow's packet to send next. Notice that if only one flow has data to send, then it can send a sequence of packets back-to-back. However, should more than one of the flows have data to send, then their packets are interleaved on the link. Figure 1.5 depicts a switch multiplexing packets from multiple sources onto a single shared link.

The decision as to which packet to send next on a shared link can be made in a number of different ways. For example, in a network consisting of switches interconnected by links such as the one in Figure 1.4, the decision would be made by the switch that transmits packets onto the shared link. (As we will see later, not all packet-switched networks actually involve switches, and they may use other mechanisms to determine whose packet goes onto the link next.) Each switch in a packet-switched network makes this decision independently, on a packet-by-packet basis. One of the issues that faces a network designer is how to make this decision in a fair manner. For example, a switch could be designed to service packets on a first-in-first-out (FIFO) basis. Another approach would be to service the different flows in a round-robin manner, just as in STDM. This might be done to ensure that certain flows receive a particular share of the link's bandwidth, or that they never have

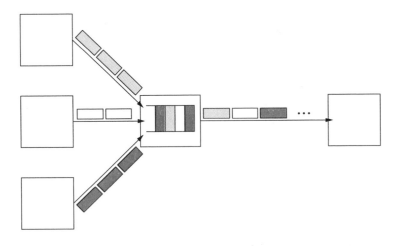

Figure 1.5   A switch multiplexing packets from multiple sources onto one shared link.

their packets delayed in the switch for more than a certain length of time. A network that allows flows to request such treatment is said to support *quality of service* (QoS).

Also, notice in Figure 1.5 that since the switch has to multiplex three incoming packet streams onto one outgoing link, it is possible that the switch will receive packets faster than the shared link can accommodate. In this case, the switch is forced to buffer these packets in its memory. Should a switch receive packets faster than it can send them for an extended period of time, then the switch will eventually run out of buffer space, and some packets will have to be dropped. When a switch is operating in this state, it is said to be *congested*.

The bottom line is that statistical multiplexing defines a cost-effective way for multiple users (e.g., host-to-host flows of data) to share network resources (links and nodes) in a fine-grained manner. It defines the packet as the granularity with which the links of the network are allocated to different flows, with each switch able to schedule the use of the physical links it is connected to on a per-packet basis. Fairly allocating link capacity to different flows and dealing with congestion when it occurs are the key challenges of statistical multiplexing.

1.1.3   Support for Common Services

While the previous section outlined the challenges involved in providing cost-effective connectivity among a group of hosts, it is overly simplistic to view a computer network as simply delivering packets among a collection of computers. It is more accurate to think of a network as providing the means for a set of application processes

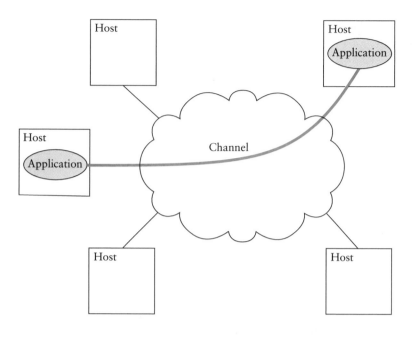

Figure 1.6 Processes communicating over an abstract channel.

that are distributed over those computers to communicate. In other words, the next requirement of a computer network is that the application programs running on the hosts connected to the network must be able to communicate in a meaningful way.

When two application programs need to communicate with each other, there are a lot of complicated things that need to happen beyond simply sending a message from one host to another. One option would be for application designers to build all that complicated functionality into each application program. However, since many applications need common services, it is much more logical to implement those common services once and then to let the application designer build the application using those services. The challenge for a network designer is to identify the right set of common services. The goal is to hide the complexity of the network from the application without overly constraining the application designer.

Intuitively, we view the network as providing logical *channels* over which application-level processes can communicate with each other; each channel provides the set of services required by that application. In other words, just as we use a cloud to abstractly represent connectivity among a set of computers, we now think of a channel as connecting one process to another. Figure 1.6 shows a pair of application-level processes communicating over a logical channel that is, in turn, implemented on top of a cloud that connects a set of hosts. We can think of the channel as being like a pipe connecting two applications, so that a sending application can put data in one end and expect that data to be delivered by the network to the application at the other end of the pipe.

The challenge is to recognize what functionality the channels should provide to application programs. For example, does the application require a guarantee that messages sent over the channel are delivered, or is it acceptable if some messages fail to arrive? Is it necessary that messages arrive at the recipient process in the same order in which they are sent, or does the recipient not care about the order in which messages arrive? Does the network need to ensure that no third parties are able to eavesdrop on the channel, or is privacy not a concern? In general, a network provides a variety of different types of channels, with each application selecting the type that best meets its needs. The rest of this section illustrates the thinking involved in defining useful channels.

Identifying Common Communication Patterns

Designing abstract channels involves first understanding the communication needs of a representative collection of applications, then extracting their common communication requirements, and finally incorporating the functionality that meets these requirements in the network.

One of the earliest applications supported on any network is a file access program like FTP (File Transfer Protocol) or NFS (Network File System). Although many details vary—for example, whether whole files are transferred across the network or only single blocks of the file are read/written at a given time—the communication component of remote file access is characterized by a pair of processes, one that requests that a file be read or written and a second process that honors this request. The process that requests access to the file is called the *client*, and the process that supports access to the file is called the *server*.

Reading a file involves the client sending a small request message to a server and the server responding with a large message that contains the data in the file. Writing works in the opposite way—the client sends a large message containing the data to be written to the server, and the server responds with a small message confirming that the write to disk has taken place.

A more recent application class that behaves like remote file access is a digital library program. As exemplified by the World Wide Web, the kind of data being retrieved from a digital library may vary—for example, it may be a small text file, a very large digital image, or some sort of multimedia object—but the communication pattern looks very similar to the file transfer described above: A client process makes a request, and a server process responds by returning the requested data.

A third class of applications that differs substantially from these first two involves playing video over the network. While an entire video file could first be fetched from a remote machine using a file access application and then played at the local machine, this would entail waiting for the last second of the video file to be delivered before starting to look at it. Consider instead the case in which the sender and the receiver are, respectively, the source and the sink for the video stream. That is, the source generates a video stream that is sent across the network in messages and then displayed at the destination as it is received.

Video, in and of itself, is not an application. It is a type of data. One example video application is video-on-demand, which reads a preexisting movie from disk and transmits it over the network. Another kind of application is videoconferencing, which is actually the more interesting case to consider. To participate in a videoconference, you need special hardware, called a *frame grabber*, which takes the sequence of images output by a video camera and digitizes them so that they can be fed into a computer. The size of each image, which is called a *frame*, depends on the resolution of the picture. For example, an image one quarter the size of a standard TV image would have a resolution of 352 by 240 pixels; a pixel corresponds to one dot on a display. If each pixel is represented by 24 bits of information, as would be the case for 24-bit color, then the size of each frame would be

$$(352 \times 240 \times 24)/8 = 247.5 \text{ kilobytes (KB)}.$$

The rate at which images are taken is called the *frame rate* and needs to be about 25–30 frames per second to provide video quality that is as good as television. Frame rates of 15 frames per second are still tolerable, while update rates of greater than 30 frames per second cannot be perceived by a human and are therefore not very useful. In practice, video applications usually run at a slower speed, on the order of 10 frames a second, to reduce the rate at which data is sent, because both the computers involved in the conference and the network in between are typically unable to handle data at such high rates with today's commodity technology. In any case, digital images, once provided to the sending host by the frame grabber, are sent over the network as a stream of messages (frames) to a receiving host. The receiving host then displays the received frames on its monitor at the same rate as they were captured. So as to use less network capacity, the frames are usually compressed before they are transmitted, and then decompressed at the receiver.

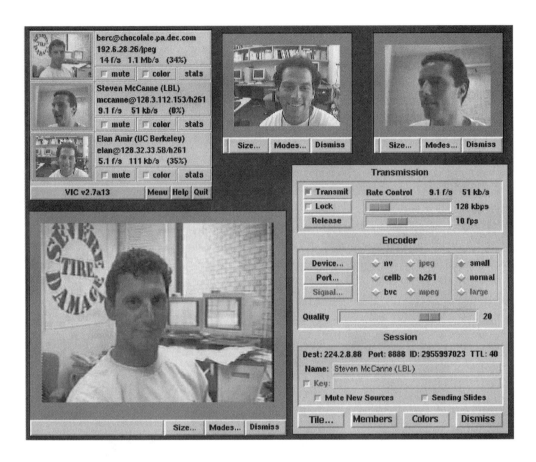

Figure 1.7   The vic video application.

The Unix application vic is an example of a popular videoconferencing tool. Figure 1.7 shows the control panel for a vic session. Note that vic is actually one of a suite of conferencing tools designed at Lawrence Berkeley Laboratory and UC Berkeley. The others include a whiteboard application (wb) that allows users to send sketches and slides to each other, a visual audio tool called vat, and a session directory (sdr) that is used to create and advertise videoconferences. All these tools run on Unix—hence their lowercase names—and are freely available on the Internet. Similar tools are available for other operating systems.

Although video-on-demand and videoconferencing are similar, there is a major difference. In the case of video-on-demand, there are no serious timing constraints; if it takes 10 seconds from the time the user starts the video until the first frame is displayed, then the service is still deemed satisfactory. In contrast, a teleconferencing system has very tight timing constraints. Just as when using the telephone, the interactions among the participants must be timely. When a person at one end gestures, then the corresponding video frame must be displayed at the other end as quickly as possible. Added delay makes the system unusable. Also, interactive video implies that frames are flowing in both directions, while a video-on-demand application is most likely sending frames in only one direction.

Using these four applications as a representative sample, we might decide to provide the following two types of channels: *request/reply* channels and *message stream* channels. The request/reply channel would be used by the file transfer and digital library applications. It would guarantee that every message sent by one side is received by the other side and that only one copy of each message is delivered. The request/reply channel might also protect the privacy and integrity of the data that flows over it, so that unauthorized parties cannot read or modify the data being exchanged between the client and server processes.

The message stream channel could be used by both the video-on-demand and videoconferencing applications, provided it is parameterized to support both one-way and two-way traffic and to support different delay properties. The message stream channel might not need to guarantee that all messages are delivered, since a video application can operate adequately even if some frames are not received. It would, however, need to ensure that those messages that are delivered arrive in the same order in which they were sent, to avoid displaying frames out of sequence. Like the request/reply channel, the message stream channel might want to ensure the privacy and integrity of the video data. Finally, the message stream channel might need to support multicast, so that multiple parties can participate in the teleconference or view the video.

While it is common for a network designer to strive for the smallest number of abstract channel types that can serve the largest number of applications, there is a danger in trying to get away with too few channel abstractions. Simply stated, if you have a hammer, then everything looks like a nail. For example, if all you have are message stream and request/reply channels, then it is tempting to use them for the next application that comes along, even if neither type provides exactly the semantics needed by the application. Thus, network designers will probably be inventing new types of channels—and adding options to existing channels—for as long as application programmers are inventing new applications.

Also note that independent of exactly *what* functionality a given channel provides, there is the question of *where* that functionality is implemented. In many cases, it is easiest to view the host-to-host connectivity of the underlying network as simply providing a *bit pipe*, with any high-level communication semantics provided at the end hosts. The advantage of this approach is it keeps the switches in the middle of the network as simple as possible—they simply forward packets—but it requires the end hosts to take on much of the burden of supporting semantically rich process-to-process channels. The alternative is to push additional functionality onto the switches, thereby allowing the end hosts to be "dumb" devices (e.g., telephone handsets). We will see this question of how various network services are partitioned between the packet switches and the end hosts (devices) as a reoccurring issue in network design.

Reliability

As suggested by the examples just considered, reliable message delivery is one of the most important functions that a network can provide. It is difficult to determine how to provide this reliability, however, without first understanding how networks can fail. The first thing to recognize is that computer networks do not exist in a perfect world. Machines crash and later are rebooted, fibers are cut, electrical interference corrupts bits in the data being transmitted, switches run out of buffer space, and if these sorts of physical problems aren't enough to worry about, the software that manages the hardware sometimes forwards packets into oblivion. Thus, a major requirement of a network is to mask (hide) certain kinds of failures, so as to make the network appear more reliable than it really is to the application programs using it.

There are three general classes of failure that network designers have to worry about. First, as a packet is transmitted over a physical link, *bit errors* may be introduced into the data; that is, a 1 is turned into a 0 or vice versa. Sometimes single bits are

Bandwidth and Throughput

Bandwidth and *throughput* are two of the most confusing terms used in networking. While we could try to give you a precise definition of each term, it is important that you know how other people might use them and for you to be aware that they are often used interchangeably. First of all, bandwidth is literally a measure of the width of a frequency band. For example, a voice-grade telephone line supports a frequency band ranging from 300 to 3300 Hz; it is said to have a bandwidth of 3300 Hz − 300 Hz = 3000 Hz. If you see the word "bandwidth" used in a situation in which it is being measured in hertz, then it probably refers to the range of signals that can be accommodated.

When we talk about the bandwidth of a communication link, we normally refer to the number of bits per second that can be transmitted on the link. We might say that the bandwidth of an Ethernet is 10 Mbps. A useful distinction might be made, however, between

corrupted, but more often than not, a *burst error* occurs—several consecutive bits are corrupted. Bit errors typically occur because outside forces, such as lightning strikes, power surges, and microwave ovens, interfere with the transmission of data. The good news is that such bit errors are fairly rare, affecting on average only one out of every 10^6 to 10^7 bits on a typical copper-based cable and one out of every 10^{12} to 10^{14} bits on a typical optical fiber. As we will see, there are techniques that detect these bit errors with high probability. Once detected, it is sometimes possible to correct for such errors—if we know which bit or bits are corrupted, we can simply flip them—while in other cases the damage is so bad that it is necessary to discard the entire packet. In such a case, the sender may be expected to retransmit the packet.

the bandwidth that is available on the link and the number of bits per second that we can actually transmit over the link in practice. We tend to use the word "throughput" to refer to the *measured performance* of a system. Thus, because of various inefficiencies of implementation, a pair of nodes connected by a link with a bandwidth of 10 Mbps might achieve a throughput of only 2 Mbps. This would mean that an application on one host could send data to the other host at 2 Mbps.

Finally, we often talk about the bandwidth *requirements* of an application. This is the number of bits per second that it needs to transmit over the network to perform acceptably. For some applications, this might be "whatever I can get"; for others, it might be some fixed number (preferably no more than the available link bandwidth); and for others, it might be a number that varies with time. We will provide more on this topic later in this section.

The second class of failure is at the packet, rather than the bit, level; that is, a complete packet is lost by the network. One reason this can happen is that the packet contains an uncorrectable bit error and therefore has to be discarded. A more likely reason, however, is that one of the nodes that has to handle the packet—for example, a switch that is forwarding it from one link to another—is so overloaded that it has no place to store the packet, and therefore is forced to drop it. This is the problem of congestion mentioned in Section 1.1.2. Less commonly, the software running on one of the nodes that handles the packet makes a mistake. For example, it might incorrectly forward a packet out on the wrong link, so that the packet never finds its way to the ultimate destination. As we will see, one of the main difficulties in dealing with lost packets is distinguishing between a packet that is indeed lost and one that is merely late in arriving at the destination.

The third class of failure is at the node and link level; that is, a physical link is cut, or the computer it is connected to crashes. This can be caused by software that crashes, a power failure, or a reckless backhoe operator. While such failures can eventually be corrected, they can have a dramatic effect on the network for an extended period of time. However, they need not totally disable the network. In a packet-switched network, for example, it is sometimes possible to route around a failed node or link. One of the difficulties in dealing with this third class of failure is distinguishing between a failed computer and one that is merely slow, or in the case of a link, between one that has been cut and one that is very flaky and therefore introducing a high number of bit errors.

The key idea to take away from this discussion is that defining useful channels involves both understanding the applications' requirements and recognizing the limitations of the underlying technology. The challenge is to fill in the gap between what the application expects and what the underlying technology can provide. This is sometimes called the *semantic gap*.

1.1.4 Performance

Like any computer system, computer networks are expected to exhibit high performance, and often more importantly, high performance per unit cost. Computations distributed over multiple machines use networks to exchange data. The effectiveness of these computations often depends directly on the efficiency with which the network delivers that data. While the old programming adage "first get it right and then make it fast" is valid in many settings, in networking it is usually necessary to "design for performance." It is therefore important to understand the various factors that impact network performance.

Bandwidth and Latency

Network performance is measured in two fundamental ways: *bandwidth* (also called *throughput*) and *latency* (also called *delay*). The bandwidth of a network is given by the number of bits that can be transmitted over the network in a certain period of time. For example, a network might have a bandwidth of 10 million bits/second (Mbps), meaning that it is able to deliver 10 million bits every second. It is sometimes useful to think of bandwidth in terms of how long it takes to transmit each bit of data. On a 10-Mbps network, for example, it takes 0.1 microsecond (μs) to transmit each bit.

While you can talk about the bandwidth of the network as a whole, sometimes you want to be more precise, focusing, for example, on the bandwidth of a single physical link or of a logical process-to-process channel. At the physical level, bandwidth is constantly improving, with no end in sight. Intuitively, if you think of a second of time as a distance you could measure with a ruler, and bandwidth as how many bits fit in that distance, then you can think of each bit as a pulse of some width. For example,

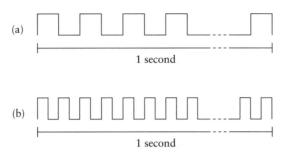

(a)

1 second

(b)

1 second

Figure 1.8 **Bits transmitted at a particular bandwidth can be regarded as having some width: (a) bits transmitted at 1 Mbps (each bit 1 μs wide); (b) bits transmitted at 2 Mbps (each bit 0.5 μs wide).**

each bit on a 1-Mbps link is 1 μs wide, while each bit on a 2-Mbps link is 0.5 μs wide, as illustrated in Figure 1.8. The more sophisticated the transmitting and receiving technology, the narrower each bit can become, and thus, the higher the bandwidth. For logical process-to-process channels, bandwidth is also influenced by other factors, including how many times the software that implements the channel has to handle, and possibly transform, each bit of data.

The second performance metric, latency, corresponds to how long it takes a message to travel from one end of a network to the other. (As with bandwidth, we could be focused on the latency of a single link or an end-to-end channel.) Latency is measured strictly in terms of time. For example, a transcontinental network might have a latency of 24 milliseconds (ms); that is, it takes a message 24 ms to travel from one end of North America to the other. There are many situations in which it is more important to know how long it takes to send a message from one end of a network to the other and back, rather than the one-way latency. We call this the *round-trip time* (RTT) of the network.

We often think of latency as having three components. First, there is the speed-of-light propagation delay. This delay occurs because nothing, including a bit on a wire, can travel faster than the speed of light. If you know the distance between two points, you can calculate the speed-of-light latency, although you have to be careful because light travels across different mediums at different speeds: It travels at 3.0×10^8 m/s in a vacuum, 2.3×10^8 m/s in a cable, and 2.0×10^8 m/s in a fiber. Second, there is the amount of time it takes to transmit a unit of data. This is a function of the network bandwidth and the size of the packet in which the data is carried. Third, there may be queuing delays inside the network, since packet switches generally need to store packets for some time before forwarding them on an outbound link, as discussed in Section 1.1.2. So, we could define the total latency as

$$\text{Latency} = \text{Propagation} + \text{Transmit} + \text{Queue}$$

$$\text{Propagation} = \text{Distance}/\text{SpeedOfLight}$$

$$\text{Transmit} = \text{Size}/\text{Bandwidth}$$

where Distance is the length of the wire over which the data will travel, SpeedOfLight is the effective speed of light over that wire, Size is the size of the packet, and Bandwidth is the bandwidth at which the packet is transmitted. Note that if the message contains only one bit and we are talking about a single link (as opposed to a whole network), then the Transmit and Queue terms are not relevant, and latency corresponds to the propagation delay only.

Bandwidth and latency combine to define the performance characteristics of a given link or channel. Their relative importance, however, depends on the application. For some applications, latency dominates bandwidth. For example, a client that sends a 1-byte message to a server and receives a 1-byte message in return is latency bound. Assuming that no serious computation is involved in preparing the response, the application will perform much differently on a transcontinental channel with a 100-ms RTT than it will on an across-the-room channel with a 1-ms RTT. Whether the channel is 1 Mbps or 100 Mbps is relatively insignificant, however, since the former implies that the time to transmit a byte (Transmit) is 8 μs and the latter implies Transmit $= 0.08$ μs.

In contrast, consider a digital library program that is being asked to fetch a 25-megabyte (MB) image—the more bandwidth that is available, the faster it will be able to return the image to the user. Here, the bandwidth of the channel dominates performance. To see this, suppose that the channel has a bandwidth of 10 Mbps. It will take 20 seconds to transmit the image, making it relatively unimportant if the image is on the other side of a 1-ms channel or a 100-ms channel; the difference between a 20.001-second response time and a 20.1-second response time is negligible.

Figure 1.9 gives you a sense of how latency or bandwidth can dominate performance in different circumstances. The graph shows how long it takes to move objects of various sizes (1 byte, 2 KB, 1 MB) across networks with RTTs ranging from 1 to 100 ms and link speeds of either 1.5 or 10 Mbps. We use logarithmic scales to show relative performance. For a 1-byte object (say, a keystroke), latency remains almost exactly equal to the RTT, so that you cannot distinguish between a 1.5-Mbps network and a 10-Mbps network. For a 2-KB object (say, an email message), the link speed makes quite a difference on a 1-ms-RTT network but a negligible difference on a 100-ms-RTT network. And for a 1-MB object (say, a digital image), the RTT makes no difference—it is the link speed that dominates performance across the full range of RTT.

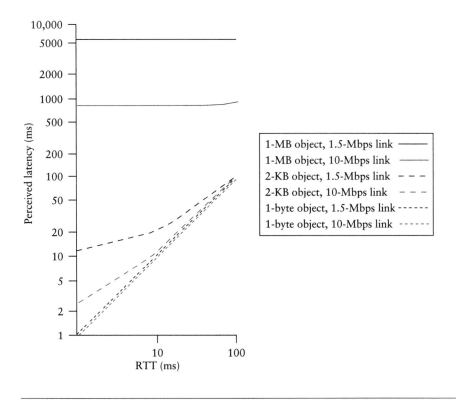

Figure 1.9 Perceived latency (response time) versus round-trip time for various object sizes and link speeds.

Note that throughout this book we use the terms *latency* and *delay* in a generic way, that is, to denote how long it takes to perform a particular function such as delivering a message or moving an object. When we are referring to the specific amount of time it takes a signal to propagate from one end of a link to another, we use the term *propagation delay*. Also, we make it clear in the context of the discussion whether we are referring to the one-way latency or the round-trip time.

As an aside, computers are becoming so fast that when we connect them to networks, it is sometimes useful to think, at least figuratively, in terms of *instructions per mile*. Consider what happens when a computer that is able to execute 200 million instructions per second sends a message out on a channel with a 100-ms RTT. (To make the math easier, assume that the message covers a distance of 5000 miles.) If that computer sits idle the full 100 ms waiting for a reply message, then it has forfeited the ability to execute 20 million instructions, or 4000 instructions per mile. It had better have been worth going over the network to justify this waste.

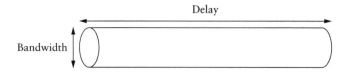

Figure 1.10 Network as a pipe.

Delay × Bandwidth Product

It is also useful to talk about the product of these two metrics, often called the *delay × bandwidth product*. Intuitively, if we think of a channel between a pair of processes as a hollow pipe (see Figure 1.10), where the latency corresponds to the

length of the pipe and the bandwidth gives the diameter of the pipe, then the delay × bandwidth product gives the volume of the pipe—the number of bits it holds. Said another way, if latency (measured in time) corresponds to the length of the pipe, then given the width of each bit (also measured in time), you can calculate how many bits fit in the pipe. For example, a transcontinental channel with a one-way latency of 50 ms and a bandwidth of 45 Mbps is able to hold

$$50 \times 10^{-3} \text{ sec} \times 45 \times 10^6 \text{ bits/sec}$$

$$= 2.25 \times 10^6 \text{ bits}$$

or approximately 280 KB of data. In other words, this example channel (pipe) holds as many bytes as the memory of a personal computer from the early 1980s could hold.

The delay × bandwidth product is important to know when constructing high-performance networks because it corresponds to how many bits the sender must transmit before the first bit arrives at the receiver. If the sender is expecting the re-

How Big Is a Mega?

There are several pitfalls you need to be aware of when working with the common units of networking— MB, Mbps, KB, and Kbps. The first is to distinguish carefully between bits and bytes. Throughout this book, we always use a lowercase *b* for bits and a capital *B* for bytes. The second is to be sure you are using the appropriate definition of mega (M) and kilo (K). *Mega*, for example, can mean either 2^{20} or 10^6. Similarly, *kilo* can be either 2^{10} or 10^3. What is worse, in networking we typically use both definitions. Here's why.

Network bandwidth, which is often specified in terms of Mbps, is typically governed by the speed of the clock that paces the transmission of the bits. A clock that is running at 10 MHz is used to transmit bits at 10 Mbps. Because the *mega*

ceiver to somehow signal that bits are starting to arrive, and it takes another channel latency for this signal to propagate back to the sender (i.e., we are interested in the channel's RTT rather than just its one-way latency), then the sender can send up to two delay × bandwidths worth of data before hearing from the receiver that all is well. The bits in the pipe are said to be "in flight," which means that if the receiver tells the sender to stop transmitting, it might receive up to a delay × bandwidth's worth of data before the sender manages to respond. In our example above, that amount corresponds to 5.5×10^6 bits (560 KB) of data. On the other hand, if the sender does not fill the pipe—send a whole delay × bandwidth product's worth of data before it stops to wait for a signal—the sender will not fully utilize the network.

Note that most of the time we are interested in the RTT scenario, which we simply refer to as the delay × bandwidth product, without explicitly saying that this product is multiplied by two. Again, whether the "delay" in "delay × bandwidth" means one-way latency or RTT is made clear by the context.

in MHz means 10^6 hertz, Mbps is usually also defined as 10^6 bits per second. (Similarly, Kbps is 10^3 bits per second.) On the other hand, when we talk about a message that we want to transmit, we often give its size in kilobytes. Because messages are stored in the computer's memory, and memory is typically measured in powers of two, the K in KB is usually taken to mean 2^{10}. (Similarly, MB usually means 2^{20}.) When you put the two together, it is not uncommon to talk about sending a 32-KB message over a 10-Mbps channel, which should be interpreted to mean $32 \times 2^{10} \times 8$ bits are being transmitted at a rate of 10×10^6 bits per second. This is the interpretation we use throughout the book, unless explicitly stated otherwise.

High-Speed Networks

The bandwidths available on today's networks are increasing at a dramatic rate, and there is eternal optimism that network bandwidth will continue to improve. This causes network designers to start thinking about what happens in the limit, or stated another way, what is the impact on network design of having infinite bandwidth available.

Although high-speed networks bring a dramatic change in the bandwidth available to applications, in many respects their impact on how we think about networking comes in what does *not* change as bandwidth increases: the speed of light. To quote Scotty from *Star Trek*, "You cannae change the laws of physics." In other words, "high speed" does not mean that latency improves at the same rate as bandwidth; the transcontinental RTT of a 1-Gbps link is the same 100 ms as it is for a 1-Mbps link.

To appreciate the significance of ever-increasing bandwidth in the face of fixed latency, consider what is required to transmit a 1-MB file over a 1-Mbps network versus over a 1-Gbps network, both of which have an RTT of 100 ms. In the case of the 1-Mbps network, it takes 100 round-trip times to transmit the file; during each RTT, 1% of the file is sent. In contrast, the same 1-MB file doesn't even come close to filling 1 RTT's worth of the 1-Gbps link, which has a delay × bandwidth product of 12.5 MB.

Figure 1.11 illustrates the difference between the two networks. In effect, the 1-MB file looks like a stream of data that needs to be transmitted across a 1-Mbps network, while it looks like a single packet on a 1-Gbps network. To help drive this point home, consider that a 1-MB file is to a 1-Gbps network what a 1-KB *packet* is to a 1-Mbps network.

Another way to think about the situation is that more data can be transmitted during each RTT on a high-speed network, so much so that a single RTT becomes a significant amount of time. Thus, while you wouldn't think twice about the difference between a file transfer taking 101 RTTs rather than 100 RTTs (a relative difference of only 1%), suddenly the difference between 1 RTT and 2 RTTs is significant—a 100% increase. In other words, latency, rather than throughput, starts to dominate our thinking about network design.

Perhaps the best way to understand the relationship between throughput and latency is to return to basics. The effective end-to-end throughput that can be achieved over a network is given by the simple relationship

The good news is that many times we are satisfied with a back-of-the-envelope calculation, in which case it is perfectly reasonable to pretend that a byte has 10 bits in it (making it easy to convert between bits and bytes) and that 10^6 is really equal to 2^{20} (making it easy to convert between the two definitions of mega). Notice that the first approximation introduces a 20% error, while the latter introduces only a 5% error.

To help you in your quick-and-dirty calculations, 100 ms is a reasonable number to use for a cross-country round-trip time—at least when the country in question is the United States—and 1 ms is a good approximation of an RTT across a local area network. In the case of the former, we increase the 48-ms round-trip time implied by the speed of light over a fiber to 100 ms because there are, as we have said, other sources of delay, such as the processing time in the switches inside the network. You can also be sure that the path taken by the fiber between two points will not be a straight line.

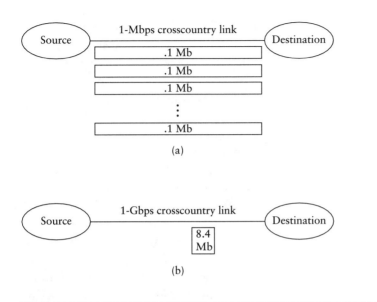

Figure 1.11 Relationship between bandwidth and latency. With an 8.4-Mb file, (a) the 1-Mbps link has 84 pipes full of data; (b) the 1-Gbps link has 1/12 of one pipe full of data.

$$\text{Throughput} = \text{TransferSize}/\text{TransferTime}$$

where TransferTime includes not only the elements of one-way Latency identified earlier in this section, but also any additional time spent requesting or setting up the transfer. Generally, we represent this relationship as

$$\text{TransferTime} = \text{RTT} + 1/\text{Bandwidth} \times \text{TransferSize}$$

We use RTT in this calculation to account for a request message being sent across the network and the data being sent back. For example, consider a situation where a user wants to fetch a 1-MB file across a 1-Gbps network with a round-trip time of 100 ms. The TransferTime includes both the transmit time for 1 MB (1/1 Gbps × 1 MB = 8 ms), and the 100-ms RTT, for a total transfer time of 108 ms. This means that the effective throughput will be

$$1 \text{ MB}/108 \text{ ms} = 74.1 \text{ Mbps}$$

not 1 Gbps. Clearly, transferring a larger amount of data will help improve the effective throughput, where in the limit, an infinitely large transfer size will cause the effective throughput to approach the network bandwidth. On the other hand, having to endure more than 1 RTT—for example, to retransmit missing packets—will hurt the effective throughput for any transfer of finite size and will be most noticeable for small transfers.

Application Performance Needs

The discussion in this section has taken a network-centric view of performance; that is, we have talked in terms of what a given link or channel will support. The unstated assumption has been that application programs have simple needs—they want as much bandwidth as the network can provide. This is certainly true of the aforementioned digital library program that is retrieving a 25-MB image; the more bandwidth that is available, the faster the program will be able to return the image to the user. However, some applications are able to state an upper limit on how much bandwidth they need. For example, a video application that needs to transmit a 128-KB video frame 30 times a second might request a throughput rate of 32 Mbps. The ability of the network to provide more bandwidth is of no interest to such an application because it has only so much data to transmit in a given period of time.

Unfortunately, the situation is not as simple as this example suggests. Because the difference between any two adjacent frames in a video stream is often small, it is possible to compress the video by transmitting only the differences between adjacent frames. This compressed video does not flow at a constant rate, but varies with time according to factors such as the amount of action and detail in the picture and the compression algorithm being used. Therefore, it is possible to say what the average bandwidth requirement will be, but the instantaneous rate may be more or less.

The key issue is the time interval over which the average is computed. Suppose that this example video application can be compressed down to the point that it needs only 2 Mbps, on average. If it transmits 1 megabit in a 1-second interval and 3 megabits in the following 1-second interval, then over the 2-second interval it is transmitting at an average rate of 2 Mbps; however, this will be of little consolation to a channel that was engineered to support no more than 2 megabits in any one second. Clearly, just knowing the average bandwidth needs of an application will not always suffice.

Generally, however, it is possible to put an upper bound on how big of a burst an application like this is likely to transmit. A burst might be described by some peak rate that is maintained for some period of time. Alternatively, it could be described as the number of bytes that can be sent at the peak rate before reverting to the average rate or some lower rate. If this peak rate is higher than the available channel capacity, then the excess data will have to be buffered somewhere, to be transmitted later. Knowing how big of a burst might be sent allows the network designer to allocate sufficient buffer capacity to hold the burst. We will return to the subject of describing bursty traffic accurately in Chapter 6.

Analogous to the way an application's bandwidth needs can be something other than "all it can get," an application's delay requirements may be more complex than simply "as little delay as possible." In the case of delay, it sometimes doesn't matter so much whether the one-way latency of the network is 100 ms or 500 ms as how much the latency varies from packet to packet. The variation in latency is called *jitter*.

Consider the situation in which the source sends a packet once every 33 ms, as would be the case for a video application transmitting frames 30 times a second. If the packets arrive at the destination spaced out exactly 33 ms apart, then we can deduce that the delay experienced by each packet in the network was exactly the same. If the spacing between when packets arrive at the destination—sometimes called the *interpacket gap*—is variable, however, then the delay experienced by the sequence of packets must have also been variable, and the network is said to have introduced jitter into the packet stream. Such variation is generally not introduced in a single physical link, but it can happen when packets experience different queuing delays in a multihop packet-switched network. This queuing delay corresponds to the Queue component of latency defined earlier in this section, which varies with time.

To understand the relevance of jitter, suppose that the packets being transmitted over the network contain video frames, and in order to display these frames on the screen the receiver needs to receive a new one every 33 ms. If a frame arrives early, then it can simply be saved by the receiver until it is time to display it. Unfortunately, if a frame arrives late, then the receiver will not have the frame it needs in time to update the screen, and the video quality will suffer; it will not be smooth. Note that it is not necessary to eliminate jitter, only to know how bad it is. The reason for this is that if the receiver knows the upper and lower bounds on the latency that a packet can experience, it can delay the time at which it starts playing back the video (i.e., displays the first frame) long enough to ensure that in the future it will always have a frame to display when it needs it. The receiver delays the frame, effectively smoothing out the jitter, by storing it in a buffer. We return to the topic of jitter in Chapter 9.

1.2 Network Architecture

In case you hadn't noticed, the previous section established a pretty substantial set of requirements for network design—a computer network must provide general, cost-effective, fair, robust, and high-performance connectivity among a large number of computers. As if this weren't enough, networks do not remain fixed at any single point in time, but must evolve to accommodate changes in both the underlying technologies

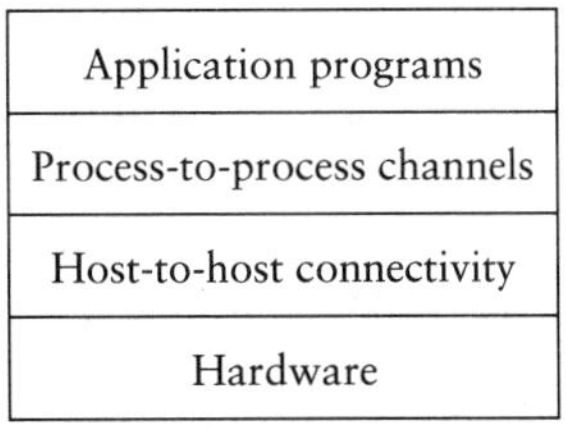

Application programs
Process-to-process channels
Host-to-host connectivity
Hardware

Figure 1.12   Example of a layered network system.

upon which they are based as well as changes in the demands placed on them by application programs. Designing a network to meet these requirements is no small task.

To help deal with this complexity, network designers have developed general blueprints—usually called a *network architecture*—that guide the design and implementation of networks. This section defines more carefully what we mean by a network architecture by introducing the central ideas that are common to all network architectures. It also introduces two of the most widely referenced architectures—the OSI architecture and the Internet architecture.

1.2.1 Layering and Protocols

When the system gets complex, the system designer introduces another level of abstraction. The idea of an abstraction is to define a unifying model that can capture some important aspect of the system, encapsulate this model in an object that provides an interface that can be manipulated by other components of the system, and hide the details of how the object is implemented from the users of the object. The challenge is to identify abstractions that simultaneously provide a service that proves useful in a large number of situations and that can be efficiently implemented in the underlying system. This is exactly what we were doing when we introduced the idea of a channel in the previous section: We were providing an abstraction for applications that hides the complexity of the network from application writers.

Abstractions naturally lead to layering, especially in network systems. The general idea is that you start with the services offered by the underlying hardware, and then add a sequence of layers, each providing a higher (more abstract) level of service. The services provided at the high layers are implemented in terms of the services provided by the low layers. Drawing on the discussion of requirements given in the previous section, for example, we might imagine a network as having two layers of abstraction sandwiched between the application program and the underlying hardware, as illustrated in Figure 1.12. The layer immediately above the hardware in this

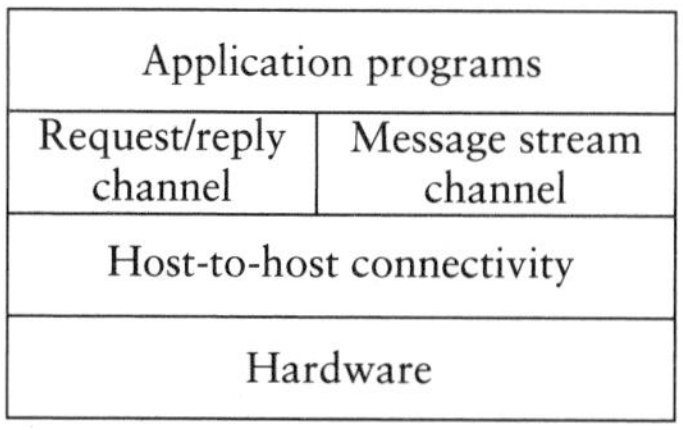

Application programs	
Request/reply channel	Message stream channel
Host-to-host connectivity	
Hardware	

Figure 1.13 Layered system with alternative abstractions available at a given layer.

case might provide host-to-host connectivity, abstracting away the fact that there may be an arbitrarily complex network topology between any two hosts. The next layer up builds on the available host-to-host communication service and provides support for process-to-process channels, abstracting away the fact that the network occasionally loses messages, for example.

Layering provides two nice features. First, it decomposes the problem of building a network into more manageable components. Rather than implementing a monolithic piece of software that does everything you will ever want, you can implement several layers, each of which solves one part of the problem. Second, it provides a more modular design. If you decide that you want to add some new service, you may only need to modify the functionality at one layer, reusing the functions provided at all the other layers.

Thinking of a system as a linear sequence of layers is an oversimplification, however. Many times there are multiple abstractions provided at any given level of the system, each providing a different service to the higher layers but building on the same low-level abstractions. To see this, consider the two types of channels discussed in Section 1.1.3: One provides a request/reply service and one supports a message stream service. These two channels might be alternative offerings at some level of a multilevel networking system, as illustrated in Figure 1.13.

Using this discussion of layering as a foundation, we are now ready to discuss the architecture of a network more precisely. For starters, the abstract objects that make up the layers of a network system are called *protocols*. That is, a protocol provides a communication service that higher-level objects (such as application processes, or perhaps higher-level protocols) use to exchange messages. For example, we could imagine a network that supports a request/reply protocol and a message stream protocol, corresponding to the request/reply and message stream channels discussed above.

Each protocol defines two different interfaces. First, it defines a *service interface* to the other objects on the same computer that want to use its communication services.

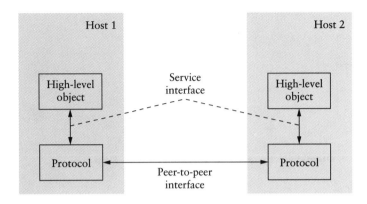

Figure 1.14 Service and peer interfaces.

This service interface defines the operations that local objects can perform on the protocol. For example, a request/reply protocol would support operations by which an application can send and receive messages. Second, a protocol defines a *peer interface* to its counterpart (peer) on another machine. This second interface defines the form and meaning of messages exchanged between protocol peers to implement the communication service. This would determine the way in which a request/reply protocol on one machine communicates with its peer on another machine. In other words, a protocol defines a communication service that it exports locally, along with a set of rules governing the messages that the protocol exchanges with its peer(s) to implement this service. This situation is illustrated in Figure 1.14.

Except at the hardware level where peers directly communicate with each other over a link, peer-to-peer communication is indirect—each protocol communicates with its peer by passing messages to some lower-level protocol, which in turn delivers the message to *its* peer. In addition, there are potentially multiple protocols at any given level, each providing a different communication service. We therefore represent the suite of protocols that make up a network system with a *protocol graph*. The nodes of the graph correspond to protocols, and the edges represent a *depends on* relation. For example, Figure 1.15 illustrates a protocol graph for the hypothetical layered system we have been discussing—protocols RRP (Request/Reply Protocol) and MSP (Message Stream Protocol) implement two different types of process-to-process channels, and both depend on HHP (Host-to-Host Protocol), which provides a host-to-host connectivity service.

In this example, suppose that the file access program on host 1 wants to send a message to its peer on host 2 using the communication service offered by protocol

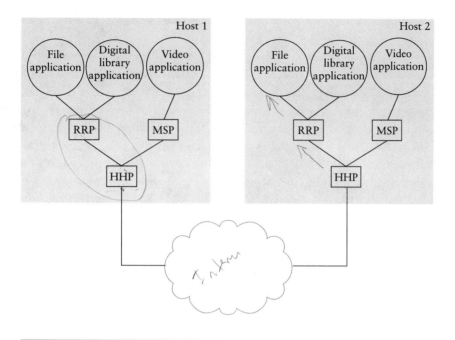

Figure 1.15 Example of a protocol graph.

RRP. In this case, the file application asks RRP to send the message on its behalf. To communicate with its peer, RRP then invokes the services of HHP, which in turn transmits the message to its peer on the other machine. Once the message has arrived at protocol HHP on host 2, HHP passes the message up to RRP, which in turn delivers the message to the file application. In this particular case, the application is said to employ the services of the *protocol stack* RRP/HHP. [7]

Note that the term *protocol* is used in two different ways. Sometimes it refers to the abstract interfaces—that is, the operations defined by the service interface and the form and meaning of messages exchanged between peers—and sometimes it refers to the module that actually implements these two interfaces. To distinguish between the interfaces and the module that implements these interfaces, we generally refer to the former as a *protocol specification*. Specifications are generally expressed using a combination of prose, pseudocode, state transition diagrams, pictures of packet formats, and other abstract notations. It should be the case that a given protocol can be implemented in different ways by different programmers, as long as each adheres to the specification. The challenge is ensuring that two different implementations of the same specification can successfully exchange messages. Two or more protocol modules that do accurately implement a protocol specification are said to *interoperate* with each other.

We can imagine many different protocols and protocol graphs that satisfy the communication requirements of a collection of applications. Fortunately, there exist standardization bodies, such as the International Standards Organization (ISO) and the Internet Engineering Task Force (IETF), that establish policies for a particular protocol graph. We call the set of rules governing the form and content of a protocol graph a *network architecture*. Although beyond the scope of this book, standardization bodies such as the ISO and the IETF have established well-defined procedures for introducing, validating, and finally approving protocols in their respective architectures. We briefly describe the architectures defined by the ISO and the IETF shortly, but first there are two additional things we need to explain about the mechanics of a protocol graph.

Encapsulation

Consider what happens in Figure 1.15 when one of the application programs sends a message to its peer by passing the message to protocol RRP. From RRP's perspective, the message it is given by the application is an uninterpreted string of bytes. RRP does not care that these bytes represent an array of integers, an email message, a digital image, or whatever; it is simply charged with sending them to its peer. However, RRP must communicate control information to its peer, instructing it how to handle the message when it is received. RRP does this by attaching a *header* to the message. Generally speaking, a header is a small data structure—from a few bytes to a few dozen bytes—that is used among peers to communicate with each other. As the name suggests, headers are usually attached to the front of a message. In some cases, however, this peer-to-peer control information is sent at the end of the message, in which case it is called a *trailer*. The exact format for the header attached by RRP is defined by its protocol specification. The rest of the message—that is, the data being transmitted on behalf of the application—is called the message's *body* or *payload*. We say that the application's data is *encapsulated* in the new message created by protocol RRP. (Request Reply Protocol)

This process of encapsulation is then repeated at each level of the protocol graph; for example, HHP encapsulates RRP's message by attaching a header of its own. If we now assume that HHP sends the message to its peer over some network, then when the message arrives at the destination host, it is processed in the opposite order: HHP first strips its header off the front of the message, interprets it (i.e., takes whatever action is appropriate given the contents of the header), and passes the body of the message up to RRP, which removes the header that its peer attached, takes whatever action is indicated by that header, and passes the body of the message up to the application program. The message passed up from RRP to the application on host 2 is exactly the

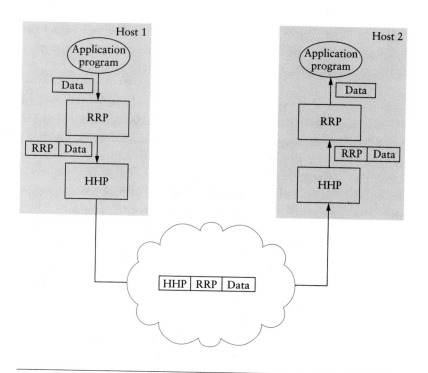

Figure 1.16 High-level messages are encapsulated inside of low-level messages.

same message as the application passed down to RRP on host 1; the application does not see any of the headers that have been attached to it to implement the lower-level communication services. This whole process is illustrated in Figure 1.16. Note that in this example, nodes in the network (e.g., switches and routers) may inspect the HHP header at the front of the message.

Note that when we say a low-level protocol does not interpret the message it is given by some high-level protocol, we mean that it does not know how to extract any meaning from the data contained in the message. It is sometimes the case, however, that the low-level protocol applies some simple transformation to the data it is given, such as to compress or encrypt it. In this case, the protocol is transforming the entire body of the message, including both the original application's data and all the headers attached to that data by higher-level protocols.

Multiplexing and Demultiplexing

Recall from Section 1.1.2 that a fundamental idea of packet switching is to multiplex multiple flows of data over a single physical link. This same idea applies up and down the protocol graph, not just to switching nodes. In Figure 1.15, for example, we can think of RRP as implementing a logical communication channel, with messages from two different applications multiplexed over this channel at the source host and then demultiplexed back to the appropriate application at the destination host.

Practically speaking, all this means is that the header that RRP attaches to its messages contains an identifier that records the application to which the message belongs. We call this identifier RRP's *demultiplexing key*, or *demux key* for short. At the source host, RRP includes the appropriate demux key in its header. When the message is delivered to RRP on the destination host, it strips its header, examines the demux key, and demultiplexes the message to the correct application.

RRP is not unique in its support for multiplexing; nearly every protocol implements this mechanism. For example, HHP has its own demux key to determine which messages to pass up to RRP and which to pass up to MSP. However, there is no uniform agreement among protocols—even those within a single network architecture—on exactly what constitutes a demux key. Some protocols use an 8-bit field (meaning they can support only 256 high-level protocols), and others use 16- or 32-bit fields. Also, some protocols have a single demultiplexing field in their header, while others have a pair of demultiplexing fields. In the former case, the same demux key is used on both sides of the communication, while in the latter case, each side uses a different key to identify the high-level protocol (or application program) to which the message is to be delivered.

1.2.2 OSI Architecture

The ISO was one of the first organizations to formally define a common way to connect computers. Their architecture, called the *Open Systems Interconnection* (OSI) architecture and illustrated in Figure 1.17, defines a partitioning of network functionality into seven layers, where one or more protocols implement the functionality assigned to a given layer. In this sense, the schematic given in Figure 1.17 is not a protocol graph, per se, but rather a *reference model* for a protocol graph. The ISO, usually in conjunction with a second standards organization known as the International Telecommunications Union (ITU),[1] publishes a series of protocol specifications based on the OSI architecture. This series is sometimes called the "X dot" series since the protocols are given names like X.25, X.400, X.500, and so on. There have been several networks based on these standards, including the public X.25 network and private networks like Tymnet.

Starting at the bottom and working up, the *physical* layer handles the transmission of raw bits over a communications link. The *data link* layer then collects a stream

---

[1] A subcommittee of the ITU on telecommunications (ITU-T) replaces an earlier subcommittee of the ITU, which was known by its French name, Comité Consultatif International de Télégraphique et Téléphonique (CCITT).

Software program

Format of data

holds stream of data together

message

Packet

frame — ✗

bits —

Basic switches on any device that is attach to the network

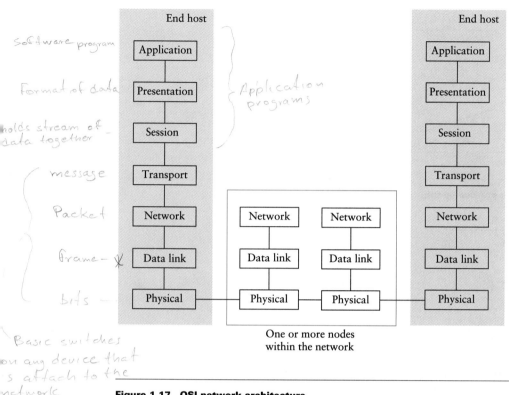

Application programs

Figure 1.17 OSI network architecture.

of bits into a larger aggregate called a *frame*. Network adaptors, along with device drivers running in the node's OS, typically implement the data link level. This means that frames, not raw bits, are actually delivered to hosts. The *network* layer handles routing among nodes within a packet-switched network. At this layer, the unit of data exchanged among nodes is typically called a *packet* rather than a frame, although they are fundamentally the same thing. The lower three layers are implemented on all network nodes, including switches within the network and hosts connected along the exterior of the network. The *transport* layer then implements what we have up to this point been calling a process-to-process channel. Here, the unit of data exchanged is commonly called a *message* rather than a packet or a frame. The transport layer and higher layers typically run only on the end hosts and not on the intermediate switches or routers.

There is less agreement about the definition of the top three layers. Skipping ahead to the top (seventh) layer, we find the *application* layer. Application layer protocols include things like the File Transfer Protocol (FTP), which defines a protocol

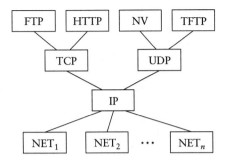

Figure 1.18 Internet protocol graph.

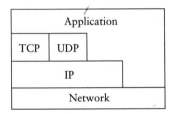

Figure 1.19 Alternative view of the Internet architecture.

by which file transfer applications can interoperate. Below that, the *presentation* layer is concerned with the format of data exchanged between peers, for example, whether an integer is 16, 32, or 64 bits long and whether the most significant bit is transmitted first or last, or how a video stream is formatted. Finally, the *session* layer provides a name space that is used to tie together the potentially different transport streams that are part of a single application. For example, it might manage an audio stream and a video stream that are being combined in a teleconferencing application.

1.2.3 Internet Architecture

The Internet architecture, which is also sometimes called the TCP/IP architecture after its two main protocols, is depicted in Figure 1.18. An alternative representation is given in Figure 1.19. The Internet architecture evolved out of experiences with an earlier packet-switched network called the ARPANET. Both the Internet and the ARPANET were funded by the Advanced Research Projects Agency (ARPA), one of the R&D funding agencies of the U.S. Department of Defense. The Internet and ARPANET were around before the OSI architecture, and the experience gained from building them was a major influence on the OSI reference model.

While the seven-layer OSI model can, with some imagination, be applied to the Internet, a four-layer model is often used instead. At the lowest level are a wide variety of network protocols, denoted NET_1, NET_2, and so on. In practice, these protocols are implemented by a combination of hardware (e.g., a network adaptor) and software (e.g., a network device driver). For example, you might find Ethernet or Fiber Distributed Data Interface (FDDI) protocols at this layer. (These protocols in turn may actually involve several sublayers, but the Internet architecture does not presume anything about them.) The second layer consists of a single protocol—the *Internet Protocol* (IP). This is the protocol that supports the interconnection of multiple networking technologies into a single, logical internetwork. The third layer contains two main protocols—the *Transmission Control Protocol* (TCP) and the *User Datagram Protocol* (UDP). TCP and UDP provide alternative logical channels to application programs: TCP provides a reliable byte-stream channel, and UDP provides an unreliable datagram delivery channel (*datagram* may be thought of as a synonym for message). In the language of the Internet, TCP and UDP are sometimes called *end-to-end* protocols, although it is equally correct to refer to them as transport protocols.

Running above the transport layer are a range of application protocols, such as FTP, TFTP (Trivial File Transport Protocol), Telnet (remote login), and SMTP (Simple Mail Transfer Protocol, or electronic mail), that enable the interoperation of popular applications. To understand the difference between an application layer protocol and an application, think of all the different World Wide Web browsers that are available (e.g., Mosaic, Netscape, Internet Explorer, Lynx, etc.). There is a similarly

OSI versus Internet Architecture

While there have been countless spirited discussions over the past 15–20 years about the technical advantages of the ISO protocols versus the Internet protocols, such debates are no longer relevant. This is because the ISO protocols, with a handful of exceptions, are largely ignored, while the Internet thrives. (This statement does not imply that the OSI reference architecture is worthless; on the contrary, it continues to be somewhat influential by providing a model for understanding networks, even though the ISO protocols themselves have been a commercial failure.)

One explanation for the success of one and the failure of the other is that some of the technical arguments made against the OSI architecture during these debates were on the mark. There is a more likely explanation, however, one that is surprisingly pragmatic in nature: An implementation of the TCP/IP protocol suite was bundled

large number of different implementations of Web servers. The reason that you can use any one of these application programs to access a particular site on the Web is because they all conform to the same application layer protocol: HTTP (HyperText Transport Protocol). Confusingly, the same word sometimes applies to both an application and the application layer protocol that it uses (e.g., FTP).

The Internet architecture has three features that are worth highlighting. First, as best illustrated by Figure 1.19, the Internet architecture does not imply strict layering. The application is free to bypass the defined transport layers and to directly use IP or one of the underlying networks. In fact, programmers are free to define new channel abstractions or applications that run on top of any of the existing protocols.

Second, if you look closely at the protocol graph in Figure 1.18, you will notice an hourglass shape—wide at the top, narrow in the middle, and wide at the bottom. This shape actually reflects the central philosophy of the architecture. That is, IP serves as the focal point for the architecture—it defines a common method for exchanging packets among a wide collection of networks. Above IP can be arbitrarily many transport protocols, each offering a different channel abstraction to application programs. Thus, the issue of delivering messages from host to host is completely separated from the issue of providing a useful process-to-process communication service. Below IP, the architecture allows for arbitrarily many different network technologies, ranging from Ethernet to FDDI to ATM to single point-to-point links.

with the popular Unix operating system distributed by the University of California at Berkeley in the early 1980s. People are more likely to use software that is readily available than software that requires effort to acquire, and the widespread availability of Berkeley Unix allowed the TCP/IP architecture to achieve a critical mass.

To expand on this point a bit further, the ISO/ITU culture has always been to "specify first and implement later." As the specification process is a long and tedious one, especially when you do not have any working code with which to experiment, the implementation of ISO protocols were always a long time in arriving. In contrast, the Internet culture has been to "implement as you go." In fact, to quote a T-shirt commonly worn at IETF meetings:

We reject kings, presidents, and voting. We believe in rough consensus and running code. (Dave Clark)

A final attribute of the Internet architecture (or more accurately, of the IETF culture) is that in order for someone to propose a new protocol to be included in the architecture, they must produce both a protocol specification and at least one (and preferably two) representative implementations of the specification. The existence of working implementations is required for standards to be adopted by the IETF. This cultural assumption of the design community helps to ensure that the architecture's protocols can be efficiently implemented. Even with this requirement, the implementations of the protocols in the Internet architecture have evolved quite significantly over time as researchers and practitioners have gained experience using them.

1.3 Implementing Network Software

Network architectures and protocol specifications are essential things, but a good blueprint is not enough to explain the phenomenal success of the Internet: The number of computers connected to the Internet has been doubling every year since 1981, and now stands at approximately 30 million; the number of people that use the Internet is estimated at well over 100 million; and it is expected that the number of bits transmitted over the Internet will surpass the corresponding figure for the voice phone system around the year 2001.

What explains the success of the Internet? There are certainly many contributing factors (including a good architecture), but one thing that has made the Internet such a runaway success is the fact that so much of its functionality is provided by software running in general-purpose computers. The significance of this is that new functionality can be added readily with "just a small

To understand just how important running code is, we observe that it is even more powerful than the U.S. government. In 1988, the National Institute for Standards and Technology (NIST), an agency within the U.S. government's Department of Commerce, approved a mandate that required government agencies to procure equipment that could run the ISO protocols. (The agencies did not have to use the ISO protocols, but the vendors had to support it or at least demonstrate how their systems could support it.) Since the U.S. government is such a big consumer of computers, this mandate was expected to push the commercial sector toward adopting the ISO protocol suite. In reality, however, computers were shipped with ISO-compliant code, but people kept using TCP/IP. To make a long story short, the mandate was officially rescinded in September 1994.

matter of programming." As a result, new applications and services—electronic commerce, videoconferencing, and packet telephony, to name a few—have been showing up at a phenomenal pace.

A related factor is the massive increase in computing power available in commodity machines. Although computer networks have always been capable in principle of transporting any kind of information, such as digital voice samples, digitized images, and so on, this potential was not particularly interesting if the computers sending and receiving that data were too slow to do anything useful with the information. Virtually all of today's computers are capable of playing back digitized voice at full speed and can display video at a speed and resolution that is useful for some (but by no means all) applications. Thus, today's networks have begun to support multimedia, and their support for it will only improve as computing hardware becomes faster.

The point to take away from this is that knowing how to implement network software is an essential part of understanding computer networks. With this in mind, this section first introduces some of the issues involved in implementing an application program on top of a network, and then goes on to identify the issues involved in implementing the protocols running within the network. In many respects, network applications and network protocols are very similar—the way an application engages the services of the network is pretty much the same as the way a high-level protocol invokes the services of a low-level protocol. As we will see later in the section, however, there are a couple important differences.

A word of warning: If you find some of the concepts described in this section a little challenging, you should feel free to move through it quickly now and refer back to it as needed when we discuss implementation issues later in the book.

1.3.1 Application Programming Interface (Sockets)

The place to start when implementing a network application is the interface exported by the network. Since most network protocols are implemented in software (especially those high in the protocol stack), and nearly all computer systems implement their network protocols as part of the operating system, when we refer to the interface "exported by the network," we are generally referring to the interface that the OS provides to its networking subsystem. This interface is often called the network *application programming interface* (API).

Although each operating system is free to define its own network API (and most have), over time certain of these APIs have become widely supported; that is, they have been ported to operating systems other than their native system. This is what has happened with the *socket interface* originally provided by the Berkeley distribution of Unix, which is now supported in virtually all popular operating systems. The advantage of industrywide support for a single API is that applications can be easily ported from one OS to another. It is important to keep in mind, however, that application programs typically interact with many parts of the OS other than the network; for example, they read and write files, fork concurrent processes, and output to the graphical display. Just because two systems support the same network API does not mean that their file system, process, or graphic interfaces are the same. Still, understanding a widely adopted API like Unix sockets gives us a good place to start.

Before describing the socket interface, it is important to keep two concerns separate in your mind. Each protocol provides a certain set of *services*, and the API provides a *syntax* by which those services can be invoked in this particular OS. The implementation is then responsible for mapping the tangible set of operations and objects defined by the API onto the abstract set of services defined by the protocol. If you have done a good job of defining the interface, then it will be possible to use the syntax of the interface to invoke the services of many different protocols. Such generality was certainly a goal of the socket interface, although it's far from perfect.

The main abstraction of the socket interface, not surprisingly, is the *socket*. A good way to think of a socket is as the point where a local application process attaches to the network. The interface defines operations for creating a socket, attaching the socket to the network, sending/receiving messages through the socket, and closing the socket. To simplify the discussion, we will limit ourselves to showing how sockets are used with TCP.

The first step is to create a socket, which is done with the following operation:

```
int socket(int domain, int type, int protocol)
```

The reason that this operation takes three arguments is that the socket interface was designed to be general enough to support any underlying protocol suite. Specifically, the domain argument specifies the protocol *family* that is going to be used. PF_INET is used to denote the Internet family; PF_UNIX is an alternative that denotes the Unix pipe facility. The type argument indicates the semantics of the communication. SOCK_STREAM is used to denote a byte stream. SOCK_DGRAM is an alternative that denotes a message-oriented service, such as that provided by UDP. The protocol argument identifies the specific protocol that is going to be used. In our case, this argument is UNSPEC because the combination of PF_INET and SOCK_STREAM implies TCP. Finally, the return value from socket is a *handle* for the newly created socket, that is, an identifier by which we can refer to the socket in the future. It is given as an argument to subsequent operations on this socket.

The next step depends on whether you are a client or a server. On a server machine, the application process performs a *passive* open—the server says that it is prepared to accept connections, but it does not actually establish a connection. The server does this by invoking the following three operations:

```
int bind(int socket, struct sockaddr *address, int addr_len)
int listen(int socket, int backlog)
int accept(int socket, struct sockaddr *address, int *addr_len)
```

The bind operation, as its name suggests, binds the newly created socket to the specified address. This is the network address of the *local* participant—the server. Note that, when used with the Internet protocols, address is a data structure that includes both the IP address of the server and a TCP port number. (As we will see in Chapter 5, ports are used to indirectly identify processes. They are a form of *demux keys* as defined in Section 1.2.1.) The port number is usually some well-known number specific to the service being offered; for example, Web servers commonly accept connections on port 80.

The listen operation then defines how many connections can be pending on the specified socket. Finally, the accept operation carries out the passive open. It is a blocking operation that does not return until a remote participant has established a connection, and when it does complete, it returns a *new* socket that corresponds to this just-established connection, and the address argument contains the *remote* participant's address. Note that when accept returns, the original socket that was given as an argument still exists and still corresponds to the passive open; it is used in future invocations of accept.

On the client machine, the application process performs an *active* open; that is, it says who it wants to communicate with by invoking the following single operation:

```
int connect(int socket, struct sockaddr *address, int addr_len)
```

This operation does not return until TCP has successfully established a connection, at which time the application is free to begin sending data. In this case, address contains the remote participant's address. In practice, the client usually specifies only the remote participant's address and lets the system fill in the local information. Whereas a server usually listens for messages on a well-known port, a client typically does not care which port it uses for itself; the OS simply selects an unused one.

Once a connection is established, the application processes invoke the following two operations to send and receive data:

```
int send(int socket, char *message, int msg_len, int flags)
int recv(int socket, char *buffer, int buf_len, int flags)
```

The first operation sends the given message over the specified socket, while the second operation receives a message from the specified socket into the given buffer. Both operations take a set of flags that control certain details of the operation.

1.3.2 Example Application

We now show the implementation of a simple client/server program that uses the socket interface to send messages over a TCP connection. The program also uses other Unix networking utilities, which we introduce as we go. Our application allows a user on one machine to type in and send text to a user on another machine. It is a simplified version of the Unix talk program, which is similar to the program at the core of a Web chat room.

Client

We start with the client side, which takes the name of the remote machine as an argument. It calls the Unix utility gethostbyname to translate this name into the remote host's IP address. The next step is to construct the address data structure (sin) expected by the socket interface. Notice that this data structure specifies that we'll be using the socket to connect to the Internet (AF_INET). In our example, we use TCP port 5432 as the well-known server port; this happens to be a port that has not been assigned to any other Internet service. The final step in setting up the connection is to call socket and connect. Once the connect operation returns, the connection is established and the client program enters its main loop, which reads text from standard input and sends it over the socket.

```c
#include <stdio.h>
#include <sys/types.h>
#include <sys/socket.h>
#include <netinet/in.h>
#include <netdb.h>

#define SERVER_PORT 5432
#define MAX_LINE 256

int
main(int argc, char * argv[])
{
  FILE *fp;
  struct hostent *hp;
  struct sockaddr_in sin;
  char *host;
  char buf[MAX_LINE];
  int s;
  int len;
```

```
if (argc==2) {
  host = argv[1];
}
else {
  fprintf(stderr, "usage: simplex-talk host\n");
  exit(1);
}

/* translate host name into peer's IP address */
hp = gethostbyname(host);
if (!hp) {
  fprintf(stderr, "simplex-talk: unknown host: %s\n", host);
  exit(1);
}

/* build address data structure */
bzero((char *)&sin, sizeof(sin));
sin.sin_family = AF_INET;
bcopy(hp->h_addr, (char *)&sin.sin_addr, hp->h_length);
sin.sin_port = htons(SERVER_PORT);

/* active open */
if ((s = socket(PF_INET, SOCK_STREAM, 0)) < 0) {
  perror("simplex-talk: socket");
  exit(1);
}
if (connect(s, (struct sockaddr *)&sin, sizeof(sin)) < 0) {
  perror("simplex-talk: connect");
  close(s);
  exit(1);
}
/* main loop: get and send lines of text */
while (fgets(buf, sizeof(buf), stdin)) {
  buf[MAX_LINE-1] = '\0';
  len = strlen(buf) + 1;
  send(s, buf, len, 0);
}
}
```

Server

The server is equally simple. It first constructs the address data structure by filling in its own port number (SERVER_PORT). By not specifying an IP address, the application program is willing to accept connections on any of the local host's IP addresses. Next, the server performs the preliminary steps involved in a passive open: creates the socket, binds it to the local address, and sets the maximum number of pending connections to be allowed. Finally, the main loop waits for a remote host to try to connect, and when one does, receives and prints out the characters that arrive on the connection.

```
#include <stdio.h>
#include <sys/types.h>
#include <sys/socket.h>
#include <netinet/in.h>
#include <netdb.h>

#define SERVER_PORT   5432
#define MAX_PENDING   5
#define MAX_LINE      256

int
main()
{
  struct sockaddr_in sin;
  char buf[MAX_LINE];
  int len;
  int s, new_s;

  /* build address data structure */
  bzero((char *)&sin, sizeof(sin));
  sin.sin_family = AF_INET;
  sin.sin_addr.s_addr = INADDR_ANY;
  sin.sin_port = htons(SERVER_PORT);

  /* setup passive open */
  if ((s = socket(PF_INET, SOCK_STREAM, 0)) < 0) {
    perror("simplex-talk: socket");
    exit(1);
  }
```

```
if ((bind(s, (struct sockaddr *)&sin, sizeof(sin))) < 0) {
  perror("simplex-talk: bind");
  exit(1);
}
listen(s, MAX_PENDING);

/* wait for connection, then receive and print text */
while(1) {
  if ((new_s = accept(s, (struct sockaddr *)&sin, &len)) < 0) {
    perror("simplex-talk: accept");
    exit(1);
  }
  while (len = recv(new_s, buf, sizeof(buf), 0))
    fputs(buf, stdout);
  close(new_s);
}
}
```

1.3.3 Protocol Implementation Issues

As mentioned at the beginning of this section, the way application programs interact with the underlying network is similar to the way a high-level protocol interacts with a low-level protocol. For example, TCP needs an interface to send outgoing messages to IP, and IP needs to be able to deliver incoming messages to TCP. This is exactly the service interface introduced in Section 1.2.1.

Since we already have a network API (e.g., sockets), we might be tempted to use this same interface between every pair of protocols in the protocol stack. Although certainly an option, in practice the socket interface is not used in this way. The reason is that there are inefficiencies built into the socket interface that protocol implementers are not willing to tolerate. Application programmers tolerate them because they simplify their programming task, and because the inefficiency only has to be tolerated once, but protocol implementers are often obsessed with performance and must worry about getting a message through several layers of protocols. The rest of this section discusses the two primary differences between the network API and the protocol-to-protocol interface found lower in the protocol graph. It also introduces library routines commonly used by protocol implementations.

Process Model

Most operating systems provide an abstraction called a *process*, or alternatively, a *thread*. Each process runs largely independently of other processes, and the OS is

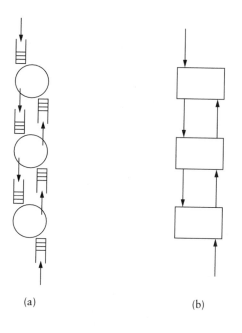

Figure 1.20 Alternative process models: (a) process-per-protocol; (b) process-per-message.

responsible for making sure that resources, such as address space and CPU cycles, are allocated to all the current processes. The process abstraction makes it fairly straightforward to have a lot of things executing concurrently on one machine; for example, each user application might execute in its own process, and various things inside the OS might execute as other processes. When the OS stops one process from executing on the CPU and starts up another one, we call the change a *context switch*.

When designing the network subsystem, one of the first questions to answer is, "Where are the processes?" There are essentially two choices, as illustrated in Figure 1.20. In the first, which we call the *process-per-protocol* model, each protocol is implemented by a separate process. This means that as a message moves up or down the protocol stack, it is passed from one process/protocol to another—the process that implements protocol i processes the message, then passes it to protocol $i - 1$, and so on. How one process/protocol passes a message to the next process/protocol depends on the support the host OS provides for interprocess communication. Typically, there is a simple mechanism for enqueuing a message with a process. The important point, however, is that a context switch is required at each level of the protocol graph— typically a time-consuming operation.

The alternative, which we call the *process-per-message* model, treats each protocol as a static piece of code and associates the processes with the messages. That is, when a message arrives from the network, the OS dispatches a process that it makes responsible for the message as it moves up the protocol graph. At each level, the procedure that implements that protocol is invoked, which eventually results in the procedure for the next protocol being invoked, and so on. For outbound messages, the application's process invokes the necessary procedure calls until the message is delivered. In both directions, the protocol graph is traversed in a sequence of procedure calls.

Although the process-per-protocol model is sometimes easier to think about—I implement my protocol in my process, and you implement your protocol in your process—the process-per-message model is generally more efficient for a simple reason: A procedure call is an order of magnitude more efficient than a context switch on most computers. The former model requires the expense of a context switch at each level, while the latter model costs only a procedure call per level.

Now think about the relationship between the service interface as defined above and the process model. For an outgoing message, the high-level protocol invokes a send operation on the low-level protocol. Because the high-level protocol has the message in hand when it calls send, this operation can be easily implemented as a procedure call; no context switch is required. For incoming messages, however, the high-level protocol invokes the receive operation on the low-level protocol, and then must wait for a message to arrive at some unknown future time; this basically forces a context switch. In other words, the process running in the high-level protocol receives a message from the process running in the low-level protocol. This isn't a big deal if only the application process receives messages from the network subsystem—in fact, it's the right interface for the network API since application programs already have a process-centric view of the world—but it does have a significant impact on performance if such a context switch occurs at each layer of the protocol stack.

It is for this reason that most protocol implementations replace the receive operation with a deliver operation. That is, the low-level protocol does an *upcall*—a procedure call up the protocol stack—to deliver the message to the high-level protocol. Figure 1.21 shows the resulting interface between two adjacent protocols, TCP and IP in this case. In general, messages move down the protocol graph through a sequence of send operations, and up the protocol graph through a sequence of deliver operations.

In summary, we use the operations

```
int send(Protocol llp, Msg *message)
int deliver(Protocol hlp, Msg *message)
```

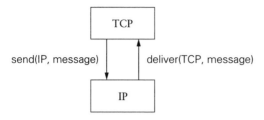

Figure 1.21 Protocol-to-protocol interface.

in code fragments throughout the book, where llp denotes the low-level protocol on top of which the calling protocol is configured, and hlp denotes the high-level protocol configured on top of the calling protocol. Note that our use of type Protocol and variables llp and hlp is a bit of a simplification—they hide details about how protocols are configured in the protocol graph, and how a high-level protocol opens a connection on a low-level protocol. (To see all that is involved in this process, consult the x-kernel references given at the end of this chapter.)

Message Buffers

A second inefficiency of the socket interface is that the application process provides the buffer that contains the outbound message when calling send, and similarly it provides the buffer into which an incoming message is copied when invoking the receive operation. This forces the topmost protocol to copy the message from the application's buffer into a network buffer, and vice versa, as shown in Figure 1.22. It turns out that copying data from one buffer to another is one of the most expensive things a protocol implementation can do. This is because while processors are becoming faster at an incredible pace, memory is not getting faster as quickly as processors are.

Instead of copying message data from one buffer to another at each layer in the protocol stack, most network subsystems define a message abstraction that is shared by all protocols in the protocol graph. Not only does this abstraction permit messages to be passed up and down the protocol graph without copying, but it usually provides copy-free ways of manipulating messages in other ways, such as adding and stripping headers, fragmenting large messages into a set of small messages, and reassembling a collection of small messages into a single large message. The exact form of this message abstraction differs from OS to OS, but it generally looks something like the abstraction we use throughout this book.

We denote this abstraction with the C type definition Msg. The message abstraction can best be viewed as a byte string of some length, and the various message

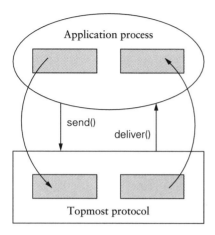

Figure 1.22 Copying incoming/outgoing messages between application buffer and network buffer.

operations can be viewed as string manipulations. For example, as outgoing messages move down the protocol graph, each protocol attaches its header onto the front of the message. Similarly, as an incoming message moves up the protocol graph, each protocol strips its header from the front of the message. The message abstraction supports the following two operations for adding and stripping headers:

```
msgAddHdr(Msg *message, char *hdr, int length)
char *msgStripHdr(Msg *message, int length)
```

The first operation attaches a header (hdr) of length bytes to the front of the message. In the case of msgStripHdr, length bytes are removed from the front of the message, and a pointer to the location of the stripped bytes (the header) is returned. The protocol can then read the header available at the returned memory location. Figures 1.23 and 1.24 illustrate the semantics of the two operations.

Fragmenting and reassembling messages is another common activity in network protocols. The following two operations support this activity:

```
void msgFragment(Msg *original, Msg *fragment, int length)
void msgReassemble(Msg *new, Msg *fragment1, Msg *fragment2)
```

The first operation creates a pair of messages by breaking length bytes off the front of the original message and placing them in (fragment). After the operation returns, original contains the sequence of bytes that remains after length bytes are removed. The second operation attaches fragment1 to the front of fragment2, producing

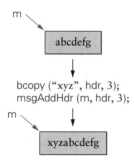

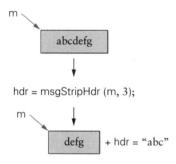

Figure 1.23 Effects of msgAddHdr operation.

Figure 1.24 Effects of msgStripHdr operation.

new. The arguments to msgReassemble need not refer to distinct messages. One common use of msgReassemble is to attach a fragment to the end of a larger message, in which case the first two arguments are the same (the larger message) and the third argument is the fragment. These two operations are illustrated in Figures 1.25 and 1.26.

Finally, the message abstraction typically includes the following operations:

```
void msgSaveCopy(Msg *m1, Msg *m2)
void msgCreate(Msg *m, char  *buffer, int length)
void msgDestroy(Msg *m)
int msgLength(Msg *m)
int msgTruncate(Msg *m, int length)
```

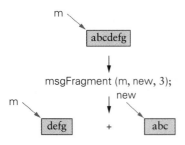

Figure 1.25   Effects of msgFragment operation.

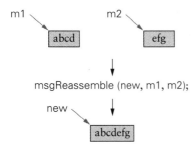

Figure 1.26   Effects of msgReassemble operation.

The first operation saves a copy of message m2 in message m1. This is usually a "logical" copy, and so does not involve copying the contents of the message from one buffer to another. The second operation is used to create a new message m from the data contained in the specified buffer. The next two operations destroy a message and return the length of the message, respectively. The last operation truncates message m at length bytes; that is, it truncates the right end of the message. There is no special operation to truncate the bytes off the left end of a message since this is exactly what the msgStripHdr operation does.

Other Common Library Routines

The message abstraction is an example of a support library that is used by all protocols in the network system. It is not uncommon for an operating system to provide other support routines that implement services needed by all protocols.

For example, another common activity for protocols is to schedule an event to happen some time in the future. To understand how a protocol might use such events, consider the situation in which a network sometimes fails to deliver a message to the destination. A protocol that wants to offer a reliable channel across such a network might, after sending a message, schedule an event that is to occur after a certain period of time. If the protocol has not received confirmation that the message was delivered by the time this event happens, then the protocol retransmits the message. In this case, the event implements a *timeout;* we will see several examples of protocols that use timeouts in later chapters. Note that another use for events is to perform periodic maintenance functions, such as garbage collection.

Because this is such a common activity, the network subsystem often defines an event manager that allows a protocol to schedule a procedure that is to be called after a certain period of time. The event manager defines a single object—the Event—and the following operation:

Event evSchedule(EvFunc function, void *argument, int time)

This operation schedules an event that executes the specified function with the given argument after a delay of time microseconds. (EvFunc is a pointer to function that returns a void.) A handle to the event is returned, which can be used to cancel the event at some later time. When an event is executed, a new process is created to run the specified function; that is, the event runs asynchronously with respect to the rest of the system. Since each event occurs at most one time, if the protocol wants an event to repeat, then the next incarnation of the event should be rescheduled using evSchedule as the last action taken in the event handling function.

A second operation

void evCancel(Event event)

is used to cancel the given Event. evCancel is called, for example, because a source has received confirmation that a message it sent was successfully delivered, and so there is no reason for it to retransmit the message.

As another example, the network subsystem sometimes provides an id mapper that maintains a set of bindings between identifiers. The id mapper supports operations for adding new bindings to the set, removing bindings from the set, and mapping one identifier into another. Protocol implementations use these operations to translate identifiers extracted from message headers (e.g., addresses, demultiplexing keys) into capabilities for (pointers to) internal objects such as a data structure that implements the local state associated with a connection. A common situation in which these operations would be used is when a network node receives a packet that it needs to forward; a map could be used to determine the correct output on which to send a packet that contains a certain destination address.

The id mapper supports two main objects: *maps* and *bindings*, denoted by the types Map and Binding, respectively. A map is simply a table of bindings, where each binding is given by the pair ⟨ external key, internal id ⟩. An external key is a variable-length byte string, and an internal id is a fixed-size identifier (e.g., a 32- or 64-bit memory address). Typically, an external key is constructed from various fields in a message header, and an internal id is a pointer to a local data structure. Three operations are typically defined on maps:

```
Binding mapBind(Map map, void *key, void *id)
Boolean mapResolve(Map map, void *key, void **id)
Boolean mapRemove(Map map, Binding b)
```

The first operation inserts a binding of key to id into the specified map. The second operation returns the internal id bound to the specified key in the given map. If the key is not found in the map, then mapResolve returns FALSE. The third operation removes a binding from a map.

Protocols generally maintain two maps: an active map and a passive map. Active maps are used to implement active opens: They map keys found in incoming messages into the connection that will process the message. Passive maps are used to implement passive opens: They map keys found in incoming messages into the information needed to create a new connection.

1.4 Summary

Computer networks like the Internet have experienced explosive growth over the past decade and are now positioned to provide a wide range of services—remote file access, digital libraries, videoconferencing—to hundreds of millions of users. Much of this growth can be attributed to the general-purpose nature of computer networks, and in particular to the ability to add new functionality to the network by writing software that runs on affordable, high-performance computers. With this in mind, the overriding goal of this book is to describe computer networks in such a way that when you finish reading it, you should feel that if you had an army of programmers at your disposal, you could actually build a fully functional computer network from the ground up. This chapter lays the foundation for realizing this goal.

The first step we have taken toward this goal is to carefully identify exactly what we expect from a network. For example, a network must first provide cost-effective connectivity among a set of computers. This is accomplished through a nested interconnection of nodes and links, and by sharing this hardware base through the use of statistical multiplexing. This results in a packet-switched network, on top of which we then define a collection of process-to-process communication services. Finally, the network as a whole must offer high performance, where the two performance metrics we are most interested in are latency and throughput.

The second step is to define a layered architecture that will serve as a blueprint for our design. The central objects of this architecture are network protocols. Protocols both provide a communication service to higher-level protocols and define the form and meaning of messages exchanged with their peers running on other machines. We have briefly surveyed two of the most widely used architectures: the OSI architecture and the Internet architecture. This book most closely follows the Internet architecture, both in its organization and as a source of examples.

The third step is to implement the network's protocols and application programs, usually in software. Both protocols and applications need an interface by which they invoke the services of other protocols in the network subsystem. The socket interface is the most widely used interface between application programs and the network subsystem, but a slightly different interface is typically used within the network subsystem. The network subsystem also provides a collection of support routines that implement services used by virtually all protocols.

There is little doubt that computer networks are on the brink of becoming an integral part of the everyday lives of vast numbers of people. What began over 20 years ago as experimental systems like the ARPANET— connecting mainframe computers

O P E N   I S S U E
Ubiquitous Networking

over long-distance telephone lines—has turned into big business. And where there is big business, there are lots of players. In this case, there is the computing industry, which has become increasingly involved in supporting packet-switched networking products; the telephone carriers, which recognize the market for carrying all sorts of data, not just voice; and the cable TV industry, which currently owns the entertainment portion of the market.

Assuming that the goal is ubiquitous networking—to bring the network into every household—the first problem that must be addressed is how to establish the necessary physical links. Although it could be argued that the ultimate answer is to bring an optical fiber into every home, at an estimated $1000 per house and 100 million homes in the U.S. alone, this is a $100 billion proposition. The most widely discussed alternatives make use of either the existing cable TV facilities or the copper pairs used to deliver telephone service. Each of these approaches has its own set of problems. For example, today's cable facilities are asymmetric—you can deliver 150 channels into every home, but the outgoing bandwidth is severely limited. Such asymmetry implies that there are a small number of information providers, but that most of us are simply information consumers. Many people would argue that in a democracy we should all have an equal opportunity to provide information. Digital subscriber line (DSL) technology need not be asymmetric, but can only offer high-bandwidth connections to a subset of consumers over the existing telephone wires.

How the struggle between the computer companies, the telephone companies, and the cable industry will play out in the marketplace is anyone's guess. (If we knew the answer, we'd be charging a lot more for this book.) All we know is that there are many technical obstacles—issues of connectivity, levels of service, performance, reliability, and fairness—that stand between the current state of the art and the sort of global, ubiquitous, heterogeneous network that we believe is possible and desirable. It is these challenges that are the focus of this book.

FURTHER READING

Computer networks are not the first communication-oriented technology to have found their way into the everyday fabric of our society. For example, the early part of this century saw the introduction of the telephone, and then during the 1950s television became widespread. When considering the future of networking—how widely it will spread and how we will use it—it is instructive to study this history. Our first reference is a good starting point for doing this (the entire issue is devoted to the first 100 years of telecommunications).

The second and third papers are the seminal papers on the OSI and Internet architectures, respectively. The Zimmerman paper introduces the OSI architecture, and the Clark paper is a retrospective. The final two papers are not specific to networking, but ones that every systems person should read. The Saltzer et al. paper motivates and describes one of the most widely applied rules of system design—the *end-to-end argument*. The paper by Mashey describes the thinking behind RISC architectures; as we will soon discover, making good judgments about where to place functionality in a complex system is what system design is all about.

- ■ Pierce, J. Telephony—A personal view. *IEEE Communications* 22(5):116–120, May 1984.

- ■ Zimmerman, H. OSI reference model—The ISO model of architecture for open systems interconnection. *IEEE Transactions on Communications* COM-28(4):425–432, April 1980.

- Clark, D. The design philosophy of the DARPA Internet protocols. *Proceedings of the SIGCOMM '88 Symposium*, pages 106–114, August 1988.

- Saltzer, J., D. Reed, and D. Clark. End-to-end arguments in system design. *ACM Transactions on Computer Systems* 2(4):277–288, November 1984.

- Mashey, J. RISC, MIPS, and the motion of complexity. *UniForum 1986 Conference Proceedings*, pages 116–124, 1986.

Several texts offer an introduction to computer networking: Stallings gives an encyclopedic treatment of the subject, with an emphasis on the lower levels of the OSI hierarchy [Sta96]; Tanenbaum uses the OSI architecture as an organizational model [Tan96]; Comer gives an overview of the Internet architecture [Com95]; and Bertsekas and Gallager discuss networking from a performance modeling perspective [BG92].

To put computer networking into a larger context, two books—one dealing with the past and the other looking toward the future—are must reading. The first is Holzmann and Pehrson's *The Early History of Data Networks* [HP95]. Surprisingly, many of the ideas covered in the book you are now reading were invented during the 1700s. The second is *Realizing the Information Future: The Internet and Beyond*, a book prepared by the Computer Science and Telecommunications Board of the National Research Council [NRC94].

To follow the history of the Internet from its beginning, the reader is encouraged to peruse the Internet's *Request for Comments* (RFC) series of documents. These documents, which include everything from the TCP specification to April Fools' jokes, are retrievable at http://www.ietf.org/rfc.html. For example, the protocol specifications for TCP, UDP, and IP are available in RFC 793, 768, and 791, respectively.

To gain a better appreciation for the Internet philosophy and culture, two references are must reading; both are also quite entertaining. Padlipsky gives a good description of the early days, including a pointed comparison of the Internet and OSI architectures [Pad85]. For a more up-to-date account of what really happens behind the scenes at the Internet Engineering Task Force, we recommend Boorsook's article [Boo95].

There are a wealth of articles discussing various aspects of protocol implementations. A good starting point is to understand two complete protocol implementation environments: the Stream mechanism from System V Unix [Rit84] and the *x*-kernel [HP91]. In addition, [LMKQ89] and [SW95] describe the widely used Berkeley Unix implementation of TCP/IP.

More generally, there is a large body of work addressing the issue of structuring and optimizing protocol implementations. Clark was one of the first to discuss the relationship between modular design and protocol performance [Cla82]. Later papers then introduce the use of upcalls in structuring protocol code [Cla85] and study the processing overheads in TCP [CJRS89]. Finally, [WM87] describes how to gain efficiency through appropriate design and implementation choices.

Several papers have introduced specific techniques and mechanisms that can be used to improve protocol performance. For example, [HMPT89] describes some of the mechanisms used in the *x*-kernel, [MD93] discusses various implementations of demultiplexing tables, [VL87] introduces the timing wheel mechanism used to manage protocol events, and [DP93] describes an efficient buffer management strategy. Also, the performance of protocols running on parallel processors—locking is a key issue in such environments—is discussed in [BG93] and [NYKT94].

Because many aspects of protocol implementation depend on an understanding of the basics of operating systems, we recommend Finkel [Fin88], Bic and Shaw [BS88], and Tanenbaum [Tan92] for an introduction to OS concepts.

Finally, we conclude the Further Reading section of each chapter with a set of live references, that is, URLs for locations on the World Wide Web where you can learn more about the topics discussed in that chapter. Since these references are live, it is possible that they will not remain active for an indefinite period of time. For this reason, we limit the set of live references at the end of each chapter to sites that either export software, provide a service, or report on the activities of an ongoing working group or standardization body. In other words, we only give URLs for the kinds of material that cannot easily be referenced using standard citations. For this chapter, we include four live references:

- ■ http://www.mkp.com: information about this book, including supplements, addendums, and so on

- ■ http://www.acm.org/sigcomm/sos.html: status of various networking standards, including those of the IETF, ISO, and IEEE

- ■ http://www.ietf.org/: information about the IETF and its working groups

- ■ http://www.cs.columbia.edu/˜hgs/netbib/: searchable bibliography of network-related research papers

EXERCISES

1 Use anonymous FTP to connect to ftp.isi.edu (directory in-notes), and retrieve the RFC index. Also retrieve the protocol specifications for TCP, IP, and UDP.

2 Look up the Web site

http://www.cs.princeton.edu/nsg

Here you can read about current network research under way at Princeton University and see a picture of author Larry Peterson. Follow links to find a picture of author Bruce Davie.

3 Use a Web search tool to locate useful, general, and noncommercial information about the following topics: MBone, ATM, MPEG, IPv6, and Ethernet.

4 The Unix utility whois can be used to find the domain name corresponding to an organization, or vice versa. Read the man page documentation for whois and experiment with it. Try whois princeton.edu and whois princeton, for starters.

5 Calculate the total time required to transfer a 1000-KB file in the following cases, assuming an RTT of 100 ms, a packet size of 1 KB data, and an initial 2 × RTT of "handshaking" before data is sent.

(a) The bandwidth is 1.5 Mbps, and data packets can be sent continuously.

(b) The bandwidth is 1.5 Mbps, but after we finish sending each data packet we must wait one RTT before sending the next.

(c) The bandwidth is "infinite," meaning that we take transmit time to be zero, and up to 20 packets can be sent per RTT.

(d) The bandwidth is infinite, and during the first RTT we can send one packet (2^{1-1}), during the second RTT we can send two packets (2^{2-1}), during the third we can send four (2^{3-1}), and so on. (A justification for such an exponential increase will be given in Chapter 6.)

6 Consider a LAN with a maximum distance of 2 km. At what bandwidth would propagation delay (at a speed of 2×10^8 m/s) equal transmit delay for 100-byte packets? What about 512-byte packets?

7 What properties of postal addresses would be likely to be shared by a network addressing scheme? What differences might you expect to find? What properties of telephone numbering might be shared by a network addressing scheme?

8 One property of addresses is that they are unique; if two nodes had the same address it would be impossible to distinguish between them. What other properties might be useful for network addresses to have? Can you think of any situations in which network (or postal or telephone) addresses might *not* be unique?

9 Give an example of a situation in which multicast addresses might be beneficial.

10 What differences in traffic patterns account for the fact that STDM is a cost-effective form of multiplexing for a voice telephone network and FDM is a cost-effective form of multiplexing for television and radio networks, yet we reject both as not being cost-effective for a general-purpose computer network?

11 How "wide" is a bit on a 1-Gbps link? How long is a bit in copper wire, where the speed of propagation is 2.3×10^8 m/s?

12 How long does it take to transmit x KB over a y-Mbps link? Give your answer as a ratio of x and y.

13 Suppose a 100-Mbps point-to-point link is being set up between the earth and a new lunar colony. The distance from the moon to the earth is approximately 385,000 km, and data travels over the link at the speed of light—3×10^8 m/s.

(a) Calculate the minimum RTT for the link.

(b) Using the RTT as the delay, calculate the delay × bandwidth product for the link.

(c) What is the significance of the delay × bandwidth product computed in (b)?

(d) A camera on the lunar base takes pictures of the earth and saves them in digital format to disk. Suppose Mission Control on earth wishes to download the most current image, which is 25 MB. What is the minimum amount of time that will elapse between when the request for the data goes out and the transfer is finished?

14 For each of the following operations on a remote file server, discuss whether they are more likely to be delay sensitive or bandwidth sensitive.

(a) Open a file.

(b) Read the contents of a file.

(c) List the contents of a directory.

(d) Display the attributes of a file.

15 Calculate the latency (from first bit sent to last bit received) for the following:

(a) 10-Mbps Ethernet with a single store-and-forward switch in the path, and a packet size of 5000 bits. Assume that each link introduces a propagation delay of 10 μs, and that the switch begins retransmitting immediately after it has finished receiving the packet.

Figure 1.27   Diagram for Exercise 18.

(b) Same as (a) but with three switches.

(c) Same as (a) but assume the switch implements "cut-through" switching: It is able to begin retransmitting the packet after the first 200 bits have been received.

16 Calculate the effective bandwidth for the following cases. For (a) and (b) assume there is a steady supply of data to send; for (c) simply calculate the average over 12 hours.

(a) 10-Mbps Ethernet through three store-and-forward switches as in Exercise 15(b). Switches can send on one link while receiving on the other.

(b) Same as (a) but with the sender having to wait for a 50-byte acknowledgment packet after sending each 5000-bit data packet.

(c) Overnight (12-hour) shipment of 100 compact disks (650 MB each).

17 Calculate the bandwidth × delay product for the following links. Use one-way delay, measured from first bit sent to first bit received.

(a) 10-Mbps Ethernet with a delay of 10 μs.

(b) 10-Mbps Ethernet with a single store-and-forward switch like that of Exercise 15(a), packet size 5000 bits, and 10 μs per link propagation delay.

(c) 1.5-Mbps T1 link, with a transcontinental one-way delay of 50 ms.

(d) 1.5-Mbps T1 link through a satellite in geosynchronous orbit, 35,900 km high. The only delay is speed-of-light propagation delay.

18 Hosts A and B are each connected to a switch S via 10-Mbps links as in Figure 1.27. The propagation delay on each link is 20 μs. S is a store-and-forward device; it begins retransmitting a received packet 35 μs after it has finished receiving it. Calculate the total time required to transmit 10,000 bits from A to B

(a) as a single packet

(b) as two 5,000-bit packets sent one right after the other

19 Suppose a host has a 1-MB file that is to be sent to another host. The file takes 1 second of CPU time to compress 50%, or 2 seconds to compress 60%.

(a) Calculate the bandwidth at which each compression option takes the same total compression + transmission time.

(b) Explain why latency does not affect your answer.

20 Suppose that a certain communications protocol involves a per-packet overhead of 100 bytes for headers and framing. We send 1 million bytes of data using this protocol; however, one data byte is corrupted and the entire packet containing it is thus lost. Give the total number of overhead + loss bytes for packet data sizes of 1000, 5000, 10,000, and 20,000 bytes. Which size is optimal?

21 Consider a closed-loop network (e.g., token ring) with bandwidth 100 Mbps and propagation speed 2×10^8 m/s. What would the circumference of the loop be to exactly contain one 250-byte packet, assuming nodes do not introduce delay? What would the circumference be if there was a node every 100 m, and each node introduced 10 bits of delay?

22 Compare the channel requirements for voice traffic with the requirements for the real-time transmission of music, in terms of bandwidth, delay, and jitter. What would have to improve? By approximately how much? Could any channel requirements be relaxed?

23 For the following, assume that no data compression is done; this would in practice almost never be the case. For (a)–(c), calculate the bandwidth necessary for transmitting in real time:

(a) Video at a resolution of 640 × 480, 3 bytes/pixel, 30 frames/second.

(b) 160 × 120 video, 1 byte/pixel, 5 frames/second.

(c) CD-ROM music, assuming one CD holds 75 minutes' worth and takes 650 MB.

(d) Assume a fax transmits an 8 × 10-inch black-and-white image at a resolution of 72 pixels per inch. How long would this take over a 14.4-Kbps modem?

24 Discuss the relative performance needs of the following applications, in terms of average bandwidth, peak bandwidth, latency, jitter, and loss tolerance:

(a) file server

(b) print server

(c) digital library

(d) routine monitoring of remote weather instruments

(e) voice

(f) video monitoring of a waiting room

(g) television broadcasting

25 Suppose a shared medium M offers to hosts $A_1, A_2, \ldots, A_N$ in round-robin fashion an opportunity to transmit one packet; hosts that have nothing to send immediately relinquish M. How does this differ from STDM? How does network utilization of this scheme compare with STDM?

26 Consider a simple protocol for transferring files over a link. After some initial negotiation, A sends data packets of size 1 KB to B; B then replies with an acknowledgment. A always waits for each ACK before sending the next data packet; this is known as *stop-and-wait*. Packets that are overdue are presumed lost and are retransmitted.

(a) In the absence of any packet losses or duplications, explain why it is not necessary to include any "sequence number" data in the packet headers.

(b) Suppose that the link can lose occasional packets, but that packets that do arrive always arrive in the order sent. Is a 2-bit sequence number (that is, N mod 4) enough for A and B to detect and resend any lost packets? Is a 1-bit sequence number enough?

(c) Now suppose that the link can deliver out of order, and that sometimes a packet can be delivered as much as 1 minute after subsequent packets. How does this change the sequence number requirements?

27 Suppose hosts A and B are connected by a link. Host A continuously transmits the current time from a high-precision clock, at a regular rate, fast enough to consume all the available bandwidth. Host B reads these time values and writes them each paired with its own time from a local clock synchronized with A's. Give qualitative examples of B's output assuming the link has

(a) high bandwidth, high latency, low jitter

(b) low bandwidth, high latency, high jitter

(c) high bandwidth, low latency, low jitter, occasional lost data

For example, a link with zero jitter, a bandwidth high enough to write on every other clock tick, and a latency of 1 tick might yield something like (0000, 0001), (0002, 0003), (0004, 0005).

28 Obtain and build the simplex-talk sample socket program shown in the text. Start one server and one client, in separate windows. While the first client is running, start 10 other clients that connect to the same server; these other clients should most likely be started in the background with their input redirected from a file. What happens to these 10 clients? Do their connect()s fail, or time out, or succeed? Do any other calls block? Now let the first client exit. What happens? Try this with the server value MAX_PENDING set to 1 as well.

29 Modify the simplex-talk socket program so that each time the client sends a line to the server, the server sends the line back to the client. The client (and server) will now have to make alternating calls to recv() and send().

30 Modify the simplex-talk socket program so that it uses UDP as the transport protocol, rather than TCP. You will have to change SOCK_STREAM to SOCK_DGRAM in both client and server. Then, in the server, remove the calls to listen() and accept(), and replace the two nested loops at the end with a single loop that calls recv() with socket s. Finally, see what happens when two such UDP clients simultaneously connect to the same UDP server, and compare this to the TCP behavior.

31 The Unix utility ping can be used to find the RTT to various Internet hosts. Read the man page for ping, and use it to find the RTT to www.cs.princeton.edu in New Jersey and www.cisco.com in California. Measure the RTT values at different times of day, and compare the results. What do you think accounts for the differences?

32 The Unix utility traceroute, or its Windows equivalent tracert, can be used to find the sequence of routers through which a message is routed. Use this to find the path from your site to some others. How well does the number of hops correlate with the RTT times from ping? How well does the number of hops correlate with geographical distance?

33 Use traceroute, above, to map out some of the routers within your organization (or to verify none are used).

The simplest network possible is one in which all the hosts are directly connected by some physical medium. This may be a wire or a fiber, and it may cover a small area (e.g., an office building) or a wide area (e.g., transcontinental). Connecting two or more nodes with a suitable medium is only the first step, however. There are five additional problems that must be addressed before the nodes can successfully exchange packets.

The first is *encoding* bits onto the wire or fiber so that they can be understood by a receiving host. Second is the matter of delineating the sequence of bits transmitted over the link into complete messages that can be delivered to the end node. This is called the *framing* problem, and the messages delivered to the end hosts are often called *frames*. Third, because frames are sometimes corrupted during transmission, it is necessary to detect these errors and take the appropriate action; this is the *error detection* problem. The fourth issue is making a link appear reliable in spite of the fact that it corrupts frames from time to time. Finally, in those cases where the link is shared by multiple hosts—as opposed to a simple point-to-point link—it is necessary to mediate access to this link. This is the *media access control* problem.

Although these five issues—encoding, framing, error detection, reliable delivery, and access mediation—can be discussed in the abstract, they are very real problems that are addressed in different ways by different networking technologies. This chapter considers these issues in the context of four specific network technologies: point-to-point links, Carrier Sense Multiple Access (CSMA) networks (of which Ethernet is the most famous example), token rings (of which IEEE Standard 802.5 and FDDI are the most famous examples), and wireless (for which 802.11 is an emerging standard). The goal of this

P R O B L E M
Physically Connecting Hosts

It is a mistake to look too far ahead. Only one link in the chain of destiny can be handled at a time.

—Winston Churchill

chapter is simultaneously to survey the available network technology and to explore these five fundamental issues.

Before tackling the specific issues of connecting hosts, this chapter begins by examining the building blocks that will be used: nodes and links. We then explore the first three issues—encoding, framing, and error detection—in the context of a simple point-to-point link. The techniques introduced in these three sections are general and therefore apply equally well to multiple-access networks. The problem of reliable delivery is considered next. Since link-level reliability is usually not implemented in shared-access networks, this discussion focuses on point-to-point links only. Finally, we address the media access problem in the context of CSMA, token rings, and wireless.

Note that these five functions are, in general, implemented in a network adaptor—a board that plugs into a host's I/O bus on one end and into the physical medium on the other end. In other words, bits are exchanged between adaptors, but correct frames are exchanged between nodes. This adaptor is controlled by software running on the node—the device driver—which, in turn, is typically represented as the bottom protocol in a protocol graph. This chapter concludes with a concrete example of a network adaptor and sketches the device driver for such an adaptor.

2

Direct Link Networks

2.1   Hardware Building Blocks

As we saw in Chapter 1, networks are constructed from two classes of hardware
building blocks: *nodes* and *links*. This statement is just as true for the simplest possible
network—one in which a single point-to-point link connects a pair of nodes—as it
is for a worldwide internet. This section gives a brief overview of what we mean by
nodes and links and, in so doing, defines the underlying technology that we will assume
throughout the rest of this book.

2.1.1   Nodes

Nodes are often general-purpose computers, like a desktop workstation, a multiprocessor, or a PC. For our purposes, let's assume it's a workstation-class machine. This
workstation can serve as a host that users run application programs on, it might be
used inside the network as a switch that forwards messages from one link to another,
or it might be configured as a router that forwards internet packets from one network
to another. In some cases, a network node—most commonly a switch or router inside the network, rather than a host—is implemented by special-purpose hardware.
This is usually done for reasons of performance and cost: It is generally possible to
build custom hardware that performs a particular function faster and cheaper than a
general-purpose processor can perform it. When this happens, we will first describe
the basic function being performed by the node as though this function is being implemented in software on a general-purpose workstation, and then explain why and how
this functionality might instead be implemented by special hardware.

   Although we could leave it at that, it is useful to know a little bit about what a
workstation looks like on the inside. This information becomes particularly important
when we become concerned about how well the network performs. Figure 2.1 gives
a simple block diagram of the workstation-class machine we assume throughout this
book. There are three key features of this figure that are worth noting.

   First, the memory on any given machine is finite. It may be 4 MB or it may be
128 MB, but it is not infinite. As pointed out in Section 1.1.2, this is important because
memory turns out to be one of the two scarce resources in the network (the other is
link bandwidth) that must be carefully managed if we are to provide a fair amount of
network capacity to each user. Memory is a scarce resource because on a node that
serves as a switch or router, packets must be buffered in memory while waiting their
turn to be transmitted over an outgoing link.

   Second, each node connects to the network via a *network adaptor*. This adaptor
generally sits on the system's I/O bus and delivers data between the workstation's
memory and the network link. A software module running on the workstation—the
device driver—manages this adaptor. It issues commands to the adaptor, telling it, for
example, from what memory location outgoing data should be transmitted and into

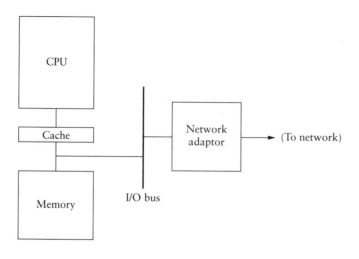

Figure 2.1 Example workstation architecture.

what memory location incoming data should be stored. Adaptors are discussed in more detail in Section 2.9.

Finally, while CPUs are becoming faster at an unbelievable pace, the same is not true of memory. Recent performance trends show processor speeds doubling every 18 months, but memory latency improving at a rate of only 7% each year. The relevance of this difference is that as a network node, a workstation runs at memory speeds, not processor speeds, to a first approximation. This means that the network software needs to be careful about how it uses memory and, in particular, about how many times it accesses memory as it processes each message. We do not have the luxury of being sloppy just because processors are becoming infinitely fast.

2.1.2 Links

Network links are implemented on a variety of different physical media, including twisted pair (the wire that your phone connects to), coaxial cable (the wire that your TV connects to), optical fiber (the medium most commonly used for high-bandwidth, long-distance links), and space (the stuff that radio waves, microwaves, and infrared beams propagate through). Whatever the physical medium, it is used to propagate *signals*. These signals are actually electromagnetic waves traveling at the speed of light. (The speed of light is, however, medium-dependent—electromagnetic waves traveling through copper and fiber do so at about two-thirds the speed of light in a vacuum.)

One important property of an electromagnetic wave is the *frequency*, measured in hertz, with which the wave oscillates. The distance between a pair of adjacent

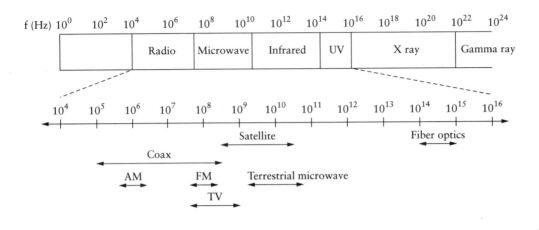

Figure 2.2 Electromagnetic spectrum.

maxima or minima of a wave, typically measured in meters, is called the wave's *wavelength*. Since all electromagnetic waves travel at the speed of light, that speed divided by the wave's frequency is equal to its wavelength. We have already seen the example of a voice-grade telephone line, which carries continuous electromagnetic signals ranging between 300 Hz and 3300 Hz; a 300-Hz wave traveling through copper would have a wavelength of

$$\text{SpeedOfLightInCopper} \div \text{Frequency}$$
$$= 2/3 \times 3 \times 10^8 \div 300$$
$$= 667 \text{ meters}$$

Generally, electromagnetic waves span a much wider range of frequencies, ranging from radio waves, to infrared light, to visible light, to X rays and gamma rays. Figure 2.2 depicts the electromagnetic spectrum and shows which media are commonly used to carry which frequency bands.

So far we understand a link to be a physical medium carrying signals in the form of electromagnetic waves. Such links provide the foundation for transmitting all sorts of information, including the kind of data we are interested in transmitting—binary data (1s and 0s). We say that the binary data is *encoded* in the signal. The problem of encoding binary data onto electromagnetic signals is a complex topic. To help make the topic more manageable, we can think of it as being divided into two layers. The lower layer is concerned with *modulation*—varying the frequency, amplitude, or phase of the signal to effect the transmission of information. A simple example of modulation is to vary the power (amplitude) of a single wavelength. Intuitively, this is equivalent to turning a light on and off. Because the issue of modulation is secondary to our discussion of links as a building block for computer networks, we simply assume that it is possible to transmit a pair of distinguishable signals—think of them as a "high" signal and a "low" signal—and we consider only the upper layer, which is concerned with the much simpler problem of encoding binary data onto these two signals. Section 2.2 discusses such encodings.

Another attribute of a link is how many bit streams can be encoded on it at a given time. If the answer is only one, then the nodes connected to the link must share access to the link. This is the case for the multiple-access links described in Sections 2.6 and 2.7. For point-to-point links, however, it is often the case that two bit streams can be simultaneously transmitted over the link at the same time, one going in each direction. Such a link is said to be *full-duplex*. A point-to-point link that supports data flowing in only one direction at a time—such a link is called *half-duplex*—requires that the two nodes connected to the link alternate using it. For the purposes of this book, we assume that all point-to-point links are full-duplex.

The only other property of a link that we are interested in at this stage is a very pragmatic one—how do you go about getting one? The answer depends on how far the link needs to reach, how much money you have to spend, and whether or not you know how to operate a backhoe. The following is a survey of different link types you might use to build a computer network.

Cables

If the nodes you want to connect are in the same room, in the same building, or even on the same site (e.g., a campus), then you can buy a piece of cable and physically string it between the nodes. Exactly what type of cable you choose to install depends on the technology you plan to use to transmit data over the link; we'll see several examples later in this chapter. For now, a list of the common cable (fiber) types is given in Table 2.1.

Of these, Category 5 (Cat-5) twisted pair—it uses a thicker gauge than the twisted pair you find in your home—is quickly becoming the within-building norm. Because of the difficulty and cost in pulling new cable through a building, it is reasonable to expect that emerging technologies, such as Gigabit Ethernet, will run over Cat-5 wiring. Fiber is typically used to connect buildings at a site.

Leased Lines

If the two nodes you want to connect are on opposite sides of the country, or even across town, then it is not practical to install the link yourself. Your only option is to lease a dedicated link from the telephone company, in which case all you'll need to be

Cable	Typical Bandwidths	Distances
Category 5 twisted pair	10–100 Mbps	100 m
Thin-net coax	10–100 Mbps	200 m
Thick-net coax	10–100 Mbps	500 m
Multimode fiber	100 Mbps	2 km
Single-mode fiber	100–2400 Mbps	40 km

Table 2.1   Common types of cables and fibers available for local links.

Service	Bandwidth
DS1	1.544 Mbps
DS3	44.736 Mbps
STS-1	51.840 Mbps
STS-3	155.250 Mbps
STS-12	622.080 Mbps
STS-24	1.244160 Gbps
STS-48	2.488320 Gbps

T1

optical (fiber)

Fiber optical

Table 2.2   Common bandwidths available from the carriers.

able to do is conduct an intelligent conversation with the phone company customer service representative. Table 2.2 gives the common services that can be leased from the phone company. Again, more details are given throughout this chapter.

While these bandwidths appear somewhat arbitrary, there is actually some method to the madness. DS1 and DS3 (they are also sometimes called T1 and T3, respectively) are relatively old technologies that are defined for copper-based transmission media. DS1 is equal to the aggregation of 24 digital voice circuits of 64 Kbps each, and DS3 is equal to 30 DS1 links. All the STS-N links are for optical fiber (STS stands for Synchronous Transport Signal). STS-1 is the base link speed, and each STS-N has N times the bandwidth of STS-1. An STS-N link is also sometimes called an OC-N link (OC stands for optical carrier). The difference between STS and OC is subtle: The

Service	Bandwidth
POTS	28.8–56 Kbps
ISDN	64–128 Kbps
xDSL	16 Kbps–55.2 Mbps
CATV	20–40 Mbps

Table 2.3 Common services available to connect your home.

former refers to the *electrical* transmission on the devices connected to the link, and the latter refers to the actual *optical* signal that is propagated over the fiber.

Keep in mind that the phone company does not implement the "link" we just ordered as a single, unbroken piece of cable or fiber. Instead, it implements the link on its own network. Although the telephone network has historically looked much different from the kind of network described in this book—it was built primarily to provide a voice service and used circuit-switching technology—the current trend is toward the style of networking described in this book, including the asynchronous transfer mode (ATM) network described in Chapter 3. This is not surprising—the potential market for carrying data, voice, and video is huge.

In any case, whether the link is physical or a logical connection through the telephone network, the problem of building a computer network on top of a collection of such links remains the same. So, we will proceed as though each link is implemented by a single cable/fiber, and only when we are done will we worry about whether we have just built a computer network on top of the underlying telephone network, or the computer network we have just built could itself serve as the backbone for the telephone network.

Last-Mile Links

If you can't afford a dedicated leased line—they range in price from roughly a thousand dollars a month for a crosscountry DS1 link to "if you have to ask, you can't afford it"—then there are less expensive options available. We call these "last-mile" links because they often span the last mile from the home to a network service provider. These services, which are summarized in Table 2.3, typically connect a home to an existing network. This means they are probably not suitable for use in building a complete network from scratch, but if you've already succeeded in building a network—and "you" happen to be either the telephone company or the cable company—then you can use these links to reach millions of customers.

The first option is a conventional modem over POTS (plain old telephone service). Today it is possible to buy a modem that transmits data at 56 Kbps over a standard voice-grade line for little more than a hundred dollars. The technology is already at its bandwidth limit, however, which has led to the development of the second option: ISDN (Integrated Services Digital Network). An ISDN connection includes two 64-Kbps channels, one that can be used to transmit data and another that can be used for digitized voice. (A device that encodes analog voice into a digital ISDN link is called a CODEC, for *coder/decoder*.) When the voice channel is not in use, it can be combined with the data channel to support up to 128 Kbps of data bandwidth.

For many years ISDN was viewed as the future for modest bandwidth into the home. It now seems, however, that ISDN may be passed over by two newer technologies: xDSL (digital subscriber line) and cable modems. The former is actually a collection of technologies that are able to transmit data at high speeds over the standard twisted pair lines that currently come into most homes in the United States. The one in most widespread use today is ADSL (asymmetric digital subscriber line). As its name implies, ADSL provides a different bandwidth from the subscriber to the telephone company's central office (upstream) than it does from the central office to the subscriber (downstream). The exact bandwidth depends on the length of the line running from the subscriber to the central office. This line is called the *local loop*, as illustrated in Figure 2.3, and runs over existing copper. Downstream bandwidths range from 1.544 Mbps (18,000 feet) to 8.448 Mbps (9000 feet), while upstream bandwidths range from 16 Kbps to 640 Kbps.

An alternative technology still under development—very high data rate digital subscriber line (VDSL)—will be symmetric, with data rates ranging from 12.96 Mbps to 55.2 Mbps. VDSL will run over much shorter distances—1000 to 4500 feet—which means that it will not reach from the home to the central office. Instead, the telephone company will have to put VDSL transmission hardware in neighborhoods,

Shannon's Theorem Meets Your Modem

There has been an enormous body of work done in the related areas of signal processing and information theory, studying everything from how signals degrade over distance to how much data a given signal can effectively carry. The most notable piece of work in this area is a formula known as *Shannon's theorem*. Simply stated, Shannon's theorem gives an upper bound to the capacity of a link, in terms of bits per second (bps), as a function of the signal-to-noise ratio of the link, measured in decibels (dB).

Shannon's theorem can be used to determine the data rate at which a modem can be expected to transmit binary data over a voice-grade phone line without suffering from

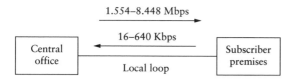

Figure 2.3 ADSL connects the subscriber to the central office via the local loop.

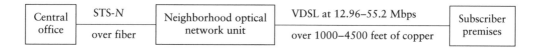

Figure 2.4 VDSL connects the subscriber to the optical network that reaches the neighborhood.

too high an error rate. For example, we assume that a voice-grade phone connection supports a frequency range of 300 Hz to 3300 Hz.

Shannon's theorem is typically given by the following formula:

$$C = B \log_2(1 + S/N)$$

where C is the achievable channel capacity measured in hertz, B is the bandwidth of the line (3300 Hz − 300 Hz = 3000 Hz), S is the average signal power, and N is the average noise power. The signal-to-noise ratio (S/N) is usually expressed in decibels, related as follows:

$$dB = 10 \times \log_{10}(S/N)$$

with some other technology (e.g., STS-N running over fiber) connecting the neighborhood to the central office, as illustrated in Figure 2.4. This is sometimes called "fiber to the neighborhood" (contrasting with more ambitious schemes such as "fiber to the home" and "fiber to the curb").

Cable modems are an alternative to xDSL. As the name suggests, this technology uses the cable TV (CATV) infrastructure, which currently reaches 95% of the households in the United States. (Only 65% of U.S. homes actually subscribe.) Although the technology is still evolving, the approach is taking on a definite shape. First, some subset of the available CATV channels will be made available for transmitting digital data, where a single CATV channel has a bandwidth of 6 MHz. Second, CATV will be used in an asymmetric way, with downstream rates much greater than upstream rates. The technology is currently able to achieve 40 Mbps downstream on a single CATV channel, with 100 Mbps as the theoretical capacity. The upstream rate is roughly half the downstream rate (i.e., 20 Mbps) due to a 1000-fold decrease in the signal-to-noise ratio. It is also the case that many fewer CATV channels will be dedicated to upstream traffic than to downstream traffic. Third, the bandwidth will be shared among all subscribers in a neighborhood. This means that some method for arbitrating access to the shared medium—similar to the 802 standards described later in this chapter—will need to be used. In fact, an IEEE 802.14 working group is starting to address this issue. Finally, like xDSL, it is unlikely that cable modems will be used to connect arbitrary node A at one site to arbitrary node B at some other site. Instead, cable modems are seen as a means to connect node A in your home to the cable company, with the cable company then defining what the rest of the network looks like.

Wireless Links

The field of wireless communication is exploding, both economically and technologically. The Advanced Mobile Phone System (AMPS) has been the standard for cellular phones in the United States for several years. AMPS, which is based on analog technology, is rapidly giving way to digital cellular—PCS (Personal Communication Services) in the United States and Canada, and GMS (Global Mobile System) in the rest of the world. All three systems currently use a system of towers to transmit signals, although significant efforts are under way to replace this infrastructure by ringing the globe with a grid of medium- and low-orbit satellites. These projects—which include ICO, Globalstar, Iridium, and Teledesic (see Table 2.4)—are exploiting the recent availability of several high-frequency bands in the electromagnetic spectrum for commercial use.

Because these systems are targeted at voice communication, they can be used to provide building block links only in the sense that they support modems just as well as POTS. One of the low-orbit satellite projects—Teledesic—is the exception. It involves a grid of 288 satellites encircling the earth at an altitude of 1350 km. Teledesic

Assuming a typical decibel ratio of 30 dB, this means that $S/N = 1000$. Thus, we have

$$C = 3000 \times \log_2(1001)$$

which equals approximately 30 Kbps, roughly the limit of a 28.8-Kbps modem.

Given this fundamental limit, why is it possible to buy 56-Kbps modems at any electronics store? One reason is that such rates depend on improved line quality, that is, a higher signal-to-noise ratio than 30 dB. Another reason is that changes within the phone system have largely eliminated analog lines that are bandwidth-limited to 3300 Hz.

All this is slowly is some

Project	Orbit (km)	Number of Satellites	Uplink Frequencies	Downlink Frequencies
ICO	10,355	10	2170–2200 MHz	1980–2010 MHz
Globalstar	1,410	48	L-band	S-band
Iridium	780	66	L-band	L-band
Teledesic	1,350	288	Ka-band	Ka-band

Table 2.4 Medium- and low-orbit satellite constellations.

plans to offer both voice and data service. Each satellite will support 1440 16-Kbps satellite-to-earth channels, which can be aggregated in groups of up to 128 to form 2.048-Mbps data channels. Each satellite will then be connected to its eight neighbors by 155.52-Mbps intersatellite channels. In other words, Teledisic will be a giant network in the sky, one that has the potential of providing a 2.048-Mbps link between any two points on the globe.

Thinking a bit less globally, frequency bands from the radio and infrared portions of the electromagnetic spectrum can be used to provide wireless links over short distances, such as office buildings, malls, building complexes, and campuses. In the case of infrared, signals with wavelengths in the 850–950-nanometer range can be used to transmit data at 1-Mbps rates over distances of about 10 m. This technology does not require line of sight, but is limited to in-building environments. In the case of radio, several different bands are currently being made available for data communication. For example, bands at 5.2 GHz and 17 GHz are allocated to HIPERLAN (High Performance European Radio LAN) in Europe. Similarly, bandwidth at 2.4 GHz is being set aside in many countries for use with the IEEE 802.11 standard for wireless LANs. (Additional bandwidth is available at 5 GHz, but unfortunately it is subject to interference from microwave ovens.) IEEE 802.11, which is an evolving standard that supports data rates of 1 and 2 Mbps, will be discussed more fully in Section 2.8.

One of the most exciting developments in the wireless arena is the Bluetooth radio interface being developed by Ericsson, Nokia, IBM, Toshiba, and Intel to operate at the 2.45-GHz frequency band. Bluetooth is being designed for short distances (on the order of 10 m) with a bandwidth of 1Mbps. Its developers envision it being used in all devices (e.g., printers, workstations, laptops, projectors, PDAs, mobile phones), thereby eliminating the need for wires and cables in the office. A network of such devices are starting to be called *piconets*.

2.2   Encoding (NRZ, NRZI, Manchester, 4B/5B)

The first step in turning nodes and links into usable building blocks is to understand how to connect them in such a way that bits can be transmitted from one node to the other. As mentioned in the preceding section, signals propagate over physical links.

The task, therefore, is to encode the binary data that the source node wants to send into the signals that the links are able to carry, and then to decode the signal back into the corresponding binary data at the receiving node. We ignore the details of modulation and assume we are working with two discrete signals: high and low. In practice, these signals might correspond to two different voltages on a copper-based link, or two different power levels on an optical link.

As we have said, most of the functions discussed in this chapter are performed by a network adaptor—a piece of hardware that connects a node to a link. The network adaptor contains a signalling component that actually encodes bits into signals at the sending node and decodes signals into bits at the receiving node. Thus, as illustrated in Figure 2.5, signals travel over a link between two signalling components, and bits flow between network adaptors.

Let's return to the problem of encoding bits onto signals. The obvious thing to do is to map the data value 1 onto the high signal and the data value 0 onto the low signal. This is exactly the mapping used by an encoding scheme called, cryptically enough, *non-return to zero* (NRZ). For example, Figure 2.6 schematically depicts the NRZ-encoded signal (bottom) that corresponds to the transmission of a particular sequence of bits (top).

The problem with NRZ is that a sequence of several consecutive 1s means that the signal stays high on the link for an

Bit Rates and Baud Rates

Many people use the terms *bit rate* and *baud rate* interchangeably, even though as we see with the Manchester encoding, they are not the same thing. While the Manchester encoding is an example of a case in which a link's baud rate is greater than its bit rate, it is also possible to have a bit rate that is greater than the baud rate. This would imply that more than one bit is encoded on each pulse sent over the link.

To see how this might happen, suppose you could transmit four distinguished signals over a link rather than just two. On an analog link, for example, these four signals might correspond to four different frequencies. Given four different signals, it is possible to encode two bits of information on each signal. That is, the first signal means 00, the second signal means 01, and so on. Now, a sender (receiver) that is able to transmit (detect) 1000 pulses per second would be able to send (receive) 2000 bits of information per second. That is, it would be a 1000-baud/2000-bps link.

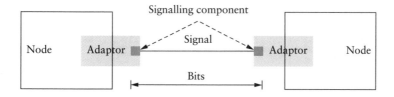

Figure 2.5 Signals travel between signalling components; bits flow between adaptors.

Figure 2.6 NRZ encoding of a bit stream.

extended period of time, and similarly, several consecutive 0s means that the signal stays low for a long time. There are two fundamental problems caused by long strings of 1s or 0s. The first is that it leads to a situation known as *baseline wander*. Specifically, the receiver keeps an average of the signal it has seen so far, and then uses this average to distinguish between low and high signals. Whenever the signal is significantly lower than this average, the receiver concludes that it has just seen a 0, and likewise, a signal that is significantly higher than the average is interpreted to be a 1. The problem, of course, is that too many consecutive 1s or 0s cause this average to change, making it more difficult to detect a significant change in the signal.

The second problem is that frequent transitions from high to low and vice versa are necessary to enable *clock recovery*. Intuitively, the clock recovery problem is that both the encoding and the decoding processes are driven by a clock—every clock cycle the sender transmits a bit and the receiver recovers a bit. The sender's and the receiver's clocks have to be precisely synchronized in order for the receiver to recover the same bits the sender transmits. If the receiver's clock is even slightly faster or slower than the sender's clock, then it does not correctly decode the signal. You could imagine sending the clock to the receiver over a separate wire, but this is typically avoided because it makes the cost of cabling twice as high. So instead, the receiver derives the clock from the received signal—the clock recovery process. Whenever the signal changes, such as on a transition from 1 to 0 or from 0 to 1, then the receiver knows it is at a clock cycle boundary, and it can resynchronize itself. However, a long period of time without such a transition leads to clock drift. Thus, clock recovery depends on having lots of transitions in the signal, no matter what data is being sent.

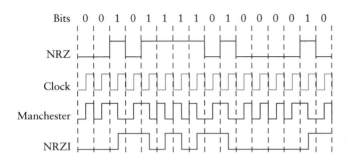

Figure 2.7   Different encoding strategies.

One approach that addresses this problem, called *non-return to zero inverted* (NRZI), has the sender make a transition from the current signal to encode a 1 and stay at the current signal to encode a 0. This solves the problem of consecutive 1s, but obviously does nothing for consecutive 0s. NRZI is illustrated in Figure 2.7. An alternative, called *Manchester encoding*, does a more explicit job of merging the clock with the signal by transmitting the exclusive-OR of the NRZ-encoded data and the clock. (Think of the local clock as an internal signal that alternates from low to high; a low/high pair is considered one clock cycle.) The Manchester encoding is also illustrated in Figure 2.7. Observe that the Manchester encoding results in 0 being encoded as a low-to-high transition and 1 being encoded as a high-to-low transition. Because both 0s and 1s result in a transition to the signal, the clock can be effectively recovered at the receiver.

The problem with the Manchester encoding scheme is that it doubles the rate at which signal transitions are made on the link, which means that the receiver has half the time to detect each pulse of the signal. The rate at which the signal changes is called the link's *baud rate*. In the case of the Manchester encoding, the bit rate is half the baud rate, so the encoding is considered only 50% efficient. Keep in mind that if the receiver had been able to keep up with the faster baud rate required by the Manchester encoding in Figure 2.7, then both NRZ and NRZI could have been able to transmit twice as many bits in the same time period.

A final encoding that we consider, called *4B/5B*, attempts to address the inefficiency of the Manchester encoding without suffering from the problem of having extended durations of high or low signals. The idea of 4B/5B is to insert extra bits into the bit stream so as to break up long sequences of 0s or 1s. Specifically, every 4 bits of actual data are encoded in a 5-bit code that is then transmitted to the receiver; hence the name 4B/5B. The 5-bit codes are selected in such a way that each one has no more

4-Bit Data Symbol	5-Bit Code
0000	11110
0001	01001
0010	10100
0011	10101
0100	01010
0101	01011
0110	01110
0111	01111
1000	10010
1001	10011
1010	10110
1011	10111
1100	11010
1101	11011
1110	11100
1111	11101

Table 2.5 4B/5B encoding.

than one leading 0 and no more than two trailing 0s. Thus, when sent back-to-back, no pair of 5-bit codes results in more than three consecutive 0s being transmitted. The resulting 5-bit codes are then transmitted using the NRZI encoding, which explains why the code is only concerned about consecutive 0s—NRZI already solves the problem of consecutive 1s. Note that the 4B/5B encoding results in 80% efficiency.

Table 2.5 gives the 5-bit codes that correspond to each of the 16 possible 4-bit data symbols. Notice that since 5 bits are enough to encode 32 different codes, and we are using only 16 of these for data, there are 16 codes left over that we can use for other purposes. Of these, code 11111 is used when the line is idle, code 00000 corresponds to when the line is dead, and 00100 is interpreted to mean halt. Of the remaining 13 codes, 7 of them are not valid because they violate the "one leading 0, two trailing 0s," rule, and the other 6 represent various control symbols. As we will see later in this chapter, some framing protocols (e.g., FDDI) make use of these control symbols.

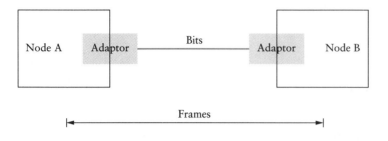

Figure 2.8   Bits flow between adaptors, frames between hosts.

2.3   Framing

Now that we have seen how to transmit a sequence of bits over a point-to-point link—from adaptor to adaptor—let's consider the scenario illustrated in Figure 2.8. Recall from Chapter 1 that we are focusing on packet-switched networks, which means that blocks of data (called frames at this level), not bit streams, are exchanged between nodes. It is the network adaptor that enables the nodes to exchange frames. When node A wishes to transmit a frame to node B, it tells its adaptor to transmit a frame from the node's memory. This results in a sequence of bits being sent over the link. The adaptor on node B then collects together the sequence of bits arriving on the link and deposits the corresponding frame in B's memory. Recognizing exactly what set of bits constitute a frame—that is, determining where the frame begins and ends—is the central challenge faced by the adaptor.

There are several ways to address the framing problem. This section uses several different protocols to illustrate the various points in the design space. Note that while we discuss framing in the context of point-to-point links, the problem is a fundamental one that must also be addressed in multiple-access networks like Ethernet and token rings.

2.3.1   Byte-Oriented Protocols (BISYNC, PPP, DDCMP)

One of the oldest approaches to framing—it has its roots in connecting terminals to mainframes—is to view each frame as a collection of bytes (characters) rather than a collection of bits. Such a *byte-oriented* approach is exemplified by the BISYNC (Binary Synchronous Communication) protocol developed by IBM in the late 1960s, and the DDCMP (Digital Data Communication Message Protocol) used in Digital Equipment Corporation's DECNET. Sometimes these protocols assume a particular character set—for example, BISYNC can support ASCII, EBCDIC, and IBM's 6-bit Transcode—but this is not necessarily the case.

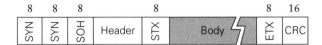

Figure 2.9 BISYNC frame format.

Although similar in many respects, these two protocols are examples of two different framing techniques, the sentinel approach and the byte-counting approach.

Sentinel Approach

The BISYNC protocol illustrates the sentinel approach to framing; its frame format is depicted in Figure 2.9. This figure is the first of many that you will see in this book that are used to illustrate frame or packet formats, so a few words of explanation are in order. We show a packet as a sequence of labeled fields. Above each field is a number indicating the length of that field in bits. Note that the packets are transmitted beginning with the leftmost field.

The beginning of a frame is denoted by sending a special SYN (synchronization) character. The data portion of the frame is then contained between special *sentinel characters*: STX (start of text) and ETX (end of text). The SOH (start of header) field serves much the same purpose as the STX field. The problem with the sentinel approach, of course, is that the ETX character might appear in the data portion of the frame. BISYNC overcomes this problem by "escaping" the ETX character by preceding it with a DLE (data-link-escape) character whenever it appears in the body of a frame; the DLE character is also escaped (by preceding it with an extra DLE) in the frame body. (C programmers may notice that this is analogous to the way a quotation mark is escaped by the backslash when it occurs inside a string.) This approach is often called *character stuffing* because extra characters are inserted in the data portion of the frame.

The frame format also includes a field labeled CRC (cyclic redundancy check) that is used to detect transmission errors; various algorithms for error detection are presented in Section 2.4. Finally, the frame contains additional header fields that are used for, among other things, the link-level reliable delivery algorithm. Examples of these algorithms are given in Section 2.5.

The more recent Point-to-Point Protocol (PPP), which is commonly run over dial-up modem links, is similar to BISYNC in that it uses character stuffing. The format for a PPP frame is given in Figure 2.10. The special start-of-text character, denoted as the Flag field in Figure 2.10, is 01111110. The Address and Control fields usually contain default values, and so are uninteresting. The Protocol field is used for demultiplexing:

8	8	8	16		16	8
Flag	Address	Control	Protocol	Payload	Checksum	Flag

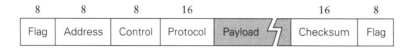

Figure 2.10 PPP frame format.

It identifies the high-level protocol such as IP or IPX (an IP-like protocol developed by Novell). The frame payload size can be negotiated, but it is 1500 bytes by default. The Checksum field is either 2 (by default) or 4 bytes long.

The PPP frame format is unusual in that several of the field sizes are negotiated rather than fixed. This negotiation is conducted by a protocol called LCP (Link Control Protocol). PPP and LCP work in tandem: LCP sends control messages encapsulated in PPP frames—such messages are denoted by an LCP identifier in the PPP Protocol field—and then turns around and changes PPP's frame format based on the information contained in those control messages. LCP is also involved in establishing a link between two peers when both sides detect the carrier signal.

Byte-Counting Approach

As every Computer Sciences 101 student knows, the alternative to detecting the end of a file with a sentinel value is to include the number of items in the file at the beginning of the file. The same is true in framing—the number of bytes contained in a frame can be included as a field in the frame header. The DECNET's DDCMP protocol uses this approach, as illustrated in Figure 2.11. In this example, the COUNT field specifies how many bytes are contained in the frame's body.

What's in a Layer?

One of the important contributions of the OSI reference model presented in Chapter 1 was to provide some vocabulary for talking about protocols and, in particular, protocol layers. This vocabulary has provided fuel for plenty of arguments along the lines of "Your protocol does function X at layer Y, and the OSI reference model says it should be done at layer Z—that's a layer violation." In fact, figuring out the right layer at which to perform a given function can be very difficult, and the reasoning is usually a lot more subtle than "What does the OSI model say?" It is partly for this reason that this book avoids a rigidly layerist approach. Instead, it shows you a lot of functions that need to be performed by protocols and looks at some ways that they have been successfully implemented.

8	8	8	14	42		16
SYN	SYN	Class	Count	Header	Body	CRC

Figure 2.11 DDCMP frame format.

One danger with this approach is that a transmission error could corrupt the count field, in which case the end of the frame would not be correctly detected. (A similar problem exists with the sentinel-based approach if the ETX field becomes corrupted.) Should this happen, the receiver will accumulate as many bytes as the bad COUNT field indicates and then use the error detection field to determine that the frame is bad. This is sometimes called a *framing error*. The receiver will then wait until it sees the next SYN character to start collecting the bytes that make up the next frame. It is therefore possible that a framing error will cause back-to-back frames to be incorrectly received.

2.3.2 Bit-Oriented Protocols (HDLC)

Unlike these byte-oriented protocols, a bit-oriented protocol is not concerned with byte boundaries—it simply views the frame as a collection of bits. These bits might come from some character set, such as ASCII, they might be pixel values in an image, or they could be instructions and operands from an executable file. The Synchronous Data Link Control (SDLC) protocol developed by IBM is an example of a bit-oriented protocol; SDLC was later standardized by the OSI as the High-Level Data Link Control (HDLC) protocol. In the following discussion, we use HDLC as an example; its frame format is given in Figure 2.12.

In spite of our nonlayerist approach, sometimes we need convenient ways to talk about classes of protocols, and the name of the layer at which they operate is often the best choice. Thus, for example, this chapter focuses primarily on link-layer protocols. (Bit encoding, described in Section 2.2, is the exception, being considered a physical-layer function.) Link-layer protocols can be identified by the fact that they run over single links—the type of network discussed in this chapter. Network-layer protocols, by contrast, run over switched networks that contain lots of links interconnected by switches or routers. Topics related to network-layer protocols are discussed in Chapters 3 and 4.

Note that protocol layers are supposed to be helpful—they provide helpful ways to talk about

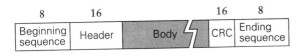

Figure 2.12 HDLC frame format.

HDLC denotes both the beginning and the end of a frame with the distinguished bit sequence 01111110. This sequence is also transmitted during any times that the link is idle so that the sender and receiver can keep their clocks synchronized. In this way, both protocols essentially use the sentinel approach. Because this sequence might appear anywhere in the body of the frame—in fact, the bits 01111110 might cross byte boundaries—bit-oriented protocols use the analog of the DLE character, a technique known as *bit stuffing*.

Bit stuffing in the HDLC protocol works as follows. On the sending side, any time five consecutive 1s have been transmitted from the body of the message (i.e., excluding when the sender is trying to transmit the distinguished 01111110 sequence), the sender inserts a 0 before transmitting the next bit. On the receiving side, should five consecutive 1s arrive, the receiver makes its decision based on the next bit it sees (i.e., the bit following the five 1s). If the next bit is a 0, it must have been stuffed, and so the receiver removes it. If the next bit is a 1, then one of two things is true: Either this is the end-of-frame marker or an error has been introduced into the bit stream. By looking at the *next* bit, the receiver can distinguish between these two cases: if it sees a 0 (i.e., the last eight bits it has looked at are 01111110), then it is the end-of-frame marker; if it sees a 1 (i.e., the last eight bits it has looked at are 01111111), then there must have been an error and the whole frame is discarded. In the latter case, the receiver has to wait for the next 01111110 before it can start receiving again, and as a consequence, there is the potential that the receiver will fail to receive two consecutive frames. Obviously, there are still ways that framing errors can go undetected, such as when an entire

classes of protocols, and they help us divide the problem of building networks into manageable subtasks. However, they are not meant to be overly restrictive—the mere fact that something is a layer violation does not end the argument about whether it is a worthwhile thing to do. In other words, layering makes a good slave, but a poor master. A particularly interesting argument about the best layer to place a certain function comes up when we look at congestion control in Chapter 6.

spurious end-of-frame pattern is generated by errors, but these failures are relatively unlikely. Robust ways of detecting errors are discussed in Section 2.4.

An interesting characteristic of bit stuffing, as well as character stuffing, is that the size of a frame is dependent on the data that is being sent in the payload of the frame. It is in fact not possible to make all frames exactly the same size, given that the data that might be carried in any frame is arbitrary. (To convince yourself of this, consider what happens if the last byte of a frame's body is the ETX character.) A form of framing that ensures that all frames are the same size is described in the next subsection.

2.3.3 Clock-Based Framing (SONET)

A third approach to framing is exemplified by the Synchronous Optical Network (SONET) standard. For lack of a widely accepted generic term, we refer to this approach simply as *clock-based framing*. SONET was first proposed by Bell Communications Research (Bellcore), and then developed under the American National Standards Institute (ANSI) for digital transmission over optical fiber; it has since been adopted by the ITU-T. Who standardized what and when is not the interesting issue though. The thing to remember about SONET is that it is the dominant standard for long-distance transmission of data over optical networks.

An important point to make about SONET before we go any further is that the full specification is substantially larger than this book. Thus, the following discussion will necessarily cover only the high points of the standard. Also, SONET addresses both the framing problem and the encoding problem. It also addresses a problem that is very important for phone companies—the multiplexing of several low-speed links onto one high-speed link. We begin with framing and discuss the other issues following.

As with the previously discussed framing schemes, a SONET frame has some special information that tells the receiver where the frame starts and ends. However, that is about as far as the similarities go. Notably, no bit stuffing is used, so that a frame's length does not depend on the data being sent. So the question to ask is, How does the receiver know where each frame starts and ends? We consider this question for the lowest-speed SONET link, which is known as STS-1 and runs at 51.84 Mbps. An STS-1 frame is shown in Figure 2.13. It is arranged as nine rows of 90 bytes each, and the first 3 bytes of each row are overhead, with the rest being available for data that is being transmitted over the link. The first 2 bytes of the frame contain a special bit pattern, and it is these bytes that enable the receiver to determine where the frame starts. However, since bit stuffing is not used, there is no reason why this pattern will not occasionally turn up in the payload portion of the frame. To guard against this, the receiver looks for the special bit pattern consistently, hoping to see it appearing once

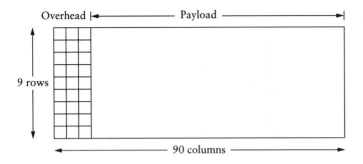

Figure 2.13   A SONET STS-1 frame.

every 810 bytes, since each frame is $9 \times 90 = 810$ bytes long. When the special pattern turns up in the right place enough times, the receiver concludes that it is in sync and can then interpret the frame correctly.

One of the things we are not describing due to the complexity of SONET is the detailed use of all the other overhead bytes. Part of this complexity can be attributed to the fact that SONET runs across the carrier's optical network, not just over a single link. (Recall that we are glossing over the fact that the carriers implement a network, and we are instead focusing on the fact that we can lease a SONET link from them and then use this link to build our own packet-switched network.) Additional complexity comes from the fact that SONET provides a considerably richer set of services than just data transfer. For example, 64 Kbps of a SONET link's capacity is set aside for a voice channel that is used for maintenance.

The overhead bytes of a SONET frame are encoded using NRZ, the simple encoding described in the previous section where 1s are high and 0s are low. However, to ensure that there are plenty of transitions to allow the receiver to recover the sender's clock, the payload bytes are *scrambled*. This is done by calculating the exclusive-OR (XOR) of the data to be transmitted and by the use of a well-known bit pattern. The bit pattern, which is 127 bits long, has plenty of transitions from 1 to 0, so that XORing it with the transmitted data is likely to yield a signal with enough transitions to enable clock recovery.

SONET supports the multiplexing of multiple low-speed links in the following way. A given SONET link runs at one of a finite set of possible rates, ranging from 51.84 Mbps (STS-1) to 2488.32 Mbps (STS-48), and beyond. (See Table 2.2 in Section 2.1 for the full set of SONET data rates.) Note that all of these rates are integer multiples of STS-1. The significance for framing is that a single SONET frame can contain subframes for multiple lower-rate channels. A second related feature is that each

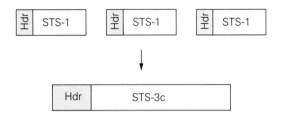

Figure 2.14 Three STS-1 frames multiplexed onto one STS-3c frame.

frame is 125 μs long. This means that at STS-1 rates, a SONET frame is 810 bytes long, while at STS-3 rates, each SONET frame is 2430 bytes long. Notice the synergy between these two features: $3 \times 810 = 2430$, meaning that three STS-1 frames fit exactly in a single STS-3 frame.

Intuitively, the STS-N frame can be thought of as consisting of N STS-1 frames, where the bytes from these frames are interleaved; that is, a byte from the first frame is transmitted, then a byte from the second frame is transmitted, and so on. The reason for interleaving the bytes from each STS-N frame is to ensure that the bytes in each STS-1 frame are evenly paced; that is, bytes show up at the receiver at a smooth 51 Mbps, rather than all bunched up during one particular 1/Nth of the 125-μs interval.

Although it is accurate to view an STS-N signal as being used to multiplex N STS-1 frames, the payload from these STS-1 frames can be linked together to form a larger STS-N payload; such a link is denoted STS-Nc (for *concatenated*). One of the fields in the overhead is used for this purpose. Figure 2.14 schematically depicts concatenation in the case of three STS-1 frames being concatenated into a single STS-3c frame. The significance of a SONET link being designated as STS-3c rather than STS-3 is that, in the former case, the user of the link can view it as a single 155.25-Mbps pipe, whereas an STS-3 should really be viewed as three 51.84-Mbps links that happen to share a fiber.

Finally, the preceding description of SONET is overly simplistic in that it assumes that the payload for each frame is completely contained within the frame. (Why wouldn't it be?) In fact, we should view the STS-1 frame just described as simply a placeholder for the frame, where the actual payload may *float* across frame boundaries. This situation is illustrated in Figure 2.15. Here we see both the STS-1 payload floating across two STS-1 frames, and the payload shifted some number of bytes to the right and, therefore, wrapped around. One of the fields in the frame overhead points to the beginning of the payload. The value of this capability is that it simplifies the task of

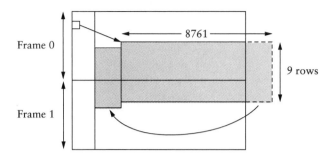

Figure 2.15   SONET frames out of phase.

synchronizing the clocks used throughout the carriers' networks, which is something that carriers spend a lot of their time worrying about.

2.4   Error Detection

As discussed in Chapter 1, bit errors are sometimes introduced into frames. This happens, for example, because of electrical interference or thermal noise. Although errors are rare, especially on optical links, some mechanism is needed to detect these errors so that corrective action can be taken. Otherwise, the end user is left wondering why the C program that successfully compiled just a moment ago now suddenly has a syntax error in it, when all that happened in the interim is that it was copied across a network file system.

There is a long history of techniques for dealing with bit errors in computer systems, dating back to Hamming and Reed/Solomon codes that were developed for use when storing data on magnetic disks and in early core memories. This section describes some of the error detection techniques most commonly used in networking.

Detecting errors is only one part of the problem. The other part is correcting errors once detected. There are two basic approaches that can be taken when the recipient of a message detects an error. One is to notify the sender that the message was corrupted so that the sender can retransmit a copy of the message. If bit errors are rare, then in all probability the retransmitted copy will be error-free. Alternatively, there are some types of error detection algorithms that allow the recipient to reconstruct the correct message even after it has been corrupted; such algorithms rely on *error-correcting codes*, discussed below.

One of the most common techniques for detecting transmission errors is a technique known as the *cyclic redundancy check* (CRC). It is used in nearly all the link-level protocols discussed in the previous section—for example, HDLC, DDCMP—as well as in the CSMA and token ring protocols described later in this chapter. Section 2.4.3

outlines the basic CRC algorithm. Before discussing that approach, we consider two simpler schemes that are also widely used: *two-dimensional parity* and *checksums*. The former is used by the BISYNC protocol when it is transmitting ASCII characters (CRC is used as the error code when BISYNC is used to transmit EBCDIC), and the latter is used by several Internet protocols.

The basic idea behind any error detection scheme is to add redundant information to a frame that can be used to determine if errors have been introduced. In the extreme, we could imagine transmitting two complete copies of the data. If the two copies are identical at the receiver, then it is probably the case that both are correct. If they differ, then an error was introduced into one (or both) of them, and they must be discarded. This is a rather poor error detection scheme for two reasons. First, it sends n redundant bits for an n-bit message. Second, many errors will go undetected—any error that happens to corrupt the same bit positions in the first and second copies of the message.

Fortunately, we can do a lot better than this simple scheme. In general, we can provide quite strong error detection capability while sending only k redundant bits for an n-bit message, where $k << n$. On an Ethernet, for example, a frame carrying up to 12,000 bits (1500 bytes) of data requires only a 32-bit CRC code, or as it is commonly expressed, uses CRC-32. Such a code will catch the overwhelming majority of errors, as we will see below.

We say that the extra bits we send are redundant because they add no new information to the message. Instead, they are derived directly from the original message using some well-defined algorithm. Both the sender and the receiver know exactly what that algorithm is. The sender applies the algorithm to the message to generate the redundant bits. It then transmits both the message and those few extra bits. When the receiver applies the same algorithm to the received message, it should (in the absence of errors) come up with the same result as the sender. It compares the result with the one sent to it by the sender. If they match, it can conclude (with high likelihood) that no errors were introduced in the message during transmission. If they do not match, it can be sure that either the message or the redundant bits were corrupted, and it must take appropriate action, that is, discarding the message, or correcting it if that is possible.

One note on the terminology for these extra bits. In general, they are referred to as error-detecting codes. In specific cases, when the algorithm to create the code is based on addition, they may be called a *checksum*. We will see that the Internet checksum is appropriately named: It is an error check that uses a summing algorithm. Unfortunately, the word "checksum" is often used imprecisely to mean any form of error-detecting code, including CRCs. This can be confusing, so we urge you to use the word "checksum" only to apply to codes that actually do use addition and to use "error-detecting code" to refer to the general class of codes described in this section.

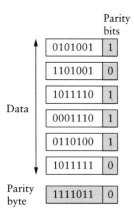

Figure 2.16   Two-dimensional parity.

2.4.1   Two-Dimensional Parity

Two-dimensional parity is exactly what the name suggests. It is based on "simple" (one-dimensional) parity, which usually involves adding one extra bit to a 7-bit code to balance the number of 1s in the byte. For example, odd parity sets the eighth bit to 1 if needed to give an odd number of 1s in the byte, and even parity sets the eighth bit to 1 if needed to give an even number of 1s in the byte. Two-dimensional parity does a similar calculation for each bit position across each of the bytes contained in the frame. This results in an extra parity byte for the entire frame, in addition to a parity bit for each byte. Figure 2.16 illustrates how two-dimensional even parity works for an example frame containing 6 bytes of data. Notice that the third bit of the parity byte is 1 since there is an odd number of 1s in the third bit across the 6 bytes in the frame. It can be shown that two-dimensional parity catches all 1-, 2-, and 3-bit errors, and most 4-bit errors. In this case, we have added 14 bits of redundant information to a 42-bit message, and yet we have stronger protection against common errors than the "repetition code" described above.

2.4.2   Internet Checksum Algorithm

A second approach to error detection is exemplified by the Internet checksum. Although it is not used at the link level, it nevertheless provides the same sort of functionality as CRCs and parity, so we discuss it here. We will see examples of its use in Sections 4.1, 5.1, and 5.2.

   The idea behind the Internet checksum is very simple—you add up all the words that are transmitted and then transmit the result of that sum. The result is called the checksum. The receiver performs the same calculation on the received data and compares the result with the received checksum. If any transmitted data, including the checksum itself, is corrupted, then the results will not match, so the receiver knows that an error occurred.

You can imagine many different variations on the basic idea of a checksum. The exact scheme used by the Internet protocols works as follows. Consider the data being checksummed as a sequence of 16-bit integers. Add them together using 16-bit ones complement arithmetic (explained below) and then take the ones complement of the result. That 16-bit number is the checksum.

In ones complement arithmetic, a negative integer $-x$ is represented as the complement of x; that is, each bit of x is inverted. When adding numbers in ones complement arithmetic, a carryout from the most significant bit needs to be added to the result. Consider, for example, the addition of -5 and -3 in ones complement arithmetic on 4-bit integers. $+5$ is 0101, so -5 is 1010; $+3$ is 0011, so -3 is 1100. If we add 1010 and 1100 ignoring the carry, we get 0110. In ones complement arithmetic, the fact that this operation caused a carry from the most significant bit causes us to increment the result, giving 0111, which is the ones complement representation of -8 (obtained by inverting the bits in 1000), as we would expect.

The following routine gives a straightforward implementation of the Internet's checksum algorithm. The count argument gives the length of buf measured in 16-bit units. The routine assumes that buf has already been padded with 0s to a 16-bit boundary.

```
u_short
cksum(u_short *buf, int count)
{
    register u_long sum = 0;

    while (count--)
    {
        sum += *buf++;
        if (sum & 0xFFFF0000)
        {
            /* carry occurred,
                so wrap around */
            sum &= 0xFFFF;
            sum++;
        }
    }
    return ~(sum & 0xFFFF);
}
```

This code ensures that the calculation uses ones complement arithmetic, rather than the twos complement that is used in most machines. Note the if statement inside the while loop. If there is a carry into the top 16 bits of sum, then we increment sum just as in the previous example.

Compared to our repetition code, this algorithm scores well for using a small number of redundant bits—only 16 for a message of any length—but it does not score extremely well for strength of error detection. For example, a pair of single-bit errors, one of which increments a word, one of which decrements another word by the same amount, will go undetected. The reason for using an algorithm like this in spite of its relatively weak protection against errors (compared to a CRC, for example) is simple: This algorithm is much easier to implement in software. Experience in the ARPANET suggested that a checksum of this form was adequate. One reason it is adequate is that this checksum is the last line of defense in an end-to-end protocol; the majority of errors are picked up by stronger error detection algorithms, such as CRCs, at the link level.

2.4.3   Cyclic Redundancy Check

It should be clear by now that a major goal in designing error detection algorithms is to maximize the probability of detecting errors using only a small number of redundant bits. Cyclic redundancy checks use some fairly powerful mathematics to achieve this goal. For example, a 32-bit CRC gives strong protection against common bit errors in messages that are thousands of bytes long. The theoretical foundation of the cyclic redundancy check is rooted in a branch of mathematics called finite fields. While this may sound daunting, the basic ideas can be easily understood.

Simple Probability Calculations

When dealing with network errors and other unlikely (we hope) events, we often have use for simple back-of-the-envelope probability estimates. A useful approximation here is that if two independent events have *small* probabilities p and q, then the probability of either event is $p + q$; the exact answer is $1 - (1 - p)(1 - q) = p + q - pq$. For $p = q = .01$, this estimate is .02, while the exact value is .0199.

For a simple application of this, suppose that the per-bit error rate on a link is 1 in 10^7. Assuming bit errors are all independent (which they aren't), we can estimate that the probability of one error in a 10,000-bit packet is $10^4 / 10^7 = 10^{-3}$. The exact answer, computed as $1 - P(\text{no errors})$, would be $1 - (1 - 10^{-7})^{10,000} = .00099950$.

For a slightly more complex application, we compute the probability of two errors in such a packet; this is the probability of

To start, think of an $(n + 1)$-bit message as being represented by an n degree polynomial, that is, a polynomial whose highest-order term is x^n. The message is represented by a polynomial by using the value of each bit in the message as the coefficient for each term in the polynomial, starting with the most significant bit to represent the highest-order term. For example, an 8-bit message consisting of the bits 10011010 corresponds to the polynomial

$$M(x) = 1 \times x^7 + 0 \times x^6 + 0 \times x^5 + 1 \times x^4$$
$$+ 1 \times x^3 + 0 \times x^2 + 1 \times x^1$$
$$+ 0 \times x^0$$
$$= x^7 + x^4 + x^3 + x^1$$

We can thus think of a sender and a receiver as exchanging polynomials with each other.

For the purposes of calculating a CRC, a sender and receiver have to agree on a *divisor* polynomial, $C(x)$. $C(x)$ is a polynomial of degree k. For example, suppose $C(x) = x^3 + x^2 + 1$. In this case, $k = 3$. The answer to the question "Where did $C(x)$ come from?" is, in most practical cases, "You look it up in a book." In fact, the choice of $C(x)$ has a significant impact on what types of errors can be reliably detected, as we discuss below. There are a handful of divisor polynomials that are very good choices for various environments, and the exact choice is normally made as part of protocol design. For example, the Ethernet standard uses a well-known polynomial of degree 32.

When a sender wishes to transmit a message $M(x)$ that is $n + 1$ bits long, what is actually sent is the $(n + 1)$-bit message

an error that would sneak past a 1-parity-bit checksum. Let E_{ij} be the event that bits i and j are bad, for $0 \leq i < j < 10^4$; the probability of this event is about $p = 10^{-7} \times 10^{-7} = 10^{-14}$. For a fixed j, the number of events E_{ij} with $i < j$ is j; adding up the number of these events for all $j < 10^4$, we get $1 + 2 + \ldots + (10^4 - 1) \approx \frac{1}{2}10^8$. The final probability is thus $\frac{1}{2}10^8 \times 10^{-14} = \frac{1}{2}10^{-6}$.

Note that had we attempted to estimate P(two errors) = P(first error) $\times$ P(second error), and taken these last two to be P(one error) = 10^{-3}, we would have obtained 10^{-6} here, which is rather far off; the problem with this approach is that not all i are equally likely to be the position of the first error. Or, looked at another way, we have overstated the true probability by a factor of two because we counted errors at positions (i, j) and (j, i) separately when they should only be counted once.

plus k bits. We call the complete transmitted message, including the redundant bits, $P(x)$. What we are going to do is contrive to make the polynomial representing $P(x)$

exactly divisible by $C(x)$; we explain how this is achieved below. If $P(x)$ is transmitted over a link and there are no errors introduced during transmission, then the receiver should be able to divide $P(x)$ by $C(x)$ exactly, leaving a remainder of zero. On the other hand, if some error is introduced into $P(x)$ during transmission, then in all likelihood the received polynomial will no longer be exactly divisible by $C(x)$, and thus the receiver will obtain a nonzero remainder implying that an error has occurred.

It will help to understand the following if you know a little about polynomial arithmetic; it is just slightly different from normal integer arithmetic. We are dealing with a special class of polynomial arithmetic here, where coefficients may be only one or zero, and operations on the coefficients are performed using modulo 2 arithmetic. This is referred to as "polynomial arithmetic modulo 2." Since this is a networking book, not a mathematics text, let's focus on the key properties of this type of arithmetic for our purposes (which we ask you to accept on faith):

- Any polynomial $B(x)$ can be divided by a divisor polynomial $C(x)$ if $B(x)$ is of higher degree than $C(x)$.

- Any polynomial $B(x)$ can be divided once by a divisor polynomial $C(x)$ if $B(x)$ is of the same degree as $C(x)$.

- The remainder obtained when $B(x)$ is divided by $C(x)$ is obtained by subtracting $C(x)$ from $B(x)$.

- To subtract $C(x)$ from $B(x)$, we simply perform the exclusive-OR (XOR) operation on each pair of matching coefficients.

For example, the polynomial $x^3 + 1$ can be divided by $x^3 + x^2 + 1$ (because they are both of degree 3) and the remainder would be $0 \times x^3 + 1 \times x^2 + 0 \times x^1 + 0 \times x^0 = x^2$ (obtained by XORing the coefficients of each term). In terms of messages, we could say that 1001 can be divided by 1101 and leaves a remainder of 0100. You should be able to see that the remainder is just the bitwise exclusive-OR of the two messages.

Now that we know the basic rules for dividing polynomials, we are able to do long division, which is necessary to deal with longer messages. An example appears below.

Recall that we wanted to create a polynomial for transmission that is derived from the original message $M(x)$, is k bits longer than $M(x)$, and is exactly divisible by $C(x)$. We can do this in the following way:

1 Multiply $M(x)$ by x^k; that is, add k zeroes at the end of the message. Call this zero-extended message $T(x)$.

2 Divide $T(x)$ by $C(x)$ and find the remainder.

3 Subtract the remainder from $T(x)$.

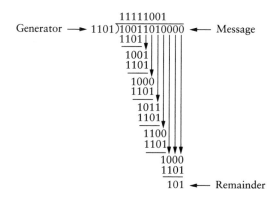

Figure 2.17 CRC calculation using polynomial long division.

It should be obvious that what is left at this point is a message that is exactly divisible by $C(x)$. We may also note that the resulting message consists of $M(x)$ followed by the remainder obtained in step 2, because when we subtracted the remainder (which can be no more than k bits long), we were just XORing it with the k zeroes added in step 1. This part will become clearer with an example.

Consider the message $x^7 + x^4 + x^3 + x^1$, or 10011010. We begin by multiplying by x^3, since our divisor polynomial is of degree 3. This gives 10011010000. We divide this by $C(x)$, which corresponds to 1101 in this case. Figure 2.17 shows the polynomial long division operation. Given the rules of polynomial arithmetic described above, the long division operation proceeds much as it would if we were dividing integers. Thus in the first step of our example, we see that the divisor 1101 divides once into the first four bits of the message (1001), since they are of the same degree, and leaves a remainder of 100 (1101 XOR 1001). The next step is to bring down a digit from the message polynomial until we get another polynomial with the same degree as $C(x)$, in this case 1001. We calculate the remainder again (100) and continue until the calculation is complete. Note that the "result" of the long division, which appears at the top of the calculation, is not really of much interest—it is the remainder at the end that matters.

You can see from the very bottom of Figure 2.17 that the remainder of the example calculation is 101. So we know that 10011010000 minus 101 would be exactly divisible by $C(x)$, and this is what we send. The minus operation in polynomial arithmetic is the logical XOR operation, so we actually send 10011010101. As noted above, this turns out to be just the original message with the remainder from the long division calculation appended to it. The recipient divides the received polynomial by $C(x)$ and, if the result is 0, concludes that there were no errors. If the result is nonzero, it may be necessary to discard the errored message; with some codes, it may be possible to *correct* a small error (e.g., if the error affected only one bit). A code that enables error correction is called an *error-correcting code* (ECC).

Now we will consider the question of where the polynomial $C(x)$ comes from. Intuitively, the idea is to select this polynomial so that it is very unlikely to divide evenly into a message that has errors introduced into it. If the transmitted message is $P(x)$, we may think of the introduction of errors as the addition of another polynomial $E(x)$, so the recipient sees $P(x) + E(x)$. The only way that an error could slip by undetected would be if the received message could be evenly divided by $C(x)$, and since we know that $P(x)$ can be evenly divided by $C(x)$, this could only happen if $E(x)$ can be divided evenly by $C(x)$. The trick is to pick $C(x)$ so that this is very unlikely for common types of errors.

One common type of error is a single-bit error, which can be expressed as $E(x) = x^i$ when it affects bit position i. If we select $C(x)$ such that the first and the last term are nonzero, then we already have a two-term polynomial that cannot divide evenly into the one term $E(x)$. Such a $C(x)$ can, therefore, detect all single-bit errors. In general, it is possible to prove that the following types of errors can be detected by a $C(x)$ with the stated properties:

> **Error Detection or Error Correction?**
>
> We have mentioned that it is possible to use codes that not only detect the presence of errors but also enable errors to be corrected. Since the details of such codes require yet more complex mathematics than that required to understand CRCs, we will not dwell on them here. However, it is worth considering the merits of correction versus detection.
>
> At first glance, it would seem that correction is always better, since with detection we are forced to throw away the message and, in general, ask for another copy to be transmitted. This uses up bandwidth and may introduce latency while waiting for the retransmission. However, there is a downside to correction: it generally requires a greater number of redundant bits to send an error-correcting code that is as strong (that is, able to

- All single-bit errors, as long as the x^k and x^0 terms have nonzero coefficients.

- All double-bit errors, as long as $C(x)$ has a factor with at least three terms.

- Any odd number of errors, as long as $C(x)$ contains the factor $(x + 1)$.

- Any "burst" error (i.e., sequence of consecutive errored bits) for which the length of the burst is less than k bits. (Most burst errors of larger than k bits can also be detected.)

Six versions of $C(x)$ are widely used in link-level protocols (shown in Table 2.6). For example, the Ethernet and 802.5 networks described later in this chapter use CRC-32, while HDLC uses CRC-CCITT. ATM, as described in Chapter 3, uses CRC-8, CRC-10, and CRC-32.

Finally, we note that the CRC algorithm, while seemingly complex, is easily implemented in hardware using a k-bit shift register and XOR gates. The number of bits in the shift register equals the degree of the generator polynomial (k). Figure 2.18 shows the hardware that would be used for the generator $x^3 + x^2 + 1$ from our previous example. The message is shifted in from the left, beginning with the most significant bit and ending with the string of k zeroes that is attached to the message, just as in the long division example. When all the bits have been shifted in and appropriately XORed, the register contains the remainder, that is, the CRC (most significant bit on the right). The position of the XOR gates is determined as follows: If the bits in the shift register are labelled 0 through $k - 1$, left to right, then put a shift register in front of bit n if there is a term x^n in the generator polynomial. Thus, we see an XOR gate in front of positions 0 and 2 for the generator $x^3 + x^2 + x^0$.

cope with the same range of errors) as a code that only detects errors. Thus, while error detection requires more bits to be sent when errors occur, error correction requires more bits to be sent *all the time*. As a result, error correction tends to be most useful when (1) errors are quite probable, as they may be, for example, in a wireless environment, or (2) the cost of retransmission is too high, for example, because of the latency involved retransmitting a packet over a satellite link.

The use of error-correcting codes in networking is sometimes referred to as *forward error correction* (FEC) because the correction of errors is handled "in advance" by sending extra information, rather than waiting for errors to happen and dealing with them later by retransmission.

2.5 Reliable Transmission

As we saw in the previous section, frames are sometimes corrupted while in transit, with an error code like CRC used to detect such errors. While some error codes are strong enough also to correct errors, in practice the state of the art in error-correcting codes is not advanced enough to handle the range of bit and burst errors that can be introduced on a network link without introducing excessive overhead. As a result, corrupt frames generally must be discarded. A link-level protocol that wants to deliver frames reliably must somehow recover from these discarded (lost) frames.

CRC	$C(x)$
CRC-8	$x^8 + x^2 + x^1 + 1$
CRC-10	$x^{10} + x^9 + x^5 + x^4 + x^1 + 1$
CRC-12	$x^{12} + x^{11} + x^3 + x^2 + 1$
CRC-16	$x^{16} + x^{15} + x^2 + 1$
CRC-CCITT	$x^{16} + x^{12} + x^5 + 1$
CRC-32	$x^{32} + x^{26} + x^{23} + x^{22} + x^{16} + x^{12} + x^{11}$ $+ x^{10} + x^8 + x^7 + x^5 + x^4 + x^2 + x + 1$

Table 2.6   Common CRC polynomials.

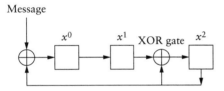

Figure 2.18   CRC calculation using shift register.

This is usually accomplished using a combination of two fundamental mechanisms—*acknowledgments* and *timeouts*. An acknowledgment (ACK for short) is a small control frame that a protocol sends back to its peer saying that it has received an earlier frame. By control frame we mean a header without any data, although a protocol can *piggyback* an ACK on a data frame it just happens to be sending in the opposite direction. The receipt of an acknowledgment indicates to the sender of the original frame that its frame was successfully delivered. If the sender does not receive an acknowledgment after a reasonable amount of time, then it *retransmits* the original frame. This action of waiting a reasonable amount of time is called a *timeout*.

The general strategy of using acknowledgments and timeouts to implement reliable delivery is sometimes called *automatic repeat request* (normally abbreviated ARQ). This section describes three different ARQ algorithms using generic language; that is, we do not give detailed information about a particular protocol's header fields.

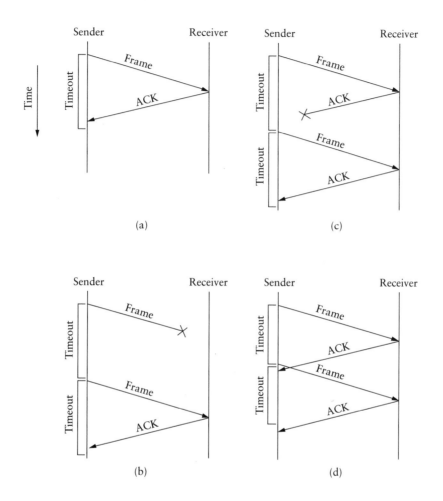

Figure 2.19 Timeline showing four different scenarios for the stop-and-wait algorithm. (a) The ACK is received before the timer expires; (b) the original frame is lost; (c) the ACK is lost; (d) the timeout fires too soon.

2.5.1 Stop-and-Wait

The simplest ARQ scheme is the *stop-and-wait* algorithm. The idea of stop-and-wait is straightforward: After transmitting one frame, the sender waits for an acknowledgment before transmitting the next frame. If the acknowledgment does not arrive after a certain period of time, the sender times out and retransmits the original frame.

Figure 2.19 illustrates four different scenarios that result from this basic algorithm. This figure is a timeline, a common way to depict a protocol's behavior. The sending side is represented on the left, the receiving side is depicted on the right, and

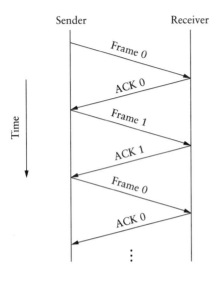

Figure 2.20   Timeline for stop-and-wait with 1-bit sequence number.

time flows from top to bottom. Figure 2.19(a) shows the situation in which the ACK is received before the timer expires, (b) and (c) show the situation in which the original frame and the ACK, respectively, are lost, and (d) shows the situation in which the timeout fires too soon. Recall that by "lost" we mean that the frame was corrupted while in transit, that this corruption was detected by an error code on the receiver, and that the frame was subsequently discarded.

There is one important subtlety in the stop-and-wait algorithm. Suppose the sender sends a frame and the receiver acknowledges it, but the acknowledgment is either lost or delayed in arriving. This situation is illustrated in timelines (c) and (d) of Figure 2.19. In both cases, the sender times out and retransmits the original frame, but the receiver will think that it is the next frame, since it correctly received and acknowledged the first frame. This has the potential to cause duplicate copies of a frame to be delivered. To address this problem, the header for a stop-and-wait protocol usually includes a 1-bit sequence number—that is, the sequence number can take on the values 0 and 1—and the sequence numbers used for each frame alternate, as illustrated in Figure 2.20. Thus, when the sender retransmits frame 0, the receiver can determine that it is seeing a second copy of frame 0 rather than the first copy of frame 1 and therefore can ignore it (the receiver still acknowledges it).

The main shortcoming of the stop-and-wait algorithm is that it allows the sender to have only one outstanding frame on the link at a time, and this may be far below

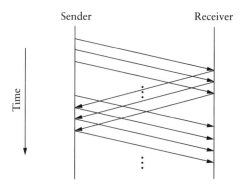

Figure 2.21 Timeline for the sliding window algorithm.

the link's capacity. Consider, for example, a 1.5-Mbps link with a 45-ms round-trip time. This link has a delay × bandwidth product of 67.5 Kb, or approximately 8 KB. Since the sender can send only one frame per RTT, and assuming a frame size of 1 KB, this implies a maximum sending rate of

$$\text{BitsPerFrame} \div \text{TimePerFrame}$$
$$= 1024 \times 8 \div 0.045$$
$$= 182 \text{ Kbps}$$

or about one-eighth of the link's capacity. To use the link fully, then, we'd like the sender to be able to transmit up to eight frames before having to wait for an acknowledgment.

The significance of the bandwidth × delay product is that it represents the amount of data that could be in transit. We would like to be able to send this much data without waiting for the first acknowledgment. The principle at work here is often referred to as *keeping the pipe full*. The algorithms presented in the following two subsections do exactly this.

2.5.2 Sliding Window

Consider again the scenario in which the link has a delay × bandwidth product of 8 KB and frames are of 1-KB size. We would like the sender to be ready to transmit the ninth frame at pretty much the same moment that the ACK for the first frame arrives. The algorithm that allows us to do this is called *sliding window*, and an illustrative timeline is given in Figure 2.21.

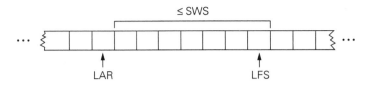

Figure 2.22 Sliding window on sender.

The Sliding Window Algorithm

The sliding window algorithm works as follows. First, the sender assigns a *sequence number*, denoted SeqNum, to each frame. For now, let's ignore the fact that SeqNum is implemented by a finite-size header field and instead assume that it can grow infinitely large. The sender maintains three variables: The *send window size*, denoted SWS, gives the upper bound on the number of outstanding (unacknowledged) frames that the sender can transmit; LAR denotes the sequence number of the *last acknowledgment received*; and LFS denotes the sequence number of the *last frame sent*. The sender also maintains the following invariant:

$$\text{LFS} - \text{LAR} \leq \text{SWS}$$

This situation is illustrated in Figure 2.22.

When an acknowledgment arrives, the sender moves LAR to the right, thereby allowing the sender to transmit another frame. Also, the sender associates a timer with each frame it transmits, and it retransmits the frame should the timer expire before an ACK is received. Notice that the sender has to be willing to buffer up to SWS frames since it must be prepared to retransmit them until they are acknowledged.

The receiver maintains the following three variables: The *receive window size*, denoted RWS, gives the upper bound on the number of out-of-order frames that the receiver is willing to accept; LAF denotes the sequence number of the *largest acceptable frame*; and LFR denotes the sequence number of the *last frame received*. The receiver also maintains the following invariant:

$$\text{LAF} - \text{LFR} \leq \text{RWS}$$

This situation is illustrated in Figure 2.23.

When a frame with sequence number SeqNum arrives, the receiver takes the following action. If SeqNum $\leq$ LFR or SeqNum $>$ LAF, then the frame is outside the receiver's window and it is discarded. If LFR $<$ SeqNum $\leq$ LAF, then the frame is within the receiver's window and it is accepted. Now the receiver needs to decide

Figure 2.23 Sliding window on receiver.

whether or not to send an ACK. Let SeqNumToAck denote the largest sequence number not yet acknowledged, such that all frames with sequence numbers less than or equal to SeqNumToAck have been received. The receiver acknowledges the receipt of SeqNumToAck, even if higher-numbered packets have been received. This acknowledgment is said to be cumulative. It then sets LFR = SeqNumToAck and adjusts LAF = LFR + RWS.

For example, suppose LFR = 5 (i.e., the last ACK the receiver sent was for sequence number 5), and RWS = 4. This implies that LAF = 9. Should frames 7 and 8 arrive, they will be buffered because they are within the receiver's window. However, no ACK needs to be sent since frame 6 is yet to arrive. Frames 7 and 8 are said to have arrived out of order. (Technically, the receiver could resend an ACK for frame 5 when frames 7 and 8 arrive.) Should frame 6 then arrive—perhaps it is late because it was lost the first time and had to be retransmitted, or perhaps it was simply delayed—the receiver acknowledges frame 8, bumps LFR to 8, and sets LAF to 12. If frame 6 was in fact lost, then a timeout will have occurred at the sender, causing it to retransmit frame 6.

We observe that when a timeout occurs, the amount of data in transit decreases, since the sender is unable to advance its window until frame 6 is acknowledged. This means that when packet losses occur, this scheme is no longer keeping the pipe full. The longer it takes to notice that a packet loss has occurred, the more severe this problem becomes.

Notice that in this example, the receiver could have sent a *negative acknowledgment* (NAK) for frame 6 as soon as frame 7 arrived. However, this is unnecessary since the sender's timeout mechanism is sufficient to catch this situation, and sending NAKs adds additional complexity to the receiver. Also, as we mentioned, it would have been legitimate to send additional acknowledgments of frame 5 when frames 7 and 8 arrived; in some cases, a sender can use duplicate ACKs as a clue that a frame was lost. Both approaches help to improve performance by allowing early detection of packet losses.

Yet another variation on this scheme would be to use *selective acknowledgments*. That is, the receiver could acknowledge exactly those frames it has received, rather than just the highest-numbered frame received in order. So, in the above example, the receiver could acknowledge the receipt of frames 7 and 8. Giving more information to the sender makes it potentially easier for the sender to keep the pipe full, but adds complexity to the implementation.

The sending window size is selected according to how many frames we want to have outstanding on the link at a given time; SWS is easy to compute for a given delay × bandwidth product.[1] On the other hand, the receiver can set RWS to whatever it wants. Two common settings are RWS = 1, which implies that the receiver will not buffer any frames that arrive out of order, and RWS = SWS, which implies that the receiver can buffer any of the frames the sender transmits. It makes no sense to set RWS > SWS since it's impossible for more than SWS frames to arrive out of order.

Finite Sequence Numbers and Sliding Window

We now return to the one simplification we introduced into the algorithm—our assumption that sequence numbers can grow infinitely large. In practice, of course, a frame's sequence number is specified in a header field of some finite size. For example, a 3-bit field means that there are eight possible sequence numbers, 0 . . . 7. This makes it necessary to reuse sequence numbers or, stated another way, sequence numbers wrap around. This introduces the problem of being able to distinguish between different incarnations of the same sequence numbers, which implies that the number of possible sequence numbers must be larger than the number of outstanding frames allowed. For example, stop-and-wait allowed one outstanding frame at a time and had two distinct sequence numbers.

Suppose we have one more number in our space of sequence numbers than we have potentially outstanding frames; that is, SWS $\leq$ MaxSeqNum − 1, where MaxSeqNum is the number of available sequence numbers. Is this sufficient? The answer depends on RWR. If RWS = 1, then MaxSeqNum $\geq$ SWS + 1 is sufficient. If RWS is equal to SWS, then having a MaxSeqNum just one greater than the sending window size is not good enough. To see this, consider the situation in which we have the eight sequence numbers 0 through 7, and SWS = RWS = 7. Suppose the sender transmits frames 0..6, they are successfully received, but the ACKs are lost. The receiver is now expecting frames 7, 0..5, but the sender times out and sends frames 0..6. Unfortunately, the receiver is expecting the second incarnation of frames 0..5, but gets the first incarnation of these frames. This is exactly the situation we wanted to avoid.

---

[1] Easy, that is, if we know the delay and the bandwidth. Sometimes we do not, and estimating them well is a challenge to protocol designers. We discuss this further in Chapter 5.

It turns out that the sending window size can be no more than half as big as the number of available sequence numbers when RWS = SWS, or stated more precisely,

$$SWS \leq (MaxSeqNum + 1)/2$$

Intuitively, what this is saying is that the sliding window protocol alternates between the two halves of the sequence number space, just as stop-and-wait alternates between sequence numbers 0 and 1. The only difference is that it continually slides between the two halves rather than discretely alternating between them.

Note that this rule is specific to the situation where RWS = SWS. We leave it as an exercise to determine the more general rule that works for arbitrary values of RWS and SWS. Also note that the relationship between the window size and the sequence number space depends on an assumption that is so obvious that it is easy to overlook, namely, that frames are not reordered in transit. This cannot happen on a direct point-to-point link since there is no way for one frame to overtake another during transmission. However, we will see the sliding window algorithm used in a different environment in Chapter 5, and we will need to devise another rule.

Implementation of Sliding Window

The following routines illustrate how we might implement the sending and receiving sides of the sliding window algorithm. The routines are taken from a working protocol named, appropriately enough, Sliding Window Protocol (SWP). So as not to concern ourselves with the adjacent protocols in the protocol graph, we denote the protocol sitting above SWP as HLP (high-level protocol) and the protocol sitting below SWP as LINK (link-level protocol).

We start by defining a pair of data structures. First, the frame header is very simple: It contains a sequence number (SeqNum) and an acknowledgment number (AckNum). It also contains a Flags field that indicates whether the frame is an ACK or carries data.

```
typedef u_char   SwpSeqno;

typedef struct {
    SwpSeqno   SeqNum;    /* sequence number of this frame */
    SwpSeqno   AckNum;    /* ack of received frame */
    u_char     Flags;     /* up to 8 bits worth of flags */
} SwpHdr;
```

Next, the state of the sliding window algorithm has the following structure. For the sending side of the protocol, this state includes variables LAR and LFS, as described earlier in this section, as well as a queue that holds frames that have been transmitted but not yet acknowledged (sendQ). The sending state also includes a *counting semaphore* called sendWindowNotFull. We will see how this is used below, but generally a semaphore is a synchronization primitive that supports semWait and semSignal operations. Every invocation of semSignal increments the semaphore by 1, and every invocation of semWait decrements s by 1, with the calling process blocked (suspended) should decrementing the semaphore cause its value to become less than 0. A process that is blocked during its call to semWait will be allowed to resume as soon as enough semSignal operations have been performed to raise the value of the semaphore above 0.

For the receiving side of the protocol, the state includes the variable NFE, as described earlier in this section, plus a queue that holds frames that have been received out of order (recvQ). Finally, although not shown, the sender and receiver sliding window sizes are defined by constants SWS and RWS, respectively.

```
typedef struct {
    /* sender side state: */
    SwpSeqno    LAR;        /* seqno of last ACK received */
    SwpSeqno    LFS;        /* last frame sent */
    Semaphore   sendWindowNotFull;
    SwpHdr      hdr;        /* pre-initialized header */
    struct sendQ_slot {
        Event   timeout;   /* event associated with send-timeout */
        Msg     msg;
    } sendQ[SWS];

    /* receiver side state: */
    SwpSeqno    NFE;        /* seqno of next frame expected */
    struct recvQ_slot {
        int     received;  /* is msg valid? */
        Msg     msg;
    } recvQ[RWS];
} SwpState;
```

The sending side of SWP is implemented by procedure sendSWP. This routine is rather simple. First, semWait causes this process to block on a semaphore until it is OK to send another frame. Once allowed to proceed, sendSWP sets the sequence number in the frame's header, saves a copy of the frame in the transmit queue (sendQ), schedules a timeout event to handle the case in which the frame is not acknowledged, and sends the frame to the next-lower-level protocol, which we denote as LINK.

One detail worth noting is the call to store_swp_hdr just before the call to msgAddHdr. This routine translates the C structure that holds the SWP header (state->hdr) into a byte string that can be safely attached to the front of the message (hbuf). This routine (not shown) must translate each integer field in the header into network byte order and remove any padding that the compiler has added to the C structure. The issue of byte order is discussed more fully in Section 7.1, but for now it is enough to assume that this routine places the most significant bit of a multiword integer in the byte with the highest address.

Another piece of complexity in this routine is the use of semWait and the sendWindowNotFull semaphore. sendWindowNotFull is initialized to the size of the sender's sliding window, SWS (this initialization is not shown). Each time the sender transmits a frame, the semWait operation decrements this count and blocks the sender should the count go to 0. Each time an ACK is received, the semSignal operation invoked in deliverSWP (see below) increments this count, thus unblocking any waiting sender.

```
static int
sendSWP(SwpState *state, Msg *frame)
{
    struct sendQ_slot *slot;
    hbuf[HLEN];

    /* wait for send window to open */
    semWait(&state->sendWindowNotFull);
    state->hdr.SeqNum = ++state->LFS;
    slot = &state->sendQ[state->hdr.SeqNum % SWS];
    store_swp_hdr(state->hdr, hbuf);
    msgAddHdr(frame, hbuf, HLEN);
    msgSaveCopy(&slot->msg, frame);
    slot->timeout = evSchedule(swpTimeout, slot,
        SWP_SEND_TIMEOUT);
    return send(LINK, frame);
}
```

Before continuing to the receive side of SWP, we need to reconcile a seeming inconsistency. On the one hand, we have been saying that a high-level protocol invokes the services of a low-level protocol by calling the send operation, so we would expect that a protocol that wants to send a message via SWP would call send(SWP, packet). On the other hand, the procedure that implements SWP's send operation is called sendSWP, and its first argument is a state variable (SwpState). What gives? The answer is that the operating system provides glue code that translates the generic call to send into a protocol-specific call to sendSWP. This glue code maps the first argument to send (the magic protocol variable SWP) into both a function pointer to sendSWP, and a pointer to the protocol state that SWP needs to do its job. The reason we have the high-level protocol indirectly invoke the protocol-specific function through the generic function call is that we want to limit how much information the high-level protocol has coded in it about the low-level protocol. This makes it easier to change the protocol graph configuration at some time in the future.

Now to SWP's protocol-specific implementation of the deliver operation, which is given in procedure deliverSWP. This routine actually handles two different kinds of incoming messages: ACKs for frames sent earlier from this node and data frames arriving at this node. In a sense, the ACK half of this routine is the counterpart to the sender side of the algorithm given in sendSWP. A decision as to whether the incoming message is an ACK or a data frame is made by checking the Flags field in the header. Note that this particular implementation does not support piggybacking ACKs on data frames.

When the incoming frame is an ACK, deliverSWP simply finds the slot in the transmit queue (sendQ) that corresponds to the ACK, cancels the timeout event, and frees the frame saved in that slot. This work is actually done in a loop since the ACK may be cumulative. The only other thing to notice about this case is the call to subroutine swpInWindow. This subroutine, which is given below, ensures that the sequence number for the frame being acknowledged is within the range of ACKs that the sender currently expects to receive.

When the incoming frame contains data, deliverSWP first calls msgStripHdr and load_swp_hdr to extract the header from the frame. Routine load_swp_hdr is the counterpart to store_swp_hdr discussed earlier; it translates a byte string into the C data structure that holds the SWP header. deliverSWP then calls swpInWindow to make sure the sequence number of the frame is within the range of sequence numbers that it expects. If it is, the routine loops over the set of consecutive frames it has received and passes them up to the higher-level protocol by invoking the deliverHLP routine. It also sends a cumulative ACK back to the sender, but does so by looping over the receive queue (it does not use the SeqNumToAck variable used in the prose description given earlier in this section).

```
static int
deliverSWP(SwpState state, Msg *frame)
{
```

```
SwpHdr   hdr;
char     *hbuf;

hbuf = msgStripHdr(frame, HLEN);
load_swp_hdr(&hdr, hbuf)
if (hdr->Flags & FLAG_ACK_VALID)
{
    /* received an acknowledgment---do SENDER side */
    if (swpInWindow(hdr.AckNum, state->LAR + 1,
        state->LFS))
    {
        do
        {
            struct sendQ_slot *slot;

            slot = &state->sendQ[++state->LAR % SWS];
            evCancel(slot->timeout);
            msgDestroy(&slot->msg);
            semSignal(&state->sendWindowNotFull);
        } while (state->LAR != hdr.AckNum);
    }
}

if (hdr.Flags & FLAG_HAS_DATA)
{
    struct recvQ_slot *slot;

    /* received data packet---do RECEIVER side */
    slot = &state->recvQ[hdr.SeqNum % RWS];
    if (!swpInWindow(hdr.SeqNum, state->NFE,
        state->NFE + RWS - 1))
    {
        /* drop the message */
        return SUCCESS;
    }
    msgSaveCopy(&slot->msg, frame);
    slot->received = TRUE;
    if (hdr.SeqNum == state->NFE)
    {
        Msg m;
```

```
        while (slot->received)
        {
            deliver(HLP, &slot->msg);
            msgDestroy(&slot->msg);
            slot->received = FALSE;
            slot = &state->recvQ[++state->NFE % RWS];
        }
        /* send ACK: */
        prepare_ack(&m, state->NFE - 1);
        send(LINK, &m);
        msgDestroy(&m);
    }
}
return SUCCESS;
}
```

Finally, **swpInWindow** is a simple subroutine that checks to see if a given sequence number falls between some minimum and maximum sequence number.

```
static bool
swpInWindow(SwpSeqno seqno, SwpSeqno min, SwpSeqno max)
{
    SwpSeqno pos, maxpos;

    pos    = seqno - min;       /* pos *should* be in range [0..MAX) */
    maxpos = max - min + 1;     /* maxpos is in range [0..MAX] */
    return pos < maxpos;
}
```

Frame Order and Flow Control

The sliding window protocol is perhaps the best-known algorithm in computer networking. What is easily confusing about the algorithm, however, is that it can be used to serve three different roles. The first role is the one we have been concentrating on in this section—to reliably deliver frames across an unreliable link. (In general, the algorithm can be used to reliably deliver messages across an unreliable network.) This is the core function of the algorithm.

The second role that the sliding window algorithm can serve is to preserve the order in which frames are transmitted. This is easy to do at the receiver—since each frame has a sequence number, the receiver just makes sure that it does not pass a frame up to the next-higher-level protocol until it has already passed up all frames with a smaller sequence number. That is, the receiver buffers (i.e., does not pass along) out-of-order frames. The version of the sliding window algorithm described in this section does preserve frame order, although we could imagine a variation in which the receiver passes frames to the next protocol without waiting for all earlier frames to be delivered. A question we should ask ourselves is whether we really need the sliding window protocol to keep the frames in order, or whether, instead, this is unnecessary functionality at the link level. Unfortunately, we have not yet seen enough of the network architecture to answer this question; we first need to understand how a sequence of point-to-point links is connected by switches to form an end-to-end path.

The third role that the sliding window algorithm sometimes plays is to support *flow control*—a feedback mechanism by which the receiver is able to throttle the sender. Such a mechanism is used to keep the sender from overrunning the receiver, that is, from transmitting more data than the receiver is able to process. This is usually accomplished by augmenting the sliding window protocol so that the receiver not only acknowledges frames it has received, but also informs the sender of how many frames it has room to receive. The number of frames that the receiver is capable of receiving corresponds to how much free buffer space it has. As in the case of ordered delivery, we need to make sure that flow control is necessary at the link level before incorporating it into the sliding window protocol.

One important concept to take away from this discussion is the system design principle we call *separation of concerns*. That is, you must be careful to distinguish between different functions that are sometimes rolled together in one mechanism, and you must make sure that each function is necessary and being supported in the most effective way. In this particular case, reliable delivery, ordered delivery, and flow control are sometimes combined in a single sliding window protocol, and we should ask ourselves if this is the right thing to do at the link level. With this question in mind, we revisit the sliding window algorithm in Chapter 3 (we show how X.25 networks use it to implement hop-by-hop flow control) and in Chapter 5 (we describe how TCP uses it to implement a reliable byte-stream channel).

2.5.3 Concurrent Logical Channels

The data link protocol used in the ARPANET provides an interesting alternative to the sliding window protocol, in that it is able to keep the pipe full while still using the simple stop-and-wait algorithm. One important consequence of this approach is that the frames sent over a given link are not kept in any particular order. The protocol also implies nothing about flow control.

The idea underlying the ARPANET protocol, which we refer to as *concurrent logical channels*, is to multiplex several logical channels onto a single point-to-point link and to run the stop-and-wait algorithm on each of these logical channels. There is no relationship maintained among the frames sent on any of the logical channels, yet because a different frame can be outstanding on each of the several logical channels, the sender can keep the link full.

More precisely, the sender keeps 3 bits of state for each channel: a boolean, saying whether the channel is currently busy; the 1-bit sequence number to use the next time a frame is sent on this logical channel; and the next sequence number to expect on a frame that arrives on this channel. When the node has a frame to send, it uses the lowest idle channel, and otherwise it behaves just like stop-and-wait.

In practice, the ARPANET supported 8 logical channels over each ground link and 16 over each satellite link. In the ground-link case, the header for each frame included a 3-bit channel number and a 1-bit sequence number, for a total of 4 bits. This is exactly the number of bits the sliding window protocol requires to support up to eight outstanding frames on the link when RWS = SWS.

2.6 Ethernet (802.3)

The Ethernet is easily the most successful local area networking technology of the last 20 years. Developed in the mid-1970s by researchers at the Xerox Palo Alto Research Center (PARC), the Ethernet is a working example of the more general Carrier Sense, Multiple Access with Collision Detect (CSMA/CD) local area network technology.

As indicated by the CSMA name, the Ethernet is a multiple-access network, meaning that a set of nodes send and receive frames over a shared link. You can, therefore, think of an Ethernet as being like a bus that has multiple stations plugged into it. The "carrier sense" in CSMA/CD means that all the nodes can distinguish between an idle and a busy link, and "collision detect" means that a node listens as it transmits and can therefore detect when a frame it is transmitting has interfered (collided) with a frame transmitted by another node.

The Ethernet has its roots in an early packet radio network, called Aloha, developed at the University of Hawaii to support computer communication across the Hawaiian Islands. Like the Aloha network, the fundamental problem faced by the Ethernet is how to mediate access to a shared medium fairly and efficiently (in Aloha the medium was the atmosphere, while in Ethernet the medium is a coax cable). That is, the core idea in both Aloha and the Ethernet is an algorithm that controls when each node can transmit.

Digital Equipment Corporation and Intel Corporation joined Xerox to define a 10-Mbps Ethernet standard in 1978. This standard then formed the basis for IEEE standard 802.3. With one exception that we will see in Section 2.6.2, it is fair to view the 1978 Ethernet standard as a proper subset of the 802.3 standard; 802.3 additionally defines a much wider collection of physical media over which Ethernet

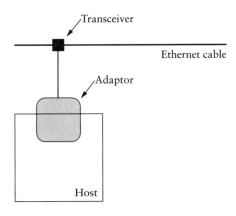

Figure 2.24 Ethernet tranceiver and adaptor.

can operate, and more recently, it has been extended to include a 100-Mbps version called Fast Ethernet, and a 1000-Mbps version called Gigabit Ethernet. The rest of this section focuses on 10-Mbps Ethernet since it is typically used in multiple-access mode, and we are interested in how multiple hosts share a single link. Both 100-Mbps and 1000-Mbps Ethernets are designed to be used in full-duplex, point-to-point configurations, which means that they are typically used in switched networks, as described in the next chapter.

2.6.1 Physical Properties

An Ethernet segment is implemented on a coaxial cable of up to 500 m. This cable is similar to the type used for cable TV, except that it typically has an impedance of 50 ohms instead of cable TV's 75 ohms. Hosts connect to an Ethernet segment by tapping into it; taps must be at least 2.5 m apart. A *transceiver*—a small device directly attached to the tap—detects when the line is idle and drives the signal when the host is transmitting. It also receives incoming signals. The transceiver is, in turn, connected to an Ethernet adaptor, which is plugged into the host. All the logic that makes up the Ethernet protocol, as described in this section, is implemented in the adaptor (not the transceiver). This configuration is shown in Figure 2.24.

Multiple Ethernet segments can be joined together by *repeaters*. A repeater is a device that forwards digital signals, much like an amplifier forwards analog signals. However, no more than four repeaters may be positioned between any pair of hosts, meaning that an Ethernet has a total reach of only 2500 m. For example, using just two repeaters between any pair of hosts supports a configuration similar to the one illustrated in Figure 2.25, that is, a segment running down the spine of a building with

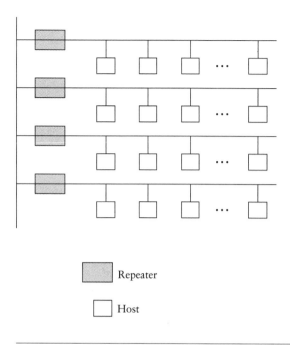

Repeater

Host

Figure 2.25 Ethernet repeater.

a segment on each floor. All told, an Ethernet is limited to supporting a maximum of 1024 hosts.

Any signal placed on the Ethernet by a host is broadcast over the entire network; that is, the signal is propagated in both directions, and repeaters forward the signal on all outgoing segments. Terminators attached to the end of each segment absorb the signal and keep it from bouncing back and interfering with trailing signals. The Ethernet uses the Manchester encoding scheme described in Section 2.2.

In addition to the system of segments and repeaters just described, alternative technologies have been introduced over the years. For example, rather than using a 50-ohm coax cable, an Ethernet can be constructed from a thinner cable known as 10Base2; the original cable is called 10Base5 (the two cables are commonly called *thin-net* and *thick-net*, respectively). The "10" in 10Base2 means that the network operates at 10 Mbps, "Base" refers to the fact that the cable is used in a *baseband* system, and the "2" means that a given segment can be no longer than 200 m (a segment of the original 10Base5 cable can be up to 500 m long). Today an even newer technology is commonly used, called 10BaseT, where the "T" stands for twisted pair. Typically, Category 5 twisted pair wiring is used. A 10BaseT segment is usually limited to under

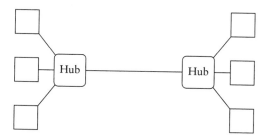

Figure 2.26 Ethernet hub.

100 m in length. (Both 100-Mbps and 1000-Mbps Ethernets also run up over Category 5 twisted pair, up to distances of 100 m.)

Because the cable is so thin, you do not tap into a 10Base2 or 10BaseT cable in the same way as you would with 10Base5 cable. With 10Base2, a T-joint is spliced into the cable. In effect, 10Base2 is used to daisy-chain a set of hosts together. With 10BaseT, the common configuration is to have several point-to-point segments coming out of a multiway repeater, sometimes called a *hub*, as illustrated in Figure 2.26. Multiple 100-Mbps Ethernet segments can also be connected by a hub, but the same is not true of 1000-Mbps segments.

It is important to understand that whether a given Ethernet spans a single segment, a linear sequence of segments connected by repeaters, or multiple segments connected in a star configuration by a hub, data transmitted by any one host on that Ethernet reaches all the other hosts. This is the good news. The bad news is that all these hosts are competing for access to the same link, and as a consequence, they are said to be in the same *collision domain*.

2.6.2 Access Protocol

We now turn our attention to the algorithm that controls access to the shared Ethernet link. This algorithm is commonly called the Ethernet's *media access control* (MAC). It is typically implemented in hardware on the network adaptor. We will not describe the hardware per se, but instead focus on the algorithm it implements. First, however, we describe the Ethernet's frame format and addresses.

Frame Format

Each Ethernet frame is defined by the format given in Figure 2.27. The 64-bit preamble allows the receiver to synchronize with the signal; it is a sequence of alternating 0s and 1s. Both the source and destination hosts are identified with a 48-bit address. The packet type field serves as the demultiplexing key; that is, it identifies to which

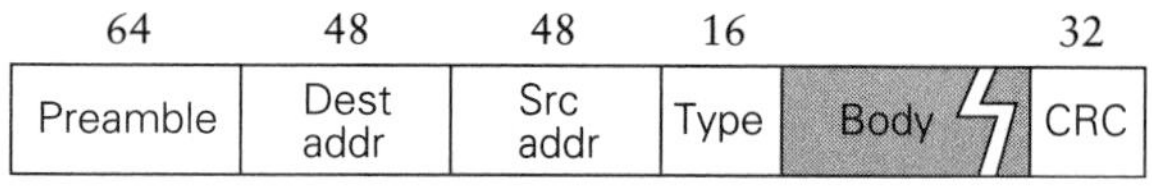

64	48	48	16		32
Preamble	Dest addr	Src addr	Type	Body	CRC

Figure 2.27   Ethernet frame format.

of possibly many higher-level protocols this frame should be delivered. Each frame contains up to 1500 bytes of data. Minimally, a frame must contain at least 46 bytes of data, even if this means the host has to pad the frame before transmitting it. The reason for this minimum frame size is that the frame must be long enough to detect a collision; we discuss this more below. Finally, each frame includes a 32-bit CRC. Like the HDLC protocol described in Section 2.3.2, the Ethernet is a bit-oriented framing protocol. Note that from the host's perspective, an Ethernet frame has a 14-byte header: two 6-byte addresses and a 2-byte type field. The sending adaptor attaches the preamble, CRC, and postamble before transmitting, and the receiving adaptor removes them.

The frame format just described is taken from the Digital-Intel-Xerox Ethernet standard. The 802.3 frame format is exactly the same, except it substitutes a 16-bit length field for the 16-bit type field. 802.3 is usually paired with an encapsulation standard that defines a type field used to demultiplex incoming frames. This type field is the first thing in the data portion of the 802.3 frames; that is, it immediately follows the 802.3 header. Fortunately, since the Ethernet standard has avoided using any type values less than 1500 (the maximum length found in an 802.3 header), and the type and length fields are in the same location in the header, it is possible for a single device to accept both formats, and for the device driver running on the host to interpret the last 16 bits of the header as either a type or a length. In practice, most hosts follow the Digital-Intel-Xerox format and interpret this field as the frame's type.

Addresses

Each host on an Ethernet—in fact, every Ethernet host in the world—has a unique Ethernet address. Technically, the address belongs to the adaptor, not the host; it is usually burned into ROM. Ethernet addresses are typically printed in a form humans can read as a sequence of six numbers separated by colons. Each number corresponds to 1 byte of the 6-byte address and is given by a pair of hexadecimal digits, one for each of the 4-bit nibbles in the byte; leading 0s are dropped. For example, 8:0:2b:e4:b1:2 is the human-readable representation of Ethernet address

```
00001000   00000000   00101011
11100100   10110001   00000010
```

To ensure that every adaptor gets a unique address, each manufacturer of Ethernet devices is allocated a different prefix that must be prepended to the address on every adaptor they build. For example, Advanced Micro Devices has been assigned the 24-bit prefix x080020 (or 8:0:20). A given manufacturer then makes sure the address suffixes it produces are unique.

Each frame transmitted on an Ethernet is received by every adaptor connected to that Ethernet. Each adaptor recognizes those frames addressed to its address and passes only those frames on to the host. (An adaptor can be programmed to run in *promiscuous* mode, in which case it delivers all received frames to the host.) In addition to these *unicast* addresses, an Ethernet address consisting of all 1s is treated as a *broadcast* address; all adaptors pass frames addressed to the broadcast address up to the host. Similarly, an address that has the first bit set to 1 but is not the broadcast address is called a *multicast* address. A given host can program its adaptor to accept some set of multicast addresses. Multicast addresses are used to send messages to some subset of the hosts on an Ethernet (e.g., all file servers). To summarize, an Ethernet adaptor receives all frames and accepts

- frames addressed to its own address

- frames addressed to the broadcast address

- frames addressed to a multicast address, if it has been instructed to listen to that address

- all frames, if it has been placed in promiscuous mode

It passes to the host only the frames that it accepts.

Transmitter Algorithm

As we have just seen, the receiver side of the Ethernet protocol is simple; the real smarts are implemented at the sender's side. The transmitter algorithm is defined as follows.

When the adaptor has a frame to send and the line is idle, it transmits the frame immediately; there is no negotiation with the other adaptors. The upper bound of 1500 bytes in the message means that the adaptor can occupy the line for only a fixed length of time.

When an adaptor has a frame to send and the line is busy, it waits for the line to go idle and then transmits immediately.[2] The Ethernet is said to be a *1-persistent* protocol because an adaptor with a frame to send transmits with probability 1 whenever a busy line goes idle. In general, a *p-persistent* algorithm transmits with probability

---

[2] To be more precise, all adaptors wait 9.6 μs after the end of one frame before beginning to transmit the next frame. This is true for both the sender of the first frame, as well as those nodes listening for the line to become idle.

$0 \leq p \leq 1$ after a line becomes idle, and defers with probability $q = 1 - p$. The reasoning behind choosing a $p < 1$ is that there might be multiple adaptors waiting for the busy line to become idle, and we don't want all of them to begin transmitting at the same time. If each adaptor transmits immediately with a probability of, say, 33%, then up to three adaptors can be waiting to transmit and the odds are that only one will begin transmitting when the line becomes idle. Despite this reasoning, an Ethernet adaptor always transmits immediately after noticing that the network has become idle and has been very effective in doing so.

To complete the story about p-persistent protocols for the case when $p < 1$, you might wonder how long a sender that loses the coin flip (i.e., decides to defer) has to wait before it can transmit. The answer for the Aloha network, which originally developed this style of protocol, was to divide time into discrete slots, with each slot corresponding to the length of time it takes to transmit a full frame. Whenever a node has a frame to send and it senses an empty (idle) slot, it transmits with probability p and defers until the next slot with probability $q = 1 - p$. If that next slot is also empty, the node again decides to transmit or defer, with probabilities p and q, respectively. If that next slot is not empty—that is, some other station has decided to transmit—then the node simply waits for the next idle slot and the algorithm repeats.

Returning to our discussion of the Ethernet, because there is no centralized control it is possible for two (or more) adaptors to begin transmitting at the same time, either because both found the line to be idle or because both had been waiting for a busy line to become idle. When this happens, the two (or more) frames are said to *collide* on the network. Each sender, because the Ethernet supports collision detection, is able to determine that a collision is in progress. At the moment an adaptor detects that its frame is colliding with another, it first makes sure to transmit a 32-bit jamming sequence and then stops the transmission. Thus, a transmitter will minimally send 96 bits in the case of a collision: 64-bit preamble plus 32-bit jamming sequence.

One way that an adaptor will send only 96 bits—which is sometimes called a *runt frame*—is if the two hosts are close to each other. Had the two hosts been farther apart, they would have had to transmit longer, and thus send more bits, before detecting the collision. In fact, the worst-case scenario happens when the two hosts are at opposite ends of the Ethernet. To know for sure that the frame it just sent did not collide with another frame, the transmitter may need to send as many as 512 bits. Not coincidentally, every Ethernet frame must be 512 bits (64 bytes) long: 14 bytes of header plus 46 bytes of data plus 4 bytes of CRC.

Why 512 bits? The answer is related to another question you might ask about an Ethernet: Why is its length limited to only 2500 m? Why not 10 or 1000 km? The answer to both questions has to do with the fact that the farther apart two nodes are, the longer it takes for a frame sent by one to reach the other, and the network is vulnerable to a collision during this time.

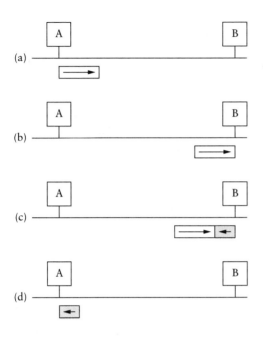

Figure 2.28 Worst-case scenario: (a) A sends a frame at time *t*; (b) A's frame arrives at B at time *t* + *d*; (c) B begins transmitting at time *t* + *d* and collides with A's frame; (d) B's runt (32-bit) frame arrives at A at time *t* + 2*d*.

Figure 2.28 illustrates the worst-case scenario, where hosts A and B are at opposite ends of the network. Suppose host A begins transmitting a frame at time *t*, as shown in (a). It takes it one link latency (let's denote the latency as *d*) for the frame to reach host B. Thus, the first bit of A's frame arrives at B at time *t* + *d*, as shown in (b). Suppose an instant before host A's frame arrives (i.e., B still sees an idle line), host B begins to transmit its own frame. B's frame will immediately collide with A's frame, and this collision will be detected by host B (c). Host B will send the 32-bit jamming sequence, as described above. (B's frame will be a runt.) Unfortunately, host A will not know that the collision occurred until B's frame reaches it, which will happen one link latency later, at time *t* + 2 × *d*, as shown in (d). Host A must continue to transmit until this time in order to detect the collision. In other words, host A must transmit for 2 × *d* to be sure that it detects all possible collisions. Considering that a maximally configured Ethernet is 2500 m long, and that there may be up to four repeaters between any two hosts, the round-trip delay has been determined to be 51.2 μs, which on a 10-Mbps Ethernet corresponds to 512 bits. The other way to look at this situation is that we need to limit the Ethernet's maximum latency to a fairly small value (e.g.,

51.2 μs) for the access algorithm to work; hence, an Ethernet's maximum length must be something on the order of 2500 m.

Once an adaptor has detected a collision and stopped its transmission, it waits a certain amount of time and tries again. Each time it tries to transmit but fails, the adaptor doubles the amount of time it waits before trying again. This strategy of doubling the delay interval between each retransmission attempt is a general technique known as *exponential backoff*. More precisely, the adaptor first delays either 0 or 51.2 μs, selected at random. If this effort fails, it then waits 0, 51.2, 102.4, or 153.6 μs (selected randomly) before trying again; this is $k \times 51.2$ for $k = 0..3$. After the third collision, it waits $k \times 51.2$ for $k = 0..2^3 - 1$, again selected at random. In general, the algorithm randomly selects a k between 0 and $2^n - 1$ and waits $k \times 51.2$ μs, where n is the number of collisions experienced so far. The adaptor gives up after a given number of tries and reports a transmit error to the host. Adaptors typically retry up to 16 times, although the backoff algorithm caps n in the above formula at 10.

2.6.3   Experience with Ethernet

Because Ethernets have been around for so many years and are so popular, we have a great deal of experience in using them. One of the most important observations people have made about Ethernets is that they work best under lightly loaded conditions. This is because under heavy loads—typically, a utilization of over 30% is considered heavy on an Ethernet—too much of the network's capacity is wasted by collisions.

Fortunately, most Ethernets are used in a far more conservative way than the standard allows. For example, most Ethernets have fewer than 200 hosts connected to them, which is far fewer than the maximum of 1024. (See if you can discover a reason for this upper limit of around 200 hosts in Chapter 4.) Similarly, most Ethernets are far shorter than 2500 m, with a round-trip delay of closer to 5 μs than 51.2 μs. Another factor that makes Ethernets practical is that, even though Ethernet adaptors do not implement link-level flow control, the hosts typically provide an end-to-end flow-control mechanism. As a result, it is rare to find situations in which any one host is continuously pumping frames onto the network.

Finally, it is worth saying a few words about why Ethernets have been so successful, so that we can understand the properties we should emulate with any LAN technology that tries to replace it. First, an Ethernet is extremely easy to administer and maintain: There are no switches that can fail, no routing or configuration tables that have to be kept up-to-date, and it is easy to add a new host to the network. It is going to be a major challenge to make any of the switch-based networks described in the next chapter this simple to operate. Second, it is inexpensive: Cable is cheap, and the only other cost is the network adaptor on each host. Again, any switch-based

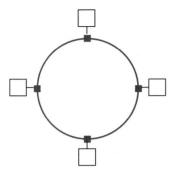

Figure 2.29   Token ring network.

approach will involve an investment in an expensive infrastructure (the switches), in addition to the incremental cost of each adaptor.

2.7   Token Rings (802.5, FDDI)

Alongside the Ethernet, token rings are the other significant class of shared-media network. There are more different types of token rings than there are types of Ethernet; this section will discuss the most prevalent type, known as the IBM Token Ring. Like the Xerox Ethernet, IBM's Token Ring has a nearly identical IEEE standard, known as 802.5. Where necessary, we note the differences between the IBM and 802.5 token rings.

Most of the general principles of token ring networks can be understood once the IBM and 802.5 standards have been discussed. However, the FDDI (Fiber Distributed Data Interface) standard—a newer, faster type of token ring—warrants some discussion, which we provide at the end of this section.

As the name suggests, a token ring network consists of a set of nodes connected in a ring (see Figure 2.29). Data always flows in a particular direction around the ring, with each node receiving frames from its upstream neighbor and then forwarding them to its downstream neighbor. This ring-based topology is in contrast to the Ethernet's bus topology. Like the Ethernet, however, the ring is viewed as a single shared medium; it does not behave as a collection of independent point-to-point links that just happen to be configured in a loop. Thus, a token ring shares two key features with an Ethernet: First, it involves a distributed algorithm that controls when each node is allowed to transmit, and second, all nodes see all frames, with the node identified in the frame header as the destination saving a copy of the frame as it flows past.

The word "token" in token ring comes from the way access to the shared ring is managed. The idea is that a token, which is really just a special sequence of bits,

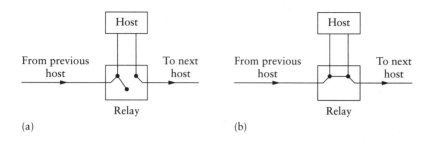

Figure 2.30 Relay used on a token ring: (a) relay open—host active; (b) relay closed—host bypassed.

circulates around the ring; each node receives and then forwards the token. When a node that has a frame to transmit sees the token, it takes the token off the ring (i.e., it does not forward the special bit pattern) and instead inserts its frame into the ring. Each node along the way simply forwards the frame, with the destination node saving a copy and forwarding the message onto the next node on the ring. When the frame makes its way back around to the sender, this node strips its frame off the ring (rather than continuing to forward it) and reinserts the token. In this way, some node downstream will have the opportunity to transmit a frame. The media access algorithm is fair in the sense that as the token circulates around the ring, each node gets a chance to transmit. Nodes are serviced in a round-robin fashion.

2.7.1 Physical Properties

One of the first things you might worry about with a ring topology is that any link or node failure would render the whole network useless. This problem is addressed by connecting each station into the ring using an electromechanical relay. As long as the station is healthy, the relay is open and the station is included in the ring. If the station stops providing power, the relay closes and the ring automatically bypasses the station. This is illustrated in Figure 2.30.

Several of these relays are usually packed into a single box, known as a multi-station access unit (MSAU). This has the interesting effect of making a token ring actually look more like a star topology, as shown in Figure 2.31. It also makes it very easy to add stations to and remove stations from the network, since they can just be plugged into or unplugged from the nearest MSAU, while the overall wiring of the network can be left unchanged. One of the small differences between the IBM Token Ring specification and 802.5 is that the former actually requires the use of MSAUs, while the latter does not. In practice, MSAUs are almost always used because of the need for robustness and ease of station addition and removal.

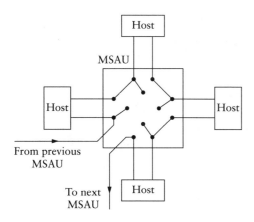

Figure 2.31 Multistation access unit.

There are a few other physical details to know about 802.5 and IBM token rings. The data rate may be either 4 Mbps or 16 Mbps. The encoding of bits uses differential Manchester encoding, as described in Section 2.2. IBM token rings may have up to 260 stations per ring, while 802.5 sets the limit at 250. The physical medium is twisted pair for IBM, but is not specified in 802.5.

2.7.2 Token Ring Media Access Control

It is now time to look a little more closely at how the MAC protocol operates on a token ring. The network adaptor for a token ring contains a receiver, a transmitter, and one or more bits of data storage between them. When none of the stations connected to the ring has anything to send, the token circulates around the ring. Obviously, the ring has to have enough "storage capacity" to hold an entire token. For example, the 802.5 token is 24 bits long. If every station could hold only 1 bit (as is the norm for 802.5 networks), and the stations were close enough together that the time for a bit to propagate from one station to another was negligible, we would need to have at least 24 stations on the ring before it would operate correctly. This situation is avoided by having one designated station, called the *monitor*, add some additional bits of delay to the ring if necessary. The operation of the monitor is described in more detail below.

As the token circulates around the ring, any station that has data to send may "seize" the token, that is, drain it off the ring and begin sending data. In 802.5 networks, the seizing process involves simply modifying 1 bit in the second byte token; the first 2 bytes of the modified token now become the preamble for the subsequent data packet. Once a station has the token, it is allowed to send one or more packets— exactly how many more depends on some factors described below.

Each transmitted packet contains the destination address of the intended receiver; it may also contain a multicast (or broadcast) address if it is intended to reach more than one (or all) receivers. As the packet flows past each node on the ring, each node looks inside the packet to see if it is the intended recipient. If so, it copies the packet into a buffer as it flows through the network adaptor, but it does not remove the packet from the ring. The sending station has the responsibility of removing the packet from the ring. For any packet that is longer than the number of bits that can be stored in the ring, the sending station will be draining the first part of the packet from the ring while still transmitting the latter part.

One issue we must address is how much data a given node is allowed to transmit each time it possesses the token, or said another way, how long a given node is allowed to hold the token. We call this the *token holding time* (THT). If we assume that most nodes on the network do not have data to send at any given time—a reasonable assumption, and certainly one that the Ethernet takes advantage of—then we could make a case for letting a node that possesses the token transmit as much data as it has before passing the token on to the next node. This would mean setting the THT to infinity. It would be silly in this case to limit a node to sending a single message and to force it to wait until the token circulates all the way around the ring before getting a chance to send another message. Of course, "as much data as it has" would be dangerous because a single station could keep the token for an arbitrarily long time, but we could certainly set the THT to significantly more than the time to send one packet.

It is easy to see that the more bytes a node can send each time it has the token, the better the utilization of the ring you can achieve in the situation in which only a single node has data to send. The downside, of course, is that this strategy does not work well when multiple nodes have data to send—it favors nodes that have a lot of data to send over nodes that have only a small message to send, even when it is important to get this small message delivered as soon as possible. The situation is analogous to finding yourself in line at the bank behind a customer who is taking out a car loan, even though you simply want to cash a check. In 802.5 networks, the default THT is 10 ms.

There is a little subtlety to the use of the THT. Before putting each packet onto the ring, the station must check that the amount of time it would take to transmit the packet would not cause it to exceed the token holding time. This means keeping track of how long it has already held the token, and looking at the length of the next packet that it wants to send.

From the token holding time we can derive another useful quantity, the *token rotation time* (TRT), which is the amount of time it takes a token to traverse the ring as viewed by a given node. It is easy to see that

$$TRT \leq ActiveNodes \times THT + RingLatency$$

where RingLatency denotes how long it takes the token to circulate around the ring when no one has data to send, and ActiveNodes denotes the number of nodes that have data to transmit.

The 802.5 protocol provides a form of reliable delivery using 2 bits in the packet trailer, the A and C bits. These are both 0 initially. When a station sees a frame for which it is the intended recipient, it sets the A bit in the frame. When it copies the frame into its adaptor, it sets the C bit. If the sending station sees the frame come back over the ring with the A bit still 0, it knows that the intended recipient is not functioning or absent. If the A bit is set but not the C bit, this implies that for some reason, (e.g., lack of buffer space) the destination could not accept the frame. Thus, the frame might reasonably be retransmitted later in the hope that buffer space had become available.

Another detail of the 802.5 protocol concerns the support of different levels of priority. The token contains a 3-bit priority field, so we can think of the token having a certain priority n at any time. Each device that wants to send a packet assigns a priority to that packet, and the device can only seize the token to transmit a packet if the packet's priority is at least as great as the token's. The priority of the token changes over time due to the use of three *reservation* bits in the frame header. For example, a station X waiting to send a priority n packet may set these bits to n if it sees a data frame going past and the bits have not already been set to a higher value. This causes the station that currently holds the token to elevate its priority to n when it releases it. Station X is responsible for lowering the token priority to its old value when it is done.

Note that this is a *strict* priority scheme, in the sense that no lower-priority packets get sent when higher-priority packets are waiting. This may cause lower-priority packets to be locked out of the ring for extended periods if there is a sufficient supply of high-priority packets.

One final issue will complete our discussion of the MAC protocol, which is the matter of exactly when the sending node releases the token. As illustrated in Figure 2.32, the sender can insert the token back onto the ring immediately following its frame (this is called *early release*) or after the frame it transmits has gone all the way around the ring and been removed (this is called *delayed release*). Clearly early release allows better bandwidth utilization, especially on large rings. 802.5 originally used delayed token release, but support for early release was subsequently added.

2.7.3 Token Ring Maintenance

As we noted above, token rings have a designated monitor station. The monitor's job is to ensure the health of the ring. Any station on the ring can become the monitor,

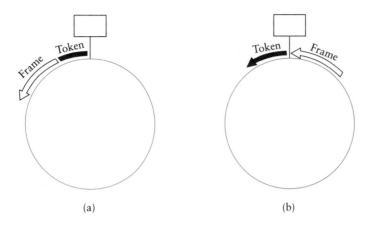

Figure 2.32   Token release: (a) early versus (b) delayed.

and there are defined procedures by which the monitor is elected when the ring is first connected or on the failure of the current monitor. A healthy monitor periodically announces its presence with a special control message; if a station fails to see such a message for some period of time, it will assume that the monitor has failed and will try to become the monitor. The procedures for electing a monitor are the same whether the ring has just come up or the active monitor has just failed.

When a station decides that a new monitor is needed, it transmits a "claim token" frame, announcing its intent to become the new monitor. If that token circulates back to the sender, it can assume that it is OK for it to become the monitor. If some other station is also trying to become the monitor at the same instant, the sender might see a claim token message from that other station first. In this case, it will be necessary to break the tie using some well-defined rule like "highest address wins."

Once the monitor is agreed upon, it plays a number of roles. We have already seen that it may need to insert additional delay into the ring. It is also responsible for making sure that there is always a token somewhere in the ring, either circulating or currently held by a station. It should be clear that a token may vanish for several reasons, such as a bit error, or a crash on the part of a station that was holding it. To detect a missing token, the monitor watches for a passing token and maintains a timer equal to the maximum possible token rotation time. This interval equals

$$NumStations \times THT + RingLatency$$

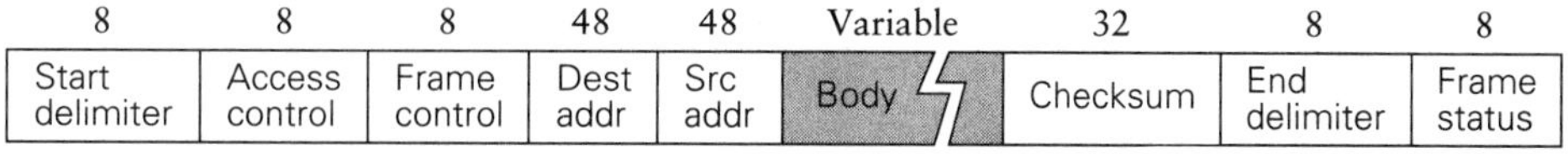

8	8	8	48	48	Variable	32	8	8
Start delimiter	Access control	Frame control	Dest addr	Src addr	Body	Checksum	End delimiter	Frame status

Figure 2.33 802.5/token ring frame format.

where NumStations is the number of stations on the ring, and RingLatency is the total propagation delay of the ring. If the timer expires without the monitor seeing a token, it creates a new one.

The monitor also checks for corrupted or orphaned frames. The former have checksum errors or invalid formats, and without monitor intervention, they could circulate forever on the ring. The monitor drains them off the ring before reinserting the token. An orphaned frame is one that was transmitted correctly onto the ring but whose "parent" died; that is, the sending station went down before it could remove the frame from the ring. These are detected using another header bit, the "'monitor'" bit. This is 0 on transmission and set to 1 the first time the packet passes the monitor. If the monitor sees a packet with this bit set, it knows the packet is going by for the second time and it drains the packet off the ring.

One additional ring maintenance function is the detection of dead stations. The relays in the MSAU can automatically bypass a station that has been disconnected or powered down, but may not detect more subtle failures. If any station suspects a failure on the ring, it can send a *beacon* frame to the suspect destination. Based on how far this frame gets, the status of the ring can be established, and malfunctioning stations can be bypassed by the relays in the MSAU.

2.7.4 Frame Format

We are now ready to define the 802.5 frame format, which is depicted in Figure 2.33. As noted above, 802.5 uses Manchester encoding. This fact is used by the frame format, which uses "illegal" Manchester codes in the start and end delimiters. After the start delimiter comes the access control byte, which includes the frame priority and the reservation priority mentioned above. The frame control byte is a demux key that identifies the higher-layer protocol.

Similar to the Ethernet, 802.5 addresses are 48 bits long. The standard actually allows for smaller 16-bit addresses, but 48-bit addresses are typically used. When 48-bit addresses are used, they are interpreted in exactly the same way as on an Ethernet. The frame also includes a 32-bit CRC. This is followed by the frame status byte, which includes the A and C bits for reliable delivery.

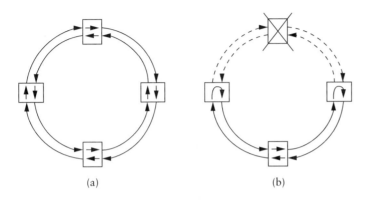

                    (a)   (b)

Figure 2.34   Dual-fiber ring: (a) normal operation; (b) failure of the primary ring.

2.7.5   FDDI

In many respects, FDDI is similar to 802.5 and IBM Token Rings. However, there are significant differences—some arising because it runs on fiber, not copper, and some arising from innovations that were made subsequent to the invention of the IBM Token Ring. We discuss some of the significant differences below.

Physical Properties

Unlike 802.5 networks, an FDDI network consists of a dual ring—two independent rings that transmit data in opposite directions, as illustrated in Figure 2.34(a). The second ring is not used during normal operation but instead comes into play only if the primary ring fails, as depicted in Figure 2.34(b). That is, the ring loops back on the secondary fiber to form a complete ring, and as a consequence, an FDDI network is able to tolerate a single break in the cable or the failure of one station.

Because of the expense of the dual-ring configuration, FDDI allows nodes to attach to the network by means of a single cable. Such nodes are called *single attachment stations* (SAS); their dual-connected counterparts are called, not surprisingly, *dual attachment stations* (DAS). A concentrator is used to attach several SASs to the dual ring, as illustrated in Figure 2.35. Notice how the single-cable (two-fiber) connection into an SAS forms a connected piece of the ring. Should this SAS fail, the concentrator detects this situation and uses an *optical bypass* to isolate the failed SAS, thereby keeping the ring connected. This is analogous to the relays inside MSAUs used in 802.5 rings. Note that in this illustration, the second (backup) ring is denoted with a dotted line.

As in 802.5, each network adaptor holds some number of bits between its input and output interfaces. Unlike 802.5, however, the buffer can be of different sizes in different stations, although never less than 9 bits nor more than 80 bits. It is also

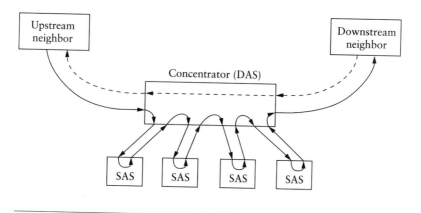

Figure 2.35 SASs connected to a concentrator.

possible for a station to start transmitting bits out of this buffer before it is full. Of course, the total time it takes for a token to pass around the network is a function of the size of these buffers. For example, because FDDI is a 100-Mbps network, it has a 10-nanosecond (ns) bit time (each bit is 10 ns wide). If each station implements a 10-bit buffer, and waits for the buffer to be half full before starting to transmit, then each station introduces a 5×10 ns $= 50$-ns delay into the total ring rotation time.

FDDI has other physical characteristics. For example, the standard limits a single network to at most 500 stations (hosts), with a maximum distance of 2 km between any pair of stations. Overall, the network is limited to a total of 200 km of fiber, which means that, because of the dual nature of the ring, the total amount of cable connecting all stations is limited to 100 km. Also, although the "F" in FDDI implies that optical fiber serves as the underlying physical medium, the standard has been defined to run over a number of different physical media, including coax and twisted pair. Of course, you still have to be careful about the total distance covered by the ring. As we will see below, the amount of time it takes the token to traverse the network plays an important role in the access control algorithm.

FDDI uses 4B/5B encoding, as discussed in Section 2.2 of this chapter. Since FDDI was the first popular networking technology to use fiber, and 4B/5B chip sets operating at FDDI rates became widely available, 4B/5B has enjoyed considerable popularity as an encoding scheme for fiber.

Timed-Token Algorithm

The rules governing token holding times are a little more complex in FDDI than in 802.5. The THT for each node is defined as before and is configured to some suitable value. In addition, to ensure that a given node has the opportunity to transmit within a certain amount of time—that is, to put an upper bound on the TRT observed by any node—we define a *target token rotation time* (TTRT), and all nodes agree to live within the limits of the TTRT. (How the nodes agree to a particular TTRT is described in the next subsection.) Specifically, each node measures the time between successive arrivals of the token. We call this the node's *measured* TRT. If this measured TRT is greater than the agreed upon TTRT, then the token is late, and the node does not transmit any data. If this measured TRT is less than the TTRT, then the token is early, and the node is allowed to hold the token for the difference between TTRT and the measured TRT.

Although it may seem that we are now done, the algorithm we have just developed does not ensure that a node concerned with sending a frame with a bounded delay will actually be able to do so. The problem is that a node with lots of data to send has the opportunity, upon seeing an early token, to hold the token for so long that by the time a downstream node gets the token, its measured TRT is equal to or exceeds the TTRT, meaning that it still cannot transmit its frame. To account for this possibility, FDDI defines two classes of traffic: *synchronous* and *asynchronous*.[3] When a node receives a token, it is always allowed to send synchronous data, without regard for whether the token is early or late. In contrast, a node can send asynchronous traffic only when the token is early.

Note that the terms *synchronous* and *asynchronous* are somewhat misleading. By synchronous, FDDI means that the traffic is delay sensitive. For example, you would send voice or video as synchronous traffic on an FDDI network. In contrast, asynchronous means that the application is more interested in throughput than delay. A file transfer application would be asynchronous FDDI traffic.

Are we done yet? Not quite. Because synchronous traffic can transmit without regard to whether the token is early or late, it would seem that if each node had a sizable amount of synchronous data to send, then the target rotation time would again be meaningless. To account for this, the total amount of synchronous data that can be sent during one token rotation is also bounded by TTRT. This means that in the worst case, the nodes with asynchronous traffic first use up one TTRT's worth of time, and then the nodes with synchronous data consume another TTRT's worth of time, meaning that it is possible for the measured TRT at any given node to be as much as $2 \times$ TTRT. Note that if the synchronous traffic has already consumed one TTRT's worth of time, then the nodes with asynchronous traffic will not send any data because the token will be late. Thus, while it is possible for a single rotation of the token to

---

[3] Originally, FDDI defined two subclasses of asynchronous traffic: *restricted* and *unrestricted*. In practice, however, the restricted asynchronous case is not supported, and so we describe only the unrestricted case and refer to it simply as "asynchronous."

take as long as 2 × TTRT, it is not possible to have back-to-back rotations that take 2 × TTRT amount of time.

One final detail concerns precisely how a node determines if it can send asynchronous traffic. As stated above, a node sends if the measured TRT is less than the TTRT. The question then arises: What if the measured TRT is less than the TTRT, but by such a small amount that it's not possible to send the full message without exceeding the TTRT? The answer is that the node is allowed to send in this case. As a consequence, the measured TRT is actually bounded by TTRT plus the time it takes to send a full FDDI frame.

Token Maintenance

The FDDI mechanisms for ensuring that a valid token is always in circulation are also different from those in 802.5, as they are intertwined with the process of setting the TTRT. First, all nodes on an FDDI ring monitor the ring to be sure that the token has not been lost. Observe that in a correctly functioning ring, each node should see a valid transmission—either a data frame or the token—every so often. The greatest idle time between valid transmissions that a given node should experience is equal to the ring latency plus the time it takes to transmit a full frame, which on a maximally sized ring is a little less than 2.5 ms. Therefore, each node sets a timer event that fires after 2.5 ms. If this timer expires, the node suspects that something has gone wrong and transmits a "claim" frame. Every time a valid transmission is received, however, the node resets the timer back to 2.5 ms.

The claim frames in FDDI differ from those in 802.5 because they contain the node's *bid* for the TTRT, that is, the token rotation time that the node needs so that the applications running on the node can meet their timing constraints. A node can send a claim frame without holding the token and typically does so whenever it suspects a failure or when it first joins the network. If this claim frame makes it all the way around the ring, then the sender removes it, knowing that its TTRT bid was the lowest. That node now holds the token—that is, it is responsible for inserting a valid token on the ring—and may proceed with the normal token algorithm.

When a node receives a claim frame, it checks to see if the TTRT bid in the frame is less than its own. If it is, then the node resets its local definition of the TTRT to that contained in the claim frame and forwards the frame to the next node. If the bid TTRT is greater than that node's minimum required TTRT, then the claim frame is removed from the ring and the node enters the bidding process by putting its own claim frame on the ring. Should the bid TTRT be equal to the node's required TTRT, the node compares the address of the claim frame's sender with its own and the higher address wins. Thus, if a claim frame makes it all the way back around to the original sender, that node knows that it is the only active bidder and that it can safely claim the token.

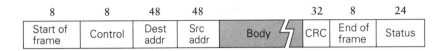

Figure 2.36 FDDI frame format.

At the same time, all nodes are now in agreement about the TTRT that will be short enough to keep all nodes happy.

Frame Format

The FDDI frame format, depicted in Figure 2.36, differs in very few ways from that for 802.5. Because FDDI uses 4B/5B encoding instead of Manchester, it uses 4B/5B control symbols rather than illegal Manchester symbols in the start and end of frame markers. The other significant difference is the presence of a bit in the header to distinguish synchronous from asynchronous traffic, and the lack of the access control bits of 802.5.

2.8 Wireless (802.11)

Wireless networking is a rapidly evolving technology for connecting computers. As we saw earlier in this chapter, the possibilities for building wireless networks are almost endless, ranging from using infrared signals within a single building, to constructing a global network from a grid of low-orbit satellites. This section takes a closer look at a specific technology centered around the emerging IEEE 802.11 standard. Like its Ethernet and token ring siblings, 802.11 is designed for use in a limited geographical area (homes, office buildings, campuses), and its primary challenge is to mediate access to a shared communication medium—in this case, signals propagating through space. 802.11 supports additional features (e.g., time-bounded services, power management, and security mechanisms), but we focus our discussion on its base functionality.

2.8.1 Physical Properties

802.11 was designed to run over three different physical media—two based on spread spectrum radio and one based on diffused infrared, all three of which run at either 1 or 2 Mbps.

The idea behind spread spectrum is to spread the signal over a wider frequency band than normal, so as to minimize the impact of interference from other devices. (Spread spectrum was originally designed for military use, so these "other devices" were often attempting to jam the signal.) For example, *frequency hopping* is a spread spectrum technique that involves transmitting the signal over a random sequence of frequencies; that is, first transmitting at one frequency, then a second, then a third,

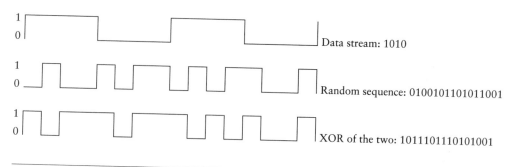

Figure 2.37 Example 4-bit chipping sequence.

and so on. The sequence of frequencies is not truly random, but is instead computed algorithmically by a pseudorandom number generator. The receiver uses the same algorithm as the sender—and initializes it with the same seed—and hence is able to hop frequencies in sync with the transmitter to correctly receive the frame.

A second spread spectrum technique, called *direct sequence*, achieves the same effect by representing each bit in the frame by multiple bits in the transmitted signal. For each bit the sender wants to transmit, it actually sends the exclusive-OR of that bit and n random bits. As with frequency hopping, the sequence of random bits is generated by a pseudorandom number generator known to both the sender and the receiver. The transmitted values, known as an n-bit *chipping code*, spread the signal across a frequency band that is n times wider than the frame would have otherwise required. Figure 2.37 gives an example of a 4-bit chipping sequence.

802.11 defines one physical layer using frequency hopping (over 79 1-MHz-wide frequency bandwidths) and a second using direct sequence (using an 11-bit chipping sequence). Both standards run in the 2.4-GHz frequency band of the electromagnetic spectrum. In both cases, spread spectrum also has the interesting characteristic of making the signal look like noise to any receiver that does not know the pseudorandom sequence.

The third physical standard for 802.11 is based on infrared signals. The transmission is diffused, meaning that the sender and receiver do not have to be aimed at each other and do not need a clear line of sight. This technology has a range of up to about 10 m and is limited to the inside of buildings only.

2.8.2 Collision Avoidance

At first glance, it might seem that a wireless protocol would follow exactly the same algorithm as the Ethernet—wait until the link becomes idle before transmitting and back off should a collision occur—and to a first approximation, this is exactly what 802.11

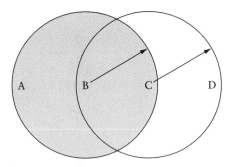

Figure 2.38   Example wireless network.

does. The problem is more complicated in a wireless network, however, because not all nodes are always within reach of each other.

Consider the situation depicted in Figure 2.38, where each of four nodes is able to send and receive signals that reach just the nodes to its immediate left and right. For example, B can exchange frames with A and C but it cannot reach D, while C can reach B and D but not A. (A and D's reach is not shown in the figure.) Suppose both A and C want to communicate with B and so they each send it a frame. A and C are unaware of each other since their signals do not carry that far. These two frames collide with each other at B, but unlike an Ethernet, neither A nor C is aware of this collision. A and C are said to be *hidden nodes* with respect to each other.

A related problem, called the *exposed node problem*, occurs under the following circumstances. Suppose B is sending to A in Figure 2.38. Node C is aware of this communication because it hears B's transmission. It would be a mistake for C to conclude that it cannot transmit to anyone just because it can hear B's transmission. For example, suppose C wants to transmit to node D. This is not a problem since C's transmission to D will not interfere with A's ability to receive from B. (It would interfere with A sending to B, but B is transmitting in our example.)

802.11 addresses these two problems with an algorithm called Multiple Access with Collision Avoidance (MACA). The idea is for the sender and receiver to exchange control frames with each other before the sender actually transmits any data. This exchange informs all nearby nodes that a transmission is about to begin. Specifically, the sender transmits a *Request to Send* (RTS) frame to the receiver; the RTS frame includes a field that indicates how long the sender wants to hold the medium (i.e., it specifies the length of the data frame to be transmitted). The receiver then replies with a *Clear to Send* (CTS) frame; this frame echoes this length field back to the sender. Any node that sees the CTS frame knows that it is close to the receiver, and therefore cannot transmit for the period of time it takes to send a frame of the specified length. Any node that sees the RTS frame but not the CTS frame is not close enough to the receiver to interfere with it, and so is free to transmit.

There are two more details to complete the picture. First, the receiver sends an ACK to the sender after successfully receiving a frame. All nodes must wait for this ACK before trying to transmit.[4] Second, should two or more nodes detect an idle link and try to transmit an RTS frame at the same time, their RTS frames will collide with each other. 802.11 does not support collision detection, but instead the senders realize the collision has happened when they do not receive the CTS frame after a period of time, in which case they each wait a random amount of time before trying again. The amount of time a given node delays is defined by the same exponential backoff algorithm used on the Ethernet (see Section 2.6.2).

2.8.3 Distribution System

As described so far, 802.11 would be suitable for an ad hoc configuration of nodes that may or may not be able to communicate with all other nodes, depending on how far apart they are. Moreover, since one of the advantages of a wireless network is that nodes are free to move around—they are not tethered by wire—the set of directly reachable nodes may change over time. To help deal with this mobility and partial connectivity, 802.11 defines additional structure on a set of nodes. Nodes are free to directly communicate with each other as just described, but in practice, they operate within this structure.

Instead of all nodes being created equal, some nodes are allowed to roam (e.g., your laptop) and some are connected to a wired network infrastructure. The latter are called *access points* (AP) and, they are connected to each other by a so-called *distribution system*. Figure 2.39 illustrates a distribution system that connects three access points, each of which services the nodes in some region. Each of these regions is analogous to a cell in a cellular phone system, with the APs playing the same role as a base station. The details of the distribution system are not important to this discussion—it could be an Ethernet or a token ring, for example.

Although two nodes can communicate directly with each other if they are within reach of each other, the idea behind this configuration is that each node associates itself with one access point. For node A to communicate with node E, for example, A first sends a frame to its access point (AP-1), which forwards the frame across the distribution system to AP-3, which finally transmits the frame to E. How AP-1 knew to forward the message to AP-3 is beyond the scope of 802.11; it may have used the

---

[4] This ACK was not part of the original MACA algorithm, but was instead proposed in an extended version called MACAW: MACA for *Wireless* LANs.

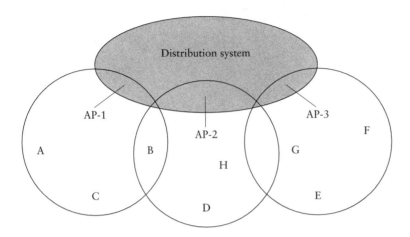

Figure 2.39   Access points connected to a distribution network.

bridging protocol described in the next chapter (Section 3.2). What 802.11 does specify is how nodes select their access points and, more interestingly, how this algorithm works in light of nodes moving from one cell to another.

The technique for selecting an AP is called *scanning* and involves the following four steps:

1 The node sends a Probe frame.

2 All APs within reach reply with a Probe Response frame.

3 The node selects one of the access points, and sends that AP an Association Request frame.

4 The AP replies with an Association Response frame.

A node engages this protocol whenever it joins the network, as well as when it becomes unhappy with its current AP. This might happen, for example, because the signal from its current AP has weakened due to the node moving away from it. Whenever a node acquires a new AP, the new AP notifies the old AP of the change (this happens in step 4) via the distribution system.

Consider the situation shown in Figure 2.40, where node C moves from the cell serviced by AP-1 to the cell serviced by AP-2. As it moves, it sends Probe frames, which eventually result in Probe Response frames from AP-2. At some point, C prefers AP-2 over AP-1, and so it associates itself with that access point.

The mechanism just described is called active scanning since the node is actively searching for an access point. APs also periodically send a Beacon frame that advertises

Distribution system
AP-1
AP-2
AP-3
A
B
C
C
D
E
F
G
H

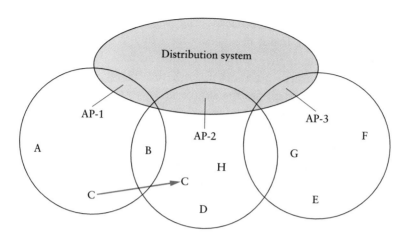

Figure 2.40 Node mobility.

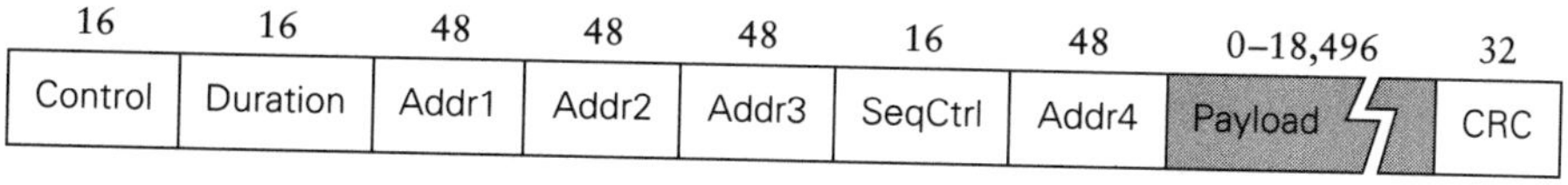

16
16
48
48
48
16
48
0–18,496
32
Control
Duration
Addr1
Addr2
Addr3
SeqCtrl
Addr4
Payload
CRC

Figure 2.41 802.11 frame format.

the capabilities of the access point; these include the transmission rates supported by the AP. This is called passive scanning, and a node can change to this AP based on the Beacon frame simply by sending it an Association Request frame back to the access point.

2.8.4 Frame Format

Most of the 802.11 frame format, which is depicted in Figure 2.41, is exactly what we would expect. The frame contains the source and destination node addresses, each of which are 48 bits long; up to 2312 bytes of data; and a 32-bit CRC. The Control field contains three subfields of interest (not shown): a 6-bit Type field that indicates whether the frame carries data, is an RTS or CTS frame, or is being used by the scanning algorithm; and a pair of 1-bit fields—called ToDS and FromDS—that are described below.

The peculiar thing about the 802.11 frame format is that it contains four, rather than two, addresses. How these addresses are interpreted depends on the settings of the ToDS and FromDS bits in the frame's Control field. This is to account for the possibility that the frame had to be forwarded across the distribution system, which would mean that the original sender is not necessarily the same as the most recent transmitting node. Similar reasoning applies to the destination address. In the simplest case, when one node is sending directly to another, both the DS bits are 0, Addr1 identifies the target node, and Addr2 identifies the source node. In the most complex case, both DS bits are set to 1, indicating that the message went from a wireless node onto the distribution system, and then from the distribution system to another wireless node. With both bits set, Addr1 identifies the ultimate destination, Addr2 identifies the immediate sender (the one that forwarded the frame from the distribution system to the ultimate destination), Addr3 identifies the intermediate destination (the one that accepted the frame from a wireless node and forwarded it across the distribution system), and Addr4 identifies the original source. In terms of the example given in Figure 2.39, Addr1 corresponds to E, Addr2 identifies AP-3, Addr3 corresponds to AP-1, and Addr4 identifies A.

2.9 Network Adaptors

Nearly all the networking functionality described in this chapter is implemented in the network adaptor: framing, error detection, and the media access protocol. The only exceptions are the point-to-point automatic repeat request (ARQ) schemes described in Section 2.5, which are typically implemented in the lowest-level protocol running on the host. We conclude this chapter by describing the design of a generic network adaptor, and the device driver software that controls it.

When reading this section, keep in mind that no two network adaptors are exactly alike; they vary in countless small details. Our focus, therefore, is on their general characteristics, although we do include some examples from an actual adaptor to make the discussion more tangible.

2.9.1 Components

A network adaptor serves as an interface between the host and the network, and as a result, it can be thought of as having two main components: a bus interface that understands how to communicate with the host and a link interface that speaks the correct protocol on the network. There must also be a communication path between these two components, over which incoming and outgoing data is passed. A simple block diagram of a network adaptor is depicted in Figure 2.42.

Network adaptors are always designed for a specific I/O bus, which often precludes moving an adaptor from one vendor's machine to another.[5] Each bus, in effect,

---

[5] Fortunately, there are standards in bus design just as there are in networking, so some adaptors can be used on machines from several vendors.

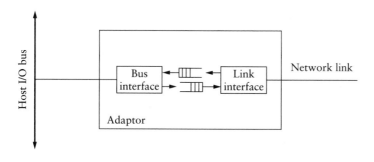

Figure 2.42   Block diagram of a typical network adaptor.

defines a protocol that is used by the host's CPU to program the adaptor, by the adaptor to interrupt the host's CPU, and by the adaptor to read and write memory on the host. One of the main features of an I/O bus is the data transfer rate that it supports. For example, a typical bus might have a 32-bit-wide data path (i.e., it can transfer 32 bits of data in parallel) running at 25 MHz (i.e., the bus's cycle time is 40 ns), giving it a peak transfer rate of 800 Mbps, which would be enough to support a (unidirectional) 622-Mbps STS-12 link. Of course, the peak rate tells us almost nothing about the average rate, which may be much lower.

The link half of the adaptor implements the link-level protocol. For fairly mature technologies like Ethernet, the link half of the adaptor is implemented by a chip set that can be purchased on the commodity market. For newer link technologies, however, the link-level protocol may be implemented in software on a general-purpose microprocessor or perhaps with some form of programmable hardware, such as a field-programmable gate array (FPGA). These approaches generally add to the cost of the adaptor but make it more flexible—it is easier to modify software than hardware and easier to reprogram FPGAs than to redesign boards.

Because the host's bus and the network link are, in all probability, running at different speeds, there is a need to put a small amount of buffering between the two halves of the adaptor. Typically, a small FIFO (byte queue) is enough to hide the asynchrony between the bus and the link.

2.9.2 View from the Host

Since we have spent most of this chapter discussing various protocols that are implemented by the link half of the adaptor, we now turn our attention to the host's view of the network adaptor.

Control Status Register

A network adaptor, like any other device, is ultimately programmed by software running on the CPU. From the CPU's perspective, the adaptor exports a *control status register* (CSR) that is readable and writable from the CPU. The CSR is typically located at some address in the memory, thereby making it possible for the CPU to read and write just like any other memory location. The CPU writes to the CSR to instruct it to transmit and/or receive a frame and reads from the CSR to learn the current state of the adaptor.

The following is an example CSR from the Lance Ethernet device, which is manufactured by Advanced Microsystem Devices (AMD). The Lance device actually has four different control status registers; the following shows the bit masks used to interpret the 16-bit CSR0. To set a bit on the adaptor, the CPU does an inclusive-OR of CSR0 and the mask corresponding to the bit it wants to set. To determine if a particular bit is set, the CPU compares the AND of the contents of CSR0 and the mask against 0.

```
/*
 * Control and status bits for CSR0.
 *
 * Legend:
 *   RO  - Read Only
 *   RC  - Read/Clear (writing 1 clears, writing 0 has no effect)
 *   RW  - Read/Write
 *   W1  - Write-1-only (writing 1 sets, writing 0 has no effect)
 *   RW1 - Read/Write-1-only (writing 1 sets, writing 0 has no effect)
 */

#define LE_ERR    0x8000    /* RO BABL | CERR | MISS | MERR */
#define LE_BABL   0x4000    /* RC transmitted too many bits */
#define LE_CERR   0x2000    /* RC No Heartbeat */
#define LE_MISS   0x1000    /* RC Missed an incoming packet */
#define LE_MERR   0x0800    /* RC Memory Error; no acknowledge */
#define LE_RINT   0x0400    /* RC Received packet Interrupt */
#define LE_TINT   0x0200    /* RC Transmitted packet Interrupt */
#define LE_IDON   0x0100    /* RC Initialization Done */
#define LE_INTR   0x0080    /* RO BABL|MISS|MERR|RINT|TINT|IDON */
#define LE_INEA   0x0040    /* RW Interrupt Enable */
#define LE_RXON   0x0020    /* RO Receiver On */
#define LE_TXON   0x0010    /* RO Transmitter On */
```

```
#define LE_TDMD     0x0008      /* W1 Transmit Demand (send it now) */
#define LE_STOP     0x0004      /* RW1 Stop */
#define LE_STRT     0x0002      /* RW1 Start */
#define LE_INIT     0x0001      /* RW1 Initialize */
```

This definition says, for example, that the host writes a 1 to the least significant bit of CSR0 (0x0001) to initialize the Lance chip. Similarly, if the host sees a 1 in the sixth significant bit (0x0020) and in the fifth significant bit (0x0010), then it knows that the Lance chip is enabled to receive and transmit frames, respectively.

Interrupts

The host CPU could sit in a tight loop reading the adaptor's control status register until something interesting happens and then take the appropriate action. On the Lance chip, for example, it could continually watch for a 1 in the 11th significant bit (0x0400), which would indicate that a frame has just arrived. This is called *polling*, and although it is not an unreasonable design in certain situations (e.g., a network router that has nothing better to do than wait for the next frame), it is not typically done on end hosts that could better spend their time running application programs.

Instead of polling, most hosts only pay attention to the network device when the adaptor interrupts the host. The device raises an interrupt when an event that requires host intervention occurs—for example, a frame has been successfully transmitted or received, or an error occurred when the device was attempting to transmit or receive a frame. The host's architecture includes a mechanism that causes a particular procedure inside the operating system to be invoked when such an interrupt occurs. This procedure is known as an *interrupt handler*, and it inspects the CSR to determine the cause of the interrupt and then takes the appropriate action.

While servicing an interrupt, the host typically *disables* additional interrupts. This keeps the device driver from having to service multiple interrupts at one time. Because interrupts are disabled, the device driver must finish its job quickly (it does not have the time to execute the entire protocol stack), and under no circumstances can it afford to block (that is, suspend execution while awaiting some event). For example, this might be accomplished by having the interrupt handler dispatch a process to take care of the frame and then return. Thus, the handler makes sure that the frame will get processed without having to spend valuable time actually processing the frame itself.

Direct Memory Access versus Programmed I/O

One of the most important issues in network adaptor design is how the bytes of a frame are transferred between the adaptor and the host memory. There are two basic mechanisms: *direct memory access* (DMA) and *programmed I/O* (PIO). With DMA, the adaptor directly reads and writes the host's memory without any CPU involvement;

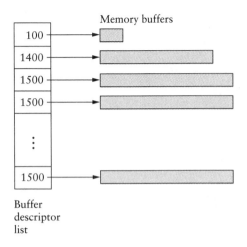

Figure 2.43   Buffer descriptor list.

the host simply gives the adaptor a memory address and the adaptor reads to (writes from) it. With PIO, the CPU is directly responsible for moving data between the adaptor and the host memory: To send a frame, the CPU sits in a tight loop that first reads a word from host memory and then writes it to the adaptor; to receive a frame, the CPU reads words from the adaptor and writes them to memory. We now consider DMA and PIO in more detail.

When using DMA, there is no need to buffer frames on the adaptor; the adaptor reads and writes host memory. (A few bytes of buffering are needed to stage data between the bus and the link, as described above, but complete frames are not buffered on the adaptor.) The CPU is therefore responsible for giving the adaptor a pair of *buffer descriptor lists:* one to transmit out of and one to receive into. A buffer descriptor list is an array of address/length pairs, as illustrated in Figure 2.43.

When receiving frames, the adaptor uses as many buffers as it needs to hold the incoming frame. For example, the descriptor illustrated in Figure 2.43 would cause an Ethernet adaptor that was attempting to receive a 1450-byte frame to put the first 100 bytes in the first buffer and the next 1350 bytes in the second buffer. If a second 1500-byte frame arrived immediately after the first, it would be placed entirely in the third buffer. That is, separate frames are placed in separate buffers, although a single frame may be scattered across multiple buffers. This latter feature is usually called *scatter-read*. In practice, scatter-read is used when the network's maximum frame size is so large that it is wasteful to allocate all buffers big enough to contain the largest possible arriving frame. A mechanism like the **Msg** data structure described

Frames, Buffers, and Messages

As this section has suggested, the network adaptor is the place where the network comes in physical contact with the host. It also happens to be the place where three different worlds intersect: the network, the host architecture, and the host operating system. It turns out that each of these has a different terminology for talking about the same thing. It is important to recognize when this is happening.

From the network's perspective, the adaptor transmits *frames* from the host and receives *frames* into the host. Most of this chapter has been presented from the network perspective, so you should have a good understanding of what the term "frame" means. From the perspective of the host architecture, each frame is received into or transmitted from a *buffer*, which is simply a region of main memory of some length and starting at some address. Finally, from the operating system's perspective, a *message* is an abstract object that holds network frames. Messages are implemented by a data structure that includes pointers to different memory locations (buffers). We saw an example of a message data structure in Chapter 1.

in Section 1.3.3 would then be used to link together all the buffers that make up a single frame. Scatter-read is typically not used on an Ethernet because preallocating 1500-byte buffers does not excessively waste memory.

Output works in a similar way. When the host has a frame to transmit, it puts a pointer to the buffer that contains the frame in the transmit descriptor list. Devices that support *gather-write* allow the frame to be fragmented across multiple physical buffers. In practice, gather-write is more widely used than scatter-read because outgoing frames are often constructed in a piecemeal fashion, with more than one protocol contributing a buffer. For example, by the time a message makes it down the protocol stack and is ready to be transmitted, it consists of a buffer that contains the aggregate header (the collection of headers attached by various protocols that processed the message) and a separate buffer that contains the application's data.

In the case of PIO, the network adaptor must contain some amount of buffering—the CPU copies frames between host memory and this adaptor memory, as illustrated in Figure 2.44. The basic fact that necessitates buffering is that, with most operating systems, you can never be sure when the CPU will get around to doing something, so you need to be prepared to wait for it. One important question that must be addressed is how much memory is needed on the adaptor. There certainly needs to be at least one frame's worth of memory in both the transmit and the receive direction. In addition, adaptors that use PIO usually have additional memory that can

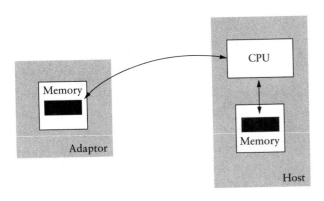

Figure 2.44 Programmed I/O.

be used to hold a small number of incoming frames until the CPU can get around to copying them into host memory. Although the computer system axiom that "memory is cheap" would seem to suggest putting a huge amount of memory on the adaptor, this memory must be of the more expensive dual-ported type because both the CPU and the adaptor read/write it. PIO-based adaptors typically have something on the order of 64 to 256 KB of adaptor memory, although there are adaptors with as much as 1 MB of memory.

2.9.3 Device Drivers

A device driver is a collection of operating system routines that effectively anchor the protocol graph to the network hardware. It typically includes routines to initialize the device, transmit frames on the link, and field interrupts. The code is often difficult to read because it's full of device-specific details, but the overall logic is actually quite simple. For example, the following routine is called to transmit a message on the Lance Ethernet device. We've hidden most of the ugly details in the subroutines next_xmit_desc and prepare_xmit_desc, which return the next available buffer descriptor and translate the OS's representation of a message into the format prescribed by the device's buffer descriptor, respectively.

```
#define  csr    ((u_int *) 0xffff3579 /* magic CSR address */
lance_transmit(Msg *msg)
{
    Descriptor *d;
```

```
        semWait(xmit_queue);
        semWait(mutex);
        disable_interrupts();
        d = next_xmit_desc();
        prepare_xmit_desc(d, msg);
        csr = LE_TDMD | LE_INEA;
        enable_interrupts();
        semSignal(mutex);
    }
```

The routine first waits on a counting semaphore that ensures that there is a free transmit buffer on the device to handle this message. This semaphore (xmit_queue) is initialized to the number of transmit buffers supported by this device, typically 64. This means that up to 64 messages can be queued at any one time on the transmit list (and the calling process allowed to return), and it's not until a process tries to enqueue the 65th message that it is blocked. Any number of processes can block on this semaphore while trying to enqueue their message on the transmit list.

Once there is an available transmit buffer, the invoking process protects itself from other transmitting processes by waiting on a mutual exclusion (mutex) semaphore and from the device by disabling interrupts. The routine then calls the aforementioned subroutines to translate the message from the internal format to that expected by the device, sets the CSR to instruct the device to transmit, enables interrupts, and signals the mutex semaphore.

The logic for the interrupt handler is equally simple, as shown in routine lance_interrupt_handler. It first disables additional interrupts that might interfere with the processing of this interrupt. It then inspects the CSR to determine what caused the interrupt. There are three possibilities: (1) an error has occurred, (2) a transmit request has completed, or (3) a frame has been received. In the first case, the handler prints a message and clears the error bits. In the second case, we know that a transmit request that was queued earlier by lance_transmit has completed, meaning that there is now a free transmit buffer that can be reused. Thus, we signal semaphore xmit_queue, which permits another process blocked in lance_transmit to proceed. In the third case, the handler calls routine lance_receive to extract the incoming frame from the receive buffer list and place it in the OS's internal message data structure, and then start a process to shepherd the message up the protocol graph. As mentioned before, it is important that lance_receive return as quickly as possible since interrupts are disabled; it cannot afford to process the entire protocol stack itself.

```
lance_interrupt_handler()
{
    disable_interrupts();

    /* some error occurred */
    if (csr & LE_ERR)
    {
        print_error(csr);
        /* clear error bits */
        csr = LE_BABL | LE_CERR | LE_MISS | LE_MERR | LE_INEA;
        enable_interrupts();
        return();
    }


    /* transmit interrupt */
    if (csr & LE_TINT)
    {
        /* clear interrupt */
        csr = LE_TINT | LE_INEA;

        /* signal blocked senders */
        semSignal(xmit_queue);

        enable_interrupts();
        return(0);
    }


    /* receive interrupt */
    if (csr & LE_RINT)
    {
        /* clear interrupt */
        csr = LE_RINT | LE_INEA;

    /* process received frame */
    lance_receive();
        enable_interrupts();
        return();
    }
}
```

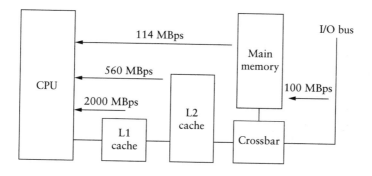

Figure 2.45   Memory bandwidth on an Alpha workstation.

2.9.4   Memory Bottleneck

As discussed in Section 2.1.1, host memory performance is often the limiting factor in network performance. Nowhere is this possibility more critical than at the host/adaptor interface. To help drive this point home, consider Figure 2.45. This diagram shows the bandwidth available between various components of an Alpha workstation, which is representative of workstation-class machines. While the I/O bus is fast enough to transfer frames between the network adaptor and host memory at, say, STS-12 rates (622 Mbps), there are two potential problems.

The first is that the advertised I/O bus speed corresponds to its peak bandwidth. The real limitation is the size of the data block that is being transferred across the I/O bus, since there is a certain amount of overhead involved in each bus transfer. On this particular architecture, for example, it takes 8 clock cycles to acquire the bus for the purpose of transferring data from the adaptor to host memory. This overhead is independent of the number of data bytes transferred. Thus, if you want to transfer a 48-byte payload across the I/O bus—this happens to be the size of an ATM cell— then the whole transfer takes 20 cycles: 8 cycles to acquire the bus and 12 cycles to transfer the data. (The bus is 32 bits wide, which means that it can transfer a 4-byte word during each clock cycle; 48 bytes divided by 4 bytes per cycle equals 12 cycles.) This means that the maximum bandwidth you can achieve is

$$12 \div (8 + 12) \times 800 = 480 \text{ Mbps}$$

not the peak 800 Mbps.

The second problem is that the memory/CPU bandwidth, which is 114 MBps (956 Mbps), is only slightly more than the bandwidth of the I/O bus. Fortunately, this is a measured number rather than an advertised peak rate, meaning that it reflects the fact that data is always transferred between main memory and the higher levels of the memory hierarchy in cache lines (e.g., 64 bytes on this machine). The principal ramification of this memory/CPU number is that it is of the same order of magnitude as the range of network bandwidths this machine can support. Thus, while it is possible to deliver frames across the I/O bus and into memory and then to load the data from memory into the CPU's registers at network bandwidths, it is impractical for the device driver, operating system, and application to go to memory multiple times for each word of data in a network packet, possibly because it needs to copy the data from one buffer to another. In particular, if the memory/CPU path is crossed n times—in either direction, read or write—then the best throughput you can hope for is 114 MBps/n. For example, if the various software layers need to copy the message from one buffer to another five times—not an uncommon situation in today's systems—then the best throughput the application can hope for is just 22 MBps (176 Mbps), a far cry from the 800 Mbps we thought this machine could support.

▶   As an aside, it is important to recognize that there are many parallels between moving a message to and from memory and moving a message across a network. In particular, the effective throughput of the memory system is defined by the same two formulas given in Section 1.1.4.

$$\text{Throughput} = \text{TransferSize}/\text{TransferTime}$$

$$\text{TransferTime} = \text{RTT} + 1/\text{Bandwidth} \times \text{TransferSize}$$

In the case of the memory system, however, the transfer size corresponds to how big a unit of data we can move across the bus in one transfer (i.e., cache line versus small cells versus large message), and the RTT corresponds to the memory latency, that is, whether the memory is on-chip cache, off-chip cache, or main memory. Just as in the case of the network, the larger the transfer size and the smaller the latency, the better the effective throughput. Also similar to a network, the effective memory throughput does not necessarily equal the peak memory bandwidth (i.e., the bandwidth that can be achieved with an infinitely large transfer).

The main point of this discussion is that we must be aware of the limits memory bandwidth places on network performance. If carefully designed, the system can work around these limits. For example, it is possible to integrate the buffers used by the device driver, the operating system, and the application in a way that minimizes data copies. The system also needs to be aware of when data is brought into cache, so it can perform all necessary operations on the data before it gets bumped from the cache. The details of how this is accomplished are beyond the scope of this book, but can be found in papers referenced at the end of the chapter.

2.10 Summary

This chapter introduced the hardware building blocks of a computer network—nodes and links—and discussed the five key problems that must be solved so that two or more nodes that are directly connected by a physical link can exchange messages with each other.

First, physical links carry signals. It is therefore necessary to encode the bits that make up a binary message into the signal at the source node and then to recover the bits from the signal at the receiving node. This is the encoding problem, and it is made challenging by the need to keep the sender's and receiver's clocks synchronized. We discussed four different encoding techniques—NRZ, NRZI, Manchester, and 4B/5B—which differ largely in how they encode clock information along with the data being transmitted. One of the key attributes of an encoding scheme is its efficiency, that is, the ratio of signal pulses to encoded bits.

Once it is possible to transmit bits between nodes, the next step is to figure out how to package these bits into frames. This is the framing problem, and it boils down to being able to recognize the beginning and end of each frame. Again, we looked at several different techniques, including byte-oriented protocols, bit-oriented protocols, and clock-based protocols.

Assuming that each node is able to recognize the collection of bits that make up a frame, the third problem is to determine if those bits are in fact correct, or if they have possibly been corrupted in transit. This is the error detection problem, and we looked at three different approaches: cyclic redundancy check, two-dimensional parity, and checksums. Of these, the CRC approach gives the strongest guarantees and is the most widely used at the link level.

Given that some frames will arrive at the destination node containing errors and thus will have to be discarded, the next problem is how to recover from such losses. The goal is to make the link appear reliable. The general approach to this problem is called ARQ and involves using a combination of acknowledgments and timeouts. We looked at three specific ARQ algorithms: stop-and-wait, sliding window, and concurrent channels. What makes these algorithms interesting is how effectively they use the link, with the goal being to keep the pipe full.

The final problem is not relevant to point-to-point links, but it is the central issue in multiple-access links: how to mediate access to a shared link so that all nodes eventually have a chance to transmit their data. In this case, we looked at three different media access protocols—Ethernet, token ring, and wireless—which have been put to practical use in building local area networks. What these technologies have in common is that control over the network is distributed over all the nodes connected to the network; there is no dependence on a central arbitrator.

We concluded the chapter by observing that, in practice, most of the algorithms that address these five problems are implemented on the adaptor that connects the host to the link. It turns out that the design of this adaptor is of critical importance in how well the network, as a whole, performs.

O P E N   I S S U E

Does It Belong in Hardware?

One of the most important questions in the design of any computer system is, What belongs in hardware and what belongs in software? In the case of networking, the network adaptor finds itself at the heart of this question. For example, why is the Ethernet algorithm, presented in Section 2.6 of this chapter, typically implemented on the network adaptor, while the higher-level protocols discussed later in this book are not?

It is certainly possible to put a general-purpose microprocessor on the network adaptor, which gives you the opportunity to move high-level protocols there, such as TCP/IP. The reason that this is typically not done is complicated, but it comes down to the economics of computer design: the host processor is usually the fastest processor on a computer, and it would be a shame if this fast host processor had to wait for a slower adaptor processor to run TCP/IP when it could have done the job faster itself. On the flip side, some protocol processing does belong on the network adaptor. The general rule of thumb is that any processing for which a fixed processor can keep pace with the link speed—that is, a faster processor would not improve the situation—is a good candidate for being moved to the adaptor. In other words, any function that is already limited by the link speed, as opposed to the processor at the end of the link, might be effectively implemented on the adaptor.

In general, making the call as to what functionality belongs on the network adaptor and what belongs on the host computer is a difficult one, and it is a problem that is reexamined each time someone designs a new network adaptor.

Independent of exactly what protocols are implemented on the network adaptor, generally the data will eventually find its way onto the main computer, and when it does, the efficiency with which the data is moved between the adaptor and the computer's memory is very important. Recall from Section 2.9.4 that memory bandwidth—the rate at which data can be moved from one memory location to another—is typically the limiting factor in how a workstation-class machine performs. An inefficient host/adaptor data transfer mechanism can, therefore, limit the throughput rate seen by application programs running on the host. First, there is the issue of whether DMA or programmed I/O is used; each has advantages in different situations. Second, there is the issue of how well the network adaptor is integrated with the operating system's buffer mechanism; a carefully integrated system is usually able to avoid copying data at a higher level of the protocol graph, thereby improving application-to-application throughput.

FURTHER READING

One of the most important contributions in computer networking over the last 20 years is the original paper by Metcalf and Boggs (1976) introducing the Ethernet. Many years later, Boggs, Mogul, and Kent (1988) reported their practical experiences with Ethernet, debunking many of the myths that had found their way into the literature over the years. Both papers are must reading. The third and fourth papers discuss the issues involved in integrating high-speed network adaptors with system software.

- Metcalf, R., and D. Boggs. Ethernet: Distributed packet switching for local computer networks. *Communications of the ACM* 19(7):395–403, July 1976.

- Boggs, D., J. Mogul, and C. Kent. Measured capacity of an Ethernet. *Proceedings of the SIGCOMM '88 Symposium*, pages 222–234, August 1988.

- Metcalf, R. Computer/network interface design lessons from Arpanet and Ethernet. *IEEE Journal of Selected Areas in Communication (JSAC)* 11(2):173–180, February 1993.

- Druschel, P., M. Abbot, M. Pagels, and L. L. Peterson. Network subsystem design. *IEEE Network (Special Issue on End-System Support for High Speed Networks)* 7(4):8–17, July 1993.

There are countless textbooks with a heavy emphasis on the lower levels of the network hierarchy, with a particular focus on *telecommunications*—networking from the phone company's perspective. Books by Spragins et al. [SHP91] and Minoli [Min93] are two good examples. Several other books concentrate on various local area network technologies. Of these, Stallings's book is the most comprehensive [Sta90], while Jain gives a thorough description of FDDI [Jai94]. Jain's book also gives a good introduction to the low-level details of optical communication. Also, a comprehensive overview of FDDI can be found in Ross's article [Ros86].

For an introduction to information theory, Blahut's book is a good place to start [Bla87], along with Shannon's seminal paper on link capacity [Sha48].

For a general introduction to the mathematics behind error codes, Rao and Fujiwara [RF89] is recommended. For a detailed discussion of the mathematics of

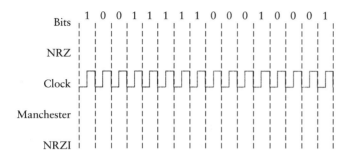

Figure 2.46   Diagram for exercise 1.

CRCs in particular, along with some more information about the hardware used to calculate them, see Peterson and Brown [PB61].

On the topic of network adaptor design, much work was done in the early 1990s by researchers trying to connect hosts to networks running at higher and higher rates. In addition to the two examples given in the reading list, see Traw and Smith [TS93], Ramakrishnan [Ram93], Edwards et al. [EWL+94], Druschel et al. [DPD94], Kanakia and Cheriton [KC88], Cohen et al. [CFFD93], and Steenkiste [Ste94a].

For general information on computer architecture, Hennessy and Patterson's book [HP96] is an excellent reference, while Sites [Sit92] explains the DEC Alpha architecture in detail. (Many of the performance experiments discussed in this book were run on the DEC Alpha.)

Finally, we recommend the following live reference:

■ http://standards.ieee.org/: status of various IEEE network-related standards

EXERCISES

1 Show the NRZ, Manchester, and NRZI encodings for the bit pattern shown in Figure 2.46. Assume that the NRZI signal starts out low.

2 Show the 4B/5B encoding, and the resulting NRZI signal, for the following bit sequence:

   1110 0101 0000 0011

3 In the 4B/5B encoding (Table 2.5), only two of the 5-bit codes used end in two 0s. How many possible 5-bit sequences are there (used by the existing code or not)

that meet the stronger restriction of having at most one leading and at most one trailing 0? Could all 4-bit sequences be mapped to such 5-bit sequences?

4 Assuming a framing protocol that uses bit stuffing, show the bit sequence transmitted over the link when the frame contains the following bit sequence:

   11010111110101111101011111110

   Mark the stuffed bits.

5 Suppose the following sequence of bits arrives over a link:

   1101011111010111110010111110110

   Show the resulting frame after any stuffed bits have been removed. Indicate any errors that might have been introduced into the frame.

6 Suppose you want to send some data using the BISYNC framing protocol, and the last 2 bytes of your data are DLE and ETX. What sequence of bytes would be transmitted immediately prior to the CRC?

7 For each of the following framing protocols, give an example of a byte/bit sequence that should never appear in a transmission.
   (a) BISYNC
   (b) HDLC

8 Assume that a SONET receiver resynchronizes its clock whenever a 1 bit appears; otherwise, the receiver samples the signal in the middle of what it believes is the bit's timeslot.
   (a) What relative accuracy of the sender's and receiver's clocks is required in order to receive correctly 48 zero-bytes (one ATM AAL5 cell's worth) in a row?
   (b) Consider a forwarding station A on a SONET STS-1 line, receiving frames from the downstream end B and retransmitting them upstream. What relative accuracy of A's and B's clocks is required to keep A from accumulating more than one extra frame per minute?

9 Show that two-dimensional parity allows detection of all 3-bit errors.

10 Give an example of a 4-bit error that would not be detected by two-dimensional parity, as illustrated in Figure 2.16. What is the general set of circumstances under which 4-bit errors will be undetected?

11 Show that two-dimensional parity provides the receiver enough information to correct any 1-bit error (assuming the receiver knows only 1 bit is bad), but not any 2-bit error.

12 Show that the Internet checksum will never be 0xFFFF (that is, the final value of sum will not be 0x0000) unless every byte in the buffer is 0. (Internet specifications in fact require that a checksum of 0x0000 be transmitted as 0xFFFF; the value 0x0000 is then reserved for an omitted checksum. Note that, in ones complement arithmetic, 0x0000 and 0xFFFF are both representations of the number 0.)

13 Suppose that one byte in a buffer covered by the Internet checksum algorithm needs to be decremented (e.g., a header hop count field). Give an algorithm to compute the revised checksum without rescanning the entire buffer. Your algorithm should consider whether the byte in question is low order or high order.

14 Show that the Internet checksum can be computed by first taking the 32-bit ones complement sum of the buffer in 32-bit units, then taking the 16-bit ones complement sum of the upper and lower halfwords, and finishing as before by complementing the result. (To take a 32-bit ones complement sum on 32-bit twos complement hardware, you need access to the "overflow" bit.)

15 Suppose we want to transmit the message 11001001 and protect it from errors using the CRC polynomial $x^3 + 1$.

   (a) Use polynomial long division to determine the message that should be transmitted.

   (b) Suppose the leftmost bit of the message is inverted due to noise on the transmission link. What is the result of the receiver's CRC calculation? How does the receiver know that an error has occurred?

16 The CRC algorithm as presented in this chapter requires lots of bit manipulations. It is, however, possible to do polynomial long division taking multiple bits at a time, via a table-driven method, that enables efficient software implementations of CRC. We outline the strategy here for long division 3 bits at a time (see Table 2.7); in practice we would divide 8 bits at a time, and the table would have 256 entries.

p	$q = p \frown 000 \div C$	$C \times q$
000	000	000 000
001	001	001 101
010	011	010 ____
011	0____	011 ____
100	111	100 011
101	110	101 110
110	100	110 ____
111	____	111 ____

Table 2.7 Table-driven CRC calculation.

Let the divisor polynomial $C = C(x)$ be $x^3 + x^2 + 1$, or 1101. To build the table for C, we take each 3-bit sequence, p, append three trailing 0s, and then find the quotient $q = p \frown 000 \div C$, ignoring the remainder. The third column is the product $C \times q$, the first 3 bits of which should equal p.

(a) Verify, for $p = 110$, that the quotients $p \frown 000 \div C$ and $p \frown 111 \div C$ are the same; that is, it doesn't matter what the trailing bits are.

(b) Fill in the missing entries in the table.

(c) Use the table to divide 101 001 011 001 100 by C. Hint: The first 3 bits of the dividend are $p = 101$, so from the table the corresponding first 3 bits of the quotient are $q = 110$. Write the 110 above the second 3 bits of the dividend, and subtract $C \times q = 101$ 110, again from the table, from the first 6 bits of the dividend. Keep going in groups of 3 bits. There should be no remainder.

17 With 1 parity bit we can detect all 1-bit errors. Show that at least one generalization fails, as follows:

(a) Show that if messages m are 8 bits long, then there is no error detection code $e = e(m)$ of size 2 bits that can detect all 2-bit errors. Hint: Consider the set M of all 8-bit messages with a single 1 bit; note that any message from M can be transmuted into any other with a 2-bit error, and show that some pair of messages m_1 and m_2 in M must have the same error code e.

(b) Find an N (not necessarily minimal) such that no 32-bit error detection code applied to N-bit blocks can detect all errors altering up to 8 bits.

18 Consider an ARQ protocol that uses only negative acknowledgments (NAKs), but no positive acknowledgments (ACKs). Describe what timeouts would need to be scheduled. Explain why an ACK-based protocol is usually preferred to a NAK-based protocol.

19 Consider an ARQ algorithm running over a 20-km point-to-point fiber link.

(a) Compute the propagation delay for this link, assuming that the speed of light is 2×10^8 m/s in the fiber.

(b) Suggest a suitable timeout value for the ARQ algorithm to use.

(c) Why might it still be possible for the ARQ algorithm to time out and retransmit a frame, given this timeout value?

20 Suppose you are designing a sliding window protocol for a 1-Mbps point-to-point link to the moon, which has a one-way latency of 1.25 seconds. Assuming that each frame carries 1 KB of data, what is the minimum number of bits you need for the sequence number?

21 The text suggests that the sliding window protocol can be used to implement flow control. We can imagine doing this by having the receiver delay ACKs, that is, not send the ACK until there is free buffer space to hold the next frame. In doing so, each ACK would simultaneously acknowledge the receipt of the last frame and tell the source that there is now free buffer space available to hold the next frame. Explain why implementing flow control in this way is not a good idea.

22 Implicit in the stop-and-wait scenarios of Figure 2.19 is the notion that the receiver will retransmit its ACK immediately on receipt of the duplicate data frame. Suppose instead that the receiver keeps its own timer, and retransmits its ACK only after the next expected frame has not arrived within the timeout interval. Draw timelines illustrating the scenarios in Figure 2.19(b)–(d); assume the receiver's timeout value is twice the sender's. Also redraw (c) assuming the receiver's timeout value is half the sender's.

23 In stop-and-wait transmission, suppose that both sender and receiver retransmit their last frame immediately on receipt of a duplicate ACK or data frame; such a strategy is superficially reasonable because receipt of such a duplicate is most likely to mean the other side has experienced a timeout.

(a) Draw a timeline showing what will happen if the first data frame is somehow duplicated, but no frame is lost. How long will the duplications continue? This situation is known as the Sorcerer's Apprentice bug.

(b) Suppose that, like data, ACKs are retransmitted if there is no response within the timeout period. Suppose also that both sides use the same timeout interval. Identify a reasonably likely scenario for triggering the Sorcerer's Apprentice bug.

24 Give some details of how you might augment the sliding window protocol with flow control by having ACKs carry additional information that reduces the SWS as the receiver runs out of buffer space. Illustrate your protocol with a timeline for a transmission; assume the initial SWS and RWS are 4, the link speed is instantaneous, and the receiver can free buffers at the rate of one per second (i.e., the receiver is the bottleneck). Show what happens at $T = 0, T = 1, \ldots, T = 4$ seconds.

25 Describe a protocol combining the sliding window algorithm with selective ACKs. Your protocol should retransmit promptly, but not if a frame simply arrives one or two positions out of order. Your protocol should also make explicit what happens if several consecutive frames are lost.

26 Draw a timeline diagram for the sliding window algorithm with SWS = RWS = 3 frames, for the following two situations. Use a timeout interval of about 2 × RTT.

(a) Frame 4 is lost.

(b) Frames 4–6 are lost.

27 Suppose that we attempt to run the sliding window algorithm with SWS = RWS = 3 and with MaxSeqNum = 5. The Nth packet DATA[N] thus actually contains N mod 5 in its sequence number field. Give an example in which the algorithm becomes confused; that is, a scenario in which the receiver expects DATA[5] and accepts DATA[0]—which has the same transmitted sequence number—in its stead. No packets may arrive out of order. Note this implies MaxSeqNum ≥ 6 is necessary as well as sufficient.

28 Consider the sliding window algorithm with SWS = RWS = 3, with no out-of-order arrivals, and with infinite-precision sequence numbers.

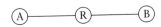

Figure 2.47   Diagram for Exercises 30–32.

(a) Show that if DATA[6] is in the receive window, then DATA[0] (or in general any older data) cannot arrive at the receiver (and hence that MaxSeqNum = 6 would have sufficed).

(b) Show that if ACK[6] may be sent (or, more literally, that DATA[5] is in the sending window), then ACK[2] (or earlier) cannot be received.

These amount to a proof of the formula given in Section 2.5.2, particularized to the case SWS = 3. Note that part (b) implies that the scenario of the previous problem cannot be reversed to involve a failure to distinguish ACK[0] and ACK[5].

29 Suppose that we run the sliding window algorithm with SWS = 5 and RWS = 3, and no out-of-order arrivals.

(a) Find the smallest value for MaxSeqNum. You may assume that it suffices to find the smallest MaxSeqNum such that if DATA[MaxSeqNum] is in the receive window, then DATA[0] can no longer arrive.

(b) Give an example showing that MaxSeqNum − 1 is not sufficient.

(c) State a general rule for the minimum MaxSeqNum in terms of SWS and RWS.

30 Suppose A is connected to B via an intermediate router R, as shown in Figure 2.47. The A–R and R–B links each accept and transmit only one packet per second in each direction (so two packets take 2 seconds), and the two directions transmit independently. Assume A sends to B using the sliding window protocol with SWS = 4.

(a) For Time = 0, 1, 2, 3, 4, 5, state what packets arrive at and leave each node, or label them on a timeline.

(b) What happens if the links have a propagation delay of 1.0 seconds, but accept immediately as many packets as are offered (i.e., latency = 1 second but bandwidth is infinite)?

31 Suppose A is connected to B via an intermediate router R, as in the previous problem. The A–R link is instantaneous, but the R–B link transmits only one packet each second, one at a time (so two packets take 2 seconds). Assume A sends to B using the sliding window protocol with SWS = 4. For Time = 0, 1, 2, 3, 4, state

Item	Delay
Coaxial cable	propagation speed .77c
Link/drop cable	propagation speed .65c
Repeaters	approximately 0.6 μs each
Transceivers	approximately 0.2 μs each

Table 2.8 Typical delays associated with various devices (Exercise 34).

what packets arrive at and are sent from A and B. How large does the queue at R grow?

32 Consider the situation in the previous exercise, except this time assume that the router has a queue size of 1; that is, it can hold one packet in addition to the one it is sending (in each direction). Let A's timeout be 5 seconds, and let SWS again be 4. Show what happens at each second from $T = 0$ until all four packets from the first windowful are successfully delivered.

33 Why is it important for protocols configured on top of the Ethernet to have a length field in their header, indicating how long the message is?

34 The 1982 Ethernet specification allowed between any two stations up to 1500 m of coaxial cable, 1000 m of other point-to-point link cable, and two repeaters. Each station or repeater connects to the coaxial cable via up to 50 m of "drop cable." Typical delays associated with each device are given in Table 2.8 (where c = speed of light in a vacuum = 3×10^8 m/s).

What is the worst-case round-trip propagation delay, measured in bits, due to the sources listed? (This list is not complete; other sources of delay include sense time and signal rise time.)

35 Coaxial cable Ethernet was limited to a maximum of 500 m between repeaters, which regenerate the signal to 100% of its original amplitude. Along one 500-m segment, the signal could decay to no less than 14% of its original value (8.5 dB). Along 1500 m, then, the decay might be $(0.14)^3 = 0.3\%$. Such a signal, even along 2500 m, is still strong enough to be read; why then are repeaters required every 500 m?

36 Suppose the round-trip propagation delay for Ethernet is 46.4 μs. This yields a minimum packet size of 512 bits (464 bits corresponding to propagation delay + 48 bits of jam signal).

(a) What happens to the minimum packet size if the delay time is held constant, and the signaling rate rises to 100 Mbps?

(b) What are the drawbacks to so large a minimum packet size?

(c) If compatibility were not an issue, how might the specifications be written so as to permit a smaller minimum packet size?

37 Let A and B be two stations attempting to transmit on an Ethernet. Each has a steady queue of frames ready to send; A's frames will be numbered A_1, A_2, and so on, and B's similarly. Let $T = 51.2$ μs be the exponential backoff base unit.

Suppose A and B simultaneously attempt to send frame 1, collide, and happen to choose backoff times of $0 \times T$ and $1 \times T$, respectively, meaning A wins the race and transmits A_1 while B waits. At the end of this transmission, B will attempt to retransmit B_1 while A will attempt to transmit A_2. These first attempts will collide, but now A backs off for either $0 \times T$ or $1 \times T$, while B backs off for time equal to one of $0 \times T, \ldots, 3 \times T$.

(a) Give the probability that A wins this second backoff race immediately after this first collision; that is, A's first choice of backoff time $k \times 51.2$ is less than B's.

(b) Suppose A wins this second backoff race. A transmits A_3, and when it is finished, A and B collide again as A tries to transmit A_4 and B tries once more to transmit B_1. Give the probability that A wins this third backoff race immediately after the first collision.

(c) Give a reasonable lower bound for the probability that A wins all the remaining backoff races.

(d) What then happens to the frame B_1?

This scenario is known as the Ethernet *capture effect*.

38 Suppose the Ethernet transmission algorithm is modified as follows: After each successful transmission attempt, a host waits one or two slot times before attempting to transmit again, and otherwise backs off the usual way.

(a) Explain why the capture effect of the previous exercise is now much less likely.

(b) Show how the strategy above can now lead to a pair of hosts capturing the Ethernet, alternating transmissions, and locking out a third.

(c) Propose an alternative approach, for example, by modifying the exponential backoff. What aspects of a station's history might be used as parameters to the modified backoff?

39 Suppose A, B, and C all make their first carrier sense, as part of an attempt to transmit, while a fourth station D is transmitting. Draw a timeline showing one possible sequence of transmissions, attempts, collisions, and exponential backoff choices. Your timeline should also meet the following criteria: (i) initial transmission attempts should be in the order A, B, C but successful transmissions should be in the order C, B, A, and (ii) there should be at least four collisions.

40 Repeat the previous exercise, now with the assumption that Ethernet is p-persistent with $p = 0.33$ (that is, a waiting station transmits immediately with probability p when the line goes idle, and otherwise defers one 51.2-μs slot time and repeats the process). Your timeline should meet criterion (i) of the previous problem, but in lieu of criterion (ii), you should show at least one collision and at least one run of four deferrals on an idle line. Again, note that many solutions are possible.

41 Suppose Ethernet physical addresses are chosen at random (using true random bits).

(a) What is the probability that on a 1024-host network, two addresses will be the same?

(b) What is the probability that the above event will occur on some one or more of 2^{20} networks?

(c) What is the probability that of the 2^{30} hosts in all the networks of (b), some pair has the same address?

Hint: The calculation for (a) and (c) is a variant of that used in solving the so-called Birthday Problem: Given N people, what is the probability that two of their birthdays (addresses) will be the same? The second person has probability $1 - \frac{1}{365}$ of having a different birthday from the first, the third has probability $1 - \frac{2}{365}$ of having a different birthday from the first two, and so on. The probability all birthdays are different is thus

$$\left(1 - \frac{1}{365}\right) \times \left(1 - \frac{2}{365}\right) \times \cdots \times \left(1 - \frac{N-1}{365}\right)$$

which for smallish N is about

$$1 - \frac{1 + 2 + \cdots + (N-1)}{365}$$

42 Suppose five stations are waiting for another packet to finish on an Ethernet. All transmit at once when the packet is finished and collide.

(a) Simulate this situation up until the point when one of the five waiting stations succeeds. Use coin flips or some other genuine random source to determine backoff times. Make the following simplifications: Ignore interframe spacing, ignore variability in collision times (so that retransmission is always after an exact integral multiple of the 51.2-μs slot time), and assume that each collision uses up exactly one slot time.

(b) Discuss the effect of the listed simplifications in your simulation versus the behavior you might encounter on a real Ethernet.

43 Write a program to implement the simulation discussed above, this time with N stations waiting to transmit. Again model time as an integer, T, in units of slot times, and again treat collisions as taking one slot time (so a collision at time T followed by a backoff of $k = 0$ would result in a retransmission attempt at time T + 1). Find the average delay before *one* station transmits successfully, for $N = 20$, $N = 40$, and $N = 100$. Does your data support the notion that the delay is linear in N? Hint: For each station, keep track of that station's NextTimeToSend and CollisionCount. You are done when you reach a time T for which there is only one station with NextTimeToSend == T. If there is no such station, increment T. If there are two or more, schedule the retransmissions and try again.

44 Suppose that N Ethernet stations, all trying to send at the same time, require $N/2$ slot times to sort out who transmits next. Assuming the average packet size is 5 slot times, express the available bandwidth as a function of N.

45 Consider the following Ethernet model. Transmission attempts are at random times with an average spacing of λ slot times; specifically, the interval between consecutive attempts is an exponential random variable $x = -\lambda \log u$, where u is chosen randomly in the interval $0 \leq u \leq 1$. An attempt at time t results in a collision if there is another attempt in the range from $t - 1$ to $t + 1$, where t is measured in units of the 51.2-μs slot time; otherwise the attempt succeeds.

(a) Write a program to simulate, for a given value of λ, the average number of slot times needed before a successful transmission, called the *contention interval*. Find the minimum value of the contention interval. Note that you will have to find one attempt past the one that succeeds, in order to determine if there was a collision. Ignore retransmissions, which probably do not fit the random model above.

(b) The Ethernet alternates between contention intervals and successful transmissions. Suppose the average successful transmission lasts 8 slot times (512 bytes). Using your minimum length of the contention interval from above, what fraction of the theoretical 10-Mbps bandwidth is available for transmissions?

46 What conditions would have to hold for a corrupted frame to circulate forever on a token ring without a monitor? How does the monitor fix this problem?

47 An IEEE 802.5 token ring has five stations and a total wire length of 230 m. How many bits of delay must the monitor insert into the ring? Do this for both 4 Mbps and 16 Mbps; use a propagation rate of 2.3×10^8 m/s.

48 Consider a token ring network like FDDI in which a station is allowed to hold the token for some period of time (the *token holding time*, or THT). Let RingLatency denote the time it takes the token to make one complete rotation around the network when none of the stations have any data to send.

(a) In terms of THT and RingLatency, express the efficiency of this network when only a single station is active.

(b) What setting of THT would be optimal for a network that had only one station active (with data to send) at a time?

(c) In the case where N stations are active, give an upper bound on the token rotation time, or TRT, for the network.

49 Consider a token ring with a ring latency of 200 μs. Assuming that the delayed token release strategy is used, what is the effective throughput rate that can be achieved if the ring has a bandwidth of 4 Mbps? What is the effective throughput rate that can be achieved if the ring has a bandwidth of 100 Mbps? Answer for both a single active host and for "many" hosts; for the latter, assume there are sufficiently many hosts transmitting that the time spent advancing the token can be ignored. Assume a packet size of 1 KB.

50 For a 100-Mbps token ring network with a token rotation time of 200 μs and that allows each station to transmit one 1-KB packet each time it possesses the token, calculate the maximum effective throughput rate that any one host can achieve. Do this assuming (a) immediate release and (b) delayed release.

51 Suppose a 100-Mbps delayed-release token ring has 10 stations, a ring latency of 30 μs, and an agreed-on TTRT of 350 μs.

(a) How many synchronous frame bytes could each station send, assuming all are allocated the same amount?

(b) Assume stations A, B, C are in increasing order on the ring. Due to uniform synchronous traffic, the TRT without asynchronous data is 300 μs. B sends a 200-μs (2.5-Kb) asynchronous frame. What TRT will A, B, and C then see on their next measurement? Who may transmit such a frame next?

T he directly connected networks described in the previous chapter suffer from two limitations. First, there is a limit to how many hosts can be attached. For example, only two hosts can be attached to a point-to-point link, and an Ethernet can connect up to only 1024 hosts. Second, there is a limit to how large of a geographic area a single network can serve. For example, an Ethernet can span only 1500 m, and even though point-to-point links can be quite long, they do not really serve the area between the two ends. Since our goal is to build networks that can be global in scale, the next problem is therefore to enable communication between hosts that are not directly connected.

This problem is not unlike the one addressed in the telephone network: Your phone is not directly connected to every person you might want to call, but instead is connected to an exchange that contains a *switch*. It is the switches that create the impression that you have a connection to the person at the other end of the call. Similarly, computer networks use *packet switches* (as distinct from the *circuit switches* used for telephony) to enable packets to travel from one host to another, even when no direct connection exists between those hosts. This chapter introduces the major concepts of packet switching, which lies at the heart of computer networking.

A packet switch is a device with several inputs and outputs leading to and from the hosts that the switch interconnects. The core job of a switch is to take packets that arrive on an input and *forward* (or *switch*) them to the right output so that they will reach their appropriate destination. There are a variety of ways that the switch can determine the "right" output for a packet, which can be broadly categorized as connectionless and connection-oriented approaches.

A key problem that a switch must deal with is the finite bandwidth of its outputs. If packets destined for a certain output arrive at a switch and their arrival rate exceeds the capacity of that output, then we have a problem of *contention*. The switch queues (buffers) packets until the contention subsides, but if it lasts too long, the switch will run out of buffer space and be forced to discard packets. When packets are discarded too frequently, the switch is said to be *congested*. The ability of a switch to handle contention is a key aspect of its performance, and many high-performance switches use exotic hardware to reduce the effects of contention.

This chapter introduces the issues of forwarding and contention in packet switches. For the most part, these discussions apply to a wide range of packet-switched technologies. However, two particular technologies warrant detailed examination. The first is *LAN switching*, which has evolved from Ethernet *bridging* to become one of the dominant technologies in today's LAN environments. The second noteworthy switching technology is *asynchronous transfer mode* (ATM), which is popular in wide area networks. The chapter concludes with a discussion of the hardware that can be used to implement a packet switch. This discussion of switches focuses on contention; we postpone the related problem of congestion until Chapter 6.

3

Packet
Switching

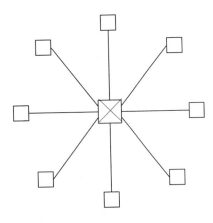

Figure 3.1 A switch provides a star topology.

3.1 Switching and Forwarding

In the simplest terms, a switch is a mechanism that allows us to interconnect links to form a larger network. A switch is a multi-input, multi-output device, which transfers packets from an input to one or more outputs. Thus, a switch adds the star topology (see Figure 3.1) to the point-to-point link, bus (Ethernet), and ring (802.5 and FDDI) topologies established in the last chapter. There are several nice features of a star topology:

- Even though a switch has a fixed number of inputs and outputs, which limits the number of hosts that can be connected to a single switch, large networks can be built by interconnecting a number of switches.

- We can connect switches to each other and to hosts using point-to-point links, which typically means that we can build networks of large geographic scope.

- Adding a new host to the network by connecting it to a switch does not necessarily mean that the hosts already connected will get worse performance from the network.

This last claim cannot be made for the shared-media networks discussed in the last chapter. For example, it is impossible for two hosts on the same Ethernet to transmit continuously at 10 Mbps because they share the same transmission medium. Every host on a switched network has its own link to the switch, so it may be entirely possible for many hosts to transmit at the full link speed (bandwidth), provided that the switch is designed with enough aggregate capacity. Providing high aggregate throughput is one of the design goals for a switch; we return to this topic in Section 3.4.

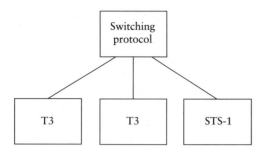

Figure 3.2 Example protocol graph running on a switch. ← Detail protocol

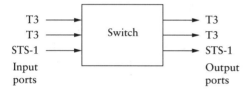

Figure 3.3 Example switch with three input and output ports.

In general, switched networks are considered more *scalable* (i.e., more capable of growing to large numbers of nodes) than shared-media networks because of this ability to support many hosts at full speed.

A switch is connected to a set of links and, for each of these links, runs the appropriate data link protocol to communicate with the node at the other end of the link. A switch's primary job is to receive incoming packets on one of its links and to transmit them on some other link. This function is sometimes referred to as either *switching* or *forwarding*, and in terms of the OSI architecture, it is the main function of the network layer. Figure 3.2 shows the protocol graph that would run on a switch that is connected to two T3 links and one STS-1 SONET link. A representation of this same switch is given in Figure 3.3. In this figure, we have split the input and output halves of each link, and we refer to each input or output as a *port*. (In general, we assume that each link is bidirectional, and hence supports both input and output.) In other words, this example switch has three input ports and three output ports.

The question then is, how does the switch decide which output port to place each packet on? The general answer is that it looks at the header of the packet for an identifier that it uses to make the decision. The details of how it uses this identifier vary, but there are two common approaches. The first is the *datagram* or *connectionless* approach. The second is the *virtual circuit* or *connection-oriented* approach. A third approach, *source routing*, is less common than these other two, but it is simple to explain and does have some useful applications.

One thing that is common to all networks is that we need to have a way to identify the end nodes. Such identifiers are usually called addresses. We have already seen examples of addresses in the previous chapter, for example, the 48-bit address used for Ethernet. The only requirement for Ethernet addresses is that no two nodes on a network have the same address. This is accomplished by making sure that all Ethernet cards are assigned a *globally unique* identifier. For the following discussions, we assume that each host has a globally unique address. Later on, we consider other useful properties that an address might have, but global uniqueness is adequate to get us started.

Another assumption that we need to make is that there is some way to identify the input and output ports of each switch. There are at least two sensible ways to identify ports: One is to number each port, and the other is to identify the port by the name of the node (switch or host) to which it leads. For now, we use numbering of the ports.

3.1.1 Datagrams   or (connectionless)

The idea behind datagrams is incredibly simple: You just make sure that every packet contains enough information to enable any switch to decide how to get it to its destination. That is, every packet contains the complete destination address. Consider the example network illustrated in Figure 3.4, in which the hosts have addresses A, B, C, and so on. To decide how to forward a packet, a switch consults a *forwarding table* (often called a *routing table*), an example of which is depicted in Table 3.1. This particular table shows the forwarding information that switch 2 needs to forward datagrams in the example network. It is pretty easy to figure out such a table when you have a complete map of a simple network like that depicted here; we could imagine a network operator configuring the tables statically. It is a lot harder to create the forwarding tables in large, complex networks with dynamically changing topologies and multiple paths between destinations. That harder problem is known as *routing* and is the topic of Section 4.2. We can think of routing as a process that takes place in the background so that, when a data packet turns up, we will have the right information in the forwarding table to be able to forward, or switch, the packet.

Connectionless (datagram) networks have the following characteristics:

■ A host can send a packet anywhere at any time, since any packet that turns up at a switch can be immediately forwarded (assuming a correctly populated forwarding table). As we will see, this contrasts with most connection-oriented

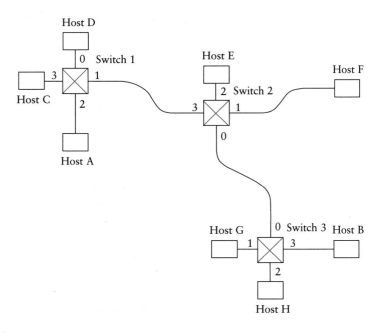

Figure 3.4   Datagram forwarding: an example network.

Destination	Port
A	3
B	0
C	3
D	3
E	2
F	1
G	0
H	0

Table 3.1   Forwarding table for switch 2.

networks, in which some "connection state" needs to be established before the first data packet is sent.

■ When a host sends a packet, it has no way of knowing if the network is capable of delivering it or if the destination host is even up and running.

■ Each packet is forwarded independently of previous packets that might have been sent to the same destination. Thus, two successive packets from host A to host B may follow completely different paths (perhaps because of a change in the forwarding table at some switch in the network).

■ A switch or link failure might not have any serious effect on communication if it is possible to find an alternate route around the failure and to update the forwarding table accordingly.

This last fact is particularly important to the history of datagram networks. One of the important goals of the ARPANET, forerunner to the Internet, was to develop networking technology that would be robust in a military environment, where you might expect links and nodes to fail because of active attacks such as bombing. It was the ability to route around failures that led to a datagram-based design.

3.1.2 Virtual Circuit Switching

A widely used technique for packet switching, which differs significantly from the datagram model, uses the concept of a *virtual circuit* (VC). This approach, which is also called a connection-oriented model, requires that we first set up a virtual connection from the source host to the destination host. To understand how this works, consider Figure 3.5, where host A again wants to send packets to host B. We can think of this as a two-stage process. The first stage is "connection setup." The second is data transfer. We consider each in turn.

In the connection setup phase, it is necessary to establish "connection state" in each of the switches between the source and destination hosts. There are two broad classes of approach to establishing this state. One is to have a network administrator configure the state, in which case the virtual circuit is "permanent." Of course, it can also be deleted by the administrator, so a permanent virtual circuit (PVC) might best be thought of as a long-lived VC. Alternatively, a host can send messages into the network to cause the state to be established. This is referred to as *signalling*, and the resulting virtual circuits are said to be *switched*. The salient characteristic of a switched virtual circuit (SVC) is that a host may set up and delete such a VC dynamically without the involvement of a network administrator. Note that an SVC should more accurately be called a "signalled" VC, since it is the use of signalling (not switching) that distinguishes an SVC from a PVC.

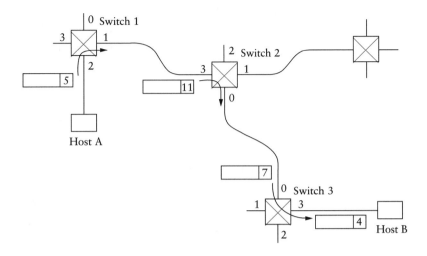

Figure 3.5   An example of a virtual circuit network.

Let us first consider how a PVC could be established. The connection state required in a virtual circuit switch consists of an entry in a VC table for each connection. One entry contains

■ an incoming interface on which packets for this VC arrive

■ a *virtual circuit identifier* (VCI) that will be carried in the arriving packets

■ an outgoing interface in which packets for this VC leave the switch

■ a VCI that will be used for outgoing packets

Note that the combination of incoming interface and incoming VCI uniquely identifies the virtual connection. Thus, whenever we create a new connection, we need to ensure that it is assigned a VCI that is not currently in use on the interface on which its packets will arrive. Also, we observe that the incoming and outgoing VCI values are generally not the same. Thus, the VCI is not a globally significant identifier for the VC; rather, it has significance only on a given link.

To establish a VC from host A to host B, the network administrator picks VCI values that are currently unused on each link for the connection. For the purposes of our example, let's suppose that the VCI value 5 is chosen for the link from A to switch 1; 11 is chosen for the link from switch 1 to switch 2; 7 for the link from switch 2 to switch 3; and 4 for the link to host B. In that case, each switch needs to be configured with VC table entries as shown in Table 3.2. Note that what is shown here is one line from each of three separate switch tables.

Incoming Interface	Incoming VCI	Outgoing Interface	Outgoing VCI
2	5	1	11
⋮	⋮	⋮	⋮

VC table at switch 1

Incoming Interface	Incoming VCI	Outgoing Interface	Outgoing VCI
3	11	0	7
⋮	⋮	⋮	⋮

VC table at switch 2

Incoming Interface	Incoming VCI	Outgoing Interface	Outgoing VCI
0	7	3	4
⋮	⋮	⋮	⋮

VC table at switch 3

Table 3.2 Virtual circuit table entries for three switches.

Once the VC tables have been set up, the data transfer phase can proceed. For any packet that it wants to send to host B, A puts the VCI value of 5 in the packet and sends it to switch 1. Switch 1 receives any such packet on interface 2, and it uses the combination of the interface and the VCI to find the appropriate VC table entry. As shown in Table 3.2, the table entry in this case tells switch 1 to forward the packet out of interface 1 and to use the VCI value 11 when the packet is sent. Thus, the packet will arrive at switch 2 on interface 3 bearing VCI 11 and will thus be switched appropriately, and so on until it arrives at host B with the VCI value of 4 in the packet. To host B, this identifies the packet as having come from host A.

In real networks of reasonable size, the burden of configuring VC tables correctly in a large number of switches would quickly become excessive using the above procedures. Thus, some sort of signalling is almost always used, even when setting up "permanent" VCs. In the case of PVCs, signalling is done by the network administrator, while SVCs are usually set up using signalling by one of the hosts. We consider now how the same VC just described could be set up by signalling.

To start the signalling process, host A sends a setup message into the network, that is, to switch 1. The setup message contains, among other things, the complete destination address of host B. The setup message needs to get all the way to B to create the necessary connection state in every switch along the way. We can see that getting the setup message to B is a lot like getting a datagram to B, in that the switches have to know which output to send the setup message to so that it eventually reaches B. For now, let's just assume that the switches are able to figure out how to do that, so that the setup message flows on to switches 2 and 3 before finally reaching host B.

When switch 1 receives the connection request, in addition to sending it on to switch 2, it creates a new entry in its virtual circuit table for this new connection. The important things in this entry are the port on which the setup message arrived (port 2), the port on which it was sent to continue on to B (port 1), an incoming VCI, and an outgoing VCI. The switch picks a value for the incoming VCI subject to the constraint that it must be a value that is not currently in use for that port. In this example, the switch picks the value 5. The virtual circuit table now has the following information: "When packets arrive on port 2 with identifier 5, send them out on port 1." Of course, the switch will have to tell host A to put the VCI value of 5 in packets that it wants to send to B; we will see how that happens below.

When switch 2 receives the setup message, it performs a similar process; in this example it picks the value 11 as the incoming VCI value. Similarly switch 3 picks 7 as the value for its incoming VCI. Each switch can pick any number it likes, as long as that number is not currently in use for some other connection on that port of that switch. As noted above, VCIs have "link-local scope"; that is, they have no global significance.

Finally the setup message arrives as host B. Assuming that B is healthy and willing to accept a connection from host A, it too allocates an incoming VCI value, in this case 4. This VCI value can be used by B to identify all packets coming from host A.

Now, to complete the connection, everyone needs to be told what their down-stream neighbor is using as the VCI for this connection. Host B sends an acknowledgment of the connection setup to switch 3 and includes in that message the VCI that it chose (4). Now switch 3 can complete the virtual circuit table entry for this connection, since it knows the outgoing value must be 4. Switch 3 sends the acknowledgment on to switch 2, specifying a VCI of 7. Switch 2 sends the message on to switch 1, specifying a VCI of 11. Finally, switch 1 passes the acknowledgment on to host A, telling it to use the VCI of 5 for this connection.

At this point, everyone knows all that is necessary to allow traffic to flow from host A to host B. Each switch has a complete virtual circuit table entry for the connection. Furthermore, host A has a firm acknowledgment that everything is in place all the way to host B. At this point, the connection table entries are in place in all three switches just as in the administratively configured example above, but the whole process happened automatically in response to the signalling message sent from A. The data transfer phase can now begin and is identical to that used in the PVC case.

When host A no longer wants to send data to host B, it tears down the connection by sending a teardown message to switch 1. The switch removes the relevant entry from its table and forwards the message on to the other switches in the path, which similarly delete the appropriate table entries. At this point, if host A were to send a packet with a VCI of 5 to switch 1, it would be dropped as if the connection had never existed.

There are several things to note about virtual circuit switching:

■ Since host A has to wait for the connection request to reach the far side of the network and return before it can send its first data packet, there is at least one RTT of delay before data is sent.[1]

■ While the connection request contains the full address for host B (which might be quite large, being a global identifier on the network), each data packet contains only a small identifier, which is only unique on one link. Thus, the per-packet overhead caused by the header is reduced.

■ If a switch or a link in a connection fails, the connection is broken and a new one will need to

Introduction to Congestion

Recall the distinction between contention and congestion: Contention occurs when multiple packets have to be queued at a switch because they are competing for the same output link, while congestion means that the switch has so many packets queued that it runs out of buffer space and has to start dropping packets. We return to the topic of congestion in Chapter 6, after we have seen the transport protocol component of the network architecture. At this point, however, we observe that the decision as to whether your network uses virtual circuits or datagrams has an impact on how you deal with congestion.

On the one hand, suppose that each switch allocates enough buffers to handle the packets belonging to each virtual circuit it supports, as is done in an X.25 network. In this case, the network has defined away the problem of congestion—a switch never encounters a situation in which it has more packets to queue than it has buffer space, since it does not allow the connection to be established in the first place unless it can dedicate

---

[1] This is not strictly true. Some people have proposed "optimistically" sending a data packet immediately after sending the connection request. However, most current implementations wait for connection setup to complete before sending data.

be established. Also, the old one needs to be torn down to free up table storage space in the switches.

■ The issue of how a switch decides which link to forward the connection request on has been glossed over. We discuss this issue in Section 4.2.

enough resources to it to avoid this situation. The problem with this approach, however, is that it is extremely conservative—it is unlikely that all the circuits will need to use all of their buffers at the same time, and as a consequence, the switch is potentially underutilized.

On the other hand, the datagram model seemingly invites congestion—you do not know that there is enough contention at a switch to cause congestion until you run out of buffers. At that point, it is too late to prevent the congestion, and your only choice is to try to recover from it. The good news, of course, is that you are likely to get much better utilization out of your switches since you are not holding buffers in reserve for a worst-case scenario that is unlikely to happen.

As is quite often the case, nothing is strictly black and white—there are design advantages for defining congestion away (as the X.25 model does) and for doing nothing about congestion until after it happens (as the simple datagram model does). We describe some of these design points in Chapter 6.

One of the nice aspects of virtual circuits is that by the time the host gets the go-ahead to send data, it knows quite a lot about the network—for example, that there really is a route to the receiver and that the receiver is willing and able to receive data. It is also possible to allocate resources to the virtual circuit at the time it is established. For example, an X.25 network—a packet-switched network that uses the connection-oriented model—employs the following three-part strategy:

1 Buffers are allocated to each virtual circuit when the circuit is initialized.

2 The sliding window protocol is run between each pair of nodes along the virtual circuit, and this protocol is augmented with flow control to keep the sending node from overrunning the buffers allocated at the receiving node.

3 The circuit is rejected by a given node if not enough buffers are available at that node when the connection request message is processed.

In doing these three things, each node is ensured of having the buffers it needs to queue the packets that arrive on that circuit. This basic strategy is usually called *hop-by-hop flow control*.

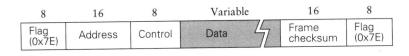

8	16	8	Variable		16	8
Flag (0x7E)	Address	Control	Data		Frame checksum	Flag (0x7E)

Figure 3.6 Frame Relay packet format.

By comparison, a datagram network has no connection establishment phase, and each switch processes each packet independently, making it less obvious how a datagram network would allocate resources in a meaningful way. Instead, each arriving packet competes with all other packets for buffer space. If there are no free buffers, the incoming packet must be discarded. We observe, however, that even in a datagram-based network, a source host often sends a sequence of packets to the same destination host. It is possible for each switch to distinguish among the set of packets it currently has queued, based on the source/destination pair, and thus for the switch to ensure that the packets belonging to each source/destination pair are receiving a fair share of the switch's buffers. We discuss this idea in much greater depth in Chapter 6.

In the virtual circuit model, we could imagine providing each circuit with a different *quality of service* (QoS). In this setting, the term "quality of service" is usually taken to mean that the network gives the user some kind of performance-related guarantee, which in turn implies that switches set aside the resources they need to meet this guarantee. For example, the switches along a given virtual circuit might allocate a percentage of each outgoing link's bandwidth to that circuit. As another example, a sequence of switches might ensure that packets belonging to a particular circuit not be delayed (queued) for more than a certain amount of time. We return to the topic of quality of service in Section 6.5.

The most popular examples of virtual circuit technologies are X.25, Frame Relay, and asynchronous transfer mode (ATM). ATM has a number of interesting properties that we discuss in Section 3.3. Frame Relay is a rather straightforward implementation of virtual circuit technology, and its simplicity has made it extremely popular. Many network service providers offer Frame Relay PVC services. One of the applications of Frame Relay is the construction of *virtual private networks* (VPNs), a subject discussed in Section 4.1.8.

Frame Relay provides some basic quality of service and congestion-avoidance features, but these are rather lightweight compared to X.25 and ATM. The Frame Relay packet format (see Figure 3.6) provides a good example of a packet used for virtual circuit switching.

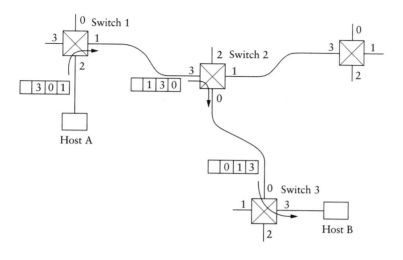

Figure 3.7 Source routing in a switched network (where the switch reads the rightmost number).

3.1.3 Source Routing

A third approach to switching that uses neither virtual circuits nor conventional datagrams is known as source routing. The name derives from the fact that all the information about network topology that is required to switch a packet across the network is provided by the source host.

There are various ways to implement source routing. One would be to assign a number to each output of each switch and to place that number in the header of the packet. The switching function is then very simple: For each packet that arrives on an input, the switch would read the port number in the header and transmit the packet on that output. However, since there will in general be more than one switch in the path between the sending and the receiving host, the header for the packet needs to contain enough information to allow every switch in the path to determine which output the packet needs to be placed on. One way to do this would be to put an ordered list of switch ports in the header and to rotate the list so that the next switch in the path is always at the front of the list. Figure 3.7 illustrates this idea.

In this example, the packet needs to traverse three switches to get from host A to host B. At switch 1, it needs to exit on port 1, at the next switch it needs to exit at port 0, and at the third switch it needs to exit at port 3. Thus, the original header when the packet leaves host A contains the list of ports (3, 0, 1), where we assume that each switch reads the rightmost element of the list. To make sure that the next switch gets the appropriate information, each switch rotates the list after it has read its own entry. Thus, the packet header as it leaves switch 1 en route to switch 2 is now

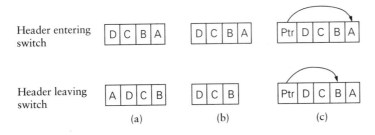

Figure 3.8 Three ways to handle headers for source routing: (a) rotation; (b) stripping; (c) pointer. The labels are read right to left.

(1, 3, 0); switch 2 performs another rotation and sends out a packet with (0, 1, 3) in the header. Although not shown, switch 3 performs yet another rotation, restoring the header to what it was when host A sent it.

There are several things to note about this approach. First, it assumes that host A knows enough about the topology of the network to form a header that has all the right directions in it for every switch in the path. This is somewhat analogous to the problem of building the forwarding tables in a datagram network or figuring out where to send a setup packet in a virtual circuit network. Second, observe that we cannot predict how big the header needs to be, since it must be able to hold one word of information for every switch on the path. This implies that headers are probably of variable length with no upper bound, unless we can predict with absolute certainty the maximum number of switches through which a packet will ever need to pass. Third, there are some variations on this approach. For example, rather than rotate the header, each switch could just strip the first element as it uses it. Rotation has an advantage over stripping, however: Host B gets a copy of the complete header, which may help it figure out how to get back to host A. Yet another alternative is to have the header carry a pointer to the current "next port" entry, so that each switch just updates the pointer rather than rotating the header; this may be more efficient to implement. We show these three approaches in Figure 3.8. In each case, the entry that this switch needs to read is A, and the entry that the next switch needs to read is B.

Source routing can be used in both datagram networks and virtual circuit networks. For example, the Internet Protocol, which is a datagram protocol, includes a source route option that allows selected packets to be source routed, while the majority are switched as conventional datagrams. Source routing is also used in some virtual circuit networks as the means to get the initial setup request along the path from source to destination.

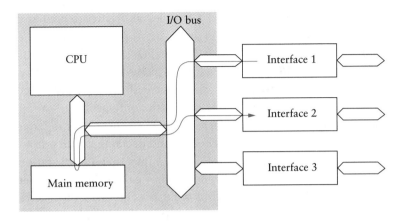

Figure 3.9 A workstation used as a packet switch.

Finally, we note that source routing suffers from a scaling problem. In any reasonably large network, it is very hard for a host to get the complete path information it needs to construct correct headers.

3.1.4 Implementation and Performance

So far, we have talked about what a switch must do without discussing how to do it. There is a very simple way to build a switch: Buy a general-purpose workstation and equip it with a number of network interfaces. Such a device, equipped with suitable software, can receive packets, perform any of the switching functions described above, and send packets out over its interfaces. This is, in fact, a popular way to build experimental switches when you want to be able to do things like develop new routing protocols because it offers extreme flexibility and a familiar programming environment.

Figure 3.9 shows a workstation with three network interfaces used as a switch. The figure shows a path that a packet might take from the time it arrives on interface 1 until it is output on interface 2. We have assumed here that the workstation has a mechanism to move data directly from an interface to its main memory without having to be directly copied by the CPU, that is, direct memory access (DMA) as described in Section 2.9. Once the packet is in memory, the CPU examines its header to determine which interface the packet should be sent out on. It then uses DMA to move the packet out to the appropriate interface. Note that Figure 3.9 does not show the packet going to the CPU because the CPU inspects only the header of the packet; it does not have to read every byte of data in the packet.

The main problem with using a workstation as a switch is that its performance is limited by the fact that all packets must pass through a single point of contention:

In the example shown, each packet crosses the I/O bus twice and is written to and read from main memory once. The upper bound on aggregate throughput of such a device (the total sustainable data rate summed over all inputs) is, thus, either half the main memory bandwidth or half the I/O bus bandwidth, whichever is less. (Usually, it's the I/O bus bandwidth.) For many applications, this limit will make performance too low. This upper bound also assumes that moving data is the only problem—a fair approximation for long packets but a bad one when packets are short. In the latter case, the cost of processing each packet—parsing its header and deciding which output link to transmit it on—is likely to dominate. Suppose, for example, that a workstation could switch 100,000 packets each second. This is sometimes called the packet per second (pps) rate. (This number is at the high end of what is achievable on today's high-end PCs.) If the average packet is short, say, 64 bytes, this would imply

$$\text{Throughput} = \text{pps} \times (\text{BitsPerPacket})$$
$$= 100 \times 10^3 \times 64 \times 8$$
$$= 51.2 \times 10^6$$

that is, a throughput of 51.2 Mbps—substantially below the range that users are demanding from their networks today. Bear in mind that this 51.2 Mbps would be shared by all users connected to the switch, just as the 10 Mbps of an Ethernet (or the 100 Mbps of an FDDI ring) is shared among all users connected to the shared medium.

To address this problem, hardware designers have come up with a large array of switch designs that reduce the amount of contention and provide high aggregate throughput. Note that some contention is unavoidable: If every input has data to send to a single output, then they cannot all send it at once. However, if data destined for different outputs is arriving at different inputs, a well-designed switch will be able to move data from inputs to outputs in parallel, thus increasing the aggregate throughput. We discuss some approaches to handling contention in Section 3.4.

3.2 Bridges and LAN Switches

Having discussed some of the basic ideas behind switching, we now focus more closely on some specific switching technologies. We begin by considering a class of switch that is used to forward packets between shared-media LANs such as Ethernets. Such switches are sometimes known by the obvious name of LAN switches; historically they have also been referred to as bridges.

Suppose you have a pair of Ethernets that you want to interconnect. One approach you might try is to put a repeater between them, as described in Chapter 2. This would not be a workable solution, however, if doing so exceeded the physical limitations of the Ethernet. (Recall that no more than two repeaters between any pair

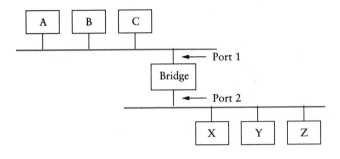

Figure 3.10   Illustration of a learning bridge.

of hosts and no more than a total of 2500 m in length is allowed.) An alternative would be to put a node between the two Ethernets and have the node forward frames from one Ethernet to the other. This node would be in promiscuous mode, accepting all frames transmitted on either of the Ethernets, so it could forward them to the other.

The node we have just described is typically called a *bridge*, and a collection of LANs connected by one or more bridges is usually said to form an *extended LAN*. In their simplest variants, bridges simply accept LAN frames on their inputs and forward them out on all other outputs. This simple strategy was used by early bridges, but has since been refined to make bridges a more effective mechanism for interconnecting a set of LANs. The rest of this section fills in the more interesting details.

Note that a bridge meets our definition of a switch from the previous section: a multi-input, multi-output device, which transfers packets from an input to one or more outputs. And recall that this provides a way to increase the total bandwidth of a network. For example, while a single Ethernet segment can carry only 10 Mbps of total traffic, an Ethernet bridge can carry as much as $10n$ Mbps, where n is the number of ports (inputs and outputs) on the bridge.

3.2.1 Learning Bridges

The first optimization we can make to a bridge is to observe that it need not forward all frames that it receives. Consider the bridge in Figure 3.10. Whenever a frame from host A that is addressed to host B arrives on port 1, there is no need for the bridge to forward the frame out over port 2. The question, then, is, How does a bridge come to learn on which port the various hosts reside?

One option would be to have a human download a table into the bridge similar to the one given in Table 3.3. Then, whenever the bridge receives a frame on port 1 that is addressed to host A, it would not forward the frame out on port 2; there would be no need because host A would have already directly received the frame on the LAN

Host	Port
A	1
B	1
C	1
X	2
Y	2
Z	2

Table 3.3   Forwarding table maintained by a bridge.

connected to port 1. Anytime a frame addressed to host A was received on port 2, the bridge would forward the frame out on port 1.

Note that a bridge using such a table would be using the datagram (or connectionless) model of forwarding described in Section 3.1.1. Each packet carries a global address, and the bridge decides which output to send a packet on by looking up that address in a table.

Having a human maintain this table is quite a burden, especially considering that there is a simple trick by which a bridge can learn this information for itself. The idea is for each bridge to inspect the *source* address in all the frames it receives. Thus, when host A sends a frame to a host on either side of the bridge, the bridge receives this frame and records the fact that a frame from host A was just received on port 1. In this way, the bridge can build a table just like Table 3.3.

When a bridge first boots, this table is empty; entries are added over time. Also, a timeout is associated with each entry, and the bridge discards the entry after a specified period of time. This is to protect against the situation in which a host—and as a consequence, its LAN address—is moved from one network to another. Thus, this table is not necessarily complete. Should the bridge receive a frame that is addressed to a host not currently in the table, it goes ahead and forwards the frame out on all the other ports. In other words, this table is simply an optimization that filters out some frames; it is not required for correctness.

Implementation

The code that implements the learning bridge algorithm is quite simple, and we sketch it here. Structure BridgeEntry defines a single entry in the bridge's forwarding table; these are stored in a Map structure (see Section 1.3.3) to enable entries to be efficiently located when packets arrive from sources already in the table. The constant MAX_TTL specifies how long an entry is kept in the table before it is discarded.

```
#define BRIDGE_TAB_SIZE    1024   /* max. size of bridging table */
#define MAX_TTL             120   /* time (in seconds) before
                                     an entry is flushed */


typedef struct {
    MacAddr      destination;     /* MAC address of a node */
    int          ifnumber;        /* interface to reach it */
    u_short      TTL;             /* time to live */
    Binding      binding;         /* binding in the Map */
} BridgeEntry;


int     numEntries = 0;
Map     bridgeMap = mapCreate(BRIDGE_TAB_SIZE,
                              sizeof(BridgeEntry));
```

The routine that updates the forwarding table when a new packet arrives is given
by updateTable. The arguments passed are the source MAC address contained in the
packet and the interface number on which it was received. Another routine, not shown
here, is invoked at regular intervals, scans the entries in the forwarding table, and
decrements the TTL (time to live) field of each entry, discarding any entries whose TTL
has reached 0. Note that the TTL is reset to MAX_TTL every time a packet arrives to
refresh an existing table entry, and that the interface on which the destination can be
reached is updated to reflect the most recently received packet.

```
void
updateTable (MacAddr src, int inif)
{
    BridgeEntry        *b;

    if (mapResolve(bridgeMap, &src, (void **)&b) == FALSE )
    {
        /* this address is not in the table, so try to add it */
        if (numEntries < BRIDGE_TAB_SIZE)
        {
            b = NEW(BridgeEntry);
            b->binding = mapBind( bridgeMap, &src, b);
            /* use source address of packet as dest. address in table */
            b->destination = src;
            numEntries++;
        }
```

```
        else
        {
            /* can't fit this address in the table now, so give up */
            return;
        }
    }
    /* reset TTL and use most recent input interface */
    b->TTL = MAX_TTL;
    b->ifnumber = inif;
}
```

Note that this implementation adopts a simple strategy in the case where the bridge table has become full to capacity—it simply fails to add the new address. Recall that completeness of the bridge table is not necessary for correct forwarding, it just optimizes performance. If there is some entry in the table that is not currently being used, it will eventually time out and be removed, creating space for a new entry. An alternative approach would be to invoke some sort of cache replacement algorithm on finding the table full; for example, we might locate and remove the entry with the smallest TTL to accommodate the new entry.

3.2.2 Spanning Tree Algorithm

The preceding strategy works just fine until the extended LAN has a loop in it, in which case it fails in a horrible way—frames potentially loop through the extended LAN forever. This is easy to see in the example depicted in Figure 3.11, where, for example, bridges B1, B4, and B6 form a loop. How does an extended LAN come to have a loop in it? One possibility is that the network is managed by more than one administrator, for example, because it spans multiple departments in an organization. In such a setting, it is possible that no single person knows the entire configuration of the network, meaning that a bridge that closes a loop might be added without anyone knowing. A second, more likely scenario is that loops are built into the network on purpose—to provide redundancy in case of failure.

Whatever the cause, bridges must be able to correctly handle loops. This problem is addressed by having the bridges run a distributed *spanning tree* algorithm. If you think of the extended LAN as being represented by a graph that possibly has loops (cycles), then a spanning tree is a subgraph of this graph that covers (spans) all the vertices, but contains no cycles. That is, a spanning tree keeps all of the vertices of the original graph, but throws out some of the edges. For example, Figure 3.12 shows a cyclic graph on the left and one of possibly many spanning trees on the right.

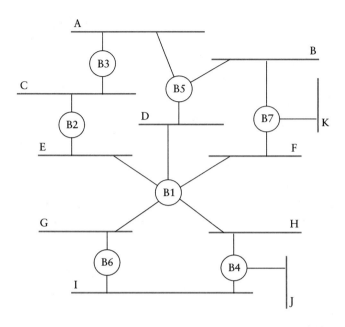

Figure 3.11 Extended LAN with loops.

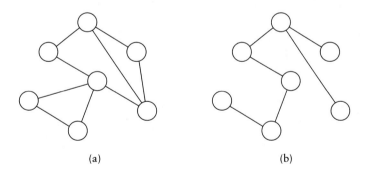

(a)　　　　　　　　(b)

Figure 3.12 Example of (a) a cyclic graph; (b) a corresponding spanning tree.

The spanning tree algorithm, which was developed by Radia Perlman at Digital, is a protocol used by a set of bridges to agree upon a spanning tree for a particular extended LAN. (The IEEE 802.1 specification for LAN bridges is based on this algorithm.) In practice, this means that each bridge decides the ports over which it is and is not willing to forward frames. In a sense, it is by removing ports from the topology that the extended LAN is reduced to an acyclic tree.[2] It is even possible that an entire bridge will not participate in forwarding frames, which seems kind of strange when you consider that the one reason we intentionally have loops in the network in the first place is to provide redundancy. The algorithm is dynamic, however, meaning that the bridges are always prepared to reconfigure themselves into a new spanning tree should some bridge fail.

The main idea of the spanning tree is for the bridges to select the ports over which they will forward frames. The algorithm selects ports as follows. Each bridge has a unique identifier; for our purposes, we use the labels B1, B2, B3, and so on. The algorithm first elects the bridge with the smallest id as the root of the spanning tree; exactly how this election takes place is described below. The root bridge always forwards frames out over all of its ports. Next, each bridge computes the shortest path to the root and notes which of its ports is on this path. This port is also selected as the bridge's preferred path to the root. Finally, all the bridges connected to a given LAN elect a single *designated* bridge that will be responsible for forwarding frames toward the root bridge. Each LAN's designated bridge is the one that is closest to the root, and if two or more bridges are equally close to the root, then the bridges' identifiers are used to break ties; the smallest id wins. Of course, each bridge is connected to more than one LAN, so it participates in the election of a designated bridge for each LAN it is connected to. In effect, this means that each bridge decides if it is the designated bridge relative to each of its ports. The bridge forwards frames over those ports for which it is the designated bridge.

Figure 3.13 shows the spanning tree that corresponds to the extended LAN shown in Figure 3.11. In this example, B1 is the root bridge, since it has the smallest id. Notice that both B3 and B5 are connected to LAN A, but B5 is the designated bridge since it is closer to the root. Similarly, both B5 and B7 are connected to LAN B, but in this case, B5 is the designated bridge since it has the smaller id; both are an equal distance from B1.

While it is possible for a human to look at the extended LAN given in Figure 3.11 and to compute the spanning tree given in Figure 3.13 according to the rules given above, the bridges in an extended LAN do not have the luxury of being able to see the topology of the entire network, let alone peek inside other bridges to see their ids.

---

[2] Representing an extended LAN as an abstract graph is a bit awkward. Basically, you let both the bridges and the LANs correspond to the vertices of the graph, and the ports correspond to the graph's edges. However, the spanning tree we are going to compute for this graph needs to span only those nodes that correspond to networks. It is possible that nodes corresponding to bridges will be disconnected from the rest of the graph. This corresponds to a situation in which all the ports connecting a bridge to various networks get removed by the algorithm.

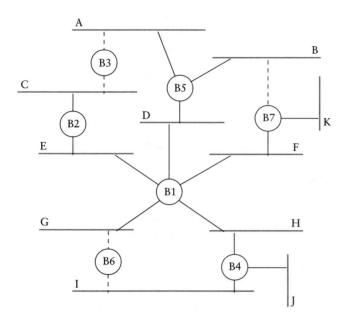

Figure 3.13 Spanning tree with some ports not selected.

Instead, the bridges have to exchange configuration messages with each other and then decide whether or not they are the root or a designated bridge based on these messages.

Specifically, the configuration messages contain three pieces of information:

1 the id for the bridge that is sending the message

2 the id for what the sending bridge believes to be the root bridge

3 the distance, measured in hops, from the sending bridge to the root bridge

Each bridge records the current "best" configuration message it has seen on each of its ports ("best" is defined below), including both messages it has received from other bridges and messages that it has itself transmitted.

Initially, each bridge thinks it is the root, and so it sends a configuration message out on each of its ports identifying itself as the root and giving a distance to the root of 0. Upon receiving a configuration message over a particular port, the bridge checks to see if that new message is better than the current best configuration message recorded for that port. The new configuration message is considered "better" than the currently recorded information if

■ it identifies a root with a smaller id or

■ it identifies a root with an equal id but with a shorter distance or

■ the root id and distance are equal, but the sending bridge has a smaller id.

If the new message is better than the currently recorded information, the bridge discards the old information and saves the new information. However, it first adds 1 to the distance-to-root field since the bridge is one hop farther away from the root than the bridge that sent the message.

When a bridge receives a configuration message indicating that it is not the root bridge—that is, a message from a bridge with a smaller id—the bridge stops generating configuration messages on its own and instead only forwards configuration messages from other bridges, after first adding 1 to the distance field. Likewise, when a bridge receives a configuration message that indicates it is not the designated bridge for that port—that is, a message from a bridge that is closer to the root or equally far from the root but with a smaller id—the bridge stops sending configuration messages over that port. Thus, when the system stabilizes, only the root bridge is still generating configuration messages, and the other bridges are forwarding these messages only over ports for which they are the designated bridge.

To make this more concrete, consider what would happen in Figure 3.13 if the power had just been restored to the building housing this network, so that all the bridges boot at about the same time. All the bridges would start off by claiming to be the root. We denote a configuration message from node X in which it claims to be distance d from root node Y as (Y, d, X). Focusing on the activity at node B3, a sequence of events would unfold as follows:

1 B3 receives (B2, 0, B2).

2 Since $2 < 3$, B3 accepts B2 as root.

3 B3 adds one to the distance advertised by B2 (0) and thus sends (B2, 1, B3) toward B5.

4 Meanwhile, B2 accepts B1 as root because it has the lower id, and it sends (B1, 1, B2) toward B3.

5 B5 accepts B1 as root and sends (B1, 1, B5) toward B3.

6 B3 accepts B1 as root, and it notes that both B2 and B5 are closer to the root than it is. Thus B3 stops forwarding messages on both its interfaces.

This leaves B3 with both ports not selected, as shown in Figure 3.13.

Even after the system has stabilized, the root bridge continues to send configuration messages periodically, and the other bridges continue to forward these messages as described in the previous paragraph. Should a particular bridge fail, the downstream bridges will not receive these configuration messages, and after waiting a specified period of time, they will once again claim to be the root, and the algorithm just described will kick in again to elect a new root and new designated bridges.

One important thing to notice is that although the algorithm is able to reconfigure the spanning tree whenever a bridge fails, it is not able to forward frames over alternative paths for the sake of routing around a congested bridge.

3.2.3 Broadcast and Multicast

The preceding discussion has focused on how bridges forward unicast frames from one LAN to another. Since the goal of a bridge is to transparently extend a LAN across multiple networks, and since most LANs support both broadcast and multicast, then bridges must also support these two features. Broadcast is simple—each bridge forwards a frame with a destination broadcast address out on each active (selected) port other than the one on which the frame was received.

Multicast can be implemented in exactly the same way, with each host deciding for itself whether or not to accept the message. This is exactly what is done in practice. Notice, however, that since not all the LANs in an extended LAN necessarily have a host that is a member of a particular multicast group, it is possible to do better. Specifically, the spanning tree algorithm can be extended to prune networks over which multicast frames need not be forwarded. Consider a frame sent to group M by a host on LAN A in Figure 3.13. If there is no host on LAN J that belongs to group M, then there is no need for bridge B4 to forward the frames over that network. On the other hand, not having a host on LAN H that belongs to group M does not necessarily mean that bridge B1 can avoid forwarding multicast frames onto LAN H. It all depends on whether or not there are members of group M on LANs I and J.

How does a given bridge learn whether it should forward a multicast frame over a given port? It learns exactly the same way that a bridge learns whether it should forward a unicast frame over a particular port—by observing the *source* addresses that it receives over that port. Of course, groups are not typically the source of frames, so we have to cheat a little. In particular, each host that is a member of group M must periodically send a frame with the address for group M in the source field of the frame header. This frame would have as its destination address the multicast address for the bridges.

Note that while the multicast extension just described has been proposed, it is not widely adopted. Instead, multicast is implemented in exactly the same way as broadcast on today's extended LANs.

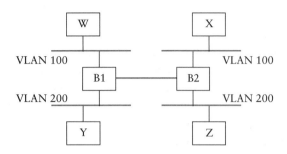

Figure 3.14 Two virtual LANs share a common backbone.

3.2.4 Limitations of Bridges

The bridge-based solution just described is meant to be used in only a fairly limited setting—to connect a handful of similar LANs. The main limitations of bridges become apparent when we consider the issues of scale and heterogeneity.

On the issue of scale, it is not realistic to connect more than a few LANs by means of bridges, where in practice "few" typically means "tens of." One reason for this is that the spanning tree algorithm scales linearly; that is, there is no provision for imposing a hierarchy on the extended LAN. A second reason is that bridges forward all broadcast frames. While it is reasonable for all hosts within a limited setting (say, a department) to see each other's broadcast messages, it is unlikely that all the hosts in a larger environment (say, a large company or university) would want to have to be bothered by each other's broadcast messages. Said another way, broadcast does not scale, and as a consequence, extended LANs do not scale.

One approach to increasing the scalability of extended LANs is the *virtual LAN* (VLAN). VLANs allow a single extended LAN to be partitioned into several seemingly separate LANs. Each virtual LAN is assigned an identifier (sometimes called a *color*), and packets can only travel from one segment to another if both segments have the same identifier. This has the effect of limiting the number of segments in an extended LAN that will receive any given broadcast packet.

We can see how VLANs work with an example. Figure 3.14 shows four hosts on four different LAN segments. In the absence of VLANs, any broadcast packet from any host will reach all the other hosts. Now let's suppose that we define the segments connected to hosts W and X as being in one VLAN, which we'll call VLAN 100. We also define the segments that connect to hosts Y and Z as being in VLAN 200. To do this, we need to configure a VLAN ID on each port of bridges B1 and B2. The link between B1 and B2 is considered to be in both VLANs.

When a packet sent by host X arrives at bridge B2, the bridge observes that it came in a port that was configured as being in VLAN 100. It inserts a VLAN header between the Ethernet header and its payload. The interesting part of the VLAN header is the VLAN ID; in this case, that ID is set to 100. The bridge now applies its normal rules for forwarding to the packet, with the extra restriction that the packet may not be sent out an interface that is not part of VLAN 100. Thus, under no circumstances will the packet—even a broadcast packet—be sent out the interface to host Z, which is in VLAN 200. The packet is, however, forwarded on to bridge B1, which follows the same rules, and thus may forward the packet to host W but not to host Y.

An attractive feature of VLANs is that it is possible to change the logical topology without moving any wires or changing any addresses. For example, if we wanted to make the segment that connects to host Z be part of VLAN 100, and thus enable X, W, and Z to be on the same virtual LAN, we would just need to change one piece of configuration on bridge B2.

On the issue of heterogeneity, bridges are fairly limited in the kinds of networks they can interconnect. In particular, bridges make use of the network's frame header and so can support only networks that have exactly the same format for addresses. Thus, bridges can be used to connect Ethernets to Ethernets, 802.5 to 802.5, and Ethernets to 802.5 rings, since both networks support the same 48-bit address format. Bridges do not readily generalize to other kinds of networks, such as ATM.[3]

Despite their limitations, bridges are a very important part of the complete networking picture. Their main advantage is that they allow multiple LANs to be transparently connected; that is, the networks can be connected without the end hosts having to run any additional protocols (or even be aware, for that matter). The one potential exception is when the hosts are expected to announce their membership in a multicast group, as described in Section 3.2.3.

Notice, however, that this transparency can be dangerous. If a host, or more precisely, the application and transport protocol running on that host, is programmed under the assumption that it is running on a single LAN, then inserting bridges between the source and destination hosts can have unexpected consequences. For example, if a bridge becomes congested, it may have to drop frames; in contrast, it is rare that a single Ethernet ever drops a frame. As another example, the latency between any pair of hosts on an extended LAN becomes both larger and more highly variable; in contrast, the physical limitations of a single Ethernet make the latency both small and predictable. As a final example, it is possible (although unlikely) that frames will be

---

[3] As we will see in Section 3.3.5, there are techniques to make ATM networks look more like "conventional" LANs such as Ethernets, and bridges do have a role in this environment.

reordered in an extended LAN; in contrast, frame order is never shuffled on a single Ethernet. The bottom line is that it is never safe to design network software under the assumption that it will run over a single Ethernet segment. Bridges happen.

3.3 Cell Switching (ATM)

Another switching technology that deserves special attention is *asynchronous transfer mode* (ATM). ATM became an important technology in the 1980s and early 1990s for a variety of reasons, not the least of which is that it was embraced by the telephone industry, which has historically been less than active in data communications except as a supplier of links on top of which other people have built networks. ATM also happened to be in the right place at the right time, as a high-speed switching technology that appeared on the scene just when shared media like Ethernet and 802.5 were starting to look a bit too slow for many users of computer networks. In some ways ATM is a competing technology with Ethernet switching, but the areas of application for these two technologies only partially overlap.

ATM is a connection-oriented, packet-switched technology, which is to say, it uses virtual circuits very much in the manner described in Section 3.1.2. In ATM terminology, the connection setup phase is called *signalling*. The main ATM signalling protocol is known as Q.2931. In addition to discovering a suitable route across an ATM network, Q.2931 is also responsible for allocating resources at the switches along the circuit. This is done in an effort to ensure the circuit a particular quality of service. Indeed, the QoS capabilities of ATM are one of its greatest strengths. We return to this topic in Chapter 6, where we discuss it in the context of similar efforts to implement QoS.

When any virtual connection is set up, it is necessary to put the address of the destination in the signalling message. In ATM, this address can be in one of several formats, the most common ones being E.164 and NSAP (network service access point); the details are not terribly important here, except to note that they are different from the MAC addresses used in traditional LANs.

One thing that makes ATM really unusual is that the packets that are switched in an ATM network are of fixed length. That length happens to be 53 bytes—5 bytes of header followed by 48 bytes of payload—a rather interesting choice that is discussed in more detail below. To distinguish these fixed-length packets from the more common variable-length packets normally used in computer networks, they are given a special name: *cells*. ATM may be thought of as the canonical example of cell switching.

3.3.1 Cells

All the packet-switching technologies we have looked at so far have used variable-length packets. Variable-length packets are normally constrained to fall within some bounds. The lower bound is set by the minimum amount of information that needs to be contained in the packet, which is typically a header with no optional extensions. The upper bound may be set by a variety of factors; the maximum FDDI packet size, for example, determines how long each station is allowed to transmit without passing on the token, and thus determines how long a station might have to wait for the token to reach it. Cells, in contrast, are both fixed in length and small in size. While this seems like a simple enough design choice, there are actually a lot of factors involved, as explained in the following paragraphs.

Cell Size

Variable-length packets have some nice characteristics. If you only have 1 byte to send (e.g., to acknowledge the receipt of a packet), you put it in a minimum-sized packet. If you have a large file to send, however, you break it up into as many maximum-sized packets as you need. You do not need to send any extraneous padding in the first case, and in the second, you drive down the ratio of header to data bytes, thus increasing bandwidth efficiency. You also minimize the total number of packets sent, thereby minimizing the total processing incurred by per-packet operations. This can be particularly important in obtaining high throughput, since many network devices are limited not by how many *bits* per second they can process but rather by the number of *packets* per second.

So, why use fixed-length cells? One of the main reasons was to facilitate the implementation of hardware switches. When ATM was being created in the mid- and late 1980s, 10-Mbps Ethernet was the cutting-edge technology in terms of speed. To go much faster, most people thought in terms of hardware. Also, in the telephone world, people think big when they think of switches—telephone switches often serve tens of thousands of customers. Fixed-length packets turn out to be a very helpful thing if you want to build fast, highly scalable switches. There are two main reasons for this:

1 It is easier to build hardware to do simple jobs, and the job of processing packets is simpler when you already know how long each one will be.

2 If all packets are the same length, then you can have lots of switching elements all doing much the same thing in parallel, each of them taking the same time to do its job.

This second reason, the enabling of parallelism, greatly improves the scalability of switch designs. We will examine a highly scalable, parallel switch in Section 3.4.5. It would be overstating the case to say that fast parallel hardware switches can only be built using fixed-length cells. However, it is certainly true that cells ease the task of building such hardware and that there was a lot of knowledge available about how to build cell switches in hardware at the time the ATM standards were being defined.

Another nice property of cells relates to the behavior of queues. Queues build up in a switch when traffic from several inputs may be heading for a single output. In general, once you extract a packet from a queue and start transmitting it, you need to continue until the whole packet is transmitted; it is not practical to preempt the transmission of a packet. The longest time that a queue output can be tied up is equal to the time it takes to transmit a maximum-sized packet. Fixed-length cells mean that a queue output is never tied up for more than the time it takes to transmit one cell, which is almost certainly shorter than the maximum-sized packet on a variable-length packet network. Thus, if tight control over the latency that is being experienced by cells when they pass through a queue is important, cells provide some advantage. Of course, long queues can still build up, and there is no getting around the fact that some cells will have to wait their turn. What you get from cells is not much-shorter queues but potentially finer control over the behavior of queues.

An example will help to clarify this idea. Imagine a network with variable-length packets, where the maximum packet length is 4 KB and the link speed is 100 Mbps. The time to transmit a maximum-sized packet is $4096 \times 8/100 = 327.68$ μs. Thus, a high-priority packet that arrives just after the switch starts to transmit a 4-KB packet will have to sit in the queue 327.68 μs waiting for access to the link. In contrast, if the switch were forwarding 53-byte cells, the longest wait would be $53 \times 8/100 = 4.24$ μs. This may not seem like a big deal, but the ability to control delay and especially to control its variation with time (jitter) can be important for some applications.

Queues of cells also tend to be a little shorter than queues of packets, for the following reason. When a packet begins to arrive in an empty queue, it is typical for the switch to have to wait for the whole packet to arrive before it can start transmitting the packet on an outgoing link. This means that the link sits idle while the packet arrives. However, if you imagine a large packet being replaced by a "train" of small cells, then as soon as the first cell in the train has entered the queue, the switch can transmit it. Imagine in the example above what would happen if two 4-KB packets arrived in a queue at about the same time. The link would sit idle for 327.68 μs while these two packets arrive, and at the end of that period we would have 8 KB in the queue. Only then could the queue start to empty. If those same two packets were sent as trains of cells, then transmission of the cells could start 4.24 μs after the first train started to arrive. At the end of 327.68 μs, the link would have been active for a little over 323 μs, and there would be just over 4 KB of data left in the queue, not 8 KB as before. Shorter queues mean less delay for all the traffic.

Having decided to use small, fixed-length packets, the next question is, What is the right length to fix them at? If you make them too short, then the amount of header information that needs to be carried around relative to the amount of data that fits in one cell gets larger, so the percentage of link bandwidth that is actually used to

A Compromise of 48 Bytes

The explanation for why the payload of an ATM cell is 48 bytes is an interesting one and is an excellent case study in the process of standardization. As the ATM standard was evolving, the U.S. telephone companies were pushing for a 64-byte cell size, while the European companies were advocating 32-byte cells. The reason that the Europeans wanted the smaller size was that since the countries they served were of a small enough size, they would not have to install echo cancelers if they were able to keep the latency induced by generating a complete cell small enough. Thirty-two-byte cells were adequate for this purpose. In contrast, the United States is a large enough country that the phone companies had to install echo cancelers anyway, and so the larger cell size reflected a desire to improve the header-to-payload ratio.

Averaging is a classic form of compromise—48 bytes is simply the average of 64 bytes and 32 bytes. So as not to leave the false impression that this use of compromise-by-averaging is an isolated incident, we note that the seven-layer OSI model was actually a compromise between six and eight layers.

carry data goes down. Even more seriously, if you build a device that processes cells at some maximum number of cells per second, then as cells get shorter, the total data rate drops in direct proportion to cell size. An example of such a device might be a network adaptor that reassembles cells into larger units before handing them up to the host. The performance of such a device depends directly on cell size. On the other hand, if you make the cells too big, then there is a problem of wasted bandwidth caused by the need to pad transmitted data to fill a complete cell. If the cell payload size is 48 bytes and you want to send 1 byte, you'll need to send 47 bytes of padding. If this happens a lot, then the utilization of the link will be very low.

Efficient link utilization is not the only factor that influences cell size. For example, cell size has a particular effect on voice traffic, and since ATM grew out of the telephony community, one of the major concerns was that it be able to carry voice effectively. The standard digital encoding of voice is done at 64 Kbps (8-bit samples taken at 8 KHz). To maximize efficiency, you want to collect a full cell's worth of voice samples before transmitting a cell. A sampling rate of 8 KHz means that 1 byte is sampled every 125 μs, so the time it takes to fill an n-byte cell with samples is $n \times 125$ μs. If cells are, say, 1000 bytes long, it would take 125 ms just to collect a full cell of samples before you even start to transmit it to the receiver. That amount of latency starts to be quite noticeable to a human listener. Even considerably smaller latencies create problems for voice, particularly in the form

4	8	16	3	1	8	384 (48 bytes)
GFC	VPI	VCI	Type	CLP	HEC (CRC-8)	Payload

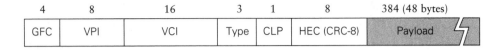

Figure 3.15 ATM cell format at the UNI.

of echoes. Echoes can be eliminated by a piece of technology called an echo canceler, but this adds cost to a telephone network that many network operators would rather avoid.

All of the above factors caused a great deal of debate in the international standards bodies when ATM was being standardized, and the fact that no length was perfect in all cases was used by those opposed to ATM to argue that fixed-length cells were a bad idea in the first place. As is so often the case with standards, the end result was a compromise that pleased almost no one: 48 bytes was chosen as the length for the ATM cell payload. Probably the greatest tragedy of this choice is that it is not a power of two, which means that it is quite a mismatch to most things that computers handle, like pages and cache lines. Rather less controversially, the header was fixed at 5 bytes. The format of an ATM cell is shown in Figure 3.15; note that this figure shows the field lengths in bits.

Cell Format

The ATM cell actually comes in two different formats, depending on where you look in the network. The one shown in Figure 3.15 is called the UNI (user-network interface) format; the alternative is the NNI (network-network interface). The UNI format is used, of course, at the user-to-network interface. This is likely to be the interface between a telephone company and one of its customers. The network-to-network interface is likely to be between a pair of phone companies. The only significant difference in cell formats is that the NNI format replaces the GFC field with 4 extra bits of VPI. Clearly, understanding all the three-letter acronyms (TLAs) is a key part of understanding ATM.

Starting from the leftmost byte of the cell (which is the first one transmitted), the UNI cell has 4 bits for generic flow control (GFC). These bits have not been widely used, but they were intended to have local significance at a site and could be overwritten in the network. The basic idea behind the GFC bits was to provide a means to arbitrate access to the link if the local site used some shared medium to connect to ATM.

The next 24 bits contain an 8-bit virtual path identifier (VPI) and a 16-bit virtual circuit identifier (VCI). The difference between the two is explained below, but for now it is adequate to think of them as a single 24-bit identifier that is used to identify a virtual connection, just as in Section 3.1.2. Following the VPI/VCI is a 3-bit Type field that has eight possible values. Four of them, when the first bit in the field is set, relate to management functions. When that bit is clear, it means that the cell contains user data. In this case, the second bit is the "explicit forward congestion indication" (EFCI) bit and the third is the "user signalling" bit. The former can be set by a congested switch to tell an end node that it is congested; it has its roots in the DECbit described in Section 6.4.1; in ATM, it is used for congestion control in conjunction with the available bit rate (ABR) service class described in Section 6.5.4. The third bit is used primarily in conjunction with ATM Adaptation Layer 5 to delineate frames, as discussed below.

Next is a bit to indicate cell loss priority (CLP); a user or network element may set this bit to indicate cells that should be dropped preferentially in the event of overload. For example, a video coding application could set this bit for cells that, if dropped, would not dramatically degrade the quality of the video. A network element might set this bit for cells that have been transmitted by a user in excess of the amount that was negotiated.

The last byte of the header is an 8-bit CRC, known as the header error check (HEC). It uses the CRC-8 polynomial given in Section 2.4.3 and provides error detection and single-bit error correction capability on the cell header only. Protecting the cell header is particularly important because an error in the VCI will cause the cell to be misdelivered.

3.3.2 Segmentation and Reassembly

Up to this point, we have assumed that a low-level protocol could just accept the packet handed down to it by a high-level protocol, attach its own header, and pass the packet on down. This is not possible with ATM, however, since the packets handed down from above are often larger than 48 bytes, and thus, will not fit in the payload of an ATM cell. The solution to this problem is to *fragment* the high-level message into low-level packets at the source, transmit the individual low-level packets over the network, and then reassemble the fragments back together at the destination. This general technique is usually called *fragmentation and reassembly*. In the case of ATM, however, it is often called *segmentation and reassembly* (SAR).

Segmentation is not unique to ATM, but it is much more of a problem than in a network with a maximum packet size of, say, 1500 bytes. To address the issue, a protocol layer was added that sits between ATM and the variable-length packet protocols that might use ATM, such as IP. This layer is called the ATM Adaptation Layer (AAL), and to a first approximation, the AAL header simply contains the information needed by the destination to reassemble the individual cells back into

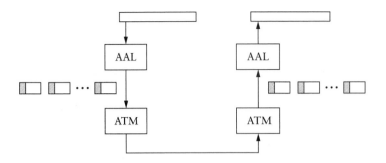

Figure 3.16 Segmentation and reassembly in ATM.

the original message. The relationship between the AAL and ATM is illustrated in Figure 3.16.

Because ATM was designed to support all sorts of services, including voice, video, and data, it was felt that different services would have different AAL needs. Thus, four adaptation layers were originally defined: 1 and 2 were designed to support applications, like voice, that require guaranteed bit rates, while 3 and 4 were intended to provide support for packet data running over ATM. The idea was that AAL3 would be used by connection-oriented packet services (such as X.25) and AAL4 would be used by connectionless services (such as IP). Eventually, the reasons for having different AALs for these two types of service were found to be insufficient, and the AALs merged into one that is inconveniently known as AAL3/4. Meanwhile, some perceived shortcomings in AAL3/4 caused a fifth AAL to be proposed, called AAL5. Thus, there are now four AALs: 1, 2, 3/4, and 5. The two that support computer communications are described below.

ATM Adaptation Layer 3/4

The main function of AAL3/4 is to provide enough information to allow variable-length packets to be transported across the ATM network as a series of fixed-length cells. That is, the AAL supports the segmentation and reassembly process. Since we are now working at a new layer of the network hierarchy, convention requires us to introduce a new name for a packet—in this case, we call it a *protocol data unit* (PDU). The task of segmentation/reassembly involves two different packet formats. The first of these is the *convergence sublayer protocol data unit* (CS-PDU), as depicted in Figure 3.17. The CS-PDU defines a way of encapsulating variable-length PDUs prior to segmenting them into cells. The PDU passed down to the AAL layer is encapsulated by adding a header and a trailer, and the resultant CS-PDU is segmented into ATM cells.

8	8	16	< 64 KB	0–24	8	8	16
CPI	Btag	BASize	User data	Pad	0	Etag	Len

Figure 3.17 ATM Adaptation Layer 3/4 packet format.

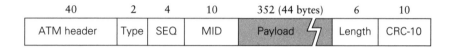

40	2	4	10	352 (44 bytes)	6	10
ATM header	Type	SEQ	MID	Payload	Length	CRC-10

Figure 3.18 ATM cell format for AAL3/4.

The CS-PDU format begins with an 8-bit common part indicator (CPI), which indicates which version of the CS-PDU format is in use. Only the value 0 is currently defined. The next 8 bits contain the beginning tag (Btag), which is supposed to match the end tag (Etag) for a given PDU. This protects against the situation in which the loss of the last cell of one PDU and the first cell of another causes two PDUs to be inadvertently joined into a single PDU and passed up to the next layer in the protocol stack. The buffer allocation size (BASize) field is not necessarily the length of the PDU (which appears in the trailer); it is supposed to be a hint to the reassembly process as to how much buffer space to allocate for the reassembly. The reason for not including the actual length here is that the sending host might not have known how long the CS-PDU was when it transmitted the header. Before adding the CS-PDU trailer, the user data is padded to a multiple of 3 bytes, by adding up to 3 bytes of padding. This padding, plus the 0-filled byte, ensures that the trailer is aligned on a 32-bit boundary, making for more efficient processing. The CS-PDU trailer itself contains the Etag and the real length of the PDU (Len).

In addition to the CS-PDU header and trailer, AAL3/4 specifies a header and trailer that are carried in each cell, as depicted in Figure 3.18. Thus, the CS-PDU is actually segmented into 44-byte chunks; an AAL3/4 header and trailer is attached to each one, bringing it up to 48 bytes, which is then carried as the payload of an ATM cell.

The first two bits of the AAL3/4 header contain the Type field, which indicates if this is the first cell of a CS-PDU, the last cell of a CS-PDU, a cell in the middle of a CS-PDU, or a single-cell PDU (in which case it is both first and last). The official names for these four conditions are shown in Table 3.4, along with the bit encodings.

Value	Name	Meaning
10	BOM	Beginning of message
00	COM	Continuation of message
01	EOM	End of message
11	SSM	Single-segment message

Table 3.4 AAL3/4 Type field.

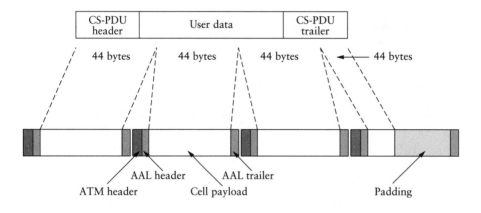

Figure 3.19 Encapsulation and segmentation for AAL3/4.

Next is a 4-bit sequence number (SEQ), which is intended simply to detect cell loss or misordering so that reassembly can be aborted. Clearly, a sequence number this small can miss cell losses if the number of lost cells is large enough. This is followed by a multiplexing identifier (MID), which can be used to multiplex several PDUs onto a single connection. The 6-bit Length field shows the number of bytes of PDU that are contained in the cell; it must equal 44 for BOM and COM cells. Finally, a 10-bit CRC is used to detect errors anywhere in the 48-byte cell payload.

Figure 3.19 shows the entire encapsulation and segmentation process for AAL3/4. At the top, the user data is encapsulated with the CS-PDU header and trailer. The CS-PDU is then segmented into 44-byte payloads, which are encapsulated as ATM cells by adding the AAL3/4 header and trailer as well as the 5-byte ATM header. Note that the last cell is only partially filled whenever the CS-PDU is not an exact multiple of 44 bytes.

< 64 KB	0–47 bytes	16	16	32
Data	Pad	Reserved	Len	CRC-32

Figure 3.20   ATM Adaptation Layer 5 packet format.

One thing to note about AAL3/4 is that it exacerbates the fixed per-cell overhead that we discussed above. With 44 bytes of data to 9 bytes of header, the best possible bandwidth utilization would be 83%. Note that the efficiency can be considerably less than that, as illustrated by Figure 3.19, because of the CS-PDU encapsulation and the partial filling of the last cell.

ATM Adaptation Layer 5

One thing you may have noticed in the discussion of AAL3/4 is that it seems to take a lot of fields and thus a lot of overhead to perform the conceptually simple function of segmentation and reassembly. This observation was, in fact, made by several people in the early days of ATM, and numerous competing proposals arose for an AAL to support computer communications over ATM. There was a movement, known informally as "Back the Bit," that argued that if we could just have 1 bit in the ATM header (as opposed to the AAL header) to delineate the end of a frame, then segmentation and reassembly could be accomplished without using any of the 48-byte ATM payload for segmentation/reassembly information. This movement eventually led to the definition of the user signalling bit described above and to the standardization of AAL5.

What AAL5 does is replace the 2-bit Type field of AAL3/4 with 1 bit of framing information in the ATM cell header. By setting that 1 bit, we can identify the last cell of a PDU; the next cell is assumed to be the first cell of the next PDU, and subsequent cells are assumed to be COM cells until another cell is received with the user signalling bit set. All the pieces of AAL3/4 that provide protection against lost, corrupt, or misordered cells, including the loss of an EOM cell, are provided by the AAL5 CS-PDU packet format depicted in Figure 3.20.

The AAL5 CS-PDU consists simply of the data portion (the PDU handed down by the higher-layer protocol) and an 8-byte trailer. To make sure that the trailer always falls at the tail end of an ATM cell, there may be up to 47 bytes of padding between the data and the trailer. It is necessary to force the trailer to be at the end of a cell, as otherwise there would be no way for the entity performing reassembly of the CS-PDU to find the trailer. The first 2 bytes of the trailer are currently reserved and must be 0. The length field (Len) is the number of bytes carried in the PDU, not including the trailer or any padding before the trailer. Finally, there is a 32-bit CRC.

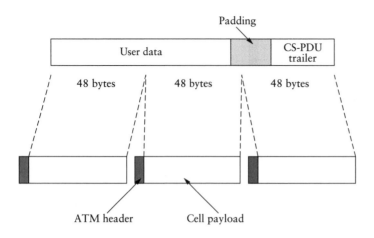

Figure 3.21   Encapsulation and segmentation for AAL5.

Figure 3.21 shows the encapsulation and segmentation process for AAL5. Just like AAL3/4, the user data is encapsulated to form a CS-PDU (although using only a trailer in this case). The resulting PDU is then cut up into 48-byte chunks, which are carried directly inside the payload of ATM cells without any further encapsulation.

Somewhat surprisingly, AAL5 provides almost the same functionality as AAL3/4 without using an extra 4 bytes out of every cell. For example, the CRC-32 detects lost or misordered cells as well as bit errors in the data. In fact, having a checksum over the entire PDU rather than doing it on a per-cell basis as in AAL3/4 provides stronger protection. For example, it protects against the loss of 16 consecutive cells, an event that would not be picked up by the sequence number checking of AAL3/4. Also, a 32-bit CRC protects against longer burst errors than a 10-bit CRC.

The main feature missing from AAL5 is the ability to provide an additional layer of multiplexing onto one virtual circuit using the MID. It is not clear whether this is a significant loss. It is still possible to multiplex traffic from many applications and higher-layer protocols onto a single VC using AAL5 by carrying a demux key of the sort described in Section 1.2.1. It just becomes necessary to do the multiplexing on a packet-by-packet, rather than a cell-by-cell, basis. The details of such multiplexing are described in Section 3.3.5.

There are positive and negative aspects to multiplexing traffic from a lot of different applications onto a single VC. For example, if you are being charged for every virtual circuit you set up across a network, then multiplexing traffic from lots of different applications onto one connection might be a plus. However, this approach has the drawback that all applications will have to live with whatever quality of service

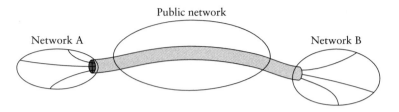

Public network

Network A

Network B

Figure 3.22 Example of a virtual path.

(e.g., delay and bandwidth guarantees) has been chosen for that one connection, which may mean that some applications are not receiving appropriate service.

In general, AAL5 has been wholeheartedly embraced by the computer communications community (at least by that part of the community that has embraced ATM at all). For example, it is the preferred AAL in the IETF for transmitting IP datagrams over ATM. Its more efficient use of bandwidth and simple design are the main features that make it more appealing than AAL3/4.

3.3.3 Virtual Paths

As mentioned above, ATM uses a 24-bit identifier for virtual circuits, and these circuits operate almost exactly like the ones described in Section 3.1.2. The one twist is that the 24-bit identifier is split into two parts: an 8-bit virtual path identifier (VPI) and a 16-bit virtual circuit identifier (VCI). This effectively creates a two-level hierarchy of virtual connections. To understand how such a hierarchy might work, consider the following example. (We ignore the fact that in some places there might be a network-network interface with a different-sized VPI; just assume that 8-bit VPIs are used everywhere.)

Suppose that a corporation has two sites that connect to a public ATM network, and that at each site the corporation has a network of ATM switches. We could imagine establishing a virtual path between two sites using only the VPI field. Thus, the switches in the public network would use the VPI as the only field on which to make forwarding decisions. From their point of view, this is a virtual circuit network with 8-bit circuit identifiers. The 16-bit VCI is of no interest to these public switches, and they neither use the field for switching nor remap it. Within the corporate sites, however, the full 24-bit space is used for switching. Any traffic that needs to flow between the two sites is routed to a switch that has a connection to the public network, and its top 8 bits (the VPI) are mapped onto the appropriate value to get the data to the other site. This idea is illustrated in Figure 3.22. Note that the virtual path acts like a fat pipe that contains a bundle of virtual circuits, all of which have the same 8 bits in their most significant byte.

The advantage of this approach is clear: Although there may be thousands or millions of virtual connections across the public network, the switches in the public network behave as if there is only one connection. This means that there needs to be much less connection-state information stored in the switches, avoiding the need for big, expensive tables of per-VCI information.

3.3.4 Physical Layers for ATM

While the layered approach to protocol design might lead you to think that we do not need to worry about what type of point-to-point link ATM runs on top of, this turns out not to be the case. From a simple pragmatic point of view, when you buy an ATM adaptor for a workstation or an ATM switch, it comes with some physical medium over which ATM cells will be sent. Of course, this is also true for other networking protocols such as 802.5 and Ethernet. Like these protocols, ATM can also run over several different physical media and physical-layer protocols.

From early in the process of standardizing ATM, it was assumed that ATM would run on top of a SONET physical layer (see Section 2.3.3). Some people even get ATM and SONET confused because they have been so tightly coupled for so long. While it is true that standard ways of carrying ATM cells inside a SONET frame have been defined, and that you can now buy ATM-over-SONET products, the two are entirely separable. For example, you can lease a SONET link from a phone company and send whatever you want over it, including variable-length packets. Also, you can send ATM cells over many other physical layers instead of SONET, and standards have been (or are being) defined for these encapsulations. A notable early physical layer for ATM was TAXI, the physical layer used in FDDI (Section 2.7). Wireless physical layers for ATM are also being defined.

When you send ATM cells over some physical medium, the main issue is how to find the boundaries of the ATM cells; this is exactly the framing problem described in Chapter 2. With SONET, there are two easy ways to find the boundaries. One of the overhead bytes in the SONET frame can be used as a pointer into the SONET payload to the start of an ATM cell. Having found the start of one cell, it is known that the next cell starts 53 bytes further on in the SONET payload, and so on. In theory, you only need to read this pointer once, but in practice, it makes sense to read it every time the SONET overhead goes by so that you can detect errors or resynchronize if needed.

The other way to find the boundaries of ATM cells takes advantage of the fact that every cell has a CRC in the fifth byte of the cell. Thus, if you run a CRC calculation over the last 5 bytes received and the answer comes out to indicate no errors, then it is probably true that you have just read an ATM header. If this happens several times in a row at 53-byte intervals, you can be pretty sure you have found the cell boundary.

3.3.5 ATM in the LAN

As we mentioned above, ATM grew out of the telephony community, who envisioned it as a way to build large public networks that could transport voice, video, and data traffic. However, it was subsequently embraced by the computer and data communications industries as a technology to be used in LANs—a replacement for Ethernet and 802.5. Its popularity in this realm can be attributed to two main factors:

■ ATM is a switched technology, compared to Ethernet and 802.5, which are shared-media technologies.

■ ATM was designed to operate on links with speeds of 155 Mbps and above.

When ATM switches first became available, these were significant advantages over the existing solutions. In particular, switched networks have a big performance advantage over shared-media networks: A single shared-media network has a fixed total bandwidth that must be shared among all hosts, whereas each host gets its own dedicated link to the switch in a switched network. Thus the performance of switched networks scales better than that of shared-media networks.

However, it should be apparent that the distinction between shared-media and switched networks is not all that clear-cut. A bridge that connects a number of shared-media networks together is also a switch, and it is possible (and quite common) to connect only one host to each segment, giving it dedicated access to that bandwidth. At the same time as ATM switches were appearing on the scene, high-performance Ethernet switches became available. These devices have large numbers of ports and high total throughput. The 100-Mbps Ethernet standard was defined, and so the link speed of Ethernet—which could be achieved over copper—began to approach that of ATM.

All this was not enough to kill off ATM in the LAN. One advantage of ATM over Ethernet that remains is the lack of distance limitation for ATM links. Also, 622-Mbps ATM links have become available. This makes ATM fairly popular for the high-performance "backbone" of larger LANs. It is common to find hosts connected to Ethernet switches, which in turn are interconnected by ATM switches, as depicted in Figure 3.23. High-performance servers might also be connected directly to the ATM switch, as with host H7 in this example.

More recently, a technology that will compete strongly with ATM for LAN backbones and server connections has emerged in the form of Gigabit Ethernet. Gigabit Ethernet links are point-to-point fiber (mostly) and can run over relatively long distances (up to several kilometers).

The problem with running ATM in a LAN is that it doesn't look like a "traditional" LAN. Because most LANs (i.e., Ethernets and token rings) are shared-media

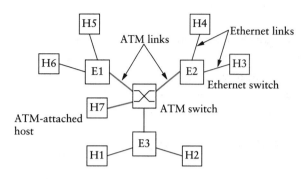

Figure 3.23 ATM used as a LAN backbone.

networks (i.e., every node on the LAN is connected to the same link), it is easy to implement broadcast (sending to everybody) and multicast (sending to a group). Thus, many of the protocols that people depend on in their LANs—for example, the Address Resolution Protocol (ARP) described in Section 4.1.5—depend in turn on the ability of the LAN to support multicast and broadcast. However, because of its connection-oriented and switched nature, ATM behaves rather differently than a shared-media LAN. For example, how can you broadcast to all nodes on an ATM LAN if you don't know all their addresses and set up VCs to all of them?

There are two possible solutions to this problem, and both of them have been explored. One is to redesign the protocols that make assumptions about LANs that are not in fact true of ATM. Thus, for example, there is a new protocol called ATMARP that, unlike traditional ARP, does not depend on broadcast. The alternative is to make ATM behave more like a shared-media LAN—in the sense of supporting multicast and broadcast—without losing the performance advantages of a switched network. This approach has been specified by the ATM Forum as "LAN emulation" or LANE (which might be more correctly called "shared-media emulation"). This approach aims to add functionality to ATM LANs so that anything that runs over a shared-media LAN can operate over an ATM LAN.

One aspect of LAN emulation that can be confusing is the variety of different addresses and identifiers that are used. All ATM devices must have an ATM address, which is used when signalling to establish a VC. As noted above, these addresses are different from the standard IEEE 802 MAC addresses used in Ethernets, token rings, and so on. If we want to emulate the behavior of these types of LANs, each device will also need to have a standard (48-bit, globally unique) MAC address. And finally, recall that a virtual circuit identifier is very different from an address. It is the shorthand

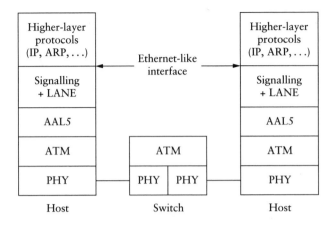

Figure 3.24   Protocol layers in LAN emulation.

that is used to get cells along an established connection, but you must first establish a connection, and to do that you need an ATM address.

LAN emulation does not actually change the functionality of ATM switches, but adds functionality to the network through the addition of a number of servers. Devices that connect to the ATM network—hosts, bridges, routers—are referred to as LAN emulation clients (LECs). The interactions between LECs and the various servers result in network behavior that, from the point of view of any higher-layer protocol, is indistinguishable from that of an Ethernet or token ring network. Figure 3.24 illustrates the protocol layers in the case where a pair of hosts communicate across an ATM network that is emulating a LAN. By "Ethernet-like interface," we mean that the services offered up to higher layers are like those of an Ethernet: Frames can be delivered to any MAC address on the LAN, frames can be broadcast to all destinations on the LAN, and so on.

The servers that are required to build an emulated LAN are

■ the LAN emulation configuration server (LECS)

■ the LAN emulation server (LES)

■ the broadcast and unknown server (BUS)

These servers can be physically located in one or more devices, perhaps in one of the hosts or other devices connected to the ATM network. The LECS and LES primarily perform configuration functions, while the BUS has a central role in making data transfer in an ATM network resemble that of a shared-media LAN.

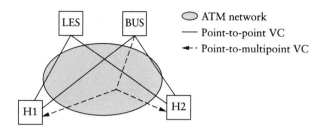

Figure 3.25   Servers and clients in an emulated LAN.

The LECS enables a newly attached or rebooted LAN emulation client (e.g., a host) to get some essential information. First, the client must find the LECS, which it may do by using a well-known, predefined VC that is always set up; alternatively, the client must have prior knowledge of the ATM address of the LECS so it can set up a VC to it. Once connected to the LECS, the client provides the LECS with its ATM address, and the LECS responds by telling the client what type of LAN is being emulated (Ethernet or token ring), what the maximum packet size is, and the ATM address of the LES. One LECS might support many separate emulated LANs.

The client now signals for a connection to the LES whose ATM address it just learned. Once connected to the LES, the client registers its MAC and ATM addresses with the LES. Among other things, the LES provides the client with the ATM address of the BUS.

The BUS maintains a single point-to-multipoint VC that connects it to all registered clients. It should be apparent that the BUS and this multipoint VC are crucial to LAN emulation: They enable the broadcast capability of traditional LANs to be emulated in a virtual circuit environment. Once a LEC has the ATM address of the BUS, it signals for a connection to the BUS. The BUS in turn adds the LEC to the point-to-multipoint VC. At this point, everything is ready for the LEC to participate in data transfer. The arrangement where two hosts have connected to the LES and the BUS, and the BUS has formed the point-to-multipoint VC to both of them, is shown in Figure 3.25. The LECS is not shown.

This might seem like a lot of work to get the LEC connected to the BUS, but the separation of functions among servers is helpful from a network management standpoint. For example, a great deal of information can be centralized in a single LECS rather than having to be distributed to many LESs, and the amount of special configuration needed in each host is kept to a bare minimum.

It should be clear that the BUS is the place to send any packet that needs to be broadcast to all clients on the LAN. While it could also be used for delivery of unicast packets, this would be inefficient. Delivery of unicast packets operates as follows. Assume that a host has a packet that it wants to deliver to a particular MAC address. In a traditional LAN, the packet could be placed on the wire and would be picked up by the intended recipient. In an emulated LAN, the packet needs to be delivered to the recipient over a virtual circuit. But a newly attached host would only have a VC to the LES and the BUS, not the recipient. To make matters worse, it would not even know the ATM address of the recipient, which is required to set up a VC. Thus, the host performs the following steps:

- It sends the packet to the BUS, which it knows can deliver the packet to the destination using its point-to-multipoint VC.

- It sends an "address resolution" request to the LES, of the form "What ATM address corresponds to this MAC address?"

Since all clients should have registered their MAC and ATM addresses with the LES, the LES should be able to answer the query and provide an ATM address to the client. The client can now signal for a VC to the recipient, which it may use to forward *subsequent* frames to the destination. The reason for using the BUS to send the first packet is to minimize delay, since it may take some time to get a response from the LES and establish a VC.

One detail in this process is that LANs are not supposed to deliver frames out of order, and an emulated LAN should be no different. But if some frames are sent via the BUS and then later frames are sent on a direct connection, misordering may occur. LAN emulation procedures include a "flush" mechanism to ensure that the last packet sent down one path has arrived before another one is sent on a new path, thus ensuring in-order delivery.

With the above process, a client would eventually end up with direct VCs to all destinations that it has ever sent data to. This might be an excessive number of VCs, and so a client may use a caching algorithm to dispose of VCs that are no longer carrying traffic. A "cache miss" (i.e., the arrival of a packet that needs to be sent to a destination for which no VC exists) will be handled by sending the packet to the BUS.

3.4 Switching Hardware

Whether a switch has to handle virtual circuits or datagrams, variable-length packets or fixed-length cells, many of the basic issues that have to be addressed in its design remain the same. A switch is a multi-input, multi-output device, and its job is to get as many packets as possible from the inputs to the appropriate outputs. Most of what we have talked about in the previous sections of this chapter has revolved around deciding which output to send a particular packet to. In this section, we look at how to make the process of getting packets from the inputs to the outputs as fast as possible.

Recall from Section 3.1.4 that the performance of a switch implemented in software on a general-purpose processor is limited by the bandwidth of the machine's I/O bus (among other factors). When you consider that each packet must traverse the bus twice—once from the adaptor to memory and once from memory to the adaptor—it is easy to see that a processor with a 1-Gbps I/O bus would be able to handle at most 10 T3 (45-Mbps) links, up to three STS-3 (155-Mbps) links, and not even one STS-12 (622-Mbps) link. Considering that the whole purpose of a switch is to connect reasonably large numbers of links, this is not an ideal situation. Fortunately, switches can be implemented by special-purpose hardware, as we now discuss.

This section is probably the most hardware-oriented in the book. The reason for this focus on hardware is that switches (and their close relatives, routers) are such fundamental building blocks of packet-switched networks that it is hard to fully understand networking without some grasp of the limitations of switching hardware. Indeed, the success or failure of a new protocol—such as ATM or a new version of IP—may very much depend on whether it takes advantage of things that switches do well, or whether it burdens the switches with excessively complex tasks. An important goal of this section is to provide enough information about how switches are built to serve as background for later discussions of protocol design issues. Note that the technology described in this section is applicable to some devices we have already discussed, such as Ethernet switches and ATM switches, and also to some devices that we will be focusing on in the next chapter, notably routers. Routers are the canonical example of a datagram switch.

3.4.1 Design Goals

There are three major challenges in the design of a packet switch. The first is throughput—the number of packets the switch can forward each second. The second is size or scalability—how many inputs/outputs it can connect. And the third is cost, which tends to preclude designs that depend on being cooled in liquid nitrogen, for example. Thus, we are interested in metrics like performance per unit cost, and cost per port of a given speed.

Before we discuss these challenges, we need one item of terminology. We normally describe a switch in terms of the number of inputs and outputs it has; an $n \times m$ (read "n by m") switch is one with n inputs and m outputs. It is often (but not always) the case that $n = m$; this configuration obviously makes sense if the links to the switch are bidirectional. Another interesting special case is the one in which all link speeds are the same, but it is sometimes the case that a switch will have links of various speeds.

Throughput

It turns out to be very difficult to define the throughput of a switch. Intuitively, we might think that if a switch has n inputs that each support a link speed of s_n, then the throughput would just be the sum of all the s_n. This is actually the best possible throughput that such a switch could provide, but virtually no real switch can guarantee that level of performance. The reason for this is simple to understand. Suppose that, for some period of time, all the traffic arriving at the switch needed to be sent to the same output. As long as the bandwidth of that output is less than the sum of the input bandwidths, then some of the traffic will need to be either buffered or dropped. With this particular traffic pattern, the switch could not provide a sustained throughput higher than the link speed of that one output. However, a switch might be able to handle traffic arriving at the full link speed on all inputs if it is distributed across all the outputs evenly; this would be considered optimal.

Another factor that affects the performance of switches is the size of packets arriving on the inputs. For an ATM switch, this is normally not an issue because all "packets" (cells) are the same length. But for Ethernet switches or IP routers, packets of widely varying sizes are possible. Some of the operations that a switch must perform have a constant overhead per packet, so a switch is likely to perform differently depending on whether all arriving packets are very short, very long, or mixed. For this reason, routers or switches that forward variable-length packets are often characterized by a *packet per second* (pps) rate as well as a throughput in bits per second. The pps rate is usually measured with minimum-sized packets.

The first thing to notice about this discussion is that the throughput of the switch is a function of the traffic to which it is subjected. One of the things that switch designers spend a lot of their time doing is trying to come up with traffic models that approximate the behavior of real data traffic. It turns out that it is extremely difficult to achieve accurate models. There are several elements to a traffic model. The main ones are (1) when do packets arrive, (2) what outputs are they destined for, and (3) how big are they.

Traffic modeling is a well-established science that has been extremely successful in the world of telephony, enabling telephone companies to engineer their networks to carry expected loads quite efficiently. This is partly because the way people use the phone network does not change that much over time: The frequency with which calls are placed, the amount of time taken for a call, and the tendency of everyone to make calls on Mother's Day have stayed fairly constant for many years.[4] By contrast, the rapid evolution of computer communications, where a new application like the

---

[4] This statement has recently become less true with the advent of fax machines and modem connections to the Internet.

World Wide Web can change the traffic patterns almost overnight, has made effective modeling of computer networks much more difficult. Nevertheless, there are some excellent books and articles on the subject that we list at the end of the chapter.

Aside from the difficulty of obtaining good traffic models, the main problem that we run up against in switch design is *contention*. The above example (sending all traffic to the same output) illustrates the problem of output contention. This sort of contention is pretty much unavoidable: You cannot fit more traffic into an output link than that link will carry. However, most switch designs are also subject to some degree of internal contention, and the amount of contention under different traffic loads determines the performance of the switch.

To give you a sense of the range of throughputs that designers need to be concerned about, a high-end router used in the Internet at the time of writing might support 16 OC-48 links for a throughput of approximately 40 Gbps. The networking trade press is full of articles about forthcoming "terabit routers," which will presumably offer 10^{12} bps total throughput, a 25-fold increase on the state of the art today. Note that a 40-Gbps switch, if called upon to handle a steady stream of 64-byte packets, would need a packet per second rate of

$$40 \times 10^9 \div (64 \times 8) = 78 \times 10^6 \text{ pps}$$

Scalability

The other issue that switch designers tend to be concerned about is scalability. Typically, the amount of hardware needed to build a switch is a function of the number of inputs and outputs. The question is, How fast does hardware cost rise with increasing n? For example, a switch design for which the hardware cost increases in proportion to n^2 would be considered more scalable than one that increases in proportion to n^3. Furthermore, most switch designs run into problems at some maximum number of inputs and outputs, for example, because some piece of wire gets too long to run at full speed or the fanout of a device is exceeded. Thus, scalability can be measured in terms of both the rate of increase in cost and the maximum possible switch size.

One of the reasons that scalability has been a big issue for ATM switches is that ATM was originally conceived as the technology that would replace current telephone switching technology. Telephone switches, since they are bought by companies with millions of subscribers, tend to have very large numbers of ports—tens of thousands are common. Thus, many designers were thinking in terms of similarly huge ATM switches. Interestingly, the thing that caused ATM to take off was the availability of small switches, on the order of 16 to 32 ports. These switches can use less-scalable designs, which may lead to simpler implementation for a small switch. It remains to

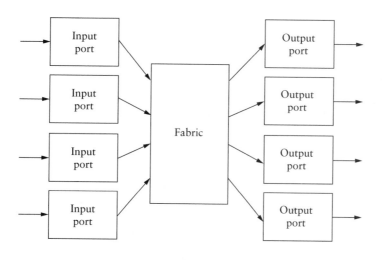

Figure 3.26 A 4 × 4 switch.

be seen whether very large switches will be commercially successful or whether large networks will be built from many small switches.

The next few sections look at a number of switch designs. Each has advantages and disadvantages in terms of its ability to handle contention, its complexity, and its scalability. Before examining them, however, we need to look in a little more detail at the component parts of a switch.

3.4.2 Ports and Fabrics

Most switches look conceptually similar to the one shown in Figure 3.26. They consist of a number of *input ports* and *output ports* and a *fabric*. The ports have to communicate with the outside world. They may contain fiber optic receivers and lasers, buffers to hold packets (cells) that are waiting to be switched or transmitted, and often a significant amount of other circuitry that enables the switch to function. The fabric has a very simple and well-defined job: When presented with a packet, deliver it to the right output.

One of the jobs of the ports, then, is to deal with the complexity of the real world in such a way that the fabric can do its relatively simple job. For example, suppose that this switch is supporting a virtual circuit model of communication. In general, the process of setting up and managing virtual circuits is handled in the ports. The ports maintain tables of virtual circuit identifiers that are currently in use, with information about what output a packet should be sent out on for each VCI and how the VCI needs to be remapped to ensure uniqueness on the outgoing link. Similarly, the ports of an Ethernet switch may store tables that map between Ethernet addresses and output ports (bridge forwarding tables as described in Section 3.2). In general, when a packet is handed from an input port to the fabric, the port has figured out where the packet needs to go, and either the port sets up the fabric accordingly by communicating some control information to it, or it attaches enough information to the packet itself (e.g., an output port number) to allow the fabric to do its job automatically. Fabrics that operate in this way are referred to as "self-routing," since they require no external control to route packets.

The input port is the first place to look for performance bottlenecks. The input port has to receive a steady stream of packets, analyze information in the header of each one to determine which output port (or ports) the packet must be sent to, and pass the packet on to the fabric. The type of header analysis that it performs can range from a simple table lookup on a VCI to complex matching algorithms that examine many fields in the header. This is the type of operation that sometimes becomes a problem when the average packet size is very small.

Another key function of ports is buffering. While some fabrics have internal buffering, some do not, and in almost all cases it is necessary to provide some if not most of the buffering on the ports. The design of these buffers, in terms of both their capacity and the way data is managed in them, can have a profound impact on the performance of the switch. It is worth noting that although there have been many more papers published on fabrics than on ports, a switch's functionality, size, and cost often depend more on the ports than on the fabric.

Observe that buffering can happen in either the input or the output port; it can also happen within the fabric. In the latter case, it is called *internal buffering*. In the switch examples that follow, internal and output buffering are discussed; none of the designs use input buffering. One reason for this is that input buffering has some serious limitations. The simplest way to build an input buffer is to use a FIFO. As packets arrive at the switch, they are placed in the input buffer. The switch then tries to forward the packets at the front of each FIFO to their appropriate output port. However, if the packets at the front of several different input ports are destined for the same output port at the same time, then only one of them can be forwarded;[5] the rest must stay in their input buffers.

The drawback of this feature is that those packets left at the front of the input buffer prevent other packets further back in the buffer from getting a chance to go to their chosen outputs, even though there may be no contention for those outputs.

---

[5] For a simple input-buffered switch, one packet at a time can be sent to a given output port. It is possible to design switches that can forward more than one packet to the same output at once, at a cost of higher switch complexity, but there is always some upper limit on the number.

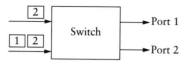

Figure 3.27 Simple illustration of head-of-line blocking.

This phenomenon is called *head-of-line blocking*. A simple example of head-of-line blocking is given in Figure 3.27, where we see a packet destined for port 1 blocked behind a packet contending for port 2. It can be shown that when traffic is uniformly distributed among outputs, head-of-line blocking limits the throughput of an input-buffered switch to 59% of the theoretical maximum (which is the sum of the link bandwidths for the switch). Thus, the vast majority of switches use either pure output buffering or a mixture of internal and output buffering.

Buffers actually perform a more complex task than just holding onto packets that are waiting to be transmitted. The buffers are also the main place where the quality of service characteristics of a switch are determined. For example, if a certain packet has been sent along a VC that has a guaranteed delay, it cannot afford to sit in a buffer for very long. This means that the buffers, in general, must be managed using packet scheduling and discard algorithms that meet a wide range of QoS requirements. We talk more about these issues in Chapter 6.

3.4.3 Crossbar Switches

Crossbar switches are a good place to start in our discussion of switch designs because they are conceptually very simple. The only contention problem they exhibit is the output port contention we mentioned above. Figure 3.28 shows a 4×4 crossbar switch.

Note that every input is connected to every output. The complexity of the switch lies primarily in the deceptively small box sitting in front of each output. (We consider this box part of the output port, not the fabric.) The main function of this box is to deal with the contention that arises when multiple packets are sent to the same output simultaneously.

In general, the complexity of the output port grows in proportion to or faster than the number of inputs n, and since there are also n outputs, that means that the complexity of the switch as a whole grows at least as fast as n^2. However, it takes some clever design work to come up with an output port that only grows linearly with n. One example of such a design is the Knockout switch developed by Yeh, Hluchyj, and Acampora, which we now examine in more detail.

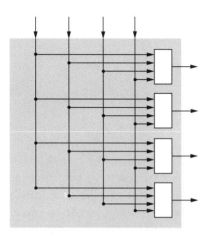

Figure 3.28   A 4 × 4 crossbar switch.

The Knockout Switch

The Knockout switch is in fact not quite a "perfect" crossbar—some assumptions about traffic are made to reduce the complexity of the output ports. A true crossbar would be able to deal with the situation in which every switch input had a packet to send to a given output at exactly the same time. For a small switch like the one in Figure 3.28, this might be easy enough to implement; for a large switch, it would not only be quite difficult, it would be overkill. For most reasonable traffic scenarios, the likelihood that many inputs would all need to send to the same output simultaneously is very small. So, the idea is to design an output port that can accept l packets simultaneously, with $l < n$. We would clearly like to pick l to be small enough to keep our cost down, yet large enough that the likelihood of more than l packets arriving all at once is acceptably small. Here again we are in the realm of traffic models; it is relatively easy to figure out a good value of l if you assume that the traffic arriving at each input port is independent of the traffic arriving at all other ports. Sadly, that may be a bad assumption if someone has just connected a popular Web site to one output of the switch. The phenomenon of traffic collecting to "beat up" on one port of a switch is referred to as a *hot spot*, and it is likely to be quite common in an environment where many clients communicate with a server. We do not delve deeper into this problem, except to note that ignoring it when you calculate l might be a bad idea.

The output port of the Knockout switch, then, is made up of three parts:

■ a set of packet filters that recognize packets destined for this port

- the "Knockout" part, called a *concentrator*, that selects up to *l* packets from those destined for this port and discards any excess packets on the (hopefully) rare occasions when they occur

- a queue that accepts up to *l* packets at a time and buffers them while they await transmission

The filters use simple matching hardware to identify the packets that contain the right output port number. The concentrator's job turns out to be the hard part, primarily because of the need to ensure fairness: We need to be sure that no one input port is singled out for bad treatment every time the output is overloaded. Fairness is achieved by "playing" the packets against each other in a form of Knockout "tournament" to select *l* winners from *n* contestants. One game in the tournament involves two packets. These two packets compete by entering a 2×2 switching element, which randomly selects a winner. Picking the overall winner is easy—it is exactly the way the winner is picked in a Knockout tennis tournament, that is, you play $\log_2 n$ rounds and the losers of each round are knocked out until only one winner remains. To pick *l* winners is a bit more complicated—the process is illustrated in Figure 3.29 in the case in which $n = 8$ and $l = 4$. For the following discussion, we assume that packets are all of the same length, as they would be in an ATM switch.

We can think of the tournament as having *l* sections designed to pick a winner, a runner-up, a third-place finisher, and so on, up to the *l*th-place finisher. The first section is the traditional Knockout tournament, which selects one winner. All the losers from that section go to compete to be runner-up. Any packet that loses in the second section goes on to the third, and so on. If a packet loses in *l* sections, it is dropped. Since each section selects just one packet as the winner of that section, we end up selecting *l* packets and dropping all the rest, if there were in fact more than *l* packets submitted.

This process is much easier to understand when you look at an example like the one in Figure 3.29. The leftmost section looks like the quarterfinal round at Wimbledon, and selects one winner. The first-round losers from this section go straight to the second section and play off against each other, to be joined at later stages by second- and third-round losers from the first section. With each loss, a packet moves right to another section of competition, while each win advances it further within its current section. With enough losses, a packet is eliminated; if it goes undefeated in a given section, it reaches the output of that box. Sometimes at a particular stage a section has an odd number of players, so one packet needs to wait in a delay element, marked D, before moving on to the next round. Delay elements are also used to ensure that all winning packets exit at the same time in spite of the different tournament lengths.

Inputs

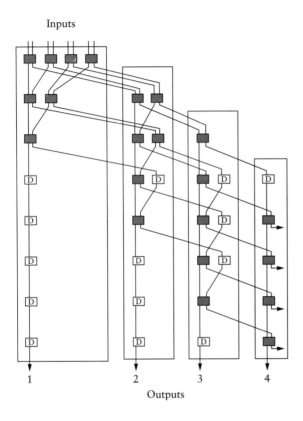

Figure 3.29 An 8-to-4 Knockout concentrator.

Now that we have discussed the Knockout fabric, we turn our attention to the design of the output ports, which are also quite novel. Each output port has a buffer that must accept up to l packets in a single cycle and then transmit one packet each cycle. Since there are as many buffers as there are switch ports (n), it is important to focus on complexity here as well as in the fabric.

Rather than implementing the output buffer as a FIFO with an input that runs l times faster than the output, which would be expensive, the Knockout designers used an array of l buffers preceded by a shifter, as shown in Figure 3.30. The shifter moves arriving packets into different buffers to ensure that they are filled in round-robin order, and thus that they never differ by more than one packet in their level of occupancy. At the same time, packets are read out one at a time, also in round-robin order, so that packet order is preserved. Clearly, if the number of packets arriving in each cycle is more than one for a significant period of time, the buffer will overflow. In

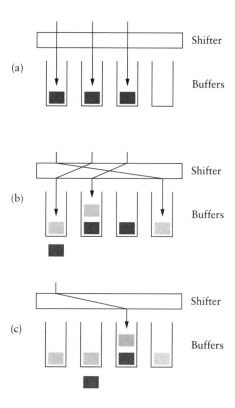

Figure 3.30 **The shared buffer of a Knockout switch: (a) three packets arrive; (b) three packets arrive, one leaves; (c) one packet arrives, one leaves.**

Figure 3.30(a), three packets arrive and are placed in the first three buffers. In the next cycle, Figure 3.30(b), three more arrive and are shifted right by three positions, while the first packet is sent out from the first buffer. Finally, in Figure 3.30(c), one packet arrives, is shifted right by two positions (6 mod 4, since 6 packets arrived previously) and stored, while a packet is transmitted from the second buffer.

Let's consider the complexity of this switch for large values of n (the number of inputs and outputs) in order to evaluate its scalability. First, note that l, the number of packets that can simultaneously be delivered to an output, can remain fixed at some reasonably small value, such as 8, and still provide quite good performance. Since the shared buffer scales with l, its cost is constant. The complexity of the concentrator for a large n value approaches $n \times l$, so it scales with n. The number of packet filters needed per port is clearly n. Thus, the complexity of the output port, most of which

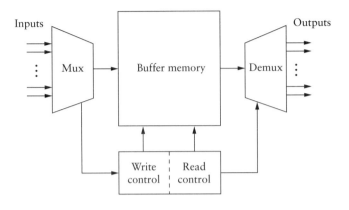

Figure 3.31   A shared-memory switch.

is in the concentrator, is proportional to n. Since there are n output ports, the total switch complexity is roughly proportional to n^2—not great, but not awful either.

Probably the greatest flaw of the Knockout switch is that it rests on the assumption that traffic arriving at different ports is uncorrelated and equally likely to go to any output. Its n^2 cost is also a drawback. Self-routing fabrics are the type of switch design that has generally achieved greatest scalability, as we discuss in Section 3.4.5. First, however, we look at another simple class of switch.

3.4.4   Shared-Media Switches

In Section 3.1.4, we described how to build a sort of switch using a PC. Such a switch is an example of a shared-media design. The shared media in this case are the PC's bus and memory. As we saw in that example, shared-media switches tend not to scale terribly well, since the shared resource either gets more overloaded or needs to get faster as the switch size grows. However, there are many existence proofs of reasonably high-throughput switches that use such an approach. We consider one example of a shared-media switch here—a shared-memory switch, as illustrated in Figure 3.31.

The nice thing about a shared-memory switch is that it is basically one big buffer, which can be built out of off-the-shelf memory chips. It can be made to work like a perfect crossbar, only better: Since the buffering is shared among all the output ports, you can get better utilization out of the buffering. To understand why utilization is better, recall that an output-buffered crossbar only loses packets when the rate at which packets are arriving at one output exceeds the rate at which they can be transmitted, for a long enough period to overflow the buffer at that output. As a consequence, you need to provide enough buffering at each output to make this overflow a rare occurrence. But the likelihood that all your outputs will be simultaneously overloaded

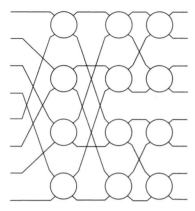

Figure 3.32 An eight-input banyan network.

is very low, so it would be nice if you could borrow unused buffer space from another output and give it to the overloaded output. This is exactly what a shared-buffer memory does for you.

The memory switch in Figure 3.31 is only capable of writing one packet into the shared memory at a time. This means that the bus connecting the multiplexer to the memory must run n times faster than the line speed of a single link, which would typically be achieved by making it a very wide bus. Each arriving packet has its header passed to the write-control logic. Upon examining the output port number, the write control gets an address of a free location from a free list, writes the packet to this address, and links the packet to a linked list associated with the appropriate output port. Similarly, the read control takes packets from the linked list for each output, sends them to the appropriate port through the demultiplexer, and returns the memory addresses to the free list.

Note that the main limitation on size for this sort of switch is the rate at which the control logic can operate, since unlike the buffer memory, the control logic cannot be made faster by widening it.

3.4.5 Self-Routing Fabrics

Self-routing fabrics are a class of switches made up of many small, interconnected switching elements in which packets find their own way through the fabric based on a sequence of local switching decisions made at each small switching element. Figure 3.32 shows a self-routing fabric of the type known as a *banyan network*, so called because of its similarity to the banyan tree. It may seem strange to call this a banyan "network," but in a sense the fabric is a miniature network inside the switch.

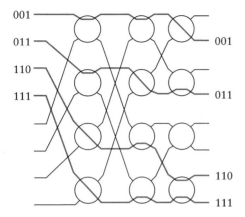

001

011

110

111

001

011

110

111

Figure 3.33 Routing packets through a banyan network.

The general principle behind self-routing fabrics is that each packet carries enough information in its header to allow the small switching elements to make a local decision, without consulting any other elements or any central controller. This is normally done by having the input port add an extra (internal) header to the packet before it arrives at the fabric, and then having the output port remove this header before the packet is transmitted to the next switch. This header is called a *self-routing header*. In a virtual circuit switch, for example, the virtual circuit number in an arriving packet is used to look up the appropriate switch output port, and this port number is then placed in the self-routing header. (Notice the similarity between a self-routing header and source routing, as described in Section 3.1.3.)

Banyan Networks
Self-routing fabrics are often made from simple 2×2 switching elements that switch based on just 1 bit in the self-routing header. For example, the 2×2 switches in the banyan network just look at 1 bit in each packet header and route toward the upper output if it is clear or toward the lower output if it is set. Obviously, if two packets arrive at a banyan element at the same time and both have this bit set to the same value, then they want to be routed to the same output and a collision will occur. Either preventing or dealing with these collisions is a main challenge for self-routing switch design. The banyan network is a clever arrangement of 2×2 switching elements that routes all packets to the correct output without collisions if the packets are presented in ascending order. We can see how this works in an example, as shown in Figure 3.33.

In this example, the switch elements in the first column look at the most significant bit of the output port number contained in the self-routing header and route

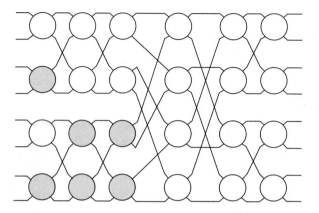

Figure 3.34   An 8 × 8 Batcher network. The elements that send the higher number to the top output are shaded.

packets to the top if that bit is a 0 or the bottom if it is a 1. Switch elements in the second column look at the second bit, and those in the last column look at the least significant bit. You can see from this example that the packets are routed to the correct destination port without collisions. Notice how the top outputs from the first column of switches all lead to the top half of the network, thus getting packets with port numbers 0–3 into the right half of the network. The next column gets packets to the right quarter of the network, and the final column gets them to the right output port. The clever part is the way switches are arranged to avoid collisions. Part of the arrangement includes the "perfect shuffle" wiring pattern at the start of the network.

From this discussion it should be apparent that a banyan network with n inputs needs to have $\log_2 n$ stages, each of which has $n/2$ switching elements, so that the complexity is on the order of $n \log_2 n$.

Batcher Networks

Since a banyan network can route a set of packets without collisions when those packets are presented in ascending order, one thing you might think of doing—and which has been done successfully in several switches—is to precede a banyan network with a different sort of self-routing network that sorts packets into order. The *Batcher network*, named after its inventor, is just such a network. An example Batcher network is illustrated in Figure 3.34. When you put a Batcher network in front of a banyan network, you get a Batcher-banyan fabric, which has the property that it is *nonblocking*; that is, there will be no collisions as long as the packets presented to it are all destined for unique output ports.

The 2×2 switching element of a Batcher network differs substantially from that of a banyan network. It does a complete comparison of the self-routing headers, routing the packet with the numerically greater tag to one output and the one with the lesser tag to the other output. If the tags are equal, it makes a random choice. There are actually two types of switch elements in a Batcher network: those that sort "up" (i.e., send the higher number to the top output) and those that sort "down" (i.e., send the higher number to the bottom output). In the figure, the "up" elements are shaded.

In essence, the Batcher network implements a recursive merge-sort algorithm in hardware. You can see how this works by looking first at the six switching elements in the top left corner of Figure 3.34. The basic 2×2 element can sort two packets, so if we take a "down" element and an "up" element, we get a pair of two-member ordered lists—one in ascending order and one in descending order. Using two more columns of "down" elements, we can merge these two lists into a four-member list in ascending order. (By "ascending," we mean that the numbers get bigger as you go down the figure.) Meanwhile, the six switching elements in the bottom left corner are just like the ones in the top left except all the "up" sorters have been replaced by "down" sorters and vice versa. Thus, they provide a list of packets sorted in *descending* order. With three more columns of "down" sorters, we can merge our two four-member lists into one eight-member list. By now, it should be fairly clear how you could build arbitrarily large Batcher networks. For example, a 16-input version would be made from two 8-input versions followed by four rows of sorters to do the merge function. While it may not be totally obvious, this means that the number of stages in an n-input Batcher network is $\log_2 n \times (1 + \log_2 n)/2$. Since there are $n/2$ switching elements per stage, the total complexity is on the order of $n \log_2^2 n$, which is actually better (i.e., grows less quickly) than n^2.

The important idea behind how merging works is that the merger depends on the fact that it is presented with a pair of ordered lists, one in ascending order and one in descending order. Without going into the details, you should note that the first column of the merger (the fourth column from the left in the figure) sends packets to the correct half of the network (top or bottom), the next column sends them to the correct quarter, and the final column sends them to the correct output.

To make this concrete, consider the smaller example in Figure 3.35. In this network, the one shaded element sorts packets "up," so that the higher-numbered packet comes out on top; the rest sort down. Four packets, carrying labels 7, 3, 6, and 1, are presented to the inputs of a four-input Batcher network. Packets 7 and 3 are sorted down, so that 3 comes out on top, 7 on the bottom. Packets 6 and 1 are sorted up, so 6 comes out on top. Coming out of the first stage, we have an ascending list 3, 7, which must be merged with a descending list 6, 1. The second stage begins the merge, sorting the higher element from the second list (6) against the lower element of

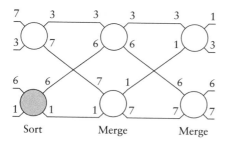

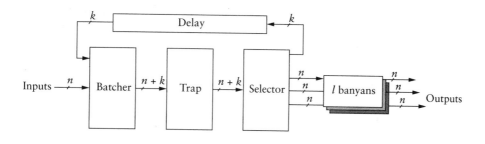

Figure 3.35 Routing packets through a Batcher network.

Figure 3.36 The Sunshine switch.

the first list (3): 6 comes out on the bottom, 3 on top. Similarly, 7 is sorted against 1, so 7 comes out on the bottom and 1 on the top. In the final stage, 1 is sorted against 3, and 6 against 7, and the packets come out of the final stage in correct ascending order.

Sunshine Switch

With a combination of Batcher and banyan networks, we can construct a fabric that delivers all packets to the right output port, as long as there are no duplicate packets heading for the same port. Unfortunately, that is a rather severe restriction. A switch this simple would need to drop packets every time two or more were destined for the same output. There have been many switch architectures designed around Batcher-banyan networks that aim to deal with this limitation. An interesting one that uses a combination of techniques to avoid collisions is the Sunshine switch, depicted in Figure 3.36.

The Sunshine switch complements the Batcher and banyan networks with three additional elements: a trap, a selector, and a set of delay boxes. It also uses multiple parallel banyans. The multiple banyans enable multiple packets to go to one output at the same time. Like the Knockout switch, this means that the output port (not shown) must be able to accept l packets at once if there are l parallel banyans. When more than l packets are destined for a single output in the same cycle, they are recirculated through the delay box and resubmitted to the switch in the next cycle. This means that the Batcher network needs to be able to sort $n + k$ packets—n from the input ports and up to k that have been recirculated. The trap network identifies those packets that will be able to exit the switch through the banyans (up to l of them per output port) and marks the rest for recirculation. The selector makes sure that if l packets are going to the same output, they get sent to separate banyans to avoid collisions, and any extras get sent to the recirculator. The packets include a priority field that is incremented each time they get recirculated, which ensures that "older" packets have a better chance of getting out through the banyans than newly arrived packets; this feature ensures that packet order is preserved through the switch, a requirement for ATM networks.

The Sunshine switch turns out to be a very good compromise design. It has lower complexity than the Knockout switch, and rather than discarding the extra packets when more than l are destined for one output, it recirculates the extras. The only way packets get dropped before reaching the output is when the number of packets getting recirculated is greater than k. The Sunshine designers simulated and analyzed the design for a very wide range of traffic scenarios and found that with well-chosen values for l and k they could make these losses very rare.

3.5 Summary

This chapter has started to look at some of the issues involved in building large scalable networks by using switches, rather than just links, to interconnect hosts. There are several different ways to decide how to switch packets; the two main ones are the datagram (connectionless) model and the virtual circuit (connection-oriented) model.

An important application of switching is the interconnection of shared-media LANs. LAN switches, or bridges, use techniques such as source address learning to improve forwarding efficiency, and spanning tree algorithms to avoid looping.

The most widespread uses of virtual circuit switching are in Frame Relay and ATM switches. ATM introduces some particular challenges through the use of cells, short fixed-length packets. The availability of relatively high-throughput ATM switches has contributed to the acceptance of the technology, although it has certainly not swept all other technologies aside as some predicted. To increase the usefulness of ATM in the LAN environment, it has been necessary to define some fairly complex procedures, known as LAN emulation, to make ATM networks behave more like traditional shared-media LANs.

Independent of the specifics of the switching technology, switches need to forward packets from inputs to outputs at a high rate, and in some circumstances, switches need to grow to a large size to accommodate hundreds or thousands of ports. Building switches that both scale and offer high performance at acceptable cost is complicated by the problem of contention, and as a consequence, switches often employ special-purpose hardware rather than being built from general-purpose workstations. Some switch designers have targeted the "central office switch" for design improvement, which would allow the telephone companies to provide ATM instead of a simple voice telephone line to everyone's home. Building such large, fast switches is a tough problem that has yielded a wealth of clever switch architectures. Much of this work also applies to router design, to be discussed in the next chapter.

In addition to the issues of contention discussed here, we observe that the related problem of congestion has come up throughout this chapter. We will postpone our discussion of congestion control until Chapter 6, after we have seen more of the network architecture. We do this because it is impossible to fully appreciate congestion (both the problem and how it to address it) without understanding both what happens inside the network (the topic of this and the next chapter) and what happens at the edges of the network (the topic of Chapter 5).

ATM was originally envisioned by many of its proponents as the foundation for the "Broadband Integrated Services Digital Network," and it was predicted in some quarters that ATM would displace all other networking technologies.

O P E N   I S S U E

The Future of ATM

Hosts would acquire ATM adaptors instead of Ethernet ports, enabling "ATM to the desktop." Phone companies everywhere would deploy ATM, and as the technology that supports all media types—voice, video, and data—it would remove the need for any other type of network.

It is now apparent that this scenario is unlikely to play out. The success of Ethernet switches in particular has largely killed off the ATM-to-the-desktop movement. Only a few servers directly attached to ATM backbones keep the market for workstation ATM adaptors alive, and new technologies such as Gigabit Ethernet threaten this segment as well.

Another factor that has limited the acceptance of ATM has been the success of the Internet. It seems to be a fact of life now that consumers are willing to pay for Internet access, and that means selling a service that delivers IP packets. While ATM can be used to help deliver that service, simply selling ATM connections to customers is not going to meet their needs. The notable exception is corporate customers looking to interconnect many sites, where an ATM VC may be just the right thing to economically replace a leased line.

ATM certainly has a niche as a backbone technology, primarily because it already runs over fiber at speeds of 0.6–2.4 Gbps. It is widely used in both campus networks and Internet service providers for just that purpose. And the sophisticated QoS features of today's ATM switches still make it very attractive in some environments where strict QoS guarantees are needed. It remains to be seen whether ATM can expand its domain of applicability in the face of competition from Gigabit Ethernet, multigigabit IP routers, and other emerging technologies.

FURTHER READING

The seminal paper on bridges, in particular the spanning tree algorithm, is the article by Perlman below. There is a wealth of survey papers on ATM; the article by Lyles and Swinehart is a good early example, partly because it discusses ATM from the perspective of the desktop rather than from the perspective of the telephone company. Finally, the last paper describes the Sunshine switch and is especially interesting because it provides insights into the important role of traffic analysis in switch design. In particular, the Sunshine designers were among the first to realize that cells were unlikely to arrive at a switch in a totally uncorrelated way and thus were able to factor these correlations into their design.

- Perlman, R. An algorithm for distributed computation of spanning trees in an extended LAN. *Proceedings of the Ninth Data Communications Symposium*, pages 44–53, September 1985.

- Lyles, J., and D. Swinehart. The emerging gigabit environment and the role of the local ATM. *IEEE Communications* 30(4):52–58, April 1992.

- Giacopelli, J. N., et al. Sunshine: A high-performance self-routing broadband packet-switched architecture. *IEEE Journal of Selected Areas in Communications (JSAC)* 9(8):1289–1298, October 1991.

A good general overview of bridges can be found in another work by Perlman [Per92]. For a detailed description of many aspects of ATM, with a focus on building real networks, we recommend the book by Ginsburg [Gin96]. For more information on ATM, a useful overview book is the one by De Prycker [DeP95]. Also, as one of the key ATM standards-setting bodies, the ATM Forum produces new specifications for

ATM; the User Network Interface (UNI) specification, version 4.0, is the most recent at the time of this writing. (See the live reference below.)

There have been literally thousands of papers published on switch architectures. One early paper that explains Batcher networks well is, not surprisingly, one by Batcher himself [Bat68]. Sorting networks are explained by Drysdale and Young [DY75], and the Knockout switch is described by Yeh et al. [YHA87]. A survey of ATM switch architectures appears in Partridge [Par94], and a good overview of the performance of different switching fabrics can be found in Robertazzi [Rob93]. An example of a modern non-ATM switch can be found in Gopal and Guerin [GG94].

An excellent text to read if you want to learn about the mathematical analysis of network performance is by Kleinrock [Kle75], one of the pioneers of the ARPANET. Many papers have been published on the applications of queuing theory to packet switching. We recommend the article by Paxson and Floyd [PF94] as a recent contribution focused on the Internet, and one by Leland et al. [LTWW94], a significant paper that introduces the important concept of "long-range dependence" and shows the inadequacy of many traditional approaches to traffic modeling.

Finally, we recommend the following live reference:

■ http://www.atmforum.com: current activities of the ATM Forum

E X E R C I S E S

1 Using the example network given in Figure 3.37, give the virtual circuit tables for all the switches after each of the following connections is established. Assume that the sequence of connections is cumulative; that is, the first connection is still up when the second connection is established, and so on. Also assume that the VCI assignment always picks the lowest unused VCI on each link, starting with 0.

(a) Host A connects to host B.

(b) Host C connects to host G.

(c) Host E connects to host I.

(d) Host D connects to host B.

(e) Host F connects to host J.

(f) Host H connects to host A.

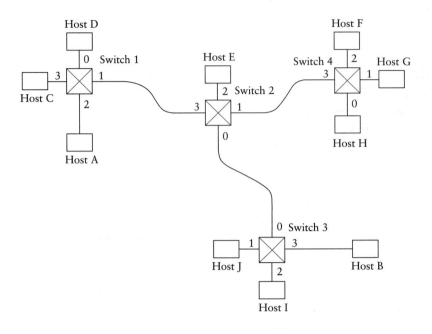

Figure 3.37 Example network for Exercise 1.

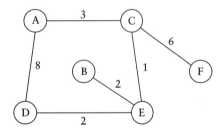

Figure 3.38 Network for Exercise 2.

2 For the network given in Figure 2, give the datagram forwarding table for each node. The links are labelled with relative costs; your tables should forward each packet via the lowest-cost path to its destination.

3 Give forwarding tables for switches S1–S4 in Figure 3.39. Each switch should have a "default" routing entry, chosen to forward packets with unrecognized destina-

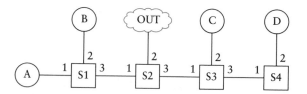

Figure 3.39   Diagram for Exercise 3.

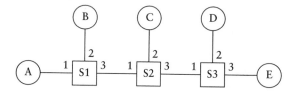

Figure 3.40   Diagram for Exercise 4.

Switch S1				Switch S2				Switch S3			
Port	VCI	Port	VCI	Port	VCI	Port	VCI	Port	VCI	Port	VCI
1	2	3	1	1	1	3	3	1	3	2	1
1	1	2	3	1	2	3	2	1	2	3	1
2	1	3	2								

Table 3.5   VCI tables for switches in Figure 3.40.

tion addresses toward OUT. Any specific-destination table entries duplicated by the default entry should then be eliminated.

4 Consider the virtual circuit switches in Figure 3.40. Table 3.5 lists, for each switch, what ⟨port, VCI⟩ (or ⟨VCI, interface⟩) pairs are connected to what other. Connections are bidirectional. List all endpoint-to-endpoint connections.

5 In the source routing example of Section 3.1.3, the address received by B is not reversible and doesn't help B know how to reach A. Propose a modification to the delivery mechanism that does allow for reversibility. Your mechanism should *not* require giving all switches globally unique names.

6 Propose a mechanism that virtual circuit switches might use so that if one switch loses all its state regarding connections, then a sender of packets along a path through that switch is informed of the failure.

7 Propose a mechanism that might be used by datagram switches so that if one switch loses all or part of its forwarding table, affected senders are informed of the failure.

8 The virtual circuit mechanism described in Section 3.1.2 assumes that each link is point-to-point. Extend the forwarding algorithm to work in the case that links are shared-media connections, for example, Ethernet.

9 Suppose, in Figure 3.4, that a new link has been added, connecting switch 3 port 1 (where G is now) and switch 1 port 0 (where D is now); neither switch is "informed" of this link. Furthermore, switch 3 mistakenly thinks that host B is reached via port 1.
  (a) What happens if host A attempts to send to host B, using datagram forwarding?
  (b) What happens if host A attempts to connect to host B, using the virtual circuit setup mechanism discussed in the text?

10 Give an example of a working virtual circuit whose path traverses some link twice. Datagrams sent along this path should *not*, however, circulate indefinitely.

11 In Section 3.1.2, each switch chose the VCI value for the incoming link. Show that it is also possible for each switch to choose the VCI value for the outbound link, and that the same VCI values will be chosen by each approach. If each switch chooses the outbound VCI, is it still necessary to wait one RTT before data is sent?

12 Given the extended LAN shown in Figure 3.41, indicate which ports are not selected by the spanning tree algorithm.

13 Consider the arrangement of learning bridges shown in Figure 3.42. Assuming all are initially empty, give the forwarding tables for each of the bridges B1–B4 after the following transmissions:
  • A sends to C.
  • C sends to A.
  • D sends to C.

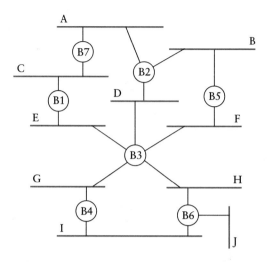

Figure 3.41 Network for Exercise 12.

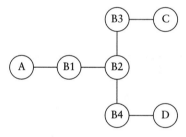

Figure 3.42 Diagram for Exercise 13.

Identify ports with the unique neighbor reached directly from that port; that is, the ports for B1 are to be labelled "A" and "B2".

14 Consider hosts X, Y, Z, W and learning bridges B1, B2, B3, with initially empty forwarding tables, as in Figure 3.43.

(a) Suppose X sends to Z. Which bridges learn where X is? Does Y's network interface see this packet?

(b) Suppose Z now sends to X. Which bridges learn where Z is? Does Y's network interface see this packet?

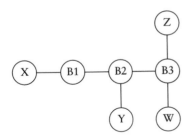

Figure 3.43   Diagram for Exercise 14.

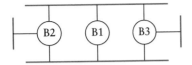

Figure 3.44   Extended LAN for Exercise 15.

(c) Suppose Y now sends to X. Which bridges learn where Y is? Does Z's network interface see this packet?

(d) Finally, suppose Z sends to Y. Which bridges learn where Z is? Does W's network interface see this packet?

15 Give the spanning tree generated for the extended LAN shown in Figure 3.44, and discuss how any ties are resolved.

16 Suppose two learning bridges B1 and B2 form a loop as shown in Figure 3.45, and do *not* implement the spanning tree algorithm. Each bridge maintains a single table of ⟨address, interface⟩ pairs.

(a) What will happen if M sends to L?

(b) Suppose a short while later L replies to M. Give a sequence of events that leads to one packet from M and one packet from L circling the loop in opposite directions.

17 Suppose that M in Figure 3.45 sends to itself (this normally would never happen). State what would happen, assuming

(a) the bridges' learning algorithm is to install (or update) the new ⟨sourceaddress, interface⟩ entry *before* searching the table for the destination address.

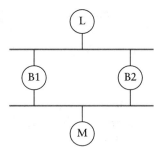

Figure 3.45 Loop for Exercises 16 and 17.

(b) the new source address was installed *after* destination address lookup.

18 Consider the extended LAN of Figure 3.11. What happens in the spanning tree algorithm if bridge B1 does not participate and

(a) simply forwards all spanning tree algorithm messages?

(b) drops all spanning tree messages?

19 Suppose some repeaters (hubs), rather than bridges, are connected into a loop.

(a) What will happen when somebody transmits?

(b) Why would the spanning tree mechanism be difficult or impossible to implement for repeaters?

(c) Propose a mechanism by which repeaters might detect loops and shut down some ports to break the loop. Your solution is not required to work 100% of the time.

20 Suppose a bridge has two of its ports on the same network. How might the bridge detect and correct this?

21 What percentage of an ATM link's total bandwidth is consumed by the ATM cell headers? What percentage of the total bandwidth is consumed by all nonpayload bits in AAL3/4 and AAL5, when the user data is 512 bytes long?

22 Explain why AAL3/4 will not detect the loss of 16 consecutive cells of a single PDU.

23 The IP datagram for a TCP ACK message is 40 bytes long: it contains 20 bytes of TCP header and 20 bytes of IP header. Assume that this ACK is traversing an ATM network that uses AAL5 to encapsulate IP packets. How many ATM packets will it take to carry the ACK? What if AAL3/4 is used instead?

24 The CS-PDU for AAL5 contains up to 47 bytes of padding, while the AAL3/4 CS-PDU only contains up to 3 bytes of padding. Explain why the effective bandwidth of AAL5 is always the same as, or higher than, that of AAL3/4, given a PDU of a particular size.

25 How reliable does an ATM connection have to be in order to maintain a loss rate of less than one per million for a higher-level PDU of size 20 cells? Assume AAL5.

26 Assuming the 20-cell AAL5 packet from the previous problem, suppose a final cell is tacked on the end of the PDU, and that this cell is the XOR of all the previous cells in the PDU. This allows recovery from any one lost cell. What cell loss rate now would yield a net one-per-million loss rate for 20-data-cell PDUs?

27 Recall that AAL3/4 has a CRC-10 checksum at the end of each cell, while AAL5 has a single CRC-32 checksum at the end of the PDU. If a PDU is carried in 12 AAL3/4 cells, then AAL3/4 devotes nearly four times as many bits to error detection as AAL5.

(a) Suppose errors are known to come in bursts, where each burst is small enough to be confined to a single cell. Find the probability that AAL3/4 fails to detect an error, given that it is known that exactly two cells are affected. Do the same for three cells. Under these conditions is AAL3/4 more or less reliable than AAL5? Assume that an N-bit CRC fails to detect an error with probability $1/2^N$ (which is strictly true only when all errors are equally likely).

(b) Can you think of any error distribution in which the AAL3/4 would be more likely than AAL5 to detect an error? Do you think such circumstances are likely?

28 Cell switching methods essentially always use virtual circuit routing rather than datagram routing. Give a specific argument why this is so.

29 Suppose a workstation has an I/O bus speed of 800 Mbps and memory bandwidth of 2 Gbps. Assuming DMA in and out of main memory, how many interfaces to 45-Mbps T3 links could a switch based on this workstation handle?

30 Suppose a switch can forward packets at a rate of 100,000 per second, regardless (within limits) of size. Assuming the workstation parameters described in the previous problem, at what packet size would the bus bandwidth become the limiting factor?

31 Give a schematic for a 16-to-6 Knockout concentrator, similar to the one given in Figure 3.29.

32 Suppose that the numbers $7, \ldots, 0$, in descending order, are presented as input values from top to bottom, to the 8×8 Batcher network of Figure 3.34. Show the outputs of each sorter.

33 Suppose someone has built the first three columns of an 8×8 Batcher network, as in Figure 3.34, except that they failed to reverse the sense of the sorters in the bottom two rows. Thus, the output of the bottom two rows is sorted in ascending order. Show how to wire between the above three sorter columns and the existing merger columns (columns 4–6) so that the fabric works correctly.

34 Give the wiring between the first two columns of the "merger" section of a 16×16 Batcher network.

35 A stage of an $n \times n$ banyan network consists of $(n/2)$ 2×2 switching elements. The first stage directs packets to the correct half of the network, the next stage to the correct quarter, and so on, until the packet is routed to the correct output. Derive an expression for the number of 2×2 switching elements needed to make an $n \times n$ banyan network. Verify your answer for $n = 8$.

36 An $n \times n$ Batcher network can be made from two Batcher networks of size $n/2 \times n/2$ plus a merge network of size $n/2 \log_2 n$. Assuming that a 2×2 Batcher network has a complexity of 1 (i.e., it has one switching element), derive the expression for the complexity (number of switching elements) of an $n \times n$ Batcher network. Check your result for $n = 8$ against Figure 3.34.

37 An Ethernet switch is simply a bridge that has the ability to forward some number of packets in parallel, assuming the input and output ports are all distinct. Supposes two such N-port switches, for a large value of N, are each able to forward individually up to three packets in parallel. They are then connected to one another in series by joining a pair of ports, one from each switch; the joining link is the bottleneck as it can, of course, carry only one packet at a time.

(a) Suppose we choose two connections through this combined switch at random. What is the probability that both connections can be forwarded in parallel? Hint: This is the probability that at most one of the connections crosses the link.

(b) What if three connections are chosen at random?

38 Suppose a 10-Mbps Ethernet hub (repeater) is replaced by a 10-Mbps switch, in an environment where all traffic is between a single server and N "clients." Because all traffic must still traverse the server-switch link, nominally there is no improvement in bandwidth.

(a) Would you expect *any* improvement in bandwidth? If so, why? Hint: See Exercises 43 and 44 in Chapter 2.

(b) What would your answer be if the original hub were token ring rather than Ethernet?

(c) What other advantages and drawbacks might a switch offer versus a hub?

DV (Distance Vector)

- Info exchange with neighbors
- Info about all nodes and routers.

1. A link state packet contains ID of the node that crosses that LSP node
2. Cost of link to each directly connected neighbor
3. Contains a sequence number (time to live) TTL.

Reliable Flooding — To store the most recent LSP from each node. Then forward LSP to all nodes, except the one that sent it. Each node generates a new LSP periodically and the sequences number. All sequences numbers start at zero when a node is rebooted. Finally TTL is reduced at every node until it becomes zero, at which time the packet is discarded.

The original metric of ARPANET measures the number of packets that were "queue" at each link. It did not take into account earlier latency or bandwidth.

IP is a collection of networks interconnected to provide host to host packet delivery service. It is a logical network built on physical networks. It is the concatenation of networks. Multiple networks are connected to each other using routers.

IP (Internet protocol) is a set of software programs that enable communication functionality.

Layers of internet architecture

Physical layer — IP — TCP

IP supports formal connection (connectionless model)

g. - Phone system → connection oriented

IP best effort model → unreliable service

IP is a connectionless.

IP does not provide reliable service delivery. Meaning that packets, can be lost packets. Packets can be delivered out of sequence. Packets can be delayed for any time.

Fragmentation and Reasembly

MTU (Maximum transmission Unit) - Every network has got an upper limit in the size of the data packet that can travel on it. This upper limit is called MTU. If a network's MTU is less than the size of the packets, then the packet needs to be broken down into smaller pieces. This process is called Fragmentation and these pieces are called fragments. Fragmentation does not occur at the source host. It occurs to the routers. If fragmentation is possible.

The process of putting together fragments and recreating the original packet is called reasembly. Reasembly happens at the destination host.

No IP addresses are equal. They are unique. IP addresses are also hierchical.

Routing and Forwarding

Forwarding is the act of selecting an output based on destination address and routing tables.

Routing is the process by which a routing table is built.

there are 2 types of routers protocols

Cost of infinity means that this node does not know how to get to its destination

Routing table always are dinamic. The name, the distance vector and the link state

Each node mantains a set of tripods destination cost.

Next hop. Each node exchanges updates with its directed connected neighbors.

This updates are a list of pairs-node destination cost. these updates are sent out periodically (every couple of seconds) or whenever the table changes. The receiving node updates its own position table. If a better router is found, meaning that the cost is smaller, nodes refresh routing tables periodically. If a node does not receive any information regarding about routing destination, that entry is deleted from the routing table.

There is a certain scale of duties, there is a certain Hierarchy of upper and lower commands.

—John Milton

We have now seen how to build a single network using point-to-point links, shared media, and switches. The problem is that lots of people have built networks with these various technologies and they all want to be able to communicate with each other, not just with the other users of a single network. This chapter is about the problem of interconnecting different networks.

There are two important problems that must be addressed when connecting networks: *heterogeneity* and *scale*. Simply stated, the problem of heterogeneity is that users on one type of network want to be able to communicate with users on other types of networks. To further complicate matters, establishing connectivity between hosts on two different networks may require traversing several other networks in between, each of which may be of yet another type. These different networks may be Ethernets, token rings, point-to-point links, or switched networks of various kinds, and each of them is likely to have its own addressing scheme, media access protocols, service model, and so on. The challenge of heterogeneity is to provide a useful and fairly predictable host-to-host service over this hodgepodge of different networks. To understand the problem of scaling, it is worth considering the growth of the Internet, which has roughly doubled in size each year for 20 years. This sort of growth forces us to face a number of challenges. One of these is *routing*: How can you find an efficient path through a network with millions, or perhaps billions, of nodes? Closely related to this is the problem of *addressing*, the task of providing suitable identifiers for all those nodes.

This chapter looks at a series of approaches to interconnecting networks, and the problems that must be solved. In doing so, we trace the evolution of the TCP/IP Internet in an effort to understand the problems of heterogeneity and scale in detail, along with the general techniques that can be applied to them.

The first section introduces the Internet Protocol (IP) and shows how it can be used to build a scalable, heterogeneous internetwork. This section includes a discussion of the Internet's service model, which is the key to its ability to handle heterogeneity. It also describes how the Internet's hierarchical addressing scheme has helped the Internet to scale to a modestly large size.

A central aspect of building large heterogeneous internetworks is the problem of finding efficient, loop-free paths through the constituent networks. The second section introduces the principles of routing and explores the scaling issues of routing protocols, using some of the Internet's routing protocols as examples.

The third section discusses several of the problems (growing pains) that the Internet has experienced over the past several years and introduces a variety of techniques that have been employed to address these problems. The experience gained from using these techniques has led to the design of a new version of IP, which is known as Next Generation IP, or IP version 6 (IPv6). Throughout all these discussions, we see the importance of hierarchy in building scalable networks.

The chapter concludes by considering a significant enhancement to the Internet's service model: multicast packet delivery. We show how multicast—the ability to deliver packets efficiently to a set of receivers—can be incorporated into an internet, and we describe several of the routing protocols that have been developed to support multicast.

Internetworking

4

Local Area Network

4.1 Simple Internetworking (IP)

In the previous chapter, we saw that it was possible to build reasonably large LANs using bridges and LAN switches, but that such approaches were limited in their ability to scale and to handle heterogeneity. In this chapter, we explore some ways to go beyond the limitations of bridged networks, enabling us to build large, highly heterogeneous networks with reasonably efficient routing. We refer to such networks as *internetworks*. In the following sections, we make a steady progression toward larger and larger internetworks. We start with the basic functionality of the currently deployed version of the Internet Protocol (IP), and then we examine various techniques that have been developed to extend the scalability of the Internet in Section 4.3. This discussion culminates with a description of IP version 6 (IPv6), also known as the "next generation" IP. Before delving into the details of an internetworking protocol, however, let's consider more carefully what the word "internetwork" means.

4.1.1 What Is an Internetwork?

We use the term "internetwork," or sometimes just "internet" with a lowercase *i*, to refer to an arbitrary collection of networks interconnected to provide some sort of host-to-host packet delivery service. For example, a corporation with many sites might construct a private internetwork by interconnecting the LANs at their different sites with point-to-point links leased from the phone company. When we are talking about the widely used, global internetwork to which a large percentage of networks are now connected, we call it the "Internet" with a capital *I*. In keeping with the first-principles approach of this book, we mainly want you to learn about the principles of "lowercase *i*" internetworking, but we illustrate these ideas with real-world examples from the "big *I* " Internet.

Another piece of terminology that can be confusing is the difference between networks, subnetworks, and internetworks. We are going to avoid subnetworks (or subnets) altogether until Section 4.3. For now, we use *network* to mean either a directly connected or a switched network of the kind that was discussed in the last two chapters. Such a network uses one technology, such as 802.5, Ethernet, or ATM. An *internetwork* is an interconnected collection of such networks. Sometimes, to avoid ambiguity, we refer to the underlying networks that we are interconnecting as *physical* networks. An internet is a *logical* network built out of a collection of physical networks. In this context, a collection of Ethernets connected by bridges or switches would still be viewed as a single network.

Figure 4.1 shows an example internetwork. An internetwork is often referred to as a "network of networks" because it is made up of lots of smaller networks. In this figure, we see Ethernets, an FDDI ring, and a point-to-point link. Each of these is a single-technology network. The nodes that interconnect the networks are called

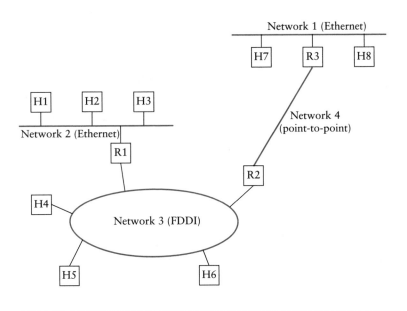

Figure 4.1 A simple internetwork. Hn = host; Rn = router.

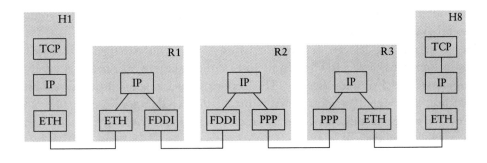

Figure 4.2 A simple internetwork, showing the protocol layers used to connect H1 to H8 in Figure 4.1. ETH is the protocol that runs over Ethernet.

routers. They are also sometimes called *gateways,* but since this term has several other connotations, we restrict our usage to router.

The Internet Protocol is the key tool used today to build scalable, heterogeneous internetworks. It was originally known as the Kahn-Cerf protocol after its inventors. One way to think of IP is that it runs on all the nodes (both hosts and routers) in a collection of networks and defines the infrastructure that allows these nodes and networks to function as a single logical internetwork. For example, Figure 4.2 shows how hosts H1 and H8 are logically connected by the internet in Figure 4.1, including the protocol graph running on each node. Note that higher-level protocols, such as TCP and UDP, typically run on top of IP on the hosts.

Most of the rest of this chapter is about various aspects of IP. While it is certainly possible to build an internetwork that does not use IP—for example, Novell supports an internetworking protocol called IPX, which is in turn based on the XNS internet designed by Xerox—IP is the most interesting case to study simply because of the size of the Internet. Said another way, it is only the IP Internet that has really faced the issue of scale. Thus it provides the best case study of a scalable internetworking protocol.

4.1.2 Service Model

A good place to start when you build an internetwork is to define its *service model*, that is, the host-to-host services you want to provide. The main concern in defining a service model for an internetwork is that we can provide a host-to-host service only if this service can somehow be provided over each of the underlying physical networks. For example, it would be no good deciding that our internetwork service model was going to provide guaranteed delivery of every packet in 1 ms or less if there were underlying network technologies that could arbitrarily delay packets. The philosophy used in defining the IP service model, therefore, was to make it undemanding enough that just about any network technology that might turn up in an internetwork would be able to provide the necessary service.

The IP service model can be thought of as having two parts: an addressing scheme, which provides a way to identify all hosts in the internetwork, and a datagram (connectionless) model of data delivery. This service model is sometimes called *best effort* because, although IP makes every effort to deliver datagrams, it makes no guarantees. We postpone a discussion of the addressing scheme for now and look first at the data delivery model.

Datagram Delivery

The IP datagram is fundamental to the Internet Protocol. Recall from Section 3.1.1 that a datagram is a type of packet that happens to be sent in a connectionless manner over a network. Every datagram carries enough information to let the network forward the packet to its correct destination; there is no need for any advance setup mechanism to tell the network what to do when the packet arrives. You just send it, and the network makes its best effort to get it to the desired destination. The "best-effort" part means that if something goes wrong and the packet gets lost, corrupted, misdelivered, or in any way fails to reach its intended destination, the network does nothing—it made its best effort, and that is all it has to do. It does not make any attempt to recover from the failure. This is sometimes called an *unreliable* service.

Best-effort, connectionless service is about the simplest service you could ask for from an internetwork, and this is a great strength. For example, if you provide best-effort service over a network that provides a reliable service, then that's fine—you end up with a best-effort service that just happens to always deliver the packets. If, on the other hand, you had a reliable service model over an unreliable network, you would have to put lots of extra functionality into the routers to make up for the deficiencies of the underlying network. Keeping the routers as simple as possible was one of the original design goals of IP.

The ability of IP to "run over anything" is frequently cited as one of its most important characteristics. It is noteworthy that many of the technologies over which IP runs today did not exist when IP was invented. So far, no networking technology has been invented that has proven too bizarre for IP; it has even been claimed that IP can run over a network that consists of two tin cans and a piece of string.

Best-effort delivery does not just mean that packets can get lost. Sometimes they can get delivered out of order, and sometimes the same packet can get delivered more than once. The higher-level protocols or applications that run above IP need to be aware of all these possible failure modes.

Packet Format

Clearly, a key part of the IP service model is the type of packets that can be carried. The IP datagram, like most packets, consists of a header followed by a number of bytes of data. The format of the header is shown in Figure 4.3. Note that we have adopted a different style of representing packets than the one we used in previous chapters. This is because packet formats at the internetworking layer and above, where we will be focusing our attention for the next few chapters, are almost invariably designed to align on 32-bit boundaries to simplify the task of processing them in software. Thus, the common way of representing them (used in Internet Requests for Comments, for example) is to draw them as a succession of 32-bit words. The top word is the one transmitted first, and the leftmost byte of each word is the one transmitted first. In this representation, you can easily recognize fields that are a multiple of 8 bits long. On the odd occasion when fields are not an even multiple of 8 bits, you can determine the field lengths by looking at the bit positions marked at the top of the packet.

Looking at each field in the IP header, we see that the "simple" model of best-effort datagram delivery still has some subtle features. The Version field specifies the version of IP. The current version of IP is 4, and it is sometimes called IPv4.[1] Observe that putting this field right at the start of the datagram makes it easy for everything

---

[1] Next Generation IP, which is discussed later in this chapter, has a new version number 6 and is known as IPv6. The version number 5 was used for an experimental protocol called ST-II.

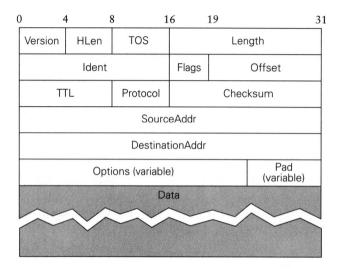

Figure 4.3   IPv4 packet header.

else in the packet format to be redefined in subsequent versions; the header processing software starts off by looking at the version and then branches off to process the rest of the packet according to the appropriate format. The next field, HLen, specifies the length of the header in 32-bit words. When there are no options, which is most of the time, the header is 5 words (20 bytes) long. The 8-bit TOS (type of service) field has had a number of different definitions over the years, but its basic function is to allow packets to be treated differently based on application needs. For example, the TOS value might determine whether or not a packet should be placed in a special queue that receives low delay. We discuss the use of this field (and a new name for it) in more detail in Section 6.5.3.

The next 16 bits of the header contain the Length of the datagram, including the header. Unlike the HLen field, the Length field counts bytes rather than words. Thus, the maximum size of an IP datagram is 65,535 bytes. The physical network over which IP is running, however, may not support such long packets. For this reason, IP supports a fragmentation and reassembly process. The second word of the header contains information about fragmentation, and the details of its use are presented under "Fragmentation and Reassembly" below.

Moving on to the third word of the header, the next byte is the TTL (time to live) field. Its name reflects its historical meaning rather than the way it is commonly used today. The intent of the field is to catch packets that have been going around in routing loops and discard them, rather than let them consume resources indefinitely. Originally,

TTL was set to a specific number of seconds that the packet would be allowed to live, and routers along the path would decrement this field until it reached 0. However, since it was rare for a packet to sit for as long as 1 second in a router, and routers did not all have access to a common clock, most routers just decremented the TTL by 1 as they forwarded the packet. Thus, it became more of a hop count than a timer, which is still a perfectly good way to catch packets that are stuck in routing loops. One subtlety is in the initial setting of this field by the sending host: Set it too high and packets could circulate rather a lot before getting dropped; set it too low and they may not reach their destination. The value 64 is the current default.

The Protocol field is simply a demultiplexing key that identifies the higher-level protocol to which this IP packet should be passed. There are values defined for TCP (6), UDP (17), and many other protocols that may sit above IP in the protocol graph.

The Checksum is calculated by considering the entire IP header as a sequence of 16-bit words, adding them up using ones complement arithmetic, and taking the ones complement of the result. This is the IP checksum algorithm described in Section 2.4. Thus, if any bit in the header is corrupted in transit, the checksum will not contain the correct value upon receipt of the packet. Since a corrupted header may contain an error in the destination address—and, as a result, may have been misdelivered—it makes sense to discard any packet that fails the checksum. It should be noted that this type of checksum does not have the same strong error detection properties as a CRC, but it is much easier to calculate in software.

The last two required fields in the header are the SourceAddr and the DestinationAddr for the packet. The latter is the key to datagram delivery: Every packet contains a full address for its intended destination so that forwarding decisions can be made at each router. The source address is required to allow recipients to decide if they want to accept the packet and to enable them to reply. IP addresses are discussed in Section 4.1.3—for now, the important thing to know is that IP defines its own global address space, independent of whatever physical networks it runs over. As we will see, this is one of the keys to supporting heterogeneity.

Finally, there may be a number of options at the end of the header. The presence or absence of options may be determined by examining the header length (HLen) field. While options are used fairly rarely, a complete IP implementation must handle them all.

Fragmentation and Reassembly

One of the problems of providing a uniform host-to-host service model over a heterogeneous collection of networks is that each network technology tends to have its own idea of how large a packet can be. For example, an Ethernet can accept packets up to 1500 bytes long, while FDDI packets may be 4500 bytes long. This leaves two choices for the IP service model: make sure that all IP datagrams are small enough to fit inside one packet on any network technology, or provide a means by which packets can be fragmented and reassembled when they are too big to go over a given network technology. The latter turns out to be a good choice, especially when you consider the fact that new network technologies are always turning up, and IP needs to run over all of them; this would make it hard to pick a suitably small bound on datagram size. This also means that a host will not send needlessly small packets, which wastes bandwidth and consumes processing resources by requiring more headers per byte of data sent. For example, two hosts connected to FDDI networks that are interconnected by a point-to-point link would not need to send packets small enough to fit on an Ethernet.

The central idea here is that every network type has a *maximum transmission unit* (MTU), which is the largest IP datagram that it can carry in a frame. Note that this value is smaller than the largest packet size on that network because the IP datagram needs to fit in the *payload* of the link-layer frame. Also, note that in ATM networks, the "frame" is the CS-PDU, not the ATM cell; the fact that CS-PDUs get segmented into cells is not visible to IP.

When a host sends an IP datagram, therefore, it can choose any size that it wants. A reasonable choice is the MTU of the network to which the host is directly attached. Then, fragmentation will only be necessary if the path to the destination includes a network with a smaller MTU. Should the transport protocol that sits on top of IP give IP a packet larger than the local MTU, however, then the source host must fragment it.

Fragmentation typically occurs in a router when it receives a datagram that it wants to forward over a network that has an MTU that is smaller than the received datagram. To enable these fragments to be reassembled at the receiving host, they all carry the same identifier in the Ident field. This identifier is chosen by the sending host and is intended to be unique among all the datagrams that might arrive at the destination from this source over some reasonable time period. Since all fragments of the original datagram contain this identifier, the reassembling host will be able to recognize those fragments that go together. Should all the fragments not arrive at the receiving host, the host gives up on the reassembly process and discards the fragments that did arrive. IP does not attempt to recover from missing fragments.

To see what this all means, consider what happens when host H1 sends a datagram to host H8 in the example internet shown in Figure 4.1. Assuming that the MTU is 1500 bytes for the two Ethernets, 4500 bytes for the FDDI network, and 532 bytes for the point-to-point network, then a 1420-byte datagram (20-byte IP header plus 1400 bytes of data) sent from H1 makes it across the first Ethernet and the FDDI network without fragmentation but must be fragmented into three datagrams at router R2. These three fragments are then forwarded by router R3 across the second Ethernet to the destination host. This situation is illustrated in Figure 4.4. This figure also serves to reinforce two important points:

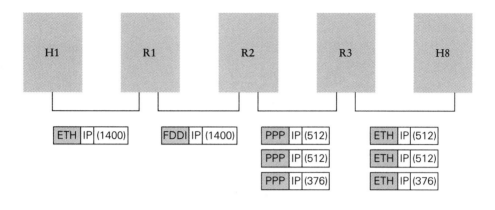

Figure 4.4 IP datagrams traversing the sequence of physical networks graphed in Figure 4.1.

1 Each fragment is itself a self-contained IP datagram that is transmitted over a sequence of physical networks, independent of the other fragments.

2 Each IP datagram is reencapsulated for each physical network over which it travels.

The fragmentation process can be understood in detail by looking at the header fields of each datagram, as is done in Figure 4.5. The unfragmented packet, shown at the top, has 1400 bytes of data and a 20-byte IP header. When the packet arrives at router R2, which has an MTU of 532 bytes, it has to be fragmented. A 532-byte MTU leaves 512 bytes for data after the 20-byte IP header, so the first fragment contains 512 bytes of data. The router sets the M bit in the Flags field (see Figure 4.3), meaning that there are more fragments to follow, and it sets the Offset to 0, since this fragment contains the first part of the original datagram. The data carried in the second fragment starts with the 513th byte of the original data, so the Offset field in this header is set to 512, and again the M bit is set. In the third fragment go the last 376 bytes of data, and the offset is now $2 \times 512 = 1024$. Since this is the last fragment, the M bit is not set. A minor detail that we have not mentioned up to this point is that the Offset field counts 8-byte units of data, not individual bytes. This means that a datagram must be fragmented on 8-byte boundaries, which happens to be the case in this example. We leave it as an exercise for you to figure out why the Offset field specifies 8-byte chunks of data rather than individual bytes.

Observe that the fragmentation process is done in such a way that it could be repeated if a fragment arrived at another network with an even smaller MTU. Fragmentation produces smaller, valid IP datagrams that can be readily reassembled

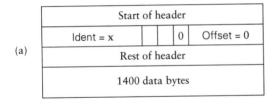

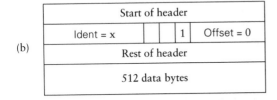

Figure 4.5   Header fields used in IP fragmentation. (a) Unfragmented packet; (b) fragmented packets.

into the original datagram upon receipt, independent of the order of their arrival.
Reassembly is done at the receiving host and not at each router.

Implementation

We conclude this discussion of IP fragmentation and reassembly by giving a fragment
of code that performs reassembly. One reason we give this particular piece of code is
that it is representative of a large proportion of networking software—it does little
more than tedious and unglamorous bookkeeping.

First, we define the key data structure (FragList) that is used to hold the individual fragments that arrive at the destination. Incoming fragments are saved in this data structure until all the fragments in the original datagram have arrived, at which time they are reassembled into a complete datagram and passed up to some higher-level protocol. Note that each element in FragList contains either a fragment or a hole.

```
#define FRAGOFFMASK          0x1fff
#define FRAGOFFSET(fragflag)  ((fragflag) & FRAGOFFMASK)
#define INFINITE_OFFSET      0xffff

/* structure to hold the fields that uniquely identify fragments
   of the same IP datagram */

typedef struct fid {
    IpHost  source;
    IpHost  dest;
    u_char  prot;
    u_char  pad;
    u_short ident;
} FragId;

typedef struct hole {
    u_int   first;
    u_int   last;
} Hole;

#define HOLE  1
#define FRAG  2

/* structure to hold a fragment or a hole */

typedef struct fragif {
    u_char type;
    union {
        Hole    hole;
        Msg     frag;
    } u;
    struct fragif *next, *prev;
} FragInfo;
```

```
/* structure to hold all the fragments and holes for a
   single IP datagram being reassembled */

typedef struct FragList {
    u_short      nholes;
    FragInfo     head;   /* dummy header node */
    Binding      binding;
    bool         gcMark; /* garbage collection flag */
} FragList;
```

The reassembly routine, ipReassemble, takes an incoming datagram (dg) and the IP header for that datagram (hdr) as arguments. The third argument, fragMap, is a Map structure (Section 1.3.3) used to efficiently map the incoming datagram into the appropriate FragList. (Recall that the group of fragments that are being reassembled together are uniquely identified by several fields in the IP header, as defined by structure FragId given above.)

The actual work done in ipReassemble is straightforward; as stated above, it is mostly bookkeeping. First, the routine extracts the fields from the IP header that uniquely identify the datagram to be reassembled, constructs a key from these fields, and looks this key up in fragMap to find the appropriate FragList. If this is the first fragment for the datagram, a new FragList must be created and initialized. Next, the routine inserts the new fragment into this FragList. This involves comparing the sum of the offset and length of this fragment with the offset of the next fragment in the list. Some of this work is done in subroutine hole_create, which is given below. Finally, ipReassemble checks to see if all the holes are filled. If all the fragments are present, it calls the routine msgReassemble to actually reassemble the fragments into a whole datagram and then calls deliver to pass this datagram up the protocol graph to some high-level protocol identified as HLP.

```
ipReassemble(Msg *dg, IpHdr *hdr, Map fragMap)
{
    FragId       fragid;
    FragList     *list;
    FragInfo     *fi, *prev;
    Hole         *hole;
    u_short      offset, len;

    /* extract fragmentation info from header
       (offset and fragment length) */
    offset = FRAGOFFSET(hdr->frag)*8;
```

```
len = hdr->dlen - GET_HLEN(hdr) * 4;

/*  Create the unique id for this fragment */
bzero((char *)&fragid, sizeof(FragId));
fragid.source = hdr->source;
fragid.dest = hdr->dest;
fragid.prot = hdr->prot;
fragid.ident = hdr->ident;

/* find reassembly list for this frag; create one if none exists */
if (mapResolve( fragMap, &fragid, (void **)&list) == FALSE )
{
    /* first fragment of datagram - need new FragList */
    list = NEW(FragList);

    /* insert it into the Map structure */
    list->binding = mapBind( fragMap, &fragid, list );

    /* initialize list with a single hole spanning the
       whole datagram */
    list->nholes = 1;
    list->head.next = fi = NEW(FragInfo);
    fi->next = 0;
    fi->type = HOLE;
    fi->u.hole.first = 0;
    fi->u.hole.last = INFINITE_OFFSET;
}

/* mark the current FragList as ineligible for garbage collection */
list->gcMark = FALSE;

/* walk through the FragList to find the right hole for this frag */
prev = &list->head;
for ( fi = prev->next; fi != 0; prev = fi, fi = fi->next )
{
    if ( fi->type == FRAG )
    {
        continue;
    }
    hole = &fi->u.hole;
```

```
    if ( (offset < hole->last) && ((offset + len) > hole->first) )
    {
        /* check to see if frag overlaps previously
           received frags */
        if ( offset < hole->first )
        {
            /* truncate message from left */
            msgStripHdr(dg, hole->first - offset);
            offset = hole->first;
        }
        if ( (offset + len) > hole->last )
        {
            /* truncate message from right */
            msgTruncate(dg, hole->last - offset);
            len = hole->last - offset;
        }

        /* now check to see if new hole(s) need to be made */
        if (((offset + len) < hole->last) &&
            (hdr->frag & MOREFRAGMENTS))
        {
            /* creating new hole above */
            hole_create(prev, fi, (offset+len), hole->last);
            list->nholes++;
        }
        if ( offset > hole->first )
        {
            /* creating new hole below */
            hole_create(fi, fi->next, hole->first, (offset));
            list->nholes++;
        }

        /* change this FragInfo structure to be FRAG */
        list->nholes--;
        fi->type = FRAG;
        msgSaveCopy(&fi->u.frag, dg);
        break;
    } /* if found a hole */
} /* for loop */
```

```
    /* check to see if we're done, and if so, pass datagram up */
    if ( list->nholes == 0 )
    {
        Msg fullMsg;

        /* now have a full datagram */
        for( fi = list->head.next; fi != 0; fi = fi->next )
        {
            msgReassemble(&fullMsg, &fi->u.frag, &fullMsg);
        }

        /* get rid of FragList and its Map entry */
        mapRemove(fragMap, list->binding);
        ipFreeFragList(list);
        deliver(HLP, &fullMsg);
        msgDestroy(&fullMsg);
    }
    return SUCCESS;
}
```

Subroutine hole_create creates a new hole in the fragment list that begins at offset first and continues to offset last. It makes use of the utility NEW, which creates an instance of the given structure.

```
static int
hole_create(FragInfo *prev, FragInfo *next, u_int first, u_int last)
{
    FragInfo    *fi;

    /* creating new hole from first to last */
    fi = NEW(FragInfo);
    fi->type = HOLE;
    fi->u.hole.first = first;
    fi->u.hole.last = last;
    fi->next = next;
    prev->next = fi;
}
```

Finally, note that these routines do not capture the entire picture of reassembly. What is not shown is a background process that periodically checks to see if there has been any recent activity on this datagram (it looks at field gcMark), and if not, it deletes the corresponding FragList. IP does not attempt to recover from the situation in which one or more of the fragments does not arrive; it simply gives up and reclaims the memory that was being used for reassembly.

One thing to notice from this code is that IP reassembly is far from a simple process. Note, for example, that if a single fragment is lost, the receiver will still attempt to reassemble the datagram, and it will eventually give up and have to garbage-collect the resources that were used to perform the failed reassembly. For this reason, among others, IP fragmentation is generally considered a good thing to avoid. Hosts are now strongly encouraged to perform "path MTU discovery," a process by which fragmentation is avoided by sending packets that are small enough to traverse the link with the smallest MTU in the path from sender to receiver.

4.1.3 Global Addresses

In the above discussion of the IP service model, we mentioned that one of the things that it provides is an addressing scheme. After all, if you want to be able to send data to any host on any network, there needs to be a way of identifying all the hosts. Thus, we need a global addressing scheme—one in which no two hosts have the same address. Global uniqueness is the first property that should be provided in an addressing scheme.

Ethernet addresses are globally unique, but that alone does not suffice for an addressing scheme in a large internetwork. Ethernet addresses are also *flat*, which means that they have no structure and provide very few clues to routing protocols.[2] In contrast, IP addresses are *hierarchical*, by which we mean that they are made up of several parts that correspond to some sort of hierarchy in the internetwork. Specifically, IP addresses consist of two parts, a network part and a host part. This is a fairly logical structure for an internetwork, which is made up of many interconnected networks. The network part of an IP address identifies the network to which the host is attached; all hosts attached to the same network have the same network part in their IP address. The host part then identifies each host uniquely on that particular network. Thus, in the simple internetwork of Figure 4.1, the addresses of the hosts on network 1, for example, would all have the same network part and different host parts.

Note that the routers in Figure 4.1 are attached to two networks. They need to have an address on each network, one for each interface. For example, router R1, which sits between network 2 and network 3, has an IP address on the interface to

---

[2] In fact, as we noted, Ethernet addresses do have a structure for the purposes of *assignment*—the first 24 bits identify the manufacturer—but this provides no useful information to routing protocols since this structure has nothing to do with network topology.

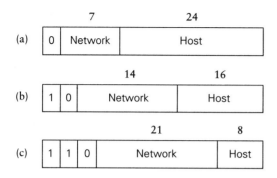

Figure 4.6   IP addresses: (a) class A; (b) class B; (c) class C.

network 2 that has the same network part as the hosts on network 2, and it has an IP address on the interface to network 3 that has the same network part as the hosts on network 3. Thus, bearing in mind that a router might be implemented as a host with two network interfaces, it is more precise to think of IP addresses as belonging to interfaces than to hosts.

Now, what do these hierarchical addresses look like? Unlike some other forms of hierarchical address, the sizes of the two parts are not the same for all addresses. Instead, IP addresses are divided into three different classes, as shown in Figure 4.6, each of which defines different-sized network and host parts. (There are also class D addresses that specify a multicast group, discussed in Section 4.4, and class E addresses that are currently unused.) In all cases, the address is 32 bits long.

The class of an IP address is identified in the most significant few bits. If the first bit is 0, it is a class A address. If the first bit is 1 and the second is 0, it is a class B address. If the first two bits are 1 and the third is 0, it is a class C address. Thus, of the approximately 4 billion possible IP addresses, half are class A, one-quarter are class B, and one-eighth are class C. Each class allocates a certain number of bits for the network part of the address and the rest for the host part. Class A networks have 7 bits for the network part and 24 bits for the host part, meaning that there can be only 126 class A networks (the values 0 and 127 are reserved), but each of them can accommodate up to $2^{24} - 2$ (about 16 million) hosts (again, there are two reserved values). Class B addresses allocate 14 bits for the network and 16 bits for the host, meaning that each class B network has room for 65,534 hosts. Finally, class C addresses have only 8 bits for the host and 21 for the network part. Therefore, a class C network can have only 256 unique host identifiers, which means only 254 attached hosts (one host identifier, 255, is reserved for broadcast, and 0 is not a valid host number). However, the addressing scheme supports 2^{21} class C networks.

On the face of it, this addressing scheme has a lot of flexibility, allowing networks of vastly different sizes to be accommodated fairly efficiently. The original idea was that the Internet would consist of a small number of wide area networks (these would be class A networks), a modest number of site- (campus-) sized networks (these would be class B networks), and a large number of LANs (these would be class C networks). However, as we shall see in Section 4.3, additional flexibility has been needed, and some innovative ways to provide it are now in use. Because one of these techniques actually removes the distinction between address classes, the addressing scheme just described is now known as "classful" addressing to distinguish it from the newer "classless" approach.

Before we look at how IP addresses get used, it is helpful to look at some practical matters, such as how you write them down. By convention, IP addresses are written as four *decimal* integers separated by dots. Each integer represents the decimal value contained in 1 byte of the address, starting at the most significant. For example, the address of the computer on which this sentence was typed is 171.69.210.245.

It is important not to confuse IP addresses with Internet domain names, which are also hierarchical. Domain names tend to be ASCII strings separated by dots, such as cs.princeton.edu. We will be talking about those in Section 9.1. The important thing about IP addresses is that they are what is carried in the headers of IP packets, and it is those addresses that are used to make forwarding decisions.

4.1.4 Datagram Forwarding in IP

We are now ready to look at the basic mechanism by which IP routers forward datagrams in an internetwork. Recall from Chapter 3 that *forwarding* is the process of taking a packet from an input and sending it out on the appropriate output, while *routing* is the process of building up the tables that allow the correct output for a packet to be determined. The discussion here focuses on forwarding; we take up routing in Section 4.2.

The main points to bear in mind as we discuss the forwarding of IP datagrams are the following:

- Every IP datagram contains the IP address of the destination host.

- The "network part" of an IP address uniquely identifies a single physical network that is part of the larger Internet.

- All hosts and routers that share the same network part of their address are connected to the same physical network and can thus communicate with each other by sending frames over that network.

■ Every physical network that is part of the Internet has at least one router that, by definition, is also connected to at least one other physical network; this router can exchange packets with hosts or routers on either network.

Forwarding IP datagrams can therefore be handled in the following way. A datagram is sent from a source host to a destination host, possibly passing through several routers along the way. Any node, whether it is a host or a router, first tries to establish whether it is connected to the same physical network as the destination. To do this, it compares the network part of the destination address with the network part of the address of each of its network interfaces. (Hosts normally have only one interface, while routers normally have two or more, since they are typically connected to two or more networks.) If a match occurs, then that means that the destination lies on the same physical network as the interface, and the packet can be directly delivered over that network. Section 4.1.5 explains some of the details of this process.

If the node is not connected to the same physical network as the destination node, then it needs to send the datagram to a router. In general, each node will have a choice of several routers, and so it needs to pick the best one, or at least one that has a reasonable chance of getting the datagram closer to its destination. The router that it chooses is known as the *next hop* router. The router finds the correct next hop by consulting its forwarding table. The forwarding table is conceptually just a list of (NetworkNum, NextHop) pairs. (As we will see below, forwarding tables in practice often contain some additional information related to the next hop.) Normally, there is also a default router that is used if none of the entries in the table match the destination's network number. For a host, it may be quite acceptable to have a default router and nothing else—this means that all datagrams destined for hosts not on the physical network to which the sending host is attached will be sent out through the default router.

We can describe the datagram forwarding algorithm in the following way:

```
if (NetworkNum of destination = NetworkNum of one of my interfaces) then
    deliver packet to destination over that interface
else
    if (NetworkNum of destination is in my forwarding table) then
        deliver packet to NextHop router
    else
        deliver packet to default router
```

For a host with only one interface and only a default router in its forwarding table, this simplifies to

NetworkNum	NextHop
1	R3
2	R1

Table 4.1 **Example forwarding table for router R2 in Figure 4.1.**

```
if (NetworkNum of destination = my NetworkNum) then
    deliver packet to destination directly
else
    deliver packet to default router
```

Let's see how this works in the example internetwork of Figure 4.1. First, suppose that H1 wants to send a datagram to H2. Since they are on the same physical network, H1 and H2 have the same network number in their IP address. Thus, H1 deduces that it can deliver the datagram directly to H2 over the Ethernet. The one issue that needs to be resolved is how H1 finds out the correct Ethernet address for H2—this is the address resolution mechanism described in Section 4.1.5.

Now suppose H1 wants to send a datagram to H8. Since these hosts are on different physical networks, they have different network numbers, so H1 deduces that it needs to send the datagram to a router. R1 is the only choice—the default router—so H1 sends the datagram over the Ethernet to R1. Similarly, R1 knows that it cannot deliver a datagram directly to H8 because neither of R1's interfaces is on the same network as H8. Suppose R1's default router is R2; R1 then sends the datagram to R2 over the token ring network. Assuming R2 has the forwarding table shown in Table 4.1, it looks up H8's network number (network 1)

Bridges, Switches, and Routers

It is easy to become confused about the distinction between bridges, switches, and routers. There is good reason for such confusion, since at some level, they all forward messages from one link to another. One distinction people make is based on layering: Bridges are link-level nodes (they forward frames from one link to another to implement an extended LAN), switches are network-level nodes (they forward packets from one link to another to implement a packet-switched network), and routers are internet-level nodes (they forward datagrams from one network to another to implement an internet). In some sense, however, this is an artificial distinction. It is certainly the case that networking companies do not ask the layering police for permission to

NetworkNum	NextHop
1	R3
2	R1
3	Interface 1
4	Interface 0

Table 4.2 Complete forwarding table for router R2 in Figure 4.1.

sell new products that do not fit neatly into one layer or another.

For example, we have already seen that a multiport bridge is often called an Ethernet switch or LAN switch. Thus the distinction between bridges and switches is far from clear. For this reason, bridges and switches are often grouped together as "layer 2 devices," where layer 2 in this context means "above the physical layer, below the internet layer."

There is, however, an important distinction between LAN switches (or bridges) and ATM switches (and other switches that are used in WANs, such as Frame Relay and X.25 switches). LAN switches and bridges depend on the spanning tree algorithm, while WAN switches generally run routing protocols that allow each

and forwards the datagram to R3. Finally, R3, since it is on the same network as H8, forwards the datagram directly to H8.

Note that it is possible to include the information about directly connected networks in the forwarding table. For example, we could label the network interfaces of router R2 as interface 0 for the point-to-point link (network 4) and interface 1 for the token ring (network 3). Then R2 would have the forwarding table shown in Table 4.2.

Thus, for any network number that R2 encounters in a packet, it knows what to do. Either that network is directly connected to R2, in which case the packet can be delivered to its destination over that network, or the network is reachable via some next hop router that R2 can reach over a network to which it is connected. In either case, R2 will use ARP, described below, to find the MAC address of the node to which the packet is to be sent next.

The forwarding table used by R2 is simple enough that it could be manually configured. Usually, however, these tables are more complex and would be built up by running a routing protocol such as one of those described in Section 4.2. Also note that, in practice, the network numbers are usually longer (e.g., 128.96).

We can now see how hierarchical addressing—splitting the address into network and host parts—has improved the scalability of a large network. Routers now contain forwarding tables that list only a set of network numbers, rather than all the nodes in the network. In our simple example, that meant that R2 could store the information needed to reach all the hosts in the network (of which there were eight) in a four-entry table. Even if there were 100 hosts on each physical network, R2 would still only need those same four entries. This is a good first step (although by no means the last) in achieving scalability.

This illustrates one of the most important principles of building scalable networks: To achieve scalability, you need to reduce the amount of information that is stored in each node and that is exchanged between nodes. The most common way to do that is *hierarchical aggregation*. IP introduces a two-level hierarchy, with networks at the top level and nodes at the bottom level. We have aggregated information by letting routers deal only with reaching the right network; the information that a router needs to deliver a datagram to any node on a given network is represented by a single aggregated piece of information.

4.1.5 Address Translation (ARP)

In the previous section we talked about how to get IP datagrams to the right physical network, but glossed over the issue of how to get a datagram to a particular host or router on that network. The main issue is

switch to learn the topology of the whole network. This is an important distinction because knowing the whole network topology allows the switches to discriminate among different routes, while in contrast, the spanning tree algorithm locks in a single tree over which messages are forwarded. It is also the case that the spanning tree approach does not scale as well.

What about switches and routers? Are they fundamentally the same thing, or are they different in some important way? Here, the distinction is much less clear. For starters, since a single point-to-point link is itself a legitimate network, a router can be used to connect a set of such links. In such a situation, a router looks just like a switch. It just happens to be a switch that forwards IP packets using a datagram forwarding model and IP routing protocols.

One big difference between an ATM network built from switches and the Internet built from routers is that the Internet is able to accommodate heterogeneity, whereas ATM consists of homogeneous links. This support for heterogeneity is one of the key reasons why the Internet is so widely deployed.

that IP datagrams contain IP addresses, but the physical interface hardware on the host or router to which you want to send the datagram only understands the addressing scheme of that particular network. Thus, we need to translate the IP address to a link-level address that makes sense on this network (e.g., a 48-bit Ethernet address). We can then encapsulate the IP datagram inside a frame that contains that link-level address and send it either to the ultimate destination or to a router that promises to forward the datagram toward the ultimate destination.

One simple way to map an IP address into a physical network address is to encode a host's physical address in the host part of its IP address. For example, a host with physical address **00010001 00101001** (which has the decimal value 33 in the upper byte and 81 in the lower byte) might be given the IP address **128.96.33.81**. While this solution has been used on some networks, it is limited in that the network's physical addresses can be no more than 16 bits long in this example; they can be only 8 bits long on a class C network. This clearly will not work for 48-bit Ethernet addresses.

A more general solution would be for each host to maintain a table of address pairs; that is, the table would map IP addresses into physical addresses. While this table could be centrally managed by a system administrator and then copied to each host on the network, a better approach would be for each host to dynamically learn the contents of the table using the network. This can be accomplished using the Address Resolution Protocol (ARP). The goal of ARP is to enable each host on a network to build up a table of mappings between IP addresses and link-level addresses. Since these mappings may change over time (e.g., because an Ethernet card in a host breaks and is replaced by a new one with a new address), the entries are timed out periodically and removed. This happens on the order of every 15 minutes. The set of mappings currently stored in a host is known as the ARP cache or ARP table.

ARP takes advantage of the fact that many link-level network technologies, such as Ethernet and token ring, support broadcast. If a host wants to send an IP datagram to a host (or router) that it knows to be on the same network (i.e., the sending and receiving node have the same IP network number), it first checks for a mapping in the cache. If no mapping is found, it needs to invoke the Address Resolution Protocol over the network. It does this by broadcasting an ARP query onto the network. This query contains the IP address in question (the "target IP address"). Each host receives the query and checks to see if it matches its IP address. If it does match, the host sends a response message that contains its link-layer address back to the originator of the query. The originator adds the information contained in this response to its ARP table.

The query message also includes the IP address and link-layer address of the sending host. Thus, when a host broadcasts a query message, each host on the network can learn the sender's link-level and IP addresses and place that information in its ARP table. However, not every host adds this information to its ARP table. If the host

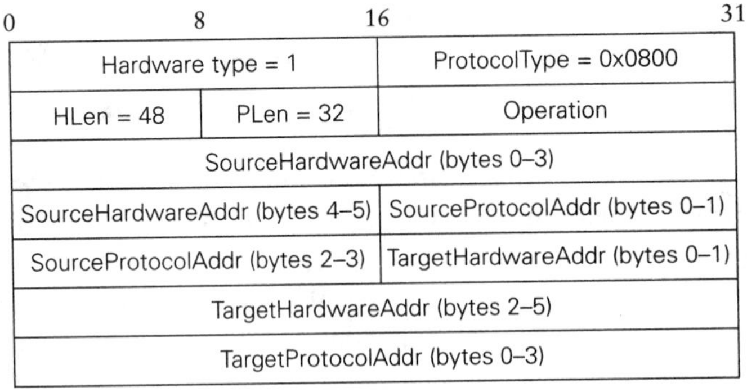

0	8	16	31
Hardware type = 1		ProtocolType = 0x0800	
HLen = 48	PLen = 32	Operation	
SourceHardwareAddr (bytes 0–3)			
SourceHardwareAddr (bytes 4–5)		SourceProtocolAddr (bytes 0–1)	
SourceProtocolAddr (bytes 2–3)		TargetHardwareAddr (bytes 0–1)	
TargetHardwareAddr (bytes 2–5)			
TargetProtocolAddr (bytes 0–3)			

Figure 4.7 ARP packet format for mapping IP addresses into Ethernet addresses.

already has an entry for that host in its table, it "refreshes" this entry; that is, it resets the length of time until it discards the entry. If that host is the target of the query, then it adds the information about the sender to its table, even if it did not already have an entry for that host. This is because there is a good chance that the source host is about to send it an application-level message, and it may eventually have to send a response or ACK back to the source; it will need the source's physical address to do this. If a host is not the target and does not already have an entry for the source in its ARP table, then it does not add an entry for the source. This is because there is no reason to believe that this host will ever need the source's link-level address; there is no need to clutter its ARP table with this information.

Figure 4.7 shows the ARP packet format for IP-to-Ethernet address mappings. In fact, ARP can be used for lots of other kinds of mappings—the major differences are in the address sizes. In addition to the IP and link-layer addresses of both sender and target, the packet contains

- a HardwareType field, which specifies the type of physical network (e.g., Ethernet)

- a ProtocolType field, which specifies the higher-layer protocol (e.g., IP)

- HLen ("hardware" address length) and PLen ("protocol" address length) fields, which specify the length of the link-layer address and higher-layer protocol address, respectively

- an Operation field, which specifies whether this is a request or a response

- the source and target hardware (Ethernet) and protocol (IP) addresses

Note that the results of the ARP process can be added as an extra column in a forwarding table like the one in Table 4.1. Thus, for example, when R2 needs to forward a packet to network 2, it not only finds that the next hop is R1, but also finds the MAC address to place on the packet to send it to R1.

ATMARP

It should be clear that if an ATM network is to operate as part of an IP internetwork, then it too must provide a form of ARP. However, the procedure just described will clearly not work on a simple ATM network, because it depends on the fact that ARP packets can be broadcast to all hosts on a single network. One solution to this problem is to use the LAN emulation procedures described in Section 3.3.5. Since the goal of these procedures is to make an ATM network behave just like a shared-media LAN, which includes support for broadcast, the effect is to reduce ARP to a previously solved problem.

There are, however, situations where it may not be desirable to treat an ATM network as an emulated LAN. In particular, LAN emulation can be quite inefficient in a large, wide area ATM network. Recall that in an emulated LAN many packets may need to be sent to the broadcast and unknown server, which then floods those packets to all nodes on the emulated LAN. Clearly there are limits to how far this can scale. The problem here is that adding broadcast capabilities to an intrinsically nonbroadcast network, while useful in some circumstances, is really overkill if the only reason you need broadcast is to enable address resolution.

For this reason, there is a different ARP procedure that may be used in an ATM network and that does not depend on broadcast or LAN emulation. This procedure is known as ATMARP, and is part of the *Classical IP over ATM* model. The reason for calling the model "classical" will become apparent shortly. Like LAN emulation, ATMARP relies on the use of a server to resolve addresses—in this case, it is called an ARP server, and its behavior is described below.

A key concept in the Classical IP over ATM model is the *logical IP subnet* (LIS). The LIS abstraction allows us to take one large ATM network and subdivide it into several smaller subnets. (We define "subnet" precisely in Section 4.3.1, but in this case a subnet behaves much like a single network.) All nodes on the same subnet have the same IP network number. And just as in "classical" IP, two nodes (hosts or routers) that are on the same subnet can communicate directly over the ATM network, whereas two nodes that are on different subnets will have to communicate via one or more routers. An example of an ATM network divided into two LISs appears in Figure 4.8. Note that the IP address of host H1 has a network number of 10, as does the router interface that connects to the left-hand LIS, while H2 has a network number of 12, as does the

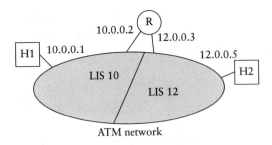

Figure 4.8   Logical IP subnets.

right-hand interface on the router. That is, H1 and the router connect to the same LIS (LIS 10) while H2 is on a different subnet (LIS 12) to which the router also connects.

An advantage of the LIS model is that we can connect a large number of hosts and routers to a big ATM network without necessarily giving them all addresses from the same IP network. This may make it easier to manage address assignment, for example, in the case where not all nodes connected to the ATM network are under the control of the same administrative entity. The division of the ATM network into a number of LISs also improves scalability by limiting the number of nodes that must be supported by a single ARP server.

The basic job of an ARP server is to enable nodes on a LIS to resolve IP addresses to ATM addresses without using broadcast. Each node in the LIS must be configured with the ATM address of the ARP server, so that it can establish a VC to the server when it boots. Once it has a VC to the server, the node sends a registration message to the ARP server that contains both the IP and ATM addresses of the registering node. Thus the ARP server builds up a complete database of all the ⟨IP address, ATM address⟩ pairs. Once this is in place, any node that wants to send a packet to some IP address can ask the ARP server to provide the corresponding ATM address. Once this is received, the sending node can use ATM signalling to set up a VC to that ATM address, and then send the packet. Just like conventional ARP, a cache of IP-to-ATM address mappings can be maintained. In addition, the node can keep a VC established to that ATM destination as long as there is enough traffic flowing to justify it, thus avoiding the delay of setting up the VC again when the next packet arrives.

An interesting consequence of the Classical IP over ATM model is that two nodes on the same ATM network cannot establish a direct VC between themselves if they are on different subnets. This would violate the rule that communication from one subnet to another must pass through a router. For example, host H1 and host H2 in Figure 4.8 cannot establish a direct VC under the classical model. Instead, each needs to have a

VC to router R. The simple explanation for this rule is that IP routing is known to work well when that rule is obeyed, as it is in non-ATM networks. New techniques to work around that rule have been developed, but they have introduced considerable complexity and problems of robustness.

We have now seen the basic mechanisms that IP provides for dealing with both heterogeneity and scale. On the issue of heterogeneity, IP begins by defining a best-effort service model that makes minimal assumptions about the underlying networks; most notably, this service model is based on unreliable datagrams. IP then makes two important additions to this starting point: (1) a common packet format (fragmentation/reassembly is the mechanism that makes this format work over networks with different MTUs) and (2) a global address space for identifying all hosts (ARP is the mechanism that makes this global address space work over networks with different physical addressing schemes). On the issue of scale, IP uses hierarchical aggregation to reduce the amount of information needed to forward packets. Specifically, IP addresses are partitioned into network and host components, with packets first routed toward the destination network and then delivered to the correct host on that network.

4.1.6 Host Configuration (DHCP)

In Section 2.6 we observed that Ethernet addresses are configured into the network adaptor by the manufacturer, and this process is managed in such a way to ensure that these addresses are globally unique. This is clearly a sufficient condition to ensure that any collection of hosts connected to a single Ethernet (including an extended LAN) will have unique addresses. Furthermore, uniqueness is all we ask of Ethernet addresses.

IP addresses, by contrast, must be not only unique on a given internetwork, but also must reflect the structure of the internetwork. As noted above, they contain a network part and a host part, and the network part must be the same for all hosts on the same network. Thus, it is not possible for the IP address to be configured once into a host when it is manufactured, since that would imply that the manufacturer knew which hosts were going to end up on which networks, and it would mean that a host, once connected to one network, could never move to another. For this reason, IP addresses need to be reconfigurable.

In addition to an IP address, there are some other pieces of information a host needs to have before it can start sending packets. The most notable of these is the address of a default router—the place to which it can send packets whose destination address is not on the same network as the sending host.

Most host operating systems provide a way for a system administrator, or even a user, to manually configure the IP information needed by a host. However, there are some obvious drawbacks to such manual configuration. One is that it is simply a lot of work to configure all the hosts in a large network directly, especially when you consider that such hosts are not reachable over a network until they are configured. Even more importantly, the configuration process is very error-prone, since it is necessary to ensure that every host gets the correct network number and that no two hosts receive the same IP address. For these reasons, automated configuration methods are required. The primary method uses a protocol known as the Dynamic Host Configuration Protocol (DHCP).

DHCP relies on the existence of a DHCP server that is responsible for providing configuration information to hosts. There is at least one DHCP server for an administrative domain. At the simplest level, the DHCP server can function just as a centralized repository for host configuration information. Consider, for example, the problem of administering addresses in the internetwork of a large company. DHCP saves the network administrators from having to walk around to every host in the company with a list of addresses and network map in hand and configuring each host manually. Instead, the configuration information for each host could be stored in the DHCP server and automatically retrieved by each host when it is booted or connected to the network. However, the administrator would still pick the address that each host is to receive; he would just store that in the server. In this model, the configuration information for each host is stored in a table that is indexed by some form of unique client identifier, typically the "hardware address" (e.g., the Ethernet address of its network adaptor).

A more sophisticated use of DHCP saves the network admininstrator from even having to assign addresses to individual hosts. In this model, the DHCP server maintains a pool of available addresses that it hands out to hosts on demand. This considerably reduces the amount of configuration an administrator must do, since now it is only necessary to allocate a range of IP addresses (all with the same network number) to each network.

Since the goal of DHCP is to minimize the amount of manual configuration required for a host to function, it would rather defeat the purpose if each host had to be configured with the address of a DHCP server. Thus, the first problem faced by DHCP is that of server discovery.

To contact a DHCP server, a newly booted or attached host sends a DHCPDISCOVER message to a special IP address (255.255.255.255) that is an IP broadcast address. This means it will be received by all hosts and routers on that network. (Routers do not forward such packets onto other networks, preventing broadcast to the entire Internet.) In the simplest case, one of these nodes is the DHCP server for the network. The server would then reply to the host that generated the discovery message (all the other nodes would ignore it). However, it is not really desirable to require one DHCP server on every network, because this still creates a potentially large number of servers that need to be correctly and consistently configured. Thus, DHCP uses the concept of a *relay agent*. There is at least one relay agent on each network, and it is configured with just one piece of information: the IP address of the DHCP server. When

Unicast to server
DHCP relay
Other networks
DHCP server
Broadcast
Host

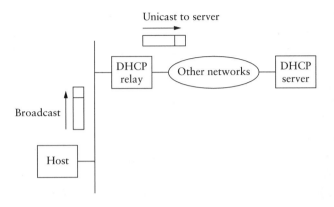

Figure 4.9 A DHCP relay agent receives a broadcast DHCPDISCOVER message from a host and sends a unicast DHCPDISCOVER to the DHCP server.

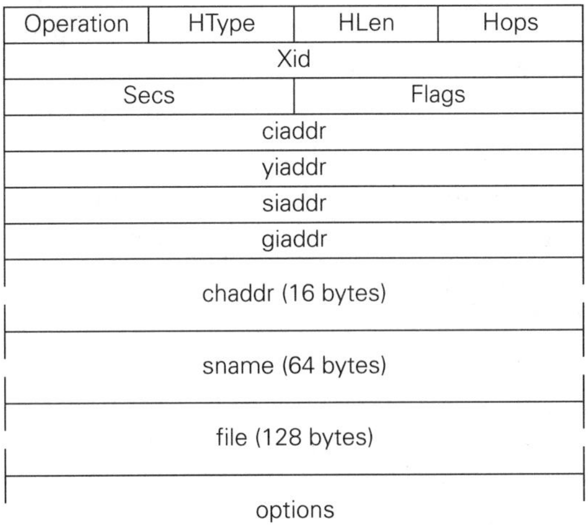

Operation
HType
HLen
Hops
Xid
Secs
Flags
ciaddr
yiaddr
siaddr
giaddr
chaddr (16 bytes)
sname (64 bytes)
file (128 bytes)
options

Figure 4.10 DHCP packet format.

a relay agent receives a DHCPDISCOVER message, it unicasts it to the DHCP server and awaits the response, which it will then send back to the requesting client. The process of relaying a message from a host to a remote DHCP server is shown in Figure 4.9.

Figure 4.10 shows the format of a DHCP message. The message is actually sent using a protocol called UDP (the User Datagram Protocol) that runs over IP. UDP is discussed in detail in the next chapter, but the only interesting thing it does in this context is to provide a demultiplexing key that says, "This is a DHCP packet."

DHCP is derived from an earlier protocol called BOOTP, and some of the packet fields are thus not strictly relevant to host configuration. When trying to obtain configuration information, the client puts its hardware address (e.g., its Ethernet address) in the chaddr field. The DHCP server replies by filling in the yiaddr ("your" IP address) field and sending it to the client. Other information such as the default router to be used by this client can be included in the options field.

In the case where DHCP dynamically assigns IP addresses to hosts, it is clear that hosts cannot keep addresses indefinitely, as this would eventually cause the server to exhaust its address pool. At the same time, a host cannot be depended upon to give back its address, since it might have crashed, been unplugged from the network, or been turned off. Thus, DHCP allows addresses to be "leased" for some period of time. Once the lease expires, the server is free to return that address to its pool. A host with a leased address clearly needs to renew the lease periodically if in fact it is still connected to the network and functioning correctly.

▶　 DHCP illustrates an important aspect of scaling: the scaling of network management. While discussions of scaling often focus on keeping the state in network devices from growing too fast, it is important to pay attention to growth of network management complexity. By allowing network managers to configure a range of IP addresses per network rather than one IP address per host, DHCP improves the manageability of a network.

Note that DHCP may also introduce some more complexity into network management, since it makes the binding between physical hosts and IP addresses much more dynamic. This may make the network manager's job more difficult if, for example, it becomes necessary to locate a malfunctioning host.

4.1.7　Error Reporting (ICMP)

The next issue is how the Internet treats errors. While IP is perfectly willing to drop datagrams when the going gets tough—for example, when a router does not know how to forward the datagram or when one fragment of a datagram fails to arrive at the destination—it does not fail silently. IP is always configured with a companion protocol, known as the Internet Control Message Protocol (ICMP), that defines a collection of error messages that are sent back to the source host whenever a router or host is unable to process an IP datagram successfully. For example, ICMP defines error messages indicating that the destination host is unreachable (perhaps due to a link failure), that the reassembly process failed, that the TTL had reached 0, that the IP header checksum failed, and so on.

ICMP also defines a handful of control messages that a router can send back to a source host. One of the most useful control messages, called an ICMP-Redirect, tells the source host that there is a better route to the destination. ICMP-Redirects are used in the following situation. Suppose a host is connected to a network that has two routers attached to it, called R1 and R2, where the host uses R1 as its default router. Should R1 ever receive a datagram from the host, where based on its forwarding table it knows that R2 would have been a better choice for a particular destination address, it sends an ICMP-Redirect back to the host, instructing it to use R2 for all future datagrams addressed to that destination. The host then adds this new route to its forwarding table.

4.1.8 Virtual Networks and Tunnels

We conclude our introduction to IP by considering an issue you might not have anticipated, but one that is becoming increasingly important. Our discussion up to this point has focused on making it possible for nodes on different networks to communicate with each other in an unrestricted way. This is the usually the goal in the Internet—everybody wants to be able to send email to everybody, and the creator of a new Web site wants to reach the widest possible audience. However, there are many situations where more controlled connectivity is required. An important example of such a situation is the *virtual private network* (VPN).

The term "VPN" is heavily overused and definitions vary, but intuitively we can define a VPN by considering first the idea of a private network. Corporations with many sites often build private networks by leasing transmission lines from the phone companies and using those lines to interconnect sites. In such a network, communication is restricted to take place only among the sites of that corporation, which is often desirable for security reasons. To make a private network *virtual*, the leased transmission lines—which are not shared with any other corporations—would be replaced by some sort of shared network. A virtual circuit is a very reasonable replacement for a leased line because it still provides a logical point-to-point connection between the corporation's sites. For example, if corporation X has a VC from site A to site B, then clearly it can send packets between sites A and B. But there is no way that corporation Y can get its packets delivered to site B without first establishing its own virtual circuit to site B, and the establishment of such a VC can be administratively prevented, thus preventing unwanted connectivity between corporation X and corporation Y.

Figure 4.11(a) shows two private networks for two separate corporations. In Figure 4.11(b) they are both migrated to a virtual circuit network. The limited connectivity of a real private network is maintained, but since the private networks now share the same transmission facilities and switches we say that two virtual private networks have been created.

In Figure 4.11, a Frame Relay or ATM network is used to provide the controlled connectivity among sites. It is also possible to provide a similar function using an IP network—an internetwork—to provide the connectivity. However, we cannot just

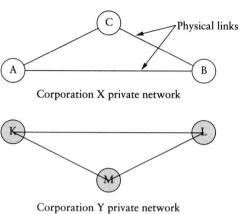

Corporation X private network

Corporation Y private network

(a)

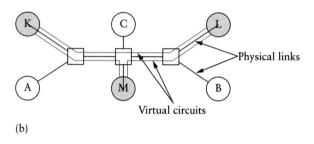

(b)

Figure 4.11 An example of virtual private networks: (a) Two separate private networks; (b) two virtual private networks sharing common switches.

connect the various corporations' sites to a single internetwork because that would provide connectivity between corporation X and corporation Y, which we wish to avoid. To solve this problem, we need to introduce a new concept, the *IP tunnel*.

We can think of an IP tunnel as a virtual point-to-point link between a pair of nodes that are actually separated by an arbitrary number of networks. The virtual link is created within the router at the entrance to the tunnel by providing it with the IP address of the router at the far end of the tunnel. Whenever the router at the entrance of the tunnel wants to send a packet over this virtual link, it encapsulates the packet inside an IP datagram. The destination address in the IP header is the address of the router at the far end of the tunnel, while the source address is that of the encapsulating router.

In the forwarding table of the router at the entrance to the tunnel, this virtual link looks much like a normal link. Consider, for example, the network in Figure 4.12.

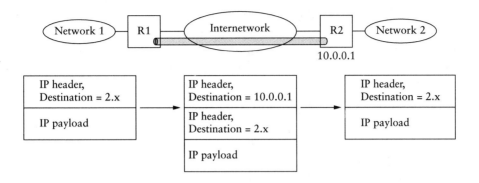

Figure 4.12   A tunnel through an internetwork.

NetworkNum	NextHop
1	Interface 0
2	Virtual interface 0
Default	Interface 1

Table 4.3   Forwarding table for router R1 in Figure 4.12.

A tunnel has been configured from R1 to R2 and assigned a virtual interface number of 0. The forwarding table in R1 might therefore look like Table 4.3.

R1 has two physical interfaces. Interface 0 connects to network 1; interface 1 connects to a large internetwork and is thus the default for all traffic that does not match something more specific in the forwarding table. In addition, R1 has a virtual interface, which is the interface to the tunnel. Suppose R1 receives a packet from network 1 that contains an address in network 2. The forwarding table says this packet should be sent out virtual interface 0. In order to send a packet out this interface, the router takes the packet, adds an IP header addressed to R2, and then proceeds to forward the packet as if it had just been received. R2's address is 10.0.0.1; since the network number of this address is 10, not 1 or 2, a packet destined for R2 will be forwarded out the default interface into the internetwork.

Once the packet leaves R1, it looks to the rest of the world like a normal IP packet destined to R2, and it is forwarded accordingly. All the routers in the internetwork forward it using normal means, until it arrives at R2. When R2 receives the packet, it finds that it carries its own address, so it removes the IP header and looks at the payload of the packet. What it finds is an inner IP packet whose destination address is in network 2. R2 now processes this packet like any other IP packet it receives. Since R2 is directly connected to network 2, it forwards the packet on to that network. Figure 4.12 shows the change in encapsulation of the packet as it moves across the network.

While R2 is acting as the endpoint of the tunnel, there is nothing to prevent it from performing the normal functions of a router. For example, it might receive some packets that are not tunneled, but which are addressed to networks that it knows how to reach, and it would forward them in the normal way.

You might wonder why anyone would want to go to all the trouble of creating a tunnel and changing the encapsulation of a packet as it goes across an internetwork. One reason is security, which we will discuss in more detail in Chapter 8. Supplemented with encryption, a tunnel can become a very private sort of link across a public network. Another reason may be that R1 and R2 have some capabilities that are not widely available in the intervening networks, such as multicast routing. By connecting these routers with a tunnel, we can build a virtual network in which all the routers with this capability appear to be directly connected. This in fact is how the MBone (multicast backbone) is built, as we will see in Section 4.4. A third reason to build tunnels is to carry packets from protocols other than IP across an IP network. As long as the routers at either end of the tunnel know how to handle these other protocols, the IP tunnel looks to them like a point-to-point link over which they can send non-IP packets. Thus, we see that tunneling is a powerful and quite general technique for building virtual links across internetworks.

Tunneling does have its downsides. One is that it increases the length of packets, which might be significant for short packets (which are common in audio applications, for example). There may also be performance implications for the routers at either end of the tunnel. Finally, there is a management cost for the administrative entity that is responsible for setting up the tunnels and making sure they are correctly handled by the routing protocols.

4.2 Routing

In both this and the previous chapter we have assumed that the switches and routers have enough knowledge of the network topology so they can choose the right port onto which each packet should be output. In the case of virtual circuits, routing is an issue only for the connection request packet; all subsequent packets follow the same path as the request. In datagram networks, including IP networks, routing is an issue for every packet. In either case, a switch or router needs to be able to look at the packet's destination address and then to determine which of the output ports is the best choice to get the packet to that address. As we saw in Section 3.1.1, the switch makes this decision by consulting a forwarding table. The fundamental problem of routing is, How do switches and routers acquire the information in their forwarding tables?

▶ We restate an important distinction, which is often neglected, between *forwarding* and *routing*. Forwarding consists of taking a packet, looking at its destination address, consulting a table, and sending the packet in a direction determined by that table. We saw several examples of forwarding in the preceding section. Routing is the process by which forwarding tables are built. We also note that forwarding is a relatively well-defined process performed locally at a node, whereas routing depends on complex distributed algorithms that have continued to evolve throughout the history of networking.

While the terms *forwarding table* and *routing table* are sometimes used interchangeably, we will make a distinction between them here. The forwarding table is used when a packet is being forwarded and so must contain enough information to accomplish the forwarding function. This means that a row in the forwarding table contains the mapping from a network number to an outgoing interface and some MAC information, such as the Ethernet address of the next hop. The routing table, on the other hand, is the table that is built up by the routing algorithms as a precursor to building the forwarding table. It generally contains mappings from network numbers to next hops. It may also contain information about how this information was learned, so that the router will be able to decide when it should discard some information.

Whether the routing table and forwarding table are actually separate data structures is something of an implementation choice, but there are numerous reasons to keep them separate. For example, the forwarding table needs to be structured to optimize the process of looking up a network number when forwarding a packet, while the routing table needs to be optimized for the purpose of calculating changes in topology. In some cases, the forwarding table may even be implemented in specialized hardware, whereas this is rarely if ever done for the routing table. Table 4.4 provides an example of a row from each sort of table. In this case, the routing table tells us that network number 10 is to be reached by a next hop router with the IP address 171.69.245.10, while the forwarding table contains the information about exactly how to forward a packet to that next hop: Send it out interface number 0 with a MAC address of 8:0:2b:e4:b:1:2. Note that the last piece of information is provided by the Address Resolution Protocol.

Before getting into the details of routing, we need to remind ourselves of the key question we should be asking anytime we try to build a mechanism for the Internet: "Does this solution scale?" The answer for the algorithms and protocols described in this section is no. They are designed for networks of fairly modest size—fewer than a hundred nodes, in practice. However, the solutions we describe do serve as

Network Number	Next Hop
10	171.69.245.10

(a)

Network Number	Interface	MAC Address
10	if0	8:0:2b:e4:b:1:2

(b)

Table 4.4   Example rows from (a) routing and (b) forwarding tables

a building block for a hierarchical routing infrastructure that is used in the Internet today. Specifically, the protocols described in this section are collectively known as *intradomain* routing protocols, or *interior gateway protocols* (IGPs). To understand these terms, we need to define a routing *domain*: A good working definition is an internetwork in which all the routers are under the same adminstrative control (e.g., a single university campus). The relevance of this definition will become apparent in the next section when we look at *interdomain* routing protocols. For now, the important thing to keep in mind is that we are considering the problem of routing in the context of small to midsized networks, not for a network the size of the Internet.

4.2.1 Network as a Graph

Routing is, in essence, a problem of graph theory. Figure 4.13 shows a graph representing a network. The nodes of the graph, labeled A through F, may be either hosts, switches, routers, or networks. For our initial discussion, we will focus on the case where the nodes are routers. The edges of the graph correspond to the network links. Each edge has an associated *cost*, which gives some indication of the desirability of sending traffic over that link. A discussion of how edge costs are assigned is given in Section 4.2.4.[3]

The basic problem of routing is to find the lowest-cost path between any two nodes, where the cost of a path equals the sum of the costs of all the edges that make up the path. For a simple network like the one in Figure 4.13, you could imagine just

---

[3] In the example networks (graphs) used throughout this chapter, we use undirected edges and assign each edge a single cost. This is actually a slight simplification. It is more accurate to make the edges directed, which typically means that there would be a pair of edges between each node—one flowing in each direction, and each with its own edge cost.

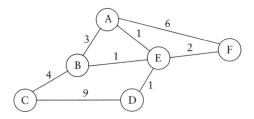

Figure 4.13 Network represented as a graph.

calculating all the shortest paths and loading them into some nonvolatile storage on each node. Such a static approach has several shortcomings:

- It does not deal with node or link failures.

- It does not consider the addition of new nodes or links.

- It implies that edge costs cannot change, even though we might reasonably wish to temporarily assign a high cost to a link that is heavily loaded.

For these reasons, routing is achieved in most practical networks by running routing protocols among the nodes. These protocols provide a distributed, dynamic way to solve the problem of finding the lowest-cost path in the presence of link and node failures and changing edge costs. Note the word "distributed" in the last sentence: Centralization is the enemy of scalability, so all good routing protocols are distributed.

The distributed nature of routing algorithms is one of the main reasons why this has been such a rich field of research and development—there are a lot of challenges in making distributed algorithms work well. For example, distributed algorithms raise the possibility that two routers will at one instant have different ideas about the shortest path to some destination. In fact, each one may think that the other one is closer to the destination, and decide to send packets to the other one. Clearly such packets will be stuck in a loop until the discrepancy between the two routers is resolved, and it would be good to resolve it as soon as possible. This is just one example of the type of problem routing protocols must address.

To begin our analysis, we assume that the edge costs in the network are known. We will examine the two main classes of routing protocols: *distance vector* and *link state*. In Section 4.2.4 we return to the problem of calculating edge costs in a meaningful way.

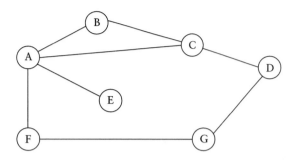

Figure 4.14   Distance-vector routing: an example network.

4.2.2 Distance Vector (RIP)

The idea behind the distance-vector algorithm is suggested by its name:[4] Each node constructs a one-dimensional array (a vector) containing the "distances" (costs) to all other nodes and distributes that vector to its immediate neighbors. The starting assumption for distance-vector routing is that each node knows the cost of the link to each of its directly connected neighbors. A link that is down is assigned an infinite cost.

To see how a distance-vector routing algorithm works, it is easiest to consider an example like the one depicted in Figure 4.14. In this example, the cost of each link is set to 1, so that a least-cost path is simply the one with the fewest hops. (Since all edges have the same cost, we do not show the costs in the graph.) We can represent each node's knowledge about the distances to all other nodes as a table like the one given in Table 4.5. Note that each node only knows the information in one row of the table (the one that bears its name in the left column). The global view that is presented here is not available at any single point in the network.

We may consider each row in Table 4.5 as a list of distances from one node to all other nodes, representing the current beliefs of that node. Initially, each node sets a cost of 1 to its directly connected neighbors and ∞ to all other nodes. Thus, A initially believes that it can reach B in one hop and that D is unreachable. The routing table stored at A reflects this set of beliefs and includes the name of the next hop that A would use to reach any reachable node. Initially, then, A's routing table would look like Table 4.6.

---

[4] The other common name for this class of algorithm is Bellman-Ford, after its inventors.

Information	Distance to Reach Node						
Stored at Node	A	B	C	D	E	F	G
A	0	1	1	∞	1	1	∞
B	1	0	1	∞	∞	∞	∞
C	1	1	0	1	∞	∞	∞
D	∞	∞	1	0	∞	∞	1
E	1	∞	∞	∞	0	∞	∞
F	1	∞	∞	∞	∞	0	1
G	∞	∞	∞	1	∞	1	0

Table 4.5 Initial distances stored at each node (global view).

Destination	Cost	NextHop
B	1	B
C	1	C
D	∞	—
E	1	E
F	1	E
G	∞	—

Table 4.6 Initial routing table at node A.

The next step in distance-vector routing is that every node sends a message to its directly connected neighbors containing its personal list of distances. For example, node F tells node A that it can reach node G at a cost of 1; A also knows it can reach F at a cost of 1, so it adds these costs to get the cost of reaching G by means of F. This total cost of 2 is less than the current cost of infinity, so A records that it can reach G at a cost of 2 by going through F. Similarly, A learns from C that D can be reached from C at a cost of 1; it adds this to the cost of reaching C (1) and decides that D can be reached via C at a cost of 2, which is better than the old cost of infinity. At the same time, A learns from C that B can be reached from C at a cost of 1, so it concludes that

Destination	Cost	NextHop
B	1	B
C	1	C
D	2	C
E	1	E
F	1	E
G	2	F

Table 4.7   Final routing table at node A.

Information Stored at Node	Distance to Reach Node						
	A	B	C	D	E	F	G
A	0	1	1	2	1	1	2
B	1	0	1	2	2	2	3
C	1	1	0	1	2	2	2
D	2	2	1	0	3	2	1
E	1	2	2	3	0	2	3
F	1	2	2	2	2	0	1
G	2	3	2	1	3	1	0

Table 4.8   Final distances stored at each node (global view).

the cost of reaching B via C is 2. Since this is worse than the current cost of reaching B (1), this new information is ignored.

At this point, A can update its routing table with costs and next hops for all nodes in the network. The result is shown in Table 4.7.

In the absence of any topology changes, it only takes a few exchanges of information between neighbors before each node has a complete routing table. The process of getting consistent routing information to all the nodes is called *convergence*. Table 4.8 shows the final set of costs from each node to all other nodes when routing has converged. We must stress that there is no one node in the network that has all the information in this table—each node only knows about the contents of its own routing table. The beauty of a distributed algorithm like this is that it enables all nodes to achieve a consistent view of the network in the absence of any centralized authority.

There are a few details to fill in before our discussion of distance-vector routing is complete. First we note that there are two different circumstances under which a given node decides to send a routing update to its neighbors. One of these circumstances is the *periodic* update. In this case, each node automatically sends an update message every so often, even if nothing has changed. This serves to let the other nodes know that this node is still running. It also makes sure that they keep getting information that they may need if their current routes become unviable. The frequency of these periodic updates varies from protocol to protocol, but it is typically on the order of several seconds to several minutes. The second mechanism, sometimes called a *triggered* update, happens whenever a node receives an update from one of its neighbors that causes it to change one of the routes in its routing table. That is, whenever a node's routing table changes, it sends an update to its neighbors, which may lead to a change in their tables, causing them to send an update to their neighbors.

Now consider what happens when a link or node fails. The nodes that notice first send new lists of distances to their neighbors, and normally the system settles down fairly quickly to a new state. As to the question of how a node detects a failure, there are a couple of different answers. In one approach, a node continually tests the link to another node by sending a control packet and seeing if it receives an acknowledgment. In another approach, a node determines that the link (or the node at the other end of the link) is down if it does not receive the expected periodic routing update for the last few update cycles.

To understand what happens when a node detects a link failure, consider what happens when F detects that its link to G has failed. First, F sets its new distance to G to infinity and passes that information along to A. Since A knows that its 2-hop path to G is through F, A would also set its distance to G to infinity. However, with the next update from C, A would learn that C has a 2-hop path to G. Thus A would know that it could reach G in 3 hops through C, which is less than infinity, and so A would update its table accordingly. When it advertises this to F, node F would learn that it can reach G at a cost of 4 through A, which is less than infinity, and the system would again become stable.

Unfortunately, slightly different circumstances can prevent the network from stabilizing. Suppose, for example, that the link from A to E goes down. In the next round of updates, A advertises a distance of infinity to E, but B and C advertise a distance of 2 to E. Depending on the exact timing of events, the following might happen: Node B, upon hearing that E can be reached in 2 hops from C, concludes that it can reach E in 3 hops and advertises this to A; node A concludes that it can reach E in 4 hops and advertises this to C; node C concludes that it can reach E in 5 hops; and so on. This cycle stops only when the distances reach some number that is large enough to be considered infinite. In the meantime, none of the nodes actually knows that E is unreachable, and the routing tables for the network do not stabilize. This situation is known as the *count to infinity* problem.

There are several partial solutions to this problem. The first one is to use some relatively small number as an approximation of infinity. For example, we might decide that the maximum number of hops to get across a certain network is never going to be more than 16, and so we could pick 16 as the value that represents infinity. This at least bounds the amount of time that it takes to count to infinity. Of course, it could also present a problem if our network grew to a point where some nodes were separated by more than 16 hops.

One technique to improve the time to stabilize routing is called *split horizon*. The idea is that when a node sends a routing update to its neighbors, it does not send those routes it learned from each neighbor back to that neighbor. For example, if B has the route (E, 2, A) in its table, then it knows it must have learned this route from A, and so whenever B sends a routing update to A, it does not include the route (E, 2) in that update. In a stronger variation of split horizon, called *split horizon with poison reverse*, B actually sends that route back to A, but it puts negative information in the route to ensure that A will not eventually use B to get to E. For example, B sends the route (E, ∞) to A. The problem with both of these techniques is that they only work for routing loops that involve two nodes. For larger routing loops, more drastic measures are called for. Continuing the above example, if B and C had waited for a while after hearing of the link failure from A before advertising routes to E, they would have found that neither of them really had a route to E. Unfortunately, this approach delays the convergence of the protocol; speed of convergence is one of the key advantages of its competitor, link-state routing, the subject of Section 4.2.3.

Implementation

The code that implements this algorithm is very straightforward; we give only some of the basics here. Structure Route defines each entry in the routing table, and constant MAX_TTL specifies how long an entry is kept in the table before it is discarded.

```
#define MAX_ROUTES     128     /* maximum size of routing table */
#define MAX_TTL        120     /* time (in seconds) until route expires
*/

typedef struct {
    NodeAddr    Destination;    /* address of destination */
```

```
        NodeAddr     NextHop;          /* address of next hop */
        int          Cost;             /* distance metric */
        u_short      TTL;              /* time to live */
    } Route;


int      numRoutes = 0;
Route    routingTable[MAX_ROUTES];
```

The routine that updates the local node's routing table based on a new route is given by mergeRoute. Although not shown, a timer function periodically scans the list of routes in the node's routing table, decrements the TTL (time to live) field of each route, and discards any routes that have a time to live of 0. Notice, however, that the TTL field is reset to MAX_TTL any time the route is reconfirmed by an update message from a neighboring node.

```
void
mergeRoute (Route *new)
{
    int i;

    for (i = 0; i < numRoutes; ++i)
    {
        if (new->Destination == routingTable[i].Destination)
        {
            if (new->Cost + 1 < routingTable[i].Cost)
            {
                /* found a better route: */
                break;
            } else if (new->NextHop == routingTable[i].NextHop) {
                /* metric for current next-hop may have changed: */
                break;
            } else {
                /* route is uninteresting---just ignore it */
                return;
            }
        }
    }
```

```
    if (i == numRoutes)
    {
        /* this is a completely new route; is there room for it? */
        if (numRoutes < MAXROUTES)
        {
            ++numRoutes;
        } else {
            /* can't fit this route in table so give up */
            return;
        }
    }
    routingTable[i] = *new;
    /* reset TTL */
    routingTable[i].TTL = MAX_TTL;
    /* account for hop to get to next node */
    ++routingTable[i].Cost;


}
```

Finally, the procedure updateRoutingTable is the main routine that calls
mergeRoute to incorporate all the routes contained in a routing update that is received
from a neighboring node.

```
void
updateRoutingTable (Route *newRoute, int numNewRoutes)
{
    int i;

    for (i=0; i < numNewRoutes; ++i)
    {
        mergeRoute(&newRoute[i]);
    }
}
```

Routing Information Protocol (RIP)

One of the most widely used routing protocols in IP networks is the Routing Information Protocol (RIP). Its widespread use is due in no small part to the fact that it was
distributed along with the popular Berkeley Software Distribution (BSD) version of
Unix, from which many commercial versions of Unix were derived. It is also extremely
simple. RIP is the canonical example of a routing protocol built on the distance-vector
algorithm just described.

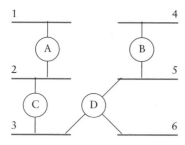

Figure 4.15 Example network running RIP.

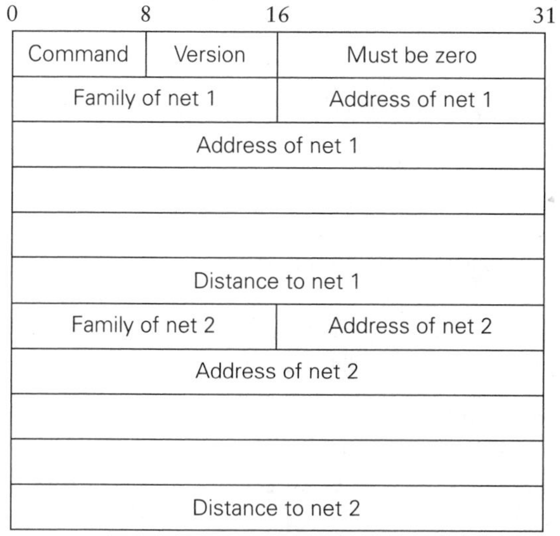

0	8	16	31
Command	Version	Must be zero	
Family of net 1		Address of net 1	
Address of net 1			
Distance to net 1			
Family of net 2		Address of net 2	
Address of net 2			
Distance to net 2			

Figure 4.16 RIP packet format.

Routing protocols in internetworks differ very slightly from the idealized graph model described above. In an internetwork, the goal of the routers is to learn how to forward packets to various *networks*. Thus, rather than advertising the cost of reaching other routers, the routers advertise the cost of reaching networks. For example, in Figure 4.15, router C would advertise to router A the fact that it can reach networks 2 and 3 (to which it is directly connected) at a cost of 0; networks 5 and 6 at cost 1; and network 4 at cost 2.

We can see evidence of this in the RIP packet format in Figure 4.16. The majority of the packet is taken up with ⟨network-address, distance⟩ pairs. However, the principles of the routing algorithm are just the same. For example, if router A learns from router B that network X can be reached at a lower cost via B than via the existing next hop in the routing table, A updates the cost and next hop information for the network number accordingly.

RIP is in fact a fairly straightforward implementation of distance-vector routing. Routers running RIP send their advertisements every 30 seconds; a router also sends an update message whenever an update from another router causes it to change its routing table. One point of interest is that it supports multiple address families, not just IP. The network-address part of the advertisements is actually represented as a ⟨family, address⟩ pair. RIP version 2 (RIPv2) also has some features related to scalability that we will discuss in the next section.

As we will see below, it is possible to use a range of different metrics or costs for the links in a routing protocol. RIP takes the simplest approach, with all link costs being equal to 1, just as in our example above. Thus it always tries to find the minimum hop route. Valid distances are 1 through 15, with 16 representing infinity. This also limits RIP to running on fairly small networks—those with no paths longer than 15 hops.

4.2.3 Link State (OSPF)

Link-state routing is the second major class of intradomain routing protocol. The starting assumptions for link-state routing are rather similar to those for distance-vector routing. Each node is assumed to be capable of finding out the state of the link to its neighbors (up or down) and the cost of each link. Again, we want to provide each node with enough information to enable it to find the least-cost path to any destination. The basic idea behind link-state protocols is very simple: Every node knows how to reach its directly connected neighbors, and if we make sure that the totality of this knowledge is disseminated to every node, then every node will have enough knowledge of the network to build a complete map of the network. This is clearly a sufficient condition (although not a necessary one) for finding the shortest path to any point in the network. Thus, link-state routing protocols rely on two mechanisms: reliable dissemination of link-state information, and the calculation of routes from the sum of all the accumulated link-state knowledge.

Reliable Flooding ✓ *(LSP) Link-State-Information*

Definition → *Reliable flooding* is the process of making sure that all the nodes participating in the routing protocol get a copy of the link-state information from all the other nodes. As the term "flooding" suggests, the basic idea is for a node to send its link-state information out on all of its directly connected links, with each node that receives this information forwarding it out on all of *its* links. This process continues until the information has reached all the nodes in the network.

More precisely, each node creates an update packet, also called a link-state packet (LSP), that contains the following information:

- the ID of the node that created the LSP
- a list of directly connected neighbors of that node, with the cost of the link to each one
- a sequence number
- a time to live for this packet $-(TTL)$ Time to live

The first two items are needed to enable route calculation; the last two are used to make the process of flooding the packet to all nodes reliable. Reliability includes making sure that you have the most recent copy of the information, since there may be multiple, contradictory LSPs from one node traversing the network. Making the flooding reliable has proven to be quite difficult. (For example, an early version of link-state routing used in the ARPANET caused that network to fail in 1981.)

Flooding works in the following way. First, the transmission of LSPs between adjacent routers is made reliable using acknowledgments and retransmissions just as in the reliable link-layer protocol described in Section 2.5. However, there are several more steps needed to reliably flood an LSP to all nodes in a network.

Consider a node X that receives a copy of an LSP that originated at some other node Y. Note that Y may be any other router in the same routing domain as X. X checks to see if it has already stored a copy of an LSP from Y. If not, it stores the LSP. If it already has a copy, it compares the sequence numbers; if the new LSP has a larger sequence number, it is assumed to be the more recent, and that LSP is stored, replacing the old one. A smaller (or equal) sequence number would imply an LSP older (or not newer) than the one stored, so it would be discarded and no further action would be needed. If the received LSP was the newer one, X then sends a copy of that LSP to all of its neighbors except the neighbor from which the LSP was just received. The fact that the LSP is not sent back to the node from which it was received helps to bring an end to the flooding of an LSP. Since X passes the LSP on to all its neighbors, who then turn around and do the same thing, the most recent copy of the LSP eventually reaches all nodes.

Figure 4.17 shows an LSP being flooded in a small network. Each node becomes shaded as it stores the new LSP. In Figure 4.17(a) the LSP arrives at node X, which sends it to neighbors A and C in Figure 4.17(b). A and C do not send it back to X, but send it on to B. Since B receives two identical copies of the LSP, it will accept whichever arrived first and ignore the second as a duplicate. It then passes the LSP onto D, who has no neighbors to flood it to, and the process is complete.

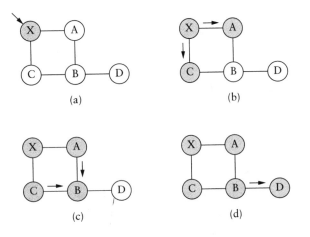

Figure 4.17 Flooding of link-state packets. (a) LSP arrives at node X; (b) X floods LSP to A and C; (c) A and C flood LSP to B (but not X); (d) flooding is complete.

Just as in RIP, each node generates LSPs under two circumstances. Either the expiry of a periodic timer or a change in topology can cause a node to generate a new LSP. However, the only topology-based reason for a node to generate an LSP is if one of its directly connected links or immediate neighbors has gone down. The failure of a link can be detected in some cases by the link-layer protocol. The demise of a neighbor or loss of connectivity to that neighbor can be detected using periodic "hello" packets. Each node sends these to its immediate neighbors at defined intervals. If a sufficiently long time passes without receipt of a "hello" from a neighbor, the link to that neighbor will be declared down, and a new LSP will be generated to reflect this fact.

One of the important design goals of a link-state protocol's flooding mechanism is that the newest information must be flooded to all nodes as quickly as possible, while old information must be removed from the network and not allowed to circulate. In addition, it is clearly desirable to minimize the total amount of routing traffic that is sent around the network; after all, this is just "overhead" from the perspective of those who actually use the network for their applications. The next few paragraphs describe some of the ways that these goals are accomplished.

One easy way to reduce overhead is to avoid generating LSPs unless absolutely necessary. This can be done by using very long timers—often on the order of hours—for the periodic generation of LSPs. Given that the flooding protocol is truly reliable when topology changes, it is safe to assume that messages saying "nothing has changed" do not need to be sent very often.

To make sure that old information is replaced by newer information, LSPs carry sequence numbers. Each time a node generates a new LSP, it increments the sequence number by 1. Unlike most sequence numbers used in protocols, these sequence numbers are not expected to wrap, so the field needs to be quite large (say, 64 bits). If a node goes down and then comes back up, it starts with a sequence number of 0. If the node was down for a long time, all the old LSPs for that node will have timed out (as described below); otherwise, this node will eventually receive a copy of its own LSP with a higher sequence number, which it can then increment and use as its own sequence number. This will ensure that its new LSP replaces any of its old LSPs left over from before the node went down.

LSPs also carry a time to live. This is used to ensure that old link-state information is eventually removed from the network. A node always decrements the TTL of a newly received LSP before flooding it to its neighbors. It also "ages" the LSP while it is stored in the node. When the TTL reaches 0, the node refloods the LSP with a TTL of 0, which is interpreted by all the nodes in the network as a signal to delete that LSP.

Route Calculation

Once a given node has a copy of the LSP from every other node, it is able to compute a complete map for the topology of the network, and from this map it is able to decide the best route to each destination. The question, then, is exactly how it calculates routes from this information. The solution is based on a well-known algorithm from graph theory—Dijkstra's shortest-path algorithm.

We first define Dijkstra's algorithm in graph-theoretic terms. Imagine that a node takes all the LSPs it has received and constructs a graphical representation of the network, in which N denotes the set of nodes in the graph, $l(i, j)$ denotes the nonnegative cost (weight) associated with the edge between nodes $i, j \in N$, and $l(i, j) = \infty$ if no edge connects i and j. In the following description, we let $s \in N$ denote this node, that is, the node executing the algorithm to find the shortest path to all the other nodes in N. Also, the algorithm maintains the following two variables: M denotes the set of nodes incorporated so far by the algorithm, and $C(n)$ denotes the cost of the path from s to each node n. Given these definitions, the algorithm is defined as follows:

```
M = {s}
for each n in N − {s}
    C(n) = l(s, n)
while (N ≠ M)
    M = M ∪ {w} such that C(w) is the minimum for all w in (N − M)
    for each n in (N − M)
        C(n) = MIN(C(n), C(w) + l(w, n))
```

Basically, the algorithm works as follows. We start with M containing this node s and then initialize the table of costs (the $C(n)$s) to other nodes using the known costs to

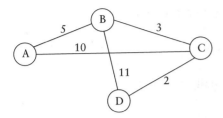

Figure 4.18 Link-state routing: an example network.

directly connected nodes. We then look for the node that is reachable at the lowest cost (w) and add it to M. Finally, we update the table of costs by considering the cost of reaching nodes through w. In the last line of the algorithm, we choose a new route to node n that goes through node w if the total cost of going from the source to w and then following the link from w to n is less than the old route we had to n. This procedure is repeated until all nodes are incorporated in M.

In practice, each switch computes its routing table directly from the LSPs it has collected using a realization of Dijkstra's algorithm called the *forward search* algorithm. Specifically, each switch maintains two lists, known as Tentative and Confirmed. Each of these lists contains a set of entries of the form (Destination, Cost, NextHop). The algorithm works as follows:

1 Initialize the Confirmed list with an entry for myself; this entry has a cost of 0.

2 For the node just added to the Confirmed list in the previous step, call it node Next, select its LSP.

3 For each neighbor (Neighbor) of Next, calculate the cost (Cost) to reach this Neighbor as the sum of the cost from myself to Next and from Next to Neighbor.

   (a) If Neighbor is currently on neither the Confirmed nor the Tentative list, then add (Neighbor, Cost, NextHop) to the Tentative list, where NextHop is the direction I go to reach Next.

   (b) If Neighbor is currently on the Tentative list, and the Cost is less than the currently listed cost for Neighbor, then replace the current entry with (Neighbor, Cost, NextHop), where NextHop is the direction I go to reach Next.

4 If the Tentative list is empty, stop. Otherwise, pick the entry from the Tentative list with the lowest cost, move it to the Confirmed list, and return to step 2.

This will become a lot easier to understand when we look at an example. Consider the network depicted in Figure 4.18. Note that, unlike our previous example, this

Step	Confirmed	Tentative	Comments
1	(D,0,-)		Since D is the only new member of the confirmed list, look at its LSP.
2	(D,0,-)	(B,11,B) (C,2,C)	D's LSP says we can reach B through B at cost 11, which is better than anything else on either list, so put it on **Tentative** list; same for C.
3	(D,0,-) (C,2,C)	(B,11,B)	Put lowest-cost member of **Tentative** (C) onto **Confirmed** list. Next, examine LSP of newly confirmed member (C).
4	(D,0,-) (C,2,C)	(B,5,C) (A,12,C)	Cost to reach B through C is 5, so replace (B,11,B). C's LSP tells us that we can reach A at cost 12.
5	(D,0,-) (C,2,C) (B,5,C)	(A,12,C)	Move lowest-cost member of **Tentative** (B) to **Confirmed**, then look at its LSP.
6	(D,0,-) (C,2,C) (B,5,C)	(A,10,C)	Since we can reach A at cost 5 through B, replace the **Tentative** entry.
7	(D,0,-) (C,2,C) (B,5,C) (A,10,C)		Move lowest-cost member of **Tentative** (A) to **Confirmed**, and we are all done.

Table 4.9 Steps for building routing table for node D (Figure 4.18).

network has a range of different edge costs. Table 4.9 traces the steps for building the routing table for node D. We denote the two outputs of D by using the names of the nodes to which they connect, B and C. Note the way the algorithm seems to head off on false leads (like the 11-unit cost path to B that was the first addition to the **Tentative** list) but ends up with the least-cost paths to all nodes.

The link-state routing algorithm has many nice properties: It has been proven to stabilize quickly, it does not generate much traffic, and it responds rapidly to topology changes or node failures. On the downside, the amount of information stored at each node (one LSP for every other node in the network) can be quite large. This is one of the fundamental problems of routing and is an instance of the more general problem of scalability. Some solutions to both the specific problem (the amount of storage potentially required at each node) and the general problem (scalability) will be discussed in the next section.

Thus, the difference between the distance-vector and link-state algorithms can be summarized as follows. In distance vector, each node talks only to its directly connected neighbors, but it tells them everything it has learned (i.e., distance to all nodes). In link state, each node talks to all other nodes, but it tells them only what it knows for sure (i.e., only the state of its directly connected links).

The Open Shortest Path First Protocol (OSPF)

One of the most widely used link-state routing protocols is OSPF. The first word, "Open," refers to the fact that it is an open, nonproprietary standard, created under the auspices of the IETF. The "SPF" part comes from an alternative name for link-state routing. OSPF adds quite a number of features to the basic link-state algorithm described above, including the following:

■ Authentication of routing messages: This is a nice feature, since it is all too common for some misconfigured host to decide that it can reach every host in the universe at a cost of 0. When the host advertises this fact, every router in the surrounding neighborhood updates its forwarding tables to point to that host, and said host receives a vast amount of data that, in reality, it has no idea what to do with. It typically drops it all, bringing the network to a halt. Such disasters can be averted in many cases by requiring routing updates to be authenticated. Early versions of OSPF used a simple 8-byte password for authentication. This is not a strong enough form of authentication to prevent dedicated malicious users, but it alleviates many problems caused by misconfiguration. (A similar form of authentication was added to RIP in version 2.) Strong cryptographic authentication of the sort discussed in Section 8.2.1 was later added.

■ Additional hierarchy: Hierarchy is one of the fundamental tools used to make systems more scalable. OSPF introduces another layer of hierarchy into routing by allowing a domain to be partitioned into *areas*. This means that a router within a domain does not necessarily need to know how to reach every network within that domain—it may be able to get by knowing only how to get to the right area. Thus, there is a reduction in the amount of information that

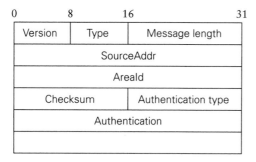

0	8	16	31

Version	Type	Message length
SourceAddr		
AreaId		
Checksum		Authentication type
Authentication		

Figure 4.19 OSPF header format.

must be transmitted to and stored in each node. We examine areas in detail in Section 4.3.4.

- Load balancing: OSPF allows multiple routes to the same place to be assigned the same cost and will cause traffic to be distributed evenly over those routes.

There are several different types of OSPF messages, but all begin with the same header, as shown in Figure 4.19. The Version field is currently set to 2, and the Type field may take the values 1 through 5. The SourceAddr identifies the sender of the message, and the AreaId is a 32-bit identifier of the area in which the node is located. The entire packet, except the authentication data, is protected by a 16-bit checksum using the same algorithm as the IP header (see Section 2.4). The Authentication type is 0 if no authentication is used; otherwise it may be 1, implying a simple password is used, or 2, which indicates that a cryptographic authentication checksum, of the sort described in Section 8.2.1, is used. In the latter cases the Authentication field carries the password or cryptographic checksum.

Of the five OSPF message types, type 1 is the "hello" message, which a router sends to its peers to notify them that it is still alive and connected as described above. The remaining types are used to request, send, and acknowledge the receipt of link-state messages. The basic building block of link-state messages in OSPF is known as the link-state advertisement (LSA). One message may contain many LSAs. We provide a few details of the LSA here.

Like any internetwork routing protocol, OSPF must provide information about how to reach networks. Thus, OSPF must provide a little more information than the simple graph-based protocol described above. Specifically, a router running OSPF may generate link-state packets that advertise one or more of the networks that are directly connected to that router. In addition, a router that is connected to another router by

LS Age		Options	Type=1
Link state ID			
Advertising router			
LS sequence number			
LS checksum		Length	
0	Flags	0	Number of links
Link ID			
Link data			
Link type	Num_TOS	Metric	
Optional TOS information			
More links			

Figure 4.20 OSPF link-state advertisement.

some link must advertise the cost of reaching that router over the link. These two types of advertisements are necessary to enable all the routers in a domain to determine the cost of reaching all networks in that domain and the appropriate next hop for each network.

Figure 4.20 shows the packet format for a "type 1" link-state advertisement. Type 1 LSAs advertise the cost of links between routers. Type 2 LSAs are used to advertise networks to which the advertising router is connected, while other types are used to support additional hierarchy as described in the next section. Many fields in the LSA should be familiar from the preceding discussion. The LS Age is the equivalent of a time to live, except that it counts up and the LSA expires when the age reaches a defined maximum value. The Type field tells us that this is a type 1 LSA.

In a type 1 LSA, the Link state ID and the Advertising router field are identical. Each carries a 32-bit identifier for the router that created this LSA. While a number of assignment strategies may be used to assign this ID, it is essential that it be unique in the routing domain and that a given router consistently uses the same router ID. One way to pick a router ID that meets these requirements would be to pick the lowest IP address among all the IP addresses assigned to that router. (Recall that a router may have a different IP address on each of its interfaces.)

The LS sequence number is used exactly as described above, to detect old or duplicate LSAs. The LS checksum is similar to others we have seen in Section 2.4 and in other protocols; it is of course used to verify that data has not been corrupted. It covers all fields in the packet except LS Age, so that it is not necessary to recompute a checksum every time LS Age is incremented. Length is the length in bytes of the complete LSA.

Now we get to the actual link-state information. This is made a little complicated by the presence of TOS (type of service) information. Ignoring that for a moment, each link in the LSA is represented by a Link ID, some Link Data, and a metric. The first two of these fields identify the link; a common way to do this would be to use the router ID of the router at the far end of the link as the Link ID, and then use the Link Data to disambiguate among multiple parallel links if necessary. The metric is of course the cost of the link. Type tells us something about the link, for example, if it is a point-to-point link.

The TOS information is present to allow OSPF to choose different routes for IP packets based on the value in their TOS field. Instead of assigning a single metric to a link, it is possible to assign different metrics depending on the TOS value of the data. For example, if we had a link in our network that was very good for delay-sensitive traffic, we could give it a low metric for the TOS value representing low delay, and a high metric for everything else. OSPF would then pick a different shortest path for those packets that had their TOS field set to that value. It is worth noting that, at the time of writing, this capability has not been widely deployed.

4.2.4 Metrics

The preceding discussion assumes that link costs, or metrics, are known when we execute the routing algorithm. In this section, we look at some ways to calculate link costs that have proven effective in practice. One example that we have seen already, which is quite reasonable and very simple, is to assign a cost of 1 to all links—the least-cost route will then be the one with the fewest hops. Such an approach has several drawbacks, however. First, it does not distinguish between links on a latency basis. Thus, a satellite link with 250-ms latency looks just as attractive to the routing protocol as a terrestrial link with 1-ms latency. Second, it does not distinguish between routes on a capacity basis, making a 9.6-Kbps link look just as good as a 45-Mbps link. Finally, it does not distinguish between links based on their current load, making it impossible to route around overloaded links. It turns out that this last problem is the hardest because you are trying to capture the complex and dynamic characteristics of a link in a single scalar cost.

The ARPANET was the testing ground for a number of different approaches to link-cost calculation. (It was also the place where the superior stability of link-state over distance-vector routing was demonstrated; the original mechanism used distance vector while the later version used link state.) The following discussion traces the evolution of the ARPANET routing metric and, in so doing, explores the subtle aspects of the problem.

The original ARPANET routing metric measured the number of packets that were queued waiting to be transmitted on each link, meaning that a link with 10 packets queued waiting to be transmitted was assigned a larger cost weight than a link with 5 packets queued for transmission. Using queue length as a routing metric did not work well, however, since queue length is an artificial measure of load—it moves packets toward the shortest queue rather than toward the destination, a situation all too familiar to those of us who hop from line to line at the grocery store. Stated more precisely, the original ARPANET routing mechanism suffered from the fact that it did not take either the bandwidth or the latency of the link into consideration.

Note →

A second version of the ARPANET routing algorithm, sometimes called the "new routing mechanism," took both link bandwidth and latency into consideration and used delay, rather than just queue length, as a measure of load. This was done as follows. First, each incoming packet was timestamped with its time of arrival at the router (ArrivalTime); its departure time from the router (DepartTime) was also recorded. Second, when the link-level ACK was received from the other side, the node computed the delay for that packet as

$$\text{Delay} = (\text{DepartTime} - \text{ArrivalTime}) + \text{TransmissionTime} + \text{Latency}$$

where TransmissionTime and Latency were statically defined for the link and captured the link's bandwidth and latency, respectively. Notice that in this case, DepartTime − ArrivalTime represents the amount of time the packet was delayed (queued) in the node due to load. If the ACK did not arrive, but instead the packet timed out, then DepartTime was reset to the time the packet was *retransmitted*. In this case, DepartTime − ArrivalTime captures the reliability of the link—the more frequent the retransmission of packets, the less reliable the link, and the more we want to avoid it. Finally, the weight assigned to each link was derived from the average delay experienced by the packets recently sent over that link.

Although an improvement over the original mechanism, this approach also had a lot of problems. Under light load, it worked reasonably well, since the two static factors of delay dominated the cost. Under heavy load, however, a congested link would start to advertise a very high cost. This caused all the traffic to move off that link, leaving it idle, so then it would advertise a low cost, thereby attracting back all the traffic, and so on. The effect of this instability was that, under heavy load, many links would in fact spend a great deal of time being idle, which is the last thing you want under heavy load.

Another problem was that the range of link values was much too large. For example, a heavily loaded 9.6-Kbps link could look 127 times more costly than a lightly loaded 56-Kbps link. This means that the routing algorithm would choose a path with 126 hops of lightly loaded 56-Kbps links in preference to a 1-hop 9.6-Kbps path. While shedding some traffic from an overloaded line is a good idea, making it

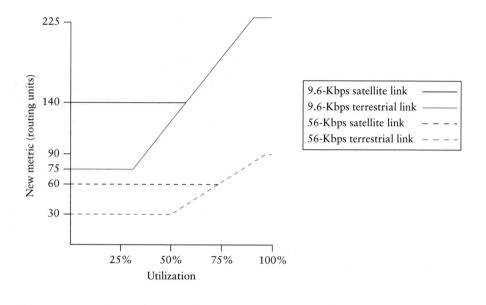

Figure 4.21 Revised ARPANET routing metric versus link utilization.

look so unattractive that it loses all its traffic is excessive. Using 126 hops when 1 hop will do is in general a bad use of network resources. Also, satellite links were unduly penalized, so that an idle 56-Kbps satellite link looked considerably more costly than an idle 9.6-Kbps terrestrial link, even though the former would give better performance for high-bandwidth applications.

A third approach, called the "revised ARPANET routing metric," addressed these problems. The major changes were to compress the dynamic range of the metric considerably, to account for the link type, and to smooth the variation of the metric with time.

The smoothing was achieved by several mechanisms. First, the delay measurement was transformed to a link utilization, and this number was averaged with the last reported utilization to suppress sudden changes. Second, there was a hard limit on how much the metric could change from one measurement cycle to the next. By smoothing the changes in the cost, the likelihood that all nodes would abandon a route at once is greatly reduced.

The compression of the dynamic range was achieved by feeding the measured utilization, the link type, and the link speed into a function that is shown graphically in Figure 4.21. Observe the following:

■ A highly loaded link never shows a cost of more than three times its cost when idle.

■ The most expensive link is only seven times the cost of the least expensive.

■ A high-speed satellite link is more attractive than a low-speed terrestrial link.

■ Cost is a function of link utilization only at moderate to high loads.

All these factors mean that a link is much less likely to be universally abandoned, since a threefold increase in cost is likely to make the link unattractive for some paths while letting it remain the best choice for others. The slopes, offsets, and breakpoints for the curves in Figure 4.21 were arrived at by a great deal of trial and error, and they were carefully tuned to provide good performance.

There is one final issue related to calculating edge weights—the frequency with which each node calculates the weights on its links. There are two things to keep in mind. First, none of the metrics are instantaneous. That is, whether a node is measuring queue length, delay, or utilization, it is actually computing an average over a period of time. Second, just because a metric changes does not mean that the node sends out an update message. In practice, updates are sent only when the change to an edge weight is larger than some threshold.

4.2.5 Routing for Mobile Hosts

Looking back over the preceding discussion of how IP addressing and routing works,

Monitoring Routing Behavior

Given the complexity of routing packets through a network of the scale of the Internet, we might wonder how well the system works. We know it works some of the time because we are able to connect to sites all over the world. We suspect it doesn't work all the time, though, because sometimes we are unable to connect to certain sites. The real problem is determining what part of the system is at fault when our connections fail: Has some routing machinery failed to work properly, is the remote server too busy, or has some link or machine simply gone down?

This is really an issue of network management, and while there are tools that system administrators use to keep tabs on their own networks—for example, see the Simple Network Management Protocol (SNMP) described in Section 9.2.3—it is a largely unresolved problem for the Internet as a whole. In fact, the Internet has grown so large and complex that, even though it is constructed from a collection of man-made, largely deterministic parts, we have come to view it almost as a living organism or natural phenomenon that is

you might notice that there is an implicit assumption about the mobility of hosts, or rather the lack of it. A host's address consists of a network number and a host part, and the network number tells us which network the host is attached to. IP routing algorithms tell the routers how to get packets to the correct network, thus enhancing the scalability of the routing system by keeping host-specific information out of the routers. So what would happen if a host were disconnected from one network and connected to another? If we didn't change the IP address of the host, then it would become unreachable. Any packet destined for this host would be sent to the network that has the appropriate network number, but when the router(s) on that network tried to deliver the packet to the host, the host would not be there to receive it.

The obvious solution to this problem is to provide the host with a new address when it attaches to a new network. Techniques such as DHCP (described in Section 4.1.6) can make this a relatively simple process. In many situations this solution is adequate, but in others it is not. For example, suppose that a user of a PC equipped with a wireless network interface is running some application while she roams the countryside. The PC might detach itself from one network and attach to another with some frequency, but the user would want to be oblivious to this. In particular, the applications that were running when the PC was attached to network A should continue to run without interruption when it attaches to network B. If the PC simply changes its IP address in the middle of running the application, the application cannot simply keep working, because the remote end has

to be studied. That is, we try to understand the Internet's dynamic behavior by performing experiments on it and proposing models that explain our observations.

An excellent example of this kind of study has been conducted by Vern Paxson, now at the AT&T Center for Internet Research. Paxson used the Unix traceroute tool to study 40,000 end-to-end routes between 37 Internet sites in 1995. He was attempting to answer questions about how routes fail, how stable routes are over time, and whether or not they are symmetric. Among other things, Paxson found that the likelihood of a user encountering a serious end-to-end routing problem was 1 in 30, and that such problems usually lasted about 30 seconds. He also found that two-thirds of the Internet's routes persisted for days or weeks, and that about one-third of the time the route used to get from host A to host B included at least one different routing domain than the route used to get from host B to host A. Paxson's overall conclusion was that Internet routing was becoming less and less predictable over time.

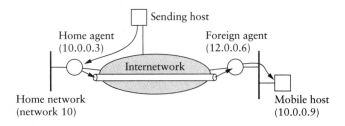

Figure 4.22   Mobile host and mobility agents.

no way of knowing that it must now send the packets to a new IP address. Ideally, we want the movement of the PC to be transparent to the remote application. The procedures that are designed to address this problem are usually referred to as "Mobile IP" (named after the IETF working group that defined them).

The Mobile IP working group made some important design decisions at the outset. In particular, it was a requirement that the solution would work without any changes to the software of nonmobile hosts or the majority of routers in the Internet. This sort of approach is frequently adopted in the Internet. Any new technology that requires a majority of routers or hosts to be modified before it can work is likely to face an uphill battle for acceptance.

While the majority of routers remain unchanged, mobility support does require some new functionality in at least one router, known as the *home agent* of the mobile node. This router is located on the "home" network of the mobile host. The mobile host is assumed to have a permanent IP address, called its *home address*, which has a network number equal to that of the home network, and thus of the home agent. This is the address that will be used by other hosts when they send packets to the mobile host; since it does not change, it can be used by long-lived applications as the host roams.

In many cases, a second router with enhanced functionality, the *foreign agent,* is also required. This router is located on a network to which the mobile node attaches itself when it is away from its home network. We will consider first the operation of Mobile IP when a foreign agent is used. An example network with both home and foreign agents is shown in Figure 4.22.

Both home and foreign agents periodically announce their presence on the networks to which they are attached using agent advertisement messages. A mobile host may also solicit an advertisement when it attaches to a new network. The advertisement by the home agent enables a mobile host to learn the address of its home agent before it leaves its home network. When the mobile host attaches to a foreign network, it hears an advertisement from a foreign agent and registers with the agent, providing the address of its home agent. The foreign agent then contacts the home agent, providing a *care-of address*. This is usually the IP address of the foreign agent.

At this point, we can see that any host that tries to send a packet to the mobile host will send it with a destination address equal to the home address of that node. Normal IP forwarding will cause that packet to arrive on the home network of the mobile node, on which the home agent is sitting. Thus, we can divide the problem of delivering the packet to the mobile node into three parts:

1 How does the home agent intercept a packet that is destined for the mobile node?

2 How does the home agent then deliver the packet to the foreign agent?

3 How does the foreign agent deliver the packet to the mobile node?

The first problem might look easy if you just look at Figure 4.22, in which the home agent is clearly the only path between the sending host and the home network, and thus must receive packets that are destined to the mobile node. But what if the sending node were on network 10, or what if there were another router connected to network 10 that tried to deliver the packet without its passing through the home agent? To address this problem, the home agent actually impersonates the mobile node, using a technique called "proxy ARP." This works just like ARP as described in Section 4.1.5, except that the home agent inserts the IP address of the mobile node, rather than its own, in the ARP messages. It uses its own hardware address, so that all the nodes on the same network learn to associate the hardware address of the home agent with the IP address of the mobile node. One subtle aspect of this process is the fact that ARP information may be cached in other nodes on the network. To make sure that these caches are invalidated in a timely way, the home agent issues an ARP message as soon as the mobile node registers with a foreign agent. Because the ARP message is not a response to a normal ARP request, it is termed a "gratuitous ARP."

The second problem is the delivery of the intercepted packet to the foreign agent. Here we use the tunneling technique described in Section 4.1.8. The home agent simply "wraps" the packet inside an IP header that is destined for the foreign agent and transmits it into the internetwork. All the intervening routers just see an IP packet destined for the IP address of the foreign agent. Another way of looking at this is that an IP tunnel is established between the home agent and the foreign agent, and the home agent just drops packets destined for the mobile node into that tunnel.

When a packet finally arrives at the foreign agent, it strips the extra IP header and finds inside an IP packet destined for the mobile node. Clearly the foreign agent cannot treat this like any old IP packet because this would cause it to send it back to the home network. Instead, it has to recognize the address as that of a registered mobile node. It then delivers the packet to the *hardware* address of the mobile node (e.g., its Ethernet address), which was learned as part of the registration process.

One observation that can be made about these procedures is that it is possible for the foreign agent and the mobile node to be in the same box; that is, a mobile node can perform the foreign agent function itself. To make this work, however, the mobile node must be able to dynamically acquire an IP address that is located in the address space of the foreign network. This address will then be used as the care-of address. In our example, this would have to be an address with a network number of 12. We have already seen one way in which a host can dynamically acquire a correct IP address, using DHCP (Section 4.1.6). This approach has the desirable feature of allowing mobile nodes to attach to networks that don't have foreign agents; thus, mobility can be achieved with only the addition of a home agent and some new software on the mobile node (assuming DHCP is used on the foreign network).

What about traffic in the other direction (i.e., from mobile node to fixed node)? This turns out to be much easier. The mobile node just puts the IP address of the fixed node in the destination field of its IP packets, while putting its permanent address in the source field, and the packets are forwarded to the fixed node using normal means. Of course, if both nodes in a conversation are mobile, then the procedures described above are used in each direction.

Route Optimization in Mobile IP

There is one significant drawback to the above approach, which may be familiar to users of cellular telephones. The route from sending node to mobile node can be significantly suboptimal. One of the most extreme examples is when a mobile node and the sending node are on the same network, but the home network for the mobile node is on the far side of the Internet. The sending node addresses all packets to the home network; they traverse the Internet to reach the home agent, which then tunnels them back across the Internet to reach the foreign agent. Clearly it would be nice if the sending node could find out that the mobile node is actually on the same network and deliver the packet directly. In the more general case, the goal is to deliver packets as directly as possible from sending node to mobile node without passing through a home agent. This is sometimes referred to as the "triangle routing problem" since the path from sender to mobile node via home agent takes two sides of a triangle, rather than the third side that is the direct path.

The basic idea behind the solution to triangle routing is to let the sending node know the care-of address of the mobile node. The sending node can then create its own tunnel to the foreign agent. This is treated as an optimization of the process just described. If the sender has been equipped with the necessary software to learn the care-of address and create its own tunnel, then the route can be optimized; if not, packets just follow the suboptimal route.

When a home agent sees a packet destined for one of the mobile nodes that it supports, it can deduce that the sender is not using the optimal route. Therefore, it sends a "binding update" message back to the source, in addition to forwarding the data packet to the foreign agent. The source, if capable, uses this binding update to create an entry in a "binding cache," which consists of a list of mappings from mobile node addresses to care-of addresses. The next time this source has a data packet to send to that mobile node, it will find the binding in the cache and can tunnel the packet directly to the foreign agent.

There is an obvious problem with this scheme, which is that the binding cache may become out-of-date if the mobile host moves to a new network. If an out-of-date cache entry is used, the foreign agent will receive tunneled packets for a mobile node that is no longer registered on its network. In this case, it sends a "binding warning" message back to the sender to tell it to stop using this cache entry. This scheme works only in the case where the foreign agent is not the mobile node itself, however. For this reason, cache entries need to be deleted after some period of time; the exact amount is specified in the binding update message.

Mobile routing provides some interesting security challenges. For example, an attacker wishing to intercept the packets destined to some other node in an internetwork could contact the home agent for that node and announce itself as the new foreign agent for the node. Thus it is clear that some authentication mechanisms are required. We discuss such mechanisms in Chapter 8.

Finally, we note that there are many open issues in mobile networking. For example, the security and performance aspects of mobile networks might require routing algorithms to take account of several factors when finding a route to a mobile host; for example, it might be desirable to find a route that doesn't pass through some untrusted network. There is also the problem of "ad hoc" mobile networks—enabling a group of mobile nodes to form a network in the absence of any fixed nodes. These continue to be areas of active research.

4.3 Global Internet

At this point, we have seen how to connect a heterogeneous collection of networks to create an internetwork and how to use the simple hierarchy of the IP address to make routing in an internet somewhat scalable. We say "somewhat" scalable because even though each router does not need to know about all the hosts connected to the internet, it does, in the model described so far, need to know about all the networks connected to the internet. Today's Internet has tens of thousands of networks connected to it.

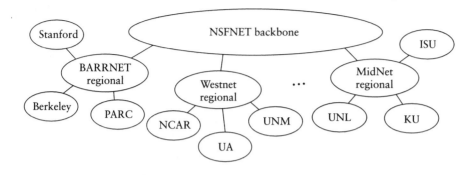

Figure 4.23   The tree structure of the Internet in 1990.

Routing protocols such as those we have just discussed do not scale to those kinds of numbers. This section looks at a variety of techniques that greatly improve scalability and that have enabled the Internet to grow as far as it has.

Before getting to these techniques, we need to have a general picture in our heads of what the global Internet looks like. It is not just a random interconnection of Ethernets, but instead it takes on a shape that reflects the fact that it interconnects many different organizations. Figure 4.23 gives a simple depiction of the state of the Internet in 1990. Since that time, the Internet's topology has grown much more complex than this figure suggests—we present a more accurate picture of the current Internet in Section 4.3.3 and Figure 4.28—but this picture will do for now.

One of the salient features of this topology is that it consists of "end user" sites (e.g., Stanford University) that connect to "service provider" networks (e.g., BARRNET was a provider network that served sites in the San Francisco Bay Area). In 1990, many providers served a limited geographic region and were thus known as regional networks. The regional networks were, in turn, connected by a nationwide backbone. In 1990, this backbone was funded by the National Science Foundation (NSF) and was therefore called the NSFNET backbone. Although the detail is not shown in this figure, the provider networks are typically built from a large number of point-to-point links (e.g., DS-3 or OC-3 links) that connect to routers; similarly, each end user site is typically not a single network, but instead consists of multiple physical networks connected by routers and bridges.

Notice in Figure 4.23 that each provider and end user is likely to be an administratively independent entity. This has some significant consequences on routing. For example, it is quite likely that different providers will have different ideas about the best routing protocol to use within their network, and on how metrics should be assigned to links in their network. Because of this independence, each provider's network is usually a single *autonomous system* (AS). We will define this term more precisely in Section 4.3.3, but for now it is adequate to think of an AS as a network that is administered independently of other ASs.

The fact that the Internet has a discernible structure can be used to our advantage as we tackle the problem of scalability. In fact, we need to deal with two related scaling issues. The first is the scalability of routing. We need to find ways to minimize the number of network numbers that get carried around in routing protocols and stored in the routing tables of routers. The second is address utilization—that is, making sure that the IP address space does not get consumed too quickly.

Throughout this section, we will see the principle of hierarchy used again and again to improve scalability. We begin with subnetting, which primarily deals with address space utilization. Next we introduce classless routing or supernetting, which tackles both address utilization and routing scalability. We then look at how hierarchy can be used to improve the scalability of routing, both through interdomain routing and within a single domain. Our final subsection looks at the emerging standards for IP version 6, the invention of which was largely the result of scalability concerns.

4.3.1 Subnetting

The original intent of IP addresses was that the network part would uniquely identify exactly one physical network. It turns out that this approach has a couple of drawbacks. Imagine a large campus that has lots of internal networks and that decides to connect to the Internet. For every network, no matter how small, the site needs at least a class C network address. Even worse, for any network with more than 255 hosts, they need a class B address. This may not seem like a big deal, and indeed it wasn't when the Internet was first envisioned, but there are only a finite number of network numbers, and there are far fewer class B addresses than class Cs. Class B addresses tend to be in particularly high demand because you never know if your network might expand beyond 255 nodes, so it is easier to use a class B address from the start than to have to renumber every host when you run out of room on a class C network. The problem we observe here is address assignment inefficiency: A network with two nodes uses an entire class C network address, thereby wasting 253 perfectly useful addresses; a class B network with slightly more than 255 hosts wastes over 64,000 addresses.

Assigning one network number per physical network, therefore, uses up the IP address space potentially much faster than we would like. While we would need to connect over 4 billion hosts to use up all the valid addresses, we only need to connect 2^{14} (about 16,000) class B networks before that part of the address space runs out. Therefore, we would like to find some way to use the network numbers more efficiently.

Assigning many network numbers has another drawback that becomes apparent when you think about routing. Recall that the amount of state that is stored in a node participating in a routing protocol is proportional to the number of other nodes, and that routing in an internet consists of building up forwarding tables that tell a router how to reach different networks. Thus, the more network numbers there are in use, the bigger the forwarding tables get. Big forwarding tables add cost to routers, and they are slower to search than smaller tables for a given technology, so they degrade router performance. This provides another motivation for assigning network numbers carefully.

Subnetting provides an elegantly simple way to reduce the total number of network numbers that are assigned. The idea is to take a single IP network number and allocate the IP addresses with that network number to several physical networks, which are now referred to as *subnets*. Several things need to be done to make this work. First, the subnets should be close to each other. This is because at a distant point in the Internet, they will all look like a single network, having only one network number between them. This means that a router will only be able to select one route to reach any of the subnets, so they had better all be in the same general direction. A perfect situation in which to use subnetting is a large campus or corporation that has many physical networks. From outside the campus, all you need to know to reach any subnet inside the campus is where the campus connects to the rest of the Internet. This is often at a single point, so one entry in your forwarding table will suffice. Even if there are multiple points at which the campus is connected to the rest of the Internet, knowing how to get to one point in the campus network is still a good start.

The mechanism by which a single network number can be shared among multiple networks involves configuring all the nodes on each subnet with a *subnet mask*. With simple IP addresses, all hosts on the same network must have the same network number. The subnet mask enables us to introduce a *subnet number*; all hosts on the same physical network will have the same subnet number, which means that hosts may be on different physical networks but share a single network number.

What the subnet mask effectively does is introduce another level of hierarchy into the IP address. For example, suppose that we want to share a single class B address among several physical networks. We could use a subnet mask of 255.255.255.0. (Subnet masks are written down just like IP addresses; this mask is therefore all 1s in the upper 24 bits and 0s in the lower 8 bits.) In effect, this means that the top 24 bits (where the mask has 1s) are now defined to be the network number, and the lower 8 bits (where the mask has 0s) are the host number. Since the top 16 bits identify the network in a class B address, we may now think of the address as having not two parts but three: a network part, a subnet part, and a host part. That is, we have divided what used to be the host part into a subnet part and a host part. This is shown in Figure 4.24.

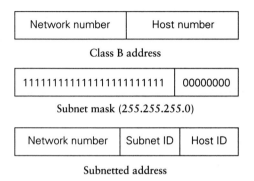

Figure 4.24 Subnet addressing.

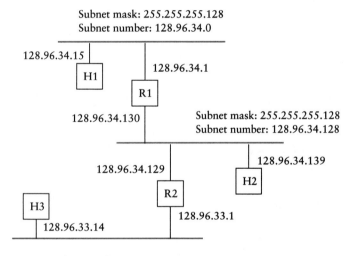

Figure 4.25 An example of subnetting.

What subnetting means to a host is that it is now configured with both an IP address and a subnet mask for the subnet to which it is attached. For example, host H1 in Figure 4.25 is configured with an address of 128.96.34.15 and a subnet mask of 255.255.255.128. (All hosts on a given subnet are configured with the same mask; i.e., there is exactly one subnet mask per subnet.) The bitwise AND of these two numbers defines the subnet number of the host and of all other hosts on the same subnet. In this

SubnetNumber	SubnetMask	NextHop
128.96.34.0	255.255.255.128	Interface 0
128.96.34.128	255.255.255.128	Interface 1
128.96.33.0	255.255.255.0	R2

Table 4.10   Example forwarding table with subnetting for Figure 4.25.

case, 128.96.34.15 AND 255.255.255.128 equals 128.96.34.0, so this is the subnet number for the topmost subnet in the figure.

When the host wants to send a packet to a certain IP address, the first thing it does is to perform a bitwise AND between its own subnet mask and the destination IP address. If the result equals the subnet number of the sending host, then it knows that the destination host is on the same subnet and the packet can be delivered directly over the subnet. If the results are not equal, the packet needs to be sent to a router to be forwarded to another subnet. For example, if H1 is sending to H2, then H1 ANDs its subnet mask (255.255.255.128) with the address for H2 (128.96.34.139) to obtain 128.96.34.128. This does not match the subnet number for H1 (128.96.34.0) so H1 knows that H2 is on a different subnet. Since H1 cannot deliver the packet to H2 directly over the subnet, it sends the packet to its default router R1.

Note that ARP is largely unaffected by the change in address structure. Once a host or router figures out which node it needs to deliver a packet to on one of the networks to which it is attached, it performs ARP to find the MAC address for that node if necessary.

The job of a router also changes when we introduce subnetting. Recall that, for simple IP, a router has a forwarding table that consists of entries of the form ⟨NetworkNum, NextHop⟩. To support subnetting, the table must now hold entries of the form ⟨SubnetNumber, SubnetMask, NextHop⟩. To find the right entry in the table, the router ANDs the packet's destination address with the SubnetMask for each entry in turn; if the result matches the SubnetNumber of the entry, then this is the right entry to use, and it forwards the packet to the next hop router indicated. In the example network of Figure 4.25, router R1 would have the entries shown in Table 4.10.

Continuing with the example of a datagram from H1 being sent to H2, R1 would AND H2's address (128.96.34.139) with the subnet mask of the first entry (255.255.255.128) and compare the result (128.96.34.128) with the network number for that entry (128.96.34.0). Since this is not a match, it proceeds to the next entry.

This time a match does occur, so R1 delivers the datagram to H2 using interface 1, which is the interface connected to the same network as H2.

We can now describe the datagram forwarding algorithm in the following way:

```
D = destination IP address
for each forwarding table entry ⟨SubnetNumber, SubnetMask, NextHop⟩
    D1 = SubnetMask & D
    if D1 = SubnetNumber
        if NextHop is an interface
            deliver datagram directly to destination
        else
            deliver datagram to NextHop (a router)
```

Although not shown in this example, a default router would usually be included in the table and would be used if no explicit matches were found. We note in passing that a naive implementation of this algorithm—one involving repeated ANDing of the destination address with a subnet mask that may not be different every time, and a linear table search—would be very inefficient.

A few fine points about subnetting need to be mentioned. We have already seen that the subnet mask does not need to align with a byte boundary, with the example mask of 255.255.255.128 (25 1s followed by 7 0s) used above. More confusingly, it is not even necessary for all the 1s in a subnet mask to be contiguous. For example, it would be quite possible to use a subnet mask of 255.255.1.0. All of the mechanisms described above should continue to work, but now you can't look at a contiguous part of the IP address and say, "That is the subnet number." This makes administration more difficult. It may also fail to work with implementations that assume that no one would use noncontiguous masks, and so it is not recommended in practice.

We can also put multiple subnets on a single physical network. The effect of this would be to force hosts on the same network to talk to each other through a router, which might be useful for administrative purposes; for example, to provide isolation between different departments sharing a LAN.

A third point to which we have alluded is that different parts of the internet see the world differently. From outside our hypothetical campus, routers see a single network. In the example above, routers outside the campus see the collection of networks in Figure 4.25 as just the network 128.96, and they keep one entry in their forwarding tables to tell them how to reach it. Routers within the campus, however, need to be able to route packets to the right subnet. Thus, not all parts of the internet see exactly the same routing information. The next section takes a closer look at how the propagation of routing information is done in the Internet.

▶   The bottom line is that subnetting helps solve our scalability problems in two ways. First, it improves our address assignment efficiency by letting us not use up an entire class C or class B address every time we add a new physical network. Second, it helps us aggregate information. From a reasonable distance, a complex collection of physical networks can be made to look like a single network, so that the amount of information that routers need to store to deliver datagrams to those networks can be reduced.

4.3.2 Classless Routing (CIDR)

Classless interdomain routing (CIDR, pronounced "cider") is a technique that addresses two scaling concerns in the Internet: the growth of backbone routing tables as more and more network numbers need to be stored in them, and the potential for the 32-bit IP address space to be exhausted well before the 4 billionth host is attached to the Internet. We have already mentioned the problem that would cause this address space exhaustion: address assignment inefficiency. The inefficiency arises because the IP address structure, with class A, B, and C addresses, forces us to hand out network address space in fixed-sized chunks of three very different sizes. A network with two hosts needs a class C address, giving an address assignment efficiency of $2/255 = 0.78\%$; a network with 256 hosts needs a class B address, for an efficiency of only $256/65,535 = 0.39\%$. Even though subnetting can help us to assign addresses carefully, it does not get around the fact that any autonomous system with more than 255 hosts, or an expectation of eventually having that many, wants a class B address.

As it turns out, exhaustion of the IP address space centers on exhaustion of the class B network numbers. One way to deal with that would seem to be saying no to any AS that requests a class B address unless they can show a need for something close to 64K addresses, and instead giving them an appropriate number of class C addresses to cover the expected number of hosts. Since we would now be handing out address space in chunks of 256 addresses at a time, we could more accurately match the amount of address space consumed to the size of the AS. For any AS with at least 256 hosts (which means the majority of ASs), we can guarantee an address utilization of at least 50%.

This solution, however, raises a problem that is at least as serious: excessive storage requirements at the routers. If a single AS has, say, 16 class C network numbers assigned to it, that means every Internet backbone router needs 16 entries in its routing tables for that AS. This is true even if the path to every one of those networks is the same. If we had assigned a class B address to the AS, the same routing information could be stored in one table entry. However, our address assignment efficiency would then be only $16 \times 255/65,536 = 6.2\%$.

CIDR, therefore, tries to balance the desire to minimize the number of routes that a router needs to know against the need to hand out addresses efficiently. To do this, CIDR helps us to *aggregate* routes. That is, it lets us use a single entry in a forwarding table to tell us how to reach a lot of different networks. As you may have guessed from the name, it does this by breaking the rigid boundaries between address classes. To understand how this works, consider our hypothetical AS with 16 class C network numbers. Instead of handing out 16 addresses at random, we can hand out a block of *contiguous* class C addresses. Suppose we assign the class C network numbers from 192.4.16 through 192.4.31. Observe that the top 20 bits of all the addresses in this range are the same (11000000 00000100 0001). Thus, what we have effectively created is a 20-bit network number—something that is between a class B network number and a class C number in terms of the number of hosts that it can support. In other words, we get both the high address efficiency of handing out addresses 256 nodes at a time and a single network prefix that can be used in forwarding tables. Observe that for this scheme to work, we need to hand out blocks of class C addresses that share a common prefix, which means that each block must contain a number of class C networks that is a power of two.

All we need now to make CIDR solve our problems is a routing protocol that can deal with these "classless" addresses, which means that it must understand that a network number may be of any length. Modern routing protocols (such as BGP-4, described below) do exactly that. The network numbers that are carried in such a routing protocol are represented simply by ⟨length, value⟩ pairs, where the length gives the number of bits in the network prefix—20 in the above example. Note that representing a network address in this way is similar to the ⟨mask, value⟩ approach used in subnetting, as long as masks consist of contiguous bits starting from the most significant bit. Also note that we used subnetting to share one address among multiple physical networks, while CIDR aims to collapse the multiple addresses that would be assigned to a single AS onto one address. The similarity between the two approaches is reflected in the original name for CIDR—supernetting.

In fact, the ability to aggregate routes in the way that we have just shown is only the first step. Imagine an Internet service provider network, whose primary job is to provide Internet connectivity to a large number of corporations and campuses. If we assign network numbers to the corporations in such a way that all the different corporations connected to the provider network share a common address prefix, then we can get even greater aggregation of routes. Consider the example in Figure 4.26. The two corporations served by the provider network have been assigned adjacent 20-bit network prefixes. Since both of the corporations are reachable through the same provider network, it can advertise a single route to both of them by just advertising the common 19-bit prefix they share. In general, it is possible to aggregate routes

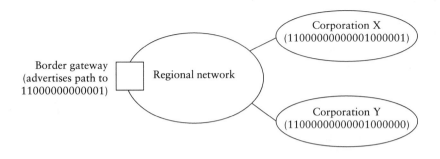

Figure 4.26 Route aggregation with CIDR.

repeatedly if addresses are assigned carefully. This means that we need to pay attention to which provider a corporation is attached to before assigning it an address if this scheme is to work. One way to accomplish that is to assign a portion of address space to the provider and then to let the network provider assign addresses from that space to its customers.

IP Forwarding Revisited

In all our discussion of IP forwarding so far, we have assumed that we could find the network number in a packet and then look up that number in a forwarding table. However, now that we have introduced CIDR, we need to reexamine this assumption. CIDR means that prefixes may be of any length, from 2 to 32 bits. Furthermore, it is sometimes possible to have prefixes in the forwarding table that "overlap," in the sense that some addresses may match more than one prefix. For example, we might find both 171.69 (a 16-bit prefix) and 171.69.10 (a 24-bit prefix) in the forwarding table of a single router. In this case, a packet destined to, say, 171.69.10.5 clearly matches both prefixes. The rule in this case is based on the principle of "longest match"; that is, the packet matches the longest prefix, which would be 171.69.10 in this example. On the other hand, a packet destined to 171.69.20.5 would match 171.69 and *not* 171.69.10, and in the absence of any other matching entry in the routing table, 171.69 would be the longest match.

The task of efficiently finding the longest match between an IP address and the variable-length prefixes in a forwarding table has been a fruitful field of research in recent years, and the Further Reading section of this chapter provides some references. The most well-known algorithm uses an approach known as a PATRICIA tree, which was actually developed well in advance of CIDR.

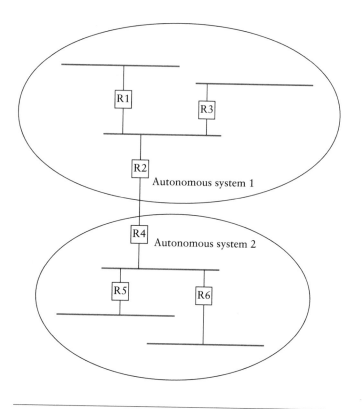

Figure 4.27 **A network with two autonomous systems.**

4.3.3 Interdomain Routing (BGP)

At the beginning of this section we introduced the notion that the Internet is organized as autonomous systems, each of which is under the control of a single administrative entity. A corporation's complex internal network might be a single AS, as may the network of a single Internet service provider. Figure 4.27 shows a simple network with two autonomous systems.

The basic idea behind autonomous systems is to provide an additional way to hierarchically aggregate routing information in a large internet, thus improving scalability. We now divide the routing problem into two parts: routing within a single autonomous system and routing between autonomous systems. Since another name for autonomous systems in the Internet is routing *domains*, we refer to the two parts of the routing problem as interdomain routing and intradomain routing. In addition to improving scalability, the AS model decouples the intradomain routing that takes place in one AS from that taking place in another. Thus, each AS can run whatever intradomain routing protocols it chooses. It can even use static routes or multiple protocols if desired. The interdomain routing problem is then one of having different ASs share reachability information with each other.

One feature of the autonomous system idea is that it enables some ASs to dramatically reduce the amount of routing information they need to care about by using *default routes*. For example, if a corporate network is connected to the rest of the Internet by a single router (this router is typically called a *border router* since it sits at the boundary between the AS and the rest of the Internet), then it is pretty easy for a host or router *inside* the autonomous system to figure out where it should send packets that are headed for a destination *outside* of this AS—they first go to the AS's border router. This is the default route. Similarly, a regional Internet service provider can keep track of how to reach the networks of all its directly connected customers and can have a default route to some other provider (typically a backbone provider) for everyone else. Of course, this passing of the buck has to stop at some point; eventually the packet should reach a router connected to a backbone network that knows how to reach everything. Managing the amount of routing information in the backbones is an important issue that we discuss below.

There have been two major interdomain routing protocols in the recent history of the Internet. The first was the Exterior Gateway Protocol (EGP). EGP had a number of limitations, perhaps the most severe of which was that it constrained the topology of the Internet rather significantly. EGP basically forced a treelike topology onto the Internet, or to be more precise, it was designed when the Internet had a treelike topology, such as that illustrated in Figure 4.23. EGP did not allow for the topology to become more general. Note that in this simple treelike structure, there is a single backbone, and autonomous systems are connected only as parents and children and not as peers.

The replacement for EGP is the Border Gateway Protocol (BGP), which is in its fourth version at the time of this writing (BGP-4). BGP is also known for being rather complex. This section presents the highlights of BGP-4.

As a starting position, BGP assumes that the Internet is an arbitrarily interconnected set of ASs. This model is clearly general enough to accommodate non-tree-structured internetworks, like the simplified picture of today's multibackbone Internet shown in Figure 4.28.[5]

Unlike the simple tree-structured Internet shown in Figure 4.23, today's Internet consists of an interconnection of multiple backbone networks (they are usually called

---

[5] In an interesting stretch of metaphor, the Internet now has multiple backbones, having had only one for most of its early life. The authors know of no other animal that has this characteristic.

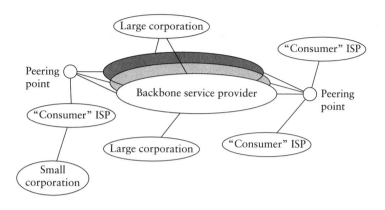

Figure 4.28 Today's multibackbone Internet.

service provider networks, and they are operated by private companies rather than the government), and sites are connected to each in arbitrary ways. Some large corporations connect directly to one or more of the backbones, while others connect to smaller, nonbackbone service providers. Many service providers exist mainly to provide service to "consumers" (i.e., individuals with PCs in their homes), and these providers must also connect to the backbone providers. Often many providers arrange to interconnect with each other at a single "peering point." In short, it is hard to discern much structure at all in today's Internet.

Given this rough sketch of the Internet, if we define *local traffic* as traffic that originates at or terminates on nodes within an AS, and *transit traffic* as traffic that passes through an AS, we can classify ASs into three types:

- *stub AS:* an AS that has only a single connection to one other AS; such an AS will only carry local traffic. The small corporation in Figure 4.28 is an example of a stub AS.

- *multihomed AS:* an AS that has connections to more than one other AS but that refuses to carry transit traffic; for example, the large corporation at the top of Figure 4.28.

- *transit AS:* an AS that has connections to more than one other AS and that is designed to carry both transit and local traffic, such as the backbone providers in Figure 4.28.

Whereas the discussion of routing in Section 4.2 focused on finding optimal paths based on minimizing some sort of link metric, the problem of interdomain routing turns out to be so difficult that the goals are more modest. First and foremost, the goal is to find *any* path to the intended destination that is loop-free. That is, we are more concerned with reachability than optimality. Finding a path that is anywhere close to optimal is considered a great achievement. We will see why this is so as we look at the details of BGP.

There are a few reasons why interdomain routing is hard. The first is simply a matter of scale. An Internet backbone router must be able to forward any packet destined anywhere in the Internet. That means having a routing table that will provide a match for any valid IP address. While CIDR has helped to control the number of distinct prefixes that are carried in the Internet's backbone routing, there is inevitably a lot of routing information to pass around—on the order of 50,000 prefixes at the time of writing.

The second challenge in interdomain routing arises from the autonomous nature of the domains. Note that each domain may run its own interior routing protocols, and use any scheme they choose to assign metrics to paths. This means that it is impossible to calculate meaningful path costs for a path that crosses multiple ASs. A cost of 1000 across one provider might imply a great path, but it might mean an unacceptably bad one from another provider. As a result, interdomain routing advertises only "reachability." The concept of reachability is basically a statement that "you can reach this network through this AS." This means that for interdomain routing to pick an optimal path is essentially impossible.

The third challenge involves the issue of trust. Provider A might be unwilling to believe certain advertisements from provider B for fear that provider B will advertise erroneous routing information. For example, trusting provider B when he advertises a great route to anywhere in the Internet can be a disasterous choice if provider B turns out to have made a mistake configuring his routers or to have insufficient capacity to carry the traffic.

Closely related to this issue is the need to support very flexible policies in interdomain routing. For example, provider A might wish to implement policies that say, "Use provider B only to reach these addresses," "Use the path that crosses the fewest number of ASs," or "Use AS *x* in preference to AS *y*." The goal is to specify policies that lead to "good" paths, if not to optimal ones.

When configuring BGP, the administrator of each AS picks at least one node to be a "BGP speaker," which is essentially a spokesperson for the entire AS. That BGP speaker establishes BGP sessions to other BGP speakers in other ASs. These sessions are used to exchange reachability information among ASs.

In addition to the BGP speakers, the AS has one or more border "gateways," which need not be the same as the speakers. The border gateways are the routers through which packets enter and leave the AS. In our simple example in Figure 4.27, routers R2 and R4 would be border gateways. Note that we have avoided using the

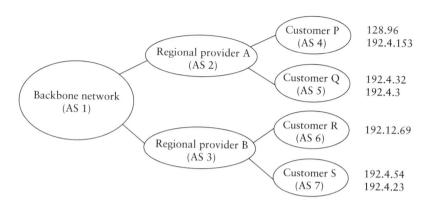

Figure 4.29 Example of a network running BGP.

word "gateway" until this point because it tends to be confusing. We can't avoid it here, given the name of the protocol we are describing. The important point to understand here is that, in the context of interdomain routing, a border gateway is simply an IP router that is charged with the task of forwarding packets between ASs.

BGP does not belong to either of the two main classes of routing protocols (distance-vector and link-state protocols) described in Section 4.2. Unlike these protocols, BGP advertises *complete paths* as an enumerated list of ASs to reach a particular network. This is necessary to enable the sorts of policy decisions described above to be made in accordance with the wishes of a particular AS. It also enables routing loops to be readily detected.

To see how this works, consider the example network in Figure 4.29. Assume that the providers are transit networks, while the customer networks are stubs. A BGP speaker for the AS of provider A (AS 2) would be able to advertise reachability information for each of the network numbers assigned to customers P and Q. Thus, it would say, in effect, "The networks 128.96, 192.4.153, 192.4.32, and 192.4.3 can be reached directly from AS 2." The backbone network, on receiving this advertisement, can advertise, "The networks 128.96, 192.4.153, 192.4.32, and 192.4.3 can be reached along the path ⟨AS 1, AS 2⟩." Similarly, it could advertise, "The networks 192.12.69, 192.4.54, and 192.4.23 can be reached along the path ⟨AS 1, AS 3⟩."

An important job of BGP is to prevent the establishment of looping paths. For example, consider three interconnected ASs, 1, 2, and 3. Suppose AS 1 learns that it can reach network 10.0.1 through AS 2, so it advertises this fact to AS 3, who in turn advertises it back to AS 2. AS 2 could now decide that AS 3 was the place to send packets destined for 10.0.1; AS 3 sends them to AS 1; AS 1 sends them back to

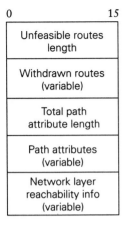

0   15

| Unfeasible routes length |
| Withdrawn routes (variable) |
| Total path attribute length |
| Path attributes (variable) |
| Network layer reachability info (variable) |

Figure 4.30   BGP-4 update packet format.

AS 2; and they would loop forever. This is prevented by carrying the complete AS path in the routing messages. In this case, the advertisement received by AS 2 from AS 3 would contain an AS path of ⟨AS 3, AS 1, AS 2⟩. AS 2 sees itself in this path, and thus concludes that this is not a useful path for it to use.

It should be apparent that the AS numbers carried in BGP need to be unique. For example, AS 2 can only recognize itself in the AS path in the above example if no other AS identifies itself in the same way. AS numbers are 16-bit numbers assigned by a central authority to assure uniqueness. While 16 bits only allows about 65,000 ASs, which might not seem like a lot, we note that stub ASs do not need a unique AS number, and this covers the overwhelming majority of nonprovider networks.

In addition to advertising paths, BGP speakers need to be able to cancel previously advertised paths if a critical link or node on a path goes down. This is done with a form of negative advertisement known as a *withdrawn route*. Both positive and negative reachability information are carried in a BGP update message, the format of which is shown in Figure 4.30. (Note that the fields in this figure are multiples of 16 bits, unlike other packet formats in this chapter.)

One point to note about BGP-4 is that it was designed to cope with the classless addresses described in Section 4.3.2. This means that the "networks" that are advertised in BGP are actually prefixes of any length. Thus, the updates contain both the prefix itself and its length in bits. When writing these down, it is common to write prefix/length. For example, a CIDR prefix that begins 192.4.16 and is 20 bits long would be written as 192.4.16/20.

We will not delve further into the details of BGP-4, except to point out that all the protocol does is specify how reachability information should be exchanged among autonomous systems. BGP speakers obtain enough information by this exchange to calculate loop-free routes to all reachable networks, but how they choose the "best" routes is largely left to the policies of the AS.

Let's return to the real question: How does all this help us to build scalable networks? First, the number of nodes participating in BGP is on the order of the number of ASs, which is much smaller than the number of networks. Second, finding a good interdomain route is only a matter of finding a path to the right border router, of which there are only a few per AS. Thus, we have neatly subdivided the routing problem into manageable parts, once again using a new level of hierarchy to increase scalability. The complexity of interdomain routing is now on the order of the number of ASs, and the complexity of intradomain routing is on the order of the number of networks in a single AS.

Integrating Interdomain and Intradomain Routing

While the preceding discussion illustrates how a BGP speaker learns interdomain routing information, the question still remains as to how all the other routers in a domain get this information. There are several ways this problem can be addressed.

We have already alluded to one very simple situation, which is also very common. In the case of a stub AS that only connects to other ASs at a single point, the border router is clearly the only choice for all routes that are outside the AS. Such a router can "inject" a default route into the intradomain routing protocol. In effect, this is a statement that any network that has not been explicitly advertised in the intradomain protocol is reachable through the border router. Recall from the discussion of IP forwarding in Section 4.1 that the default entry in the forwarding table comes after all the more specific entries, and it matches anything that failed to match a specific entry.

The next step up in complexity is to have the border routers inject specific routes they have learned from outside the AS. Consider, for example, the border router of a provider AS that connects to a customer AS. That router could learn that the network prefix 192.4.54/24 is located inside the customer AS, either through BGP or because the information is configured into the border router. It could inject a route to that prefix into the routing protocol running inside the provider AS. This would be an advertisement of the sort "I have a link to 192.4.54/24 of cost X." This would cause other routers in the provider AS to learn that this border router is the place to send packets destined for that prefix.

The final level of complexity comes in backbone networks, which learn so much routing information from BGP that it becomes too costly to inject it into the

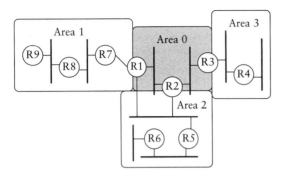

Figure 4.31 A domain divided into areas.

intradomain protocol. For example, if a border router wants to inject 10,000 prefixes that it learned about from another AS, it will have to send very big link-state packets to the other routers in that AS, and their shortest-path calculations are going to become very complex. For this reason, the routers in a backbone network use a variant of BGP called interior BGP (IBGP) to effectively redistribute the information that is learned by the BGP speakers at the edges of the AS to all the other routers in the AS. IBGP enables any router in the AS to learn the best border router to use when sending a packet to any address. At the same time, each router in the AS keeps track of how to get to each border router using a conventional intradomain protocol with no injected information. By combining these two sets of information, each router in the AS is able to determine the appropriate next hop for all prefixes.

4.3.4 Routing Areas

As if we didn't already have enough hierarchy, some link-state intradomain routing protocols—OSPF in particular—provide a means to partition a routing domain into subdomains called *areas*. By adding this extra level of hierarchy, we enable single domains to grow larger without overburdening the intradomain routing protocols.

An area is a set of routers that are administratively configured to exchange link-state information with each other. There is one special area—the backbone area, also known as area 0. An example of a routing domain divided into areas is shown in Figure 4.31. Routers R1, R2, and R3 are members of the backbone area. They are also members of at least one nonbackbone area; R1 is actually a member of both area 1 and area 2. A router that is a member of both the backbone area and a nonbackbone area is an area border router (ABR). Note that these are distinct from the routers that are at the edge of an AS, which are referred to as AS border routers for clarity.

Routing within a single area is exactly as described in Section 4.2.3. All the routers in the area send link-state advertisements to each other, and thus develop a complete, consistent map of the area. However, the link-state advertisements of routers that are not area border routers do not leave the area in which they originated. This has the effect of making the flooding and route calculation processes considerably more scalable. For example, router R4 in area 3 will never see a link-state advertisement from router R8 in area 1. As a consequence, it will know nothing about the detailed topology of areas other than its own.

How, then, does a router in one area determine the right next hop for a packet destined to a network in another area? The answer to this becomes clear if we imagine the path of a packet that has to travel from one nonbackbone area to another as being split into three parts. First, it travels from its source network to the backbone area, then it crosses the backbone, then it travels from backbone to destination network. To make this work, the area border routers summarize routing information that they have learned from one area and make it available in their advertisements to other areas. For example, R1 receives link-state advertisements from all the routers in area 1 and can thus determine the cost of reaching any network in area 1. When R1 sends link-state advertisements into area 0, it advertises the costs of reaching the networks in area 1 much as if all those networks were directly connected to R1. This enables all the area 0 routers to learn the cost to reach all networks in area 1. The area border routers then summarize this information and advertise it into the nonbackbone areas. Thus, all routers learn how to reach all networks in the domain.

Note that in the case of area 2, there are two ABRs, and that routers in area 2 will thus have to make a choice as to which one they use to reach the backbone. This is easy enough, since both R1 and R2 will be advertising costs to various networks, so that it will become clear which is the better choice as the routers in area 2 run their shortest-path algorithm. For example, it is pretty clear that R1 is going to be a better choice than R2 for destinations in area 1.

When dividing a domain into areas, the network administrator makes a trade-off between scalability and optimality of routing. The use of areas forces all packets traveling from one area to another to go via the backbone area, even if a shorter path might have been available. For example, even if R4 and R5 were directly connected, packets would not flow between them because they are in different nonbackbone areas. It turns out that the need for scalability is often more important than the need to use the absolute shortest path.

▶   This illustrates an important principle in network design. There is frequently a trade-off between some sort of optimality and scalability. When hierarchy is introduced, information is hidden from some nodes in the network, hindering their ability to make perfectly optimal decisions. However, information hiding is essential to scalability, since it saves all nodes from having global knowledge. It is invariably true in large networks that scalability is a more pressing design goal than perfect optimality.

Finally, we note that there is a trick by which network administrators can more flexibly decide which routers go in area 0. This trick uses the idea of a "virtual link" between routers. Such a virtual link is obtained by configuring a router that is not directly connected to area 0 to exchange backbone routing information with a router that is. For example, a virtual link could be configured from R8 to R1, thus making R8 part of the backbone. R8 would now participate in link-state advertisement flooding with the other routers in area 0. The cost of the virtual link from R8 to R1 is determined by the exchange of routing information that takes place in area 1. This technique can help to improve the optimality of routing.

4.3.5 IP version 6 (IPv6)

In many respects, the motivation for a new version of IP is the same as the motivation for the techniques described in the last section: to deal with scaling problems caused by the Internet's massive growth. Subnetting and CIDR have helped to contain the rate at which the Internet address space is being consumed (the address depletion problem) and have also helped to control the growth of routing table information needed in the Internet's routers (the routing information problem). However, there will come a point at which these techniques are no longer adequate. In particular, it is virtually impossible to achieve 100% address utilization efficiency, so the address space will be exhausted well before the 4 billionth host is connected to the Internet. Even if we were able to use all 4 billion addresses, it's not too hard to imagine ways that that number could be exhausted, such as the assignment of IP addresses to set-top boxes for cable TV or to electricity meters. All of these possibilities argue that a bigger address space than that provided by 32 bits will eventually be needed.

Historical Perspective

The IETF began looking at the problem of expanding the IP address space in 1991, and several alternatives were proposed. Since the IP address is carried in the header of every IP packet, increasing the size of the address dictates a change in the packet header. This means a new version of the Internet Protocol, and as a consequence, a need for new software for every host and router in the Internet. This is clearly not a trivial matter—it is a major change that needs to be thought about very carefully.

The effort to define a new version of IP was known as IP Next Generation, or IPng (the relevant IETF working groups still use this name). As the work progressed, an official IP version number was assigned, so IPng is now known as IPv6. Note that the version of IP discussed so far in this chapter is version 4 (IPv4). The apparent discontinuity in numbering is the result of version number 5 being used for an experimental protocol some years ago.

The significance of the change to a new version of IP caused a snowball effect. The general feeling among network designers was that if you are going to make a change of this magnitude, you might as well fix as many other things in IP as possible at the same time. Consequently, the IETF solicited white papers from anyone who cared to write one, asking for input on the features that might be desired in a new version of IP. In addition to the need to accommodate scalable routing and addressing, some of the other wish list items for IPng were

- support for real-time services

- security support

- autoconfiguration (i.e., the ability of hosts to automatically configure themselves with such information as their own IP address and domain name)

- enhanced routing functionality, including support for mobile hosts

It is interesting to note that while many of these features were absent from IPv4 at the time IPv6 was being designed, support for all of them has made its way into IPv4 in recent years.

In addition to the wish list, one absolutely nonnegotiable feature for IPng was that there must be a transition plan to move from the current version of IP (version 4) to the new version. With the Internet being so large and having no centralized control, it would be completely impossible to have a "flag day" on which everyone shut down their hosts and routers and installed a new version of IP. Thus, there will probably be a long transition period in which some hosts and routers will run IPv4 only, some will run IPv4 and IPv6, and some will run IPv6 only.

The IETF appointed a committee called the IPng Directorate to collect all the inputs on IPng requirements and to evaluate proposals for a protocol to become IPng. Over the life of this committee there were a number of proposals, some of which merged with other proposals, and eventually one was chosen by the Directorate to be the basis for IPng. That proposal was called SIPP (Simple Internet Protocol Plus). SIPP originally called for a doubling of the IP address size to 64 bits. When the Directorate selected SIPP, they stipulated several changes, one of which was another doubling of the address to 128 bits (16 bytes). It was around this time that the version number 6 was assigned. The rest of this section describes some of the main features of IPv6. At the time of this writing, most of the key specifications for IPv6 are Proposed or Draft Standards in the IETF.

Addresses and Routing

First and foremost, IPv6 provides a 128-bit address space, as opposed to the 32 bits of version 4. Thus, while version 4 can potentially address 4 billion nodes if address assignment efficiency reaches 100%, IPv6 can address 3.4×10^{38} nodes, again assuming 100% efficiency. As we have seen, though, 100% efficiency in address assignment is not likely. Some analysis of other addressing schemes, such as those of the French and U.S. telephone networks, as well as that of IPv4, have turned up some empirical numbers for address assignment efficiency. Based on the most pessimistic estimates of efficiency drawn from this study, the IPv6 address space is predicted to provide over 1500 addresses per square foot of the earth's surface, which certainly seems like it should serve us well even when toasters on Venus have IP addresses.

Address Space Allocation

IPv6 addresses do not have classes, but the address space is still subdivided in various ways based on the leading bits. Rather than specifying different address classes, the leading bits specify different uses of the IPv6 address. The current assignment of prefixes is listed in Table 4.11.

This allocation of the address space turns out to be easier to explain than it looks. First, the entire functionality of IPv4's three main address classes (A, B, and C) is contained inside the 001 prefix. Aggregatable Global Unicast Addresses, as we will see shortly, are a lot like classless IPv4 addresses, only much longer. These are the main ones of interest at this point, with one-eighth of the address space allocated to this important form of address. Obviously, large chunks of address space have been left unassigned to allow for future growth and new features. Two portions of the address space (0000 001 and 0000 010) have been reserved for encoding of other (non-IP) address schemes. NSAP addresses are used by the ISO protocols, and IPX addresses are used by Novell's network-layer protocol.

The idea behind "link local use" addresses is to enable a host to construct an address that will work on the network to which it is connected without being concerned about global uniqueness of the address. This may be useful for autoconfiguration, as we will see below. Similarly, the "site local use" addresses are intended to allow valid addresses to be constructed on a site (e.g., a private corporate network) that is not connected to the larger Internet; again, global uniqueness need not be an issue.

Finally, the multicast address space is for multicast, thereby serving the same role as class D addresses in IPv4. Note that multicast addresses are easy to distinguish—they start with a byte of all 1s. We will see how these addresses are used in Section 4.4.

Within the reserved address space (addresses beginning with a byte of 0s) are some important special types of addresses. A node may be assigned an "IPv4-compatible IPv6 address" by zero-extending a 32-bit IPv4 address to 128 bits. A node that is only capable of understanding IPv4 can be assigned an "IPv4-mapped IPv6 address" by prefixing the 32-bit IPv4 address with 2 bytes of all 1s and then

Prefix	Use
0000 0000	Reserved
0000 0001	Unassigned
0000 001	Reserved for NSAP allocation
0000 010	Reserved for IPX allocation
0000 011	Unassigned
0000 1	Unassigned
0001	Unassigned
001	Aggregatable Global Unicast Addresses
010	Unassigned
011	Unassigned
100	Unassigned
101	Unassigned
110	Unassigned
1110	Unassigned
1111 0	Unassigned
1111 10	Unassigned
1111 110	Unassigned
1111 1110 0	Unassigned
1111 1110 10	Link local use addresses
1111 1110 11	Site local use addresses
1111 1111	Multicast addresses

Table 4.11 Address prefix assignments for IPv6.

zero-extending the result to 128 bits. These two special address types have uses in the IPv4-to-IPv6 transition (see the sidebar on this topic).

Address Notation

Just as with IPv4, there is some special notation for writing down IPv6 addresses. The standard representation is x:x:x:x:x:x:x:x where each "x" is a hexadecimal representation of a 16-bit piece of the address. An example would be

```
47CD:1234:4422:AC02:0022:1234:A456:0124
```

Any IPv6 address can be written using this notation. Since there are a few special types of IPv6 addresses, there are some special notations that may be helpful in certain circumstances. For example, an address with a large number of contiguous 0s can be written more compactly by omitting all the 0 fields. Thus

```
47CD:0000:0000:0000:0000:0000:A456:0124
```

could be written

```
47CD::A456:0124
```

Clearly, this form of shorthand can only be used for one set of contiguous 0s in an address to avoid ambiguity.

Since there are two types of IPv6 addresses that contain an embedded IPv4 address, these have their own special notation that makes extraction of the IPv4 address easier. For example, the "IPv4-mapped IPv6 address" of a host whose IPv4 address was 128.96.33.81 could be written as

```
::00FF:128.96.33.81
```

Transition from IPv4 to IPv6

The most important idea behind the transition from IPv4 to IPv6 is that the Internet is far too big and decentralized to have a "flag day"—one specified day on which every host and router is upgraded from IPv4 to IPv6. Thus, IPv6 needs to be deployed incrementally in such a way that hosts and routers that only understand IPv4 can continue to function for as long as possible. Ideally, IPv4 nodes should be able to talk to other IPv4 nodes and some set of other IPv6-capable nodes indefinitely. Also, IPv6 hosts should be capable of talking to other IPv6 nodes even when some of the infrastructure between them may only support IPv4. Two major mechanisms have been defined to help this transition: *dual-stack operation* and *tunneling*.

The idea of dual stacks is fairly straightforward: IPv6 nodes run both IPv6 and IPv4 and use the Version field to decide which stack should process an arriving packet. In this case, the IPv6 address could be unrelated to the IPv4 address, or it could be the "IPv4-mapped IPv6 address" described earlier in this section.

The basic tunneling technique, in which an IP packet is sent as the *payload* of another IP packet, was described in Section 4.1. For IPv6 transition, tunneling is used to send an IPv6 packet over a piece of the network that only understands IPv4. This means that the IPv6 packet is encapsulated within an IPv4 header that has the address of the tunnel endpoint in its header, is transmitted across the IPv4-only piece of network, and then is decapsulated at the endpoint. The endpoint could be either a router or a host; in either case, it must be IPv6-capable to be able to process the IPv6 packet after decapsulation. If the endpoint is a host with an IPv4-mapped IPv6 address, then tunneling can be done automatically, by extracting the IPv4 address from the IPv6 address and using it to form the IPv4 header. Otherwise, the tunnel must be configured manually. In this case, the encapsulating node needs to know the IPv4 address of the other end of the tunnel, since it cannot be extracted from the IPv6 header. From the perspective of IPv6, the other end of the tunnel looks like a regular IPv6 node that is just one hop away, even though there may be many hops of IPv4 infrastructure between the tunnel endpoints.

That is, the last 32 bits are written in IPv4 notation, rather than as a pair of hexadecimal numbers separated by a colon. Note that the double colon at the front indicates the leading 0s.

Aggregatable Global Unicast Addresses

By far the most important thing that IPv6 must provide when it is deployed is plain old unicast addressing. It must do this in a way that supports the rapid rate of addition of new hosts to the Internet and that allows routing to be done in a scalable way as the number of physical networks in the Internet grows. Thus, at the heart of IPv6 is the unicast address allocation plan that determines how addresses beginning with the 001 prefix will be assigned to service providers, autonomous systems, networks, hosts, and routers.

In fact, the address allocation plan that is proposed for IPv6 unicast addresses is extremely similar to that being deployed with CIDR in IPv4. To understand how it works and how it provides scalability, it is helpful to define some new terms. We may think of a nontransit AS (i.e., a stub or multihomed AS) as a *subscriber,* and we may think of a transit AS as a *provider.* Furthermore, we may subdivide providers into *direct* and *indirect.* The former are directly connected to subscribers. The latter primarily connect other providers, are not connected directly to subscribers, and are often known as *backbone networks.*

With this set of definitions, we can see that the Internet is not just an arbitrarily interconnected set of ASs; it has some intrinsic hierarchy. The difficulty is in making use of this hierarchy without inventing mechanisms that fail when the hierarchy is not strictly observed, as happened with EGP. For example, the distinction between direct and indirect providers becomes blurred when a subscriber connects to a backbone or when a direct provider starts connecting to many other providers.

As with CIDR, the goal of the IPv6 address allocation plan is to provide aggregation of routing information to reduce the burden on intradomain routers. Again, the key idea is to use an address prefix—a set of contiguous bits at the most significant end of the address—to aggregate reachability information to a large number of networks and even to a large number of ASs. The main way to achieve this is to assign an address prefix to a direct provider and then for that direct provider to assign longer prefixes that begin with that prefix to its subscribers. This is exactly what we observed in Figure 4.26. Thus, a provider can advertise a single prefix for all of its subscribers.

Of course, the drawback is that if a site decides to change providers, it will need to obtain a new address prefix and renumber all the nodes in the site. This could be a colossal undertaking, enough to dissuade most people from ever changing providers. For this reason, there is ongoing research on other addressing schemes, such as geographic addressing, in which a site's address is a function of its location rather than the provider to which it attaches. At present, however, provider-based addressing is necessary to make routing work efficiently.

Note that while IPv6 address assignment is essentially equivalent to the way address assignment has happened in IPv4 since the introduction of CIDR, IPv6 has the significant advantage of not having a large installed base of assigned address to fit into its plans.

One question is whether it makes sense for hierarchical aggregation to take place at other levels in the hierarchy. For example, should all providers obtain their address prefixes from within a prefix allocated to the backbone to which they connect? Given that most providers connect to multiple backbones, this probably doesn't make sense. Also, since the number of providers is much smaller than the number of sites, the benefits of aggregating at this level are much less.

One place where aggregation may make sense is at the national or continental level. Continental boundaries form natural divisions in the Internet topology, and if all addresses in Europe, for example, had a common prefix, then a great deal of aggregation could be done, so that most routers in other continents would only need one routing table entry for all networks with the Europe prefix. Providers in Europe would all select their prefixes such that they began with the European prefix. Using this scheme, an IPv6 address might look like Figure 4.32. The RegistryID might be an identifier assigned to a European address registry, with different IDs assigned to other continents or countries. Note that prefixes would be of different lengths under this

3	m	n	o	p	125–m–n–o–p
010	RegistryID	ProviderID	SubscriberID	SubnetID	InterfaceID

Figure 4.32 An IPv6 provider-based unicast address.

scenario. For example, a provider with few customers could have a longer prefix (and thus less total address space available) than one with many customers.

One tricky situation could occur when a subscriber is connected to more than one provider. Which prefix should the subscriber use for his or her site? There is no perfect solution to the problem. For example, suppose a subscriber is connected to two providers X and Y. If the subscriber takes his prefix from X, then Y has to advertise a prefix that has no relationship to its other subscribers and that as a consequence cannot be aggregated. If the subscriber numbers part of his AS with the prefix of X and part with the prefix of Y, he runs the risk of having half his site become unreachable if the connection to one provider goes down. One solution that works fairly well if X and Y have a lot of subscribers in common is for them to have three prefixes between them: one for subscribers of X only, one for subscribers of Y only, and one for the sites that are subscribers of both X and Y.

Packet Format

Despite the fact that IPv6 extends IPv4 in several ways, its header format is actually simpler. This simplicity is due to a concerted effort to remove unnecessary functionality from the protocol. Figure 4.33 shows the result. (For comparison with IPv4, see the header format shown in Figure 4.3.)

As with many headers, this one starts with a Version field, which is set to 6 for IPv6. The Version field is in the same place relative to the start of the header as IPv4's Version field so that header-processing software can immediately decide which header format to look for. The TrafficClass and FlowLabel fields both relate to quality of service issues, as discussed in Section 6.5.

The PayloadLen field gives the length of the packet, excluding the IPv6 header, measured in bytes. The NextHeader field cleverly replaces both the IP options and the Protocol field of IPv4. If options are required, then they are carried in one or more special headers following the IP header, and this is indicated by the value of the NextHeader field. If there are no special headers, the NextHeader field is the demux key identifying the higher-level protocol running over IP (e.g., TCP or UDP); that is, it serves the same purpose as the IPv4 Protocol field. Also, fragmentation is now handled

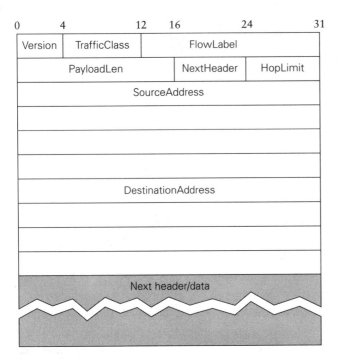

Figure 4.33 IPv6 packet header.

as an optional header, which means that the fragmentation-related fields of IPv4 are not included in the IPv6 header. The HopLimit field is simply the TTL of IPv4, renamed to reflect the way it is actually used.

Finally, the bulk of the header is taken up with the source and destination addresses, each of which is 16 bytes (128 bits) long. Thus, the IPv6 header is always 40 bytes long. Considering that IPv6 addresses are four times longer than those of IPv4, this compares quite well with the IPv4 header, which is 20 bytes long in the absence of options.

The way that IPv6 handles options is quite an improvement over IPv4. In IPv4, if any options were present, every router had to parse the entire options field to see if any of the options were relevant. This is because the options were all buried at the end of the IP header, as an unordered collection of ⟨type, length, value⟩ tuples. In contrast, IPv6 treats options as *extension headers* that must, if present, appear in a specific order. This means that each router can quickly determine if any of the options are relevant to it; in most cases, they will not be. Usually this can be determined by just looking at the NextHeader field. The end result is that option processing is much more

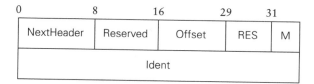

0   8   16   29   31

| NextHeader | Reserved | Offset | RES | M |

| Ident |

Figure 4.34   IPv6 fragmentation extension header.

efficient in IPv6, which is an important factor in router performance. In addition, the new formatting of options as extension headers means that they can be of arbitrary length, whereas in IPv4 they were limited to 44 bytes at most. We will see how some of the options are used below.

Each option has its own type of extension header. The type of each extension header is identified by the value of the NextHeader field in the header that precedes it, and each extension header contains a NextHeader field to identify the header following it. The last extension header will be followed by a transport-layer header (e.g., TCP) and in this case the value of the NextHeader field is the same as the value of the Protocol field would be in an IPv4 header. Thus, the NextHeader field does double duty; it may either identify the type of extension header to follow, or, in the last extension header, it serves as a demux key to identify the higher-layer protocol running over IPv6.

Consider the example of the fragmentation header, shown in Figure 4.34. This header provides functionality similar to the fragmentation fields in the IPv4 header described in Section 4.1.2, but it is only present if fragmentation is necessary. Assuming it is the only extension header present, then the NextHeader field of the IPv6 header would contain the value 44, which is the value assigned to indicate the fragmentation header. The NextHeader field of the fragmentation header itself contains a value describing the header that follows it. Again, assuming no other extension headers are present, then the next header might be the TCP header, which results in NextHeader containing the value 6, just as the Protocol field would in IPv4. If the fragmentation header were followed by, say, an authentication header, then the fragmentation header's NextHeader field would contain the value 51.

Autoconfiguration

While the Internet's growth has been impressive, one factor that has inhibited faster acceptance of the technology is the fact that getting connected to the Internet has typically required a fair amount of system administration expertise. In particular, every host that is connected to the Internet needs to be configured with a certain minimum amount of information, such as a valid IP address, a subnet mask for the link to which it attaches, and the address of a name server. Thus, it has not been possible to unpack a new computer and connect it to the Internet without some preconfiguration. One goal of IPv6, therefore, is to provide support for autoconfiguration, sometimes referred to as "plug-and-play" operation.

As we saw in Section 4.1.6, autoconfiguration is possible for IPv4, but it depends on the existence of a server that is configured to hand out addresses and other configuration information to DHCP clients. The longer address format in IPv6 helps provide a useful, new form of autoconfiguration called *stateless* autoconfiguration, which does not require a server.

Recall that IPv6 unicast addresses are hierarchical, and that the least significant portion is the interface ID. Thus, we can subdivide the autoconfiguration problem into two parts:

1 Obtain an interface ID that is unique on the link to which the host is attached.

2 Obtain the correct address prefix for this subnet.

The first part turns out to be rather easy, since every host on a link must have a unique link-level address. For example, all hosts on an Ethernet have a unique 48-bit Ethernet address. This can be turned into a valid link local use address by adding the appropriate prefix from Table 4.11 (1111 1110 10) followed by enough 0s to make up 128 bits. For some devices—for example, printers or hosts on a small routerless network that do not connect to any other

Network Address Translation

While IPv6 was motivated by a concern that increased usage of IP would lead to exhaustion of the address space, another technology has become popular as a way to conserve IP address space. That technology is network address translation (NAT), and it is possible that its widespread use will significantly delay the need to deploy IPv6. NAT is often viewed as "architecturally impure," but it is also a fact of networking life that cannot be ignored.

The basic idea behind NAT is that all the hosts that might communicate with each other over the Internet do not need to have globally unique addresses. Instead, a host could be assigned a "private address" that is not necessarily globally unique, but is unique within some more limited scope; for example, within the corporate network where the host resides. The class A network number 10 is often used for this purpose, since that network number was assigned to the ARPANET and is no longer in use as a globally unique address. As long as the host communicates only with other hosts in the corporate network, a locally unique address is sufficient. If it should want to communicate with a host

networks—this address may be perfectly adequate. Those devices that need a globally valid address depend on a router on the same link to periodically advertise the appropriate prefix for the link. Clearly, this requires that the router be configured with the correct address prefix, and that this prefix be chosen in such a way that there is enough space at the end (e.g., 48 bits) to attach an appropriate link-level address.

The ability to embed link-level addresses as long as 48 bits into IPv6 addresses was one of the reasons for choosing such a large address size. Not only does 128 bits allow the embedding, but it leaves plenty of space for the multilevel hierarchy of addressing that we discussed above.

Advanced Routing Capabilities

Another of IPv6's extension headers is the routing header. In the absence of this header, routing for IPv6 differs very little from that of IPv4 under CIDR. The routing header contains a list of IPv6 addresses that represent nodes or topological areas that the packet should visit en route to its destination. A topological area may be, for example, a backbone provider's network. Specifying that packets must visit this network would be a way of implementing provider selection on a packet-by-packet basis. Thus, a host could say that it wants some packets to go through a provider that is cheap, others through a provider that provides high reliability, and still others through a provider that the host trusts to provide security.

To provide the ability to specify topological entities rather than individual nodes, IPv6 defines an *anycast* address. An anycast

outside the corporate network, it does so via a "NAT box"—a device that is able to translate from the private address used by the host to some globally unique address that is assigned to the NAT box. Since it's likely that a small subset of the hosts in the corporation need the services of the NAT box at any one time, the NAT box might be able to get by with a small pool of globally unique addresses, much smaller than the number of addresses that would be needed if every host in the corporation had a globally unique address.

So, we can imagine a NAT box receiving IP packets from a host inside the corporation and translating the IP source address from some private address (say, 10.0.1.5) to a globally unique address (say, 171.69.210.246). When packets come back from the remote host addressed to 171.69.210.246, the NAT box translates the destination address to 10.0.1.5 and forwards the packet on toward the host.

The chief drawback of NAT is that it breaks a key assumption of the IP service model—that all nodes have globally unique addresses. It turns out that lots of applications and protocols rely on

address is assigned to a set of interfaces, and packets sent to that address will go to the "nearest" of those interfaces, with nearest being determined by the routing protocols. For example, all the routers of a backbone provider could be assigned a single anycast address, which would be used in the routing header.

The anycast address and the routing header are also expected to be used to provide enhanced routing support to mobile hosts. The detailed mechanisms for providing this support are still being defined.

Other Features

As mentioned at the beginning of this section, the primary motivation behind the development of IPv6 was to support the continued growth of the Internet. Once the IP header had to be changed for the sake of the addresses, however, the door was open for a wide variety of other changes, two of which we have just described—autoconfiguration and source-directed routing. These are among the more minor features introduced into IP, though. IPv6 includes several additional features, most of which are covered elsewhere in this book—multicast is discussed in Section 4.4, network security is the topic of Chapter 8, and a new service model proposed for the Internet is described in Section 6.5.

this assumption. In particular, many protocols that run over IP (e.g., application protocols) carry IP addresses in their messages. These addresses also need to be translated by a NAT box if the higher-layer protocol is to work properly, and thus NAT boxes become much more complex than simple IP header translators. They potentially need to understand an ever-growing number of higher-layer protocols. This in turn presents an obstacle to deployment of new applications. It is probably safe to say that networks would be better off without NAT, but its disappearance seems unlikely. Widespread deployment of IPv6 would almost certainly help.

4.4 Multicast

As we saw in Chapter 2, multiaccess networks like Ethernet and token rings implement multicast in hardware. This section describes how to extend multicast, in software, across an internetwork of such networks. The approach described in this section is based on an implementation of multicast used in the current Internet (IPv4). Multicast will also be supported in the next generation of IP (IPv6), with the major differences being restricted to the address format.

The motivation for developing multicast is that there are applications that want to send a packet to more than one destination host. Instead of forcing the source host to send a separate packet to each of the destination hosts, we want the source to be able to send a single packet to a *multicast address*, and for the network—or internet, in this case—to deliver a copy of that packet to each of a group of hosts. Hosts can then choose to join or leave this group at will, without synchronizing or negotiating with other members of the group. Also, a host may belong to more than one group at a time.

Internet multicast can be implemented on top of a collection of networks that support hardware multicast (or broadcast) by extending the routing and forwarding functions implemented by the routers that connect these networks. This section describes three such extensions: the first is based on distance-vector routing as described in Section 4.2.2; the second is based on link-state routing described in Section 4.2.3; the third can build on any underlying routing protocol and is thus called Protocol Independent Multicast (PIM).

Before looking at any of the multicast routing protocols, however, we need to look at the service model for IP multicast. We could imagine that a host wishing to send a packet to some number of internet hosts could enumerate all their addresses, but this would quickly become unscalable for large numbers of receivers—consider using the Internet to distribute a pay-per-view movie, for example. For this reason, IP multicast uses the idea of a *multicast group* that receivers may join. Each group has a specially assigned address, and senders to the group use that address as the destination address for their packets. In IPv4, these addresses are assigned in the class D address space, and IPv6 also has a portion of its address space reserved for multicast group addresses.

Hosts join multicast groups using a protocol called Internet Group Management Protocol (IGMP). They use this to notify a router on their local network of their desire to receive packets sent to a certain multicast group. The protocols described below are concerned with how packets are distributed to the appropriate routers. Delivery of packets from the "last hop" router to the host is handled by the underlying multicast capability of the network, as described in Section 2.6.

One perplexing question is how senders and receivers learn about multicast addresses. This is normally handled by out-of-band means, and there are some quite sophisticated tools to enable group addresses to be advertised on the Internet.

4.4.1 Link-State Multicast

Adding multicast to a link-state routing algorithm is fairly straightforward, so we describe it first. Recall that in link-state routing, each router monitors the state of its directly connected links and sends an update message to all of the other routers whenever the state changes. Since each router receives enough information to reconstruct the entire topology of the network, it is able to use Dijkstra's algorithm to compute

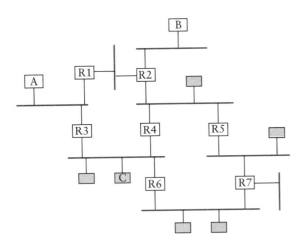

Figure 4.35 Example internet with members of group G shaded.

the shortest-path spanning tree rooted at itself and reaching all possible destinations. The router uses this tree to determine the best next hop for each packet it forwards.

All we have to do to extend this algorithm to support multicast is to add the set of groups that have members on a particular link (LAN) to the "state" for that link. The only question is how each router determines which groups have members on which links. As suggested in Section 3.2.3, the solution is to have each host periodically announce to the LAN the groups to which it belongs. The router simply monitors the LAN for such announcements. Should such announcements stop arriving after a period of time, the router then assumes that the host has left the group.

Given full knowledge of which groups have members on which links, each router is able to compute the *shortest-path multicast tree* from any source to any group, again using Dijkstra's algorithm. For example, given the internet illustrated in Figure 4.35, where the shaded hosts belong to group G, the routers would compute the shortest-path multicast trees given in Figure 4.36 for sources A, B, and C. The routers would use these trees to decide how to forward packets addressed to multicast group G. For example, router R3 would forward a packet going from host A to group G to R6.

Keep in mind that each router must potentially keep a separate shortest-path multicast tree from every source to every group. This is obviously very expensive, so instead the router just computes and stores a cache of these trees—one for each source/group pair that is currently active.

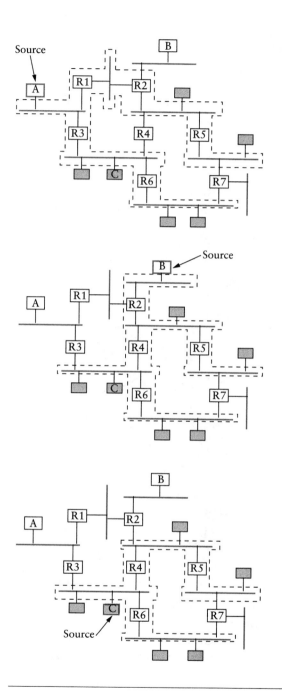

Figure 4.36   Example shortest-path multicast trees.

4.4.2 Distance-Vector Multicast

Adding multicast to the distance-vector algorithm is a bit trickier because the routers do not know the entire topology of the internet. Instead, recall that each router maintains a table of ⟨ Destination, Cost, NextHop ⟩ tuples, and exchanges a list of ⟨ Dest-ination, Cost ⟩ pairs with its directly connected neighbors. Extending this algorithm to support multicast is a two-stage process. First, we need to design a broadcast mechanism that allows a packet to be forwarded to all the networks on the internet. Second, we need to refine this mechanism so that it prunes back networks that do not have hosts that belong to the multicast group.

Reverse-Path Broadcast (RPB)

Each router knows that the current short-est path to a given destination goes through NextHop. Thus, whenever it receives a mul-ticast packet from source S, the router for-wards the packet on all outgoing links (ex-cept the one on which the packet arrived) if and only if the packet arrived over the link that is on the shortest path to S (i.e., the packet came *from* the NextHop associated with S in the routing table). This strategy ef-fectively floods packets outward from S, but does not loop packets back toward S.

> **The MBone**
>
> While multicast is not, at the time of writing, supported by many of the routers in the Internet, wide area multicast is made available via the MBone—multicast backbone. The MBone is a logical internet layered over the top of the current Internet. It uses class D addresses and tunneling. That is, multicast-enhanced routers are connected to each other via IP tunnels of the sort described in Section 4.1.8. Any regular   (non-multicast-capable) routers between two multicast-enhanced routers see only unicast IP   packets destined for the multicast-capable   routers,   and hence they never have to worry about multicast addresses or multi-cast routing.   Meanwhile, the multicast-capable routers can be-

There are two major shortcomings to this approach. The first is that it truly floods the network; it has no provision for avoid-ing LANs that have no members in the multicast group. We address this problem in the next subsection. The second limitation is that a given packet will be forwarded over a LAN by each of the routers connected to that LAN. This is due to the forwarding strategy of flooding packets on all links other than the one on which the packet arrived, without regard to whether or not those links are part of the shortest-path tree rooted at the source.

The solution to this second limitation is to eliminate the duplicate broadcast packets that are generated when more than one router is connected to a given LAN. One way to do this is to designate one router as the "parent" router for each link, relative to the source, where only the parent router is allowed to forward multicast packets from that source over the LAN. The router that has the shortest path to source S is selected as the parent; a tie between two routers would be broken according to which router has the smallest address. A given router can learn if it is the parent for the LAN (again relative to each possible source) based upon the distance-vector messages it exchanges with its neighbors.

Notice that this refinement requires that each router keep, for each source, a bit for each of its incident links indicating whether or not it is the parent for that source/link pair. Keep in mind that in an internet setting, a "source" is a network, not a host, since an internet router is only interested in forwarding packets between networks. The resulting mechanism is sometimes called reverse-path broadcast (RPB).

have as if they are connected by point-to-point links to each other. The majority of these routers use the Distance Vector Multicast Routing Protocol (DVMRP).

Like the regular Internet, the MBone has experienced exponential growth and now contains thousands of networks on at least four continents. It is used as a testbed for various applications that want to exploit its multicast capabilities.

One of the most popular applications is vic, a tool that supports multiparty videoconferencing. vic is used to broadcast both seminars and meetings across the Internet. In fact, IETF meetings—which are a week long and attract thousands of participants—are generally broadcast over the MBone.

Reverse-Path Multicast (RPM)

RPB implements shortest-path broadcast. We now want to prune the set of networks that receives each packet addressed to group G to exclude those that have no hosts that are members of G. This can be accomplished in two stages. First, we need to recognize when a *leaf* network has no group members. Determining that a network is a leaf is easy—if the parent router as described in RPB is the only router on the network, then the network is a leaf. Determining if any group members reside on the network is accomplished by having each host that is a member of group G periodically announce this fact over the network, as described in our earlier description of link-state multicast. The router then uses this information to decide whether or not to forward a multicast packet addressed to G over this LAN.

The second stage is to propagate this "no members of G here" information up the shortest-path tree. This is done by having the router augment the ⟨ Destination, Cost ⟩ pairs it sends to its neighbors with the set of groups for which the leaf network is interested in receiving multicast packets. This information can then be propagated from router to router, so that for each of its links, a given router knows for what groups it should forward multicast packets.

Note that including all of this information in the routing update is a fairly expensive thing to do. In practice, therefore, this information is exchanged only when some source starts sending packets to that group. In other words, the strategy is to use RPB, which adds a small amount of overhead to the basic distance-vector algorithm, until a particular multicast address becomes active. At that time, routers that are not interested in receiving packets addressed to that group speak up, and that information is propagated to the other routers.

4.4.3 Protocol Independent Multicast (PIM)

PIM was developed in response to the scaling problems of existing multicast routing protocols. In particular, it was recognized that the existing protocols did not scale well in environments where a relatively small proportion of routers want to receive traffic for a certain group. For example, broadcasting traffic to all routers until they explicitly ask to be removed from the distribution is not a good design choice if most routers don't want to receive the traffic in the first place. This situation is sufficiently common that PIM divides the problem space into "sparse mode" and "dense mode." Because the existing protocols were so poorly suited to the sparse environment, PIM sparse mode has received the most attention and is the focus of our discussion here.

In PIM sparse mode (PIM-SM), routers explicitly join and leave the multicast group using PIM protocol messages known as Join and Prune messages. The question that arises is where to send those messages. To address this, PIM assigns a *rendezvous point* (RP) to each group. In general, a number of routers in a domain are configured to be candidate RPs, and PIM defines a set of procedures by which all the routers in a domain can agree on the router to use as the RP for a given group. These procedures are rather complex, as they must deal with a wide variety of scenarios, such as the failure of a candidate RP and the partitioning of a domain into two separate networks due to a number of link or node failures. For the rest of this discussion, we assume that all routers in a domain know the unicast IP address of the RP for a given group.

A multicast forwarding tree is built as a result of routers sending Join messages to the RP. PIM-SM allows two types of tree to be constructed: a *shared* tree, which may be used by all senders, and a *source-specific* tree, which may be used only by a specific sending host. The normal mode of operation creates the shared tree first, followed by one or more source-specific trees if there is enough traffic to warrant it. Because building trees installs state in the routers along the tree, it is important that the default is to have only one tree for a group, not one for every sender to a group.

When a router sends a Join message toward the RP for a group G, it is sent using normal IP unicast transmission. This is illustrated in Figure 4.37(a), in which

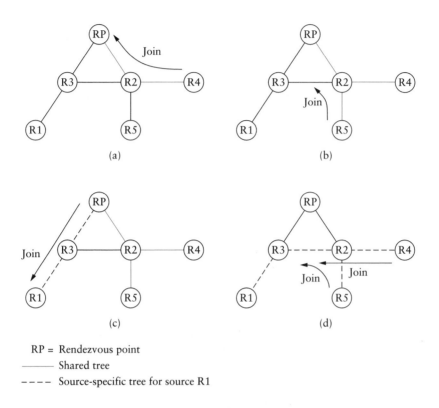

RP = Rendezvous point
——— Shared tree
- - - - Source-specific tree for source R1

Figure 4.37 PIM operation. (a) R4 sends Join to RP and joins shared tree; (b) R5 joins shared tree; (c) RP builds source-specific tree to R1 by sending Join to R1; (d) R4 and R5 build source-specific tree to R1 by sending Joins to R1.

router R4 is sending a Join to the rendezvous point for some group. The initial Join message is "wildcarded"; that is, it applies to all senders. A Join message clearly must pass through some sequence of routers before reaching the RP (e.g., R2). Each router along the path looks at the Join and creates a forwarding table entry for the shared tree, called a (*, G) entry (* meaning "all senders"). To create the forwarding table entry, it looks at the interface on which the Join arrived and marks that interface as one on which it should forward data packets for this group. It then determines which interface it will use to forward the Join toward the RP. This will be the only acceptable interface for incoming packets sent to this group. It then forwards the Join toward the RP. Eventually, the message arrives at the RP, completing the construction of the tree branch. The shared tree thus constructed is shown as a solid line from the RP to R4 in Figure 4.37(a).

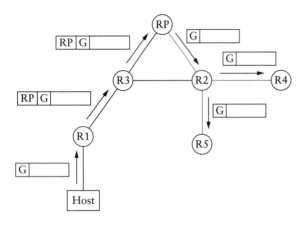

Figure 4.38 Delivery of a packet along a shared tree. R1 tunnels the packet to the RP, which forwards it along the shared tree to R4 and R5.

As more routers send Joins toward the RP, they cause new branches to be added to the tree, as illustrated in Figure 4.37(b). Note that in this case, the Join only needs to travel to R2, which can add the new branch to the tree simply by adding a new outgoing interface to the forwarding table entry created for this group. R2 need not forward the Join on to the RP. Note also that the end result of this process is to build a tree whose root is the RP.

At this point, suppose a host wishes to send a message to the group. To do so, it constructs a packet with the appropriate multicast group address as its destination and sends it to a router on its local network known as the *designated router* (DR). Suppose the DR is R1 in Figure 4.37. There is no state for this multicast group between R1 and the RP at this point, so instead of simply forwarding the multicast packet, R1 "tunnels" it to the RP. That is, R1 encapsulates the multicast packet inside a unicast IP packet that it sends to the unicast IP address of the RP. Just like a tunnel endpoint of the sort described in Section 4.1.8, the RP receives the packet addressed to it, looks at the payload of the unicast packet, and finds inside an IP packet addressed to the multicast address of this group. The RP, of course, does know what to do with such a packet—it sends it out onto the shared tree of which the RP is the root. In the example of Figure 4.37, this means that the RP sends the packet on to R2, which is able to forward it on to R4 and R5. The complete delivery of a packet from R1 to R4 and R5 is shown in Figure 4.38. We see the tunneled packet travel from R1 to the RP with an extra IP header containing the unicast address of RP, and then the multicast packet addressed to G making its way along the shared tree to R4 and R5.

At this point, we might be tempted to declare success, since all hosts can send to all receivers this way. However, there is some bandwidth inefficiency and processing cost in the encapsulation and decapsulation of packets on the way to the RP, so the RP has the option of forcing knowledge about this group into the intervening routers so that tunneling can be avoided. Its decision to exercise this option is based on the data rate of packets coming from a given source; only if this rate is high enough to warrant the effort will the RP take action. If it does, it sends a Join message toward the sending host (Figure 4.37(c)). As this Join travels toward the host, it causes the routers along the path (R3) to learn about the group, so that it will be possible for the DR to send the packet to the group as "native" (i.e., not tunneled) multicast packets.

An important detail to note at this stage is that the Join message sent by the RP to the sending host is specific to that sender, whereas the previous ones sent by R4 and R5 applied to all senders. Thus the effect of the new Join is to create *sender-specific* state in the routers between the identified source and the RP. This is referred to as (S, G) state, since it applies to one sender to one group, and contrasts with the (*, G) state that was installed between the receivers and the RP that applies to all senders. Thus, in Figure 4.37(c), we see a source-specific route from R1 to the RP (indicated by the dashed line) and a tree that is valid for all senders from the RP to the receivers (indicated by the solid line).

The next possible optimization is to replace the entire shared tree with a source-specific tree. This is desirable because the path from sender to receiver via the RP might be significantly longer than the shortest possible path. This again is likely to be triggered by a high data rate being observed from some sender. In this case, the router at the downstream end of the tree—say, R4 in our example—sends a source-specific Join toward the source. As it follows the shortest path toward the source, the routers along the way create (S, G) state for this tree, and the result is a tree that has its root at the source, rather than the RP. Assuming both R4 and R5 made the switch to the source-specific tree, we would end up with the tree shown in Figure 4.37(d). Note that this tree no longer involves the RP at all. We have removed the shared tree from this picture to simplify the diagram, but in reality all routers with receivers for a group must stay on the shared tree in case new senders show up.

We can now see why PIM is "protocol independent." All of its mechanisms for building and maintaining trees depend on whatever unicast routing protocol is used in the domain. The formation of trees is entirely determined by the paths that Join messages follow, which is determined by the choice of shortest paths made by unicast routing. Thus, to be precise, PIM is "unicast routing protocol independent," as compared to the other multicast routing protocols in this section, which are derived from either link-state or distance-vector routing. Note that PIM is very much bound up with the Internet Protocol—it is not protocol independent in terms of network-layer protocols.

The design of PIM again illustrates the challenges in building scalable networks, and how scalability is sometimes pitted against some sort of optimality. The shared tree is certainly more scalable than a source-specific tree, in the sense that it reduces the total state in routers to be on the order of the number of groups rather than the number of senders times the number of groups. However, the source-specific tree is likely to be necessary to achieve efficient routing.

4.5 Summary

The main theme of this chapter was how to build big networks by interconnecting smaller networks. We looked at bridging in the last chapter, but it is a technique that is mostly used to interconnect a small to moderate number of similar networks. What bridging does not do well is tackle the two closely related problems of building very large networks: heterogeneity and scale. The Internet Protocol is the key tool for dealing with these problems, and it provided most of the examples for this chapter.

IP tackles heterogeneity by defining a simple, common service model for an internetwork, which is based on the best-effort delivery of IP datagrams. An important part of the service model is the global addressing scheme, which enables any two nodes in an internetwork to uniquely identify each other for the purposes of exchanging data. The IP service model is simple enough to be supported by any known networking technology, and the ARP mechanism is used to translate global IP addresses into local link-layer addresses.

A crucial aspect of the operation of an internetwork is the determination of efficient routes to any destination in the internet. Internet routing algorithms solve this problem in a distributed fashion; this chapter introduced the two major classes of algorithms—link-state and distance-vector—along with examples of their application (RIP and OSPF). We also examined the extensions to IP routing that will support mobile hosts.

We then saw a succession of scaling problems and the ways that IP deals with them. The major scaling issues are the efficient use of address space and the growth of routing tables as the Internet grows. The hierarchical IP address format, with its network and host parts, gives us one level of hierarchy to manage scale. Subnetting lets us make more efficient use of network numbers and helps consolidate routing information; in effect, it adds one more level of hierarchy to the address. Classless routing (CIDR) lets us introduce more levels of hierarchy and achieve further routing aggregation. Autonomous systems allow us to partition the routing problem into two parts, interdomain and intradomain routing, each of which is much smaller than the total routing problem would be. These mechanisms have enabled today's Internet to sustain remarkable growth.

Eventually, all of these mechanisms will be unable to keep up with the Internet's growth, and a new address format will be needed. This will require a new IP datagram format and a new version of the protocol. Originally known as Next Generation IP (IPng), this new protocol is now known as IPv6, and it will provide a 128-bit address with CIDR-like addressing and routing. At the same time, it will add considerable functionality to IP, including stateless autoconfiguration, support for multicast, and advanced routing capabilities.

While we have presented IP as the only protocol for global internetworking, there have been other contenders, most notably ATM. In recent years, the enormous success of the Internet, along with the failure of ATM to displace other technologies

OPEN ISSUE
IP, ATM, and MPLS

in the local area network, has largely settled the "IP versus ATM" debates in favor of IP. ATM continues to be an important technology in the wide area and is widely used as a subnet technology over which IP runs, but is not likely to replace IP as the core protocol for global internetworking.

An interesting development in the relationship between IP and ATM is the appearance of Multiprotocol Label Switching (MPLS). This technology, which is undergoing standardization in the IETF at the time of writing, has its roots in various proprietary protocols, notably IP Switching and Tag Switching. The basic idea behind all these label switching techniques is to marry the forwarding algorithm used in ATM with the control protocols used in IP. Thus a label switching router (LSR) forwards packets by looking at a fixed-length label in its header, using that label to find the correct outgoing interface on which to forward the packet, and rewriting the label before sending the packet. This is just how an ATM switch forwards cells, and it is significantly simpler than the longest-match algorithm used to forward IP packets in conventional routers. Unlike an ATM switch, however, an LSR runs IP routing protocols like OSPF or RIP, and it uses the information in its routing table, rather than an explicit signalling protocol, to set up the entries in its forwarding table.

The exact mechanisms by which LSRs establish their forwarding tables are too complex to describe here (see the Further Reading section), but several advantages are claimed for the approach. The most common claim is that, since the label switching algorithm is so much simpler than longest match, LSRs will be dramatically cheaper at a given performance, or provide significantly higher performance at a given point in time, than conventional routers. To date, this claim has not really been born out in practice, since there are a lot of costs in a router apart from the lookup algorithm. More solid is the claim that label switching enables significant new routing capabilities, because it becomes possible to make forwarding decisions based on more complex criteria than just the IP destination address without sacrificing performance. Another emerging area for label switching is the support of virtual private networks; as we have seen, tunnels are one of the main tools for constructing VPNs today, and label switching is in many senses a form of tunneling.

It remains to be seen whether MPLS will really take off. To IP purists, it feels too much like ATM all over again. However, the claims that its proponents make are more modest than those once made for ATM. MPLS has no likelihood of replacing IP, but it may become another useful tool to expand the capabilities of IP-based networks.

FURTHER READING

Not surprisingly, there have been countless papers written on various aspects of the Internet. Of these, we recommend two as must reading: The paper by Cerf and Kahn is the one that originally introduced the TCP/IP architecture and is worth reading just for its historical perspective; the paper by Bradner and Mankin gives an informative overview on how the rapidly growing Internet has stressed the scalability of the original architecture, ultimately resulting in the next generation IP. The paper by Paxson describes a study of how routers behave in the Internet. It also happens to be a good example of how researchers are now studying the dynamic behavior of the Internet. The final two papers discuss multicast: The article by Deering and Cheriton is a seminal paper on the topic and describes the approach to multicast currently used on the MBone, while the paper by Deering et al. presents the more recent PIM protocol.

- Cerf, V., and R. Kahn. A protocol for packet network intercommunication. *IEEE Transactions on Communications* COM-22(5):637–648, May 1974.

- Bradner, S., and A. Mankin. The recommendation for the next generation IP protocol. *Request for Comments* 1752, January 1995.

■ Paxson, V. End-to-end routing behavior in the Internet. *SIGCOMM '96*, pages 25–38, August 1996.

■ Deering, S., and D. Cheriton. Multicast routing in datagram internetworks and extended LANs. ACM *Transactions on Computer Systems* 8(2):85–110, May 1990.

■ Deering, S., D. Estrin, D. Farinacci, V. Jacobson, C. Liu, and L. Wei. The PIM architecture for wide-area multicast routing. *ACM/IEEE Transactions on Networking*, April 1996.

Beyond these papers, Perlman gives an excellent explanation of routing in an internet, including coverage of both bridges and routers [Per92]. Also, the book by Lynch and Rose gives general information on the scalability of the Internet [Cha93].

Many of the techniques and protocols developed to help the Internet scale are described in RFCs: Subnetting is described in Mogul and Postel [MP85], CIDR is described in Fuller et al. [FLYV93], RIP is defined in Hedrick [Hed88] and Malkin [Mal93], OSPF is defined in Moy [Moy98], and BGP-4 is defined in Rekhter and Li [RL95]. The OSPF specification, at over 200 pages, is one of the longer RFCs around, but also contains an unusual wealth of detail about how to implement a protocol. Also, explanations of how IP and ATM can coexist are given in Heinanen [Hei93], Laubach [Lau94], and Borden et al. [BCDB95]. A collection of RFCs related to IPv6 can be found in Bradner and Mankin [BM95], and the most recent IPv6 spec is by Deering and Hinden [DH98]. The reasons to avoid IP fragmentation are examined in Kent and Mogul [KM87] and the Path MTU discovery technique is described in Mogul and Deering [MD90].

There has been a lot of work developing algorithms that can be used by routers to do fast lookup of IP addresses. (Recall that the problem is that the router needs to match the longest prefix in the forwarding table.) PATRICIA trees are one of the first algorithms applied to this problem [Mor68]. More recent work is reported in [DBCP98, WVTP97, LS98, SVSW98]. For an overview of how these algorithms can be used to build a high-speed router, see Partridge et al. [Par98]. Multiprotocol Label Switching and the related protocols that fed its development are described in Rekhter et al. [RDR+97] and Davie et al. [DDR98].

Finally, we recommend the following live references:

■ http://www.ietf.org: the IETF home page, from which you can get RFCs, internet drafts, and working group charters

■ http://playground.sun.com/pub/ipng/html/ipng-main.html: current state of IPv6

EXERCISES

1 What aspect of IP addresses makes it necessary to have one address per network interface, rather than just one per host? In light of your answer, why does IP tolerate point-to-point interfaces that have nonunique addresses or no addresses?

2 Why does the Offset field in the IP header measure the offset in 8-byte units? (Hint: Recall that the Offset field is 13 bits long.)

3 Suppose that a TCP message that contains 2048 bytes of data and 20 bytes of TCP header is passed to IP for delivery across two networks of the Internet (i.e., from the source host to a router to the destination host). The first network uses 14-byte headers and has an MTU of 1024 bytes; the second uses 8-byte headers with an MTU of 512 bytes. Each network's MTU gives the total packet size that may be sent, including the network header. Give the sizes and offsets of the sequence of fragments delivered to the network layer at the destination host. Assume all IP headers are 20 bytes.

4 Suppose an IP packet is fragmented into 10 fragments, each with a 1% (independent) probability of loss. To a reasonable approximation, this means there is a 10% chance of losing the whole packet due to loss of a fragment. What is the probability of net loss of the whole packet if the packet is transmitted twice,

   (a) assuming all fragments received must have been part of the same transmission?

   (b) assuming any given fragment may have been part of either transmission?

   (c) Explain how use of the Ident field might be applicable here.

5 Suppose the fragments of Figure 4.5(b) all pass through another router onto a link with an MTU of 380 bytes, not counting the link header. Show the fragments produced. If the packet were originally fragmented for this MTU, how many fragments would be produced?

6 What is the maximum bandwidth at which an IP host can send 576-byte packets without having the Ident field wrap around within 60 seconds? Suppose IP's maximum segment lifetime (MSL) is 60 seconds; that is, delayed packets can arrive up to 60 seconds late but no later. What might happen if this bandwidth were exceeded?

7 ATM AAL3/4 uses fields Btag/Etag, BASize/Len, Type, SEQ, MID, Length, and CRC-10 to implement fragmentation into cells. IPv4 uses Ident, Offset, and the M bit

in Flags, among others. What is the IP analog, if any, for each AAL3/4 field? Does each IP field listed here have an AAL3/4 analog? How well do these fields correspond?

8 Why do you think IPv4 has fragment reassembly done at the endpoint, rather than at the next router? Why do you think IPv6 abandoned fragmentation entirely? Hint: Think about the differences between IP-layer fragmentation and link-layer fragmentation.

9 Having ARP table entries time out after 10–15 minutes is an attempt at a reasonable compromise. Describe the problems that can occur if the timeout value is too small or too large.

10 Suppose hosts A and B have been assigned the same IP address on the same Ethernet, on which ARP is used. B starts up after A. What will happen to A's existing connections? Explain how "self-ARP" (querying the network on start-up for one's own IP address) might help with this problem.

11 Suppose an IP implementation adheres literally to the following algorithm on receipt of a packet, P, destined for IP address D:

> if (⟨Ethernet address for D is in ARP cache⟩)
>   ⟨send P⟩
> else
>   ⟨send out an ARP query for D⟩
>   ⟨put P into a queue until the response comes back⟩

   (a) If the IP layer receives a burst of packets destined for D, how might this algorithm waste resources unnecessarily?

   (b) Sketch an improved version.

   (c) Suppose we simply drop P, after sending out a query, when cache lookup fails. How would this behave? (Some early ARP implementations allegedly did this.)

12 For the network given in Figure 4.39, give global distance-vector tables like those of Tables 4.5 and 4.8 when

   (a) Each node knows only the distances to its immediate neighbors.

   (b) Each node has reported the information it had in the preceding step to its immediate neighbors.

   (c) Step (b) happens a second time.

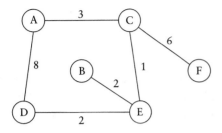

Figure 4.39 Network for Exercises 12 and 13.

A				F		
node	cost	nexthop		node	cost	nexthop
B	1	B		A	3	E
C	2	B		B	2	C
D	1	D		C	1	C
E	2	B		D	2	E
F	3	D		E	1	E

Table 4.12 Forwarding tables for Exercise 14.

13 For the network given in Figure 4.39, show how the link-state algorithm builds the routing table for node D.

14 Suppose we have the forwarding tables shown in Table 4.12 for nodes A and F, in a network where all links have cost 1. Give a diagram of the smallest network consistent with these tables.

15 For the network in Figure 4.39, suppose the forwarding tables are all established as in Exercise 12 and then the C–E link fails. Give

(a) the tables of A, B, D, and F after C and E have reported the news

(b) the tables of A and D after their next mutual exchange

(c) the table of C after A exchanges with it

16 Suppose a router has built up the routing table shown in Table 4.13. The router can deliver packets directly over interfaces 0 and 1, or it can forward packets to

SubnetNumber	SubnetMask	NextHop
128.96.39.0	255.255.255.128	Interface 0
128.96.39.128	255.255.255.128	Interface 1
128.96.40.0	255.255.255.128	R2
192.4.153.0	255.255.255.192	R3
⟨default⟩		R4

Table 4.13   Routing table for Exercise 16.

Figure 4.40   Simple network for Exercise 17.

routers R2, R3, or R4. Describe what the router does with a packet addressed to each of the following destinations:

(a) 128.96.39.10

(b) 128.96.40.12

(c) 128.96.40.151

(d) 192.4.153.17

(e) 192.4.153.90

17 Consider the simple network in Figure 4.40, in which A and B exchange distance-vector routing information. All links have cost 1. Suppose the A–E link fails.

(a) Give a sequence of routing table updates that leads to a routing loop between A and B.

(b) Estimate the probability of the scenario in (a), assuming A and B send out routing updates at random times, each at the same average rate.

(c) Estimate the probability of a loop forming if A broadcasts an updated report within 1 second of discovering the A–E failure, and B broadcasts every 60 seconds uniformly.

18 Consider the situation involving the creation of a routing loop in the network of Figure 4.14 when the A–E link goes down. List *all* sequences of table updates

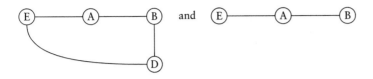

Figure 4.41 Networks for Exercise 20.

among A, B, and C, pertaining to destination E, that lead to the loop. Assume that table updates are done one at a time, that the split-horizon technique is observed by all participants, and that A sends its initial report of E's unreachability to B before C. You may ignore updates that don't result in changes.

19 Suppose a set of routers all use the split-horizon technique; we consider here under what circumstances it makes a difference if they use poison reverse in addition.

(a) Show that poison reverse makes no difference in the evolution of the routing loop in the two examples described in Section 4.2.2, given that the hosts involved use split horizon.

(b) Suppose split-horizon routers A and B somehow reach a state in which they forward traffic for a given destination X toward each other. Describe how this situation will evolve with and without the use of poison reverse.

(c) Give a sequence of events that leads A and B to a looped state as in (b), even if poison reverse is used. Hint: Suppose B and A connect through a very slow link. They each reach X through a third node, C, and simultaneously advertise their routes to each other.

20 *Hold down* is another distance-vector loop-avoidance technique, whereby hosts ignore updates for a period of time until link failure news has had a chance to propagate. Consider the networks in Figure 4.41, where all links have cost 1 except E–D with cost 10. Suppose that the E–A link breaks and B reports its loop-forming E route to A immediately afterwards (this is the false route, via A). Specify the details of a hold-down interpretation, and use this to describe the evolution of the routing loop in both networks. To what extent can hold down prevent the loop in the EAB network without delaying the discovery of the alternative route in the EABD network?

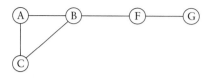

Figure 4.42   Network for Exercise 21.

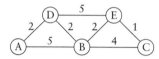

Figure 4.43   Network for Exercise 22.

21 Consider the network in Figure 4.42, using link-state routing. Suppose the B–F link fails, and the following then occur in sequence:

(a) Node H is added to the right side with a connection to G.

(b) Node D is added to the left side with a connection to C.

(c) A new link D–A is added.

The failed B–F link is now restored. Describe what link-state packets will flood back and forth. Assume that the initial sequence number at all nodes is 1, and that no packets time out, and that both ends of a link use the same sequence number in their LSP for that link, greater than any sequence number either used before.

22 Give the steps as in Table 4.9 in the forward search algorithm as it builds the routing database for node A in the network shown in Figure 4.43.

23 Suppose that nodes in the network shown in Figure 4.44 participate in link-state routing, and C receives contradictory LSPs: One from A arrives claiming the A–B link is down, but one from B arrives claiming the A–B link is up.

(a) How could this happen?

(b) What should C do? What can C expect?

Do not assume that LSPs contain any synchronized timestamp.

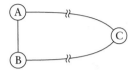

Figure 4.44 Network for Exercise 23.

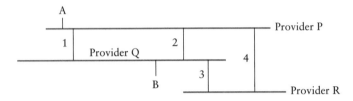

Figure 4.45 Network for Exercise 24.

24 Consider the network shown in Figure 4.45, in which horizontal lines represent transit providers and numbered vertical lines are interprovider links.

(a) How many routes to P could provider Q's BGP speakers receive?

(b) Suppose Q and P adopt the policy that outbound traffic is routed to the closest link to the destination's provider, thus minimizing their own cost. What paths will traffic from host A to host B and from host B to host A take?

(c) What could Q do to have the B⟶A traffic use the closer link 1?

(d) What could Q do to have the B⟶A traffic pass through R?

25 Give an example of an arrangement of routers grouped into autonomous systems so that the path with the fewest hops from a point A to another point B crosses the same AS twice. Explain what BGP would do with this situation.

26 Let A be the number of autonomous systems on the Internet, and let D (for diameter) be the maximum AS path length.

(a) Give a connectivity model for which D is of order $\log A$ and another for which D is of order $\sqrt{A}$.

(b) Assuming each AS number is 2 bytes and each network number is 4 bytes, give an estimate for the amount of data a BGP speaker must receive to keep track of the AS path to every network. Express your answer in terms of A, D, and the number of networks N.

27 Suppose IP routers learned about IP networks and subnets the way Ethernet learning bridges learn about hosts: by noting the appearance of new ones, and the interface by which they arrive. Compare this with existing distance-vector router learning

(a) for a leaf site with a single attachment to the Internet, and

(b) for internal use at an organization that did not connect to the Internet.

Assume that routers only receive new-network notices from other routers, and that the originating routers receive their IP network information via configuration.

28 IP hosts that are not designated routers are *required* to drop packets misaddressed to them, even if they would otherwise be able to forward them correctly. In the absence of this requirement, what would happen if a packet addressed to IP address A were inadvertently broadcast at the link layer? What other justifications for this requirement can you think of?

29 Read the man page or other documentation for the Unix/Windows utility netstat. Use netstat to display the current IP routing table on your host. Explain the purpose of each entry. What is the practical minimum number of entries?

30 Use the Unix utility traceroute (Windows tracert) to determine how many hops it is from your host to other hosts in the Internet (e.g., cs.princeton.edu or www.cisco.com). How many routers do you traverse just to get out of your local site? Read the man page or other documentation for traceroute and explain how it is implemented.

31 What will happen if traceroute is used to find the path to an unassigned address? Does it matter if the network portion or only the host portion is unassigned?

32 A site is shown in Figure 4.46. R1 and R2 are routers; R2 connects to the outside world. Individual LANs are Ethernets. RB is a *bridge-router*; it routes traffic addressed to it and acts as a bridge for other traffic. Subnetting is used inside the site; ARP is used on each subnet. Unfortunately, host A has been misconfigured and doesn't use subnets. Which of B, C, D can A reach?

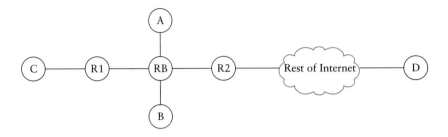

Figure 4.46   Site for Exercise 32.

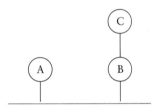

Figure 4.47   Network for Exercise 34.

33 An organization has a class C network 200.1.1 and wants to form subnets for four departments, with hosts as follows:

> A   72 hosts
>
> B   35 hosts
>
> C   20 hosts
>
> D   18 hosts

There are 145 hosts in all.

(a) Give a possible arrangement of subnet masks to make this possible.

(b) Suggest what the organization might do if department D grows to 34 hosts.

34 Suppose hosts A and B are on an Ethernet LAN with class C IP network address 200.0.0. It is desired to attach a host C to the network via a direct connection to B (see Figure 4.47). Explain how to do this with subnets; give sample subnet assignments. Assume that an additional network address is not available. What does this do to the size of the Ethernet LAN?

Net/MaskLength	nexthop
C4.50.0.0/12	A
C4.5E.10.0/20	B
C4.60.0.0/12	C
C4.68.0.0/14	D
80.0.0.0/1	E
40.0.0.0/2	F
00.0.0.0/2	G

Table 4.14   Routing table for Exercise 38.

35 An alternative method for connecting host C in Exercise 34 is to use *proxy ARP* and routing: B agrees to route traffic to and from C, and also answers ARP queries for C received over the Ethernet.

(a) Give all packets sent, with physical addresses, as A uses ARP to locate and then send one packet to C.

(b) Give B's routing table. What peculiarity must it contain?

36 Propose a plausible addressing plan for IPv6 that runs out of bits. Specifically, provide a diagram such as Figure 4.32, perhaps with additional ID fields, that adds up to more than 128 bits, together with plausible justifications for the size of each field. You may assume fields are divided on byte boundaries, and that the InterfaceID is 64 bits. Hint: Consider fields that would approach maximum allocation only under unusual circumstances. Can you do this if the InterfaceID is 48 bits?

37 Suppose two subnets share the same physical LAN; hosts on each subnet will see the other subnet's broadcast packets.

(a) How will DHCP fare if two servers, one for each subnet, coexist on the shared LAN? What problems might [*do!*] arise?

(b) Will ARP be affected by such sharing?

38 Table 4.14 is a routing table using CIDR. Address bytes are in hexadecimal. The notation "/12" in C4.50.0.0/12 denotes a netmask with 12 leading 1 bits, that is,

FF.F0.0.0. Note that the last three entries cover every address and thus serve in lieu of a default route. State to what next hop the following will be delivered.

(a) C4.5E.13.87

(b) C4.5E.22.09

(c) C3.41.80.02

(d) 5E.43.91.12

(e) C4.6D.31.2E

(f) C4.6B.31.2E

39 Suppose P, Q, and R are network service providers, with respective CIDR address allocations (using the notation of Exercise 38) C1.0.0.0/8, C2.0.0.0/8, and C3.0.0.0/8. Each provider's customers initially receive address allocations that are a subset of the provider's. P has the following customers:

> PA, with allocation C1.A3.0.0/16, and

> PB, with allocation C1.B0.0.0/12.

> Q has the following customers:

> QA, with allocation C2.0A.10.0/20, and

> QB, with allocation C2.0B.0.0/16.

Assume there are no other providers or customers.

(a) Give routing tables for P, Q, and R assuming each provider connects to both of the others.

(b) Now assume P is connected to Q and Q is connected to R, but P and R are not directly connected. Give tables for P and R.

(c) Suppose customer PA acquires a direct link to Q, and QA acquires a direct link to P, in addition to existing links. Give tables for P and Q, ignoring R.

40 In the previous problem, assume each provider connects to both others. Suppose customer PA switches to provider Q and customer QB switches to provider R. Use the CIDR longest-match rule to give routing tables for all three providers that allow PA and QB to switch without renumbering.

41 Suppose most of the Internet used some form of geographical addressing, but that a large international organization has a single IP network address and routes its internal traffic over its own links.

(a) Explain the routing inefficiency for the organization's inbound traffic inherent in this situation.

(b) Explain how the organization might solve this problem for outbound traffic.

(c) For your method above to work for inbound traffic, what would have to happen?

(d) Suppose the large organization now changes its addressing to separate geographical addresses for each office. What will its internal routing structure have to look like if internal traffic is still to be routed internally?

42 The telephone system uses geographical addressing. Why do you think this wasn't adopted as a matter of course by the Internet?

43 Suppose a site A is *multihomed*, in that it has two Internet connections from two different providers, P and Q. Provider-based addressing as in Exercise 39 is used, and A takes its address assignment from P. Q has a CIDR longest-match routing entry for A.

(a) Describe what inbound traffic might flow on the A–Q connection. Consider cases where Q does and does not advertise A to the world using BGP.

(b) What is the minimum advertising of its route to A that Q must do in order for all inbound traffic to reach A via Q if the P–A link breaks?

(c) What problems must be overcome if A is to use both links for its outbound traffic?

44 Propose a lookup algorithm for a CIDR fowarding table that does not require a linear search of the entire table to find the longest match.

45 Suppose a network N within a larger organization A acquires its own direct connection to an Internet service provider, in addition to an existing connection via A. Let R1 be the router connecting N to its own provider, and let R2 be the router connecting N to the rest of A.

(a) Assuming N remains a subnet of A, how should R1 and R2 be configured? What limitations would still exist with N's use of its separate connection? Would A be prevented from using N's connection? Specify your configuration in terms of what R1 and R2 should advertise, and with what paths. Assume a BGP-like mechanism is available.

(b) Now suppose N gets its own network number; how does this change your answer in (a)?

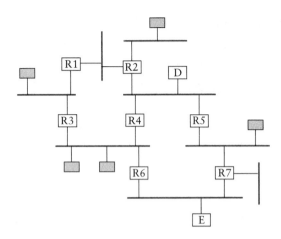

Figure 4.48 Example internet for Exercise 46.

(c) Describe a router configuration that would allow A to use N's link when its own link is down.

46 Consider the example internet shown in Figure 4.48, in which sources D and E send packets to multicast group G, whose members are shaded in gray. Show the shortest-path multicast trees for each source.

47 Suppose host A is sending to a multicast group; the recipients are leaf nodes of a tree rooted at A with depth N and with each nonleaf node having k children; there are thus k^N recipients.

(a) How many individual link transmissions are involved if A sends a multicast message to all recipients?

(b) How many individual link transmissions are involved if A sends unicast messages to each individual recipient?

(c) Suppose A sends to all recipients, but some messages are lost and retransmission is necessary. Unicast retransmissions to what fraction of the recipients is equivalent, in terms of individual link transmissions, to a multicast retransmission to all recipients?

48 Determine if your site is connected to the MBone. If so, investigate and experiment with any MBone tools, such as sdr, vat, and vic.

Design considerations for TCP

1. It can potentially connect many different hosts. This is about the network. The requirements of TCP needs explicit connection establishment and termination

2. Potentially different (RTT). The requirements of (TCP).

3. Potentially long delay on the network. TCP requirement, need to be prepared for the arrival for very old packets.

4. Potentially different capacity at the destination TCP requirements need to accomodate different node capacity

5. Potentially different network capacities. TCP requirements need to accomodate Need to be prepared for network congestion

---

Flow control is the ability of the receiver to slow down or stop the sender from sending excess of information

TCP is a connection oriented protocol, it works in both directions

TCP supports what is a byte stream, as perspective
Application writes bytes, read bytes. TCP buffers and sends segments.

There are six flags that exist in TCP, they all have different purposes

Receiving buffer stores all bytes between last byte read and last byte received.
Everything that is received but is not read has to stay in the buffer
How TCP uses sliding windows to implement control.

Max Receive Buffer ; Max Send Buffer
Last byte read and last byte received can not exceed the buffer capacity.

Advertise window = Max Received Buffer — (Last Byte Received — Last Byte Read)

Last Byte Sent — Last Byte Ack = Advertised window

Effective window = Advertise window — (Last Byte Sent — Last Byte Ack)

Last Byte Written — Last Byte Ack <= Max Send Buffer

Blast employs a strategy call (SSR) Selected Retransmission Requested which is a packet that has sent an Acknowledgement to the receiver, to the sender. (SRR) contains information about which packet had arrive and about which packet did not.

Header Format MID (Message Id) is a number that keeps together all the fragments belonging to the same message; for a given message all fragments have the same (Id).

The previous three chapters have described various technologies that can be used to connect together a collection of computers: direct links (including LAN technologies like Ethernet and token ring), packet-switched networks (including cell-based networks like ATM), and internetworks. The next problem is to turn this host-to-host packet delivery service into a process-to-process communication channel. This is the role played by the *transport* level of the network architecture, which, because it supports communication between the end application programs, is sometimes called the *end-to-end* protocol.

Two forces shape the end-to-end protocol. From above, the application-level processes that use its services have certain requirements. The following list itemizes some of the common properties that a transport protocol can be expected to provide:

- guarantees message delivery
- delivers messages in the same order they are sent
- delivers at most one copy of each message
- supports arbitrarily large messages
- supports synchronization between the sender and the receiver
- allows the receiver to apply flow control to the sender
- supports multiple application processes on each host

Victory is the beautiful, bright coloured flower. Transport is the stem without which it could never have blossomed.

—Winston Churchill

Note that this list does not include all the functionality that application processes might want from the network. For example, it does not include security, which is typically provided by protocols that sit above the transport level.

From below, the underlying network upon which the transport protocol operates has certain limitations in the level of service it can provide. Some of the more typical limitations of the network are that it may

- drop messages

- reorder messages

- deliver duplicate copies of a given message

- limit messages to some finite size

- deliver messages after an arbitrarily long delay

Such a network is said to provide a *best-effort* level of service, as exemplified by the Internet.

The challenge, therefore, is to develop algorithms that turn the less-than-desirable properties of the underlying network into the high level of service required by application programs. Different transport protocols employ different combinations of these algorithms. This chapter looks at these algorithms in the context of three representative services—a simple asynchronous demultiplexing service, a reliable byte-stream service, and a request/reply service.

In the case of the demultiplexing and byte-stream services, we use the Internet's UDP and TCP protocols, respectively, to illustrate how these services are provided in practice. In the third case, we first give a collection of algorithms that implement the request/reply (plus other related) services and then show how these algorithms can be combined to implement a Remote Procedure Call (RPC) protocol. This discussion is capped off with a description of two widely used RPC protocols—SunRPC and DCE-RPC—in terms of these component algorithms. Finally, the chapter concludes with a section that discusses the performance of the different transport protocols.

5

End-to-End Protocols

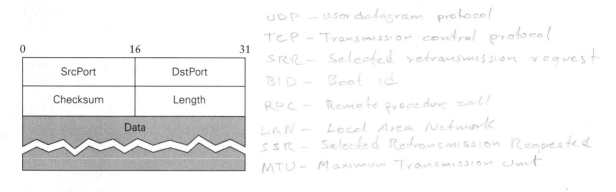

Figure 5.1   Format for UDP header.

5.1   Simple Demultiplexer (UDP)

The simplest possible transport protocol is one that extends the host-to-host delivery service of the underlying network into a process-to-process communication service. There are likely to be many processes running on any given host, so the protocol needs to add a level of demultiplexing, thereby allowing multiple application processes on each host to share the network. Aside from this requirement, the transport protocol adds no other functionality to the best-effort service provided by the underlying network. The Internet's User Datagram Protocol (UDP) is an example of such a transport protocol.

The only interesting issue in such a protocol is the form of the address used to identify the target process. Although it is possible for processes to *directly* identify each other with an OS-assigned process id (pid), such an approach is only practical in a "closed" distributed system in which a single OS runs on all hosts and assigns each process a unique id. A more common approach, and the one used by UDP, is for processes to *indirectly* identify each other using an abstract locater, often called a *port* or *mailbox*. The basic idea is for a source process to send a message to a port and for the destination process to receive the message from a port.

The header for an end-to-end protocol that implements this demultiplexing function typically contains an identifier (port) for both the sender (source) and the receiver (destination) of the message. For example, the UDP header is given in Figure 5.1. Notice that the UDP port field is only 16 bits long. This means that there are up to 64K possible ports, clearly not enough to identify all the processes on all the hosts in the Internet. Fortunately, ports are not interpreted across the entire Internet, but only on a single host. That is, a process is really identified by a port on some particular host— a ⟨port, host⟩ pair. In fact, this pair constitutes the demultiplexing key for the UDP protocol.

The next issue is how a process learns the port for the process to which it wants to send a message. Typically, a client process initiates a message exchange with a server process. Once a client has contacted a server, the server knows the client's port (it was contained in the message header) and can reply to it. The real problem, therefore, is how the client learns the server's port in the first place. A common approach is for the server to accept messages at a *well-known port*. That is, each server receives its messages at some fixed port that is widely published, much like the emergency telephone service available at the well-known phone number 911. In the Internet, for example, the Domain Name Server (DNS) receives messages at well-known port 53 on each host, the Unix **talk** program accepts messages at well-known port 517, and so on. This mapping is published periodically in an RFC and is available on most Unix systems in file /etc/services. Sometimes a well-known port is just the starting point for communication: The client and server use the well-known port to agree on some other port that they will use for subsequent communication, leaving the well-known port free for other clients.

As just mentioned, a port is purely an abstraction. Exactly how it is implemented differs from system to system, or more precisely, from OS to OS. Typically, a port is implemented by a message queue, as illustrated in Figure 5.2. When a message arrives, the protocol (e.g., UDP) appends the message to the end of the queue. Should the queue be full, the message is discarded. There is no flow-control mechanism that tells the sender to slow down. When an application process wants to receive a message, one is removed from the front of the queue. If the queue is empty, the process blocks until a message becomes available.

Finally, although UDP does not implement flow control or reliable/ordered delivery, it does a little more work than to simply demultiplex messages to some application process—it also ensures the correctness of the message by the use of a checksum. (The UDP checksum is optional in the current Internet, but it will become mandatory with IPv6.) UDP computes its checksum over the UDP header, the contents of the message body, and something called the *pseudoheader*. The pseudoheader consists of three fields from the IP header—protocol number, source IP address, and destination IP address—plus the UDP length field. (Yes, the UDP length field is included twice in the checksum calculation.) UDP uses the same checksum algorithm as IP, as defined in Section 2.4.2. The motivation behind having the pseudoheader is to verify that this message has been delivered between the correct two endpoints. For example, if the destination IP address was modified while the packet was in transit, causing the packet to be misdelivered, this fact would be detected by the UDP checksum.

5.2 Reliable Byte Stream (TCP)

In contrast to a simple demultiplexing protocol like UDP, a more sophisticated transport protocol is one that offers a reliable, connection-oriented, byte-stream service. Such a service has proven useful to a wide assortment of applications because it frees

Design consideration for

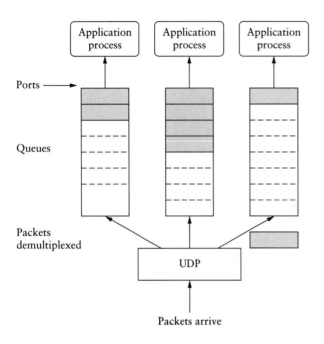

Figure 5.2 UDP message queue.

the application from having to worry about missing or reordered data. The Internet's Transmission Control Protocol (TCP) is probably the most widely used protocol of this type; it is also the most carefully tuned. It is for these two reasons that this section studies TCP in detail, although we identify and discuss alternative design choices at the end of the section.

In terms of the properties of transport protocols given in the problem statement at the start of this chapter, TCP guarantees the reliable, in-order delivery of a stream of bytes. It is a full-duplex protocol, meaning that each TCP connection supports a pair of byte streams, one flowing in each direction. It also includes a flow-control — *Flow contro* mechanism for each of these byte streams that allows the receiver to limit how much data the sender can transmit at a given time. Finally, like UDP, TCP supports a demultiplexing mechanism that allows multiple application programs on any given host to simultaneously carry on a conversation with their peers. In addition to the above features, TCP also implements a highly tuned congestion-control mechanism. The idea of this mechanism is to throttle how fast TCP sends data, not for the sake of keeping the sender from overrunning the receiver, but so as to keep the sender from overloading the network. A description of TCP's congestion-control mechanism is postponed until Chapter 6, where we discuss it in the larger context of how network resources are fairly allocated.

Since many people confuse congestion control and flow control, we restate the difference. *Flow control* involves preventing senders from overrunning the capacity of receivers. *Congestion control* involves preventing too much data from being injected into the network, thereby causing switches or links to become overloaded. Thus, flow control is an end-to-end issue, while congestion control is concerned with how hosts and networks interact.

5.2.1 End-to-End Issues

At the heart of TCP is the sliding window algorithm. Even though this is the same basic algorithm we saw in Section 2.5.2, because TCP runs over the Internet rather than a point-to-point link, there are many important differences. This subsection identifies these differences and explains how they complicate TCP. The following five subsections then describe how TCP addresses these complications.

First, whereas the sliding window algorithm presented in Section 2.5.2 runs over a single physical link that always connects the same two computers, TCP supports logical connections between processes that are running on any two computers in the Internet. This means that TCP needs an explicit connection establishment phase during which the two sides of the connection agree to exchange data with each other. This difference is analogous to having to dial up the other party, rather than having a dedicated phone line. TCP also has an explicit connection teardown phase. One of the things that happens during connection establishment is that the two parties establish some shared state to enable the sliding window algorithm to begin.

Second, whereas a single physical link that always connects the same two computers has a fixed RTT, TCP connections are likely to have widely different round-trip times. For example, a TCP connection between a host in San Francisco and a host in Boston, which are separated by several thousand kilometers, might have an RTT of 100 ms, while a TCP connection between a host in San Francisco and a host in Los Angeles, only a few hundred kilometers away, might have an RTT of only 10 ms. The same TCP protocol must be able to support both of these connections. To make matters worse, the TCP connection between hosts in San Francisco and Boston might have an RTT of 100 ms at 3 a.m., but an RTT of 500 ms at 3 p.m. Variations in the RTT are even possible during a single TCP connection that lasts only a few minutes. What this means to the sliding window algorithm is that the timeout mechanism that triggers retransmissions must be adaptive. (Certainly, the timeout for a point-to-point link must be a settable parameter, but it is not necessary to adapt this timer frequently.)

A third difference is that packets may be reordered as they cross the Internet, but this is not possible on a point-to-point link where the first packet put into one end of the link must be the first to appear at the other end. Packets that are slightly out of order do not cause a problem since the sliding window algorithm can reorder packets correctly using the sequence number. The real issue is how far out-of-order packets can get, or said another way, how late a packet can arrive at the destination. In the worst case, a packet can be delayed in the Internet until IP's time to live (TTL) field expires, at which time the packet is discarded (and hence there is no danger of it arriving late). Knowing that IP throws packets away after their TTL expires, TCP assumes that each packet has a maximum lifetime. The exact lifetime, known as the *maximum segment lifetime* (MSL), is an engineering choice. The current recommended setting is 120 seconds. Keep in mind that IP does not directly enforce this 120-second value; it is simply a conservative estimate that TCP makes of how long a packet might live in the Internet. The implication is significant—TCP has to be prepared for very old packets to suddenly show up at the receiver, potentially confusing the sliding window algorithm.

Fourth, the computers connected to a point-to-point link are generally engineered to support the link. For example, if a link's delay × bandwidth product is computed to be 8 KB—meaning that a window size is selected to allow up to 8 KB of data to be unacknowledged at a given time—then it is likely that the computers at either end of the link have the ability to buffer up to 8 KB of data. Designing the system otherwise would be silly. On the other hand, almost any kind of computer can be connected to the Internet, making the amount of resources dedicated to any one TCP connection highly variable, especially considering that any one host can potentially support hundreds of TCP connections at the same time. This means that TCP must include a mechanism that each side uses to "learn" what resources (e.g., how much buffer space) the other side is able to apply to the connection.

Fifth, because the transmitting side of a directly connected link cannot send any faster than the bandwidth of the link allows, and only one host is pumping data into the link, it is not possible to unknowingly congest the link. Said another way, the load on the link is visible in the form of a queue of packets at the sender. In contrast, the sending side of a TCP connection has no idea what links will be traversed to reach the destination. For example, the sending machine might be directly connected to a relatively fast Ethernet—and so, capable of sending data at a rate of 10 Mbps—but somewhere out in the middle of the network, a 1.5-Mbps T1 link must be traversed. And to make matters worse, data being generated by many different sources might be trying to traverse this same slow link. This leads to the problem of network congestion. Discussion of this topic is delayed until Chapter 6.

We conclude this discussion of end-to-end issues by comparing TCP's approach to providing a reliable/ordered delivery service with the approach used by X.25 networks. In TCP, the underlying IP network is assumed to be unreliable and to deliver messages out of order; TCP uses the sliding window algorithm on an end-to-end basis to provide reliable/ordered delivery. In contrast, X.25 networks use the sliding window protocol within the network, on a hop-by-hop basis. The assumption behind this approach is that if messages are delivered reliably and in order between each pair of nodes along the path between the source host and the destination host, then the end-to-end service also guarantees reliable/ordered delivery.

The problem with this latter approach is that a sequence of hop-by-hop guarantees does not necessarily add up to an end-to-end guarantee. First, if a heterogeneous link (say, across an Ethernet) is added to one end of the path, then there is no guarantee that this hop will preserve the same service as the other hops. Second, just because the sliding window protocol guarantees that messages are delivered correctly from node A to node B, and then from node B to node C, it does not guarantee that node B behaves perfectly. For example, network nodes have been known to introduce errors into messages while transferring them from an input buffer to an output buffer. They have also been known to accidentally reorder messages. As a consequence of these small windows of vulnerability, it is still necessary to provide true end-to-end checks to guarantee reliable/ordered service, even though the lower levels of the system also implement that functionality.

This discussion serves to illustrate one of the most important principles in system design—the *end-to-end argument*. In a nutshell, the end-to-end argument says that a function (in our example, providing reliable/ordered delivery) should not be provided in the lower levels of the system unless it can be completely and correctly implemented at that level. Therefore, this rule argues in favor of the TCP/IP approach. This rule is not absolute, however. It does allow for functions to be incompletely provided at a low level as a performance optimization. This is why it is perfectly consistent with the end-to-end argument to perform error detection (e.g., CRC) on a hop-by-hop basis; detecting and retransmitting a single corrupt packet across one hop is preferable to having to retransmit an entire file end-to-end.

5.2.2 Segment Format

TCP is a byte-oriented protocol, which means that the sender writes bytes into a TCP connection and the receiver reads bytes out of the TCP connection. Although "byte stream" describes the service TCP offers to application processes, TCP does not, itself, transmit individual bytes over the Internet. Instead, TCP on the source host buffers enough bytes from the sending process to fill a reasonably sized packet and then sends this packet to its peer on the destination host. TCP on the destination host then empties the contents of the packet into a receive buffer, and the receiving process reads from this buffer at its leisure. This situation is illustrated in Figure 5.3, which, for simplicity,

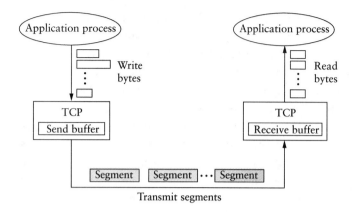

Figure 5.3 How TCP manages a byte stream.

shows data flowing in only one direction. Remember that, in general, a single TCP connection supports byte streams flowing in both directions.

The packets exchanged between TCP peers in Figure 5.3 are called *segments*, since each one carries a segment of the byte stream. One question you might ask is, How does TCP decide that it has enough bytes to send a segment? The answer is that TCP has three mechanisms to trigger the transmission of a segment. First, TCP maintains a variable, typically called the maximum segment size (**MSS**), and it sends a segment as soon as it has collected **MSS** bytes from the sending process. **MSS** is usually set to the size of the largest segment TCP can send without causing the local IP to fragment. That is, **MSS** is set to the MTU of the directly connected network, minus the size of the TCP and IP headers. The second thing that triggers TCP to transmit a segment is that the sending process has explicitly asked it to do so. Specifically, TCP supports a *push* operation, and the sending process invokes this operation to effectively flush the buffer of unsent bytes. This operation is used in terminal emulators like Telnet because each byte has to be sent as soon as it is typed. The final trigger for transmitting a segment is a timer that periodically fires; the resulting segment contains as many bytes as are currently buffered for transmission.

Each TCP segment contains the header schematically depicted in Figure 5.4. The relevance of most of these fields will become apparent throughout this section. For now, we simply introduce them.

The **SrcPort** and **DstPort** fields identify the source and destination ports, respectively, just as in UDP. These two fields, plus the source and destination IP addresses,

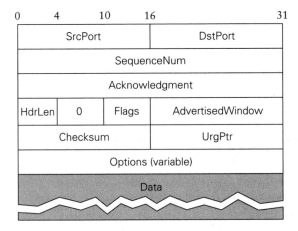

Figure 5.4 TCP header format.

combine to uniquely identify each TCP connection. That is, TCP's demux key is given by the 4-tuple

⟨ SrcPort, SrcIPAddr, DstPort, DstIPAddr ⟩

Note that because TCP connections come and go, it is possible for a connection between a particular pair of ports to be established, used to send and receive data, and closed, and then at a later time for the same pair of ports to be involved in a second connection. We sometimes refer to this situation as two different *incarnations* of the same connection.

The Acknowledgment, SequenceNum, and AdvertisedWindow fields are all involved in TCP's sliding window algorithm. Because TCP is a byte-oriented protocol, each byte of data has a sequence number; the SequenceNum field contains the sequence number for the first byte of data carried in that segment. The Acknowledgment and AdvertisedWindow fields carry information about the flow of data going in the other direction. To simplify our discussion, we ignore the fact that data can flow in both directions, and we concentrate on data that has a particular SequenceNum flowing in one direction and Acknowledgment and AdvertisedWindow values flowing in the opposite direction, as illustrated in Figure 5.5. The use of these three fields is described more fully in Section 5.2.4.

The 6-bit Flags field is used to relay control information between TCP peers. The possible flags include SYN, FIN, RESET, PUSH, URG, and ACK. The SYN and FIN flags

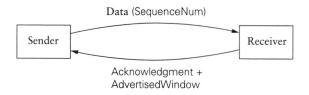

Figure 5.5 **Simplified illustration (showing only one direction) of the TCP process, with data flow in one direction and ACKs in the other.**

are used when establishing and terminating a TCP connection, respectively. Their use is described in Section 5.2.3. The ACK flag is set any time the Acknowledgment field is valid, implying that the receiver should pay attention to it. The URG flag signifies that this segment contains urgent data. When this flag is set, the UrgPtr field indicates where the nonurgent data contained in this segment begins. The urgent data is contained at the front of the segment body, up to and including a value of UrgPtr bytes into the segment. The PUSH flag signifies that the sender invoked the push operation, which indicates to the receiving side of TCP that it should notify the receiving process of this fact. We discuss these last two features more in Section 5.2.6. Finally, the RESET flag signifies that the receiver has become confused—for example, because it received a segment it did not expect to receive—and so wants to abort the connection.

Finally, the Checksum field is used in exactly the same way as for UDP—it is computed over the TCP header, the TCP data, and the pseudoheader, which is made up of the source address, destination address, and length fields from the IP header. The checksum is required for TCP in both IPv4 and IPv6. Also, since the TCP header is of variable length (options can be attached after the mandatory fields), a HdrLen field is included that gives the length of the header in 32-bit words. This field is also known as the Offset field, since it measures the offset from the start of the packet to the start of the data.

5.2.3 Connection Establishment and Termination

A TCP connection begins with a client (caller) doing an active open to a server (callee). Assuming that the server had earlier done a passive open, the two sides engage in an exchange of messages to establish the connection. (Recall from Chapter 1 that a party wanting to initiate a connection performs an active open, while a party willing to accept a connection does a passive open.) Only after this connection establishment phase is over do the two sides begin sending data. Likewise, as soon as a participant is done sending data, it closes one direction of the connection, which causes TCP to initiate a round of connection termination messages. Notice that while connection

Active participant
(client)

Passive participant
(server)

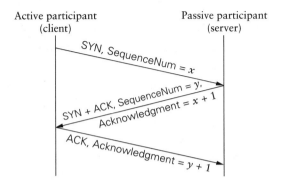

Figure 5.6 Timeline for three-way handshake algorithm.

setup is an asymmetric activity (one side does a passive open and the other side does an active open) connection teardown is symmetric (each side has to close the connection independently).[1] Therefore, it is possible for one side to have done a close, meaning that it can no longer send data, but for the other side to keep the other half of the bidirectional connection open and to continue sending data.

Three-Way Handshake

The algorithm used by TCP to establish and terminate a connection is called a *three-way handshake*. We first describe the basic algorithm and then show how it is used by TCP. The three-way handshake involves the exchange of three messages between the client and the server, as illustrated by the timeline given in Figure 5.6.

The idea is that two parties want to agree on a set of parameters, which, in the case of opening a TCP connection, are the starting sequence numbers the two sides plan to use for their respective byte streams. In general, the parameters might be any facts that each side wants the other to know about. First, the client (the active participant) sends a segment to the server (the passive participant) stating the initial sequence number it plans to use (Flags = SYN, SequenceNum = x). The server then responds with a single segment that both acknowledges the client's sequence number (Flags = ACK, Ack = $x + 1$) and states its own beginning sequence number (Flags = SYN, SequenceNum = y). That is, both the SYN and ACK bits are set in the Flags field of this second message. Finally, the client responds with a third segment that acknowledges the server's sequence number (Flags = ACK, Ack = $y + 1$). The

---

[1] To be more precise, connection setup can be symmetric, with both sides trying to open the connection at the same time, but the common case is for one side to do an active open and the other side to do a passive open.

reason that each side acknowledges a sequence number that is one larger than the one sent is that the Acknowledgment field actually identifies the "next sequence number expected," thereby implicitly acknowledging all earlier sequence numbers. Although not shown in this timeline, a timer is scheduled for each of the first two segments, and if the expected response is not received, the segment is retransmitted.

You may be asking yourself why the client and server have to exchange starting sequence numbers with each other at connection setup time. It would be simpler if each side simply started at some "well-known" sequence number, such as 0. In fact, the TCP specification requires that each side of a connection select an initial starting sequence number at random. The reason for this is to protect against two incarnations of the same connection reusing the same sequence numbers too soon, that is, while there is still a chance that a segment from an earlier incarnation of a connection might interfere with a later incarnation of the connection.

State-Transition Diagram

TCP is complex enough that its specification includes a state-transition diagram. A copy of this diagram is given in Figure 5.7. This diagram shows only the states involved in opening a connection (everything above ESTABLISHED) and in closing a connection (everything below ESTABLISHED). Everything that goes on while a connection is open—that is, the operation of the sliding window algorithm—is hidden in the ESTABLISHED state.

TCP's state-transition diagram is fairly easy to understand. Each circle denotes a state that one end of a TCP connection can find itself in. All connections start in the CLOSED state. As the connection progresses, the connection moves from state to state according to the arcs. Each arc is labeled with a tag of the form *event/action*. Thus, if a connection is in the LISTEN state and a SYN segment arrives (i.e., a segment with the SYN flag set), the connection makes a transition to the SYN_RCVD state and takes the action of replying with an ACK + SYN segment.

Notice that two kinds of events trigger a state transition: (1) a segment arrives from the peer (e.g., the event on the arc from LISTEN to SYN_RCVD), or (2) the local application process invokes an operation on TCP (e.g., the *active open* event on the arc from CLOSE to SYN_SENT). In other words, TCP's state-transition diagram effectively defines the *semantics* of both its peer-to-peer interface and its service interface, as defined in Section 1.2.1. The *syntax* of these two interfaces is given by the segment format (as illustrated in Figure 5.4), and by some application programming interface (an example of which is given in Section 1.3.1), respectively.

Now let's trace the typical transitions taken through the diagram in Figure 5.7. Keep in mind that at each end of the connection, TCP makes different transitions from state to state. When opening a connection, the server first invokes a passive

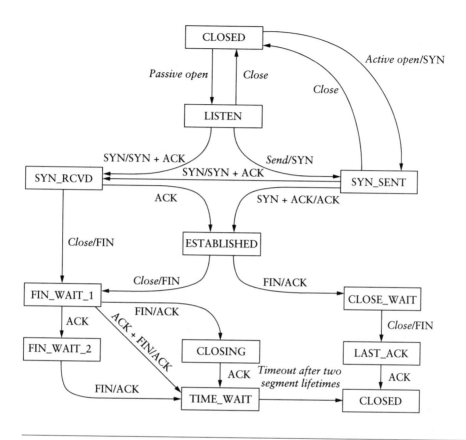

Figure 5.7 TCP state-transition diagram.

open operation on TCP, which causes TCP to move to the LISTEN state. At some later time, the client does an active open, which causes its end of the connection to send a SYN segment to the server and to move to the SYN_SENT state. When the SYN segment arrives at the server, it moves to the SYN_RCVD state and responds with a SYN + ACK segment. The arrival of this segment causes the client to move to the ESTABLISHED state and to send an ACK back to the server. When this ACK arrives, the server finally moves to the ESTABLISHED state. In other words, we have just traced the three-way handshake.

There are three things to notice about the connection establishment half of the state-transition diagram. First, if the client's ACK to the server is lost, corresponding to the third leg of the three-way handshake, then the connection still functions correctly. This is because the client side is already in the ESTABLISHED state, so the local application process can start sending data to the other end. Each of these data segments will have the ACK flag set, and the correct value in the Acknowledgment field, so the server will move to the ESTABLISHED state when the first data segment arrives. This is actually an important point about TCP—every segment reports what sequence number the sender is expecting to see next, even if this repeats the same sequence number contained in one or more previous segments.

The second thing to notice about the state-transition diagram is that there is a funny transition out of the LISTEN state whenever the local process invokes a *send* operation on TCP. That is, it is possible for a passive participant to identify both ends of the connection (i.e., itself and the remote participant that it is willing to have connect to it), and then for it to change its mind about waiting for the other side and instead actively establish the connection. To the best of our knowledge, this is a feature of TCP that no system-specific interface allows the application process to take advantage of.

The final thing to notice about the diagram is the arcs that are not shown. Specifically, most of the states that involve sending a segment to the other side also schedule a timeout that eventually causes the segment to be resent if the expected response does not happen. These retransmissions are not depicted in the state-transition diagram.

Turning our attention now to the process of terminating a connection, the important thing to keep in mind is that the application process on both sides of the connection must independently close its half of the connection. If only one side closes the connection, then this means it has no more data to send, but it is still available to receive data from the other side. This complicates the state-transition diagram because it must account for the possibility that the two sides invoke the *close* operator at the same time, as well as the possibility that first one side invokes close and then, at some later time, the other side invokes close. Thus, on any one side there are three combinations of transitions that get a connection from the ESTABLISHED state to the CLOSED state:

- This side closes first:
  ESTABLISHED → FIN_WAIT_1 → FIN_WAIT_2 → TIME_WAIT → CLOSED.

- The other side closes first:
  ESTABLISHED → CLOSE_WAIT → LAST_ACK → CLOSED.

- Both sides close at the same time:
  ESTABLISHED → FIN_WAIT_1 → CLOSING → TIME_WAIT → CLOSED.

There is actually a fourth, although rare, sequence of transitions that leads to the CLOSED state; it follows the arc from FIN_WAIT_1 to TIME_WAIT. We leave it as an exercise for you to figure out what combination of circumstances leads to this fourth possibility.

The main thing to recognize about connection teardown is that a connection in the TIME_WAIT state cannot move to the CLOSED state until it has waited for two times the maximum amount of time an IP datagram might live in the Internet (i.e., 120 seconds). The reason for this is that while the local side of the connection has sent an ACK in response to the other side's FIN segment, it does not know that the ACK was successfully delivered. As a consequence, the other side might retransmit its FIN segment, and this second FIN segment might be delayed in the network. If the connection were allowed to move directly to the CLOSED state, then another pair of application processes might come along and open the same connection (i.e., use the same pair of port numbers), and the delayed FIN segment from the earlier incarnation of the connection would immediately initiate the termination of the later incarnation of that connection.

5.2.4 Sliding Window Revisited

We are now ready to discuss TCP's variant of the sliding window algorithm, which serves several purposes: (1) it guarantees the reliable delivery of data, (2) it ensures that data is delivered in order, and (3) it enforces flow control between the sender and the receiver. TCP's use of the sliding window algorithm is the same as we saw in Section 2.5.2 in the case of the first two of these three functions. Where TCP differs from the earlier algorithm is that it folds the flow-control function in as well. In particular, rather than having a fixed-size sliding window, the receiver *advertises* a window size to the sender. This is done using the AdvertisedWindow field in the TCP header. The sender is then limited to having no more than a value of AdvertisedWindow bytes of unacknowledged data at any given time. The receiver selects a suitable value for AdvertisedWindow based on the amount of memory allocated to the connection for the purpose of buffering data. The idea is to keep the sender from overrunning the receiver's buffer. We discuss this at greater length below.

Reliable and Ordered Delivery

To see how the sending and receiving sides of TCP interact with each other to implement reliable and ordered delivery, consider the situation illustrated in Figure 5.8. TCP on the sending side maintains a send buffer. This buffer is used to store data that has been sent but not yet acknowledged, as well as data that has been written by the sending application, but not transmitted. On the receiving side, TCP maintains a receive buffer. This buffer holds data that arrives out of order, as well as data that is in the correct order (i.e., there are no missing bytes earlier in the stream) but that the application process has not yet had the chance to read.

To make the following discussion simpler to follow, we initially ignore the fact that both the buffers and the sequence numbers are of some finite size, and hence will

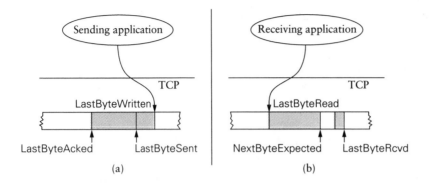

Figure 5.8 Relationship between TCP send buffer (a) and receive buffer (b).

eventually wrap around. Also, we do not distinguish between a pointer into a buffer where a particular byte of data is stored and the sequence number for that byte.

Looking first at the sending side, three pointers are maintained into the send buffer, each with an obvious meaning: **LastByteAcked**, **LastByteSent**, and **LastByteWritten**. Clearly,

$$\text{LastByteAcked} \leq \text{LastByteSent}$$

since the receiver cannot have acknowledged a byte that has not yet been sent, and

$$\text{LastByteSent} \leq \text{LastByteWritten}$$

since TCP cannot send a byte that the application process has not yet written. Also note that none of the bytes to the left of **LastByteAcked** need to be saved in the buffer because they have already been acknowledged, and none of the bytes to the right of **LastByteWritten** need to be buffered because they have not yet been generated.

A similar set of pointers (sequence numbers) are maintained on the receiving side: **LastByteRead**, **NextByteExpected**, and **LastByteRcvd**. The inequalities are a little less intuitive, however, because of the problem of out-of-order delivery. The first relationship

$$\text{LastByteRead} < \text{NextByteExpected}$$

is true because a byte cannot be read by the application until it is received *and* all preceding bytes have also been received. **NextByteExpected** points to the byte immediately after the latest byte to meet this criterion. Second,

$$\text{NextByteExpected} \leq \text{LastByteRcvd} + 1$$

since, if data has arrived in order, NextByteExpected points to the byte after LastByteRcvd, whereas if data has arrived out of order, NextByteExpected points to the start of the first gap in the data, as in Figure 5.8. Note that bytes to the left of LastByteRead need not be buffered because they have already been read by the local application process, and bytes to the right of LastByteRcvd need not be buffered because they have not yet arrived.

Flow Control

Most of the above discussion is similar to that found in Section 2.5.2; the only real difference is that this time we elaborated on the fact that the sending and receiving application processes are filling and emptying their local buffer, respectively. (The earlier discussion glossed over the fact that data arriving from an upstream node was filling the send buffer, and data being transmitted to a downstream node was emptying the receive buffer.)

You should make sure you understand this much before proceeding because now comes the point where the two algorithms differ more significantly. In what follows, we reintroduce the fact that both buffers are of some finite size, denoted MaxSendBuffer and MaxRcvBuffer, although we don't worry about the details of how they are implemented. In other words, we are only interested in the number of bytes being buffered, not in where those bytes are actually stored.

Recall that in a sliding window protocol, the size of the window sets the amount of data that can be sent without waiting for acknowledgment from the receiver. Thus, the receiver throttles the sender by advertising a window that is no larger than the amount of data that it can buffer. Observe that TCP on the receive side must keep

$$\text{LastByteRcvd} - \text{LastByteRead} \leq \text{MaxRcvBuffer}$$

to avoid overflowing its buffer. It therefore advertises a window size of

$$\text{AdvertisedWindow} = \text{MaxRcvBuffer} - (\text{LastByteRcvd} - \text{LastByteRead})$$

which represents the amount of free space remaining in its buffer. As data arrives, the receiver acknowledges it as long as all the preceding bytes have also arrived. In addition, LastByteRcvd moves to the right (is incremented), meaning that the advertised window potentially shrinks. Whether or not it shrinks depends on how fast the local application process is consuming data. If the local process is reading data just as fast as it arrives (causing LastByteRead to be incremented at the same rate as LastByteRcvd), then the advertised window stays open (i.e., AdvertisedWindow = MaxRcvBuffer). If, however, the receiving process falls behind, perhaps because it performs a very expensive operation on each byte of data that it reads, then the advertised window grows smaller with every segment that arrives, until it eventually goes to 0.

TCP on the send side must then adhere to the advertised window it gets from the receiver. This means that at any given time, it must ensure that

$$LastByteSent - LastByteAcked \leq AdvertisedWindow$$

Said another way, the sender computes an *effective* window that limits how much data it can send:

$$EffectiveWindow = AdvertisedWindow - (LastByteSent - LastByteAcked)$$

Clearly, EffectiveWindow must be greater than 0 before the source can send more data. It is possible, therefore, that a segment arrives acknowledging x bytes, thereby allowing the sender to increment LastByteAcked by x, but because the receiving process was not reading any data, the advertised window is now x bytes smaller than the time before. In such a situation, the sender would be able to free buffer space, but not to send any more data.

All the while this is going on, the send side must also make sure that the local application process does not overflow the send buffer, that is, that

$$LastByteWritten - LastByteAcked \leq MaxSendBuffer$$

If the sending process tries to write y bytes to TCP, but

$$(LastByteWritten - LastByteAcked) + y > MaxSendBuffer$$

then TCP blocks the sending process and does not allow it to generate more data.

It is now possible to understand how a slow receiving process ultimately stops a fast sending process. First, the receive buffer fills up, which means the advertised window shrinks to 0. An advertised window of 0 means that the sending side cannot transmit any data, even though data it has previously sent has been successfully acknowledged. Finally, not being able to transmit any data means that the send buffer fills up, which ultimately causes TCP to block the sending process. As soon as the receiving process starts to read data again, the receive-side TCP is able to open its window back up, which allows the send-side TCP to transmit data out of its buffer. When this data is eventually acknowledged, LastByteAcked is incremented, the buffer space holding this acknowledged data becomes free, and the sending process is unblocked and allowed to proceed.

There is only one remaining detail that must be resolved—how does the sending side know that the advertised window is no longer 0? As mentioned above, TCP *always* sends a segment in response to a received data segment, and this response contains the latest values for the Acknowledge and AdvertisedWindow fields, even if these values have not changed since the last time they were sent. The problem is this. Once the receive side has advertised a window size of 0, the sender is not permitted to send any more data, which means it has no way to discover that the advertised window is no longer 0 at some time in the future. TCP on the receive side does not spontaneously send nondata segments; it only sends them in response to an arriving data segment.

TCP deals with this situation as follows. Whenever the other side advertises a window size of 0, the sending side persists in sending a segment with 1 byte of data every so often. It knows that this data will probably not be accepted, but it tries anyway, because each of these 1-byte segments triggers a response that contains the current advertised window. Eventually, one of these 1-byte probes triggers a response that reports a nonzero advertised window.

Note that the reason the sending side periodically sends this probe segment is that TCP is designed to make the receive side as simple as possible—it simply responds to segments from the sender, and it never initiates any activity on its own. This is an example of a well-recognized (although not universally applied) protocol design rule, which, for lack of a better name, we call the *smart sender/dumb receiver* rule. Recall that we saw another example of this rule when we discussed the use of NAKs in Section 2.5.2.

Protecting against Wraparound

This subsection and the next consider the size of the SequenceNum and AdvertisedWindow fields and the implications of their sizes on TCP's correctness and performance. TCP's SequenceNum field is 32 bits long, and its AdvertisedWindow field is 16 bits long, meaning that TCP has easily satisfied the requirement of the sliding window algorithm that the sequence number space be twice as big as the window size: $2^{32} \gg 2 \times 2^{16}$. However, this requirement is not the interesting thing about these two fields. Consider each field in turn.

The relevance of the 32-bit sequence number space is that the sequence number used on a given connection might wrap around—a byte with sequence number x could be sent at one time, and then at a later time, a second byte with the same sequence number x might be sent. Once again, we assume that packets cannot survive in the Internet for longer than the recommended MSL. Thus, we currently need to make sure that the sequence number does not wrap around within a 120-second period of time. Whether or not this happens depends on how fast data can be transmitted over the Internet, that is, how fast the 32-bit sequence number space can be consumed.

Bandwidth	Time until Wraparound
T1 (1.5 Mbps)	6.4 hours
Ethernet (10 Mbps)	57 minutes
T3 (45 Mbps)	13 minutes
FDDI (100 Mbps)	6 minutes
STS-3 (155 Mbps)	4 minutes
STS-12 (622 Mbps)	55 seconds
STS-24 (1.2 Gbps)	28 seconds

Table 5.1 Time until 32-bit sequence number space wraps around.

(This discussion assumes that we are trying to consume the sequence number space as fast as possible, but of course we will be if we are doing our job of keeping the pipe full.) Table 5.1 shows how long it takes for the sequence number to wrap around on networks with various bandwidths.

As you can see, the 32-bit sequence number space is adequate for today's networks, but given that OC-48 links are currently being installed in the Internet backbone, it won't be long until individual TCP connections want to run at STS-12 speeds or higher. Fortunately, the IETF has already worked out an extension to TCP that effectively extends the sequence number space to protect against the sequence number wrapping around. This and related extensions are described in Section 5.2.7.

Keeping the Pipe Full

The relevance of the 16-bit AdvertisedWindow field is that it must be big enough to allow the sender to keep the pipe full. Clearly, the receiver is free to not open the window as large as the AdvertisedWindow field allows; we are interested in the situation in which the receiver has enough buffer space to handle as much data as the largest possible AdvertisedWindow allows.

In this case, it is not just the network bandwidth but the delay × bandwidth product that dictates how big the AdvertisedWindow field needs to be—the window needs to be opened far enough to allow a full delay × bandwidth product's worth of data to be transmitted. Assuming an RTT of 100 ms (a typical number for a crosscountry connection in the U.S.), Table 5.2 gives the delay × bandwidth product for several network technologies.

Bandwidth	Delay × Bandwidth Product
T1 (1.5 Mbps)	18 KB
Ethernet (10 Mbps)	122 KB
T3 (45 Mbps)	549 KB
FDDI (100 Mbps)	1.2 MB
STS-3 (155 Mbps)	1.8 MB
STS-12 (622 Mbps)	7.4 MB
STS-24 (1.2 Gbps)	14.8 MB

Table 5.2 Required window size for 100-ms RTT.

As you can see, TCP's AdvertisedWindow field is in even worse shape than its SequenceNum field—it is not big enough to handle even a T3 connection across the continental United States, since a 16-bit field allows us to advertise a window of only 64 KB. The very same TCP extension mentioned above (see Section 5.2.7) provides a mechanism for effectively increasing the size of the advertised window.

5.2.5 Adaptive Retransmission

Because TCP guarantees the reliable delivery of data, it retransmits each segment if an ACK is not received in a certain period of time. TCP sets this timeout as a function of the RTT it expects between the two ends of the connection. Unfortunately, given the range of possible RTTs between any pair of hosts in the Internet, as well as the variation in RTT between the same two hosts over time, choosing an appropriate timeout value is not that easy. To address this problem, TCP uses an adaptive retransmission mechanism. We now describe this mechanism and how it has evolved over time as the Internet community has gained more experience using TCP.

Original Algorithm

We begin with a simple algorithm for computing a timeout value between a pair of hosts. This is the algorithm that was originally described in the TCP specification—and the following description presents it in those terms—but it could be used by any end-to-end protocol.

The idea is to keep a running average of the RTT and then to compute the timeout as a function of this RTT. Specifically, every time TCP sends a data segment, it records the time. When an ACK for that segment arrives, TCP reads the time again, and then takes the difference between these two times as a SampleRTT. TCP then computes an EstimatedRTT as a weighted average between the previous estimate and this new sample. That is,

$$\text{EstimatedRTT} = \alpha \times \text{EstimatedRTT} + (1 - \alpha) \times \text{SampleRTT}$$

The parameter α is selected to *smooth* the EstimatedRTT. A small α tracks changes in the RTT but is perhaps too heavily influenced by temporary fluctuations. On the other hand, a large α is more stable but perhaps not quick enough to adapt to real changes. The original TCP specification recommended a setting of α between 0.8 and 0.9. TCP then uses EstimatedRTT to compute the timeout in a rather conservative way:

$$\text{TimeOut} = 2 \times \text{EstimatedRTT}$$

Karn/Partridge Algorithm

After several years of use on the Internet, a rather obvious flaw was discovered in this simple algorithm. The problem was that an ACK does not really acknowledge a transmission; it actually acknowledges the receipt of data. In other words, whenever a segment is retransmitted and then an ACK arrives at the sender, it is impossible to determine if this ACK should be associated with the first or the second transmission of the segment for the purpose of measuring the sample RTT. It is necessary to know which transmission to associate it with so as to compute an accurate SampleRTT. As illustrated in Figure 5.9, if you assume that the ACK is for the original transmission but it was really for the second, then the SampleRTT is too large (a), while if you assume that the ACK is for the second transmission but it was actually for the first, then the SampleRTT is too small (b).

The solution is surprisingly simple. Whenever TCP retransmits a segment, it stops taking samples of the RTT; it only measures SampleRTT for segments that have been sent only once. This solution is known as the Karn/Partridge algorithm, after its inventors. Their proposed fix also includes a second small change to TCP's timeout mechanism. Each time TCP retransmits, it sets the next timeout to be twice the last timeout, rather than basing it on the last EstimatedRTT. That is, Karn and Partridge proposed that TCP use exponential backoff, similar to what the Ethernet does. The motivation for using exponential backoff is simple: Congestion is the most likely cause of lost segments, meaning that the TCP source should not react too aggressively to a timeout. In fact, the more times the connection times out, the more cautious the source should become. We will see this idea again, embodied in a much more sophisticated mechanism, in Chapter 6.

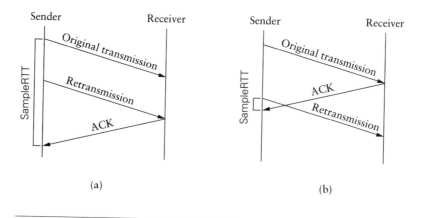

Figure 5.9 Associating the ACK with (a) original transmission versus (b) retransmission.

Jacobson/Karels Algorithm

The Karn/Partridge algorithm was introduced at a time when the Internet was suffering from high levels of network congestion. Their approach was designed to fix some of the causes of that congestion, and although it was an improvement, the congestion was not eliminated. A couple of years later, two other researchers—Jacobson and Karels— proposed a more drastic change to TCP to battle congestion. The bulk of that proposed change is described in Chapter 6. Here, we focus on the aspect of that proposal that is related to deciding when to time out and retransmit a segment.

As an aside, it should be clear how the timeout mechanism is related to congestion—if you time out too soon, you may unnecessarily retransmit a segment, which only adds to the load on the network. As we will see in Chapter 6, the other reason for needing an accurate timeout value is that a timeout is taken to imply congestion, which triggers a congestion-control mechanism. Finally, note that there is nothing about the Jacobson/Karels timeout computation that is specific to TCP. It could be used by any end-to-end protocol.

The main problem with the original computation is that it does not take the variance of the sample RTTs into account. Intuitively, if the variation among samples is small, then the EstimatedRTT can be better trusted and there is no reason for multiplying this estimate by 2 to compute the timeout. On the other hand, a large variance in the samples suggests that the timeout value should not be too tightly coupled to the EstimatedRTT.

In the new approach, the sender measures a new SampleRTT as before. It then folds this new sample into the timeout calculation as follows:

$$\text{Difference} = \text{SampleRTT} - \text{EstimatedRTT}$$

$$\text{EstimatedRTT} = \text{EstimatedRTT} + (\delta \times \text{Difference})$$

$$\text{Deviation} = \text{Deviation} + \delta(|\text{Difference}| - \text{Deviation})$$

where δ is a fraction between 0 and 1. That is, we calculate both the mean RTT and the variation in that mean.

TCP then computes the timeout value as a function of both EstimatedRTT and Deviation as follows:

$$\text{TimeOut} = \mu \times \text{EstimatedRTT} + \phi \times \text{Deviation}$$

where based on experience, μ is typically set to 1 and ϕ is set to 4. Thus, when the variance is small, TimeOut is close to EstimatedRTT; a large variance causes the Deviation term to dominate the calculation.

Implementation

There are two items of note regarding the implementation of timeouts in TCP. The first is that it is possible to implement the calculation for EstimatedRTT and Deviation without using floating-point arithmetic. Instead, the whole calculation is scaled by 2^n, with δ selected to be $1/2^n$. This allows us to do integer arithmetic, implementing multiplication and division using shifts, thereby achieving higher performance. The resulting calculation is given by the following code fragment, where $n = 3$ (i.e., $\delta = 1/8$). Note that EstimatedRTT and Deviation are stored in their scaled-up forms, while the value of SampleRTT at the start of the code and of TimeOut at the end are real, unscaled values. If you find the code hard to follow, you might want to try plugging some real numbers into it and verifying that it gives the same results as the equations above.

```
{
    SampleRTT -= (EstimatedRTT >> 3);
    EstimatedRTT += SampleRTT;
    if (SampleRTT < 0)
        SampleRTT = -SampleRTT;
    SampleRTT -= (Deviation >> 3);
    Deviation += SampleRTT;
    TimeOut = (EstimatedRTT >> 3) + (Deviation >> 1);
}
```

The second point of note is that the Jacobson/Karels algorithm is only as good as the clock used to read the current time. On a typical Berkeley Unix implementation, the clock granularity is as large as 500 ms, which is significantly larger than the average crosscountry RTT of somewhere between 100 and 200 ms. To make matters worse, the Berkeley Unix implementation of TCP only checks to see if a timeout should happen every time this 500-ms clock ticks, and it only takes a sample of the round-trip time once per RTT. The combination of these two factors quite often means that a timeout happens 1 second after the segment was transmitted. Once again, the proposed extensions to TCP include a mechanism that makes this RTT calculation a bit more precise.

5.2.6 Record Boundaries

As mentioned earlier in this section, TCP is a byte-stream protocol. This means that the number of bytes written by the sender are not necessarily the same as the number of bytes read by the receiver. For example, the application might write 8 bytes, then 2 bytes, then 20 bytes to a TCP connection, while on the receiving side, the application reads 5 bytes at a time inside a loop that iterates 6 times. TCP does not interject record boundaries between the 8th and 9th bytes, nor between the 10th and 11th bytes. This is in contrast to a message-oriented protocol, such as UDP, in which the message that is sent is exactly the same length as the message that is received.

Even though TCP is a byte-stream protocol, it has two different features that can be used by the sender to insert record boundaries into this byte stream, thereby informing the receiver how to break the stream of bytes into records. (Being able to mark record boundaries is useful, for example, in many database applications.) Both of these features were originally included in TCP for completely different reasons; they have only come to be used for this purpose over time.

The first mechanism is the urgent data feature, as implemented by the URG flag and the UrgPtr field in the TCP header. Originally, the urgent data mechanism was designed to allow the sending application to send *out-of-band* data to its peer. By "out of band" we mean data that is separate from the normal flow of data (e.g., a command to interrupt an operation already under way). This out-of-band data was identified in the segment using the UrgPtr field and was to be delivered to the receiving process as soon as it arrived, even if that meant delivering it before data with an earlier sequence number. Over time, however, this feature has not been used, so instead of signifying "urgent" data, it has come to be used to signify "special" data, such as a record marker. This use has developed because, as with the push operation, TCP on the receiving side must inform the application that "urgent data" has arrived. That is, the urgent data in itself is not important. It is the fact that the sending process can effectively send a signal to the receiver that is important.

The second mechanism for inserting end-of-record markers into a byte is the *push* operation. Originally, this mechanism was designed to allow the sending process to tell

TCP that it should send whatever bytes it had collected to its peer. This was, and still is, used by interactive applications like Telnet because each byte has to be sent as soon as it is typed. However, push can be used to implement record boundaries because the specification says that TCP must send whatever data it has buffered at the source when the application says push, and optionally, TCP at the destination notifies the application whenever an incoming segment has the PUSH flag set. If the receiving side supports this option (the socket interface does not), then the push operation can be used to break the TCP stream into records.

Of course, the application program is always free to insert record boundaries without any assistance from TCP. For example, it can send a field that indicates the length of a record that is to follow, or it can insert its own record boundary markers into the data stream.

5.2.7 TCP Extensions

We have mentioned at three different points in this section that proposed extensions to TCP may help to mitigate some problem that TCP is facing. These proposed extensions are designed to have as small an impact on TCP as possible. In particular, they are realized as options that can be added to the TCP header. (We glossed over this point earlier, but the reason that the TCP header has a HdrLen field is that the header can be of variable length; the variable part of the TCP header contains the options that have been added.) The significance of adding these extensions as options rather than changing the core of the TCP header is that hosts can still communicate using TCP even if they do not implement the options. Hosts that do implement the optional extensions, however, can take advantage of them. The two sides agree that they will use the options during TCP's connection establishment phase.

The first extension helps to improve TCP's timeout mechanism. Instead of measuring the RTT using a coarse-grained event, TCP can read the actual system clock when it is about to send a segment, and put this time—think of it as a 32-bit *timestamp*—in the segment's header. The receiver then echoes this timestamp back to the sender in its acknowledgment, and the sender subtracts this timestamp from the current time to measure the RTT. In essence, the timestamp option provides a convenient place for TCP to "store" the record of when a segment was transmitted; it stores the time in the segment itself. Note that the endpoints in the connection do not need synchronized clocks, since the timestamp is written and read at the same end of the connection.

The second extension addresses the problem of TCP's 32-bit SequenceNum field wrapping around too soon on a high-speed network. Rather than define a new 64-bit sequence number field, TCP uses the 32-bit timestamp just described to effectively extend the sequence number space. In other words, TCP decides whether to accept or reject a segment based on a 64-bit identifier that has the SequenceNum field in the low-order 32 bits and the timestamp in the high-order 32 bits. Since the timestamp is always increasing, it serves to distinguish between two different incarnations of the same sequence number. Note that the timestamp is being used in this setting only to protect against wraparound; it is not treated as part of the sequence number for the purpose of ordering or acknowledging data.

The third extension allows TCP to advertise a larger window, thereby allowing it to fill larger delay × bandwidth pipes that are made possible by high-speed networks. This extension involves an option that defines a *scaling factor* for the advertised window. That is, rather than interpreting the number that appears in the AdvertisedWindow field as indicating how many bytes the sender is allowed to have unacknowledged, this option allows the two sides of TCP to agree that the AdvertisedWindow field counts larger chunks (e.g., how many 16-byte units of data the sender can have unacknowledged). In other words, the window scaling option specifies how many bits each side should left-shift the AdvertisedWindow field before using its contents to compute an effective window.

5.2.8 Alternative Design Choices

Although TCP has proven to be a robust protocol that satisfies the needs of a wide range of applications, the design space for transport protocols is quite large. TCP is, by no means, the only valid point in that design space. We conclude our discussion of TCP by considering alternative design choices. While we offer an explanation for why TCP's designers made the choices they did, we leave it to you to decide if there might be a place for alternative transport protocols.

First, we have suggested from the very first chapter of this book that there are at least two interesting classes of transport protocols: stream-oriented protocols like TCP and request/reply protocols like RPC. In other words, we have implicitly divided the design space in half and placed TCP squarely in the stream-oriented half of the world. We could further divide the stream-oriented protocols into two groups—reliable and unreliable—with the former containing TCP and the latter being more suitable for interactive video applications that would rather drop a frame than incur the delay associated with a retransmission.

This exercise in building a transport protocol taxonomy is interesting and could be continued in greater and greater detail, but the world isn't as black and white as we might like. Consider the suitability of TCP as a transport protocol for request/reply applications, for example. TCP is a full-duplex protocol, so it would be easy to open a TCP connection between the client and server, send the request message in one direction, and send the reply message in the other direction. There are two complications, however. The first is that TCP is a *byte*-oriented protocol rather than a *message*-oriented protocol, and request/reply applications always deal with messages. (We explore the issue of bytes versus messages in greater detail in a moment.) The second complication is that in those situations where both the request message and the reply message fit in a single network packet, a well-designed request/reply protocol needs only two packets to implement the exchange, whereas TCP would need at least nine: three to establish the connection, two for the message exchange, and four to tear down the connection. Of course, if the request or reply messages are large enough to require multiple network packets (e.g., it might take 100 packets to send a 100,000-byte reply message), then the overhead of setting up and tearing down the connection is inconsequential. In other words, it isn't always the case that a particular protocol cannot support a certain functionality; it's sometimes the case that one design is more efficient than another under particular circumstances.

Second, as just suggested, you might question why TCP chose to provide a reliable *byte*-stream service rather than a reliable *message*-stream service; messages would be the natural choice for a database application that wants to exchange records. There are two answers to this question. The first is that a message-oriented protocol must, by definition, establish an upper bound on message sizes. After all, an infinitely long message is a byte stream. For any message size that a protocol selects, there will be applications that want to send larger messages, rendering the transport protocol useless and forcing the application to implement its own transportlike services. The second reason is that while message-oriented protocols are definitely more appropriate for applications that want to send records to each other, you can easily insert record boundaries into a byte stream to implement this functionality, as described in Section 5.2.6.

Third, TCP chose to implement explicit setup/teardown phases, but this is not required. In the case of connection setup, it would certainly be possible to send all necessary connection parameters along with the first data message. TCP elected to take a more conservative approach that gives the receiver the opportunity to reject the connection before any data arrives. In the case of teardown, we could quietly close a connection that has been inactive for a long period of time, but this would complicate applications like Telnet that want to keep a connection alive for weeks at a time; such applications would be forced to send out-of-band "keep alive" messages to keep the connection state at the other end from disappearing.

Finally, TCP is a window-based protocol, but this is not the only possibility. The alternative is a *rate-based* design, in which the receiver tells the sender the rate—expressed in either bytes or packets per second—at which it is willing to accept incoming data. For example, the receiver might inform the sender that it can accommodate 100 packets a second. There is an interesting duality between windows and rate, since the number of packets (bytes) in the window, divided by the RTT, is exactly the rate.

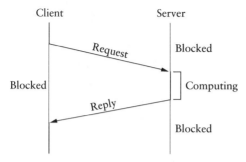

Figure 5.10   Timeline for RPC.

For example, a window size of 10 packets and a 100-ms RTT implies that the sender is allowed to transmit at a rate of 100 packets a second. It is by increasing or decreasing the advertised window size that the receiver is effectively raising or lowering the rate at which the sender can transmit. In TCP, this information is fed back to the sender in the AdvertisedWindow field of the ACK for every segment. One of the key issues in a rate-based protocol is how often the desired rate—which may change over time—is relayed back to the source: Is it for every packet, once per RTT, or only when the rate changes? While we have just now considered window versus rate in the context of flow control, it is an even more hotly contested issue in the context of congestion control, which we will discuss in Chapter 6.

5.3   Remote Procedure Call

As discussed in Chapter 1, a common pattern of communication used by application programs is the request/reply paradigm, also called message transaction: A client sends a request message to a server, the server responds with a reply message, and the client blocks (suspends execution) waiting for this response. Figure 5.10 illustrates the basic interaction between the client and server in such a message transaction.

A transport protocol that supports the request/reply paradigm is much more than a UDP message going in one direction, followed by a UDP message going in the other direction. It also involves overcoming all of the limitations of the underlying network outlined in the problem statement at the beginning of this chapter. While TCP overcomes these limitations by providing a reliable byte-stream service, it doesn't match the request/reply paradigm very well either since going to the trouble of establishing a TCP connection just to exchange a pair of messages seems like overkill. This section describes a third transport protocol—which we call Remote Procedure Call (RPC)—that more closely matches the needs of an application involved in a request/reply message exchange.

RPC is actually more than just a protocol—it is a popular mechanism for structuring distributed systems. RPC is popular because it is based on the semantics of a local procedure call—the application program makes a call into a procedure without regard for whether it is local or remote and blocks until the call returns. While this may sound simple, there are two main problems that make RPC more complicated than local procedure calls:

■ The network between the calling process and the called process has much more complex properties than the backplane of a computer. For example, it is likely to limit message sizes and has a tendency to lose and reorder messages.

■ The computers on which the calling and called processes run may have significantly different architectures and data representation formats.

Thus, a complete RPC mechanism actually involves two major components:

1 a protocol that manages the messages sent between the client and the server processes and that deals with the potentially undesirable properties of the underlying network

2 programming language and compiler support to package the arguments into a request message on the client machine and then to translate this message back into the arguments on the server machine, and likewise with the return value (this piece of the RPC mechanism is usually called a *stub compiler*)

Figure 5.11 schematically depicts what happens when a client invokes a remote procedure. First, the client calls a local stub for the procedure, passing it the arguments required by the procedure. This stub hides the fact that the procedure is remote by translating the arguments into a request message and then invoking an RPC protocol to send the request message to the server machine. At the server, the RPC protocol delivers the request message to the server stub, which translates it into the arguments to the procedure and then calls the local procedure. After the server procedure completes, it returns the answer to the server stub, which packages this return value in a reply message that it hands off to the RPC protocol for transmission back to the client. The RPC protocol on the client passes this message up to the client stub, which translates it into a return value that it returns to the client program.

This section considers just the protocol-related aspects of an RPC mechanism. That is, it ignores the stubs and focuses instead on the RPC protocol that transmits messages between client and server; the transformation of arguments into messages and vice versa is covered in Chapter 7. Furthermore, since RPC is a generic term—

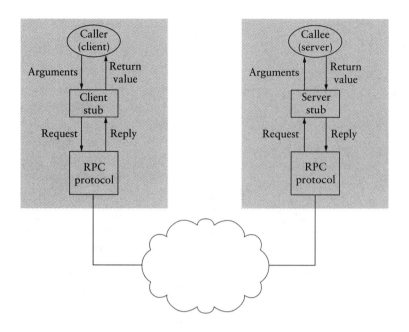

Figure 5.11 Complete RPC mechanism.

rather than a specific standard like TCP—we are going to take a different approach than we did in the previous section. Instead of organizing the discussion around an existing standard (i.e., TCP) and then pointing out alternative designs at the end, we are going to walk you through the thought process involved in designing an RPC protocol. That is, we will design our own RPC protocol from scratch—considering the design options at every step of the way—and then come back and describe some widely used RPC protocols by comparing and contrasting them to the protocol we just designed.

Before jumping in, however, we note that an RPC protocol performs a rather complicated set of functions, and so instead of treating RPC as a single, monolithic protocol, we develop it as a "stack" of three smaller protocols: BLAST, CHAN, and SELECT. Each of these smaller protocols, which we sometimes call a *microprotocol*, contains a single algorithm that addresses one of the problems outlined at the start of this chapter. As a brief overview:

- BLAST: fragments and reassembles large messages

- CHAN: synchronizes request and reply messages

- SELECT: dispatches request messages to the correct process

These microprotocols are complete, self-contained protocols that can be used in different combinations to provide different end-to-end services. Section 5.3.4 shows how they can be combined to implement RPC.

Just to be clear, BLAST, CHAN, and SELECT are not standard protocols in the sense that TCP, UDP, and IP are. They are simply protocols of our own invention, but ones that demonstrate the algorithms needed to implement RPC. Because this section is not constrained by the artifacts of what has been designed in the past, it provides a particularly good opportunity to examine the principles of protocol design.

5.3.1 Bulk Transfer (BLAST)

The first problem we are going to tackle is how to turn an underlying network that delivers messages of some small size (say, 1 KB) into a service that delivers messages of a much larger size (say, 32 KB). While 32 KB does not qualify as "arbitrarily large," it is large enough to be of practical use for many applications, including most distributed file systems. Ultimately, a stream-based protocol like TCP (see Section 5.2) will be needed to support an arbitrarily large message, since any message-oriented protocol will necessarily have some upper limit to the size of the message it can handle, and you can always imagine needing to transmit a message that is larger than this limit.

We have already examined the basic

What Layer Is RPC?

Once again, the "What layer is this?" issue raises its ugly head. To many people, especially those who adhere to the Internet architecture, RPC is implemented on top of a transport protocol (usually UDP) and so cannot itself (by definition) be a transport protocol. It is equally valid, however, to argue that the Internet should have an RPC protocol, since it offers a process-to-process service that is fundamentally different from that offered by TCP and UDP. The usual response to such a suggestion, however, is that the Internet architecture does not prohibit network designers from implementing their own RPC protocol on top of UDP. (In general, UDP is viewed as the Internet architecture's "escape hatch," since effectively it just adds a layer of demultiplexing to IP.) Whichever side of the issue of whether the Internet should have an official RPC protocol you support, the important point is that the way you implement RPC in the Internet architecture says nothing about whether RPC should be considered a transport protocol or not.

technique that is used to transmit a large message over a network that can accommodate only smaller messages—fragmentation and reassembly. We now describe the BLAST protocol, which uses this technique. One of the unique properties of BLAST is how hard it tries to deliver all the fragments of a message. Unlike the AAL

Interestingly, there are other people who believe that RPC is the most interesting protocol in the world and that TCP/IP is just what you do when you want to go "off site." This is the predominant view of the operating systems community, which has built countless OS kernels for distributed systems that contain exactly one protocol—you guessed it, RPC—running on top of a network device driver.

The water gets even muddier when you implement RPC as a combination of three different microprotocols, as is the case in this section. In such a situation, which of the three is the "transport" protocol? Our answer to this question is that any protocol that offers process-to-process service, as opposed to node-to-node or host-to-host service, qualifies as a transport protocol. Thus, RPC is a transport protocol and, in fact, can be implemented from a combination of microprotocols that are themselves valid transport protocols.

segmentation/reassembly mechanism used with ATM (see Section 3.3) or the IP fragmentation/reassembly mechanism (see Section 4.1), BLAST attempts to recover from dropped fragments by retransmitting them. However, BLAST does not go so far as to *guarantee* message delivery. The significance of this design choice will become clear later in this section.

BLAST Algorithm

The basic idea of BLAST is for the sender to break a large message passed to it by some high-level protocol into a set of smaller fragments, and then for it to transmit these fragments back-to-back over the network. Hence the name BLAST—the protocol does not wait for any of the fragments to be acknowledged before sending the next. The receiver then sends a *selective retransmission request* (SRR) back to the sender, indicating which fragments arrived and which did not. (The SRR message is sometimes called a *partial* or *selective* acknowledgment.) Finally, the sender retransmits the missing fragments. In the case in which all the fragments have arrived, the SRR serves to fully acknowledge the message. Figure 5.12 gives a representative timeline for the BLAST protocol.

We now consider the send and receive sides of BLAST in more detail. On the sending side, after fragmenting the message and transmitting each of the fragments, the sender sets a timer called DONE. Whenever an SRR arrives, the sender retransmits the requested fragments and resets timer DONE. Should the SRR indicate that all the fragments have arrived, the sender frees its copy of the message and cancels timer DONE. If timer DONE ever expires, the sender frees its copy of the message; that is, it gives up.

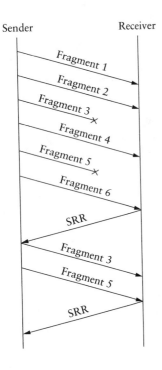

Sender   Receiver

Fragment 1
Fragment 2
Fragment 3 ✗
Fragment 4
Fragment 5 ✗
Fragment 6
SRR
Fragment 3
Fragment 5
SRR

Figure 5.12   Representative timeline for BLAST.

On the receiving side, whenever the first fragment of a message arrives, the receiver initializes a data structure to hold the individual fragments as they arrive and sets a timer LAST_FRAG. This timer counts the time that has elapsed since the last fragment arrived. Each time a fragment for that message arrives, the receiver adds it to this data structure, and should all the fragments then be present, it reassembles them into a complete message and passes this message up to the higher-level protocol. There are four exceptional conditions, however, that the receiver watches for:

■ If the last fragment arrives (the last fragment is specially marked) but the message is not complete, then the receiver determines which fragments are missing and sends an SRR to the sender. It also sets a timer called RETRY.

■ If timer LAST_FRAG expires, then the receiver determines which fragments are missing and sends an SRR to the sender. It also sets timer RETRY.

■ If timer RETRY expires for the first or second time, then the receiver determines which fragments are still missing and retransmits an SRR message.

Note it

■ If timer RETRY expires for the third time, then the receiver frees the fragments that have arrived and cancels timer LAST_FRAG; that is, it gives up.

There are three aspects of BLAST worth noting. First, two different events trigger the initial transmission of an SRR: the arrival of the last fragment and the firing of the LAST_FRAG timer. In the case of the former, because the network may reorder packets, the arrival of the last fragment does not necessarily imply that an earlier fragment is missing (it may just be late in arriving), but since this is the most likely explanation, BLAST aggressively sends an SRR message. In the latter case, we deduce that the last fragment was either lost or seriously delayed.

Second, the performance of BLAST does not critically depend on how carefully the timers are set. Timer DONE is used only to decide that it is time to give up and delete the message that is currently being worked on. This timer can be set to a fairly large value since its only purpose is to reclaim storage. Timer RETRY is only used to retransmit an SRR message. Any time the situation is so bad that a protocol is reexecuting a failure recovery process, performance is the last thing on its mind. Finally, timer LAST_FRAG has the potential to influence performance—it sometimes triggers the sending by the receiver of an SRR message—but this is an unlikely event: It only happens when the last fragment of the message happens to get dropped in the network.

Third, while BLAST is persistent in asking for and retransmitting missing fragments, it does not guarantee that the complete message will be delivered. To understand this, suppose that a message consists of only one or two fragments and that these fragments are lost. The receiver will never send an SRR, and the sender's DONE timer will eventually expire, causing the sender to release the message. To guarantee delivery, BLAST would need for the sender to time out if it does not receive an SRR and then retransmit the last set of fragments it had transmitted. While BLAST certainly could have been designed to do this, we chose not to because the purpose of BLAST is to deliver large messages, not to guarantee message delivery. Other protocols can be configured on top of BLAST to guarantee message delivery. You might wonder why we put any retransmission capability at all into BLAST if we need to put a guaranteed delivery mechanism above it anyway. The reason is that we'd prefer to retransmit only those fragments that were lost rather than having to retransmit the entire larger message whenever one fragment is lost. So we get the guarantees from the higher-level protocol but some improved efficiency by retransmitting fragments in BLAST.

BLAST Message Format

The BLAST header has to convey several pieces of information. First, it must contain some sort of message identifier so that all the fragments that belong to the same message can be identified. Second, there must be a way to identify where in the original

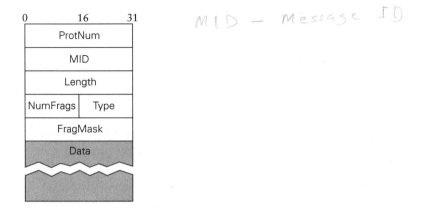

MID — Message ID

Figure 5.13   Format for BLAST message header.

message the individual fragments fit, and likewise, an SRR must be able to indicate which fragments have arrived and which are missing. Third, there must be a way to distinguish the last fragment, so that the receiver knows when it is time to check to see if all the fragments have arrived. Finally, it must be possible to distinguish a data message from an SRR message. Some of these items are encoded in a header field in an obvious way, but others can be done in a variety of different ways. Figure 5.13 gives the header format used by BLAST. The following discussion explains the various fields and considers alternative designs.

The MID field uniquely identifies this message. All fragments that belong to the same message have the same value in their MID field. The only question is how many bits are needed for this field. This is similar to the question of how many bits are needed in the SequenceNum field for TCP. The central issue in deciding how many bits to use in the MID field has to do with how long it will take before this field wraps around and the protocol starts using message ids over again. If this happens too soon—that is, the MID field is only a few bits long—then it is possible for the protocol to become confused by a message that was delayed in the network, so that an old incarnation of some message id is mistaken for a new incarnation of that same id. So, how many bits are enough to ensure that the amount of time it takes for the MID field to wrap around is longer than the amount of time a message can potentially be delayed in the network?

In the worst-case scenario, each BLAST message contains a single fragment that is 1 byte long, which means that BLAST might need to generate a new MID for every byte it sends. On a 10-Mbps Ethernet, this would mean generating a new MID roughly once every microsecond, while on a 1.2-Gbps STS-24 link, a new MID would be required once every 7 nanoseconds. Of course, this is a ridiculously conservative calculation—the overhead involved in preparing a message is going to be more than a microsecond. Thus, suppose a new MID is potentially needed once every microsecond, and a message may be delayed in the network for up to 60 seconds (our standard worst-case assumption for the Internet); then we need to ensure that there are more than 60 million MID values. While a 26-bit field would be sufficient ($2^{26} = 67,108,864$), it is easier to deal with header fields that are even multiples of a byte, so we will settle on a 32-bit MID field.

This conservative (you could say paranoid) analysis of the MID field illustrates an important point. When designing a transport protocol, it is tempting to take shortcuts, since not all networks suffer from all the problems listed in the problem statement at the beginning of this chapter. For example, messages do not get stuck in an Ethernet for 60 seconds, and similarly, it is physically impossible to reorder messages on an Ethernet segment. The problem with this way of thinking, however, is that if you want the transport protocol to work over any kind of network, then you have to *design for the worst case*. This is because the real danger is that as soon as you assume that an Ethernet does not reorder packets, someone will come along and put a bridge or a router in the middle of it.

Let's move on to the other fields in the BLAST header. The Type field indicates whether this is a DATA message or an SRR message. Notice that while we certainly don't need 16 bits to represent these two types, as a general rule we like to keep the header fields aligned on 32-bit (word) boundaries, so as to improve processing efficiency. The ProtNum field identifies the high-level protocol that is configured on top of BLAST; incoming messages are demultiplexed to this protocol. The Length field indicates how many bytes of data are in *this* fragment; it has nothing to do with the length of the entire message. The NumFrags field indicates how many fragments are in this message. This field is used to determine when the last fragment has been received. An alternative is to include a flag that is only set for the last fragment.

Finally, the FragMask field is used to distinguish among fragments. It is a 32-bit field that is used as a bit mask. For messages of Type = DATA, the ith bit is 1 (all others are 0) to indicate that this message carries the ith fragment. For messages of Type = SRR, the ith bit is 1 to indicate that the ith fragment has arrived, and it is set to 0 to indicate that the ith fragment is missing. Note that there are several ways to identify fragments. For example, the header could have contained a simple "fragment ID" field, with this field set to i to denote the ith fragment. The tricky part with this approach, as opposed to a bit-vector, is how the SRR specifies which fragments have arrived and which have not. If it takes an n-bit number to identify each missing fragment—as opposed to a single bit in a fixed-size bit-vector—then the SRR message will be of variable length, depending on how many fragments are missing. Variable-length headers are allowed, but they are a little trickier to process. On the other hand, one limitation of the BLAST header given above is that the length of the bit-vector limits each message to only 32 fragments. If the underlying network has an MTU of 1 KB, then this is sufficient to send up to 32-KB messages.

Implementation of BLAST

We conclude our discussion of BLAST by giving the C code that implements BLAST's send routine, which contains the for loop that generates and transmits all the fragments in a message. We assume that the msgFragment operation automatically makes each fragment the lesser of the specified size (FRAGMENT_SIZE) and however many bytes are left in the message, thereby freeing us from having to calculate the length of the last fragment. Also, as with other protocols presented in this text, we assume that the necessary protocol state is passed as an argument to BLAST's send operation. This state includes the last message id used (mid), a list of fragments sent in case they need to be retransmitted (frag_list), and a header template that already has the static header fields filled in (hdr_template).

```
int
sendBLAST(BlastState *state, Msg *msg)
{
    int         num_frags, i;
    Msg         *fragment;
    BlastHdr    *hdr;
    char        *hbuf;

    /* get header template and increment MID */
    hdr = state->hdr_template;
    if (state->mid == MAX_SEQ_NUM)
        state->mid = 0;
    hdr->MID = ++state->mid;

    /* check total length of message */
    if (msgLength(msg) > 32*FRAGMENT_SIZE)
        return FAILURE;

    /* determine number of fragments */
    if (msgLength(msg) <= FRAGMENT_SIZE)
        num_frags = 1;
```

```
else
    num_frags = (msgLength(msg) + FRAGMENT_SIZE - 1)/FRAGMENT_SIZE;
hdr->NumFrags = num_frags;

/* create and transmit individual fragments */
for ( i=1; i <= num_frags; i++ )
{
    /* carve a fragment off of original msg */
    msgFragment(msg, fragment, FRAGMENT_SIZE);

    /* fill in dynamic parts of header */
    hdr->len = msgLength(fragment);
    set_fragment_mask(hdr->mask, i);

    /* add header and send fragment */
    store_blast_hdr(hdr, hbuf);
    msgAddHdr(fragment, hbuf, HLEN);
    send(LLP, fragment);

    /* save copy of fragment for future retransmit */
    save_for_retransmit(state->frag_list, fragment, i);
}
/* schedule DONE timer */
state->event = evSchedule(giveup, 0, DONE);
return;
}
```

5.3.2 Request/Reply (CHAN)

The next microprotocol, CHAN, implements the request/reply algorithm that is at the core of RPC. In terms of the common properties of transport protocols given in the problem statement at the beginning of this chapter, CHAN guarantees message delivery, ensures that only one copy of each message is delivered, and allows the communicating processes to synchronize with each other. In the case of this last item, the synchronization we are after mimics the behavior of a procedure call—the caller (client) blocks while waiting for a reply from the callee (server).

At-Most-Once Semantics

The name CHAN comes from the fact that the protocol implements a logical request/reply *channel* between a pair of participants. At any given time, there can be only one message transaction active on a given channel. Like the concurrent logical channel protocol described in Section 2.5.3, the application programs have to open multiple channels if they want to have more than one request/reply transaction between them at the same time.

The most important property of each channel is that it preserves a semantics known as *at-most-once*. This means that for every request message that the client sends, at most one copy of that message is delivered to the server. Stated in terms of the RPC mechanism that CHAN is designed to support, for each time the client calls a remote procedure, that procedure is invoked at most one time on the server machine. We say "at most once" rather than "exactly once" because it is always possible that either the network or the server machine has failed, making it impossible to deliver even one copy of the request message.

As obvious as at-most-once sounds, not all RPC protocols support this behavior. Some support a semantics that is facetiously called *zero-or-more* semantics, that is, each invocation on a client results in the remote procedure being invoked zero or more times. It is not hard to understand how this would cause problems for a remote procedure that changed some local state variable (e.g., incremented a counter) or that had some externally visible side effect (e.g., launched a missile) each time it was invoked. On the other hand, if the remote procedure being invoked is *idempotent*—multiple invocations have the same effect as just one—then the RPC mechanism need not support at-most-once semantics; a simpler (possibly faster) implementation will suffice.

CHAN Algorithm

The request/reply algorithm has several subtle aspects; hence, we develop it in stages. The basic algorithm is straightforward, as illustrated by the timeline given in Figure 5.14. The client sends a request message and the server acknowledges it. Then, after executing the procedure, the server sends a reply message and the client acknowledges the reply.

Because the reply message often comes back with very little delay, and it is sometimes the case that the client turns around and makes a second request on the same channel immediately after receiving the first reply, this basic scenario can be optimized by using a technique called *implicit acknowledgments*. As illustrated in Figure 5.15, the reply message serves to acknowledge the request message, and a subsequent request acknowledges the preceding reply.

There are two factors that potentially complicate the rosy picture we have painted so far. The first is that either a message carrying data (a request message or a reply message) or the ACK sent to acknowledge that message, may be lost in the network. To account for this possibility, both client and server save a copy of each

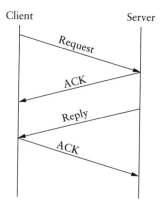

Figure 5.14 Simple timeline for CHAN.

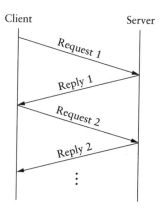

Figure 5.15 Timeline for CHAN when using implicit ACKs.

message they send until an ACK for it has arrived. Each side also sets a RETRANS-MIT timer and resends the message should this timer expire. Both sides reset this timer and try again some agreed-upon number of times before giving up and freeing the message.

Recall from Section 2.5.1 that this acknowledgment/timeout strategy means that it is possible for duplicate copies of a message to arrive—the original message arrives, the ACK is lost, and then the retransmission arrives. Thus, the receiver must remember what messages it has seen and discard any duplicates. This is done through the use of a MID field in the header. Any message whose MID field does not match the next expected

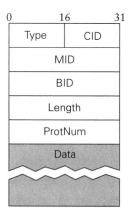

Figure 5.16 Format for CHAN message header.

MID is discarded instead of being passed up to the high-level protocol configured on top of CHAN.

The second complication is that the server may take an arbitrarily long time to produce the result, and worse yet, it may crash (either the process or the entire machine) before generating the reply. Keep in mind that we are talking about the period of time after the server has acknowledged the request but before it has sent the reply. To help the client distinguish between a slow server and a dead server, CHAN's client side periodically sends an "Are you alive?" message to the server, and CHAN's server side responds with an ACK. Alternatively, the server could send "I am still alive" messages to the client without the client having first solicited them, but we prefer the client-initiated approach because it keeps the server as simple as possible (i.e., it has one less timer to manage).

CHAN Message Format

The CHAN message format is given in Figure 5.16. As with BLAST, the Type field specifies the type of the message; in this case, the possible types are REQ, REP, ACK, and PROBE. (PROBE is the "Are you alive?" message discussed above.) Similarly, the ProtNum field identifies the high-level protocol that depends on CHAN.

The CID field uniquely identifies the logical channel to which this message belongs. This is a 16-bit field, meaning that CHAN supports up to 64K concurrent request/reply transactions between any pair of hosts. Of course, a given host can be participating in channels with many other hosts at the same time.

The MID field uniquely identifies each request/reply pair; the reply message has the same MID as the request. Note that because CHAN permits only one message transaction at a time on a given channel, you might think that a 1-bit MID field is sufficient, just as for the stop-and-wait algorithm presented in Section 2.5.1. However, as with BLAST, we have to be concerned about messages that wander around the network for an extended period of time and then suddenly appear at the destination, confusing CHAN. Thus, using much the same reasoning as we used in Section 5.3.1, CHAN uses a 32-bit MID field.

Finally, the BID field gives the *boot id* for the host. A machine's boot id is a number that is incremented each time the machine reboots; this number is read from disk, incremented, and written back to disk during the machine's start-up procedure. This number is then put in every message sent by that host. The role played by the BID field is much the same as the role played by the large MID field—it protects against old messages suddenly appearing at the destination—although in this case, the old message is not due to an arbitrary delay in the network but rather to a machine that has crashed and rebooted.

To understand the use of the boot id, consider the following pathological situation. A client machine sends a request message with MID = 0, then crashes and reboots, and then sends an unrelated request message, also with MID = 0. The server may not have been aware that the client crashed and rebooted, and upon seeing a request message with MID = 0, acknowledges it and discards it as a duplicate. To protect against this possibility, each side of CHAN makes sure that the ⟨BID, MID⟩ pair, not just the MID, matches what it is expecting. BID is also a 32-bit field, which means that if we assume that it takes at least 10 minutes to reboot a machine, it will wrap around once every 40 billion minutes (approximately 80,000 years). In effect, the BID and MID combine to form a unique 64-bit id for each transaction; the low-order 32 bits are incremented for each transaction but reset to 0 when the machine reboots, and the high-order 32 bits are incremented each time the machine reboots.

Timeouts

CHAN involves three different timers: There is a RETRANSMIT timer on both the client and server, and the client also manages a PROBE timer. The PROBE timer is not critical to performance and thus can be set to a conservatively large value—on the order of several seconds. The RETRANSMIT timer, however, does influence the performance of CHAN. If it is set too large, then CHAN might wait an unnecessarily long time before retransmitting a message that was lost by the network. This clearly hurts performance. If the RETRANSMIT timer is set too small, however, then CHAN may load the network with unnecessary traffic.

If CHAN is designed to run on a local area network only, or even over a campus-size extended LAN, then RETRANSMIT can be set to a fixed value. Something on the order of 20 milliseconds would be reasonable. This is because the RTT of a LAN is not that variable. If CHAN is expected to run over the Internet, however, then selecting a suitable value for RETRANSMIT is similar to the problem faced by TCP. Thus, CHAN would calculate the RETRANSMIT timeout using a mechanism similar to the one described in Section 5.2.5. The only difference is that CHAN has to take into account the fact that the message it is sending ranges in size from 1 B to 32 KB, whereas TCP is always transmitting segments of approximately the same size.

Synchronous versus Asynchronous Protocols

One way to characterize a protocol is by whether it is *synchronous* or *asynchronous*. These two terms have significantly different meanings, depending on where in the protocol hierarchy you use them. At the transport layer, it is most accurate to think of synchrony as a spectrum of possibilities rather than as two alternatives, where the key attribute of any point along the spectrum is how much the sender knows, after the operation to send a message returns. In other words, if we assume that an application program invokes a send operation on a transport protocol, then the question is, exactly what does the application know about the success of the operation when the send operation returns?

At the *asynchronous* end of the spectrum, the application knows absolutely nothing when send returns. It not only doesn't know if the message was received by its peer, but it doesn't even know for sure that the message has successfully left the local machine. At the *synchronous* end of the spectrum, the send operation typically returns a reply message. That is, the application not only knows that the message it sent was received by its peer, but it knows that the peer has returned an answer. Thus, synchronous protocols implement the request/reply abstraction, while asynchronous protocols are used if the sender wants to be able to transmit many messages without having to wait for a response. Using this definition, CHAN is obviously a synchronous protocol.

Although we have not discussed them in this chapter, there are interesting points between these two extremes. For example, the transport protocol might implement send so that it blocks (does not return) until the message has been successfully received at the remote machine, but returns before the sender's peer on that machine has actually processed and responded to it. This is sometimes called a *reliable datagram protocol*.

Implementation of CHAN

We conclude our discussion of CHAN by giving fragments of C code that implement its client side. Since CHAN exports a synchronous interface to higher-level protocols—the caller blocks until a reply can be returned—the send operation we have been using is not going to work. Therefore, we introduce a new interface operation, which we name call, that blocks until a reply message is available, and returns that reply message to the caller:

call(Channel chan, Msg *request, Msg *reply)

The first argument is analogous to the LLP argument given to the send operation—it encapsulates all the information needed to send the message to the correct destination. We will discuss this argument more fully in Section 5.3.3 when we look at SELECT, a protocol that invokes the call operation.

We now turn to the details of CHAN, beginning with CHAN's two key data structures: ChanHdr and ChanState. The fields in ChanHdr have already been explained. The fields in ChanState will be explained by the code that follows. As with BLAST, ChanState includes a hdr_template field, which is a copy of the CHAN header. Many of the fields in the CHAN header remain the same for all messages sent out over this channel. These fields are filled in when the channel is created (not shown); only the fields that change are modified before a given message is transmitted.

```
typedef struct {
    u_short    Type;           /* message type: REQ, REP, ACK, PROBE */
    u_short    CID;            /* unique channel id */
    int        MID;            /* unique message id */
    int        BID;            /* unique boot id */
    int        Length;         /* length of message */
    int        ProtNum;        /* high-level protocol number */
} ChanHdr;

typedef struct {
    u_char     type;           /* type of session: CLIENT or SERVER */
    u_char     status;         /* status of session: BUSY or IDLE */
    Event      event;          /* place to save timeout event */
    int        timeout;        /* timeout value */
    int        retries;        /* number of times retransmitted */
    int        ret_val;        /* place to save return value */
    Msg        *request;       /* place to save request message */
    Msg        *reply;         /* place to save reply message */
    Semaphore  reply_sem;      /* semaphore the client blocks on */
    int        mid;            /* message id for this channel */
    int        bid;            /* boot id for this channel */
    ChanHdr    hdr_template;   /* header template for this channel */
    BlastState blast;  /* pointer to BLAST protocol */
} ChanState;
```

The CHAN-specific implementation of call is given by the following routine, named callCHAN. The first thing to notice is that ChanState, which is passed as an argument to callCHAN, includes a field named status that indicates whether or not this channel is being used. If the channel is currently in use, then callCHAN returns failure. An alternative design would be to block the calling thread until the channel becomes idle. We have elected to push responsibility for blocking threads that want to use busy channels onto the higher-level protocol, in our case, SELECT.

The next thing to notice about callCHAN is that after filling out the message header and transmitting the request message via BLAST, the calling process is blocked on a semaphore (reply_sem); semWait is the semaphore operation introduced in Section 1.3. When the reply message eventually arrives, it is processed by CHAN's deliverCHAN routine (see below), which copies the reply message into state variable reply and signals this blocked process. The process then returns. Should the reply message not arrive, then timeout routine retransmit is called (see below). This event is scheduled in the body of callCHAN.

```
int
callCHAN(ChanState *state, Msg *msg, Msg *rmsg)
{
    ChanHdr    *hdr;
    char       hbuf[HLEN];

    /* ensure only one transaction per channel */
    if ((state->status != IDLE))
        return FAILURE;
    state->status = BUSY;

    /* save a copy of request msg and pointer to reply msg*/
    msgSaveCopy(&state->request, msg);
    state->reply = rmsg;

    /* fill out header fields */
    hdr = state->hdr_template;
    hdr->Length = msgLength(msg);
    if (state->mid == MAX_MID)
        state->mid = 0;
    hdr->MID = ++state->mid;

    /* attach header to msg and send it */
    store_chan_hdr(hdr, hbuf);
```

```
        msgAddHdr(msg, hdr, HLEN);
        send(BLAST, msg);

        /* schedule first timeout event */
        state->retries = 1;
        state->event = evSchedule(retransmit, state, state->timeout);

        /* block waiting for the reply msg */
        semWait(&state->reply_sem);

        /* clean up state and return */
        flush_msg(state->request);
        state->status = IDLE;
        return state->ret_val;
    }
```

The next routine, retransmit, is called whenever the retransmit timer fires. It is scheduled for the first time in callCHAN, but each time it is called, it reschedules itself. Once the request message has been retransmitted four times, CHAN gives up: It sets the return value to FAILURE and wakes up the blocked client process. Finally, each time retransmit executes and sends another copy of the request message, it needs to resave the message in state variable request. This is because we assume that each time a protocol sends a message to the lower-level protocol, it loses its reference to the message.

```
    static void
    retransmit(Event ev, int *arg)
    {
        ChanState   *state = (ChanState *)arg;
        Msg         tmp;

        /* unblock the client process if we have retried 4 times */
        if (++state->retries > 4)
        {
            state->ret_val = FAILURE;
            semSignal(state->rep_sem);
            return;
        }
```

```
/* retransmit request message */
msgSaveCopy(&tmp, &state->request);
send(BLAST, &tmp);

/* reschedule event with exponential backoff */
state->timeout = 2*state->timeout;
state->event = evSchedule(retransmit, state, state->timeout);
}
```

Finally, we consider CHAN's **deliver** routine. The first thing we observe is that CHAN is an asymmetric protocol: The code that implements CHAN on the client machine is completely distinct from the code that implements CHAN on the server machine. This fact is stored in the CHAN state variable (**type**). Thus, the first thing CHAN's **deliver** routine does is check to see whether it is running on a server (i.e., it expects **REQ** messages) or on a client (i.e., it expects **REP** messages), and then it calls the appropriate client- or server-specific routine. In this case, we show the client-specific routine, deliverClient.

```
static int
deliverClient(ChanState *state, Msg *msg)
{
    ChanHdr  hdr;
    char     *hbuf;

    /* strip header and verify correctness */
    hbuf = msgStripHdr(msg, HLEN);
    load_chan_hdr(&hdr, hbuf);
    if (!clnt_msg_ok(state, &hdr))
        return FAILURE;

    /* cancel retransmit timeout event */
    evCancel(state->event);

    /* if this is an ACK, then schedule PROBE timer and exit*/
    if (hdr.Type == ACK)
    {
        state->event = evSchedule(probe, s, PROBE);
        return SUCCESS;
    }
```

```
                    /* msg is a REP; save it and signal blocked client */
                    msgSaveCopy(state->reply, msg);
                    state->ret_val = SUCCESS;
                    semSignal(&state->reply_sem);

                    return SUCCESS;
                }
```

Routine deliverClient first checks to see if it has received the expected message, for example, that it has the right MID, the right BID, and that the message is of type REP or ACK. This check is made in subroutine clnt_msg_ok (not shown). If it is a valid acknowledgment message, then deliverClient cancels the RETRANSMIT timer and schedules the PROBE timer. The PROBE timer is not shown, but would be similar to the RETRANSMIT timer given above. If the message is a valid reply, then deliverClient cancels the RETRANSMIT timer, saves a copy of the reply message in state variable reply, and wakes up the blocked client process. It is this client process that actually returns the reply message to the high-level protocol; the process that called deliverClient simply returns back down the protocol stack.

5.3.3 Dispatcher (SELECT)

The final microprotocol, called SELECT, dispatches request messages to the appropriate procedure. It is the RPC protocol stack's version of a demultiplexing protocol like UDP; the main difference is that it is a synchronous protocol rather than an asynchronous protocol. What this means is that on the client side, SELECT is given a procedure number that the client wants to invoke, it puts this number in its header, and then it invokes the call operation on a lower-level request/reply protocol like CHAN. When this invocation returns, SELECT merely lets the return pass on through to the client; it has no real demultiplexing work to do. On the server side, SELECT uses the procedure number it finds in its header to select the right local procedure to invoke. When this procedure returns, SELECT simply returns to the low-level protocol that just invoked it. This situation is illustrated in Figure 5.17.

It may seem that SELECT is so simple that it is not worthy of being treated as a separate protocol. After all, CHAN already has its own demultiplexing field that could be used to dispatch incoming request messages to the appropriate procedure. There are two reasons why we elected to separate SELECT into a self-contained protocol.

The first is that doing so makes it possible to change the address space with which procedures are identified simply by configuring a different version of SELECT into the protocol graph. In some settings, it is sufficient to define a *flat* address space for procedures—for example, a 16-bit selector field allows you to identify 64K different

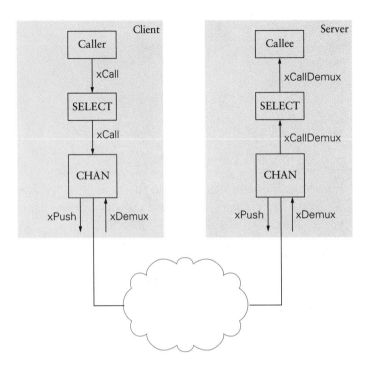

Figure 5.17   Relationship between SELECT and neighboring modules.

procedures. In other settings, however, a flat address space is hard to manage—who decides which procedure gets which procedure number? In this case, it might be better to have a hierarchical address space, that is, a two-part procedure number. First, each program could be given a program number, where a program corresponds to something like a "file server" or a "name server." Next, each program could be given the responsibility to assign unique procedure numbers to its own procedures. For example, within the file server program, read might be procedure 1, write might be procedure 2, seek might be procedure 3, and so on, whereas within the name server program, insert might be procedure 1 and lookup might be procedure 2.

The second reason we implement SELECT as its own protocol is that it provides a good place to manage concurrency. Recall that CHAN supports at-most-once channels. Suppose we want to allow applications running on this host to make multiple outstanding calls to the same remote procedure. Since CHAN allows only one outstanding call at a time, the only way to do this is to open multiple channels to the same server. Each time a calling process invokes SELECT, it sends the process out on an idle channel. If all the channels are currently active, then SELECT blocks the calling process until a channel becomes idle.

The following code gives the implementation of SELECT's call routine. It uses a stack to keep track of idle channels. We assume SELECT has already opened the channels and saved references to them in this stack; variable chan refers to the channel being used for this particular call. Think of this variable as being like a socket, as described in Section 1.3—SELECT gives it as an argument to the call operation, much in the same way an application gives a socket as an argument to the send operation in the socket API. (We do not show the details of how SELECT opens the channels, but it would be similar to how applications use the connect operation to open sockets.) Also note that the header stored in the SELECT state is the same for all outgoing messages; it contains the procedure number. Thus, there are no dynamic fields to change.

```
static int
callSELECT(SelectState *state, Msg *msg, Msg *rmsg)
{
    char     hbuf[HLEN];
    Channel  chan;

    /* prepare SELECT message */
    store_select_hdr(state->hdr, hbuf);
    msgAddHdr(msg, state->hdr, HLEN);

    /* wait for an idle channel */
    semWait(&state->available);
    chan = state->stack[--state->tos];

    /* use the channel */
    result = call(chan, msg, rmsg);

    /* free the channel */
    state->stack[state->tos++] = chan;
    semSignal(&state->available);

    return result;
}
```

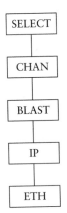

Figure 5.18   A simple RPC stack.

5.3.4   Putting It All Together (SunRPC, DCE)

We are now ready to construct an RPC stack from the microprotocols described in the three previous subsections. This section also explains two widely used RPC protocols—SunRPC and DCE-RPC—in terms of our three microprotocols.

A Simple RPC Stack

Figure 5.18 depicts a simple protocol stack that implements RPC. At the bottom are the protocols that implement the underlying network. Although this stack could contain protocols corresponding to any of the networking technologies discussed in the three previous chapters, we use IP running on top of an Ethernet for illustrative purposes.

On top of IP is BLAST, which turns the small message size of the underlying network into a communication service that supports messages of up to 32 KB in length. Notice that it is not strictly true that the underlying network provides for only small messages; IP can handle messages of up to 64 KB. However, because IP has to fragment such large messages before sending them out over the Ethernet, and BLAST's fragmentation/reassembly algorithm is superior to IP's (because it is able to selectively retransmit missing fragments), we prefer to treat IP as though it supports exactly the same MTU as the underlying physical network. This puts the fragmentation/reassembly burden on BLAST, unless IP has to perform fragmentation out in the middle of the network somewhere.

Next, CHAN implements the request/reply algorithm. Recall that we chose not to implement reliable delivery in BLAST, but instead postponed solving this issue until a higher-level protocol. In this case, CHAN's timeout and acknowledgment mechanism makes sure messages are reliably delivered. Other protocols might use different techniques to guarantee delivery or, for that matter, might choose not to implement reliable delivery at all. This is an example of the end-to-end argument at work—do not do at low levels of the system (e.g., BLAST) what has to be done at higher levels (e.g., CHAN) anyway.

Finally, SELECT defines an address space for identifying remote procedures. As suggested in Section 5.3.3, different versions of SELECT, each defining a different method for identifying procedures, could be configured on top of CHAN. In fact, it would even be possible to write a version of SELECT that mimics some existing RPC package's address space for procedures (such as SunRPC's), and then to use CHAN and BLAST underneath this new SELECT to implement the rest of the RPC stack. This new stack would not interoperate with the original protocol, but it would allow you to slide a new RPC system underneath an existing collection of remote procedures without having to change the interface. SELECT also manages concurrency.

SunRPC

SELECT, CHAN, and BLAST, although complete and correctly functioning protocols, have been neither standardized nor widely adopted. We now turn our discussion to a widely used RPC protocol—SunRPC. Ironically, SunRPC has also not been approved by any standardization body, but it has become a de facto standard, thanks to its wide distribution with Sun workstations and to the central role it plays in Sun's popular Network File System (NFS). At the time of this writing, the IETF is considering officially adopting SunRPC as a standard Internet protocol.

Fundamentally, any RPC protocol must worry about three issues: fragmenting large messages, synchronizing request and reply messages, and dispatching request messages to the appropriate procedure. SunRPC is no exception. Unlike the SELECT/CHAN/BLAST stack, however, SunRPC addresses these three functions in a different order and using slightly different algorithms. The basic SunRPC protocol graph is given in Figure 5.19.

First, SunRPC implements the core request/reply algorithm; it is CHAN's counterpart. SunRPC differs from CHAN, however, in that it does not technically guarantee at-most-once semantics; there are obscure circumstances under which a duplicate copy of a request message is delivered to the server (see below). Second, the role of SE-LECT is split between UDP and SunRPC—UDP dispatches to the correct program, and SunRPC dispatches to the correct procedure within the program. (We discuss how procedures are identified in more detail below.) Finally, the ability to send request and reply messages that are larger than the network MTU, corresponding to the functionality implemented in BLAST, is handled by IP. Keep in mind, however, that IP is not as

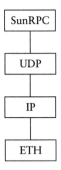

Figure 5.19 Protocol graph for SunRPC.

persistent as BLAST is in implementing fragmentation; BLAST uses selective retransmission, whereas IP does not.

As just mentioned, SunRPC uses two-tier addresses to identify remote procedures: a 32-bit program number and a 32-bit procedure number. (There is also a 32-bit version number, but we ignore that in the following discussion.) For example, the NFS server has been assigned program number x00100003, and within this program, getattr is procedure 1, setattr is procedure 2, read is procedure 6, write is procedure 8, and so on. Each program is reachable by sending a message to some UDP port. When a request message arrives at this port, SunRPC picks it up and calls the appropriate procedure.

To determine which port corresponds to a particular SunRPC program number, there is a separate SunRPC program, called the Port Mapper, that maps program numbers to port numbers. The Port Mapper itself also has a program number (x00100000) that must be translated into some UDP port. Fortunately, the Port Mapper is always present at a well-known UDP port (111). The Port Mapper program supports several procedures, one of which (procedure number 3) is the one that performs the program-to-port number mapping.

Thus, to send a request message to NFS's read procedure, a client first sends a request message to the Port Mapper at well-known UDP port 111, asking that procedure 3 be invoked to map program number x00100003 to the UDP port where the NFS program currently resides. (In practice, NFS is such an important program that it is given its own well-known UDP port, so the Port Mapper need not be involved in finding it.) The client then sends a SunRPC request message with procedure number 6 to this UDP port, and the SunRPC module listening at that port calls the NFS read procedure. The client also caches the program-to-port number mapping so that it need not go back to the Port Mapper each time it wants to talk to the NFS program.

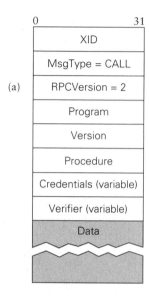

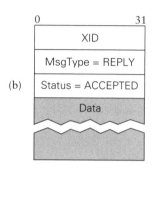

Figure 5.20 SunRPC header formats: (a) request; (b) reply.

The actual SunRPC header is defined by a complex nesting of data structures. Figure 5.20 gives the essential details for the case in which the call completes without any problems. XID is a unique transaction id, much like CHAN's MID field. The reason that SunRPC cannot guarantee at-most-once semantics is that on the server side, SunRPC does not remember that it has already seen a particular XID once it has successfully completed the transaction. This is only a problem if the client retransmits a request message as a result of a timeout and that request message is in transit at exactly the same time as the reply to the original request is on its way from the server back to the client. When the retransmitted request arrives at the server, it looks like a new transaction, since the server thinks it has already completed the transaction with this XID. Clearly, if the reply arrives at the client before the timeout, then the request will not be retransmitted. Likewise, if the retransmitted request arrives at the server before the reply has been generated, then the server will recognize that transaction XID is already in progress, and it will discard the duplicate request message. So it is really quite unlikely that this erroneous behavior will occur. Note that the server's short-term memory about XIDs also means that it cannot protect itself against messages that have been delayed for a long time in the network. This has not been a serious problem with SunRPC, however, because it was originally designed for use on a LAN.

Returning to the SunRPC header format, the request message contains variable-length Credentials and Verifier fields, both of which are used by the client to authenticate itself to the server, that is, to give evidence that the client has the right to invoke the server. How a client authenticates itself to a server is a general issue that must be addressed by any protocol that wants to provide a reasonable level of security. This topic is discussed in more detail in the next chapter.

DCE

The Distributed Computing Environment (DCE) defines another widely used RPC protocol, which we call DCE-RPC. DCE is a set of standards and software for building distributed systems. It was defined by the Open Software Foundation (OSF), a consortium of computer companies that originally included IBM, Digital, and Hewlett-Packard; today OSF goes by the name Open Group. DCE-RPC is the RPC protocol at the core of the DCE system. It can be used with the Network Data Representation (NDR) stub compiler described in Chapter 7, but it also serves as the underlying RPC protocol for the Common Object Request Broker Architecture (CORBA), which is an industrywide standard for building distributed, object-oriented systems.

DCE-RPC is designed to run on top of UDP. It is similar to SunRPC in that it defines a two-level addressing scheme: UDP demultiplexes to the correct server, DCE-RPC dispatches to a particular procedure exported by that server, and clients consult an "endpoint mapping service" (similar to SunRPC's Port Mapper) to learn how to reach a particular server. Unlike SunRPC, however, DCE-RPC implements at-most-once call semantics. It does this in a single protocol that essentially combines the algorithms in BLAST and CHAN. We focus our discussion on this aspect of DCE-RPC. (In truth, DCE-RPC supports multiple call semantics, including an idempotent semantics similar to SunRPC's, but at-most-once is the default behavior.)

Figure 5.21 gives a timeline for the typical exchange of messages, where each message is labelled by its DCE-RPC type. The pattern is similar to CHAN's: The client sends a Request message, the server eventually replies with a Response message, and the client acknowledges (Ack) the response. Instead of the server acknowledging the request messages, however, the client periodically sends a Ping message to the server, which responds with a Working message to indicate that the remote procedure is still in progress. Although not shown in the figure, other message types are also supported. For example, the client can send a Quit message to the server, asking it to abort an earlier call that is still in progress; the server responds with a Quack (quit acknowledgment) message. Also, the server can respond to a Request message with a Reject message (indicating that a call has been rejected), and it can respond to a Ping message with a Nocall message (indicating that the server has never heard of the caller).

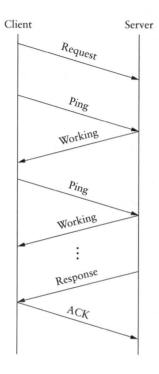

Figure 5.21 Typical DCE-RPC message exchange.

In addition to the message type, request and reply messages include four key fields that are used to implement both the fragmentation/reassembly aspects of BLAST, and the message transaction aspects of CHAN. These include ServerBoot, ActivityId, SequenceNum, and FragmentNum.

The ServerBoot field serves the same purpose as CHAN's BID (boot id) field: The server records its boot time in a global variable each time it starts up, and it includes this variable in each call it services. The ActivityId field is similar to CHAN's CID (channel id) field: It identifies a logical connection between the client and server on which a sequence of calls can be made. The SequenceNum field then distinguishes between calls made as part of the same activity; it serves the same purpose as CHAN's MID (message id) and SunRPC's xid (transaction id) fields. Like CHAN (and unlike SunRPC), DCE-RPC keeps track of the last sequence number used as part of a particular activity, so as to ensure at-most-once semantics.

Because both request and response messages may be larger than the underlying network packet size, they may be fragmented into multiple packets. The FragmentNum field uniquely identifies each fragment that makes up a given request or reply message.

Unlike BLAST, which uses a bit-vector to identify fragments, each DCE-RPC fragment is assigned a unique fragment number (e.g., 0, 1, 2, 3, and so on). Both the client and server implement a selective acknowledgment mechanism, which works as follows. (We describe the mechanism in terms of a client sending a fragmented request message to the server; the same mechanism applies when a server sends a fragment response to the client.)

First, each fragment that makes up the request message contains both a unique FragmentNum, and a flag indicating whether this packet is a fragment of a call (frag) or the last fragment of a call (last_frag); request messages that fit in a single packet carry a no_frag flag. The server knows it has received the complete request message when it has the last_frag packet and there are no gaps in the fragment numbers. Second, in response to each arriving fragment, the server sends a Fack (fragment acknowledgment) message to the client. This acknowledgment identifies the highest fragment number that the server has successfully received. In other words, the acknowledgment is cumulative, much like in TCP. In addition, however, the server selectively acknowledges any higher fragment numbers it has received out of order. It does so with a bit-vector that identifies these out-of-order fragments relative to the highest in-order fragment it has received. Finally, the client responds by retransmitting the missing fragments.

Figure 5.22 illustrates how this all works. Suppose the server has successfully received fragments up through number 20, plus fragments 23, 25, and 26. The server responds with a Fack that identifies fragment 20 as the highest in-order fragment, plus a bit-vector (SelAck) with the third ($23 = 20 + 3$), fifth ($25 = 20 + 5$), and sixth ($26 = 20 + 6$) bits turned on. So as to support an (almost) arbitrarily long bit-vector, the size of the vector (measured in 32-bit words) is given in the SelAckLen field.

Given DCE-RPC's support for very large messages—the FragmentNum field is 16 bits long, meaning it can support 64K fragments—it is not appropriate for the protocol to blast all the fragments that make up a message as fast as it can, as BLAST does, since doing so might overrun the receiver. Instead, DCE-RPC implements a flow-control algorithm that is very similar to TCP's. Specifically, each Fack message not only acknowledges received fragments, but it also informs the sender of how many fragments it may now send. This is the purpose of the WindowSize field in Figure 5.22, which serves exactly the same purpose as TCP's AdvertisedWindow field except it counts fragments rather than bytes. DCE-RPC also implements a congestion-control mechanism that is similar to TCP's, which we will see in Chapter 6.

5.4 Performance

Recall that Chapter 1 introduced the two quantitative metrics by which network performance is evaluated: latency and throughput. As mentioned in that discussion, these

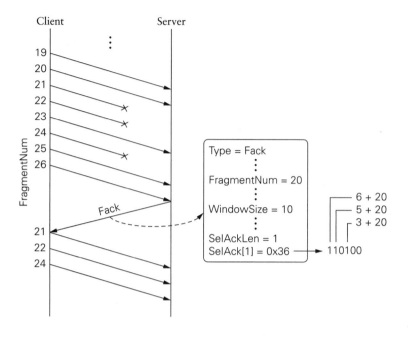

Figure 5.22 Fragmentation with selective acknowledgments.

metrics are influenced not only by the underlying hardware (e.g., propagation delay and link bandwidth) but also by software overheads. Now that we have a complete software-based protocol graph available to us that includes alternative transport protocols, we can discuss how to meaningfully measure its performance; we can hold a sort of protocol track meet. The importance of such measurements is that they represent the performance seen by application programs.

5.4.1 Experimental Method

We begin, as any report of experimental results should, by describing our experimental method. This includes the apparatus used in the experiments.

We ran our experiments on a pair of Alpha workstations connected by an isolated 10-Mbps Ethernet. Each workstation was configured with the protocol graph illustrated in Figure 5.23. Each of the protocols at the top of the protocol graph (TSTTCP, TSTUDP, TSTRPC) ran a series of independent experiments (TST stands for "test"). Each experiment involved running five identical instances of the same test. Each test, in turn, involved sending a message of some specified size back and forth between the two machines 10,000 times. The system's clock was read at the beginning and end of

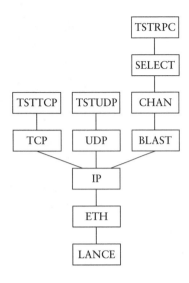

Figure 5.23 Protocol stack configuration used in performance measurements.

each test, and the difference between these two times was divided by 10,000 to determine the time taken for each round-trip. The average of these five times (the five runs of the test) is reported for each experiment below.

Each experiment involved a different-sized message. The latency numbers reported in Section 5.4.2 were for message sizes of 1 byte, 100 bytes, 200 bytes, . . . , 1000 bytes. The throughput results presented in Section 5.4.3 were for message sizes of 1 KB, 2 KB, 4 KB, 8 KB, . . . , 32 KB. The test protocol is an application program that initiates the tests and reads the system clock on the client side, and simply returns (reflects) the exact message it just received on the server side.

5.4.2 Latency

Table 5.3 gives the results of the latency test. As you would expect, latency increases with message size. Although there are sometimes special cases where you might be interested in the latency of, say, a 200-byte message, typically the most important latency number is the 1-byte case. This is because the 1-byte case represents the overhead involved in processing each message that does not depend on the amount of data contained in the message. It is typically the lower bound on latency, representing factors like the speed-of-light delay and the time taken to process headers.

We also observe that there is little difference between the latency experienced by the three different protocols (we use RPC as a shorthand for the SELECT/CHAN/

Message Size (Bytes)	UDP	TCP	RPC
1	279	365	428
100	413	519	593
200	572	691	753
300	732	853	913
400	898	1016	1079
500	1067	1185	1247
600	1226	1354	1406
700	1386	1514	1566
800	1551	1676	1733
900	1719	1845	1901
1000	1878	2015	2062

Table 5.3 Measured round-trip latencies (μs) for various message sizes and protocols.

BLAST stack). UDP is a bit faster than TCP or RPC, but this is to be expected since it provides less functionality.

Another interesting data point is how much of this round-trip latency is due to the hardware (link + adaptor) and how much can be attributed to the software that implements the protocol stack. Since it is difficult to isolate the cost of the device driver—and in any case, network hardware without a device driver isn't worth very much—we settle for knowing how much all the software above ETH contributes to the RTT. This can be done by reconfiguring the protocol stack to include only a TEST protocol, ETH, and LANCE, and then rerunning the latency experiment. In our particular case, the 1-byte latency was 216 μs, meaning that the UDP/IP stack added 58 μs to the round-trip latency. Since each round-trip involves traversing the protocol stack four times—twice outgoing and twice incoming—this means that each traversal takes on average about 15 μs. Keep in mind, however, that we do not have enough information to determine the relative times required to send and receive a message. Generally, the receive side takes longer, although the difference is small. (A similar analysis can be done for TCP and RPC.)

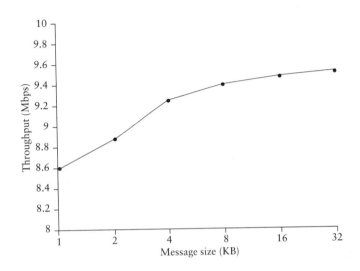

Figure 5.24 Measured throughput using UDP, for various message sizes.

5.4.3 Throughput

The results of the throughput test are given in Figure 5.24. Here, we show only the results for UDP; the performance of TCP and RPC are not noticeably different. The key thing to notice in this graph is that throughput improves as the messages get larger. This makes sense—each message involves a certain amount of overhead, so a larger message means that this overhead is amortized over more bytes. The throughput curve flattens off at about 16 KB, at which point the per-message overhead becomes insignificant when compared to the large number of bytes that the protocol stack has to process.

A second thing to notice is that the throughput curve tops out at about 9.5 Mbps. This is good news since the experiment was run on an Ethernet, which has a bandwidth of 10 Mbps. Although it can't be deduced from these measurements, it turns out that the factor preventing our system from running at the full Ethernet speed is a limitation of the network adaptor rather than the software.

5.5 Summary

This chapter has described three very different end-to-end protocols and reported on their performance. The first protocol we considered is a simple demultiplexer, as typified by UDP. All such a protocol does is dispatch messages to the appropriate application process based on a port number. It does not enhance the best-effort service model of the underlying network in any way, or said another way, it offers an unreliable, connectionless datagram service to application programs.

The second type is a reliable byte-stream protocol, and the specific example of this type that we looked at is TCP. The challenges faced with such a protocol are to recover from messages that may be lost by the network, to deliver messages in the same order in which they are sent, and to allow the receiver to do flow control on the sender. TCP uses the basic sliding window algorithm, enhanced with an advertised window, to implement this functionality. The other item of note for this protocol is the importance of an accurate timeout/retransmission mechanism.

The third transport protocol we looked at is a request/reply protocol that forms the basis for RPC. In this case, a combination of three different algorithms are employed to implement the request/reply service: a selective retransmission algorithm that is used to fragment and reassemble large messages, a synchronous channel algorithm that pairs the request message with the reply message, and a dispatch algorithm that causes the correct remote procedure to be invoked.

What should be clear after reading this chapter is that transport protocol design is a tricky business. As we have seen, getting a transport protocol right in the first place is hard enough, but changing circumstances make matters more complicated. The

OPEN ISSUE

Application-Specific Protocols

challenge is finding ways to adapt to these changes.

Our experience with using the protocol can change. As we saw with TCP's timeout mechanism, experience led to a series of refinements in how TCP decides to retransmit a segment. None of these changes affected the format of the TCP header, however, and so they could be incorporated into TCP one implementation at a time. That is, there was no need for everyone to upgrade their version of TCP on the same day.

The characteristics of the underlying network can also change. For many years, TCP's 32-bit sequence number and 16-bit advertised window were more than adequate. Recently, however, higher-bandwidth networks have meant that the sequence number is not large enough to protect against wraparound, and the advertised window is too small to allow the sender to fill the network pipe. While an obvious solution would have been to redefine the TCP header to include a 64-bit sequence number field and a 32-bit advertised window field, this would have introduced the very serious problem of how several million Internet hosts would make the transition from the current header to this new header. While such transitions have been performed on production networks, including the telephone network, they are no trivial matter. It was decided, therefore, to implement the necessary extensions as options and to allow hosts to negotiate with each other as to whether or not they will use the options for each connection.

This approach will not work indefinitely, however, since the TCP header has room for only 44 bytes of options. (This is because the HdrLen field is 4 bits long, meaning that the total TCP header length cannot exceed 16×32 bit words, or 64 bytes.) Of course, a TCP option that extends the space available for options is always a possibility, but you have to wonder how far it is worth going for the sake of backward compatibility.

Perhaps the hardest changes to accommodate are the adaptations to the level of service required by application programs. It is inevitable that some applications will have a good reason for wanting a slight variation from the standard services. For example, some applications want RPC most of the time, but occasionally want to be able to send a stream of request messages without waiting for any of the replies. While this is no longer technically the semantics of RPC, a common scenario is to modify an existing RPC protocol to allow this flexibility. As another example, because video is a stream-oriented application, it is tempting to use TCP as the transport protocol. Unfortunately, TCP guarantees reliability, which is not important to the video application. In fact, a video application would rather drop a frame (segment) than wait for it to be retransmitted. Rather than invent a new transport protocol from scratch, however, some designers have proposed that TCP should support an option that effectively turns off its reliability feature. It seems that such a protocol could hardly be called TCP anymore, but we are talking about the pragmatics of getting an application to run.

How to develop transport protocols that can evolve to satisfy diverse applications, many of which have not yet been imagined, is a hard problem. It is possible that the ultimate answer to this problem is the one-function-per-protocol style exemplified by the microprotocols we used to implement RPC, or some similar mechanism by which the application programmer is allowed to program, configure, or otherwise stylize the transport protocol.

FURTHER READING

There is no doubt that TCP is a complex protocol and that in fact it has subtleties not illuminated in this chapter. Therefore, the recommended reading list for this chapter includes the original TCP specification. Our motivation for including this specification is not so much to fill in the missing details, as to expose you to what an honest-togoodness protocol specification looks like. The other two papers in the recommended reading list focus on RPC. The paper by Birrell and Nelson is the seminal paper on the topic, while the article by O'Malley and Peterson describes the one-function-per-protocol design philosophy in more detail.

■ USC-ISI. Transmission Control Protocol. *Request for Comments* 793, September 1981.

■ Birrell, A., and B. Nelson. Implementing remote procedure calls. *ACM Transactions on Computer Systems* 2(1):39–59, February 1984.

■ O'Malley, S., and L. Peterson. A Dynamic Network Architecture. *ACM Transactions on Computer Systems* 10(2):110–143, May 1992.

Beyond the protocol specification, the most complete description of TCP, including its implementation in Berkeley Unix, can be found in Stevens [Ste94b]. Also, the third volume of Comer and Stevens's TCP/IP series of books describes how to write client/server applications on top of TCP and UDP, using both the socket interface [CS93] and the System V Unix TLI interface [CS94].

Several papers evaluate the performance of different transport protocols at a very detailed level. For example, the article by Clark et al. [CJRS89] measures the processing overheads of TCP, a paper by Mosberger et al. [MPBO96] explores the limitations of protocol processing overheads, and Thekkath and Levy [TL93] and Schroeder and Burrows [SB89] examine RPC's performance in great detail.

The original TCP timeout calculation was described in the TCP specification (see above), while the Karn/Partridge algorithm was described in [KP91] and the Jacobson/Karels algorithm was proposed in [Jac88]. The TCP extensions are defined by Jacobson et al. [JBB92], while O'Malley and Peterson [OP91] argue that extending TCP in this way is not the right approach to solving the problem.

Finally, there are several distributed operating systems that have defined their own RPC protocol. Notable examples include the V system, described by Cheriton and Zwaenepoel [CZ85]; Sprite, described by Ousterhout et al. [OCD+88]; and Amoeba, described by Mullender [Mul90]. The latest version of SunRPC, as defined by Srinivasan [Sri95a], is a proposed standard for the Internet.

E X E R C I S E S

1 If a UDP datagram is sent from host A, port P to host B, port Q, but at host B there is no process listening to port Q, then B is to send back an ICMP Port Unreachable message to A. Like all ICMP messages, this is addressed to A as a whole, not to port P on A.

(a) Give an example of when an application might want to receive such ICMP messages.

(b) Find out what an application has to do, on the operating system of your choice, to receive such messages.

(c) Why might it not be a good idea to send such messages directly back to the originating port P on A?

2 Consider a simple UDP-based protocol for requesting files (based somewhat loosely on the Trivial File Transport Protocol, TFTP). The client sends an initial file request, and the server answers (if the file can be sent) with the first data packet. Client and server then continue with a stop-and-wait transmission mechanism.

(a) Describe a scenario by which a client might request one file but get another; you may allow the client application to exit abruptly and be restarted with the same port.

(b) Propose a change in the protocol that will make this situation much less likely.

3 Design a simple UDP-based protocol for retrieving files from a server. No authentication is to be provided. Stop-and-wait transmission of the data may be used. Your protocol should address the following issues:

(a) Duplication of the first packet should not duplicate the "connection."

(b) Loss of the final ACK should not necessarily leave the server in doubt as to whether the transfer succeeded.

(c) A late-arriving packet from a past connection shouldn't be interpretable as part of a current connection.

4 This chapter explains three sequences of state transitions during TCP connection teardown. There is a fourth possible sequence, which traverses an additional arc (not shown in Figure 5.7) from FIN_WAIT_1 to TIME_WAIT and labelled FIN + ACK/ACK. Explain the circumstances that result in this fourth teardown sequence.

5 When closing a TCP connection, why is the two-segment-lifetime timeout not necessary on the transition from LAST_ACK to CLOSED?

6 A sender on a TCP connection that receives a 0 advertised window periodically probes the receiver to discover when the window becomes nonzero. Why would the receiver need an extra timer if it were responsible for reporting that its advertised window had become nonzero (i.e., if the sender did not probe)?

7 Read the man page (or Windows equivalent) for the Unix/Windows utility netstat. Use netstat to see the state of the local TCP connections. Find out how long closing connections spend in TIME_WAIT.

8 The sequence number field in the TCP header is 32 bits long, which is big enough to cover over 4 billion bytes of data. Even if this many bytes were never transferred over a single connection, why might the sequence number still wrap around from $2^{32} - 1$ to 0?

9 You are hired to design a reliable byte-stream protocol that uses a sliding window (like TCP). This protocol will run over a 100-Mbps network. The RTT of the network is 100 ms, and the maximum segment lifetime is 60 seconds.

(a) How many bits would you include in the AdvertisedWindow and Sequence-Num fields of your protocol header?

(b) How would you determine the numbers given above, and which values might be less certain?

10 Suppose a host wants to establish the reliability of a link by sending packets and measuring the percentage that are received; routers, for example, do this. Explain the difficulty doing this over a TCP connection.

11 Suppose TCP operates over a 1-Gbps link.

(a) How long would it take for the TCP sequence numbers to wrap around completely?

(b) Suppose an added 32-bit timestamp field increments 1000 times during the wraparound time you found above. How long would it take for the timestamp to wrap around?

12 If host A receives two SYN packets from the same port from remote host B, the second may be either a retransmission of the original or else, if B has crashed and rebooted, an entirely new connection request.

(a) Describe the difference as seen by host A between these two cases.

(b) Give an algorithmic description of what the TCP layer needs to do upon receiving a SYN packet. Consider the duplicate/new cases above, and the possibility that nothing is listening to the destination port.

13 Suppose x and y are two TCP sequence numbers. Write a function to determine whether x comes before y (in the notation of *Request for Comments* 793, "$x =< y$") or after y; your solution should work even when sequence numbers wrap around.

14 Suppose an idle TCP connection exists between sockets A and B. A third party has eavesdropped and knows the current sequence number at both ends.

(a) Suppose the third party sends A a forged packet ostensibly from B and with 100 bytes of new data. What happens? Hint: Look up in *Request for Comments* 793 what TCP does when it receives an ACK that is not an "acceptable ACK."

(b) Suppose the third party sends each end such a forged 100-byte data packet ostensibly from the other end. What happens now? What would happen if A later sent 200 bytes of data to B?

15 Suppose party A connects to the Internet via a dial-up IP server (e.g., using SLIP or PPP), has several open Telnet connections (using TCP), and is cut off. Party B then dials in and is assigned the same IP address that A had had. Assuming B were able to guess to what host(s) A had been connected, describe a sequence of probes that could enable B to obtain sufficient state information to continue with A's connections.

16 Diagnostic programs are commonly available that record the first 100 bytes, say, of every TCP connection to a certain ⟨host, port⟩. Outline what must be done with each received TCP packet, P, in order to determine if it contains data that belongs to the first 100 bytes of a connection to host HOST, port PORT. Assume the IP header is P.IPHEAD, the TCP header is P.TCPHEAD, and header fields are as named in Figures 4.3 and 5.4. Hint: To get initial sequence numbers (ISNs) you will have to examine every packet with the SYN bit set. Ignore the fact that sequence numbers will eventually be reused.

17 If a packet arrives at host A with B's source address, it could just as easily have been forged by any third host C. If, however, A accepts a TCP connection from B, then during the three-way handshake A sent ISN_A to B's address and received an acknowledgment of it. If C is not located so as to be able to eavesdrop on ISN_A, then it might seem that C could not have forged B's response.

However, the algorithm for choosing ISN_A does give other unrelated hosts a fair chance of guessing it. Specifically, A selects ISN_A based on a clock value at the time of connection. *Request for Comments* 793 specifies that this clock value be incremented every 4 μs; common Berkeley implementations once simplified this to incrementing by 250,000 (or 256,000) once per second.

(a) Given this simplified increment-once-per-second implementation, explain how an arbitrary host C could masquerade as B in at least the opening of a TCP connection. You may assume that B does not respond to SYN + ACK packets A is tricked into sending to it.

(b) Assuming real RTTs can be estimated to within 40 ms, about how many tries would you expect it to take to implement the strategy of part (a) with the unsimplified "increment every 4 μs" TCP implementation?

18 The Nagle algorithm, built into most TCP implementations, requires the sender to hold a partial segment's worth of data (even if PUSHed) until either a full segment accumulates or the most recent outstanding ACK arrives.

(a) Suppose the letters abcdefghi are sent, one per second, over a TCP connection with an RTT of 4.1 seconds. Draw a timeline indicating when each packet is sent and what it contains.

(b) If the above were typed over a full-duplex Telnet connection, what would the user see?

(c) Suppose that mouse position changes are being sent over the connection. Assuming that multiple position changes are sent each RTT, how would a user perceive the mouse motion with and without the Nagle algorithm?

19 The silly window syndrome denotes the situation when the sender has lots of data to send but sends it in tiny increments as the window slides forward in tiny increments. Give details of how this could happen, and suggest both sender-side and receiver-side prevention.

20 Suppose a client C repeatedly connects via TCP to a given port on a server S, and that each time it is C that initiates the close.

(a) How many TCP connections a second can C make here before it ties up all its available ports in TIME_WAIT state? Assume client ephemeral ports are in the range 1024–5119, and that TIME_WAIT lasts 60 seconds.

(b) Berkeley-derived TCP implementations typically allow a socket in TIME_WAIT state to be reopened before TIME_WAIT expires, if the highest sequence number used by the old incarnation of the connection is less than the ISN used by the new incarnation. This solves the problem of old data accepted as new; however, TIME_WAIT also serves the purpose of handling late final FINs. What would such an implementation have to do to address this and still achieve strict compliance with the TCP requirement that a FIN sent anytime before or during a connection's TIME_WAIT receive the same response?

21 Explain why TIME_WAIT is a somewhat more serious problem if the server initiates the close than if the client does. Describe a situation in which this might reasonably happen.

22 What is the justification for the exponential increase in timeout value proposed by Karn and Partridge? Why, specifically, might a linear (or slower) increase be less desirable?

23 The Jacobson/Karels algorithm sets TimeOut to be 4 mean deviations above the mean. Assume that individual packet round-trip times follow a statistical normal distribution, for which 4 mean deviations are π standard deviations. Using statistical tables, for example, what is the probability that a packet will take more than TimeOut time to arrive?

24 Suppose a TCP connection, with window size 1, loses every other packet. Those that do arrive have RTT $= 1$ second. What happens? What happens to TimeOut? Do this for two cases:

   (a) After a packet is eventually received, we pick up where we left off, resuming with EstimatedRTT initialized to its pretimeout value, and TimeOut double that.

   (b) After a packet is eventually received, we resume with TimeOut initialized to the last exponentially backed-off value used for the timeout interval.

In the following three exercises, the calculations involved are straighforward with a spreadsheet.

25 Suppose, in TCP's adaptive retransmission mechanism, that EstimatedRTT is 4.0 at some point and subsequent measured RTTs all are 1.0. How long does it take before the TimeOut value, as calculated by the Jacobson/Karels algorithm, falls below 4.0? Assume a plausible initial value of Deviation; how sensitive is your answer to this choice? Use $\delta = 1/8$.

26 Suppose TCP's measured RTT is 1.0 except that every Nth RTT is 4.0. What is the largest N, approximately, that doesn't result in timeouts in the steady state (i.e., for which the Jacobson/Karels TimeOut remains greater than 4.0)? Use $\delta = 1/8$.

27 Suppose that TCP is measuring RTTs of 1.0 second, with a mean deviation of 0.1 second. Suddenly the RTT jumps to 5.0 seconds, with no deviation. Compare the behaviors of the original and Jacobson/Karels algorithms for computing TimeOut. Specifically, how many timeouts are encountered with each algorithm? What is the largest TimeOut calculated? Use $\delta = 1/8$.

28 Suppose that, when a TCP segment is sent more than once, we take SampleRTT to be the time between the original transmission and the ACK, as in Figure 5.9(a). Show that if a connection with a 1-packet window loses every other packet (i.e., each packet is transmitted twice), then EstimatedRTT increases to infinity. Assume TimeOut = EstimatedRTT; both algorithms presented in the text always set TimeOut even larger. Hint: EstimatedRTT = EstimatedRTT + $\beta \times$ (SampleRTT − EstimatedRTT).

29 Suppose that, when a TCP segment is sent more than once, we take SampleRTT to be the time between the most recent transmission and the ACK, as in Figure 5.9(b). Assume, for definiteness, that TimeOut = 2 × EstimatedRTT. Sketch a scenario in which no packets are lost but EstimatedRTT converges to a third of the true RTT, and give a diagram illustrating the final steady state. Hint: Begin with a sudden jump in the true RTT to just over the established TimeOut.

30 Consult *Request for Comments* 793 to find out how TCP is supposed to respond if a FIN or an RST arrives with a sequence number other than NextByteExpected. Consider both when the sequence number is within the receive window and when it is not.

31 One of the purposes of TIME_WAIT is to handle the case of a data packet from a first incarnation of a connection arriving very late and being accepted as data for the second incarnation.

(a) Explain why, for this to happen (in the absence of TIME_WAIT), the hosts involved would have to exchange several packets in sequence *after* the delayed packet was sent but before it was delivered.

(b) Propose a network scenario that might account for such a late delivery.

32 Propose an extension to TCP by which one end of a connection can hand off its end to a third host; that is, if A were connected to B, and A handed off its connection to C, then afterwards C would be connected to B and A would not. Specify the new states and transitions needed in the TCP state-transition diagram, and any new packet types involved. You may assume all parties will understand this new option. What state should A go into immediately after the handoff?

33 TCP's simultaneous open feature is arguably seldom used.

(a) Propose a change to TCP in which this is disallowed. Indicate what changes would be made in the state diagram (and if necessary in the undiagrammed event responses).

(b) Could TCP reasonably disallow simultaneous close?

(c) Propose a change to TCP in which simultaneous SYNs exchanged by two hosts lead to two separate connections. Indicate what state diagram changes this entails, and also what header changes become necessary. Note that this now means that more than one connection can exist over a given pair of ⟨host, port⟩s. (You might also look up the first "Discussion" item on page 87 of *Request for Comments* 1122.)

34 TCP is a very symmetric protocol, but the client/server model is not. Consider an asymmetric TCP-like protocol in which only the server side is assigned a port number visible to the application layers. Client-side sockets would simply be abstractions that can be connected to server ports.

(a) Propose header data and connection semantics to support this. What will you use to replace the client port number?

(b) What form does TIME_WAIT now take? How would this be seen through the programming interface? Assume that a client socket could now be reconnected arbitrarily many times to a given server port, resources permitting.

(c) Look up the rsh/rlogin protocol. How would the above break this?

35 The following exercise is concerned with the TCP state FIN_WAIT_2 (see Figure 5.7).

(a) Describe how a client might leave a suitable server in state FIN_WAIT_2 indefinitely. What feature of the server's protocol is necessary here for this scenario?

(b) Try this with some appropriate existing server. Either write a stub client, or use an existing Telnet client capable of connecting to an arbitrary port. Use the netstat utility to verify that the server is in FIN_WAIT_2 state.

36 *Request for Comments* 1122 states (of TCP):

A host MAY implement a "half-duplex" TCP close sequence, so that an application that has called CLOSE cannot continue to read data from the connection. If such a host issues a CLOSE call while received data is still pending in TCP, or if new data is received after CLOSE is called, its TCP SHOULD send an RST to show that data was lost.

Sketch a scenario involving the above in which data sent by *(not to!)* the closing host is lost. You may assume that the remote host, upon receiving an RST, discards all received data still unread in buffers.

37 When TCP sends a $\langle SYN, SequenceNum = x \rangle$ or $\langle FIN, SequenceNum = x \rangle$, the consequent ACK has $Acknowledgment = x + 1$; that is, SYNs and FINs each take up one unit in sequence number space. Is this necessary? If so, give an example of an ambiguity that would arise if the corresponding Acknowledgment were x instead of $x + 1$; if not, explain why.

38 Find out the generic format for TCP header options from *Request for Comments* 793 [USC81].

(a) Outline a strategy that would expand the space available for options beyond the current limit of 44 bytes.

(b) Suggest an extension to TCP allowing the sender of an option a way of specifying what the receiver should do if the option is not understood. List several such receiver actions that might be useful, and try to give an example application of each.

39 The TCP header does not have a BID field, like CHAN does. How does TCP protect itself against the crash-and-reboot scenario that motivates CHAN's BID? Why doesn't CHAN use this same strategy?

40 Suppose we were to implement remote file system mounting using an unreliable RPC protocol that offers zero-or-more semantics. If a message reply is received, this improves to at-least-once semantics. We define read() to return the specified Nth block, rather than the next block in sequence; this way reading once is the same as reading twice and at-least-once semantics is thus the same as exactly once.

(a) For what other file system operations is there no difference between at-least-once and exactly once semantics? Consider open, create, write, seek, opendir, readdir, mkdir, delete (aka unlink), and rmdir.

(b) For the remaining operations, which can have their semantics altered to achieve equivalence of at-least-once and exactly once? What file system operations are irreconcilable with at-least-once semantics?

(c) Suppose the semantics of the rmdir system call are now that the given directory is removed if it exists, and nothing is done otherwise. How could you write a program to delete directories that distinguishes between these two cases?

41 The RPC-based "NFS" remote file system is sometimes considered to have slower than expected write performance. In NFS, a server's RPC reply to a client write request means that the data is physically written to the server's disk, not just placed in a queue.

(a) Explain the bottleneck we might expect, even with infinite bandwidth, if the client sends all its write requests through a single logical CHAN channel, and explain why using a pool of channels could help. Hint: You will need to know a little about disk controllers.

(b) Suppose the server's reply means only that the data has been placed in the disk queue. Explain how this could lead to data loss that wouldn't occur with a local disk. Note that a system crash immediately after data was enqueued doesn't count, because that would cause data loss on a local disk as well.

(c) An alternative would be for the server to respond immediately to acknowledge the write request, and to send its own separate CHAN request later to confirm the physical write. Propose different CHAN RPC semantics to achieve the same effect, but with a single logical request/reply.

42 Both the BLAST and CHAN protocols have a MID field.

(a) Under what circumstances can these be equal, for several packets in a row?

(b) In the text, these fields were sequentially incremented. Can either of these fields be a random number?

43 Suppose BLAST is used over a link with a 10% per-packet loss rate; losses are independent events. Fragments that do arrive are not reordered, however. Messages consist of six fragments.

(a) What is the probability, roughly, that LAST_FRAG expires? Assume this happens only when the last fragment is lost.

(b) What is the probability that the last fragment arrives but something else didn't, eliciting an SRR?

(c) What is the probability that no fragment arrives?

44 Consider a client and server using an RPC mechanism that includes CHAN.

(a) Give a scenario involving server reboot in which an RPC request is sent twice by the client and is executed twice by the server, with only a single ACK.

(b) How might the client become aware this had happened? Would the client be sure it had happened?

45 Suppose an RPC request is of the form "Increment the value of field X of disk block N by 10%." Specify a mechanism to be used by the executing server to guarantee that an arriving request is executed exactly once, even if the server crashes while in the middle of the operation. Assume that individual disk block writes are either complete or else the block is unchanged. You may also assume that some designated "undo log" blocks are available. Your mechanism should include how the RPC server is to behave at restart.

46 Consider a SunRPC client sending a request to a server.

(a) Under what circumstances can the client be sure its request has executed exactly once?

(b) Suppose we wished to add at-most-once semantics to SunRPC. What changes would have to be made? Explain why adding one or more fields to the existing headers would not be sufficient.

47 Suppose TCP were to be used as the underlying transport in an RPC protocol; one TCP connection is to carry a stream of requests and replies. What are the analogs, if any, to CHAN's fields CID, MID, and BID, and Type values REQ, REP, ACK, and PROBE? Which of these would the overlying RPC protocol have to provide? Would some analog of implicit acknowledgments exist?

48 Suppose BLAST runs over a 10-Mbps Ethernet, sending 32K messages.

(a) If the Ethernet packets can hold 1500 bytes of data, and optionless IP headers are used as well as BLAST headers, how many Ethernet packets are required per message?

(b) Calculate the delay due to sending a 32K message over Ethernet
  (i) directly
  (ii) broken into pieces as in (a), with one bridge

Ignore propagation delays, headers, collisions, and interpacket gaps.

49 Write a test program that uses the socket interface to send messages between a pair of Unix workstations connected by some LAN (e.g., Ethernet, ATM, or FDDI). Use this test program to perform the following experiments.

(a) Measure the round-trip latency of TCP and UDP for different message sizes (e.g., 1 byte, 100 bytes, 200 bytes, . . . , 1000 bytes).

(b) Measure the throughput of TCP and UDP for 1-KB, 2-KB, 3-KB, . . . , 32-KB messages. Plot the measured throughput as a function of message size.

(c) Measure the throughput of TCP by sending 1 MB of data from one host to another. Do this in a loop that sends a message of some size, for example, 1024 iterations of a loop that sends 1-KB messages. Repeat the experiment with different message sizes and plot the results.

B y now we have seen enough layers of the network protocol hierarchy to understand how data can be transferred among processes across heterogeneous networks. We now turn to a problem that spans the entire protocol stack—how to effectively and fairly allocate resources among a collection of competing users. The resources being shared include the bandwidth of the links and the buffers on the routers or switches where packets are queued awaiting transmission. Packets *contend* at a router for the use of a link, with each contending packet placed in a queue waiting its turn to be transmitted over the link. When too many packets are contending for the same link, the queue overflows and packets have to be dropped. When such drops become common events, the network is said to be *congested*. Most networks provide a *congestion-control* mechanism to deal with just such a situation.

Congestion control and resource allocation are two sides of the same coin. On the one hand, if the network takes an active role in allocating resources—for example, scheduling which virtual circuit gets to use a given physical link during a certain period of time—then congestion may be avoided, thereby making congestion control unnecessary. Allocating network resources with any precision is difficult, however, because the resources in question are distributed throughout the network; multiple links connecting a series of routers need to be scheduled. On the other hand, you can always let packet sources send as much data as they want, and then recover from congestion should it occur. This is the easier approach, but it can be disruptive because many packets may be discarded by the network before congestion can be controlled. Furthermore, it is precisely at those times when the network is congested—that is, resources have become scarce relative to demand—that the need for resource allocation among competing users is most keenly felt. There are also solutions in the mid-

PROBLEM

Allocating Resources

The hand that hath made you fair hath made you good.

—William Shakespeare

dle, whereby inexact allocation decisions are made, but congestion can still occur and hence some mechanism is still needed to recover from it. Whether you call such a mixed solution congestion control or resource allocation does not really matter. In some sense, it is both.

Congestion control and resource allocation involve both hosts and network elements such as routers. In network elements, various queuing disciplines can be used to control the order in which packets get transmitted and which packets get dropped. The queuing discipline can also segregate traffic, that is, to keep one user's packets from unduly affecting another user's packets. At the end hosts, the congestion-control mechanism paces how fast sources are allowed to send packets. This is done in an effort to keep congestion from occurring in the first place, and should it occur, to help eliminate the congestion.

This chapter starts with an overview of congestion control and resource allocation. We then discuss different queuing disciplines that can be implemented on the routers inside the network, followed by a description of the congestion control algorithm provided by TCP on the hosts. The fourth section explores various techniques involving both routers and hosts that aim to avoid congestion before it becomes a problem. Finally, we examine the broad area of "quality of service." We consider the needs of applications to receive different levels of resource allocation in the network, and describe a number of ways in which they can request these resources and the network can meet the requests.

6

Congestion Control and Resource Allocation

6.1 Issues in Resource Allocation

Resource allocation and congestion control are complex issues and have been the subject of much study ever since the first network was designed. They are still active areas of research. One factor that makes these issues complex is that they are not isolated to one single level of a protocol hierarchy. Resource allocation is partially implemented in the routers or switches inside the network and partially in the transport protocol running on the end hosts. End systems use signalling protocols to convey their resource requirements to network nodes, which respond with information about resource availability. One of the main goals of this chapter is to define a framework in which these mechanisms can be understood, as well as to give the relevant details about a representative sample of mechanisms.

We should clarify our terminology before going any further. By "resource allocation," we mean the process by which network elements try to meet the competing demands that applications have for network resources—primarily link bandwidth and buffer space in routers or switches. Of course, it will often not be possible to meet all the demands, meaning that some users or applications may receive fewer network resources than they want. Part of the resource allocation problem is deciding when to say no, and to whom.

We use the term "congestion control" to describe the efforts made by network nodes to prevent or respond to overload conditions. Since congestion is generally bad for everyone, the first order of business is making congestion subside, or preventing it in the first place. This might be achieved simply by persuading a few hosts to stop sending, thus improving the situation for everyone else. However, it is more common for congestion-control mechanisms to have some notion of fairness—that is, they try to share the pain among all users, rather than causing great pain to a few. Thus we see that many congestion-control mechanisms will have a notion of resource allocation built into them.

It is also important to understand the difference between flow control and congestion control. Flow control, as we have seen in Section 2.5, involves keeping a fast sender from overrunning a slow receiver. Congestion control, by contrast, is intended to keep a set of senders from sending too much data *into the network* because of lack of resources at some point. These two concepts are often confused; as we will see, they also share some mechanisms.

6.1.1 Network Model

We begin by defining three salient features of the network architecture. For the most part, this is a summary of material presented in the previous chapters that is relevant to the problem of resource allocation.

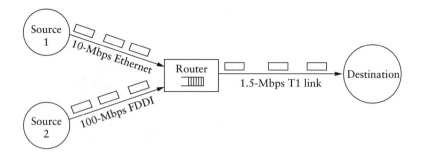

Figure 6.1 Congestion in a packet-switched network.

Packet-Switched Network

We consider resource allocation in a packet-switched network (or internet) consisting of multiple links and switches (or routers). Since most of the mechanisms described in this chapter were designed for use on the Internet, and therefore were originally defined in terms of routers rather than switches, we use the term "router" throughout our discussion. The problem is essentially the same, whether on a network or an internetwork.

In such an environment, a given source may have more than enough capacity on the immediate outgoing link to send a packet, but somewhere in the middle of a network, its packets encounter a link that is being used by many different traffic sources. Figure 6.1 illustrates this situation—two high-speed links are feeding a low-speed link. This is in contrast to shared-access networks like Ethernet and token rings, where the source can directly observe the traffic on the network and decide accordingly whether or not to send a packet. We have already seen the algorithms used to allocate bandwidth on shared-access networks (Chapter 2). These access-control algorithms are, in some sense, analogous to congestion-control algorithms in a switched network.

Note that congestion control is not the same as routing. While it is true that a congested link could be assigned a large edge weight by the route propagation protocol, and as a consequence, routers would route around it, "routing around" a congested link does not solve the congestion problem. To see this, we need look no further than the simple network depicted in Figure 6.1, where all traffic has to flow through the same router to reach the destination. Although this is an extreme example, it is common to have a certain router that it is not possible to route around.[1] This router can become congested, and there is nothing the routing mechanism can do about it. This congested router is sometimes called the *bottleneck* router.

---

[1] It is also worth noting that the complexity of routing in the Internet is such that simply obtaining a reasonably direct, loop-free route is about the best you can hope for. Routing around congestion would be considered icing on the cake.

Connectionless Flows

For much of our discussion, we assume that the network is essentially connectionless, with any connection-oriented service implemented in the transport protocol that is running on the end hosts. (We explain the qualification "essentially" in a moment.) This is precisely the model of the Internet, where IP provides a connectionless datagram delivery service and TCP implements an end-to-end connection abstraction. Note that this assumption excludes early networks like X.25, in which a virtual circuit abstraction is maintained across a set of routers (see Section 3.1.2). In such networks, a connection setup message traverses the network when a circuit is established. This setup message reserves a set of buffers for the connection at each router, thereby providing a form of congestion control—a connection is established only if enough buffers can be allocated to it at each router. The major shortcoming of this approach is that it leads to an underutilization of resources—buffers reserved for a particular circuit are not available for use by other traffic even if they were not currently being used by that circuit. The focus of this chapter is on resource allocation approaches that apply in an internetwork, and thus we focus mainly on connectionless networks. The one exception to this is our discussion of ATM quality of service in Section 6.5.4, which provides an interesting contrast to the Internet model.

We need to qualify the term "connectionless" because our classification of networks as being either connectionless or connection-oriented is a bit too restrictive; there is a gray area in between. In particular, the implication of a connectionless network that all datagrams are completely independent is too strong. The datagrams are certainly switched independently, but it is usually the case that a stream of datagrams between a particular pair of hosts flows through a particular set of routers. This idea of a *flow*—a sequence of packets sent between a source/destination host pair and following the same route through the network—is an important abstraction in the context of resource allocation; it is one that we will use in this chapter. Note that a flow is essentially the same as a channel, as we have been using that term throughout this book. The reason we introduce a new term is that a flow is visible to the routers inside the network, whereas a channel is an end-to-end abstraction. Figure 6.2 illustrates several flows passing through a series of routers.

Because multiple related packets flow through each router, it sometimes makes sense to maintain some state information for each flow, information that can be used to make resource allocation decisions about the packets that belong to the flow. This state is sometimes called *soft state*; the main difference between soft state and "hard" state is that soft state need not always be explicitly created and removed by signalling. Soft state represents a middle ground between a purely connectionless network that maintains *no* state at the routers and a purely connection-oriented network that maintains hard state at the routers. In general, the correct operation of the network does

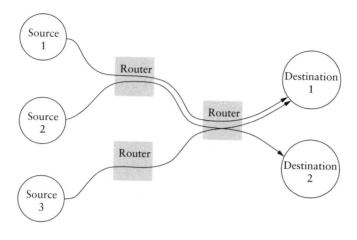

Figure 6.2 **Multiple flows passing through a set of routers.**

not depend on soft state being present (each packet is still routed correctly without regard to this state), but when a packet happens to belong to a flow for which the router is currently maintaining soft state, then the router is better able to handle the packet.

Note that a flow can be either implicitly defined or explicitly established. In the former case, each router watches for packets that happen to be traveling between the same source/destination pair—the router does this by inspecting the addresses in the header—and treats these packets as belonging to the same flow for the purpose of congestion control. In the latter case, the source sends a flow setup message across the network, declaring that a flow of packets is about to start. While explicit flows are arguably no different than a connection across a connection-oriented network, we call attention to this case because even when explicitly established, a flow does not imply any end-to-end semantics, and in particular, it does not imply the reliable and ordered delivery of a virtual circuit. It simply exists for the purpose of resource allocation. We will see examples of both implicit and explicit flows in this chapter.

Service Model

In the early part of this chapter, we will focus on mechanisms that assume the best-effort service model of the Internet. With best-effort service, each packet is treated in exactly the same way, with end hosts given no opportunity to ask the network that one of their flows be given certain guarantees. Defining a service model that supports some kind of guarantee—for example, guaranteeing the bandwidth needed for a video stream—is the subject of Section 6.5. Such a service model is said to provide multiple *qualities of service* (QoS). As we will see, there is actually a spectrum of possibilities, ranging from a purely best-effort service model to one in which individual flows receive quantitative guarantees of QoS. One of the greatest challenges is to define a service model that meets the needs of a wide range of applications and even allows for the applications that will be invented in the future.

6.1.2 Taxonomy

There are countless ways in which resource allocation mechanisms differ, making a thorough taxonomy a difficult proposition. For now, we describe three dimensions along which resource allocation mechanisms can be characterized; more subtle distinctions will be called out during the course of this chapter.

Router-Centric versus Host-Centric

Resource allocation mechanisms can be classified into two broad groups: those that address the problem from inside the network (i.e., at the routers or switches) and those that address it from the edges of the network (i.e., in the hosts, perhaps inside the transport protocol). Since it is the case that both the routers inside the network and the hosts at the edges of the network participate in resource allocation, the real issue is where the majority of the burden falls.

In a router-centric design, each router takes responsibility for deciding when packets are forwarded and selecting which packets are to dropped, as well as for informing the hosts that are generating the network traffic how many packets they are allowed to send. In a host-centric design, the end hosts observe the network conditions (e.g., how many packets they are successfully getting through the network) and adjust their behavior accordingly. Note that these two groups are not mutually exclusive. For example, a network that places the primary burden for managing congestion on routers still expects the end hosts to adhere to any advisory messages the routers send, while the routers in networks that use end-to-end congestion control still have some policy, no matter how simple, for deciding which packets to drop when their queues do overflow.

Reservation-Based versus Feedback-Based

A second way that resource allocation mechanisms are sometimes classified is according to whether they use *reservations* or *feedback*. In a reservation-based system, the end host asks the network for a certain amount of capacity at the time a flow is established. Each router then allocates enough resources (buffers and/or percentage of the link's bandwidth) to satisfy this request. If the request cannot be satisfied at some router, because doing so would overcommit its resources, then the router rejects the flow. This is analogous to getting a busy signal when trying to make a phone call. In a feedback-based approach, the end hosts begin sending data without first reserving any capacity and then adjust their sending rate according to the feedback they receive. This feedback can either be *explicit* (i.e., a congested router sends a "please slow down" message to the host) or it can be *implicit* (i.e., the end host adjusts its sending rate according to the externally observable behavior of the network, such as packet losses).

Note that a reservation-based system always implies a router-centric resource allocation mechanism. This is because each router is responsible for keeping track of how much of its capacity is currently reserved and for making sure each host lives within the reservation it made. If a host sends data faster than it claimed it would when it made the reservation, then that host's packets are good candidates for discarding, should the router become congested. On the other hand, a feedback-based system can imply either a router- or host-centric mechanism. Typically, if the feedback is explicit, then the router is involved, to at least some degree, in the resource allocation scheme. If the feedback is implicit, then almost all of the burden falls to the end host; the routers silently drop packets when they become congested.

Window-Based versus Rate-Based

A third way to characterize resource allocation mechanisms is according to whether they are *window based* or *rate based*. This is one of the areas, noted above, where similar mechanisms and terminology are used for both flow control and congestion control. Both flow-control and resource allocation mechanisms need a way to express, to the sender, how much data it is allowed to transmit. There are two general ways of doing this: with a *window* or with a *rate*. We have already seen window-based transport protocols, such as TCP, in which the receiver advertises a window to the sender. This window corresponds to how much buffer space the receiver has, and it limits how much data the sender can transmit; that is, it supports flow control. A similar mechanism—window advertisement—can be used within the network to reserve buffer space, that is, to support resource allocation. This is essentially what is done in X.25.

It is also possible to control a sender's behavior using a rate, that is, how many bits per second the receiver or network is able to absorb. Although we have not studied any rate-based transport protocols in this book because this is still an open area of research, we can imagine such a protocol used to support video: The receiver says it can process video frames at a rate of 1 Mbps, and the sender adheres to this rate. As we will see later in this chapter, rate-based characterization of flows is a logical choice in a reservation-based system that supports different qualities of service—the sender makes a reservation for so many bits per second, and each router along the path determines if it can support that rate, given the other flows it has made commitments to.

Summary of Resource Allocation Taxonomy

Classifying resource allocation approaches at two different points along each of three dimensions, as we have just done, would seem to suggest up to eight unique strategies. While eight different approaches are certainly possible, we note that in practice two general strategies seem to be most prevalent; these two strategies are tied to the underlying service model of the network.

On the one hand, a best-effort service model usually implies that feedback is being used, since such a model does not allow users to reserve network capacity. This, in turn, means that most of the responsibility for congestion control falls to the end hosts, perhaps with some assistance from the routers. In practice, such networks use window-based information. This is the general strategy adopted in the Internet and the focus of Sections 6.3 and 6.4.

On the other hand, a QoS-based service model probably implies some form of reservation.[2] Support for these reservations is likely to require significant router involvement, for example, to queue packets differently depending on the level of reserved resources they require. Moreover, it is natural to express such reservations in terms of rate, since windows are only indirectly related to how much bandwidth a user needs from the network. We discuss this topic in Section 6.5.

6.1.3 Evaluation Criteria

The final issue is one of knowing whether a resource allocation mechanism is good or not. Recall that in the problem statement at the start of this chapter we posed the question of how a network *effectively* and *fairly* allocates its resources. This suggests at least two broad measures by which a resource allocation scheme can be evaluated. We consider each in turn.

Effective Resource Allocation

A good starting point for evaluating the effectiveness of a resource allocation scheme is to consider the two principal metrics of networking: throughput and delay. Clearly, we want as much throughput and as little delay as possible. Although on the surface it might appear as though increasing throughput also means reducing delay, this is not the case. One sure way for a resource allocation algorithm to increase throughput is to allow as many packets into the network as possible, so as to drive the utilization of all the links up to 100%. We would do this to avoid the possibility of a link becoming idle because an idle link necessarily hurts throughput. The problem with this strategy

---

[2] As we will see in Section 6.5, resource reservations might be made by network managers rather than by hosts.

is that increasing the number of packets in the network also increases the length of the queues at each router. Longer queues, in turn, mean packets are delayed longer in the network.

To describe this relationship, some network designers have proposed using the ratio of throughput to delay as a metric for evaluating the effectiveness of a resource allocation scheme. This ratio is sometimes referred to as the *power* of the network:[3]

$$\text{Power} = \text{Throughput}/\text{Delay}$$

Note that it is not obvious that power is the right metric for judging resource allocation effectiveness. For one thing, the theory behind power is based on an M/M/1 queuing network[4] that assumes infinite queues; real networks have finite buffers and sometimes have to drop packets. For another, power is typically defined relative to a single connection (flow); it is not clear how it extends to multiple, competing connections. Despite these rather severe limitations, however, no alternatives have gained wide acceptance, and so power continues to be used.

The objective is to maximize this ratio, which is a function of how much load you place on the network. The load, in turn, is set by the resource allocation mechanism. Figure 6.3 gives a representative power curve, where, ideally, the resource allocation mechanism would operate at the peak of this curve. To the left of the peak, the mechanism is being too conservative; that is, it is not allowing enough packets to be sent to keep the links busy. To the right of the peak, so many packets are being allowed into the network that increases in delay due to queuing are starting to dominate any small gains in throughput.

Interestingly, this power curve looks very much like the system throughput curve in a multiprogrammed computer system. System throughput improves as more jobs are admitted into the system, until it reaches a point when there are so many jobs running that the system begins to thrash (spends all of its time swapping memory pages) and the throughput begins to drop.

As we will see in later sections of this chapter, many congestion-control schemes are able to control load in only very crude ways. That is, it is simply not possible to turn the "knob" a little and allow only a small number of additional packets into the network. As a consequence, network designers need to be concerned about what

---

[3] The actual definition is $\text{Power} = \text{Throughput}^{\alpha}/\text{Delay}$, where $0 < \alpha < 1$; $\alpha = 1$ results in power being maximized at the knee of the delay curve. Throughput is measured in units of data (e.g., bits) per second; delay in seconds.

[4] Since this is not a queuing theory book, we provide only this brief description of an M/M/1 queue. The 1 means it has a single server, and the Ms mean that the distribution of both packet arrival and service times is "Markovian," that is, exponential.

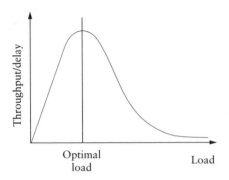

Figure 6.3   Ratio of throughput to delay as a function of load.

happens even when the system is operating under extremely heavy load—that is, at the rightmost end of the curve in Figure 6.3. Ideally, we would like to avoid the situation in which the system throughput goes to zero because the system is thrashing. In networking terminology, we want a system that is *stable*—where packets continue to get through the network even when the network is operating under heavy load. If a mechanism is not stable, the network may experience *congestion collapse*.

Fair Resource Allocation

The effective utilization of network resources is not the only criterion for judging a resource allocation scheme. We must also consider the issue of fairness. However, we quickly get into murky waters when we try to define what exactly constitutes fair resource allocation. For example, a reservation-based resource allocation scheme provides an explicit way to create controlled unfairness. With such a scheme, we might use reservations to enable a video stream to receive 1 Mbps across some link while a file transfer receives only 10 Kbps over the same link.

In the absence of explicit information to the contrary, when several flows share a particular link, we would like for each flow to receive an equal share of the bandwidth. This definition presumes that a *fair* share of bandwidth means an *equal* share of bandwidth. But even in the absence of reservations, equal shares may not equate to fair shares. Should we also consider the length of the paths being compared? For example, as illustrated in Figure 6.4, what is fair when one four-hop flow is competing with three one-hop flows?

Assuming that fair implies equal and that all paths are of equal length, Raj Jain has proposed a metric that can be used to quantify the fairness of a congestion-control mechanism. Jain's fairness index is defined as follows. Given a set of flow throughputs $(x_1, x_2, \ldots, x_n)$ (measured in consistent units such as bits/second), the

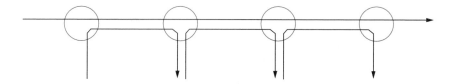

Figure 6.4 One four-hop flow competing with three one-hop flows.

following function assigns a fairness index to the flows:

$$f(x_1, x_2, \ldots, x_n) = \frac{(\sum_{i=1}^{n} x_i)^2}{n \sum_{i=1}^{n} x_i^2}$$

The fairness index always results in a number between 0 and 1, with 1 representing greatest fairness. To understand the intuition behind this metric, consider the case where all n flows receive a throughput of 1 unit of data per second. We can see that the fairness index in this case is

$$\frac{n^2}{n \times n} = 1$$

Now suppose one flow receives a throughput of $1 + \Delta$. Now the fairness index is

$$\frac{((n-1)+1+\Delta)^2}{n(n-1+(1+\Delta)^2)}$$

$$= \frac{n^2 + 2n\Delta + \Delta^2}{n^2 + 2n\Delta + n\Delta^2}$$

Note that the denominator exceeds the numerator by $(n-1)\Delta^2$. Thus whether the odd flow out was getting more or less than all the other flows (positive or negative Δ), the fairness index has now dropped below one. Another simple case to consider is where only k of the n flows receive equal throughput, and the remaining $n - k$ users receive zero throughput, in which case the fairness index drops to k/n.

6.2 Queuing Disciplines

Regardless of how simple or how sophisticated the rest of the resource allocation mechanism is, each router must implement some queuing discipline that governs how packets are buffered while waiting to be transmitted. The queuing algorithm can be thought of as allocating both bandwidth (which packets get transmitted) and buffer

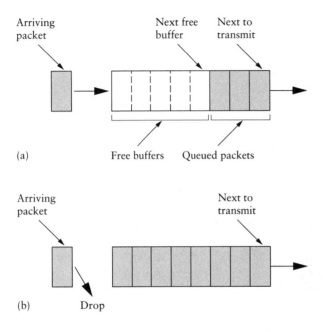

Figure 6.5   (a) FIFO queuing; (b) tail drop at a FIFO queue.

space (which packets get discarded). It also directly affects the latency experienced by a packet, by determining how long a packet waits to be transmitted. This section introduces two common queuing algorithms—FIFO and fair queuing—and identifies several variations that have been proposed.

6.2.1   FIFO

The idea of FIFO (first-in-first-out) queuing, also called first-come-first-served (FCFS) queuing, is simple: The first packet that arrives at a router is the first packet to be transmitted. This is illustrated in Figure 6.5(a), which shows a FIFO with "slots" to hold up to eight packets. Given that the amount of buffer space at each router is finite, if a packet arrives and the queue (buffer space) is full, then the router discards that packet, as shown in Figure 6.5(b). This is done without regard to which flow the packet belongs to or how important the packet is. This is sometimes called *tail drop*, since packets that arrive at the tail end of the FIFO are dropped.

Note that tail drop and FIFO are two separable ideas. FIFO is a *scheduling discipline*—it determines the order in which packets are transmitted. Tail drop is a *drop policy*—it determines which packets get dropped. Because FIFO and tail drop are the simplest instances of scheduling discipline and drop policy, respectively, they are sometimes viewed as a bundle—the vanilla queuing implementation. Unfortunately, the bundle is often referred to simply as "FIFO queuing," when it should more precisely be called "FIFO with tail drop." Section 6.4 provides an example of another drop policy, which uses a more complex algorithm than "Is there a free buffer?" to decide when to drop packets. Such a drop policy may be used with FIFO, or with more complex scheduling disciplines.

FIFO with tail drop, as the simplest of all queuing algorithms, is the most widely used in Internet routers at the time of writing. This simple approach to queuing pushes all responsibility for congestion control and resource allocation out to the edges of the network. Thus, the prevalent form of congestion control in the Internet currently assumes no help from the routers: TCP takes responsibility for detecting and responding to congestion. We will see how this works in Section 6.3.

A simple variation on basic FIFO queuing is priority queuing. The idea is to mark each packet with a priority; the mark could be carried, for example, in the IP Type of Service (TOS) field. The routers then implement multiple FIFO queues, one for each priority class. The router always transmits packets out of the highest-priority queue if that queue is nonempty before moving on to the next priority queue. Within each priority, packets are still managed in a FIFO manner. This idea is a small departure from the best-effort delivery model, but it does not go so far as to make guarantees to any particular priority class. It just allows high-priority packets to cut to the front of the line.

The problem with priority queuing, of course, is that the high-priority queue can starve out all the other queues. That is, as long as there is at least one high-priority packet in the high-priority queue, lower-priority queues do not get served. For this to be viable, there need to be hard limits on how much high-priority traffic is inserted in the queue. It should be immediately clear that we can't allow users to set their own packets to high priority in an uncontrolled way; we must either prevent them from doing this altogether, or provide some form of "pushback" on users. One obvious way to do this is to use economics—the network could charge more to deliver high-priority packets than low-priority packets. However, there are significant challenges to implementing such a scheme in a decentralized environment such as the Internet.

One situation in which priority queuing is used in the Internet is to protect the most important packets—typically the routing updates that are necessary to stabilize the routing tables after a topology change. Often there is a special queue for such packets, which can be identified by the TOS field in the IP header. This is in fact a simple case of the idea of "Differentiated Services," the subject of Section 6.5.3.

6.2.2 Fair Queuing

The main problem with FIFO queuing is that it does not discriminate between different traffic sources, or in the language introduced in the previous section, it does not separate packets according to the flow to which they belong. This is a problem at

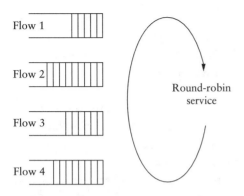

Flow 1

Flow 2

Flow 3

Flow 4

Round-robin
service

Figure 6.6 Fair queuing at a router.

two different levels. At one level, it is not clear that any congestion-control algorithm implemented entirely at the source will be able to adequately control congestion with so little help from the routers. We will suspend judgment on this point until the next section when we discuss TCP congestion control. At another level, because the entire congestion-control mechanism is implemented at the sources and FIFO queuing does not provide a means to police how well the sources adhere to this mechanism, it is possible for an ill-behaved source (flow) to capture an arbitrarily large fraction of the network capacity. Considering the Internet again, it is certainly possible for a given application not to use TCP, and as a consequence, to bypass its end-to-end congestion-control mechanism. (Applications such as Internet telephony do this today.) Such an application is able to flood the Internet's routers with its own packets, thereby causing other applications' packets to be discarded.

Fair queuing (FQ) is an algorithm that has been proposed to address this problem. The idea of FQ is to maintain a separate queue for each flow currently being handled by the router. The router then services these queues in a round-robin manner, as illustrated in Figure 6.6. When a flow sends packets too quickly, then its queue fills up. When a queue reaches a particular length, additional packets belonging to that flow's queue are discarded. In this way, a given source cannot arbitrarily increase its share of the network's capacity at the expense of other flows.

Note that FQ does not involve the router telling the traffic sources anything about the state of the router or in any way limiting how quickly a given source sends packets. In other words, FQ is still designed to be used in conjunction with an end-to-end congestion-control mechanism. It simply segregates traffic so that ill-behaved traffic sources do not interfere with those that are faithfully implementing the end-to-end algorithm. FQ also enforces fairness among a collection of flows managed by a well-behaved congestion-control algorithm.

As simple as the basic idea is, there are still a modest number of details that you have to get right. The main complication is that the packets being processed at a router are not necessarily the same length. To truly allocate the bandwidth of the outgoing link in a fair manner, it is necessary to take packet length into consideration. For example, if a router is managing two flows, one with 1000-byte packets and the other with 500-byte packets (perhaps because of fragmentation upstream from this router), then a simple round-robin servicing of packets from each flow's queue will give the first flow two-thirds of the link's bandwidth and the second flow only one-third of its bandwidth.

What we really want is bit-by-bit round-robin; that is, the router transmits a bit from flow 1, then a bit from flow 2, and so on. Clearly, it is not feasible to interleave the bits from different packets. The FQ mechanism therefore simulates this behavior by first determining when a given packet would finish being transmitted if it were being sent using bit-by-bit round-robin, and then using this finishing time to sequence the packets for transmission.

To understand the algorithm for approximating bit-by-bit round-robin, consider the behavior of a single flow and imagine a clock that ticks once each time one bit is transmitted from all of the active flows. (A flow is active when it has data in the queue.) For this flow, let P_i denote the length of packet i, let S_i denote the time when the router starts to transmit packet i, and let F_i denote the time when the router finishes transmitting packet i. If P_i is expressed in terms of how many clock ticks it takes to transmit packet i (keeping in mind that time advances 1 tick each time this flow gets 1 bit's worth of service), then it is easy to see that $F_i = S_i + P_i$.

When do we start transmitting packet i? The answer to this question depends on whether packet i arrived before or after the router finished transmitting packet $i - 1$ from this flow. If it was before, then logically the first bit of packet i is transmitted immediately after the last bit of packet $i - 1$. On the other hand, it is possible that the router finished transmitting packet $i - 1$ long before i arrived, meaning that there was a period of time during which the queue for this flow was empty, so the round-robin mechanism could not transmit any packets from this flow. If we let A_i denote the time that packet i arrives at the router, then $S_i = \max(F_{i-1}, A_i)$. Thus, we can compute

$$F_i = \max(F_{i-1}, A_i) + P_i$$

Now we move on to the situation in which there is more than one flow, and we find that there is a catch to determining A_i. We can't just read the wall clock when the

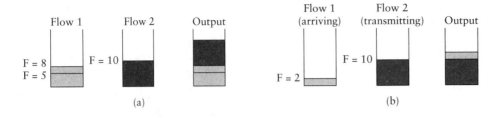

Figure 6.7 Example of fair queuing in action: (a) shorter packets are sent first; (b) sending of longer packet, already in progress, is completed first.

packet arrives. As noted above, we want time to advance by one tick each time all the active flows get one bit of service under bit-by-bit round-robin, so we need a clock that advances more slowly when there are more flows. Specifically, the clock must advance by one tick when n bits are transmitted if there are n active flows. This clock will be used to calculate A_i.

Now, for every flow, we calculate F_i for each packet that arrives using the above formula. We then treat all the F_i as timestamps, and the next packet to transmit is always the packet that has the lowest timestamp—the packet that, based on the above reasoning, should finish transmission before all others.

Note that this means that a packet can arrive on a flow, and because it is shorter than a packet from some other flow that is already in the queue waiting to be transmitted, it can be inserted into the queue in front of that longer packet. However, this does not mean that a newly arriving packet can preempt a packet that is currently being transmitted. It is this lack of preemption that keeps the implementation of FQ just described from exactly simulating the bit-by-bit round-robin scheme that we are attempting to approximate.

To better see how this implementation of fair queuing works, consider the example given in Figure 6.7. Part (a) shows the queues for two flows; the algorithm selects both packets from flow 1 to be transmitted before the packet in the flow 2 queue. In (b), the router has already begun to send a packet from flow 2 when the packet from flow 1 arrives. Though the packet arriving on flow 1 would have finished before flow 2 if we had been using perfect bit-by-bit fair queuing, the implementation does not preempt the flow 2 packet.

There are two things to notice about fair queuing. First, the link is never left idle as long as there is at least one packet in the queue. Any queuing scheme with this characteristic is said to be *work-conserving*. One effect of being work-conserving is that if I am sharing a link with a lot of flows that are not sending any data, I can use the full link capacity for my flow. As soon as the other flows start sending, however, they will start to use their share and the capacity available to my flow will drop.

The second thing to notice is that if the link is fully loaded and there are n flows sending data, I cannot use more than $1/n$th of the link bandwidth. If I try to send more than that, my packets will be assigned increasingly large timestamps, causing them to sit in the queue longer awaiting transmission. Eventually the queue will overflow—although whether it is my packets or someone else's that are dropped is a decision that is not determined by the fact that we are using fair queuing. This is determined by the drop policy; FQ is a scheduling algorithm, which, like FIFO, may be combined with various drop policies.

Because FQ is work-conserving, any bandwidth that is not used by one flow is automatically available to other flows. For example, if we have four flows passing through a router, and all of them are sending packets, then each one will receive one-quarter of the bandwidth. But if one of them is idle long enough that all its packets drain out of the router's queue, then the available bandwidth will be shared among the remaining three flows, which will each now receive one-third of the bandwidth. Thus we can think of FQ as providing a guaranteed minimum share of bandwidth to each flow, with the possibility that it can get more than its guarantee if other flows are not using their shares.

It is possible to implement a variation of FQ, called *weighted fair queuing* (WFQ), that allows a weight to be assigned to each flow (queue). This weight logically specifies how many bits to transmit each time the router services that queue, which effectively controls the percentage of the link's bandwidth that that flow will get. Simple FQ gives each queue a weight of 1, which means that logically only 1 bit is transmitted from each queue each time around. This results in each flow getting $1/n$th of the bandwidth when there are n flows. With WFQ, however, one queue might have a weight of 2, a second queue might have a weight of 1, and a third queue might have a weight of 3. Assuming that each queue always contains a packet waiting to be transmitted, the first flow will get one-third of the available bandwidth, the second will get one-sixth of the available bandwidth, and the third will get one-half of the available bandwidth.

While we have described WFQ in terms of flows, note that it could be implemented on "classes" of traffic, where classes are defined in some other way than the simple flows introduced at the start of this chapter. For example, we could use the Type of Service (TOS) bits in the IP header to identify classes, and allocate a queue and a weight to each class. This is exactly what is proposed as part of the Differentiated Services architecture described in Section 6.5.3.

Note that a router performing WFQ must learn what weights to assign to each queue from somewhere, either by manual configuration or by some sort of signalling from the sources. In the latter case, we are moving toward a reservation-based model. Just assigning a weight to a queue provides a rather weak form of reservation because these weights are only indirectly related to the bandwidth the flow receives. (The bandwidth available to a flow also depends, for example, on how many other flows are sharing the link.) We will see in Section 6.5.2 how WFQ can be used as a component of a reservation-based resource allocation mechanism.

▶ Finally, we observe that this whole discussion of queue management illustrates an important system design principle known as *separating policy and mechanism*. The idea is to view each mechanism as a black box that provides a multifaceted service that can be controlled by a set of knobs. A policy specifies a particular setting of those knobs, but does not know (or care) about how the black box is implemented. In this case, the mechanism in question is the queuing discipline, and the policy is a particular setting of which flow gets what level of service (e.g., priority or weight). We discuss some policies that can be used with the WFQ mechanism in Section 6.5.

6.3 TCP Congestion Control

This section describes the predominant example of end-to-end congestion control in use today, that implemented by TCP. The essential strategy of TCP is to send packets into the network without a reservation and then to react to observable events that occur. TCP assumes only FIFO queuing in the network's routers, but also works with fair queuing.

TCP congestion control was introduced into the Internet in the late 1980s by Van Jacobson, roughly eight years after the TCP/IP protocol stack had become operational. Immediately preceding this time, the Internet was suffering from congestion collapse—hosts would send their packets into the Internet as fast as the advertised window would allow, congestion would occur at some router (causing packets to be dropped), and the hosts would time out and retransmit their packets, resulting in even more congestion.

Broadly speaking, the idea of TCP congestion control is for each source to determine how much capacity is available in the network, so that it knows how many packets it can safely have in transit. Once a given source has this many packets in transit, it uses the arrival of an ACK as a signal that one of its packets has left the network, and that it is therefore safe to insert a new packet into the network without adding to the level of congestion. By using ACKs to pace the transmission of packets, TCP is said to be *self-clocking*. Of course, determining the available capacity in the first place is no easy task. To make matters worse, because other connections come and go, the available bandwidth changes over time, meaning that any given source must be able to adjust the number of packets it has in transit. This section describes the algorithms used by TCP to address these and other problems.

Note that although we describe these mechanisms one at a time, thereby giving the impression that we are talking about three independent mechanisms, it is only when they are taken as a whole that we have TCP congestion control.

6.3.1 Additive Increase/Multiplicative Decrease

TCP maintains a new state variable for each connection, called CongestionWindow, which is used by the source to limit how much data it is allowed to have in transit at a given time. The congestion window is congestion control's counterpart to flow control's advertised window. TCP is modified such that the maximum number of bytes of unacknowledged data allowed is now the minimum of the congestion window and the advertised window. Thus, using the variables defined in Section 5.2.4, TCP's effective window is revised as follows:

$$MaxWindow = MIN(CongestionWindow, AdvertisedWindow)$$

$$EffectiveWindow = MaxWindow - (LastByteSent - LastByteAcked).$$

That is, MaxWindow replaces AdvertisedWindow in the calculation of EffectiveWindow. Thus, a TCP source is allowed to send no faster than the slowest component—the network or the destination host—can accommodate.

The problem, of course, is how TCP comes to learn an appropriate value for CongestionWindow. Unlike the AdvertisedWindow, which is sent by the receiving side of the connection, there is no one to send a suitable CongestionWindow to the sending side of TCP. The answer is that the TCP source sets the CongestionWindow based on the level of congestion it perceives to exist in the network. This involves decreasing the congestion window when the level of congestion goes up and increasing the congestion window when the level of congestion goes down. Taken together, the mechanism is commonly called *additive increase/multiplicative decrease*; the reason for this mouthful of a name will become apparent below.

The key question, then, is how does the source determine that the network is congested and that it should decrease the congestion window? The answer is based on the observation that the main reason packets are not delivered, and a timeout results, is that a packet was dropped due to congestion. It is rare that a packet is dropped because of an error during transmission. Therefore, TCP interprets timeouts as a sign of congestion and reduces the rate at which it is transmitting. Specifically, each time a timeout occurs, the source sets CongestionWindow to half of its previous value. This halving of the CongestionWindow for each timeout corresponds to the "multiplicative decrease" part of the mechanism.

Although CongestionWindow is defined in terms of bytes, it is easiest to understand multiplicative decrease if we think in terms of whole packets. For example, suppose the CongestionWindow is currently set to 16 packets. If a loss is detected, CongestionWindow is set to 8. (Normally, a loss is detected when a timeout occurs, but as we see below, TCP has another mechanism to detect dropped packets.) Additional losses cause CongestionWindow to be reduced to 4, then 2, and finally to 1 packet.

Source   Destination

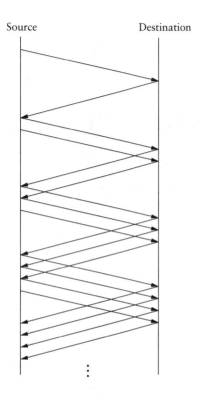

Figure 6.8   Packets in transit during additive increase, with one packet being added each RTT.

CongestionWindow is not allowed to fall below the size of a single packet, or in TCP terminology, the *maximum segment size* (MSS).

A congestion-control strategy that only decreases the window size is obviously too conservative. We also need to be able to increase the congestion window to take advantage of newly available capacity in the network. This is the "additive increase" part of the mechanism, and it works as follows. Every time the source successfully sends a CongestionWindow's worth of packets—that is, each packet sent out during the last RTT has been ACKed—it adds the equivalent of 1 packet to CongestionWindow. This linear increase is illustrated in Figure 6.8. Note that in practice, TCP does not wait for an entire window's worth of ACKs to add 1 packet's worth to the congestion window, but instead increments CongestionWindow by a little for each ACK that arrives. Specifically, the congestion window is incremented as follows each time an ACK arrives:

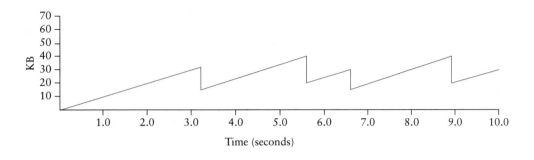

Figure 6.9 Typical TCP sawtooth pattern.

$$\text{Increment} = \text{MSS} \times (\text{MSS}/\text{CongestionWindow})$$

$$\text{CongestionWindow} += \text{Increment}$$

That is, rather than incrementing CongestionWindow by an entire MSS bytes each RTT, we increment it by a fraction of MSS every time an ACK is received. Assuming that each ACK acknowledges the receipt of MSS bytes, then that fraction is MSS/CongestionWindow.

This pattern of continually increasing and decreasing the congestion window continues throughout the lifetime of the connection. In fact, if you plot the current value of CongestionWindow as a function of time, you get a sawtooth pattern, as illustrated in Figure 6.9. The important concept to understand about additive increase/multiplicative decrease is that the source is willing to reduce its congestion window at a much faster rate than it is willing to increase its congestion window. This is in contrast to an additive increase/additive decrease strategy in which the window would be increased by 1 packet when an ACK arrives and decreased by 1 when a timeout occurs. It has been shown that additive increase/multiplicative decrease is a necessary condition for a congestion-control mechanism to be stable (see the Further Reading section). One intuitive reason to decrease the window aggressively and increase it conservatively is that the consequences of having too large a window are much worse than those of it being too small. For example, when the window is too large, packets that are dropped will be retransmitted, making congestion even worse; thus, it is important to get out of this state quickly.

Finally, since a timeout is an indication of congestion that triggers multiplicative decrease, TCP needs the most accurate timeout mechanism it can afford. We already covered TCP's timeout mechanism in Section 5.2.5, so we do not repeat it here. The two main things to remember about that mechanism are that (1) timeouts are set as a function of both the average RTT and the standard deviation in that average, and

(2) due to the cost of measuring each transmission with an accurate clock, TCP only samples the round-trip time once per RTT (rather than once per packet) using a coarse-grained (500-ms) clock.

6.3.2 Slow Start

The additive increase mechanism just described is the right approach to use when the source is operating close to the available capacity of the network, but it takes too long to ramp up a connection when it is starting from scratch. TCP therefore provides a second mechanism, ironically called *slow start*, that is used to increase the congestion window rapidly from a cold start. Slow start effectively increases the congestion window exponentially, rather than linearly.

Specifically, the source starts out by setting CongestionWindow to one packet. When the ACK for this packet arrives, TCP adds 1 to CongestionWindow and then sends two packets. Upon receiving the corresponding two ACKs, TCP increments CongestionWindow by 2—one for each ACK—and next sends four packets. The end result is that TCP effectively doubles the number of packets it has in transit every RTT. Figure 6.10 shows the growth in the number of packets in transit during slow start. Compare this to the linear growth of additive increase illustrated in Figure 6.8.

Why any exponential mechanism would be called "slow" is puzzling at first, but it can be explained if put in the proper historical context. We need to compare slow start not against the linear mechanism of the previous subsection, but against the original behavior of TCP. Consider what happens when a connection is established and the source first starts to send packets, that is, when it currently has no packets in transit. If the source sends as many packets as the advertised window allows—which is exactly what TCP did before slow start was developed—then even if there is a fairly large amount of bandwidth available in the network, the routers may not be able to consume this burst of packets. It all depends on how much buffer space is available at the routers. Slow start was therefore designed to space packets out so that this burst does not occur. In other words, even though its exponential growth is faster than linear growth, slow start is much "slower" than sending an entire advertised window's worth of data all at once.

There are actually two different situations in which slow start runs. The first is at the very beginning of a connection, at which time the source has no idea how many packets it is going to be able to have in transit at a given time. (Keep in mind that TCP runs over everything from 9600-bps links to 2.4-Gbps links, so there is no way for the source to know the network's capacity.) In this situation, slow start continues to double CongestionWindow each RTT until there is a loss, at which time a timeout causes multiplicative decrease to divide CongestionWindow by 2.

Source   Destination

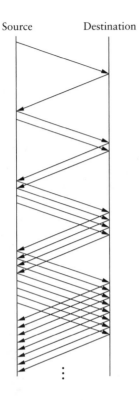

Figure 6.10 Packets in transit during slow start.

The second situation in which slow start is used is a bit more subtle; it occurs when the connection goes dead while waiting for a timeout to occur. Recall how TCP's sliding window algorithm works—when a packet is lost, the source eventually reaches a point where it has sent as much data as the advertised window allows, and so it blocks while waiting for an ACK that will not arrive. Eventually, a timeout happens, but by this time there are no packets in transit, meaning that the source will receive no ACKs to "clock" the transmission of new packets. The source will instead receive a single cumulative ACK that reopens the entire advertised window, but as explained above, the source then uses slow start to restart the flow of data rather than dumping a whole window's worth of data on the network all at once.

Although the source is using slow start again, it now knows more information than it did at the beginning of a connection. Specifically, the source has a current (and useful) value of CongestionWindow; this is the value of CongestionWindow that existed prior to the last packet loss, divided by 2 as a result of the loss. We can think of this as the "target" congestion window. Slow start is used to rapidly increase the sending rate up to this value, and then additive increase is used beyond this point. Notice that we have a small bookkeeping problem to take care of, in that we want to remember the "target" congestion window resulting from multiplicative decrease as well as the "actual" congestion window being used by slow start. To address this problem, TCP introduces a temporary variable to store the target window, typically called CongestionThreshold, that is set equal to the CongestionWindow value that results from multiplicative decrease. The variable CongestionWindow is then reset to one packet, and it is incremented by one packet for every ACK that is received until it reaches CongestionThreshold, at which point it is incremented by one packet per RTT.

In other words, TCP increases the congestion window as defined by the following code fragment:

```
{
    u_int    cw = state->CongestionWindow;
    u_int    incr = state->maxseg;

    if (cw > state->CongestionThreshold)
        incr = incr * incr / cw;
    state->CongestionWindow = MIN(cw + incr, TCP_MAXWIN);
}
```

where state represents the state of a particular TCP connection and TCP_MAXWIN defines an upper bound on how large the congestion window is allowed to grow.

Figure 6.11 traces how TCP's CongestionWindow increases and decreases over time and serves to illustrate the interplay of slow start and additive increase/ multiplicative decrease. This trace was taken from an actual TCP connection and shows the current value of CongestionWindow—the colored line—over time.

There are several things to notice about this trace. The first is the rapid increase in the congestion window at the beginning of the connection. This corresponds to the initial slow start phase. The slow start phase continues until several packets are lost at about 0.4 seconds into the connection, at which time CongestionWindow flattens out at about 34 KB. (Why so many packets are lost during slow start is discussed below.) The reason the congestion window flattens is that there are no ACKs arriving, due to the fact that several packets were lost. In fact, no new packets are sent during this time, as denoted by the lack of hash marks at the top of the graph. A timeout eventually happens at approximately 2 seconds, at which time the congestion window is divided by 2 (i.e., cut from approximately 34 KB to around 17 KB) and CongestionThreshold

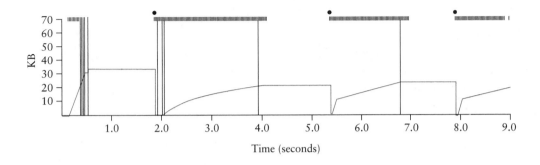

Figure 6.11 Behavior of TCP congestion control. Colored line = value of CongestionWindow over time; solid bullets at top of graph = timeouts; hash marks at top of graph = time when each packet is transmitted; vertical bars = time when a packet that was eventually retransmitted was first transmitted.

is set to this value. Slow start then causes CongestionWindow to be reset to one packet and to start ramping up from there.

There is not enough detail in the trace to see exactly what happens when a couple of packets are lost just after 2 seconds, so we jump ahead to the linear increase in the congestion window that occurs between 2 and 4 seconds. This corresponds to additive increase. At about 4 seconds, CongestionWindow flattens out, again due to a lost packet. Now, at about 5.5 seconds:

1 A timeout happens, causing the congestion window to be divided by 2, dropping it from approximately 22 KB to 11 KB, and CongestionThreshold is set to this amount.

2 CongestionWindow is reset to one packet, as the sender enters slow start.

3 Slow start causes CongestionWindow to grow exponentially until it reaches CongestionThreshold.

4 CongestionWindow then grows linearly.

The same pattern is repeated at around 8 seconds when another timeout occurs.

We now return to the question of why so many packets are lost during the initial slow start period. What TCP is attempting to do here is to learn how much bandwidth is available on the network. This is a very difficult task. If the source is not aggressive at this stage—for example, if it only increases the congestion window linearly—then it takes a long time for it to discover how much bandwidth is available. This can have a dramatic impact on the throughput achieved for this connection. On the other hand, if the source is aggressive at this stage, as TCP is during exponential growth, then the source runs the risk of having half a window's worth of packets dropped by the network.

To see what can happen during exponential growth, consider the situation in which the source was just able to successfully send 16 packets through the network, causing it to double its congestion window to 32. Suppose, however, that the network happens to have just enough capacity to support 16 packets from this source. The likely result is that 16 of the 32 packets sent under the new congestion window will be dropped by the network; actually, this is the worst-case outcome, since some of the packets will be buffered in some router. This problem will become increasingly severe as the delay × bandwidth product of networks increases. For example, a delay × bandwidth product of 500 KB means that each connection has the potential to lose up to 500 KB of data at the beginning of each connection. Of course, this assumes that both the source and the destination implement the "big windows" extension.

Some network designers have proposed alternatives to slow start, whereby the source tries to estimate the available bandwidth by more clever means of sending out groups of packets and seeing how many make it through. A technique called *packet-pair* is representative of this general strategy. In simple terms, the idea is to send a pair of packets with no spacing between them. Then, the source sees how far apart the ACKs for those two packets are. The gap between the ACKs is taken as a measure of how much congestion there is in the network, and therefore of how much increase in the congestion window is possible. The jury is still out on the effectiveness of approaches such as this, although the results seem promising.

6.3.3 Fast Retransmit and Fast Recovery

The mechanisms described so far were part of the original proposal to add congestion control to TCP. It was soon discovered, however, that the coarse-grained implementation of TCP timeouts led to long periods of time during which the connection went dead while waiting for a timer to expire. Because of this, a new mechanism called *fast retransmit* was added to TCP. Fast retransmit is a heuristic that sometimes triggers the retransmission of a dropped packet sooner than the regular timeout mechanism. The fast retransmit mechanism does not replace regular timeouts; it just enhances that facility.

The idea of fast retransmit is straightforward. Every time a data packet arrives at the receiving side, the receiver responds with an acknowledgment, even if this sequence number has already been acknowledged. Thus, when a packet arrives out of order— that is, TCP cannot yet acknowledge the data the packet contains because earlier data has not yet arrived—TCP resends the same acknowledgment it sent the last time. This second transmission of the same acknowledgment is called a *duplicate ACK*. When the sending side sees a duplicate ACK, it knows that the other side must have received a

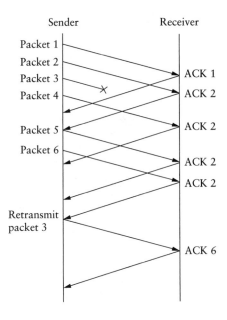

Figure 6.12 Fast retransmit based on duplicate ACKs.

packet out of order, which suggests that an earlier packet might have been lost. Since it is also possible that the earlier packet has only been delayed rather than lost, the sender waits until it sees some number of duplicate ACKs and then retransmits the missing packet. In practice, TCP waits until it has seen three duplicate ACKs before retransmitting the packet.

Figure 6.12 illustrates how duplicate ACKs lead to a fast retransmit. In this example, the destination receives packets 1 and 2, but packet 3 is lost in the network. Thus, the destination will send a duplicate ACK for packet 2 when packet 4 arrives, again when packet 5 arrives, and so on. (To simplify this example, we think in terms of packets 1, 2, 3, and so on, rather than worrying about the sequence numbers for each byte.) When the sender sees the third duplicate ACK for packet 2—the one sent because the receiver had gotten packet 6—it retransmits packet 3. Note that when the retransmitted copy of packet 3 arrives at the destination, the receiver then sends a cumulative ACK for everything up to and including packet 6 back to the source.

Figure 6.13 illustrates the behavior of a version of TCP with the fast retransmit mechanism. It is interesting to compare this trace with that given in Figure 6.11, where fast retransmit was not implemented—the long periods during which the congestion

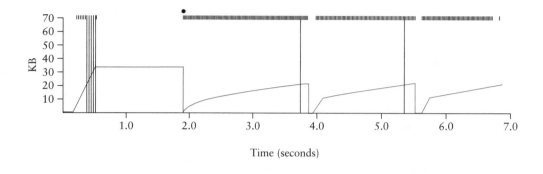

Figure 6.13 Trace of TCP with fast retransmit. Colored line = CongestionWindow; solid bullet = timeout; hash marks = time when each packet is transmitted; vertical bars = time when a packet that was eventually retransmitted was first transmitted.

window stays flat and no packets are sent has been eliminated. In general, this technique is able to eliminate about half of the coarse-grained timeouts on a typical TCP connection, resulting in roughly a 20% improvement in the throughput over what could otherwise have been achieved. Notice, however, that the fast retransmit strategy does not eliminate all coarse-grained timeouts. This is because for a small window size, there will not be enough packets in transit to cause enough duplicate ACKs to be delivered. Given enough lost packets—for example, as happens during the initial slow start phase—the sliding window algorithm eventually blocks the sender until a timeout occurs. Given the current 64-KB maximum advertised window size, TCP's fast retransmit mechanism is able to detect up to three dropped packets per window in practice.

Finally, there is one last improvement we can make. When the fast retransmit mechanism signals congestion, rather than drop the congestion window all the way back to one packet and run slow start, it is possible to use the ACKs that are still in the pipe to clock the sending of packets. This mechanism, which is called *fast recovery*, effectively removes the slow start phase that happens between when fast retransmit detects a lost packet and additive increase begins. For example, fast recovery avoids the slow start period between 3.8 and 4 seconds in Figure 6.13 and instead simply cuts the congestion window in half (from 22 KB to 11 KB) and resumes additive increase. In other words, slow start is only used at the beginning of a connection and whenever a coarse-grained timeout occurs. At all other times, the congestion window is following a pure additive increase/multiplicative decrease pattern.

6.4 Congestion-Avoidance Mechanisms

It is important to understand that TCP's strategy is to control congestion once it happens, as opposed to trying to avoid congestion in the first place. In fact, TCP repeatedly increases the load it imposes on the network in an effort to find the point at which congestion occurs, and then it backs off from this point. Said another way, TCP *needs* to create losses to find the available bandwidth of the connection. An appealing alternative, but one that has not yet been widely adopted, is to predict when congestion is about to happen and then to reduce the rate at which hosts send data just before packets start being discarded. We call such a strategy *congestion avoidance*, to distinguish it from *congestion control*.

This section describes three different congestion-avoidance mechanisms. The first two take a similar approach: They put a small amount of additional functionality into the router to assist the end node in the anticipation of congestion. The third mechanism is very different from the first two: It attempts to avoid congestion purely from the end nodes.

6.4.1 DECbit

The first mechanism was developed for use on the Digital Network Architecture (DNA), a connectionless network with a connection-oriented transport protocol. This mechanism could, therefore, also be applied to TCP and IP. As noted above, the idea here is to more evenly split the responsibility for congestion control between the routers and the end nodes. Each router monitors the load it is experiencing and explicitly notifies the end nodes when congestion is about to occur. This notification is implemented by setting a binary congestion bit in the packets that flow through the router; hence the name DECbit. The destination host then copies this congestion bit into the ACK it sends back to the source. Finally, the source adjusts its sending rate so as to avoid congestion. The following discussion describes the algorithm in more detail, starting with what happens in the router.

A single congestion bit is added to the packet header. A router sets this bit in a packet if its average queue length is greater than or equal to 1 at the time the packet arrives. This average queue length is measured over a time interval that spans the last busy + idle cycle, plus the current busy cycle. (The router is *busy* when it is transmitting and *idle* when it is not.) Figure 6.14 shows the queue length at a router as a function of time. Essentially, the router calculates the area under the curve and divides this value by the time interval to compute the average queue length. Using a queue length of 1 as the trigger for setting the congestion bit is a trade-off between significant queuing (and hence higher throughput) and increased idle time (and hence lower delay). In other words, a queue length of 1 seems to optimize the power function.

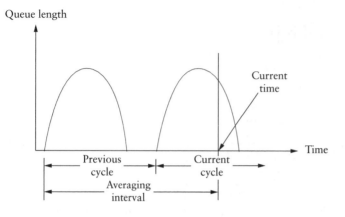

Figure 6.14 Computing average queue length at a router.

Now turning our attention to the host half of the mechanism, the source records how many of its packets resulted in some router setting the congestion bit. In particular, the source maintains a congestion window, just as in TCP, and watches to see what fraction of the last window's worth of packets resulted in the bit being set. If less than 50% of the packets had the bit set, then the source increases its congestion window by one packet. If 50% or more of the last window's worth of packets had the congestion bit set, then the source decreases its congestion window to 0.875 times the previous value. The value 50% was chosen as the threshold based on analysis that showed it to correspond to the peak of the power curve. The "increase by 1, decrease by 0.875" rule was selected because additive increase/multiplicative decrease makes the mechanism stable.

6.4.2 Random Early Detection (RED)

A second mechanism, called *random early detection* (RED), is similar to the DECbit scheme in that each router is programmed to monitor its own queue length, and when it detects that congestion is imminent, to notify the source to adjust its congestion window. RED, invented by Sally Floyd and Van Jacobson in the early 1990s, differs from the DECbit scheme in two major ways.

The first is that rather than explicitly sending a congestion notification message to the source, RED is most commonly implemented such that it *implicitly* notifies the source of congestion by dropping one of its packets. The source is, therefore, effectively notified by the subsequent timeout or duplicate ACK. In case you haven't already guessed, RED is designed to be used in conjunction with TCP, which currently detects congestion by means of timeouts (or some other means of detecting packet loss such as duplicate ACKs). As the "early" part of the RED acronym suggests, the gateway drops the packet earlier than it would have to, so as to notify the source that it should decrease its congestion window sooner than it would normally have. In other words, the router drops a few packets before it has exhausted its buffer space completely, so as to cause the source to slow down, with the hope that this will mean it does not have to drop lots of packets later on. Note that RED could easily be adapted to work with an explicit feedback scheme simply by *marking* a packet instead of *dropping* it.

The second difference between RED and DECbit is in the details of how RED decides when to drop a packet and what packet it decides to drop. To understand the basic idea, consider a simple FIFO queue. Rather than wait for the queue to become completely full and then be forced to drop each arriving packet (the tail drop policy of Section 6.2.1), we could decide to drop each arriving packet with some *drop probability* whenever the queue length exceeds some *drop level*. This idea is called *early random drop*. The RED algorithm defines the details of how to monitor the queue length and when to drop a packet.

First, RED computes an average queue length using a weighted running average similar to the one used in the original TCP timeout computation. That is, AvgLen is computed as

$$\text{AvgLen} = (1 - \text{Weight}) \times \text{AvgLen} + \text{Weight} \times \text{SampleLen}$$

where $0 < \text{Weight} < 1$ and SampleLen is the length of the queue when a sample measurement is made. In most software implementations, the queue length is measured every time a new packet arrives at the gateway. In hardware, it might be calculated at some fixed sampling interval.

The reason for using an average queue length rather than an instantaneous one is that it more accurately captures the notion of congestion. Because of the bursty nature of Internet traffic, queues can become full very quickly and then become empty again. If a queue is spending most of its time empty, then it's probably not appropriate to conclude that the router is congested and to tell the hosts to slow down. Thus, the weighted running average calculation tries to detect long-lived congestion, as indicated in the right-hand portion of Figure 6.15, by filtering out short-term changes in the queue length. You can think of the running average as a low-pass filter, where Weight determines the time constant of the filter. The question of how we pick this time constant is discussed below.

Second, RED has two queue length thresholds that trigger certain activity: MinThreshold and MaxThreshold. When a packet arrives at the gateway, RED compares the current AvgLen with these two thresholds, according to the following rules:

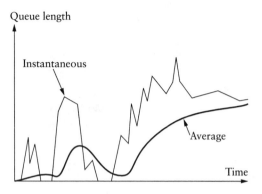

Queue length

Instantaneous

Average

Time

Figure 6.15   Weighted running average queue length.

if AvgLen ≤ MinThreshold
⟶ queue the packet

if MinThreshold < AvgLen < MaxThreshold
⟶ calculate probability P
⟶ drop the arriving packet with probability P

if MaxThreshold ≤ AvgLen
⟶ drop the arriving packet

That is, if the average queue length is smaller than the lower threshold, no action is taken, and if the average queue length is larger than the upper threshold, then the packet is always dropped. If the average queue length is between the two thresholds, then the newly arriving packet is dropped with some probability P. This situation is depicted in Figure 6.16. The approximate relationship between P and AvgLen is shown in Figure 6.17. Note that the probability of drop increases slowly when AvgLen is between the two thresholds, reaching MaxP at the upper threshold, at which point it jumps to unity. The rationale behind this is that if AvgLen reaches the upper threshold, then the gentle approach (dropping a few packets) is not working and drastic measures are called for, that is, dropping all arriving packets. Some research has suggested that a more smooth transition from random dropping to complete dropping, rather than the discontinous approach shown here, may be appropriate.

Although Figure 6.17 shows the probability of drop as a function only of AvgLen, the situation is actually a little more complicated. In fact, P is a function of both AvgLen and how long it has been since the last packet was dropped. Specifically, it is computed as follows:

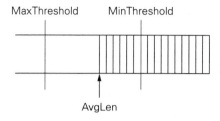

Figure 6.16 RED thresholds on a FIFO queue.

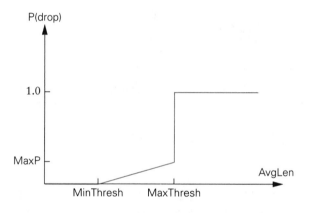

Figure 6.17 Drop probability function for RED.

$$\text{TempP} = \text{MaxP} \times (\text{AvgLen} - \text{MinThreshold})/(\text{MaxThreshold} - \text{MinThreshold})$$

$$P = \text{TempP}/(1 - \text{count} \times \text{TempP})$$

TempP is the variable that is plotted on the y-axis in Figure 6.17. count keeps track of how many newly arriving packets have been queued (not dropped) while AvgLen has been between the two thresholds. P increases slowly as count increases, thereby making a drop increasingly likely as the time since the last drop increases. This makes closely spaced drops relatively less likely than widely spaced drops. This extra step in calculating P was introduced by the inventors of RED when they observed that, without it, the packet drops were not well distributed in time, but instead tended to occur in clusters. Because packet arrivals from a certain connection are likely to arrive in bursts, this clustering of drops is likely to cause multiple drops in a single connection. This is not desirable, since only one drop per round-trip time is needed to cause a connection to reduce its window size, whereas multiple drops might send it back into slow start.

As an example, suppose that we set MaxP to 0.02 and count is initialized to zero. If the average queue length were halfway between the two thresholds, then TempP, and the initial value of P, would be half of MaxP, or 0.01. An arriving packet, of course, has a 99 in 100 chance of getting into the queue at this point. With each successive packet that is not dropped, P slowly increases, and by the time 50 packets have arrived without a drop, P would have doubled to 0.02. In the unlikely event that 99 packets arrived without loss, P reaches 1, guaranteeing that the next packet is dropped. The important thing about this part of the algorithm is that it ensures a roughly even distribution of drops over time.

Hopefully, if RED drops a small percentage of packets when AvgLen exceeds MinThreshold, the effect will be to cause a few TCP connections to reduce their window sizes, which in turn will reduce the rate at which packets arrive at the router. All going well, AvgLen will then decrease and congestion is avoided. The queue length can be kept short, while throughput remains high since few packets are dropped.

Note that, because RED is operating on a queue length averaged over time, it is possible for the instantaneous queue length to be much longer than AvgLen. In this case, if a packet arrives and there is nowhere to put it, then it will have to be dropped. When this happens, RED is operating in tail drop mode. One of the goals of RED is to prevent tail drop behavior if possible.

The random nature of RED confers an interesting property on the algorithm. Because RED drops packets randomly, the probability that RED decides to drop a particular flow's packet(s) is roughly proportional to the share of the bandwidth that that flow is currently getting at that router. This is because a flow that is sending a relatively large number of packets is providing more candidates for random dropping. Thus, there is some sense of fair resource allocation built into RED, although it is by no means precise.

▶   Note that a fair amount of analysis has gone into setting the various RED parameters—for example, MaxThreshold, MinThreshold, MaxP, and Weight—all in the name of optimizing the power function (throughput-to-delay ratio). The performance of these parameters has also been confirmed through simulation, and the algorithm has been shown not to be overly sensitive to them. It is important to keep in mind, however, that all of this analysis and simulation hinges on a particular characterization of the network workload. The real contribution of RED is a mechanism by which the router can more accurately manage its queue length. Defining precisely what constitutes an optimal queue length depends on the traffic mix and is still a subject of research, with real information now being gathered from operational deployment of RED in the Internet.

Consider the setting of the two thresholds, MinThreshold and MaxThreshold. If the traffic is fairly bursty, then MinThreshold should be sufficiently large to allow the link utilization to be maintained at an acceptably high level. Also, the difference between the two thresholds should be larger than the typical increase in the calculated average queue length in one RTT. Setting MaxThreshold to twice MinThreshold seems to be a reasonable rule of thumb given the traffic mix on today's Internet. In addition, since we expect the average queue length to hover between the two thresholds during periods of high load, there should be enough free buffer space *above* MaxThreshold to absorb the natural bursts that occur in Internet traffic without forcing the router to enter tail drop mode.

We noted above that Weight determines the time constant for the running average low-pass filter, and this gives us a clue as to how we might pick a suitable value for it. Recall that RED is trying to send signals to TCP flows by dropping packets during times of congestion. Suppose that a router drops a packet from some TCP connection and then immediately forwards some more packets from the same connection. When those packets arrive at the receiver, it starts sending duplicate ACKs to the sender. When the sender sees enough duplicate ACKs, it will reduce its window size. So from the time the router drops a packet until the time when the same router starts to see some relief from the affected connection in terms of a reduced window size, at least one round-trip time must elapse for that connection. There is probably not much point in having the router respond to congestion on time scales much less than the round-trip time of the connections passing through it. As noted previously, 100 ms is not a bad estimate of average round-trip times in the Internet. Thus, Weight should be chosen such that changes in queue length over time scales much less than 100 ms are filtered out.

We conclude our discussion of RED by considering the more general question of when it is a good idea to drop packets before you are forced to by a full buffer queue. Consider an ATM network, for example. If you are sending AAL5 packets through a congested ATM switch, and the switch is forced to drop one of the cells from that packet, then the other cells will be useless to the end host; it will have to request that the entire AAL5 packet be retransmitted. Dropping these other cells, even though the switch has enough buffer space to hold them, makes a lot of sense. This technique has in fact been proposed and is called *partial packet discard* (PPD). A switch can be made even more aggressive by combining the idea of RED with the idea of PPD. That is, when an ATM switch is nearing congestion and the first cell of a new AAL5 packet arrives, the switch drops that cell and all the others cells that belong to that AAL5 packet. This enables the whole packet, not just the last part of it, to be dropped, and is called *early packet discard* (EPD). While EPD is often confused with RED, it is important to note that EPD is specific to ATM, and that the decision to drop is usually made using a less sophisticated algorithm than RED, responding to instantaneous buffer occupancy rather than long-lived congestion.

6.4.3 Source-Based Congestion Avoidance

Unlike the two previous congestion-avoidance schemes, which depended on new mechanisms in the routers, we now describe a strategy for detecting the incipient stages of congestion—before losses occur—from the end hosts. We first give a brief overview of a collection of related mechanisms that use different information to detect the early stages of congestion, and then we describe a specific mechanism in some detail.

The general idea of these techniques is to watch for some sign from the network that some router's queue is building up and that congestion will happen soon if nothing is done about it. For example, the source might notice that as packet queues build up in the network's routers, there is a measurable increase in the RTT for each successive packet it sends. One particular algorithm exploits this observation as follows: The congestion window normally increases as in TCP, but every two round-trip delays the algorithm checks to see if the current RTT is greater than the average of the minimum and maximum RTTs seen so far. If it is, then the algorithm decreases the congestion window by one-eighth.

A second algorithm does something similar. The decision as to whether or not to change the current window size is based on changes to both the RTT and the window size. The window is adjusted once every two round-trip delays based on the product

$$(\text{CurrentWindow} - \text{OldWindow})$$
$$\times (\text{CurrentRTT} - \text{OldRTT})$$

Tahoe, Reno, and Vegas

The name "TCP Vegas" is a take-off on earlier implementations of TCP that were distributed in releases of 4.3 BSD Unix. These releases were known as Tahoe and Reno (which, like Las Vegas, are places in Nevada), and the versions of TCP became known by the names of the BSD release. TCP Tahoe, which is also known as BSD Network Release 1.0 (BNR1), corresponds to the original implementation of Jacobson's congestion-control mechanism and includes all of the mechanisms described in Section 6.3 except fast recovery. TCP Reno, which is also known as BSD Network Release 2.0 (BNR2), adds the fast recovery mechanism, along with an optimization known as *header prediction*—optimizing for the common case that segments arrive in order. TCP Reno also supports *delayed ACKs*—acknowledging every other segment rather than every segment—although this is a selectable option that is sometimes turned off. A more recent version of TCP distributed in 4.4 BSD Unix adds the "big windows" extensions described in Section 5.2.

If the result is positive, the source decreases the window size by one-eighth; if the result is negative or 0, the source increases the window by one maximum packet size. Note that the window changes during every adjustment; that is, it oscillates around its optimal point.

One point you should take away from this discussion of TCP's lineage is that TCP has been a rather fluid protocol over the last several years, especially in its congestion-control mechanism. In fact, you would not even find universal agreement about which technique was introduced in which release, due to the availability of intermediate versions of the code and the fact that patch has been layered on top of patch.

All that can be said with any certainty is that any two implementations of TCP that follow the original specification, while they should interoperate, will not necessarily perform well. Recognizing the performance implications of having TCP Tahoe interoperate with TCP Reno is a tricky business. In other words, you could argue that TCP is no longer defined by a specification, but rather by an implementation—the BSD implementation. The only question is, which BSD implementation?

Another change seen as the network approaches congestion is the flattening of the sending rate. A third scheme takes advantage of this fact. Every RTT, it increases the window size by one packet and compares the throughput achieved to the throughput when the window was one packet smaller. If the difference is less than one-half the throughput achieved when only one packet was in transit—as was the case at the beginning of the connection—the algorithm decreases the window by one packet. This scheme calculates the throughput by dividing the number of bytes outstanding in the network by the RTT.

A fourth mechanism, the one we are going to describe in more detail, is similar to this last algorithm in that it looks at changes in the throughput rate, or more specifically, changes in the sending rate. However, it differs from the third algorithm in that it calculates throughputs differently, and instead of looking for a change in the throughput slope, it compares the measured throughput rate with an expected throughput rate.

The intuition behind the algorithm, which is called TCP Vegas, can be seen in the trace of standard TCP given in Figure 6.18. (See the sidebar for an explanation of the name TCP Vegas.) The top graph shown in Figure 6.18 traces the connection's congestion window; it shows the same information as the traces given earlier in this section. The middle and bottom graphs depict new information: The middle graph shows the

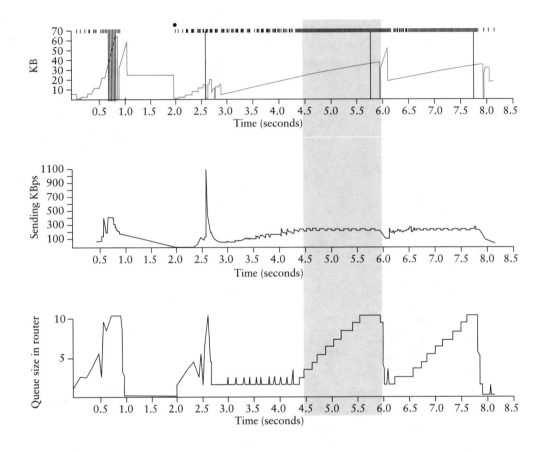

Figure 6.18 Congestion window versus observed throughput rate (the three graphs are synchro-nized). Top, congestion window; middle, observed throughput; bottom, buffer space taken up at the router. Colored line = CongestionWindow; solid bullet = timeout; hash marks = time when each packet is transmitted; vertical bars = time when a packet that was eventually retransmitted was first transmitted.

average sending rate as measured at the source, and the bottom graph shows the average queue length as measured at the bottleneck router. All three graphs are syn-chronized in time. In the period between 4.5 and 6.0 seconds (shaded region), the congestion window increases (top graph). We expect the observed throughput to also increase, but instead it stays flat (middle graph). This is because the throughput can-not increase beyond the available bandwidth. Beyond this point, any increase in the window size only results in packets taking up buffer space at the bottleneck router (bottom graph).

A useful metaphor that describes the phenomenon illustrated in Figure 6.18 is driving on ice. The speedometer (congestion window) may say that you are going 30 miles an hour, but by looking out the car window and seeing people pass you on foot (measured sending rate), you know that you are going no more than 5 miles an hour. The extra energy is being absorbed by the car's tires (router buffers).

TCP Vegas uses this idea to measure and control the amount of extra data this connection has in transit, where by "extra data" we mean data that the source would not have transmitted had it been trying to match exactly the available bandwidth of the network. The goal of TCP Vegas is to maintain the "right" amount of extra data in the network. Obviously, if a source is sending too much extra data, it will cause long delays and possibly lead to congestion. Less obviously, if a connection is sending too little extra data, it cannot respond rapidly enough to transient increases in the available network bandwidth. TCP Vegas's congestion-avoidance actions are based on changes in the estimated amount of extra data in the network, not only on dropped packets. We now describe the algorithm in detail.

First, define a given flow's BaseRTT to be the RTT of a packet when the flow is not congested. In practice, TCP Vegas sets BaseRTT to the minimum of all measured round-trip times; it is commonly the RTT of the first packet sent by the connection, before the router queues increase due to traffic generated by this flow. If we assume that we are not overflowing the connection, then the expected throughput is given by

$$ExpectedRate = CongestionWindow/BaseRTT$$

where CongestionWindow is the TCP congestion window, which we assume (for the purpose of this discussion) to be equal to the number of bytes in transit.

Second, TCP Vegas calculates the current sending rate, ActualRate. This is done by recording the sending time for a distinguished packet, recording how many bytes are transmitted between the time that packet is sent and when its acknowledgment is received, computing the sample RTT for the distinguished packet when its acknowledgment arrives, and dividing the number of bytes transmitted by the sample RTT. This calculation is done once per round-trip time.

Third, TCP Vegas compares ActualRate to ExpectedRate and adjusts the window accordingly. We let Diff = ExpectedRate − ActualRate. Note that Diff is positive or 0 by definition, since ActualRate > ExpectedRate implies that we need to change BaseRTT to the latest sampled RTT. We also define two thresholds, $\alpha < \beta$, roughly corresponding to having too little and too much extra data in the network, respectively. When Diff $< \alpha$, TCP Vegas increases the congestion window linearly during the next RTT, and when Diff $> \beta$, TCP Vegas decreases the congestion window linearly during the next RTT. TCP Vegas leaves the congestion window unchanged when $\alpha <$ Diff $< \beta$.

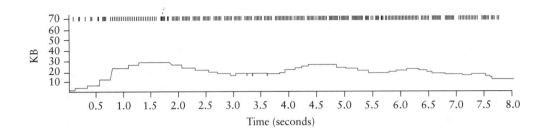

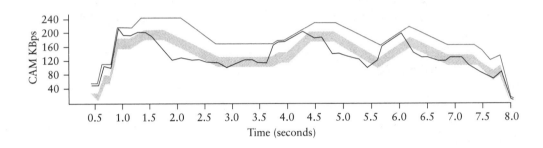

Figure 6.19 Trace of TCP Vegas congestion-avoidance mechanism. Top, congestion window; bottom, expected (colored line) and actual (black line) throughput. The shaded area is the region between the α and β thresholds.

Intuitively, we can see that the farther away the actual throughput gets from the expected throughput, the more congestion there is in the network, which implies that the sending rate should be reduced. The β threshold triggers this decrease. On the other hand, when the actual throughput rate gets too close to the expected throughput, the connection is in danger of not utilizing the available bandwidth. The α threshold triggers this increase. The overall goal is to keep between α and β extra bytes in the network.

Figure 6.19 traces the TCP Vegas congestion-avoidance algorithm. The top graph traces the congestion window, showing the same information as the other traces given throughout this chapter. The bottom graph traces the expected and actual throughput rates that govern how the congestion window is set. It is this bottom graph that best illustrates how the algorithm works. The colored line tracks the ExpectedRate, while the black line tracks the ActualRate. The wide shaded strip gives the region between the α and β thresholds; the top of the shaded strip is α KBps away from ExpectedRate, and the bottom of the shaded strip is β KBps away from ExpectedRate. The goal is to keep the ActualRate between these two thresholds, that is, within the shaded

Evaluating a New Congestion-Control Mechanism

Suppose you develop a new congestion-control mechanism and want to evaluate its performance. For example, you might want to compare it to the current mechanism running on the Internet. How do you go about measuring and evaluating your mechanism? Although at one time the Internet's primary purpose in life was to support networking research, today it is a large production network and therefore completely inappropriate for running a controlled experiment.

If your approach is purely end to end—that is, if it assumes only FIFO routers within the Internet—then it is possible to run your congestion-control mechanism on a small set of hosts and to measure the throughput your connections are able to achieve. We need to add a word of caution here, however. It is surprisingly easy to invent a congestion-control mechanism that achieves five times the throughput of TCP across the Internet. You simply blast packets into the Internet at a high rate, thereby causing congestion. All the other hosts running TCP detect this congestion and reduce the rate at which they are sending packets. Your mechanism then happily region. Whenever ActualRate falls below the shaded region (i.e., gets too far from ExpectedRate), TCP Vegas decreases the congestion window because it fears that too many packets are being buffered in the network. Likewise, whenever ActualRate goes above the shaded region (i.e., gets too close to the ExpectedRate), TCP Vegas increases the congestion window because it fears that it is underutilizing the network.

Because the algorithm, as just presented, compares the difference between the actual and expected throughput rates to the α and β thresholds, these two thresholds are defined in terms of KBps. However, it is perhaps more accurate to think in terms of how many extra *buffers* the connection is occupying in the network. For example, on a connection with a BaseRTT of 100 ms and a packet size of 1 KB, if $\alpha = 30$ KBps and $\beta = 60$ KBps, then we can think of α as specifying that the connection needs to be occupying at least 3 extra buffers in the network and β as specifying that the connection should occupy no more than 6 extra buffers in the network. In practice, a setting of α to 1 buffer and β to 3 buffers works well.

Finally, you will notice that TCP Vegas decreases the congestion window linearly, seemingly in conflict with the rule that multiplicative decrease is needed to ensure stability. The explanation is that TCP Vegas does use multiplicative decrease when a timeout occurs; the linear decrease just described is an *early* decrease in the congestion window that, hopefully, happens before congestion occurs and packets start being dropped.

6.5   Quality of Service

For many years, packet-switched networks have offered the promise of supporting multimedia applications, that is, those that combine audio, video, and data. After all, once digitized, audio and video information become like any other form of data—a stream of bits to be transmitted. One obstacle to the fulfillment of this promise has been the need for higher-bandwidth links. Recently, however, improvements in coding have reduced the bandwidth needs of audio and video applications, while at the same time link speeds have increased.

There is more to transmitting audio and video over a network than just providing sufficient bandwidth, however. Participants in a telephone conversation, for example, expect to be able to converse in such a way that one person can respond to something said by the other and be heard almost immediately. Thus, the timeliness of delivery can be very important. We refer to applications that are sensitive to the timeliness of data as *real-time applications*. Voice and video applications tend to be the canonical examples, but there are others such as industrial control—you would like a command sent to a robot arm to reach it before the arm crashes into something. Even file transfer applications can have timeliness constraints, such as a requirement that a database update complete overnight before the business that needs the data resumes on the next day.

consumes all the bandwidth. This strategy is fast but hardly fair.

Experimenting directly on the Internet, even when done carefully, will not work when your congestion-control mechanism involves changes to the routers. It is simply not practical to change the software running on thousands of routers for the sake of evaluating a new congestion-control algorithm. In this case, network designers are forced to test their systems on simulated networks or private testbed networks. For example, the TCP traces presented in this chapter were generated by an implementation of TCP that was running on an x-kernel-based network simulator. The challenge in either a simulation or a testbed is coming up with a topology and a traffic workload that are representative of the real Internet.

The distinguishing characteristic of real-time applications is that they need some sort of assurance *from the network* that data is likely to arrive on time (for some definition of "on time"). Whereas a non-real-time application can use an end-to-end retransmission strategy to make sure that data arrives *correctly*, such a strategy cannot provide timeliness: Retransmission only adds to total latency if data arrives late. Timely arrival must be provided by the network itself (the routers), not just at the network edges (the hosts). We therefore conclude that the best-effort model, in

Figure 6.20 An audio application.

which the network tries to deliver your data but makes no promises and leaves the cleanup operation to the edges, is not sufficient for real-time applications. What we need is a new service model, in which applications that need higher assurances can ask the network for them. The network may then respond by providing an assurance that it will do better or perhaps by saying that it cannot promise anything better at the moment. Note that such a service model is a superset of the current model: Applications that are happy with best-effort service should be able to use the new service model; their requirements are just less stringent. This implies that the network will treat some packets differently from others—something that is not done in the best-effort model. A network that can provide these different levels of service is often said to support quality of service (QoS).

6.5.1 Application Requirements

Before looking at the various protocols and mechanisms that may be used to provide quality of service to applications, we should try to understand what the needs of those applications are. To begin, we can divide applications into two types: real-time and non-real-time. The latter are sometimes called "traditional data" applications, since they have traditionally been the major applications found on data networks. They include most popular applications like Telnet, FTP, email, Web browsing, and so on. All of these applications can work without guarantees of timely delivery of data. Another term for this non-real-time class of applications is *elastic*, since they are able to stretch gracefully in the face of increased delay. Note that these applications can benefit from shorter-length delays, but they do not become unusable as delays increase. Also note that their delay requirements vary from the interactive applications like Telnet to more asynchronous ones like email, with interactive bulk transfers like FTP in the middle.

Real-Time Audio Example

As a concrete example of a real-time application, consider an audio application similar to the one illustrated in Figure 6.20. Data is generated by collecting samples from a microphone and digitizing them using an analog-to-digital (A→D) converter. The digital samples are placed in packets, which are transmitted across the network and received at the other end. At the receiving host, the data must be *played back* at some appropriate rate. For example, if the voice samples were collected at a rate of one per 125 μs, they should be played back at the same rate. Thus, we can think of each sample as having a particular *playback time*: the point in time at which it is needed in the receiving host. In the voice example, each sample has a playback time that is 125 μs later than the preceding sample. If data arrives after its appropriate playback time, either because it was delayed in the network or because it was dropped and subsequently retransmitted, it is essentially useless. It is the complete worthlessness of late data that characterizes real-time applications. In elastic applications, it might be nice if data turns up on time, but we can still use it when it does not.

One way to make our voice application work would be to make sure that all samples take exactly the same amount of time to traverse the network. Then, since samples are injected at a rate of one per 125 μs, they will appear at the receiver at the same rate, ready to be played back. However, it is generally difficult to guarantee that all data traversing a packet-switched network will experience exactly the same delay. Packets encounter queues in switches or routers and the lengths of these queues vary with time, meaning that the delays tend to vary with time, and as a consequence, are potentially different for each packet in the audio stream. The way to deal with this at the receiver end is to buffer up some amount of data in reserve, thereby always providing a store of packets waiting to be played back at the right time. If a packet is delayed a short time, it goes in the buffer until its playback time arrives. If it gets delayed a long time, then it will not need to be stored for very long in the receiver's buffer before being played back. Thus, we have effectively added a constant offset to the playback time of all packets as a form of insurance. We call this offset the *playback point*. The only time we run into trouble is if packets get delayed in the network for such a long time that they arrive after their playback time, causing the playback buffer to be drained.

The operation of a playback buffer is illustrated in Figure 6.21. The left-hand diagonal line shows packets being generated at a steady rate. The wavy line shows when the packets arrive, some variable amount of time after they were sent, depending on what they encountered in the network. The right-hand diagonal line shows the packets being played back at a steady rate, after sitting in the playback buffer for some period of time. As long as the playback line is far enough to the right in time, the variation in network delay is never noticed by the application. However, if we move the playback line a little to the left, then some packets will begin to arrive too late to be useful.

For our audio application, there are limits to how far we can delay playing back data. It is hard to carry on a conversation if the time between when you speak and when your listener hears you is more than 300 ms. Thus, what we want from the network in this case is a guarantee that all our data will arrive within 300 ms. If data

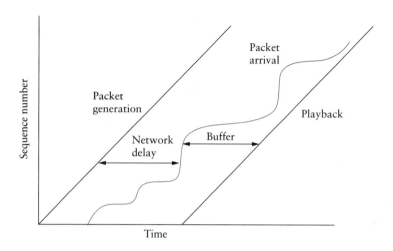

Figure 6.21 A playback buffer.

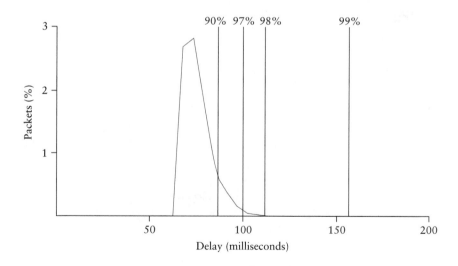

Figure 6.22 Example distribution of delays for an Internet connection.

arrives early, we buffer it until its correct playback time. If it arrives late, we have no use for it and must discard it.

To get a better appreciation of how variable network delay can be, Figure 6.22 shows the one-way delay measured over a certain path across the Internet over the course of one particular day. While the exact numbers would vary depending on the path and the date, the key factor here is the *variability* of the delay, which is consistently found on almost any path at any time. As denoted by the cumulative percentages given across the top of the graph, 97% of the packets in this case had a latency of 100 ms or less. This means that if our example audio application were to set the playback point at 100 ms, then on average, 3 out of every 100 packets would arrive too late to be of any use. One important thing to notice about this graph is that the tail of the curve—how far it extends to the right—is very long. We would have to set the playback point at over 200 ms to ensure that all packets arrived in time.

Taxonomy of Real-Time Applications

Now that we have a concrete idea of how real-time applications work, we can look at some different classes of applications, which serve to motivate our service model. The following taxonomy owes much to the work of Clark, Braden, Shenker, and Zhang, whose papers on this subject can be found in the Further Reading section for this chapter.

The first characteristic by which we can categorize applications is their tolerance of loss of data, where "loss" might occur because a packet arrived too late to be played back as well as arising from the usual causes in the network. On the one hand, one lost audio sample can be interpolated from the surrounding samples with relatively little effect on the perceived audio quality. It is only as more and more samples are lost that quality declines to the point that the speech becomes incomprehensible. On the other hand, a robot control program is likely to be an example of a real-time application that cannot tolerate loss—losing the packet that contains the command instructing the robot arm to stop is unacceptable. Thus, we can categorize real-time applications as *tolerant* or *intolerant* depending on whether they can tolerate occasional loss. (As an aside, note that many real-time applications are more tolerant of occasional loss than non-real-time applications. For example, compare our audio application to FTP, where the uncorrected loss of one bit might render a file completely useless.)

A second way to characterize real-time applications is by their adaptability. For example, an audio application might be able to adapt to the amount of delay that packets experience as they traverse the network. If we notice that packets are almost always arriving within 300 ms of being sent, then we can set our playback point accordingly, buffering any packets that arrive in less than 300 ms. Suppose that we subsequently observe that all packets are arriving within 100 ms of being sent. If we moved up our playback point to 100 ms, then the users of the application would probably perceive an improvement. The process of shifting the playback point would actually require us to play out samples at an increased rate for some period of time. With a voice application, this can be done in a way that is barely perceptible, simply by shortening the silences between words. Thus, playback point adjustment

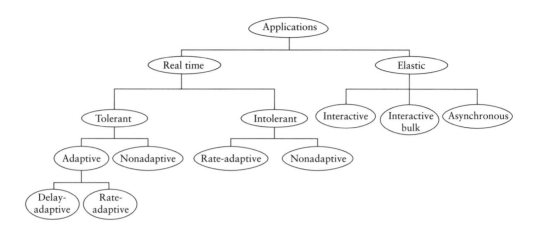

Figure 6.23 Taxonomy of applications.

is fairly easy in this case, and it has been effectively implemented for several voice applications such as the audio teleconferencing program known as **vat**. Note that playback point adjustment can happen in either direction, but that doing so actually involves distorting the played-back signal during the period of adjustment, and that the effects of this distortion will very much depend on how the end user uses the data. Intolerant applications will not, in general, be able to tolerate this distortion anymore than they can tolerate loss.

Observe that if we set our playback point on the assumption that all packets will arrive within 100 ms and then find that some packets are arriving slightly late, we will have to drop them, whereas we would not have had to drop them if we had left the playback point at 300 ms. Thus, we should advance the playback point only when it provides a perceptible advantage and only when we have some evidence that the number of late packets will be acceptably small. We may do this because of observed recent history or because of some assurance from the network.

We call applications that can adjust their playback point *delay-adaptive* applications. Another class of adaptive applications are *rate adaptive*. For example, many video coding algorithms can trade off bit rate versus quality. Thus, if we find that the network can support a certain bandwidth, we can set our coding parameters accordingly. If more bandwidth becomes available later, we can change parameters to increase the quality. While intolerant applications will not tolerate the distortion of delay adaptivity, they may be able to take advantage of rate adaptivity.

To summarize, we have the following taxonomy of applications, as illustrated in Figure 6.23. First, we have the elastic and the real time, with a range of target delays for elastic applications. Within real time, we have the intolerant, which cannot accept loss or lateness of data, and the tolerant. We also find adaptive and nonadaptive real-time applications, which may in turn be rate adaptive or delay adaptive. What the Internet and most other networks provide today is a service model that is adequate only for elastic applications. What we need is a richer service model that meets the needs of any application in this taxonomy. This leads us to a service model with not just one class (best effort), but with several classes, each available to meet the needs of some set of applications.

Approaches to QoS Support

We are now ready to look at some of the approaches that have been developed to provide a range of qualities of service. These can be divided into two broad categories:

- *fine-grained* approaches, which provide QoS to individual applications or flows

- *coarse-grained* approaches, which provide QoS to large classes of data or aggregated traffic

In the first category we find "Integrated Services," a QoS architecture developed in the IETF and often associated with RSVP (Resource Reservation Protocol). In the second category lies "Differentiated Services," which is undergoing standardization in the IETF at the time of writing. We discuss these in turn in the next two subsections.

ATM is well known for providing a rich set of QoS capabilities and is normally considered in the fine-grained category, since resources are associated with individual virtual circuits. However, a popular use of ATM is to interconnect routers, and routers may choose to send highly aggregated traffic down a single VC, so it is possible to use ATM for coarse-grained QoS as well. We discuss the details of ATM QoS in Section 6.5.4.

6.5.2   Integrated Services (RSVP)

The term "Integrated Services" refers to a body of work that was produced by the IETF around 1995–97. The Integrated Services working group developed specifications of a number of *service classes* designed to meet the needs of some of the application types described above. It also defined how RSVP could be used to make reservations using these service classes. The following paragraphs provide an overview of these specifications and the mechanisms that are used to implement them.

Service Classes

One of the service classes is designed for intolerant applications. These applications require that a packet never arrive late. The network should guarantee that the maximum delay that any packet will experience has some specified value; the application can then set its playback point so that no packet will ever arrive after its playback time. We assume that early arrival of packets can always be handled by buffering. This service is referred to as the *guaranteed* service.

In addition to the guaranteed service, the IETF considered several other services, but eventually settled on one to meet the needs of tolerant, adaptive applications. The service is known as *controlled load* and was motivated by the observation that existing applications of this type run quite well on networks that are not heavily loaded. The audio application vat, for example, adjusts its playback point as network delay varies, and produces reasonable audio quality as long as loss rates remain on the order of 10% or less.

The aim of the controlled load service is to emulate a lightly loaded network for those applications that request the service, even though the network as a whole may in fact be heavily loaded. The trick to this is to use a queuing mechanism such as WFQ (see Section 6.2) to isolate the controlled load traffic from the other traffic, and some form of admission control to limit the total amount of controlled load traffic on a link such that the load is kept reasonably low. We discuss admission control in more detail below.

Clearly, these two service classes are a subset of all the classes that might be provided. It remains to be seen as Integrated Services are deployed whether these two are adequate to meet the needs of all the application types described above.

Overview of Mechanisms

Now that we have augmented our best-effort service model with some new service classes, the next question is how we implement a network that provides these services to applications. This section outlines the key mechanisms. Keep in mind while reading this section that the mechanisms being described are still being hammered out by the Internet design community. The main thing to take away from the discussion is a general understanding of the pieces involved in supporting the service model outlined above.

First, whereas with a best-effort service we can just tell the network where we want our packets to go and leave it at that, a real-time service involves telling the network something more about the type of service we require. We may give it qualitative information such as "use a controlled load service" or quantitative information such as "I need a maximum delay of 100 ms." In addition to describing what we want, we need to tell the network something about what we are going to inject into it, since a low-bandwidth application is going to require fewer network resources than a high-bandwidth application. The set of information that we provide to the network is referred to as a *flowspec*. This name comes from the idea that a set of packets associated with a single application and that share common requirements is called a flow, consistent with our use of the term "flow" in Section 6.1.

Second, when we ask the network to provide us with a particular service, the network needs to decide if it can in fact provide that service. For example, if 10 users ask for a service in which each will consistently use 2 Mbps of link capacity, and they all share a link with 10-Mbps capacity, the network will have to say no to some of them. The process of deciding when to say no is called *admission control*.

Third, we need a mechanism by which the users of the network and the components of the network itself exchange information such as requests for service, flowspecs, and admission control decisions. This is called *signalling* in the ATM world, but since this word has several meanings, we refer to this process as *resource reservation*, and it is achieved using a resource reservation protocol.

Finally, when flows and their requirements have been described, and admission control decisions have been made, the network switches and routers need to meet the requirements of the flows. A key part of meeting these requirements is managing the way packets are queued and scheduled for transmission in the switches and routers. This last mechanism is *packet scheduling*.

Flowspecs

There are two separable parts to the flowspec: the part that describes the flow's traffic characteristics (called the *TSpec*) and the part that describes the service requested from the network (the *RSpec*). The RSpec is very service specific and relatively easy to describe. For example, with a controlled load service, the RSpec is trivial: The application just requests controlled load service with no additional parameters. With a guaranteed service, you could specify a delay target or bound. (In the IETF's guaranteed service specification, you specify not a delay but another quantity from which delay can be calculated.)

The TSpec is a little more complicated. As our example above showed, we need to give the network enough information about the bandwidth used by the flow to allow intelligent admission control decisions to be made. For most applications, however, the bandwidth is not a single number; it is something that varies constantly. A video application, for example, will generally generate more bits per second when the scene is changing rapidly than when it is still. Just knowing the long-term average bandwidth is not enough, as the following example illustrates. Suppose that we have 10 flows that arrive at a switch on separate input ports and that all leave on the same 10-Mbps link. Assume that over some suitably long interval each flow can be expected to send no more than 1 Mbps. You might think that this presents no problem. However, if these are variable bit rate applications, such as compressed video, then they will occasionally send more than their average rates. If enough sources send at above their

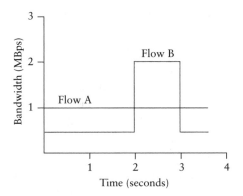

Figure 6.24 Two flows with equal average rates but different token bucket descriptions.

average rates, then the total rate at which data arrives at the switch will be greater than 10 Mbps. This excess data will be queued before it can be sent on the link. The longer this condition persists, the longer the queue will get. At the very least, while data is sitting in a queue, it is not getting closer to its destination, so it is being delayed. If packets are delayed long enough, the service that was requested will not be provided. In addition, as the queue length grows, at some point we run out of buffer space and packets must be dropped.

Exactly how we manage our queues to control delay and avoid dropping packets is something we discuss below. However, note here that we need to know something about how the bandwidth of our sources varies with time. One way to describe the bandwidth characteristics of sources is called a *token bucket* filter. Such a filter is described by two parameters: a token rate r, and a bucket depth B. It works as follows. To be able to send a byte, I must have a token. To send a packet of length n, I need n tokens. I start with no tokens and I accumulate them at a rate of r per second. I can accumulate no more than B tokens. What this means is that I can send a burst of as many as B bytes into the network as fast as I want, but over a sufficiently long interval, I can't send more than r bytes per second. It turns out that this information is very helpful to the admission control algorithm when it tries to figure out whether it can accommodate a new request for service.

Figure 6.24 illustrates how a token bucket can be used to characterize a flow's bandwidth requirements. For simplicity, assume that each flow can send data as individual bytes, rather than as packets. Flow A generates data at a steady rate of 1 MBps, so it can be described by a token bucket filter with a rate $r = 1$ MBps and a bucket depth of 1 byte. This means that it receives tokens at a rate of 1 MBps but that it cannot store more than 1 token—it spends them immediately. Flow B also sends at a rate that averages out to 1 MBps over the long term, but does so by sending at 0.5 MBps for 2 seconds and then at 2 MBps for 1 second. Since the token bucket rate r is, in a sense, a long-term average rate, flow B can be described by a token bucket with a rate of 1 MBps. Unlike flow A, however, flow B needs a bucket depth B of at least 1 MB, so that it can store up tokens while it sends at less than 1 MBps to be used when it sends at 2 MBps. For the first 2 seconds in this example, it receives tokens at a rate of 1 MBps but spends them at only 0.5 MBps, so it can save up $2 \times 0.5 = 1$ MB of tokens, which it then spends in the third second (along with the new tokens that continue to accrue in that second) to send data at 2 MBps. At the end of the third second, having spent the excess tokens, it starts to save them up again by sending at 0.5 MBps again.

It is interesting to note that a single flow can be described by many different token buckets. As a trivial example, flow A could be described by the same token bucket as flow B, with a rate of 1 MBps and a bucket depth of 1 MB. The fact that it never actually needs to accumulate tokens does not make that an inaccurate description, but it does mean that we have failed to convey some useful information to the network—the fact that flow A is actually very consistent in its bandwidth needs. In general, it is good to be as explicit about the bandwidth needs of an application as possible, to avoid overallocation of resources in the network.

Admission Control

The idea behind admission control is simple: When some new flow wants to receive a particular level of service, admission control looks at the TSpec and RSpec of the flow and tries to decide if the desired service can be provided to that amount of traffic, given the currently available resources, without causing any previously admitted flow to receive worse service than it had requested. If it can provide the service, the flow is admitted; if not, then it is denied. The hard part is figuring out when to say yes and when to say no.

Admission control is very dependent on the type of requested service and on the queuing discipline employed in the routers; we discuss the latter topic later in this section. For a guaranteed service, you need to have a good algorithm to make a definitive yes/no decision. The decision is fairly straightforward if weighted fair queuing, as discussed in Section 6.2, is used at each router. For a controlled load service, the decision may be based on heuristics, such as "The last time I allowed a flow with this TSpec into this class, the delays for the class exceeded the acceptable bound, so I'd better say no" or "My current delays are so far inside the bounds that I should be able to admit another flow without difficulty."

Admission control should not be confused with *policing*. The former is a per-flow decision to admit a new flow or not. The latter is a function applied on a per-packet basis to make sure that a flow conforms to the TSpec that was used to make the reservation. If a flow does not conform to its TSpec—for example, because it is sending twice as many bytes per second as it said it would—then it is likely to interfere with the service provided to other flows, and some corrective action must be taken. There are several options, the obvious one being to drop offending packets. However, another option would be to check if the packets really are interfering with the service of other flows. If they are not interfering, the packets could be sent on after being marked with a tag that says, in effect, "This is a nonconforming packet. Drop me first if you need to drop any packets."

Admission control is closely related to the important issue of *policy*. For example, a network administrator might wish to allow reservations made by his company's CEO to be admitted while rejecting reservations made by more lowly employees. Of course, the CEO's reservation request might still fail if the requested resources aren't available, so we see that issues of policy and resource availability may both be addressed when admission control decisions are made. The application of policy to networking is an area receiving much attention at the time of writing.

Reservation Protocol

While connection-oriented networks have always needed some sort of setup protocol to establish the necessary virtual circuit state in the switches, connectionless networks like the Internet have had no such protocols. As this section has indicated, however, we need to provide a lot more information to our network when we want a real-time service from it. While there have been a number of setup protocols proposed for the Internet, the one on which most current attention is focused is called Resource Reservation Protocol (RSVP). It is particularly interesting because it differs so substantially from conventional signalling protocols for connection-oriented networks.

One of the key assumptions underlying RSVP is that it should not detract from the robustness that we find in today's connectionless networks. Because connectionless networks rely on little or no state being stored in the network itself, it is possible for routers to crash and reboot and for links to go up and down while end-to-end connectivity is still maintained. RSVP tries to maintain this robustness by using the idea of *soft state* in the routers. Soft state—in contrast to the hard state found in connection-oriented networks—does not need to be explicitly deleted when it is no longer needed. Instead, it times out after some fairly short period (say, a minute) if it is not periodically refreshed. We will see later how this helps robustness.

Another important characteristic of RSVP is that it aims to support multicast flows just as effectively as unicast flows. This is not surprising, since the multicast applications found on the MBone, such as vat and vic, are obvious early candidates to benefit from real-time services. One of the insights of RSVP's designers is that most multicast applications have many more receivers than senders, as typified by the large audience and one speaker for a lecture carried on the MBone. Also, receivers may have different requirements. For example, one receiver might want to receive data from only one sender, while others might wish to receive data from all senders. Rather than having the senders keep track of a potentially large number of receivers, it makes more sense to let the receivers keep track of their own needs. This suggests the *receiver-oriented* approach adopted by RSVP. In contrast, connection-oriented networks usually leave resource reservation to the sender, just as it is normally the originator of a phone call who causes resources to be allocated in the phone network.

The soft state and receiver-oriented nature of RSVP give it a number of nice properties. One nice property is that it is very straightforward to increase or decrease the level of resource allocation provided to a receiver. Since each receiver periodically sends refresh messages to keep the soft state in place, it is easy to send a new reservation that asks for a new level of resources. In the event of a host crash, resources allocated by that host to a flow will naturally time out and be released. To see what happens in the event of a router or link failure, we need to look a little more closely at the mechanics of making a reservation.

Initially, consider the case of one sender and one receiver trying to get a reservation for traffic flowing between them. There are two things that need to happen before a receiver can make the reservation. First, the receiver needs to know what traffic the sender is likely to send so that it can make an appropriate reservation. That is, it needs to know the sender's TSpec. Second, it needs to know what path the packets will follow from sender to receiver, so that it can establish a resource reservation at each router on the path. Both of these requirements can be met by sending a message from the sender to the receiver that contains the TSpec. Obviously, this gets the TSpec to the receiver. The other thing that happens is that each router looks at this message (called a PATH message) as it goes past, and it figures out the *reverse path* that will be used to send reservations from the receiver back to the sender in an effort to get the reservation to each router on the path. Building the multicast tree in the first place is done by mechanisms such as those described in Section 4.4.

Having received a PATH message, the receiver sends a reservation back "up" the multicast tree in a RESV message. This message contains the sender's TSpec and an RSpec describing the requirements of this receiver. Each router on the path looks at the reservation request and tries to allocate the necessary resources to satisfy it. If the reservation can be made, the RESV request is passed on to the next router. If not, an error message is returned to the receiver who made the request. If all goes well, the correct reservation is installed at every router between the sender and the receiver. As

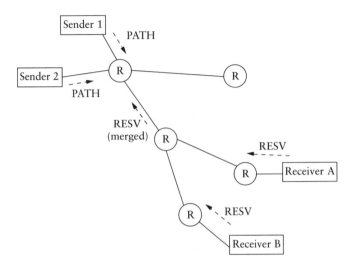

Figure 6.25   Making reservations on a multicast tree.

long as the receiver wants to retain the reservation, it sends the same RESV message about once every 30 seconds.

Now we can see what happens when a router or link fails. Routing protocols will adapt to the failure and create a new path from sender to receiver. PATH messages are sent about every 30 seconds, and may be sent sooner if a router detects a change in its forwarding table, so the first one after the new route stabilizes will reach the receiver over the new path. The receiver's next RESV message will follow the new path and (hopefully) establish a new reservation on the new path. Meanwhile, the routers that are no longer on the path will stop getting RESV messages, and these reservations will time out and be released. Thus RSVP deals quite well with changes in topology, as long as routing changes are not excessively frequent.

The next thing we need to consider is how to cope with multicast, where there may be multiple senders to a group and multiple receivers. This situation is illustrated in Figure 6.25. First, let's deal with multiple receivers for a single sender. As a RESV message travels up the multicast tree, it is likely to hit a piece of the tree where some other receiver's reservation has already been established. It may be the case that the resources reserved upstream of this point are adequate to serve both receivers. For example, if receiver A has already made a reservation that provides for a guaranteed delay of less than 100 ms, and the new request from receiver B is for a delay of less than 200 ms, then no new reservation is required. On the other hand, if the new request were for a delay of less than 50 ms, then the router would first need to see if it could accept the request, and if so, it would send the request on upstream. The next time receiver A asked for a minimum of a 100-ms delay, the router would not need to pass this request on. In general, reservations can be merged in this way to meet the needs of all receivers downstream of the merge point.

If there are also multiple senders in the tree, receivers need to collect the TSpecs from all senders and make a reservation that is large enough to accommodate the traffic from all senders. However, this may not mean that the TSpecs need to be added up. For example, in an audioconference with 10 speakers, there is not much point in allocating enough resources to carry 10 audio streams, since the result of 10 people speaking at once would be incomprehensible. Thus, we could imagine a reservation that is large enough to accommodate two speakers and no more. Calculating the correct overall TSpec from all the sender TSpecs is clearly application specific. Also, we may only be interested in hearing from a subset of all possible speakers; RSVP has different reservation "styles" to deal with such options as "Reserve resources for all speakers," "Reserve resources for any *n* speakers," and "Reserve resources for speakers A and B only."

Packet Classifying and Scheduling

Once we have described our traffic and our desired network service and have installed a suitable reservation at all the routers on the path, the only thing that remains is for the routers to actually deliver the requested service to the data packets. There are two things that need to be done:

Integrated Services and Subnet Technologies

One of the challenges to extending the best-effort service model of IP arises from the fact that IP is intended to run over any possible subnet technology. The best-effort model of IP was adopted precisely because it is the lowest common denominator offered by all subnets. Since Integrated Services moves beyond this model, there is some work to do to determine how the new service model can be operated over widely varying subnet technologies. To address this challenge, the IETF created a working group called Integrated Services over Specific Link Layers (ISSLL).

The easiest possible link layer to support is the point-to-point link, since a link of this type has completely predictable and fixed QoS characteristics. Two of the more challenging (and important) subnet technologies are Ethernet and ATM. In the case of ATM, the ISSLL group has specified how the various parameters that are used in flowspecs for Integrated Services can be mapped into ATM-specific QoS parameters on ATM virtual circuits. Because of the many similarities between ATM QoS and

Integrated Services (as discussed in Section 6.5.4), such mappings are not too difficult, although there are many details to attend to.

The case of Ethernet is made difficult by the fact that access to the link bandwidth is arbitrated in a completely decentralized way. This means, for example, that no one router can determine if it is safe to admit a new reserved flow onto an Ethernet segment because some other router may have just done the same thing for a flow that needs the entire link bandwidth. To address this issue, ISSLL defines a centralized entity responsible for arbitrating among the many devices that may request reservations. This entity is called the subnet bandwidth manager (SBM). Part of the SBM specification covers the process of automatically electing one device to be the designated SBM (DSBM) for an Ethernet, since many nodes might be capable of playing the role but it is important to have only one manager in charge at a given time. Note that there is a limit to how completely the SBM can manage bandwidth on an Ethernet because there is always the risk that nodes that are just sending packets best-effort

■ Associate each packet with the appropriate reservation so that it can be handled correctly, a process known as *classifying* packets.

■ Manage the packets in the queues so that they receive the service that has been requested, a process known as packet *scheduling*.

The first part is done by examining up to five fields in the packet: the source address, destination address, protocol number, source port, and destination port. (In IPv6, it is possible that the FlowLabel field in the header could be used to enable the lookup to be done based on a single, shorter key.) Based on this information, the packet can be placed in the appropriate class. For example, it may be classified into the controlled load classes, or it may be part of a guaranteed flow that needs to be handled separately from all other guaranteed flows. In short, there is a mapping from the flow-specific information in the packet header to a single class identifier that determines how the packet is handled in the queue. For guaranteed flows, this might be a one-to-one mapping, while for other services, it might be many to one. The details of classification are closely related to the details of queue management.

It should be clear that something as simple as a FIFO queue in a router will be inadequate to provide many different services and to provide different levels of delay within each service. Several more sophisticated queue management disciplines were discussed in Section 6.2, and some combination of these is likely to be used in a router.

The details of packet scheduling ideally should not be specified in the service model. Instead, this is an area where implementors can try to do creative things to realize the service model efficiently. In the case of guaranteed service, it has been established that a weighted fair queuing discipline, in which each flow gets its own individual queue with a certain share of the link, will provide a guaranteed end-to-end delay bound that can readily be calculated. For controlled load, simpler schemes may be used. One possibility includes treating all the controlled load traffic as a single, aggregated flow (as far as the scheduling mechanism is concerned), with the weight

(and thus have no need to talk to the SBM) might consume enough bandwidth that the reserved flows do not receive the QoS they were promised by the SBM. This problem may be partially mitigated by monitoring the current best-effort usage of the Ethernet and making reasonable predictions about how much that usage changes over time.

for that flow being set based on the total amount of traffic admitted in the controlled load class. The problem is made harder when you consider that in a single router, many different services are likely to be provided concurrently, and that each of these services may require a different scheduling algorithm. Thus, some overall queue management algorithm is needed to manage the resources between the different services.

Scalability Issues

While the Integrated Services architecture and RSVP represented a significant enhancement of the best-effort service model of IP, many Internet service providers felt that it was not the right model for them to deploy. The reason for this reticence relates to one of the fundamental design goals of IP: scalability. In the best-effort service model, routers in the Internet store little or no state about the individual flows passing through them. Thus, as the Internet grows, the only thing routers have to do to keep up with that growth is to move more bits per second and to deal with larger routing tables. But RSVP raises the possibility that every flow passing through a router might have a corresponding reservation. To understand the severity of this problem, suppose that every flow on an OC-48 (2.5-Gbps) link represents a 64-Kbps audio stream. The number of such flows is

$$2.5 \times 10^9 / 64 \times 10^3 = 39{,}000$$

Each of those reservations needs some amount of state that needs to be stored in memory and refreshed periodically. The router needs to classify, police, and queue each of those flows. Admission control decisions need to be made every time such a flow requests a reservation. And some mechanisms are needed to "push back" on users so that they don't make arbitrarily large reservations for long periods of time.[5]

These scalability concerns have, at the time of writing, prevented the widespread deployment of Integrated Services. Because of these concerns, other approaches that do not require so much "per-flow" state have been developed. The next section discusses a number of such approaches.

6.5.3 Differentiated Services

Whereas the Integrated Services architecture allocates resources to individual flows, the Differentiated Services model allocates resources to a small number of classes of traffic. In fact, some proposed approaches to Differentiated Services simply divide traffic into two classes. This is an eminently sensible approach to take: If you consider the difficulty that network operators experience just trying to keep a best-effort internet running smoothly, it makes sense to add to the service model in small increments.

Suppose that we have decided to enhance the best-effort service model by adding just one new class, which we'll call "premium." Clearly we will need some way to figure out which packets are premium and which are regular old best effort. Rather than using a protocol like RSVP to tell all the routers that some flow is sending premium packets, it would be much easier if the packets could just identify themselves to the router when they arrive. This could obviously be done by using a bit in the packet header—if that bit is a 1, the packet is a premium packet; if it's a 0, the packet is best effort. With this in mind, there are two questions we need to address:

■ Who sets the premium bit, and under what circumstances?

■ What does a router do differently when it sees a packet with the bit set?

There are many possible answers to the first question, but a common approach is to set the bit at an administrative boundary. For example, the router at the edge of an Internet service provider's network might set the bit for packets arriving on an interface that connects to a particular company's network. The Internet service provider might do this because that company has paid for a higher level of service than best effort. It is also possible that not all packets would be marked as premium; for example, the router might be configured to mark packets as premium up to some maximum rate, and to leave all excess packets as best effort.

Assuming that packets have been marked in some way, what do the routers that encounter marked packets do with them? Here again there are many answers. In fact, the Differentiated Services working group of the IETF is standardizing a set of router

---

[5] Charging per reservation would be one way to push back, consistent with the telephony model of billing for each phone call. This is not the only way to push back, and per-call billing is believed to be one of the major costs of operating the phone network.

behaviors to be applied to marked packets. These are called "per-hop behaviors" (PHBs), a term that indicates that they define the behavior of individual routers rather than end-to-end services. Because there is more than one new behavior, there is also a need for more than 1 bit in the packet header to tell the routers which behavior to apply. The IETF has decided to take the old TOS byte from the IP header, which has not been widely used, and redefine it. Six bits of this byte have been allocated for Differentiated Services code points (DSCP), where each DSCP is a 6-bit value that identifies a particular PHB to be applied to a packet.

One of the simplest PHBs to explain is known as "expedited forwarding" (EF). Packets marked for EF treatment should be forwarded by the router with minimal delay and loss. The only way that a router can guarantee this to all EF packets is if the arrival rate of EF packets at the router is strictly limited to be less than the rate at which the router can forward EF packets. For example, a router with a 100-Mbps interface needs to be sure that the arrival rate of EF packets destined for that interface never exceeds 100 Mbps. It might also want to be sure that the rate will be somewhat below 100 Mbps, so that it occasionally has time to send other packets such as routing updates.

The rate limiting of EF packets is achieved by configuring the routers at the edge of an administrative domain to allow a certain maximum rate of EF packet arrivals into the domain. A simple, albeit conservative, approach would be to ensure that the sum of the rates of all EF packets entering the domain is less than the bandwidth of the slowest link in the domain. This would ensure that, even in the worst case where all EF packets converge on the slowest link, it is not overloaded and can provide the correct behavior.

There are several possible implementation strategies for the EF behavior. One is to give EF packets strict priority over all other packets. Another is to perform weighted fair queuing between EF packets and other packets, with the weight of EF set sufficiently high that all EF packets can be delivered quickly. This has an advantage over strict priority: The non-EF packets can be assured of getting some access to the link, even if the amount of EF traffic is excessive. This might mean that the EF packets fail to get exactly the specified behavior, but it could also prevent essential routing traffic from being locked out of the network in the event of an excessive load of EF traffic.

Another PHB is known as "assured forwarding" (AF). This behavior has its roots in an approach known as "RED with In and Out" (RIO) or "Weighted RED," both of which are enhancements to the basic RED algorithm of Section 6.4.2. Figure 6.26 shows how RIO works; like Figure 6.17, we see drop probability on the y-axis increasing as average queue length increases along the x-axis. But now, for our two classes of traffic, we have two separate drop probability curves. RIO calls the two

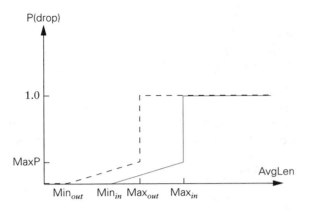

Figure 6.26   RED with In and Out drop probabilities.

classes "in" and "out" for reasons that will become clear shortly. Because the "out" curve has a lower MinThreshold than the "in" curve, it is clear that, under low levels of congestion, only packets marked "out" will be discarded by the RED algorithm. If the congestion becomes more serious, a higher percentage of "out" packets are dropped, and then if the average queue length exceeds Min_{in}, RED starts to drop "in" packets as well.

The reason for calling the two classes of packets "in" and "out" stems from the way the packets are marked. We already noted that packet marking can be performed by a router at the edge of an administrative domain. We can think of this router as being at the boundary between a network service provider and some customer of that network. The customer might be any other network, for example, the network of a corporation or of another network service provider. The customer and the network service provider agree on some sort of profile for the assured service (and perhaps the customer pays the network service provider for this profile.) The profile might be something like "Customer X is allowed to send up to y Mbps of assured traffic," or it could be significantly more complex. Whatever the profile is, the edge router can clearly mark the packets that arrive from this customer as being either in or out of profile. In the example just mentioned, as long as the customer sends less than y Mbps, all his packets will be marked "in," but once he exceeds that rate, the excess packets will be marked "out."

The combination of a "profile meter" at the edge and RIO in all the routers of the service provider's network should provide the customer with a high assurance (but not a guarantee) that packets within his profile can be delivered. In particular, if the majority of packets, including those sent by customers who have not paid extra to establish a profile, are "out" packets, then it should usually be the case that the RIO mechanism will act to keep congestion low enough that "in" packets are rarely dropped. Clearly, there must be enough bandwidth in the network so that the "in" packets alone are rarely able to congest a link to the point where RIO starts dropping "in" packets.

Just like RED, the effectiveness of a mechanism like RIO depends to some extent on correct parameter choices, and there are considerably more parameters to set for RIO. Exactly how well the scheme will work in production networks is not known at the time of writing.

One interesting property of RIO is that it does not change the order of "in" and "out" packets. For example, if a TCP connection is sending packets through a profile meter, and some packets are being marked "in" while others are marked "out," those packets will receive different drop probabilities in the router queues, but they will be delivered to the receiver in the same order in which they were sent. This is important for most TCP implementations, which perform much better when packets arrive in order, even if they are designed to cope with misordering. Note also that mechanisms such as fast retransmit can be falsely triggered when misordering happens.

The idea of RIO can be generalized to provide more than two drop probability curves, and this is the idea behind the approach known as weighted RED (WRED). In this case, the value of the DSCP field is used to pick one of several drop probability curves, so that several different classes of service can be provided.

A third way to provide Differentiated Services is to use the DSCP value to determine which queue to put a packet into in a weighted fair queuing scheduler as described in Section 6.2.2. As a very simple case, we might use one code point to indicate the "best-effort" queue and a second code point to select the "premium" queue. We then need to choose a weight for the premium queue that makes the premium packets get better service than the best-effort packets. This depends on the offered load of premium packets. For example, if we give the premium queue a weight of one and the best-effort queue a weight of four, that ensures that the bandwidth available to premium packets is

$$
\begin{aligned}
B_{premium} &= W_{premium}/(W_{premium} + W_{best\_effort}) \\
&= 1/(1 + 4) \\
&= 0.2
\end{aligned}
$$

That is, we have effectively reserved 20% of the link for premium packets, so if the offered load of premium traffic is only 10% of the link on average, then the premium traffic will behave as if it is running on a very underloaded network and the service will be very good. In particular, the delay experienced by the premium class can be kept low, since WFQ will try to transmit premium packets as soon as they arrive in this scenario. On the other hand, if the premium traffic load were 30%, it would behave like a highly loaded network, and delay could be very high for the "premium" packets—even worse than the so-called best-effort packets. Thus, knowledge of the offered load and careful setting of weights is important for this type of service. However, note that the safe approach is to be very conservative in setting the weight for the premium queue. If this weight is made very high relative to the expected load, it provides a margin of error and yet does not prevent the best-effort traffic from using any bandwidth that has been reserved for premium but is not used by premium packets.

Just as in WRED, we can generalize this WFQ-based approach to allow more than two classes represented by different code points. Furthermore, we can combine the idea of a queue selector with a drop preference. For example, with 12 code points we can have four queues with different weights, each of which has three drop preferences. This is exactly what the IETF has done in the definition of "assured service."

6.5.4 ATM Quality of Service

In many respects, the QoS capabilities that are provided in ATM networks are similar to those provided in an IP network using Integrated Services. However, the ATM standards bodies came up with a total of five service classes compared to the IETF's three.[6] The five ATM service classes are

- constant bit rate (CBR)

- variable bit rate—real-time (VBR-rt)

- variable bit rate—non-real-time (VBR-nrt)

- available bit rate (ABR)

- unspecified bit rate (UBR)

Mostly the ATM and IP service classes are quite similar, but one of them, ABR, has no real counterpart in IP. We explain this class in detail below. The remaining classes can be fairly easily understood in terms of what we have already seen.

Note that in ATM, quality of service is defined at the time a virtual circuit is set up. This is done by including information in the signalling messages that are sent at VC setup time.

---

[6] We count best effort as a service class along with controlled load and guaranteed service.

VBR-rt is very much like the guaranteed service class in IP Integrated Services. The exact parameters that are used to set up a VBR-rt VC are slightly different than those used to make a guaranteed service reservation, but the basic idea is the same. The traffic generated by the source is characterized by a token bucket, and the maximum total delay required through the network is specified.

CBR is not too different than VBR-rt, except that sources of CBR traffic are expected to send at a constant rate. Note that this is really a special case of VBR, where the source's peak rate and average rate of transmission are equal. The main reason for making this a separate class in ATM is that this special case is viewed as very important to telephone companies, since the majority of the services they offer today—voice calls and leased lines, for example—provide a pipe of fixed bandwidth to the end user. CBR also turned out to be a relatively easy service to specify and implement, so that many early ATM switches could support CBR but not VBR. The early availability of CBR in ATM products certainly helped the acceptance of ATM in the marketplace, especially since these products appeared before IP routers with any QoS features to speak of were available.

VBR-nrt bears some similarity to IP's controlled load service. Again, the source traffic is specified by a token bucket, but there is not the same hard delay guarantee of VBR-rt or IP's guaranteed service.

UBR is ATM's best-effort service. There is one small difference between UBR and the standard best-effort model provided in IP. Because ATM always requires a signalling phase before data is sent, it is possible to convey information about the source

RSVP and ATM

Now that we've seen some highlights of RSVP and ATM QoS, it is interesting to compare the two approaches. Note that, at a high level, the goals of a connection-oriented signalling protocol and RSVP are the same: to install some state information in the network nodes that forward packets so that packets get handled correctly. However, there are not many similarities beyond that high-level goal.

Table 6.1 compares RSVP with the ATM Forum's current signalling protocol, which is derived from the ITU-T protocol Q.2931. (Recall from Section 3.3 that Q.2931 defines how a virtual circuit is routed across the network, as well as how resources are reserved for that circuit.) The differences stem largely from the fact that RSVP starts with a connectionless model and tries to add functionality without going all the way to traditional connections, whereas ATM starts out from a connection-oriented model. RSVP's goal of handling multicast efficiently is also apparent in the receiver-driven approach, which aims to provide scalability for multicast groups with large numbers of receivers.

RSVP	ATM
Receiver generates reservation	Sender generates connection request
Soft state (refresh/timeout)	Hard state (explicit delete)
Separate from route establishment	Concurrent with route establishment
QoS can change dynamically	QoS is static for life of connection (although somewhat variable in ABR)
Receiver heterogeneity	Uniform QoS to all receivers

Table 6.1 Comparison of RSVP and ATM signalling.

at VC setup time. UBR allows the source to specify a maximum rate at which it will send, which may be less than the line rate. Switches may make use of this information to decide whether admitting the new VC would adversely affect previously established VCs, and thus may reject the VC setup or try to negotiate a lower peak rate with this source.

Finally, we come to ABR, which is more than just a service class; it also defines a set of congestion-control mechanisms. Having been designed by a standards body, it is rather complex, so this section covers only a few of the high points.

An ATM virtual circuit clearly has two ends, which we can call the source and the destination. VCs are usually bidirectional, so a node that is the source in one direction is generally the destination in the other. The ABR mechanisms operate over a virtual circuit by exchanging special ATM cells called resource management (RM) cells between the source and destination of the VC. The goal of sending the RM cells is to get information about the state of congestion in the network back to the source so that it can send traffic at an appropriate rate. In this respect, RM cells are an explicit congestion feedback mechanism. This is similar to the DECbit, but contrasts with TCP's use of implicit feedback, which depends on packet losses to detect congestion.

Initially, the source sends the cell to the destination and includes in it the rate at which it would like to send data cells. Switches along the path look at the requested rate and decide if sufficient resources are available to handle that rate, based on the amount of traffic being carried on other circuits. If enough resources are available, the RM cell is passed on unmodified; otherwise, the requested rate is decreased before the cell is passed along. At the destination, the RM cell is turned around and sent back to the source, which thereby learns what rate it can send at.

The intention of ABR is to allow a source to increase or decrease its allotted rate as conditions dictate. As a consequence, RM cells are sent periodically and may contain either higher or lower requested rates. Also, the rate at which a source is allowed

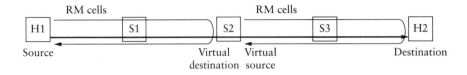

Figure 6.27   ABR VC with segmented control loops using virtual source and virtual destination.

to send decays with time if not used. This is intended to discourage a source from requesting capacity "just in case."

While we assumed so far that the source and destination of the RM cells are the endpoints of the VC, this need not be the case. ABR extends the notion of source and destination, introducing the concepts of virtual source (VS) and virtual destination (VD). They are "virtual" in the sense that they are not the true endpoints of the VC. This enables the control loop around which RM cells flow to be made shorter than the VC itself. By making the control loops shorter, the response time of the system can be reduced. Furthermore, it may reduce the buffer requirements of the switches by reducing the time between when they sense congestion and when the (virtual) source slows down. A virtual circuit that has been segmented in the middle with a virtual source and virtual destination is shown in Figure 6.27. The real source sends RM cells to the switch providing VS/VD capability, and that switch, acting as VD, turns around the RM cells. It will include in these cells the rate at which it is willing to accept traffic on this VC. In its capacity as VS, it also originates RM cells toward the real destination, which will in turn be sent back to the VS telling it at what rate it can send traffic on this VC.

There is a great deal of flexibility in how a switch actually implements ABR. In general, proprietary algorithms are used to set the rates in RM cells as they pass through the switches, based on a wide variety of information such as the current buffer occupancy and the measured arrival rates on all VCs, as well as the allotted rates on those VCs (which may not be the same as the measured rates). These algorithms, as is normal for congestion-control algorithms, seek to maximize throughput and will keep delay and loss low.

One uncertain aspect of ABR is how it interacts with TCP's congestion-avoidance mechanisms. These mechanisms are finely tuned based on experience, and they work on the premise that there is nothing fancy going on in the network—if you send too fast, packets get dropped. With ABR, you can imagine that the VS might have to drop packets while it waits for an RM cell to return, even though there is in fact no real congestion in the network. At the time of writing, most of the experience with ABR has been in simulation and laboratory conditions, and real-world experience is just beginning to be gathered.

6.6 Summary

As we have just seen, the issue of resource allocation is not only central to computer networking, it is also a very hard problem. This chapter has examined two aspects of resource allocation. The first, congestion control, is concerned with preventing overall degradation of service when the demand for resources by hosts exceeds the supply available in the network. The second aspect is the provision of different qualities of service to applications that need more assurances than those provided by the best-effort model.

Most congestion-control mechanisms are targeted at the best-effort service model of today's Internet, where the primary responsibility for congestion control falls on the end nodes of the network. Typically, the source uses feedback—either implicitly learned from the network or explicitly sent by a router—to adjust the load it places on the network; this is precisely what TCP's congestion-control mechanism does.

Independent of exactly what the end nodes are doing, the routers implement a queuing discipline that governs which packets get transmitted and which packets get dropped. Sometimes this queuing algorithm is sophisticated enough to segregate traffic (e.g., WFQ), and in other cases, the router attempts to monitor its queue length and then signals the source host when congestion is about to occur (e.g., RED gateways and DECbit).

Emerging quality of service approaches aim to do substantially more than just control congestion. Their goal is to enable applications with widely varying requirements for delay, loss, and throughput to have those requirements met through new mechanisms inside the network. The Integrated Services approach allows individual application flows to specify their needs to the routers using an explicit signalling mechanism (RSVP), while Differentiated Services assigns packets into a small number of classes that receive differentiated treatment in the routers. While the signalling used by ATM is very different from RSVP, there is considerable similarity between ATM's service classes and those of Integrated Services.

Perhaps the larger question we should be asking is how much can we expect from the network and how much responsibility will ultimately fall to the end hosts. The emerging reservation-based strategies certainly have the advantage of providing for

OPEN ISSUE

Inside versus Outside the Network

more varied qualities of service than today's feedback-based schemes; being able to support different qualities of service is a strong reason to put more functionality into the network's routers. Does this mean that the days of TCP-like end-to-end congestion control are numbered? This seems highly unlikely. TCP and the applications that use it are well entrenched, and in many cases have no need of much more help from the network. Furthermore, it is most unlikely that all the routers in a worldwide, heterogeneous network like the Internet will implement precisely the same resource reservation algorithm. Ultimately, it seems that the endpoints are going to have to look out for themselves, at least to some extent. After all, we should not forget the sound design principle underlying the Internet—do the simplest possible thing in the routers and put all the smarts at the edges where you can control it. How this all plays out in the next few years will be very interesting indeed.

In some sense, the Differentiated Services approach represents the middle ground between absolutely minimal intelligence in the network and the rather significant amount of intelligence (and stored state information) that is required in an Integrated Services network. Certainly most Internet service providers have balked at allowing their customers to make RSVP reservations inside the providers' networks. One important question is whether the Differentiated Services approach will meet the requirements of more stringent applications. For example, if a service provider is trying to offer a large-scale telephony service over an IP network, will Differentiated Services techniques be adequate to deliver the quality of service that traditional telephone users expect? It seems likely that yet more QoS options, with varying amounts of intelligence in the network, will need to be explored.

FURTHER READING

The recommended reading list for this chapter is long, reflecting the breadth of interesting work being done in congestion control and resource allocation. It includes the original papers introducing the various mechanisms discussed in this chapter. In addition to a more detailed description of these mechanisms, including thorough analysis of their effectiveness and fairness, these papers are must reading because of the insights they give into the interplay of the various issues related to congestion control. In addition, the first paper gives a nice overview of some of the early work on this topic, while the last is considered one of the seminal papers in the development of QoS capabilities in the Internet.

- Gerla, M., and L. Kleinrock. Flow control: A comparative survey. *IEEE Transactions on Communications* COM-28(4):553–573, April 1980.

- Demers, A., S. Keshav, and S. Shenker. Analysis and simulation of a fair queuing algorithm. *Proceedings of the SIGCOMM '89 Symposium*, pages 1–12, September 1989.

■ Jacobson, V. Congestion avoidance and control. *Proceedings of the SIG-COMM '88 Symposium*, pages 314–329, August 1988.

■ Ramakrishnan, K., and R. Jain. A binary feedback scheme for congestion avoidance in computer networks with a connectionless network layer. *ACM Transactions on Computer Systems* 8(2):158–181, May 1990.

■ Floyd, S., and V. Jacobson. Random early detection gateways for congestion avoidance. *IEEE/ACM Transactions on Networking* 1(4):397–413, August 1993.

■ Brakmo, L., and L. Peterson. TCP Vegas: End-to-end congestion avoidance on a global internet. *IEEE Journal of Selected Areas in Communication (JSAC)* 13(8):1465–1480, October 1995.

■ Clark, D., S. Shenker, and L. Zhang. Supporting real-time applications in an integrated services packet network: Architecture and mechanism. *Proceedings of the SIGCOMM '92 Symposium*, pages 14–26, August 1992.

Beyond these recommended papers, there is a wealth of other valuable material on resource allocation. For starters, two early papers by Kleinrock [Kle79] and Jaffe [Jaf81] set the foundation for using power as a measure of congestion-control effectiveness. Also, Jain [Jai91] gives a thorough discussion of various issues related to performance evaluation, including a description of Jain's fairness index.

More details on the various congestion-avoidance techniques introduced in Section 6.4 can be found in Wang and Crowcroft [WC92, WC91] and Jain [Jai89], with the first paper giving an especially nice overview of congestion avoidance based on a common understanding of how the network changes as it approaches congestion. Also, the packet-pair technique briefly discussed in Section 6.3.2 is more carefully described in Keshav [Kes91], and the partial packet discard technique suggested in Section 6.4.2 is described by Romanow and Floyd [RF94].

Much recent work on packet scheduling has extended the original fair queuing paper cited above. Excellent examples include articles by Stoica and Zhang [SZ97], Bennett and Zhang [BZ96], and Goyal, Vin, and Chen [GVC96].

Many additional articles have been published on the Integrated Services architecture, including an overview by Braden et al. [BCS94] and a description of RSVP by Zhang et al. [ZDE+93]. The first paper to address the topic of Differentiated Services is that of Clark [Cla97], which introduces the RIO mechanism as well as the overall architecture of Differentiated Services. A follow-on paper by Clark and Fang [CF98] presents some simulation results. [BBC+98] defines the Differentiated Services architecture.

EXERCISES

1 It is possible to define flows on either a host-to-host basis or on a process-to-process basis.

   (a) Discuss the implications of each approach to application programs.

   (b) IPv6 includes a FlowLabel field, for supplying hints to routers about individual flows. The originating host is to put here a pseudorandom hash of all the other fields serving to identify the flow; the router can thus use any subset of these bits as a hash value for fast lookup of the flow. What exactly should the FlowLabel be based on, for each of these two approaches?

2 TCP uses a host-centric, feedback-based, windows-based resource allocation model. How might TCP have been designed to use instead the following models?

   (a) Host-centric, feedback-based, and rate-based

   (b) Router-centric and feedback-based

3 Sketch curves for throughput, delay, and power, each as a function of load, for the following networks. Throughput is to be measured as a percentage of the maximum. Load is to be measured (somewhat unnaturally) as the number of stations (N) ready to send at any one time; note this implies there is always (unless $N = 0$, which you may ignore) a station ready to send. Assume each station has only one packet to send at a time.

   (a) Ethernet. Assume, as in Exercise 44 of Chapter 2, that the average packet size is 5 slot times, and that when N stations are trying to transmit, the average delay until one station succeeds is $N/2$ slot times.

   (b) Token ring, with TRT $= 0$.

4 Suppose two hosts A and B are connected via a router R. The A–R link has infinite bandwidth; the R–B link can send one packet per second. R's queue is infinite. Load is to be measured as the number of packets per second sent from A to B. Sketch the throughput-versus-load and delay-versus-load graphs, or if a graph cannot be drawn, explain why. Would another way to measure load be more appropriate?

5 Is it possible for TCP Reno to reach a state with the congestion window size much larger than (e.g., twice as large as) RTT$\times$ bandwidth? Is it likely?

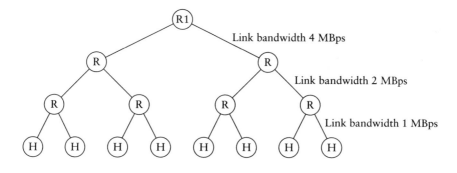

Figure 6.28 Diagram for Exercise 6.

6 Consider the arrangement of hosts H and routers R and R1 in Figure 6.28. All links are full-duplex, and all routers are faster than their links. Show that R1 cannot become congested, and for any other router R we can find a traffic pattern that congests that router alone.

7 Suppose a congestion-control scheme results in a collection of competing flows that achieve the following throughput rates: 100 KBps, 60 KBps, 110 KBps, 95 KBps, and 150 KBps.

(a) Calculate the fairness index for this scheme.

(b) Now add a flow with a throughput rate of 1000 KBps to the above, and recalculate the fairness index.

8 In fair queuing, the value F_i was interpreted as a timestamp: the time when the ith packet would finish transmitting. Give an interpretation of F_i for weighted fair queuing, and also give a formula for it in terms of F_{i-1}, arrival time A_i, packet size P_i, and weight w assigned to the flow.

9 Give an example of how nonpreemption in the implementation of fair queuing leads to a different packet transmission order from bit-by-bit round-robin service.

10 Suppose a router has three input flows and one output. It receives the packets listed in Table 6.2 all at about the same time, in the order listed, during a period in which the output port is busy but all queues are otherwise empty. Give the order in which the packets are transmitted, assuming

(a) fair queuing

Packet	Size	Flow
1	100	1
2	100	1
3	100	1
4	100	1
5	190	2
6	200	2
7	110	3
8	50	3

Table 6.2   Packets for Exercise 10.

(b) weighted fair queuing, with flow 2 having weight 2, and the other two with weight 1.

11 Suppose a router's drop policy is to drop the highest-cost packet whenever queues are full, where it defines the "cost" of a packet to be the product of its size by the time *remaining* that it will spend in the queue. (Note that in calculating cost it is equivalent to use the sum of the sizes of the earlier packets in lieu of remaining time.)

   (a) What advantages and disadvantages might such a policy offer, compared to tail drop?

   (b) Give an example of a sequence of queued packets for which dropping the highest-cost packet differs from dropping the largest packet.

   (c) Give an example where two packets exchange their relative cost ranks as time progresses.

12 Two users, one using Telnet and one sending files with FTP, both send their traffic out via router R. The outbound link from R is slow enough that both users keep packets in R's queue at all times. Discuss the relative performance seen by the Telnet user if R's queuing policy for these two flows is

   (a) round-robin service

   (b) fair queuing

   (c) modified fair queuing, where we count the cost only of data bytes, and not IP or TCP headers

Consider outbound traffic only. Assume Telnet packets have 1 byte of data, FTP packets have 512 bytes of data, and all packets have 40 bytes of headers.

13 Consider a router that is managing three flows, on which packets of constant size arrive at the following wall clock times:

> flow A: 1, 2, 4, 6, 7, 9, 10
> flow B: 2, 6, 8, 11, 12, 15
> flow C: 1, 2, 3, 5, 6, 7, 8

All three flows share the same outbound link, on which the router can transmit one packet per time unit. Assume that there is an infinite amount of buffer space.

(a) Suppose the router implements fair queuing. For each packet, give the wall clock time when it is transmitted by the router. Arrival time ties are to be resolved in order A, B, C. Note that wall clock time $T = 2$ is FQ-clock time $A_i = 1.5$.

(b) Suppose the router implements weighted fair queuing, where flows A and B are given an equal share of the capacity, and flow C is given twice the capacity of flow A. For each packet, give the wall clock time when it is transmitted.

14 Assume that TCP implements an extension that allows window sizes much larger than 64 KB. Suppose that you are using this extended TCP over a 1-Gbps link with a latency of 100 ms to transfer a 10-MB file, and the TCP receive window is 1 MB. If TCP sends 1-KB packets (assuming no congestion and no lost packets):

(a) How many RTTs does it take until slow start opens the send window to 1 MB?

(b) How many RTTs does it take to send the file?

(c) If the time to send the file is given by the number of required RTTs multiplied by the link latency, what is the effective throughput for the transfer? What percentage of the link bandwidth is utilized?

15 Consider a simple congestion-control algorithm that uses linear increase and multiplicative decrease but not slow start, that works in units of packets rather than bytes, and that starts each connection with a congestion window equal to one packet. Give a detailed sketch of this algorithm. Assume the delay is latency only, and that when a group of packets is sent, only a single ACK is returned. Plot the congestion window as a function of round-trip times for the situation in which the following packets are lost: 9, 25, 30, 38, and 50. For simplicity, assume a perfect timeout mechanism that detects a lost packet exactly 1 RTT after it is transmitted.

16 For the situation given in the previous problem, compute the effective throughput achieved by this connection. Assume that each packet holds 1 KB of data and that the RTT = 100 ms.

17 During linear increase, TCP computes an increment to the congestion window as

$$\text{Increment} = \text{MSS} \times (\text{MSS}/\text{CongestionWindow})$$

Explain why computing this increment each time an ACK arrives may not result in the correct increment. Give a more precise definition for this increment. (Hint: A given ACK can acknowledge more or less than one MSS's worth of data.)

18 Under what circumstances may coarse-grained timeouts still occur in TCP even when the fast retransmit mechanism is being used?

19 Suppose we were to add host-based congestion control to BLAST/CHAN RPC. What form might this take? Would it be better to add it to BLAST, to CHAN, or to both jointly?

20 Suppose that between A and B there is a router R. The A–R bandwidth is infinite (that is, packets are not delayed), but the R–B link introduces a bandwidth delay of 1 packet per second (that is, 2 packets take 2 seconds, etc.). Acknowledgments from B to R, though, are sent instantaneously. A sends data to B over a TCP connection, using slow start but with an arbitrarily large window size. R has a queue size of one, in addition to the packet it is sending. At each second, the sender first processes any arriving ACKs and then responds to any timeouts.

(a) Assuming a fixed TimeOut period of 2 seconds, what is sent and received for T = 0, 1, . . . , 6 seconds? Is the link ever idle due to timeouts?

(b) What changes if TimeOut is 3 seconds instead?

21 Suppose A, R, and B are as in the previous exercise, except that R's queue now has a size of three packets, in addition to the one being transmitted. A starts a connection using slow start, with an infinite receive window. Fast retransmit is done on the *second* duplicate ACK (that is, the third ACK of the same packet); the TimeOut interval is infinite. Ignore fast recovery; when a packet is lost, let the window size be 1. Give a table showing, for the first 15 seconds, what A receives, what A sends, what R sends, R's queue, and what R drops.

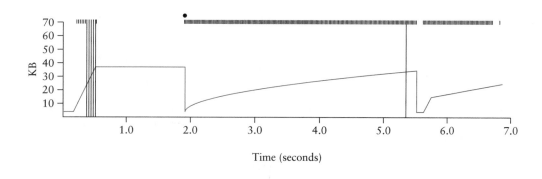

Figure 6.29 TCP trace for Exercise 25.

22 Suppose the R–B link in the previous exercise changes from a bandwidth delay to a propagation delay, so that two packets now take 1 second to send. List what is sent and received during the first 8 seconds. Assume a static timeout value of 2 seconds, that slow start is used on a timeout, and that ACKs sent at about the same time are consolidated. Note that R's queue size is now irrelevant (why?).

23 Suppose host A reaches host B via routers R1 and R2: A–R1–R2–B. Fast retransmit is not used, and A calculates TimeOut as $2 \times$ EstimatedRTT. Assume that the A–R1 and R2–B links have infinite bandwidth; the R1$\longrightarrow$R2 link, however, introduces a 1-second-per-packet bandwidth delay for data packets (though not ACKs). Describe a scenario in which the R1–R2 link is not 100% utilized, even though A always has data ready to send. Hint: Suppose A's CongestionWindow increases from N to $N + 1$, where N is R1's queue size.

24 You are an Internet service provider; your client hosts connect directly to your routers. You know some hosts are using experimental TCPs and suspect some may be using a "greedy" TCP with no congestion control. What measurements might you make at your router to establish that a client was not using slow start at all? If a client used slow start on startup but not after a timeout, could you detect that?

25 Consider the TCP trace in Figure 6.29. Identify time intervals representing slow start on startup, slow start after timeout, and linear-increase congestion avoidance. Explain what is going on from $T = 0.5$ to $T = 1.9$. The TCP version that generated this trace includes a feature absent from the TCP that generated Figure 6.11. What is this feature? This trace and the one in Figure 6.13 both lack a feature. What is it?

26 Suppose you are downloading a large file over a 3-KBps phone link. Your software displays an average-bytes-per-second counter. How will TCP congestion control and occasional packet losses cause this counter to fluctuate? Assume that only a third, say, of the total RTT is spent on the phone link.

27 Suppose TCP is used over a lossy link that loses on average one segment in four. Assume the bandwidth × delay window size is considerably larger than four segments.

(a) What happens when we start a connection? Do we ever get to the linear-increase phase of congestion avoidance?

(b) Without using an explicit feedback mechanism from the routers, would TCP have any way to distinguish such link losses from congestion losses, at least over the short term?

(c) Suppose TCP senders did reliably get explicit congestion indications from routers. Assuming links as above were common, would it be feasible to support window sizes much larger than four segments? What would TCP have to do?

28 Suppose two TCP connections share a path through a router R. The router's queue size is six segments; each connection has a stable congestion window of three segments. No congestion control is used by these connections. A third TCP connection now is attempted, also through R. The third connection does not use congestion control either. Describe a scenario in which, for at least a while, the third connection gets none of the available bandwidth, and the first two connections proceed with 50% each. Does it matter if the third connection uses slow start? How does full congestion avoidance on the part of the first two connections help solve this?

29 Suppose a TCP connection has a window size of eight segments, an RTT of 800 ms, the sender sends segments at a regular rate of one every 100 ms, and the receiver sends ACKs back at the same rate without delay. A segment is lost, and the loss is detected by the fast retransmit algorithm on the receipt of the third duplicate ACK. At the point when the ACK of the retransmitted segment finally arrives, how much total time has the sender lost (compared to lossless transmission) if

(a) the sender waits for the ACK from the retransmitted lost packet before sliding the window forward again?

(b) the sender uses the continued arrival of each duplicate ACK as an indication it may slide the window forward one segment?

30 The text states that additive increase is a necessary condition for a congestion-control mechanism to be stable. Outline a specific instability that might arise if all increases were exponential; that is, if TCP continued to use "slow" start after CongestionWindow increased beyond CongestionThreshold.

31 Discuss the relative advantages and disadvantages of marking a packet (as in the DECbit mechanism) versus dropping a packet (as in RED gateways).

32 Consider a RED gateway with $MaxP = 0.02$, and with an average queue length halfway between the two thresholds.

(a) Find the drop probability P_{count} for $count = 1$ and $count = 50$.

(b) Calculate the probability that none of the first 50 packets are dropped. Note that this is $(1 - P_1) \times \cdots \times (1 - P_{50})$.

33 Explain the intuition behind setting $MaxThreshold = 2 \times MinThreshold$ in RED gateways.

34 In RED gateways, explain why MaxThreshold is actually less than the actual size of the available buffer pool.

35 Explain the fundamental conflict between tolerating burstiness and controlling network congestion.

36 Why do you think that the drop probability P of a RED gateway does *not* simply increase linearly from $P = 0$ at MinThresh to $P = 1$ at MaxThresh?

37 In TCP Vegas, the calculation of ActualRate is done by dividing the amount of data transmitted in one RTT interval by the length of the RTT.

(a) Show that for any TCP, if the window size remains constant, then the amount of data transmitted in one RTT interval is constant once a full windowful is sent. Assume that the sender transmits each segment instantly upon receiving an ACK, packets are not lost and are delivered in order, segments are all the same size, and the first link along the path is not the slowest.

(b) Give a timeline sketch showing that the amount of data per RTT above can be less than CongestionWindow.

38 Suppose a TCP Vegas connection measures the RTT of its first packet and sets BaseRTT to that, but then a network link failure occurs and all subsequent traffic is routed via an alternative path with twice the RTT. How will TCP Vegas respond?

What will happen to the value of CongestionWindow? Assume no actual timeouts occur, and that β is much smaller than the initial ExpectedRate.

39 Consider the following two causes of a 1-second network delay (assume ACKs return instantaneously):

- One intermediate router with a 1-second outbound per-packet bandwidth delay and no competing traffic
- One intermediate router with a 100-ms outbound per-packet bandwidth delay and with a steadily replenished (from another source) 10 packets in the queue

(a) How might a transport protocol in general distinguish between these two cases?

(b) Suppose TCP Vegas sends over the above connections, with an initial CongestionWindow of 3 packets. What will happen to CongestionWindow in each case? Assume BaseRTT = 1 second and β is 1 packet per second.

40 Give an argument why the congestion-control problem is better managed at the internet level than the ATM level, at least when only part of the internet is ATM. In an exclusively IP-over-ATM network, is congestion better managed at the cell level or at the TCP level? Why?

41 Sketch how an ATM switch would implement partial packet discard and early packet discard. Is either mechanism appreciably simpler?

42 Consider the taxonomy of Figure 6.23.

(a) Give an example of a real-time application that is *intolerant/rate adaptive*.

(b) Explain why you might expect a loss tolerant application to be at least somewhat rate adaptive.

(c) Part (b) notwithstanding, give an example of an application that might be considered *tolerant/nonadaptive*. Hint: Tolerating even small losses qualifies an application as loss tolerant; you will need to interpret rate adaptive as the ability to adjust to *substantial* bandwidth changes.

43 The transmission schedule (Table 6.3) for a given flow lists for each second the number of packets sent between that time and the following second. The flow must stay within the bounds of a token bucket filter. What bucket depth does the flow need for the following token rates? Assume the bucket is initially full.

Time (seconds)	Packets Sent
0	5
1	5
2	1
3	0
4	6
5	1

Table 6.3 **Transmission schedule for Exercise 43.**

r	B
1	10
2	4
4	1

Table 6.4 **TSpecs for Exercise 44.**

    (a) 2 packets per second

    (b) 4 packets per second

44 Suppose a router has accepted flows with the TSpecs shown in Table 6.4, described in terms of token bucket filters with token rate r packets per second and bucket depth B packets. All flows are in the same direction, and the router can forward one packet every 0.1 second.

    (a) What is the maximum delay a packet might face?

    (b) What is the minimum number of packets from the third flow that the router would send over 2.0 seconds, assuming the flow sent packets at its maximum rate uniformly?

45 Suppose an RSVP router suddenly loses its reservation state, but otherwise remains running.

    (a) What will happen to the existing reserved flows if the router handles reserved and nonreserved flows via a single FIFO queue?

(b) What might happen to the existing reserved flows if the router used weighted fair queuing to segregate reserved and nonreserved traffic?

(c) Eventually the receivers on these flows will request that their reservations be renewed. Give a scenario in which these requests are denied.

46 Consider the ATM ABR virtual circuit in Figure 6.27, segmented into two control loops at switch S2.

(a) Suppose resource manager cell RM_1 departs from S2 to H1 reporting a high available rate, but right afterwards an RM cell arrives at S2 from H2 reporting a low available rate for the second half of the circuit. What problem might S2 now face?

(b) When S2 receives RM_1 from H1, it might simply hold it while it sends its own RM_2 to H2 and back. When RM_2 returns, S2 would now send back RM_1, reducing its rate specification if necessary. Why might such a strategy be undesirable? Hint: Recall the purpose of segmentation into smaller control loops.

The following exercises require the use of a network simulator. Possiblilities include the x-kernel simulator and the ns simulator. Further information about both of these can be found on this book's Web page at http://www.mkp.com.

47 Use a network simulator to measure the effect of changing TCP's additive increase/multiplicative decrease mechanism. For example, you might try changing the rate at which the congestion window is increased or decreased (e.g., decreasing by 25% on loss, rather than 50%).

48 Use a simulator to measure the effectiveness of TCP congestion control when the routers implement queuing disciplines other than FIFO (e.g., fair queuing and RED).

49 Use a simulator to measure the effectiveness of TCP Reno versus TCP Vegas at maintaining throughput in the face of congestion.

50 Use a simulator to enact the scenario of Exercise 28, perhaps with larger window sizes.

From the network's perspective, application programs send messages to each other. Each of these messages is just an uninterpreted string of bytes. From the application's perspective, however, these messages contain various kinds of *data*—arrays of integers, video frames, lines of text, digital images, and so on. In other words, these bytes have meaning. We now consider the problem of how to best encode the different kinds of data that application programs want to exchange into byte strings. In many respects, this is similar to the problem of encoding byte strings into electromagnetic signals that we saw in Section 2.2.

Thinking back to our discussion of encoding in Chapter 2, there were essentially two concerns. The first was that the receiver be able to extract the same message from the signal as the transmitter sent; this was the framing problem. The second was making the encoding as efficient as possible. Both of these concerns are present when encoding application data into network messages.

In the case of the sender and receiver seeing the same data, the issue is one of the two sides agreeing to a message format, often called the *presentation format*. If the sender wants to send the receiver an array of integers, for example, then the two sides have to agree what each integer looks like (how big it is and whether the most significant bit comes first or last) and how many elements are in the array. Section 7.1 describes various encodings of traditional computer data, such as integers, floating-point numbers, character strings, arrays, and structures. Well-established formats also exist for multimedia data: Video, for example, is typically transmitted in Moving Picture Experts Group (MPEG) format, and still images are usually transmitted in Joint Photographic Experts Group (JPEG) format or Graphical Interchange Format (GIF). Because these formats are primarily noteworthy for the compression algorithms they use, we consider them in that context in Section 7.2.

It is a capital mistake to theorize before one has data.

—Sir Arthur Conan Doyle

The second main concern of this chapter, the efficiency of the encoding, has a rich history, dating back to Shannon's pioneer work on information theory in the 1940s. In effect, there are two opposing forces at work here. In one direction, you would like as much redundancy in the data as possible so that the receiver is able to extract the right data even if errors are introduced into the message. The error detection and correcting codes we saw in Section 2.4 add redundant information to messages for exactly this purpose. In the other direction, we would like to remove as much redundancy from the data as possible so that we may encode it in as few bits as possible. This is the goal of *data compression*, which we discuss in Section 7.2.

Compression is important to the designers of networks for a wealth of reasons, not just because we rarely find ourselves with an abundance of bandwidth everywhere in the network. For example, the way we design a compression algorithm affects our sensitivity to lost or delayed data, and thus may influence the design of resource allocation mechanisms and end-to-end protocols. Conversely, if the underlying network is unable to guarantee a fixed amount of bandwidth for the duration of a videoconference, we may choose to design compression algorithms that can adapt to changing network conditions.

An important aspect of both presentation formatting and data compression is that they require the sending and receiving hosts to process every byte of data in the message. It is for this reason that presentation formatting and compression are sometimes called *data manipulation* functions. This is in contrast to most of the protocols we have seen up to this point, which process a message without ever looking at its contents. Because of this need to read, compute on, and write every byte of data in a message, data manipulations affect end-to-end throughput over the network. In fact, these manipulations can be the limiting factor.

7

End-to-End Data

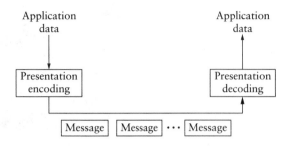

Figure 7.1 Presentation formatting involves encoding and decoding application data.

7.1 Presentation Formatting

One of the most common transformations of network data is from the representation used by the application program into a form that is suitable for transmission over a network and vice versa. This transformation is typically called *presentation formatting*. As illustrated in Figure 7.1, the sending program translates the data it wants to transmit from the representation it uses internally into a message that can be transmitted over the network; that is, the data is *encoded* in a message. On the receiving side, the application translates this arriving message into a representation that it can then process; that is, the message is *decoded*. Encoding is sometimes called *argument marshalling*, and decoding is sometimes called *unmarshalling*. This terminology comes from the RPC world, where the client thinks it is invoking a procedure with a set of arguments, but these arguments are then "brought together and ordered in an appropriate and effective way"[1] to form a network message.

You might ask what makes this problem challenging enough to warrant a name like marshalling. One reason is that computers represent data in different ways. For example, some computers represent floating-point numbers in IEEE standard 754 format, while other machines still use their own nonstandard format. Even for something as simple as integers, different architectures use different sizes (e.g., 16-bit, 32-bit, 64-bit). To make matters worse, on some machines integers are represented in *big-endian* form (the most significant bit of a word is in the byte with the highest address), while on other machines integers are represented in *little-endian* form (the most significant bit is in the byte with the lowest address). The Motorola 680x0 is an example of a big-endian architecture, and the Intel 80x86 is an example of a little-endian architecture. For example, the big-endian and little-endian representations of the integer 34,677,374 are given in Figure 7.2.

---

[1] This is a definition of *marshalling* taken from *Webster's New Collegiate Dictionary.*

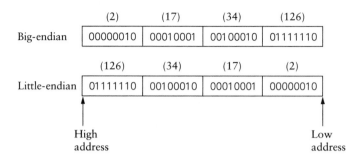

Figure 7.2 Big-endian and little-endian byte order for the integer 34,677,374.

Another reason that marshalling is difficult is that application programs are written in different languages, and even when you are using a single language, there may be more than one compiler. For example, compilers have a fair amount of latitude in how they lay out structures (records) in memory, such as how much padding they put between the fields that make up the structure. Thus, you could not simply transmit a structure from one machine to another, even if both machines were of the same architecture and the program was written in the same language, because the compiler on the destination machine might align the fields in the structure differently.

7.1.1 Taxonomy

Although anyone who has worked on argument marshalling would tell you that no rocket science is involved—it is a small matter of bit twiddling—there are a surprising number of design choices that you must address. We begin by giving a simple taxonomy for argument marshalling systems. The following is by no means the only viable taxonomy, but it is sufficient to cover most of the interesting alternatives.

Data Types

The first question is what data types the system is going to support. In general, we can classify the types supported by an argument marshalling mechanism at three levels. Each level complicates the task faced by the marshalling system.

At the lowest level, a marshalling system operates on some set of *base types*. Typically, the base types include integers, floating-point numbers, and characters. The system might also support ordinal types and booleans. As described above, the implication of the set of base types is that the encoding process must be able to convert each base type from one representation to another, for example, convert an integer from big-endian to little-endian.

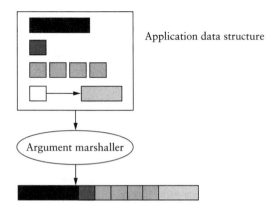

Figure 7.3 Argument marshalling: converting, packing, and linearizing.

At the next level are *flat types*—structures and arrays. While flat types might at first not appear to complicate argument marshalling, the reality is that they do. The problem is that the compilers used to compile application programs sometimes insert padding between the fields that make up the structure so as to align these fields on word boundaries. The marshalling system typically *packs* structures so that they contain no padding.

At the highest level, the marshalling system might have to deal with *complex types*—those types that are built using pointers. That is, the data structure that one program wants to send to another might not be contained in a single structure, but might instead involve pointers from one structure to another. A tree is a good example of a complex type that involves pointers. Clearly, the data encoder must prepare the data structure for transmission over the network because pointers are implemented by memory addresses, and just because a structure lives at a certain memory address on one machine does not mean it will live at the same address on another machine. In other words, the marshalling system must *serialize* (flatten) complex data structures.

In summary, depending on how complicated the type system is, the task of argument marshalling usually involves converting the base types, packing the structures, and linearizing the complex data structures, all to form a contiguous message that can be transmitted over the network. Figure 7.3 illustrates this task.

Conversion Strategy

Once the type system is established, the next issue is what conversion strategy the argument marshaller will use. There are two general options: *canonical intermediate form* and *receiver-makes-right*. We consider each, in turn.

The idea of canonical intermediate form is to settle on an external representation for each type; the sending host translates from its internal representation to this external representation before sending data, and the receiver translates from this external representation into its local representation when receiving data. To illustrate the idea, consider integer data; other types are treated in a similar manner. You might declare that the big-endian format will be used as the external representation for integers. The sending host must translate each integer it sends into big-endian form, and the receiving host must translate big-endian integers into whatever representation it uses. (This is what is done in the Internet for protocol headers.) Of course, a given host might already use big-endian form, in which case no conversion is necessary.

The alternative, which is sometimes called receiver-makes-right, has the sender transmit data in its own internal format; the sender does not convert the base types, but usually has to pack and flatten more complex data structures. The receiver is then responsible for translating the data from the sender's format into its own local format. The problem with this strategy is that every host must be prepared to convert data from all other machine architectures. In networking, this is known as an *N-by-N solution*: each of *N* machine architectures must be able to handle all *N* architectures. In contrast, in a system that uses a canonical intermediate form, each host needs to know only how to convert between its own representation and a single other representation—the external one.

Using a common external format is clearly the correct thing to do, right? This has certainly been the conventional wisdom in the networking community for the past 20 years. The answer is not cut-and-dried, however. It turns out that there are not that many different representations for the various base classes, or said another way, *N* is not that large. In addition, the most common case is for two machines of the same type to be communicating with each other. In this situation, it seems silly to translate data from that architecture's representation into some foreign external representation, only to have to translate the data back into the same architecture's representation on the receiver.

A third option, although we know of no existing system that exploits it, is to use receiver-makes-right if the sender knows that the destination has the same architecture; the sender would use some canonical intermediate form if the two machines use different architectures. How would a sender learn the receiver's architecture? It could learn this information either from a name server or by first using a simple test case to see if the appropriate result occurs.

Tags

The third issue in argument marshalling is how the receiver knows what kind of data is contained in the message it receives. There are two common approaches: *tagged* and *untagged* data. The tagged approach is most intuitive, so we describe it first.

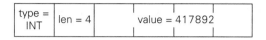

Figure 7.4   A 32-bit integer encoded in a tagged message.

A tag is any additional information included in a message—beyond the concrete representation of the base types—that helps the receiver decode the message. There are several possible tags that might be included in a message. For example, each data item might be augmented with a *type* tag. A type tag indicates that the value that follows is an integer, a floating-point number, or whatever. Another example is a *length* tag. Such a tag is used to indicate the number of elements in an array or the size of an integer. A third example is an *architecture* tag, which might be used in conjunction with the receiver-makes-right strategy to specify the architecture on which the data contained in the message was generated. Figure 7.4 depicts how a simple 32-bit integer might be encoded in a tagged message.

The alternative, of course, is not to use tags. How does the receiver know how to decode the data in this case? It knows because it was programmed to know. In other words, if you call a remote procedure that takes two integers and a floating-point number as arguments, then there is no reason for the remote procedure to inspect tags to know what it has just received. It simply assumes that the message contains two integers and a float, and decodes it accordingly. Note that while this works for most cases, the one place it breaks down is when sending variable-length arrays. In such a case, a length tag is commonly used to indicate how long the array is.

It is also worth noting that the untagged approach means that the presentation formatting is truly end to end. It is not possible for some intermediate agent to interpret the message unless the data is tagged. Why would an intermediate agent need to interpret a message, you might ask? Stranger things have happened, mostly resulting from ad hoc solutions to unexpected problems that the system was not engineered to handle. Poor network design is beyond the scope of this book.

Stubs

A stub is the piece of code that implements argument marshalling. Stubs are typically used to support RPC. On the client side, the stub marshalls the procedure arguments into a message that can be transmitted by means of the RPC protocol. On the server side, the stub converts the message back into a set of variables that can be used as arguments to call the remote procedure. Stubs can either be interpreted or compiled.

In a compilation-based approach, each procedure has a "customized" client and server stub. While it is possible to write stubs by hand, they are typically generated by

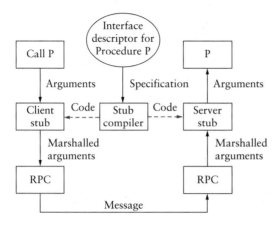

Figure 7.5 Stub compiler takes interface description as input and outputs client and server stubs.

a stub compiler, based on a description of the procedure's interface. This situation is illustrated in Figure 7.5. Since the stub is compiled, it is usually very efficient. In an interpretation-based approach, the system provides "generic" client and server stubs that have their parameters set by a description of the procedure's interface. Because it is easy to change this description, interpreted stubs have the advantage of being flexible. Compiled stubs are more common in practice.

7.1.2 Examples (XDR, ASN.1, NDR)

We now briefly describe three popular network data representations in terms of this taxonomy. We use the integer base type to illustrate how each system works.

XDR

External Data Representation (XDR) is the network format used with SunRPC. In the taxonomy just introduced, XDR

■ supports the entire C type system with the exception of function pointers

■ defines a canonical intermediate form

■ does not use tags (except to indicate array lengths)

■ uses compiled stubs

An XDR integer is a 32-bit data item that encodes a C integer. It is represented in twos complement notation, with the most significant byte of the C integer in the first byte of the XDR integer, and the least significant byte of the C integer in the fourth byte

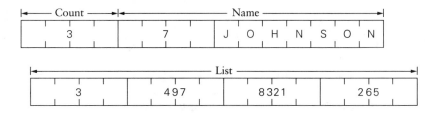

Figure 7.6 Example encoding of a structure in XDR.

of the XDR integer. That is, XDR uses big-endian format for integers. XDR supports both signed and unsigned integers, just as C does.

XDR represents variable-length arrays by first specifying an unsigned integer (4 bytes) that gives the number of elements in the array, followed by that many elements of the appropriate type. XDR encodes the components of a structure in the order of their declaration in the structure. For both arrays and structures, the size of each element/component is represented in a multiple of 4 bytes. Smaller data types are padded out to 4 bytes with 0s. The exception to this "pad to 4 bytes" rule is made for characters, which are encoded one per byte.

The following code fragment gives an example C structure (item) and the XDR routine that encodes/decodes this structure (xdr_item). Figure 7.6 schematically depicts XDR's on-the-wire representation of this structure when the field name is seven characters long and the array list has three values in it.

In this example, xdr_array, xdr_int, and xdr_string are three primitive functions provided by XDR to encode and decode arrays, integers, and character strings, respectively. Argument xdrs is a "context" variable that XDR uses to keep track of where it is in the message being processed; it includes a flag that indicates whether this routine is being used to encode or decode the message. In other words, routines like xdr_item are used on both the client and the server. Note that the application programmer can either write the routine xdr_item by hand or use a stub compiler called rpcgen (not shown) to generate this encoding/decoding routine. In the latter case, rpcgen takes the remote procedure that defines the data structure item as input, and outputs the corresponding stub.

```
#define MAXNAME 256;
#define MAXLIST 100;

struct item {
    int     count;
```

```
    char    name[MAXNAME];
    int     list[MAXLIST];
};

bool_t
xdr_item(XDR *xdrs, struct item *ptr)
{
    return(xdr_int(xdrs, &ptr->count) &&
        xdr_string(xdrs, &ptr->name, MAXNAME) &&
        xdr_array(xdrs, &ptr->list, &ptr->count, MAXLIST,
                sizeof(int), xdr_int));
}
```

Exactly how XDR performs depends, of course, on the complexity of the data. In a simple case of an array of integers, where each integer has to be converted from one byte order to another, an average of 2.75 instructions are required for each byte on an Alpha workstation, meaning that converting the whole array is a memory-bound operation. On a typical workstation-class machine, this means an upper limit on the order of 70 MBps (560 Mbps). More complex conversions that require more instructions per byte will obviously run slower.

ASN.1

Abstract Syntax Notation One (ASN.1) is an ISO standard that defines, among other things, a representation for data sent over a network. The representation-specific part of ASN.1 is called the Basic Encoding Rules (BER). ASN.1 supports the C type system without function pointers, defines a canonical intermediate form, and uses type tags. Its stubs can be either interpreted or compiled. One of the claims to fame of ASN.1 BER is that it is used by the Internet standard Simple Network Management Protocol (SNMP).

ASN.1 represents each data item with a triple of the form

⟨ tag, length, value ⟩

The tag is typically an 8-bit field, although ASN.1 allows for the definition of multibyte tags. The length field specifies how many bytes make up the value; we discuss length more below. Compound data types, such as structures, can be constructed by nesting primitive types, as illustrated in Figure 7.7.

If the value is 127 or fewer bytes long, then the length is specified in a single byte. Thus, for example, a 32-bit integer is encoded as a 1-byte type, a 1-byte length, and the 4 bytes that encode the integer, as illustrated in Figure 7.8. The value itself, in the

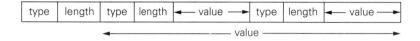

Figure 7.7 Compound types created by means of nesting in ASN.1/BER.

Figure 7.8 ASN.1/BER representation for a 4-byte integer.

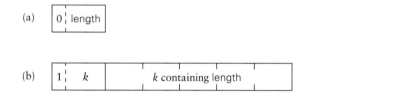

Figure 7.9 ASN.1/BER representation for length: (a) 1 byte; (b) multibyte.

case of an integer, is represented in twos complement notation and big-endian form,
just as in XDR. Keep in mind that even though the value of the integer is represented
in exactly the same way in both XDR and ASN.1, the XDR representation has neither
the type nor the length tags associated with that integer. These two tags both take up
space in the message and, more importantly, require processing during marshalling
and unmarshalling. This is one reason that ASN.1 is not as efficient as XDR. Another
is that the very fact that each data value is preceded by a length field means that the
data value is unlikely to fall on a natural byte boundary (e.g., an integer beginning on
a word boundary). This complicates the encoding/decoding process.

If the value is 128 or more bytes long, then multiple bytes are used to specify
its length. At this point you may be asking why a byte can specify a length of up to
127 bytes rather than 256. The reason is that 1 bit of the length field is used to denote
how long the length field is. A 0 in the eighth bit indicates a 1-byte length field. To
specify a longer length, the eighth bit is set to 1, and the other 7 bits indicate how
many additional bytes make up the length. Figure 7.9 illustrates a simple 1-byte length
and a multibyte length.

0	4	8	16	24	31
IntegrRep	CharRep	FloatRep	Extension 1	Extension 2	

Figure 7.10 NDR's architecture tag.

NDR

Network Data Representation (NDR) is the data-encoding standard used in the Distributed Computing Environment (DCE). Unlike XDR and ASN.1, NDR uses receiver-makes-right. It does this by inserting an architecture tag at the front of each message; individual data items are untagged. NDR uses a compiler to generate stubs. This compiler takes a description of a program written in the Interface Definition Language (IDL) and generates the necessary stubs. IDL looks pretty much like C, and so essentially supports the C type system.

Figure 7.10 illustrates the 4-byte architecture definition tag that is included at the front of each NDR-encoded message. The first byte contains two 4-bit fields. The first field, IntegrRep, defines the format for all integers contained in the message. A 0 in this field indicates big-endian integers, and a 1 indicates little-endian integers. The CharRep field indicates what character format is used: 0 means ASCII (American Standard Code for Information Interchange) and 1 means EBCDIC (an older, IBM-defined alternative to ASCII). Next, the FloatRep byte defines which floating-point representation is being used: 0 means IEEE 754, 1 means VAX, 2 means Cray, and 3 means IBM. The final 2 bytes are reserved for future use. Note that in simple cases, such as arrays of integers, NDR does the same amount of work as XDR, and so it is able to achieve the same performance.

7.2 Data Compression

Sometimes application programs need to send more data in a timely fashion than the bandwidth of the network supports. For example, a video application might have a 10-Mbps video stream that it wants to transmit, but it has only a 1-Mbps network available to it. As anyone who has used the Internet knows, it is rare that you can move data between two points in the Internet at anything close to 1 Mbps. Furthermore, the resource allocation model of the Internet at the time of writing depends heavily on the fact that individual applications do not use much more than their "fair share" of the bandwidth on a congested link. For all these reasons, it is often important to first *compress* the data at the sender, then transmit it over the network, and finally to *decompress* it at the receiver.

In many ways, compression is inseparable from data encoding. That is, in thinking about how to encode a piece of data in a set of bits, we might just as well think about how to encode the data in the smallest set of bits possible. For example, if you have a block of data that is made up of the 26 symbols A through Z, and if all of these symbols have an equal chance of occurring in the data block you are encoding, then encoding each symbol in 5 bits is the best you can do (since $2^5 = 32$ is the lowest power of 2 above 26). If, however, the symbol R occurs 50% of the time, then it would be a good idea to use fewer bits to encode the R than any of the other symbols. In general, if you know the relative probability that each symbol will occur in the data, then you can assign a different number of bits to each possible symbol in a way that minimizes the number of bits it takes to encode a given block of data. This is the essential idea of *Huffman codes*, one of the important early developments in data compression.

There are two classes of compression algorithms. The first, called *lossless compression*, ensures that the data recovered from the compression/decompression process is exactly the same as the original data. A lossless compression algorithm is used to compress file data, such as executable code, text files, and numeric data, because programs that process such file data cannot tolerate mistakes in the data. In contrast, *lossy compression* does not promise that the data received is exactly the same as the data sent. This is because a lossy algorithm removes information that it cannot later restore. Hopefully, however, the lost information will not be missed by the receiver. Lossy algorithms are used to compress still images, video, and audio. This makes sense because such data often contains more information than the human eye or ear can perceive, and for that matter, may already contain errors and imperfections that the human brain is able to compensate for. Also, lossy algorithms typically achieve much better compression ratios than do their lossless counterparts; they can be as much as an order of magnitude better.

It might seem that compressing your data before sending it would always be a good idea, since the network would be able to deliver compressed data in less time than uncompressed data. This is not necessarily the case, however. Compression/decompression algorithms often involve time-consuming computations. The question you have to ask is whether or not the time it takes to compress/ decompress the data is worthwhile given such factors as the host's processor speed and the network bandwidth. Specifically, if B_c is the average bandwidth at which data can be pushed through the compressor and decompressor (in series), B_n is the network bandwidth (including network processing costs) for uncompressed data, r is the average compression ratio, and if we assume that all the data is compressed before any of it is transmitted, then the time taken to send x bytes of uncompressed data is

$$x/B_n$$

whereas the time to compress it and send the compressed data is

$$x/B_c + x/(r B_n)$$

Thus, compression is beneficial if

$$x/B_c + x/(r B_n) < x/B_n$$

which is equivalent to

$$B_c > r/(r-1) \times B_n$$

For example, for a compression ratio of 2, B_c would have to be greater than $2 \times B_n$ for compression to make sense.

For many compression algorithms, we may not need to compress the *whole* data set before beginning transmission (videoconferencing would be impossible if we did) but rather we need to collect some amount of data (perhaps a few frames of video) first. The amount of data needed to "fill the pipe" in this case would be used as the value of x in the above equation.

Of course, when talking about lossy compression algorithms, processing resources are not the only factor. Depending on the exact application, users are willing to make very different trade-offs between bandwidth (or delay) and extent of information loss due to compression. For example, a radiologist reading a mammogram is unlikely to tolerate any significant loss of image quality and might well tolerate a delay of several hours in retrieving an image over a network. By contrast, it has become quite clear that many people will tolerate questionable audio quality in exchange for free global telephone calls (not to mention the ability to talk on the phone while driving).

7.2.1 Lossless Compression Algorithms

We begin by introducing three lossless compression algorithms. We do not describe these algorithms in much detail—we just give the essential idea—since it is the lossy algorithms used to compress image and video data that are of the greatest utility in today's network environment. We do comment, though, on how well these lossless algorithms work on digital imagery. Some of the ideas exploited by these lossless techniques show up again in later sections when we consider the lossy algorithms that are used to compress images.

Run Length Encoding

Run length encoding (RLE) is a compression technique with a brute-force simplicity. The idea is to replace consecutive occurrences of a given symbol with only one copy of the symbol, plus a count of how many times that symbol occurs—hence the name "run length." For example, the string AAABBCDDDD would be encoded as 3A2B1C4D.

RLE can be used to compress digital imagery by comparing adjacent pixel values and then encoding only the changes. For images that have large homogeneous regions, this technique is quite effective. For example, it is not uncommon that RLE can achieve compression ratios on the order of 8-to-1 for scanned text images. RLE works well on such files because they often contain a large amount of white space that can be removed. In fact, RLE is the key compression algorithm used to transmit faxes. However, for images with even a small degree of local variation, it is not uncommon for compression to actually increase the image byte size, since it takes 2 bytes to represent a single symbol when that symbol is not repeated.

Differential Pulse Code Modulation

Another simple lossless compression algorithm is Differential Pulse Code Modulation (DPCM). The idea here is to first output a reference symbol and then, for each symbol in the data, to output the difference between that symbol and the reference symbol. For example, using symbol A as the reference symbol, the string AAABBCDDDD would be encoded as A0001123333 since A is the same as the reference symbol, B has a difference of 1 from the reference symbol, and so on. Note that this simple example does not illustrate the real benefit of DPCM, which is that when the differences are small, they can be encoded with fewer bits than the symbol itself. In this example, the range of differences 0–3 can be represented with 2 bits each, rather than the 7 or 8 bits required by the full character. As soon as the difference becomes too large, a new reference symbol is selected.

DPCM works better than RLE for most digital imagery, since it takes advantage of the fact that adjacent pixels are usually similar. Due to this correlation, the dynamic range of the differences between the adjacent pixel values can be significantly less than the dynamic range of the original image, and this range can therefore be represented using fewer bits. Using DPCM, we have measured compression ratios of 1.5-to-1 on digital images.

A slightly different approach, called *delta encoding*, simply encodes a symbol as the difference from the previous one. Thus, for example, AAABBCDDDD would be represented as A001011000. Note that delta encoding is likely to work well for encoding images where adjacent pixels are similar. It is also possible to perform RLE after delta encoding, since we might find long strings of 0s if there are many similar symbols next to each other.

Dictionary-Based Methods

The final lossless compression method we consider is the dictionary-based approach, of which the Lempel-Ziv (LZ) compression algorithm is the best known. The Unix compress command uses a variation of the LZ algorithm.

The idea of a dictionary-based compression algorithm is to build a dictionary (table) of variable-length strings (think of them as common phrases) that you expect to find in the data, and then to replace each of these strings when it appears in the data with the corresponding index to the dictionary. For example, instead of working with individual characters in text data, you could treat each word as a string and output the index in the dictionary for that word. To further elaborate on this example, the word "compression" has the index 4978 in one particular dictionary; it is the 4978th word in /usr/share/dict/words. To compress a body of text, each time the string "compression" appears, it would be replaced by 4978. Since this particular dictionary has just over 25,000 words in it, it would take 15 bits to encode the index, meaning that the string "compression" could be represented in 15 bits rather than the 77 bits required by 7-bit ASCII. This is a compression ratio of 5-to-1!

Of course, this leaves the question of where the dictionary comes from. One option is to define a static dictionary, preferably one that is tailored for the data being compressed. A more general solution, and the one used by LZ compression, is to adaptively define the dictionary based on the contents of the data being compressed. In this case, however, the dictionary constructed during compression has to be sent along with the data so that the decompression half of the algorithm can do its job. Exactly how you build an adaptive dictionary has been a subject of extensive research; we discuss important papers on the subject at the end of this chapter.

A variation of the LZ algorithm is used to compress digital images in the Graphical Interchange Format (GIF). Before doing that, GIF first reduces 24-bit color images to 8-bit color images. This is done by identifying the colors used in the picture, of which there will typically be considerably fewer than 2^{24}, and then picking the 256 colors that most closely approximate the colors used in the picture. These colors are stored in a table, which can be indexed with an 8-bit number, and the value for each pixel is replaced by the appropriate index. Note that this is an example of lossy compression for any picture with more than 256 colors. GIF then runs an LZ variant over the result, treating common sequences of pixels as the strings that make up the dictionary. Using this approach, GIF is sometimes able to achieve compression ratios on the order of 10-to-1, but only when the image consists of a relatively small number of discrete colors. Images of natural scenes, which often include a more continuous spectrum of colors, cannot be compressed at this ratio using GIF. As another data point, we were able to get a 2-to-1 compression ratio when we applied the LZ-based Unix compress command to the source code for the protocols described in this book.

7.2.2 Image Compression (JPEG)

Given the increase in the use of digital imagery in the past few years—this use was spawned by the invention of graphical displays, not high-speed networks—the need

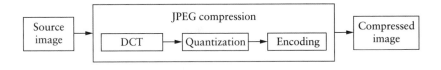

Figure 7.11 Block diagram of JPEG compression.

for compression algorithms designed for digital imagery data has grown more and more critical. In response to this need, the ISO has defined a digital image format known as JPEG, named after the Joint Photographic Experts Group that designed it. (The "Joint" in JPEG stands for a joint ISO/ITU effort.) This section describes the compression algorithm at the heart of JPEG. The next section then describes a related format—MPEG—that is used for video data.

Before describing JPEG compression, one point that needs to be made is that JPEG, GIF, and MPEG are more than just compression algorithms. They also define the *format* for image or video data, much the same way that XDR, NDR, and ASN.1 define the format for numeric and string data. However, this section concentrates on the compression aspects of these standards.

JPEG compression takes place in three phases, as illustrated in Figure 7.11. On the compression side, the image is fed through these three phases one 8×8 block at a time. The first phase applies the discrete cosine transform (DCT) to the block. If you think of the image as a signal in the spatial domain, then DCT transforms this signal into an equivalent signal in the *spatial frequency* domain. This is a lossless operation but a necessary precursor to the next, lossy step. After the DCT, the second phase applies a quantization to the resulting signal and, in so doing, loses the least significant information contained in that signal. The third phase encodes the final result, but in so doing, adds an element of lossless compression to the lossy compression achieved by the first two phases. Decompression follows these same three phases, but in reverse order.

The following discussion describes each phase in more detail. It is simplified by considering only grayscale images; color images are discussed at the end of this section. In the case of grayscale images, each pixel in the image is given by an 8-bit value that indicates the brightness of the pixel, where 0 equals white and 255 equals black.

DCT Phase

DCT is a transformation closely related to the fast Fourier transform (FFT). It takes an 8×8 matrix of pixel values as input and outputs an 8×8 matrix of frequency coefficients. You can think of the input matrix as a 64-point signal that is defined in two spatial dimensions (x and y); DCT breaks this signal into 64 spatial frequencies.

To get an intuitive feel for spatial frequency, imagine yourself moving across a picture in, say, the x direction. You would see the value of each pixel varying as some function of x. If this value changes slowly with increasing x, then it has a low spatial frequency, and if it changes rapidly, it has a high spatial frequency. So the low frequencies correspond to the gross features of the picture, while the high frequencies correspond to fine detail. The idea behind the DCT is to separate the gross features, which are essential to viewing the image, from the fine detail, which is less essential and, in some cases, might be barely perceived by the eye.

DCT, along with its inverse, which is performed during decompression, is defined by the following formulas:

$$DCT(i, j) = \frac{1}{\sqrt{2N}} C(i)C(j) \sum_{x=0}^{N-1} \sum_{y=0}^{N-1} pixel(x, y) \cos\left[\frac{(2x+1)i\pi}{2N}\right] \cos\left[\frac{(2y+1)j\pi}{2N}\right]$$

$$pixel(x, y) = \frac{1}{\sqrt{2N}} \sum_{i=0}^{N-1} \sum_{j=0}^{N-1} C(i)C(j)DCT(i, j) \cos\left[\frac{(2x+1)i\pi}{2N}\right] \cos\left[\frac{(2y+1)j\pi}{2N}\right]$$

$$C(x) = \begin{cases} \frac{1}{\sqrt{2}} & \text{if } x = 0 \\ 1 & \text{if } x > 0 \end{cases}$$

where $pixel(x, y)$ is the grayscale value of the pixel at position (x, y) in the 8×8 block being compressed; $N = 8$ in this case.

The first frequency coefficient, at location $(0,0)$ in the output matrix, is called the *DC coefficient*. Intuitively, we can see that the DC coefficient is a measure of the average value of the 64 input pixels. The other 63 elements of the output matrix are called the *AC coefficients*. They add the higher-spatial-frequency information to this average value. Thus, as you go from the first frequency coefficient toward the 64th frequency coefficient, you are moving from low-frequency information to high-frequency information, from the broad strokes of the image to finer and finer detail. These higher-frequency coefficients are increasingly unimportant to the perceived quality of the image. It is the second phase of JPEG that decides which portion of which coefficients to throw away.

Quantization Phase

The second phase of JPEG is where the compression becomes lossy. DCT does not itself lose information; it just transforms the image into a form that makes it easier to know what information to remove. (Although not lossy, per se, there is of course some loss of precision during the DCT phase because of the use of fixed-point arithmetic.)

Quantization is easy to understand—it's simply a matter of dropping the insignificant bits of the frequency coefficients.

To see how the quantization phase works, imagine that you want to compress some whole numbers less than 100, for example, 45, 98, 23, 66, and 7. If you decided that knowing these numbers truncated to the nearest multiple of 10 is sufficient for your purposes, then you could divide each number by the quantum 10 using integer arithmetic, yielding 4, 9, 2, 6, and 0. These numbers can each be encoded in 4 bits rather than the 7 bits needed to encode the original numbers.

Rather than using the same quantum for all 64 coefficients, JPEG uses a quantization table that gives the quantum to use for each of the coefficients, as specified in the formula given below. You can think of this table (Quantum) as a parameter that can be set to control how much information is lost and, correspondingly, how much compression is achieved. In practice, the JPEG standard specifies a set of quantization tables that have proven effective in compressing digital images; an example quantization table is given in Table 7.1. In tables like this one, the low coefficients have a quantum close to 1 (meaning that little low-frequency information is lost) and the high coefficients have larger values (meaning that more high-frequency information is lost). Notice that as a result of such quantization tables, many of the high-frequency coefficients end up being set to 0 after quantization, making them ripe for further compression in the third phase.

The basic quantization equation is

$$\mathsf{QuantizedValue}(i, j) = \mathsf{IntegerRound}(DCT(i, j)/\mathsf{Quantum}(i, j))$$

where

$$\mathsf{IntegerRound}(x) = \begin{cases} \lfloor x + 0.5 \rfloor & \text{if } x \geq 0 \\ \lfloor x - 0.5 \rfloor & \text{if } x < 0 \end{cases}$$

Decompression is then simply defined as

$$DCT(i, j) = \mathsf{QuantizedValue}(i, j) \times \mathsf{Quantum}(i, j)$$

For example, if the DC coefficient (i.e., DCT(0,0)) for a particular block was equal to 25, then the quantization of this value using Table 7.1 would result in

$$\lfloor 25/3 + 0.5 \rfloor = 8$$

During decompression, this coefficient would then be restored as

$$8 \times 3 = 24$$

$$
\text{Quantum} =
\begin{bmatrix}
3 & 5 & 7 & 9 & 11 & 13 & 15 & 17 \\
5 & 7 & 9 & 11 & 13 & 15 & 17 & 19 \\
7 & 9 & 11 & 13 & 15 & 17 & 19 & 21 \\
9 & 11 & 13 & 15 & 17 & 19 & 21 & 23 \\
11 & 13 & 15 & 17 & 19 & 21 & 23 & 25 \\
13 & 15 & 17 & 19 & 21 & 23 & 25 & 27 \\
15 & 17 & 19 & 21 & 23 & 25 & 27 & 29 \\
17 & 19 & 21 & 23 & 25 & 27 & 29 & 31
\end{bmatrix}
$$

Table 7.1   Example JPEG quantization table.

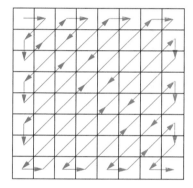

Figure 7.12   Zigzag traversal of quantized frequency coefficients.

Encoding Phase

The final phase of JPEG encodes the quantized frequency coefficients in a compact form. This results in additional compression, but this compression is lossless. Starting with the DC coefficient in position (0,0), the coefficients are processed in the zigzag sequence shown in Figure 7.12. Along this zigzag, a form of run length encoding is used—RLE is applied to only the 0 coefficients, which is significant because many of the later coefficients are 0. The individual coefficient values are then encoded using a Huffman code. (The JPEG standard allows the implementer to use an arithmetic coding instead of the Huffman code.)

In addition, because the DC coefficient contains a large percentage of the information about the 8 × 8 block from the source image, and images typically change slowly from block to block, each DC coefficient is encoded as the difference from the previous DC coefficient. This is the delta encoding approach described in Section 7.2.1.

Color Images

The preceding discussion assumed that each pixel was given by a single grayscale value. In the case of a color image, there are many different representations for each pixel to choose from. One representation, called RGB, represents each pixel with three color components: red, green, and blue. RGB is the representation of color typically supported by graphical input and output devices. Another representation, called YUV, also has three components: one luminance (Y) and two chrominance (U and V). Just like RGB, YUV is a three-dimensional coordinate system. However, compared to RGB, its coordinates are rotated to better match the human visual system. This is advantageous because the human visual system is not uniformly sensitive to colors. For example, we can distinguish the luminance (brightness) of a pixel much better than its hue (color).

Exactly why the three components in each of the two representations can be combined to produce acceptable color is an interesting question. The simple answer is that two-coordinate color systems have been defined, but they have proven inadequate for faithfully reproducing colors as perceived by humans. What is important to our discussion is that each pixel in a color image is given by three separate values. To compress such an image, each of these three components is processed independently in exactly the same way as the single grayscale value was processed. In other words, you can think of a color image as three separate images, where these separate images are overlaid on top of each other when displayed. Note that, in general, JPEG is not limited to three-component images; it is possible to compress a multispectral image using JPEG.

JPEG includes a number of variations that control how much compression you achieve versus the fidelity of the image. This can be done, for example, by using different quantization tables. These variations, plus the fact that different images have different characteristics, make it impossible to say with any precision the compression ratios that can be achieved with JPEG. The widely accepted generalization, however, is that JPEG is able to compress 24-bit color images by a ratio of roughly 30-to-1: The image can first be compressed by a factor of 3 by reducing the 24 bits of color to 8 bits of color (as described for GIF) and then by another factor of 10 by using the algorithm described in this section.

7.2.3 Video Compression (MPEG)

We now turn our attention to the MPEG format, named after the Moving Picture Experts Group that defined it. To a first approximation, a moving picture (i.e., video) is simply a succession of still images—also called *frames* or *pictures*—displayed at some video rate. Each of these frames can be compressed using the same DCT-based technique used in JPEG. Stopping at this point would be a mistake, however, because

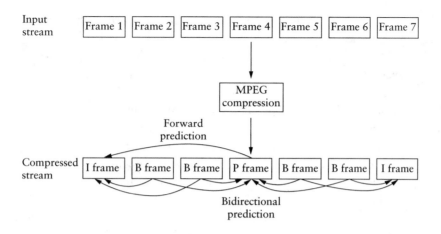

Figure 7.13 Sequence of I, P, and B frames generated by MPEG.

it fails to remove the interframe redundancy present in a video sequence. For example, two successive frames of video will contain almost identical information if there is not much motion in the scene, so it would be unnecessary to send the same information twice. Even when there is motion, there may be plenty of redundancy since a moving object may not change from one frame to the next; in some cases, only its position changes. MPEG takes this interframe redundancy into consideration. MPEG also defines a mechanism for encoding an audio signal with the video, but we consider only the video aspect of MPEG in this section.

Frame Types

MPEG takes a sequence of video frames as input and compresses them into three types of frames, called *I frames* (intrapicture), *P frames* (predicted picture), and *B frames* (bidirectional predicted picture). Each frame of input is compressed into one of these three frame types. I frames can be thought of as reference frames; they are self-contained, depending on neither earlier frames nor later frames. To a first approximation, an I frame is simply the JPEG compressed version of the corresponding frame in the video source. P and B frames are not self-contained; they specify relative differences from some reference frame. More specifically, a P frame specifies the differences from the previous I frame, while a B frame gives an interpolation between the previous and subsequent I or P frames.

Figure 7.13 illustrates a sequence of seven video frames that, after being compressed by MPEG, result in a sequence of I, P, and B frames. The two I frames stand alone; each can be decompressed at the receiver independently of any other frames.

The P frame depends on the preceding I frame; it can be decompressed at the receiver only if the preceding I frame also arrives. Each of the B frames depends on both the preceding I or P frame and the subsequent I or P frame. Both of these reference frames must arrive at the receiver before MPEG can decompress the B frame to reproduce the original video frame.

Note that because each B frame depends on a later frame in the sequence, the compressed frames are not transmitted in sequential order. Instead, the sequence I B B P B B I shown in Figure 7.13 is transmitted as I P B B I B B. Also, MPEG does not define the ratio of I frames to P and B frames; this ratio may vary depending on the required compression and picture quality. For example, it is permissible to transmit only I frames. This would be similar to using JPEG to compress the video.

In contrast to the preceding discussion of JPEG, the following focuses on the *decoding* of an MPEG stream. It is a little easier to describe, and it is the operation that is more often implemented in networking systems today, since MPEG coding is so expensive that it is normally done offline (i.e., not in real time). For example, in a video-on-demand system, the video would be encoded and stored on disk ahead of time. When a viewer wanted to watch the video, the MPEG stream would then be transmitted to the viewer's machine, which would decode and display the stream in real time.

Let's look more closely at the three frame types. As mentioned above, I frames are approximately equal to the JPEG compressed version of the source frame. The main difference is that MPEG works in units of 16×16 *macroblocks*. For a color video represented in YUV, the U and V components in each macroblock are "down sampled" into an 8×8 block. That is, each 2×2 subblock in the macroblock is given by one U value and one V value—the average of the four pixel values. The subblock still has four Y values. This can be done because the U and V components can be transmitted less accurately without visibly disturbing the image, since humans are less sensitive to color than they are to brightness. The relationship between a frame and the corresponding macroblocks is given in Figure 7.14.

The P and B frames are also processed in units of macroblocks. Intuitively, we can see that the information they carry for each macroblock captures the motion in the video; that is, it shows in what direction and how far the macroblock moved relative to the reference frame(s). The following describes how a B frame is used to reconstruct a frame during decompression; P frames are handled in a similar manner, except that they depend on only one reference frame instead of two.

Before getting to the details of how a B frame is decompressed, we first note that each macroblock in a B frame is not necessarily defined relative to both an earlier and a later frame, as suggested above, but may instead simply be specified relative to just one or the other. In fact, a given macroblock in a B frame can use the same

Color frame

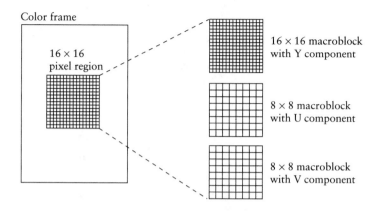

16 × 16 pixel region

16 × 16 macroblock with Y component

8 × 8 macroblock with U component

8 × 8 macroblock with V component

Figure 7.14 Each frame as a collection of macroblocks.

intracoding as is used in an I frame. This flexibility exists because if the motion picture is changing too rapidly, then it sometimes makes sense to give the intrapicture encoding rather than a forward- or backward-predicted encoding. Thus, each macroblock in a B frame includes a type field that indicates which encoding is used for that macroblock. In the following discussion, however, we consider only the general case in which the macroblock uses bidirectional predictive encoding.

In such a case, each macroblock in a B frame is represented with a 4-tuple: (1) a coordinate for the macroblock in the frame, (2) a motion vector relative to the previous reference frame, (3) a motion vector relative to the subsequent reference frame, and (4) a delta (δ) for each pixel in the macroblock (i.e., how much each pixel has changed relative to the two reference pixels). For each pixel in the macroblock, the first task is to find the corresponding reference pixel in the past and future reference frames. This is done using the two motion vectors associated with the macroblock. Then, the delta for the pixel is added to the average of these two reference pixels. Stated more precisely, if we let F_p and F_f denote the past and future reference frames, respectively, and the past/future motion vectors are given by (x_p, y_p) and (x_f, y_f), then the pixel at coordinate (x, y) in the current frame (denoted F_c) is computed as

$$F_c(x, y) = (F_p(x + x_p, y + y_p) + F_f(x + x_f, y + y_f))/2 + \delta(x, y)$$

where δ is the delta for the pixel as specified in the B frame. These deltas are encoded in the same way as pixels in I frames. That is, they are run through DCT and then quantized. Since the deltas are typically small, most of the DCT coefficients are 0 after quantization; hence they can be effectively compressed.

It should be fairly clear from the preceding discussion how encoding would be performed, with one exception. When generating a B or P frame during compression, MPEG must decide where to place the macroblocks. Recall that each macroblock in a P frame, for example, is defined relative to a macroblock in an I frame, but that the macroblock in the P frame need not be in the same part of the frame as the corresponding macroblock in the I frame—the difference in position is given by the motion vector. You would like to pick a motion vector that makes the macroblock in the P frame as similar as possible to the corresponding macroblock in the I frame, so that the deltas for that macroblock can be as small as possible. This means that you need to figure out where objects in the picture moved from one frame to the next. This is the problem of *motion estimation*, and several techniques (heuristics) for solving this problem are known. (We discuss papers that consider this problem at the end of this chapter.) The difficulty of this problem is one of the reasons that MPEG encoding takes longer than decoding on equivalent hardware. MPEG does not specify any particular technique; it only defines the format for encoding this information in B and P frames and the algorithm for reconstructing the pixel during decompression, as given above.

Effectiveness and Performance

MPEG typically achieves a compression ratio of 90-to-1, although ratios as high as 150-to-1 are not unheard of. In terms of the individual frame types, we can expect a compression ratio of approximately 30-to-1 for the I frames (this is consistent with the ratios achieved using JPEG when 24-bit color is first reduced to 8-bit color), while P and B frame compression ratios are typically three to five times smaller than the rates for the I frame. Without first reducing the 24 bits of color to 8 bits, the achievable compression with MPEG is typically between 30-to-1 and 50-to-1.

MPEG involves an expensive computation. On the compression side, it is typically done offline, which is not a problem for preparing movies for a video-on-demand service. Video can be compressed in real time using hardware today, but software implementations are quickly closing the gap. On the decompression side, low-cost MPEG video boards are available, but they do little more than YUV color lookup, which fortunately is the most expensive step. Most of the actual MPEG decoding is done in software. Until recently, processors have not been fast enough to keep pace with 30-frames-per-second video rates when decoding MPEG streams purely in software. With 400-MHz processor architectures available in 1999, however, it is possible to decompress MPEG fast enough to keep up with a 640×480 video stream running at 20 frames per second.

Other Video Encoding Standards

We conclude by noting that MPEG is not the only standard available for encoding video. For example, the ITU-T has also defined the "H series" for encoding real-time multimedia data. Generally, the H series includes standards for video, audio, control, and multiplexing (e.g., mixing audio, video, and data onto a single bit stream). Within the series, H.261 and H.263 are the first- and second-generation video encoding standards. Unlike MPEG, which is targeted at bit rates on the order of 1.5 Mbps, H.261 and H.263 are targeted at ISDN speeds. That is, they support video over links with bandwidth available in 64-Kbps increments. In principle, both H.261 and H.263 look a lot like MPEG: They use DCT, quantization, and interframe compression. The differences between H.261/H.263 and MPEG are in the details.

7.2.4 Transmitting MPEG over a Network

As suggested earlier in this chapter, MPEG not only defines how video is compressed, but it also specifies the format of an MPEG-compressed video. Similarly, JPEG and GIF define a format for still images. Focusing on MPEG, the first thing to keep in mind is that it defines the format of a video *stream*; it does not specify how this stream is broken into network packets. Thus, MPEG can be used for videos stored on disk, as well as videos transmitted over a stream-oriented network connection, like that provided by TCP. More on how you might packetize an MPEG stream in a moment.

The MPEG format is one of the most complicated of any protocols discussed in this book. This complication comes from a desire to give the encoding algorithm every possible degree of freedom in how it encodes a given video stream. It also comes from the evolution of the standard over time (i.e., MPEG-1 and MPEG-2). What we describe below is called the *main profile* of an MPEG-2 video stream. You can think of an MPEG profile as being analogous to a "version," except the profile is not explicitly specified in an MPEG header; the receiver has to deduce the profile from the combination of header fields it sees.

A main profile MPEG-2 stream has a nested structure, as illustrated in Figure 7.15. (Keep in mind that this figure hides a *lot* of messy details.) At the outermost level, the video contains a sequence of groups of pictures (GOP) separated by a SeqHdr. The sequence is terminated by a SeqEndCode (0xb7). The SeqHdr that precedes every GOP specifies—among other things—the size of each picture (frame) in the GOP (measured in both pixels and macroblocks), the interpicture period (measured in μs), and two quantization matrices for the macroblocks within this GOP: one for intracoded macroblocks (I blocks) and one for intercoded macroblocks (B and P blocks). Since this information is given for each GOP—rather than once for the entire video stream, as you might expect—it is possible to change the quantization table and frame rate at GOP boundaries throughout the video. This makes it possible to adapt the video stream over time, as we discuss below.

Each GOP is given by a GOPHdr, followed by the set of pictures that make up the GOP. The GOPHdr specifies the number of pictures in the GOP, as well as synchronization information for the GOP (i.e., when the GOP should play, relative

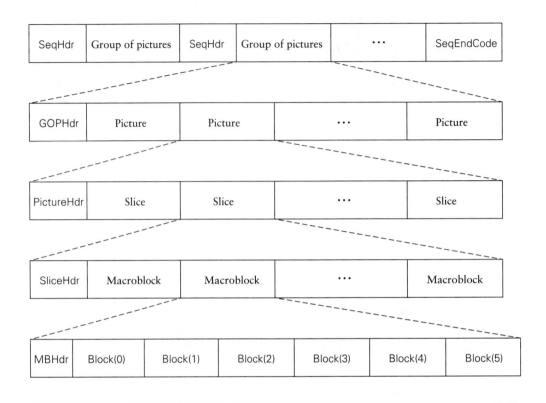

Figure 7.15 Format of an MPEG-compressed video stream.

to the beginning of the video). Each picture, in turn, is given by a PictureHdr and a set of *slices* that make up the picture. (A slice is a region of the picture, for example, one horizontal line.) The PictureHdr identifies the type of the picture (I, B, or P), as well as defines a picture-specific quantization table. The SliceHdr gives the vertical position of the slice, plus another opportunity to change the quantization table—this time by a constant scaling factor rather than by giving a whole new table. Next, the SliceHdr is followed by a sequence of macroblocks. Finally, each macroblock includes a header that specifies the block address within the picture, along with data for the six blocks within the macroblock: one for the U component, one for the V component, and four for the Y component. (Recall that the Y component is 16 × 16, while the U and V components are 8 × 8.)

It should be clear that one of the powers of the MPEG format is that it gives the encoder an opportunity to change the encoding over time. It can change the frame rate, the resolution, the mix of frame types that define a GOP, the quantization table, and the encoding used for individual macroblocks. As a consequence, it is possible to adapt

Adaptive Video Coding

We have already noted that video coding using MPEG allows a trade-off between the bandwidth consumed and the quality of the image. Conversely, it should be apparent that the output bandwidth of a video compression algorithm operating at a certain quality level will not, in general, be constant, but will vary over time depending on the amount of detail and movement in the video stream. These facts raise some interesting questions about how to design a system to transport compressed video over a packet network.

Suppose we have a video codec that outputs a compressed video stream at an average rate of R bps but occasionally bursts up to $3R$ bps. We could potentially transmit the video stream over a fixed bandwidth pipe (e.g., a leased line or CBR circuit) of capacity R, provided we passed the video stream through a "smoothing buffer" that smoothes out the instantaneous peaks in transmission rate. Now, it could happen at some point that the smoothing buffer would fill up beyond an acceptable level, perhaps due to a long action sequence in a movie causing a long period of high output from the codec. At this point, we could increase the

the rate at which a video is transmitted over a network by trading picture quality for network bandwidth. Exactly how a network protocol might exploit this adaptability is currently a subject of intense research (see sidebar).

Another interesting aspect of sending an MPEG stream over the network is exactly how the stream is broken into packets. If sent over a TCP connection, packetization is not an issue; TCP decides when it has enough bytes to send the next IP datagram. When using video interactively, however, it is rare to transmit it over TCP, since TCP's retransmission of lost segments could introduce unacceptable latency. If we are transmitting video using UDP, say, then it makes sense to break the stream at carefully selected points, for example, at macroblock boundaries. This is because we would like to confine the effects of a lost packet to a single macroblock, rather than damaging several macroblocks with a single loss. This is an example of Application Level Framing, which is discussed more fully in Section 9.3 where we consider video applications.

Packetizing the stream is only the first problem in sending MPEG-compressed video over a network. The next complication is dealing with packet loss. On the one hand, if a B frame is dropped by the network, then it is possible to simply replay the previous frame without seriously compromising the video; 1 frame out of 30 is no big deal. On the other hand, a lost I frame has serious consequences—none of the subsequent B and P frames can be processed without it. Thus, losing an I frame would result in losing multiple frames of the video. While you could retransmit the missing I frame, the resulting delay would probably not be acceptable in a real-time videoconference. One solution to this problem would be to use the Differentiated Services techniques described in Section 6.5.3 to mark the packets containing I frames with a lower drop probability than other packets.

One final observation is that how you choose to encode video depends on more than just the available network bandwidth. It also depends on the application's latency constraints. Once again, an interactive application like videoconferencing needs small latencies. The critical factor is the combination of I, P, and B frames in the GOP. Consider the following GOP:

I B B B B P B B B B I

The problem this GOP causes a videoconferencing application is that the sender has to delay the transmission of the four B frames until the P or I that follows them is available. This is because each B frame depends on the subsequent P or I frame. If the video is playing at 15 frames per second (i.e., one frame every 67 ms), this means the first B frame is delayed 4×67 ms, which is more than a quarter of a second. This delay is in addition to any propagation delay imposed by the network. A quarter of a second is far greater than the 100-ms threshold that humans are able to perceive. It is for this reason that many videoconference applications encode video using JPEG, which is often called motion-JPEG. (Motion-JPEG also addresses the problem of dropping a reference frame since all frames are able to

amount of compression for a while, thus reducing the data rate (and picture quality), and allowing the smoothing buffer to drain. When it gets close to empty, we could increase the coding quality again.

We could do pretty much the same thing over a packet-switched network, but without a smoothing buffer. Let's assume that we have some way to measure the amount of free capacity and level of congestion along a path, for example, by measuring the end-to-end loss rate. As the available bandwidth fluctuates, we can feed that information back to the codec so that it adjusts its coding parameters to back off during congestion and to send more aggressively (with a higher picture quality) when the network is idle. This is analogous to the behavior of TCP, except in the video case we are actually modifying the total amount of data sent rather than how long we take to send a fixed amount of data, since we don't want to introduce delay into a video application.

An interesting problem arises if we are *multicasting* a video stream to many receivers. How do we choose the correct rate for each receiver, since they may be experiencing wildly different levels of congestion? A cunning solution to this problem is to split the transmitted video into "layers." The first layer would have the basic level of detail needed to see some sort of useful picture, while each subsequent layer would add more detail, consisting of higher-frequency information. Each layer can then be sent to a different multicast group address, and each receiver can decide how many layers to join. If receiver A is experiencing heavy congestion, he might join only the multicast group carrying the base layer, while receiver B could join all the layers. Receiver A might periodically try to join the next layer of detail to see if more bandwidth has become available. This approach is known as receiver-driven layered multicast (RLM). An interesting research problem is how to create the right set of incentives to cause a receiver to join the appropriate number of groups rather than just joining all of them, since joining too many groups would cause unnecessary network congestion.

stand alone.) Notice, however, that an interframe encoding that depends upon only prior frames rather than later frames is not a problem. Thus, a GOP of

$$I\ P\ P\ P\ P\ I$$

would work just fine for interactive video-conferencing.

7.2.5 Audio Compression (MP3)

MPEG not only defines how video is compressed, but it also defines a standard for compressing audio. This standard can be used to compress the audio portion of a movie (in which case the MPEG standard defines how the compressed audio is interleaved with the compressed video in a single MPEG stream) or it can be used to compress stand-alone audio (for example, an audio CD).

To understand audio compression, we need to begin with the data. CD-quality audio, which is the de facto digital representation for high-quality audio, is sampled at a rate of 44.1 KHz (i.e., a sample is collected approximately once every 23 μs). Each sample is 16 bits, which means that a stereo (2-channel) audio stream results in a bit rate of

$$2 \times 44.1 \times 1000 \times 16 = 1.41 \text{ Mbps}$$

By comparison, telephone-quality voice is sampled at a rate of 8 KHz, with 8-bit samples, resulting in a bit rate of 64 Kbps, which is not coincidentally the speed of an ISDN link.

Coding	Bit Rates	Compression Factor
Layer I	384 Kbps	4
Layer II	192 Kbps	8
Layer III	128 Kbps	12

Table 7.2 MP3 compression rates.

Clearly, some amount of compression is going to be required to transmit CD-quality audio over, say, the 128-Kbps capacity of an ISDN data/voice line pair. To make matters worse, synchronization and error correction overhead require that 49 bits be used to encode each 16-bit sample, resulting in an actual bit rate of

$$49/16 \times 1.41 \text{ Mbps} = 4.32 \text{ Mbps}$$

MPEG addresses this need by defining three levels of compression, as enumerated in Table 7.2. Of these, Layer III, which is more widely known as MP3, is the most commonly used.

To achieve these compression ratios, MP3 uses techniques that are similar to those used by MPEG to compress video. First, it splits the audio stream into some number of frequency subbands, loosely analogous to the way MPEG processes the Y, U, and V components of a video stream separately. Second, each subband is broken into a sequence of blocks, which are similar to MPEG's macroblocks except they can vary in length from 64 to 1024 samples. (The encoding algorithm can vary the block size depending on certain distortion effects that are beyond our discussion.) Finally, each block is transformed using a modified DCT algorithm, quantized, and Huffman encoded, just as for MPEG video.

The trick to MP3 is how many subbands it elects to use, and how many bits it allocates to each subband, keeping in mind that it is trying to produce the highest-quality audio possible for the target bit rate. Exactly how this allocation is made is governed by psychoacoustic models that are beyond the scope of this book, but to illustrate the idea, consider that it makes sense to allocate more bits to low-frequency subbands when compressing a male voice and more bits to high-frequency subbands when compressing a female voice. Operationally, MP3 dynamically changes the quantization tables used for each subband to achieve the desired effect.

Once compressed, the subbands are packaged into fixed-size frames, and a header is attached. This header includes synchronization information, as well as the bit allocation information needed by the decoder to determine how many bits are used to encode each subband. As mentioned above, these audio frames can then be interleaved with video frames to form a complete MPEG stream. One interesting side note is that while it might work to drop B frames in the network should congestion occur, experience teaches us that it is not a good idea to drop audio frames since users are better able to tolerate bad video than bad audio.

7.3 Summary

This chapter has described how application data is encoded in network packets. Unlike the protocols described earlier in this book, which you can think of as processing *messages*, these transformations process *data*.

The first issue is presentation formatting, where the problem is formatting the different types of data that application programs compute on: integers, floating-point numbers, character strings, arrays, and structures. This involves both translating between machine and network byte order and linearizing compound data structures. We outlined the design space for presentation formatting and discussed three specific mechanisms that fall on different points in this design space: XDR, ASN.1, and NDR.

The second issue is compression, which is concerned with reducing the bandwidth required to transmit different types of data. Compression algorithms can be either lossless or lossy, with lossy algorithms being most appropriate for image and video data. JPEG, MPEG, and MP3 are examples of lossy compression protocols for still images, video, and audio data, respectively.

We've been discussing MPEG as though it were designed to compress video data so it can be transmitted over packet-switched networks. Of course this is not the case. MPEG is a general video format that is just as applicable to a movie stored on DVD

OPEN ISSUE

Computer Networks Meet Consumer Electronics

or a digital HDTV signal transmitted by NBC. What this all points to is a convergence of computers, networks, and consumer electronics.

In the not-too-distant future, we can expect to find a *media gateway* (MG) in the home. It might sit on top of the television, replacing today's set-top cable box. The MG will be connected to an Internet service provider (ISP) possibly over the CATV cable coming into the home. The MG will also support a number of ports that allow you to plug in different consumer electronic devices, such as a digital camcorder, a DVD player, a video game, and so on. As of today, it looks like Firewire, a 400-Mbps serial link developed by Apple, will serve as the common connection for these devices. Various wireless technologies are another possibility.

What will the MG be asked to do? For one thing, it will route multimedia streams between different devices, much like today's IP router forwards data packets between ports. For example, it might be possible to forward a movie of the kids captured with the digital camcorder out the ISP link and across the country to anxiously awaiting grandparents. A second thing it might have to do is translate between the TCP/IP spoken on the Internet and whatever format is supported on the devices. Of course, it's possible that camcorders will one day be full-fledged Internet nodes (i.e., have their own IP addresses), but media gateways will push the need to connect everything to the Internet indefinitely into the future.

The prospect of widespread availability of "Internet appliances" raises several interesting questions. One is the issue of address usage. IP version 6 was created with the goal of expanding the IP address space so much that assigning IP addresses to any conceivable object (toasters, water meters, etc.) would not cause address exhaustion. However, ISPs today are reluctant to deploy IPv6, and instead are handing out IPv4 addresses to their customers extremely cautiously. This has the potential to cause significant problems in the future.

Another issue is the ease of configuration of IP devices. While many of today's Internet users are comfortable setting the IP address, mask, and default gateway on their PC, it's unlikely that the average purchaser of a camcorder wants to learn how to configure anything more complex than the "record" button. "Plug-and-play" configuration of IP devices remains an important goal.

FURTHER READING

Our recommended reading list for this chapter includes two papers that give an over-view of the JPEG and MPEG standards, respectively. Their main value is in explaining the various factors that shaped the standards. We also recommend the paper on receiver-driven layered multicast as an excellent example of a systems approach to design, embracing the issues of multicast, congestion control, and video coding.

- Wallace, G. K. The JPEG still picture compression standard. *Communications of the ACM* 34(1):30–44, April 1991.

- Le Gall, D. MPEG: A video compression standard for multimedia applications. *Communications of the ACM* 34(1):46–58, April 1991.

- McCanne, S., V. Jacobson, and M. Vetterli. Receiver-driven layered multicast. *Proceedings of the SIGCOMM '96 Symposium,* pages 117–130, September 1996.

Unfortunately, there is no single paper that gives a comprehensive treatment of presentation formatting. Aside from the XDR, ASN.1/BER, and NDR specifications (see Srinivasan [Sri95b], the CCITT recommendations [CCITT92a, CCITT92b], and the Open Software Foundation [OSF94]), three other papers cover topics related to presentation formatting: those by O'Malley et al. [OPM94], Lin [Lin93], and Chen et al. [CLNZ89]. All three discuss performance-related issues.

On the topic of compression, a good place to start is with Huffman encoding, which was originally defined in [Huf52]. The original LZ algorithm is presented in Ziv and Lempel [ZL77], and an improved version of that algorithm by the same authors can be found in [ZL78]. Both of these papers are of a theoretical nature. The work that brought the LZ approach into widespread practice can be found in Welch [Wel84]. For a more complete overview of the topic of compression, Nelson's article [Nel92] is recommended. You can also learn about compression in any of several recent books on multimedia. We recommend Witten et al. [WMB94], which has an extremely high science-to-hype ratio, and Buford [Buf94], which is a collection of contributed chapters that span the range of multimedia topics. For a comprehensive description of the MPEG standard, see Mitchell et al. [MPFL96]. For a description of MP3, see Noll [Nol97].

Finally, we recommend the following live reference:

■ http://bmrc.berkeley.edu/projects/mpeg/index.html: a collection of MPEG-related programs, some of which are used in the following exercises

EXERCISES

1 Consider the following C structure definitions:

```
#define  MAXSTR 100

struct date {
    char   month[MAXSTR];
    int    day;
    int    year;
};

struct employee {
    char    name[MAXSTR];
    int     ssn;
    struct date *hireday;
```

```
int     salary_history[10];
int     num_raises;
}
```

where num_raises + 1 corresponds to the number of valid entries in array **salary_history**. Show the on-the-wire representation of structure **employee** that is generated by XDR.

2 For the data structures given in the previous problem, give the XDR routine that encodes/decodes these structures. If you have XDR available to you, run this routine and measure how long it takes to encode and decode an example instance of structure **employee**.

3 Using library functions like **htonl** and Unix's **bcopy** or Windows' **CopyMemory**, implement a routine that generates the same on-the-wire representation of the structures given in Exercise 1 as XDR does. If possible, compare the performance of your "by-hand" encoder/decoder with the corresponding XDR routines.

4 Use XDR and **htonl** to encode a 1000-element array of integers. Measure and compare the performance of each. How do these compare to a simple loop that reads and writes a 1000-element array of integers? Perform the experiment on a computer for which the native byte order is the same as the network byte order, as well as on a computer for which the native byte order and the network byte order are different.

5 Write your own implementation of **htonl**. Using both your own **htonl** and (if little-endian hardware is available) the standard library version, run appropriate experiments to determine how much longer it takes to byte-swap integers versus merely copying them.

6 Give the ASN.1 encoding for the following three integers:
   (a) 101
   (b) 10,120
   (c) 16,909,060

7 Give the big-endian and little-endian representations for the integers from the previous problem.

8 XDR is used to encode/decode the header for the SunRPC protocol illustrated by Figure 5.20. The XDR version is determined by the RPCVersion field. What potential difficulty does this present? Would it be possible for a new version of XDR to switch to little-endian integer format?

9 The presentation-formatting process is sometimes regarded as an autonomous protocol layer, separate from the application. If this is so, why might including data compression in the presentation layer be a bad idea?

10 Suppose you have a machine with a 36-bit word size. Strings are represented as five packed 7-bit characters per word. What presentation issues on this machine have to be addressed for it to exchange integer and string data with the rest of the world?

11 Using the programming language of your choice that supports user-defined automatic type conversions, define a type netint and supply conversions that enable assignments and equality comparisons between ints and netints. Can a generalization of this approach solve the problem of network argument marshalling?

12 Different architectures have different conventions on bit order as well as byte order—whether the least significant bit of a byte, for example, is bit 0 or bit 7. [Pos81] defines (in its Appendix B) the standard network bit order. Why is bit order then not relevant to presentation formatting?

13 Let $p \leq 1$ be the fraction of machines in a network that are big-endian; the remaining $1 - p$ fraction are little-endian. Suppose we choose two machines at random and send an int from one to the other. Give the average number of byte-order conversions needed for both big-endian network byte order and receiver-makes-right, for $p = 0.1$, $p = 0.5$, and $p = 0.9$. Hint: The probability that both endpoints are big-endian is p^2; the probability that the two endpoints use different byte orders is $2p(1 - p)$.

14 Experiment with a compression utility (e.g., compress, gzip, or pkzip). What compression ratios are you able to achieve? See if you can generate data files for which you can achieve 5:1 or 10:1 compression ratios.

15 Suppose a file contains the letters a, b, c, and d. Nominally we require 2 bits per letter to store such a file.

(a) Assume the letter a occurs 50% of the time, b occurs 30% of the time, and c and d each occur 10% of the time. Give an encoding of each letter as a bit string that provides optimal compression. Hint: Use a single bit for a.

(b) What is the percentage of compression you achieve above? (This is the average of the compression percentages achieved for each letter, weighted by the letter's frequency.)

(c) Repeat this, assuming a and b each occur 40% of the time, c occurs 15% of the time, and d occurs 5% of the time.

16 Suppose we have a compression function c, which takes a bit string s to a compressed string $c(s)$.

(a) Show that for any integer N there must be a string s of length N for which $\text{length}(c(s)) \geq N$; that is, no effective compression is done.

(b) Compress some already compressed files (try compressing with the same utility several times in sequence). What happens to the file size?

(c) Given a compression function c as in (a), give a function c' such that for all bit strings s, $\text{length}(c'(s)) \leq \min(\text{length}(c(s)), \text{length}(s)) + 1$; that is, in the worst case, compression with c' expands the size by only 1 bit.

17 Give an algorithm for run length encoding that requires only a single byte to represent nonrepeated symbols.

18 Write a program to construct a dictionary of all "words," defined to be runs of consecutive nonwhitespace, in a given text file. We might then compress the file (ignoring the loss of whitespace information) by representing each word as an index in the dictionary. Retrieve the file rfc791.txt containing [Pos81], and run your program on it. Give the size of the compressed file assuming first that each word is encoded with 12 bits (this should be sufficient), and then that the 128 most common words are encoded with 8 bits and the rest with 13 bits. Assume that the dictionary itself can be stored by using, for each word, $\text{length}(\text{word}) + 1$ bytes.

19 The one-dimensional discrete cosine transform is similar to the two-dimensional transform, except that we drop the second variable (j or y) and the second cosine factor. We also drop, from the inverse DCT only, the leading $1/\sqrt{2N}$ coefficient. Implement this and its inverse for $N = 8$ (a spreadsheet will do, although a language supporting matrices might be better) and answer the following:

(a) If the input data is $\langle 1, 2, 3, 5, 5, 3, 2, 1 \rangle$, which DCT coefficients are near 0?

(b) If the data is $\langle 1, 2, 3, 4, 5, 6, 7, 8 \rangle$, how many DCT coefficients must we keep so that after the inverse DCT the values are all within 1% of their original values? 10%? Assume dropped DCT coefficients are replaced with 0s.

(c) Let s_i, for $1 \le i \le 8$, be the input sequence consisting of a 1 in position i and 0 in position j, $j \ne i$. Suppose we apply the DCT to s_i, zero the last three coefficients, and then apply the inverse DCT. Which i, $1 \le i \le 8$, results in the smallest error in the ith place in the result? The largest error?

20 Compare the size of an all-white image in JPEG format with a "typical" photographic image of the same dimensions. At what stage or stages of the JPEG compression process does the white image become smaller than the photographic image?

For the next three exercises, the utilities cjpeg and djpeg may be useful and can be obtained from ftp.uu.net/graphics/jpeg. Other JPEG conversion utilities can also be used. For manual creation and examination of graphics files, the pgm portable grayscale format is recommended; see the Unix pgm(5)/ppm(5) man pages.

21 Create a grayscale image consisting of an 8×8 grid with a vertical black line in the first column. Compress into JPEG format and decompress. How far off are the resultant bytes at the default quality setting? How would you describe the inaccuracies introduced, visually? What quality setting is sufficient to recover the file exactly?

22 Create an 8×8 grayscale image consisting of a 64-character ASCII text string. Use lowercase letters only, with no whitespace or punctuation. Compress into JPEG format and decompress. How recognizable is the result, as text? Why might adding whitespace make things worse? With the quality setting at 100, would this be a plausible way of compressing text?

23 Write a program that implements forward and backward DCT, using floating-point arithmetic. Run the program on a sample grayscale image. Since DCT is lossless, the image output by the program should match the input. Now modify your program so that it zeroes some of the higher-frequency components and see how the output image is affected. How is this different from what JPEG does?

24 Express DCT(0,0) in terms of the average of the $pixel(x, y)$s.

25 Think about what functions might reasonably be expected from a video standard: fast-forward, editing capabilities, random access, and so on. (See the paper by Le Gall, "MPEG: A video compression standard for multimedia applications," given in this chapter's recommended reading list, for further ideas.) Explain MPEG's design in terms of these features.

26 Suppose you want to implement fast-forward and reverse for MPEG streams. What problems do you run into if you limit your mechanism to displaying I frames only? If you don't, then to display a given frame in the fast-forward sequence, what is the largest number of frames in the original sequence you may have to decode?

27 Use mpeg_play to play an MPEG-encoded video. Experiment with options, particularly -nob and -nop, which are used to omit the B and P frames, respectively, from the stream. What are the visible effects of omitting these frames?

28 The mpeg_stat program can be used to display statistics for video streams. Use it to determine, for several streams:

(a) number and sequence of I, B, and P frames

(b) average compression rate for the entire video

(c) average compression rate for each type of frame

29 Suppose we have a video of two white points moving toward each other at a uniform rate against a black background. We encode it via MPEG. In one I frame the two points are 100 pixels apart; in the next I frame they have merged. The final point of merger happens to lie at the center of a 16×16 macroblock.

(a) Describe how you might optimally encode the Y component of the intervening B (or P) frames.

(b) Now suppose the points are in color, and that the color changes slowly as the points move. Describe what the encoding of the U and V values might look like.

Computer networks are typically a shared resource used by many applications for many different purposes. Sometimes the data transmitted between application processes is confidential, and the applications would prefer that others not be able to read it. For example, when purchasing a product over the World Wide Web, users sometimes transmit their credit card numbers over the network. This is a dangerous thing to do since it is easy for someone to eavesdrop on the network and read all the packets that fly by. Therefore, users sometimes want to *encrypt* the messages they send, with the goal of keeping anyone who is eavesdropping on the channel from being able to read the contents of the message.

The idea of encryption is simple enough: the sender applies an *encryption* function to the original *plaintext* message, the resulting *ciphertext* message is sent over the network, and the receiver applies a reverse function (called *decryption*) to recover the original plaintext. The encryption/decryption process generally depends on a secret *key* shared between the sender and the receiver. When a suitable combination of a key and an encryption algorithm is used, it is sufficiently difficult for an eavesdropper to break the ciphertext, and the sender and receiver can rest assured that their communication is secure.

This familiar use of cryptography is designed to ensure privacy—preventing the unauthorized release of information. Privacy, however, is not the only service that cryptography provides. It can also be used to support other equally important services, including *authentication* (verifying the identity of the remote participant) and *integrity* (making sure that the message has not been altered).

This chapter first introduces the basic idea of cryptography, including a description of the three most common cryptographic algorithms: the Data Encryption Stan-

It is true greatness to have in one the frailty of a man and the security of a god.

—Seneca

dard (DES), Rivest, Shamir, and Adleman (RSA), and Message Digest 5 (MD5). It then shows how these algorithms can be used to provide authentication and integrity services. It also discusses the problem of how users get the keys they need in the first place—this is the *key distribution* problem. The chapter concludes by describing a collection of secure systems and protocols that are being built for and deployed on the Internet.

One thing to keep in mind while reading this chapter is that the various algorithms and protocols for privacy, authentication, and integrity are being described in isolation. In practice, constructing a secure system requires an intricate combination of just the right set of protocols and algorithms. This is a challenging task because each protocol is vulnerable to a different set of attacks. To make matters worse, determining when a security protocol is "good enough" is as much art and politics as science. A thorough analysis of these different attacks, and how you might build a complete system that minimizes the risk of compromise, is beyond the scope of this book.

8

Network Security

Figure 8.1 Secret key encryption.

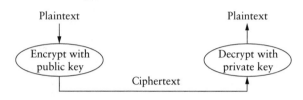

Figure 8.2 Public key encryption.

8.1 Cryptographic Algorithms

Broadly speaking, there are three types of cryptographic algorithms: *secret key* algorithms, *public key* algorithms, and *hashing* algorithms. Secret key algorithms are symmetric in the sense that both participants[1] in the communication share a single key. Figure 8.1 illustrates the use of secret key encryption to transmit data over an otherwise insecure channel. DES (Data Encryption Standard) is the best-known example of a secret key encryption function, while IDEA (International Data Encryption Algorithm) is another.

In contrast to a pair of participants sharing a single secret key, *public key* cryptography involves each participant having a *private* key that is shared with no one else and a *public* key that is published so everyone knows it. To send a secure message to this participant, you encrypt the message using the widely known public key. The participant then decrypts the message using his or her private key. This scenario is depicted in Figure 8.2. RSA—named after its inventors, Rivest, Shamir, and Adleman—is the best-known public key encryption algorithm.

The third type of cryptography algorithm is called a *hash* or *message digest* function. Unlike the preceding two types of algorithms, cryptographic hash functions

---

[1] We use the term *participant* for the parties involved in a secure communication since that is the term we have been using throughout the book to identify the two endpoints of a channel. In the security world, they are typically called *principals*.

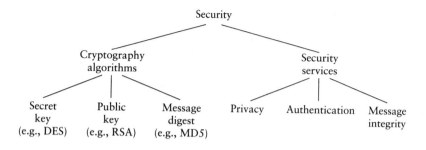

Figure 8.3   Taxonomy of network security.

involve the use of no keys.[2] Instead, the idea is to map a potentially large message into a small fixed-length number, analogous to the way a regular hash function maps values from a large space into values from a small space.

The best way to think of a cryptographic hash function is that it computes a *cryptographic checksum* over a message. That is, just as a regular checksum protects the receiver from accidental changes to the message, a cryptographic checksum protects the receiver from malicious changes to the message. This is because all cryptographic hash algorithms are carefully selected to be one-way functions—given a cryptographic checksum for a message, it is virtually impossible to figure out what message produced that checksum. Said another way, it is not computationally feasible to find two messages that hash to the same cryptographic checksum. The relevance of this property is that if you are given a checksum for a message (along with the message), and you are able to compute exactly the same checksum for that message, then it is highly likely that this message produced the checksum you were given.

The most widely used cryptographic checksum algorithm is Message Digest version 5 (MD5). An important property of MD5, in addition to those properties outlined in the previous paragraph, is that it is much more efficient to compute than either DES or RSA. We will see the relevance of this fact later in this section.

To reemphasize, cryptography algorithms like DES, RSA, and MD5 are just building blocks from which a secure system can be constructed. Figure 8.3 gives a simple taxonomy that illustrates this point. In looking at these services and building blocks, we should consider the following question: How did the participants get the various keys in the first place? This is the *key distribution* problem, one of the central problems in security, as we will see in the following sections.

---

[2] However, there are such things as *keyed* message digest functions, as we will discuss in the next section.

Before showing how cryptographic algorithms are used to build secure systems, we first describe how the three best-known algorithms—DES, RSA, and MD5—work. We will also give some insight into *why* they work, but there is only so much we can do on this front since the design principles that underlie DES are not public knowledge. In the case of RSA, a deep explanation for why it works would require a background in number theory that is beyond the scope of this book, but we can provide some intuition into the underlying principles. Before looking at details of the algorithms, however, let's step back and ask what we want from a cryptographic algorithm.

8.1.1 Requirements

The basic requirement for an encryption algorithm is that it be able to turn plaintext into ciphertext in such a way that only the intended recipient—the holder of the decryption key—can recover the plaintext. What this means is that the encryption method should be safe from attacks by people who do not hold the key. As a starting point, we should assume that the encryption algorithm itself is known and that only the key is kept secret. The reason for this assumption is that if you depend on the algorithm being kept secret, then you have to throw it out when you believe it is no longer secret. This means potentially frequent changes of algorithm, which is problematic since it takes a lot of work to develop a new algorithm. Also, one of the best ways to know that an algorithm is effective is to use it for a long time—if no one breaks it, it's probably secure. (Fortunately, there are plenty of people who will try to break algorithms and who will let it be widely known when they have succeeded, so no news is generally good news.) Thus, there is considerable risk in deploying a new algorithm. Therefore, our first requirement is that secrecy of the key, and not of the algorithm itself, is the only thing that is needed to ensure the privacy of the data.

It is important to realize that when someone receives a piece of ciphertext, they may have more information at their disposal than just the ciphertext itself. For example, they may know that the plaintext was written in English, which means that the letter *e* occurs more often in the plaintext that any other letter; the frequency of many other letters and common letter combinations can also be predicted. This information can greatly simplify the task of finding the key. Similarly, they may know something about the likely contents of the message; for example, the word "login" is likely to occur at the start of a remote login session. This may enable a "known plaintext" attack, which has a much higher chance of success than a "ciphertext only" attack. Even better is a "chosen plaintext" attack, which may be enabled by feeding some information to the sender that you know the sender is likely to transmit—such things have happened in wartime, for example.

The best cryptographic algorithms, therefore, can prevent the attacker from deducing the key even when the individual knows both the plaintext and the ciphertext.

One approach, the one taken in DES, is to make the algorithm so complicated that virtually none of the structure of the plaintext remains in the ciphertext. This leaves the attacker with no choice but to search the space of possible keys exhaustively. This can be made infeasible by choosing a suitably large key space and by making the operation of checking a key reasonably costly. As we will see, DES is now becoming only marginally secure on that basis. Some other cryptographic algorithms derive their strength from mathematics. RSA, for example, can be broken only if the attacked is able to find the factors of a number that is the product of two large primes—a problem that is known (or at least widely believed) to be very costly.

The requirements for a message digest algorithm are slightly different. These algorithms are required to be *one-way* functions, meaning that, given an output of the function, it is computationally infeasible to find an input that would produce this output. Because these algorithms produce an output that is generally shorter than the input message, there will be many different input messages that produce the same output. However, it should be computationally infeasible to find two such messages. These properties are required so that, if you were given a message m and the message digest $MD(m)$, you would not be able to find a new message $m1 \neq m$ that produced the same message digest. Thus it is not possible to modify the message m and still have the message digest function produce the same output on the modified message.

For a message digest function to meet these requirements, its outputs must be fairly randomly distributed. For example, if a digest is 128 bits long, then there are 2^{128} possible outputs. This would mean that, if the outputs are randomly distributed, you would typically need to compute the digests of about 2^{64} messages before you found two that were the same. (This fact is a version of the "birthday problem"—see the exercises for more details.) But if the outputs are not randomly distributed—that is, some outputs are much more likely than others—then you could find two messages with the same output much more easily than this, which would defeat the security of the algorithm.

The other requirement for message digests is that they be reasonably computationally efficient. If a message digest function reduces the throughput of an application by orders of magnitude, it's unlikely that many users will consider the benefits of integrity and authentication that it provides are worth the cost.

8.1.2 The Data Encryption Standard (DES)

DES encrypts a 64-bit block of plaintext using a 64-bit key. The key actually contains only 56 usable bits—the last bit of each of the 8 bytes in the key is a parity bit for that byte. Also, messages larger than 64 bits can be encrypted using DES, as described below.

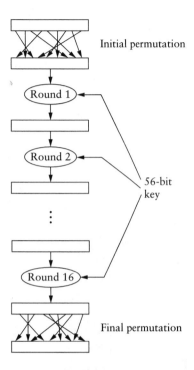

Initial permutation

56-bit
key

Final permutation

Figure 8.4 High-level outline of DES.

DES has three distinct phases:

1 The 64 bits in the block are permuted (shuffled).

2 Sixteen rounds of an identical operation are applied to the resulting data and the key.

3 The inverse of the original permutation is applied to the result.

This high-level outline of DES is depicted in Figure 8.4.

Table 8.1 represents part of the initial permutation. The final permutation is the inverse (e.g., bit 40 would be permuted to bit position 1). It is generally agreed that these two permutations add nothing to the security of DES. Some security experts speculate that they were included to make the computation take longer, but it is just as likely that they are an artifact of the initial hardware implementation, involving some restriction of pin layout, for example.

During each round, the 64-bit block is broken into two 32-bit halves, and a different 48 bits are selected from the 56-bit key. If we denote the left and right halves

Input Position	1	2	3	4	5	...	60	61	62	63	64
Output Position	40	8	48	16	56	...	9	49	17	57	25

Table 8.1 Initial (and final) DES permutation.

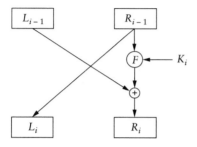

Figure 8.5 Manipulation at each round of DES.

of the block at round i as L_i and R_i, respectively, and the 48-bit key at round i as K_i, then these three pieces are combined during round i according to the following rule:

$$L_i = R_{i-1}$$

$$R_i = L_{i-1} \oplus F(R_{i-1}, K_i)$$

where F is a combiner function described below and $\oplus$ is the exclusive-OR (XOR) operator. Figure 8.5 illustrates the basic operation of each round. Note that L_0 and R_0 correspond to the left and right halves of the 64-bit block that results from the initial permutation, and that L_{16} and R_{16} are combined back together to form the 64-bit block to which the final inverse permutation is applied.

We now need to define function F and show how each K_i is derived from the 56-bit key. We start with the key. Initially, the 56-bit key is permuted according to Table 8.2. Note that every eighth bit is ignored (i.e., bit 64 is missing from the table), reducing the key from 64 bits to 56 bits. Then for each round, the current 56 bits are divided into two 28-bit halves and each half is independently rotated left either one or two bit positions, depending on the round. The extent of the rotation in bits for each round is given in Table 8.3. The 56 bits that result from this shift are used as both input for the next round (i.e., the preceding shift is repeated) and to select the 48 bits that make up the key for the current round. Table 8.4 shows how 48 of the 56 bits are selected; note that they are simultaneously selected and permuted. For example, the bit in position 9 is not selected because it is not in the table.

Input Position	1	2	3	4	5	...	59	60	61	62	63
Output Position	8	16	24	56	52	...	17	25	45	37	29

Table 8.2 DES key permutation.

Round	1	2	3	4	5	6	7	8	9	10	11	12	13	14	15	16
Rotation Amount	1	1	2	2	2	2	2	2	1	2	2	2	2	2	2	1

Table 8.3 DES key rotation amount per round.

Input Position	1	2	3	4	5	6	7	8	10	11	12	13	14	15	16	17
Output Position	5	24	7	16	6	10	20	18	12	3	15	23	1	9	19	2

Input Position	19	20	21	23	24	26	27	28	29	30	31	32	33	34	36	37
Output Position	14	22	11	13	4	17	21	8	47	31	27	48	35	41	46	28

Input Position	39	40	41	42	44	45	46	47	48	49	50	51	52	53	55	56
Output Position	39	32	25	44	37	34	43	29	36	38	45	33	26	42	30	40

Table 8.4 DES compression permutation.

Function F combines the resulting 48-bit key for round i (K_i) with the right half of the data block after round $i - 1$ (R_{i-1}), as follows. To simplify our notation, we refer to K_i and R_{i-1} as K and R, respectively. First, function F expands R from 32 bits into 48 bits so that it can be combined with the 48-bit K. It does this by breaking R into eight 4-bit chunks and expanding each chunk into 6 bits by stealing the rightmost and leftmost bit from the left and right adjacent 4-bit chunks, respectively. This expansion is illustrated in Figure 8.6, where R is treated as circular in the sense that the first and last chunks get their extra bit from each other.

Next, the 48-bit K is divided into eight 6-bit chunks, and each chunk is XORed with the corresponding chunk that resulted from the previous expansion of R. Finally, each resulting 6-bit value is fed through something called a *substitution box* (S box), which reduces each 6-bit chunk back into 4 bits. There are actually eight different S boxes, one for each of the 6-bit chunks. You can think of an S box as just performing

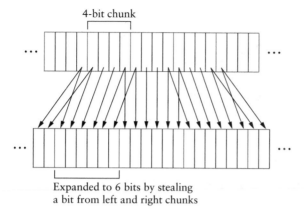

Figure 8.6 Expansion phase of DES.

Input	000000	000001	000010	000011	000100	000101	...
Output	1110	0100	1101	0001	0010	1111	...

Input	...	111010	111011	111100	111101	111110	111111
Output	...	0011	1110	1010	0000	0110	1101

Table 8.5 Example DES S box (bits 1–6).

a many-to-one mapping from 6-bit numbers to 4-bit numbers. Table 8.5 gives part of the S box function for the first chunk. We are now done with round i.

Notice that the preceding description does not distinguish between encryption and decryption. One of the nice features of DES is that both sides of the algorithm work exactly the same. The only difference is that the keys are applied in the reverse order, that is, $K_{16}, K_{15}, \ldots, K_1$.

Also keep in mind that the preceding discussion is limited to a single 64-bit data block. To encrypt a longer message using DES, a technique known as *cipher block chaining* (CBC) is typically used. The idea of CBC is simple: The ciphertext for block i is XORed with the plaintext for block $i + 1$ before running it through DES. An *initialization vector* (IV) is used in lieu of the nonexistent ciphertext for block 0. This vector IV, which is a random number generated by the sender, is sent along with the message so that the first block of plaintext can be retrieved. CBC on the encryption

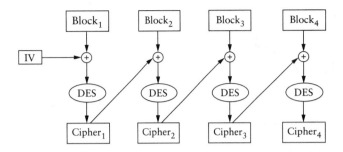

Figure 8.7   Cipher block chaining (CBC) for large messages.

side is shown in Figure 8.7 for a 256-bit (four-block) message. Decryption works in the expected way since XOR is its own inverse, with the process starting with the last block and moving toward the front of the message.

We conclude by noting that there is no published mathematical proof that DES is secure. What security it achieves it does through the application of two techniques: confusion and diffusion. (Having just plowed through the algorithm, you should now have a deep understanding of these two techniques.) What we can say is that the only known way to break DES is to exhaustively search all possible 2^{56} keys, although on average you would expect to have to search only half of the key space, or $2^{55} = 3.6 \times 10^{16}$ keys. On an Alpha workstation, it is possible to do one encryption in 4 μs, meaning that it would take $1.4 \times 10^{17} \mu$s to break a key (approximately 4500 years). While that may seem like a long time, keep in mind that searching a key space is a *highly* parallel task, meaning that if you could throw 9000 Alphas at the job, it would take only six months to break a key.

This amount of time is considered borderline-secure in many circles, especially considering that processor speeds are doubling every 18 months. For this reason, many applications now use triple-DES, that is, encrypt the data three times. This can be done with three separate keys, or with two keys: The first is used, then the second, and finally the first key is used again.

8.1.3   RSA

RSA is a much different algorithm, not only because it involves different keys for encryption (public key) and decryption (private key), but also because it is grounded in number theory. In fact, the essential aspect of RSA comes down to how these two keys are selected. The act of encrypting or decrypting a message is expressed as a simple function, although this function requires enormous computational power.

In particular, RSA commonly uses a key length of 512 bits, making it much more expensive to compute than DES; we discuss this more below.

The first task is to generate a public and private key. To do this, choose two large prime numbers p and q, and multiply them together to get n. Both p and q should be roughly 256 bits long. Next, choose the encryption key e, such that e and $(p - 1) \times (q - 1)$ are relatively prime. (Two numbers are relatively prime if they have no common factor greater than 1.) Finally, compute the decryption key d such that

$$d = e^{-1} \bmod ((p - 1) \times (q - 1))$$

The public key is constructed from the pair $\langle e, n \rangle$ and the private key is given by the pair $\langle d, n \rangle$. The original prime numbers p and q are no longer needed. They can be discarded, but they must not be disclosed.

Given these two keys, encryption is defined by the following formula:

$$c = m^e \bmod n$$

and decryption is defined by

$$m = c^d \bmod n$$

where m is the plaintext message and c is the resulting ciphertext. Note that m must be less than n, which means that it can be no more than the 512 bits long. A larger message is simply treated as the concatenation of multiple 512-bit blocks.

To see how this works, consider the following example using very small values of p and q. Suppose we pick $p = 7$ and $q = 11$. That means

$$n = 7 \times 11 = 77$$

and

$$(p - 1) \times (q - 1) = 60$$

so we need to pick a value of e that is relatively prime to 60. We choose $e = 7$; 7 and 60 have no common factor except 1. Now we need to calculate d such that

$$d = 7^{-1} \bmod ((7 - 1) \times (11 - 1))$$

which is to say

$$7 \times d = 1 \bmod 60$$

It turns out that $d = 43$, since

$$7 \times 43 = 301$$
$$= 1 \bmod 60$$

So now we have the public key $\langle e, n \rangle = \langle 7, 77 \rangle$ and the private key $\langle d, n \rangle = \langle 43, 77 \rangle$. Note that in this example it would be pretty easy to figure out p and q once you knew n, and thus figure out e from d, but if n was the product of two numbers each of which was about 256 bits long, it would be computationally infeasible to find p and q. It should be clear why p and q must not be disclosed—once they are known, it is easy to determine the private key from the public key.

Now consider a simple encryption operation. Suppose we want to encrypt a message containing the value 9. Following the encryption algorithm above:

$$c = m^e \bmod n$$
$$= 9^7 \bmod 77$$
$$= 37$$

So 37 is the ciphertext that we would send. (You can verify this calculation pretty easily with a calculator.)

On receipt of the message, the ciphertext would be decrypted as follows:

$$m = c^d \bmod n$$
$$= 37^{43} \bmod 77$$
$$= 9$$

Thus, as required, the original message is recovered. (Verifying the above calculation on a calculator is a little harder; you need to perform the exponentiation in stages and find the remainder modulo 77 after each stage to avoid dealing with integers that are too big for the calculator.)

Notice that when two participants want to encrypt data they are sending to each other using a public key algorithm like RSA, a public/private key pair is required. It doesn't work to encrypt with your private key and let the other side decrypt with the

Breaking RSA

In 1977, a challenge was issued to break a 129-digit (430-bit) message that was encrypted using RSA. It was believed that the code was impregnable, requiring 40 quadrillion years of computation using the currently known algorithms for factoring large numbers. In April 1994, a mere 17 years later, four scientists reported that they had broken the code. The hidden message was

THE MAGIC WORDS ARE
SQUEAMISH OSSIFRAGE

The task was accomplished using a factoring method that requires approximately 5000 MIP-years. This was done over an eight-month pepublic key because everyone has access to the public key and so could decrypt the message. In other words, participant *A* encrypts data it sends to participant *B* using *B*'s public key and *B* uses its private key to decrypt this data, while *B* encrypts data it sends to *A* using *A*'s public key and *A* decrypts this message using its private key. Observe that *A* cannot decrypt a message that it has sent to *B*; only *B* has the requisite private key.

RSA security comes from the premise that factoring large numbers is a computationally expensive proposition. In particular, if you could factor *n*, you could recover *p* and *q*, which would compromise *d*. The speed at which large numbers can be factored is a function of both the available processor speed and the factoring algorithm being used. It is estimated that 512-bit numbers will be factorable in the next few years, and in fact, people are already starting to use 768- and 1024-bit keys. Keep in mind that while we are concentrating on the security of data as it moves through the network—that is, the data is sometimes vulnerable for only a short period of time—in general, security people have to consider the vulnerability of data that needs to be stored in archives for tens of years.

riod of time by dividing the problem into smaller pieces and shipping these pieces, using email, to computers all over the world.

Keep in mind that it doesn't always take 5000 MIP-years to break a key, especially when the key is poorly chosen. For example, a security hole was exposed in a WWW browser that used RSA to encrypt credit card numbers that were being sent over the Internet. The problem was that the system used a highly predictable method (a combination of process ID plus time of day) to generate a random number that was, in turn, used to generate a private and public key. Such keys are easily broken.

8.1.4 Message Digest 5 (MD5)

There are a number of popular message digest algorithms known as MD*n* for various values of *n*. MD5 is the most widely used at the time of writing. The secure hash algorithm (SHA) is another well-known message digest function. All these functions do much the same thing, which is to compute a fixed-length cryptographic checksum from an arbitrarily long input message.

Mathematically, message digest algorithms tend to have more in common with DES than with RSA. That is, they don't have a formal mathematical foundation, but rely on the complexity of the algorithm to produce a random output such that the requirements outlined above are met. We provide just a brief outline of the MD5 algorithm here. The algorithm itself seems

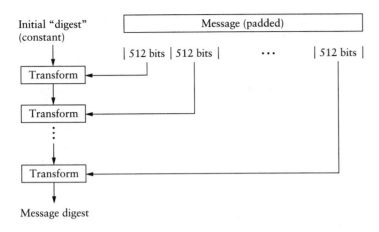

Initial "digest"
(constant)

Message (padded)

| 512 bits | 512 bits | • • • | 512 bits |

Transform

Transform

Transform

Message digest

Figure 8.8   Overview of message digest operation.

to be a random collection of transformations, so it is not surprising that it produces
suitably random outputs.[3]

The basic operation of MD4, MD5, and SHA is depicted in Figure 8.8. These
algorithms operate on a message 512 bits at a time, so the first step is to pad the
message to a multiple of 512 bits. This is done by following the message with between
1 and 512 padding bits, the first of which is a 1, the rest of which are 0s, and then
following that with a 64-bit integer that is the original message length in bits. Note
that this allows messages of arbitrary length up to 2^{64} bits.

The digest calculation begins with the digest value initialized to a constant; this
value is combined with the first 512 bits of the message to produce a new value for the
digest, using a complex transformation described below; the new value is combined
with the next 512 bits of the message using the same transformation, and so on, until
the final value of the digest is produced.

The main ingredient of the MD5 algorithm is thus the transformation that takes
as its input the current value of the 128-bit digest, plus 512 bits of message, and outputs a new 128-bit digest. MD5, like other modern digest algorithms (and unlike some
earlier ones like MD2), operates on 32-bit quantities, since these are efficiently handled in modern processors. So we can think of the current digest value as four 32-bit
words (d_0, d_1, d_2, d_3) and the piece of message currently being digested as sixteen 32-
bit words (m_0 through m_{15}).

[3] This is not to imply that any collection of random transformations will be adequate. It is necessary to verify that an
algorithm of this type truly does produce random outputs.

The basic transformation performed by MD5 can be divided into four passes. In the first pass, a new value of the digest is produced from the old value and the 16 message words using 16 steps, the first six of which are shown below:

$$d_0 = (d_0 + F(d_1, d_2, d_3) + m_0 + T_1) \hookleftarrow 7$$

$$d_3 = (d_3 + F(d_0, d_1, d_2) + m_1 + T_2) \hookleftarrow 12$$

$$d_2 = (d_2 + F(d_3, d_0, d_1) + m_2 + T_3) \hookleftarrow 17$$

$$d_1 = (d_1 + F(d_2, d_3, d_0) + m_3 + T_4) \hookleftarrow 22$$

$$d_0 = (d_0 + F(d_1, d_2, d_3) + m_4 + T_5) \hookleftarrow 7$$

$$d_1 = (d_3 + F(d_0, d_1, d_2) + m_5 + T_6) \hookleftarrow 12$$

This process continues until all 16 words have been digested. Each step causes one of the digest words to be rewritten, with the new value depending on its old value, the current value of the other three digest words, and one word of the message being digested. The function $F(a, b, c)$ is a combination of bitwise operations (OR, AND, NOT) on its arguments. The T_is are constants. The $\hookleftarrow n$ operator rotates the operand left by n bits.

The second pass looks pretty much the same as the first pass (especially if your eyes are glazing over). The differences are the following:

- F is replaced by a slightly different function G.

- The constants T_1 through T_{16} are replaced by another set (T_{17} through T_{32}).

- The amount of the left rotation is $\{5, 9, 14, 20, 5, 9, \ldots\}$ at each step.

- Instead of taking the bytes of the message in order m_0 through m_{15}, the message byte that is used at stage i is $m_{(5i+1) \bmod 16}$.

In the third pass:

- G is replaced by yet another function H, which is just the XOR of its arguments.

- Another set of constants (T_{33} through T_{48}) are used.

- The amount of the left rotation is $\{4, 11, 16, 23, 4, 11, \ldots\}$ at each step.

- The message byte that is used at stage i is $m_{(3i+5) \bmod 16}$.

The attentive reader could probably propose a fourth pass that would be as secure as the one that is actually used; for the sake of completeness, the fourth pass has the following properties:

■ H is replaced by the function I, which is a combination of bitwise XOR, OR, and NOT on its arguments.

■ Another set of constants (T_{49} through T_{64}) are used.

■ The amount of the left rotation is $\{6, 10, 16, 21, 6, 10, \ldots\}$ at each step.

■ The message byte that is used at stage i is $m_{(7i)\bmod 16}$.

After all this work, the original values of (d_0, d_1, d_2, d_3) have been thoroughly mangled in a way that, while completely dependent on the message bytes, provides no algorithmic way to find out what those message bytes were. The mangled digest is now added to the digest value that existed prior to the current stage, and that becomes the new digest value. The algorithm now proceeds to digest the next 16 bytes of the message until there is no more to be digested; the output of the last stage is the message digest.

While not quite as computationally efficient as some earlier digests, MD5 is still fairly good on this count. Note that all the operations—bitwise OR, AND, NOT, XOR, addition, and rotation—are easily implemented in modern processors.

8.1.5 Implementation and Performance

DES and MD5 are several orders of magnitude faster than RSA when implemented in software. When run on an Alpha workstation, for example, DES processes data at 36 Mbps, MD5 at 85 Mbps, and RSA at only 1 Kbps. When implemented in hardware, that is, by custom VLSI chips, it has been reported that DES and MD5 can achieve rates measured in the hundreds of Mbps, whereas RSA can achieve a whopping 64 Kbps.

Perhaps surprisingly, DES and MD5 are the more likely of the three algorithms to be implemented in hardware on a given computer. This is because even when implemented in hardware, RSA is still too slow to be of any practical use in encrypting data messages. Instead, RSA is typically used to encrypt very small amounts of data, such as a secret key or a secret number. Security protocols then use these RSA-protected secrets in conjunction with DES and MD5, possibly implemented in hardware, to provide message privacy and integrity. We will see exactly how this is accomplished in the following sections.

8.2 Security Mechanisms

Cryptographic algorithms are just one piece of the picture when it comes to providing security in a network. The next thing we need is a set of mechanisms and protocols for solving various problems. In this section we examine mechanisms that are used to authenticate participants, techniques for assuring the integrity of messages, and some approaches to solving the problem of distributing public keys.

8.2.1 Authentication Protocols

Before two participants are likely to establish a secure channel between themselves—that is, use an algorithm such as DES to encrypt messages they exchange—they will generally wish to establish that the other participant is who he or she claims to be. This is the problem of authentication. If you think about authentication in the context of a client/server relationship, say, a remote file system, then it is understandable that the server would want to establish the identity of the client: If the client is going to be allowed to modify or delete John's file, then the server is obligated to make sure that the client is, in fact, John. It is also the case, however, that the client often wants to verify the identity of the server. After all, you would not want to start writing sensitive data to what you thought was a file server, only to later discover that it was an imposter process.

This section describes three common protocols for implementing authentication. The first two use secret key cryptography (e.g., DES), while the third uses public key cryptography (e.g., RSA). Note that it is often during the process of authentication that the two participants establish the session key that is going to be used to ensure privacy during subsequent communication. The following includes a discussion of how this process gets bootstrapped.

Simple Three-Way Handshake

A simple authentication protocol is possible when the two participants who want to authenticate each other—think of them as a client and a server—already share a secret key. This situation is analogous to a user (the client) having an account on a computer system (the server), where both client and server know the password for the account.

The client and server authenticate each other using a simple three-way handshake protocol similar to the one described in Section 5.2.3. In the following, we use $E(m,k)$ to denote the encryption of message m with key k and $D(m,k)$ to denote the decryption of message m with key k.

As illustrated in Figure 8.9, the client first selects a random number x and encrypts it using its secret key, which we denote as CHK (client handshake key). The client then sends $E(x, CHK)$, along with an identifier (ClientId) for itself to the server. The server uses the key it thinks corresponds to client ClientId (call it SHK for server handshake key) to decrypt the random number. The server adds 1 to the number it recovers and sends the result back to the client. It also sends back a random number y that has been encrypted with SHK. Next, the client decrypts the first half of this message and if the result is 1 more than the random number x that it sent to the server, it knows that the server possesses its secret key. At this point, the client has authenticated the server. The client also decrypts the random number the server sent it (this should yield

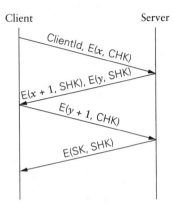

Figure 8.9   **Three-way handshake protocol for authentication.**

y), encrypts this number plus 1, and sends the result to the server. If the server is able to recover $y + 1$ then it knows the client is legitimate.

After the third message, each side has authenticated itself to the other. The fourth message in Figure 8.9 corresponds to the server sending the client a session key (SK), encrypted using SHK (which is equal to CHK). Typically, the client and server then use SK to encrypt any future data they send to each other. The advantage of using a session key is that it means that the permanent secret key is only used for a small number of messages, making it harder for an attacker to gather data that might be used to determine the key.

This only begs the question of where the client and server handshake keys came from in the first place. One possibility is that they correspond to a password that a user entered; the ClientId could be the login identifier in this situation. Because a user-selected password might not make a suitable secret key, a transformation is often performed to turn it into a legitimate 56-bit DES key, for example.

Trusted Third Party

A more likely scenario is that the two participants know nothing about each other, but both trust a third party. This third party is sometimes called an *authentication server*, and it uses a protocol to help the two participants authenticate each other. There are actually many different variations of this protocol. The one we describe is the one used in Kerberos, a TCP/IP-based security system developed at MIT.

In the following, we denote the two participants who want to authenticate each other as A and B, and we call the trusted authentication server S. The Kerberos protocol assumes that A and B each share a secret key with S; we denote these two

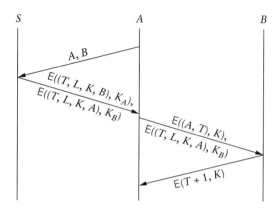

Figure 8.10   Third-party authentication in Kerberos.

keys as K_A and K_B, respectively. As before, E(m,k) denotes message m encrypted with key k.

As illustrated in Figure 8.10, participant A first sends a message to server S that identifies both itself and B. The server then generates a timestamp T, a lifetime L, and a new session key K. Timestamp T is going to serve much the same purpose as the random number in the simple three-way handshake protocol given above, plus it is used in conjunction with L to limit the amount of time that session key K is valid. Participants A and B will have to go back to server S to get a new session key when this time expires. The idea here is to limit the vulnerability of any one session key.

Server S then replies to A with a two-part message. The first part encrypts the three values T, L, and K, along with the identifier for participant B, using the key that the server shares with A. The second part encrypts the three values T, L, and K, along with participant A's identifier, but this time using the key that the server shares with B. Clearly, when A receives this message, it will be able to decrypt the first part but not the second part. A simply passes this second part on to B, along with the encryption of A and T using the new session key K. (A was able to recover T and K by decrypting the first part of the message it got from S.) Finally, B decrypts the part of the message from A that was originally encrypted by S, and in so doing, recovers T, K, and A. It uses K to decrypt the half of the message encrypted by A, and upon seeing that A and T are consistent in the two halves of the message, replies with a message that encrypts $T + 1$ using the new session key K.

A and B can now communicate with each other using the shared secret session key K to ensure privacy.

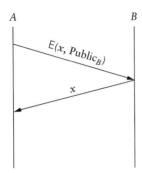

Figure 8.11 Public key authentication.

Public Key Authentication

Our final authentication protocol uses public key cryptography (e.g., RSA). The public key protocol is a useful one because the two sides need not share a secret key; they only need to know the other side's public key. As shown in Figure 8.11, participant A encrypts a random number x using participant B's public key, and B proves it knows the corresponding private key by decrypting the message and sending x back to A. A could authenticate itself to B in exactly the same way.

8.2.2 Message Integrity Protocols

Sometimes two communicating participants do not care whether an eavesdropper is able to read the messages they are sending to each other, but they are worried about the possibility of an imposter sending messages that claims to be from one of them. That is, the participants want to ensure the integrity of their messages.

One way to ensure the integrity of a message is to encrypt it using DES with cipher block chaining, and then to use the CBC *residue* (the last block output by the CBC process) as a *message integrity code* (MIC). (For the CBC example given in Figure 8.7, $cipher_4$ is the CBC residue.) The plaintext message plus the MIC would be transmitted to the receiver, with the MIC acting as a sort of checksum—if the receiver could not reproduce the attached MIC using the secret key it shares with the sender, then the message was either not sent by the sender, or it was modified since it was transmitted. Note that you would not want to use DES with CBC to both encrypt the message for privacy and to generate the MIC for integrity, because you would simply end up transmitting the CBC-encrypted message with the last block repeated. Thus, anyone who wanted to tamper with the CBC-encrypted message could take the value of the final block they wanted to send, and send it twice.

This section looks at three alternatives for ensuring message integrity. The first uses RSA to produce a digital signature. RSA used on its own tends to be slow, but it can be used in combination with MD5 to yield a much more efficient technique. The second and third approaches use MD5 (possibly in conjunction with RSA) to guarantee message integrity.

Digital Signature Using RSA

A *digital signature* is a special case of a message integrity code, where the code can have been generated only by one participant. The easiest digital signature algorithm to understand is an RSA signature, which works in the obvious way—since a given participant is the only one that knows its own private key, the participant uses this key to produce the signature. Any other participant can verify this signature using the corresponding public key. In other words, to sign a message, you encrypt it using your private key, and to verify a signature, you decrypt it using the public key of the purported sender. Clearly, this means that producing an RSA signature is as slow as RSA, which we have already seen is two or three orders of magnitude slower than DES. Observe that the use of keys is exactly reversed relative to their use for privacy: The sender encrypts with the sender's private key rather than with the receiver's public key, and the receiver decrypts with the sender's public key rather than with the receiver's private key.

Note that the National Institute for Standards and Technology (NIST) has proposed a digital signature standard known as DSS that is similar to the approach just described, except that it uses an alternative algorithm, called El Gamel, instead of RSA.

Keyed MD5

Recall that MD5 produces a cryptographic checksum for a message. This checksum does not depend on a secret key, so it does not prevent an imposter from creating a message that claims to be from someone else and computing an MD5 checksum for that message. However, there are two ways to use MD5 to implement message integrity. Both approaches overcome the performance problems inherent in using RSA alone.

The first method, which is commonly referred to as *keyed MD5*, works as follows. Suppose that we can arrange for the sender and receiver of a message to share a secret key k. This might be done by preconfiguration of the key, or by some more dynamic mechanism such as Kerberos. The sender then runs MD5 over the concatenation of the message (denoted m) and this key. In practice, the key k is attached to the end of the message for the purpose of running MD5; k is then removed from the message once MD5 is finished. The sender now transmits

$$m + \text{MD5}(m + k)$$

where MD5(s) represents applying the MD5 algorithm to string s, and $a + b$ denotes the concatenation of strings a and b.

The receiver of the message applies MD5 to the concatenation message body and the secret key k. If the result matches the checksum sent with the message, then the message must have been sent by the participant who holds that key.

Keyed MD5 itself does not depend on public key cryptography, but it can be combined with it to simplify the problem of getting the same value of the secret key k to the sender and receiver. The sender picks k at random and then encrypts it using RSA and the sender's private key. The encrypted key can now be sent to the receiver along with the original message and the MD5 checksum. The following summarizes the complete message transmitted by the sender:

$$m + \mathsf{MD5}(m + k) + \mathsf{E}(k, private)$$

The receiver recovers the random key using the purported sender's public RSA key and proceeds to run MD5 on the concatenation of the received message and k. As before, if the result matches the checksum sent with the message, then the message must have been sent by the participant who generated the random key. While this approach solves the problem of getting the secret key from sender to receiver, it still leaves the problem of getting the sender's public key reliably to the receiver; this problem is discussed in Section 8.2.3.

MD5 with RSA Signature

The second method for using MD5 for message integrity works in combination with RSA as follows. The sender runs MD5 over the original message it wants to protect, producing an MD5 checksum. It then signs this checksum with its own private RSA key. That is, the sender does not sign the entire message, it just signs the checksum. The original message, the MD5 checksum, and the RSA signature for the checksum are then transmitted. Using the same notation as above, this means that the sender transmits

$$m + \mathsf{E}(\mathsf{MD5}(m), private)$$

The receiver verifies the message by

■ running the MD5 algorithm on the received message

■ decrypting the signed checksum with the sender's public key

■ comparing the two checksums

If they match, this means that the message was not modified since the time the sender computed the MD5 checksum and signed it.

8.2.3 Public Key Distribution (X.509)

Public key cryptography is an extremely powerful technology, but it depends on the distribution of public keys. The problem of getting keys to people who need them in such a way that they can be sure that the key is legitimate (i.e., that it belongs to the entity that it purports to belong to) turns out to be an extremely challenging problem. This section examines the problem and some of the general solutions to it. Some specific systems that have attempted to solve the problem are described in Section 8.3.

Suppose participant *A* wants to convey his public key to participant *B*. He can't just use email or a bulletin board to send it, because without *A*'s public key, *B* has no way to authenticate the key as having really come from *A*. Some third party could send a public key to *B* and claim that the message came from *A*. If *A* and *B* are individuals who know each other, then they can get together in the same room and *A* can give his public key to *B* directly, perhaps on a business card. However, there are clear shortcomings to this approach, such as the inability to receive a key from someone unless you can be in the same room with them.

The basic solution to the problem relies on the use of *digital certificates*. The following sections explain what certificates are and some issues that arise in using them to achieve widespread key distribution.

Certificates

In Section 8.2.2 we introduced the notion of a *digital signature*, by which the owner of a certain key can cryptographically sign a piece of data. A digital signature proves that the data was generated by the owner of a certain key and that it has not been modified since it was signed. A certificate is just a special type of digitally signed document. The document says, in effect, "I certify that the public key in this document belongs to the entity named in this document, signed *X*." *X* in this case could be anyone with a public key. It is commonly the case that *X* would be a *certification authority* (CA),[4] that is, an administrative entity that is in the business of issuing certificates. It should be clear that this certificate is only useful to a participant who already holds the public key for *X* because that key is needed to verify the signature. Thus, certificates do not in themselves solve the key distribution problem, but they give us a way to make inroads on it. Clearly, once you have a public key for one entity *X*, you can start to accumulate more public keys from other participants if those participants can get certificates issued by *X*.

---

[4] CAs are also known as certificate authorities.

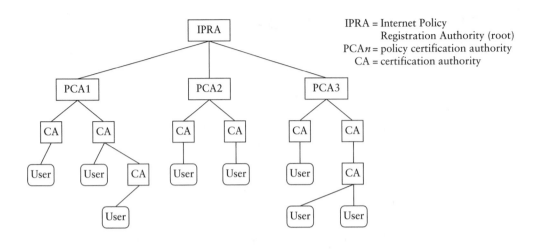

Figure 8.12   Tree-structured certification authority hierarchy for PEM (Privacy Enhanced Mail).

The idea of certificates allows the building of "chains of trust." If X certifies that a certain public key belongs to Y, and then Y goes on to certify that another public key belongs to Z, then there exists a chain of certificates from X to Z, even though X and Z may have never met. If Z wants to provide his public key to A, he can provide the complete chain of certificates—the certificate for Y's public key issued by X, and the certificate for Z's key issued by Y. If A has the public key for X, he can use the chain to verify that the public key of Z is legitimate.

With this idea of building chains of trust, public key distribution becomes somewhat more tractable. A popular way to build such chains is to arrange them in a tree-structured hierarchy, as shown in Figure 8.12. If everyone has the public key of the root CA, then any participant can provide a chain of certificates to another participant and know that it will be sufficient to build a chain of trust for that participant.

There are still significant issues with building chains of trust. First of all, even if you are certain that you have the public key of the root CA, you need to be sure that every CA from the root on down is doing its job properly. If some CA is willing to issue certificates to individuals without verifying their identity, then what looks like a valid chain of certificates becomes meaningless. Some different approaches to tackling this problem are discussed in Sections 8.3.1 and 8.3.2. In the latter approach, chains of trust form arbitrary meshes rather than a rigid tree structure.

One question to ask about certificates is, What is being certified? Since a certificate creates a binding between an identity and a public key, we should look more closely at what we mean by "identity." For example, a certificate that says, "This public key belongs to John Smith" may not be terribly useful if you can't tell which of the thousands of John Smiths is being identified. Thus certificates must use a well-defined name space for the identities being certified. For example, certificates are often issued for email addresses; a certificate might say, in effect, "This public key belongs to jsmith@acme.com ⟨John Q. Smith⟩."

Certificates can, of course, be issued for many entities other than individuals. It is particularly useful to be able to issue a certificate for a domain in the Domain Name System. For example, a certificate for the domain acme.com would be useful to enable customers visiting the acme.com Web site to be sure they had come to the real Web site and not an imposter before sending in their credit card information.

One of the major standards for certificates is known as X.509. This standard leaves a lot of details open, but specifies a basic structure for certificates. Components of a certificate clearly must include

- the name of the entity being certified

- the public key of the entity

- the name of the certificate authority

- a digital signature

X.509 certificates may use a number of different digital signature algorithms, so the certificate must specify which algorithm it uses. Another possible component is an expiration time for the certificate. We will see a particular use of this feature below.

An important point to understand about certificates is that *possession* of a certificate says nothing about your identity. Certificates can be freely copied and distributed, and indeed must be to be useful. To prove that you are the entity named in the certificate, you need to do something that shows you have the *private* key corresponding to the public key contained in the certificate. This, of course, is the authentication problem described in Section 8.2.1.

Certificate Revocation

One issue that arises with certificates is how to revoke, or undo, a certificate. Why is this important? Suppose that you suspect that someone has discovered your private key. There may be any number of certificates in the universe that assert that you are the owner of the public key corresponding to that private key. The person who discovered your private key thus has everything he needs to impersonate you: valid certificates and your private key. To solve this problem, it would be nice to be able to revoke the certificates that bind your old, compromised key to your identity, so that the impersonator will no longer be able to persuade other people that he is you.

The basic solution to the problem is simple enough. A certification authority can issue a *certificate revocation list* (CRL), which is a digitally signed list of certificates that have been revoked. The CRL is periodically updated and made publicly available. Because it is digitally signed, it can just be posted on a bulletin board. Now, when participant A receives a certificate for B that he wants to verify, A will first consult the latest CRL issued by the CA. As long as the certificate has not been revoked, it is valid. Note that if all certificates have unlimited life spans, the CRL would always be getting longer, since you could never take a certificate off the CRL for fear that some copy of the revoked certificate might be used. However, by attaching an expiration date to a certificate when it is issued, we can limit the length of time that a revoked certificate needs to stay on a CRL. As soon as its original expiration date is passed, it can be removed from the CRL.

8.3 Example Systems

At this point, we have seen many of the components that are required to build a secure system. These components include cryptographic algorithms, authentication protocols, and key distribution mechanisms. In this section we examine some complete systems that use these components.

These systems can be roughly categorized by the protocol layer at which they operate. The IPSEC (IP Security) protocols, as their name implies, operate at the IP (network) layer. Systems that operate at the application layer include Privacy Enhanced Mail (PEM) and Pretty Good Privacy (PGP). In between these are a number of protocols that operate at the transport layer, notably the IETF's Transport Layer Security (TLS) standard and the older protocol from which it derives, SSL (Secure Socket Layer). The following section describes the salient features of each of these approaches.

8.3.1 Privacy Enhanced Mail (PEM)

Privacy Enhanced Mail (PEM) was a relatively early effort in the IETF to provide a mechanism for supporting encryption, authentication, and integrity of email messages in the Internet. PEM is defined in a suite of four RFCs (completed in 1993) that specified

- the format of messages that use PEM
- a hierarchy of certification authorities
- a set of cryptographic algorithms to be used
- message formats for requesting and revoking certificates

There are a few special challenges in securing communication by email. First, most email systems expect messages to contain only ASCII characters, while cryptographic algorithms usually output binary data. Next, an email message often passes through a number of systems that have certain ideas about how long the lines of text should be and exactly how the end of a line is represented, for example, the ⟨CR⟩ (carriage-return) character only or ⟨CR⟩ followed by ⟨LF⟩ (line-feed). Simple modifications to a message, like breaking a long line in two, have no significant effect on the content of a normal email message, but could cause a signed message to appear to its recipient as invalid. While PEM solves these problems, they turn out to be exactly the problems that MIME was invented to solve in a more general setting; we describe this solution in Section 9.2.1.

Finally, email messages are frequently sent to large numbers of recipients, perhaps via a machine that performs "explosion" of a mailing list name. We will need procedures by which such messages can be sent securely to all the participants.

Perhaps the most unique aspect of PEM is its certification hierarchy. PEM uses RSA public key technology for encryption and authentication, and thus needs a mechanism to reliably distribute public keys to the participants. Recall that when participant A wants to obtain the public key of participant B, one way to do this is to obtain a certificate from someone that A trusts, called a certification authority. This certificate says, in effect, "The public key of B is K, signed CA." Rather than relying on a centralized authority (which would not scale well), PEM specifies a tree-structured hierarchy of CAs, as illustrated in Figure 8.12. As we will see in the next section, a tree is just one way to distribute certificates.

To make the process of certification scalable, a PEM certification authority is able to delegate its authority to another CA lower down in the tree. That is, CA_1, rather than signing certificates for individuals, signs certificates for other CAs, such as CA_2. Assuming I knew the public key of CA_1, I can now reliably learn the public key of CA_2. So now if CA_2 signs a certificate for B, I can be confident that this is really B's public key. By repeatedly delegating authority, we can build a tree like that shown in Figure 8.12. As long as I start out with a public key for the root CA, I can use a collection of certificates to get the public key of any leaf on the tree.

The problem with this sort of delegation, however, is the delegation of *trust* from one CA to another. The fact that CA_1 signed the certificate of CA_2 may give me high confidence that I have a legitimate public key for CA_2 (since I trust CA_1 to do its job), but it may not give me confidence in the certificates issued by CA_2, since CA_2 may be run by criminals who sign any certificate in exchange for enough money. To deal with this problem, it is necessary for the root certification authority (the Internet Policy Registration Authority) to know a lot more about any CA that it certifies than just its identity. For example, the IPRA will need to know what procedures the CA uses to ensure that its certificates are valid.

Since different CAs may go to different lengths to ensure the validity of their certificates, the PEM hierarchy allows for different types of CAs, which are certified by different policy certification authorities (PCAs). Each PCA has a set of published policies that it follows when delegating authority to CAs underneath it, and that it may require those CAs to follow in turn. Thus, if PCA1 in Figure 8.12 has very stringent policies, then I can have high confidence in the validity of any certificates issued by any CA that appears in the tree under PCA1. By contrast, when I receive a certificate from a CA that appears in the tree under a less stringent PCA, I might be willing to believe that the institution that issued the certificate is correct, but I might have some skepticism about the identity of the individual named in the certificate.

PEM certificates follow the X.509 standard. When A needs to convey his public key to B, he includes enough certificates to convince B that the key is correct. In the case where A and B work for the same organization and share the same CA, then A could just send the certificate issued by the local CA. At the other extreme, if A and B know nothing about each other, A might send a complete chain of certificates leading all the way from the root of the tree (the IPRA) to A.

When A wants to authenticate a message and send it to B, A computes a cryptographic checksum of the message (typically using MD5) and then signs the MD5 checksum using A's private key. That is, in the terminology of Section 8.2.2, A sends

$$m + \mathsf{E}(\mathsf{MD5}(m), private_A)$$

where m is the original message. The recipient of the message uses A's public key to decrypt the signed checksum; he also calculates the MD5 checksum on the received message. If these two values match, this proves both that the message was not modified in transit and that it was sent by A. Note that the only thing the recipient needs to verify the message is the public key of A, so this procedure can readily be used by any number of recipients of the message. The complete process of authenticating the message is shown in Figure 8.13.

To encrypt a message, A must first learn the public key of B, which B might have provided in an earlier email message using the appropriate certificates. A then picks a random per-message key, which he encrypts with B's public key; the result is included in the message. The per-message key is used to encrypt the body of the message using DES in CBC mode. On receipt of the message, B uses his private key to decrypt the per-message key, which he then uses to decrypt the message body. These steps are shown in Figure 8.14.

To send an encrypted message to multiple recipients, A will of course need to know the public key of each recipient. However, it is not necessary to encrypt the whole message multiple times. Note that only the per-message key is encrypted using the recipient's public key, so A includes multiple encrypted versions of the per-message key in the message, but encrypts the message body itself only once.

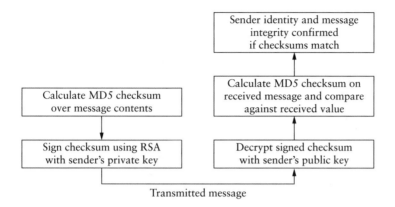

Figure 8.13 PEM message integrity and authentication.

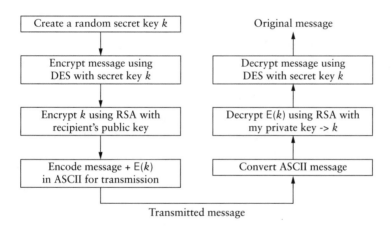

Figure 8.14 PEM message encryption.

We can see how all these pieces come together by looking at the overall structure of a PEM message, as shown in Figure 8.15. After the usual email headers (not shown) there is a well-known string that identifies this as a PEM message. This is followed by a PEM header, which provides information about the security operations that have been performed on the message. For example, the message may be authenticated, encrypted, or both. In the case where it is authenticated but not encrypted, the PEM header indicates that the message is of type "MIC-CLEAR" or of type "MIC-ONLY." In both cases, the message contains a message integrity code (MIC), for example, a signed

| ----BEGIN PRIVACY-ENHANCED MESSAGE---- |
| PEM header; includes mode (MIC-CLEAR, MIC-ONLY, ENCRYPTED) |
| Initialization vector for DES-CBC |
| Certificate of sender (signed by sender's CA) |
| Certificate of sender's CA (signed by next level CA) |
| ⋮ |
| Certificate of PCA signed by IPRA |
| Message integrity code |
| Per-message key, encrypted with recipient's public key |
| Message body (clear, encrypted, or encoded) |
| ----END PRIVACY-ENHANCED MESSAGE---- |

Figure 8.15   Structure of a PEM message.

MD5 checksum. The difference between the two modes is that, in MIC-CLEAR, the original email message is completely unmodified, whereas in MIC-ONLY the message is encoded in a way that makes it resistant to the type of modification sometimes performed by mail gateways. (This encoding is essentially the same as the encoding used by MIME, described in Section 9.2.1.) The former mode leaves the message in a form that is readable to non-PEM-capable mail readers, whereas the latter is more robust.

If the message is encrypted, and the encryption algorithm requires an initialization vector, that vector follows the PEM header. Next there may be one or more certificates, depending on how many certificates the recipient is expected to have already. In the worst case, there will need to be a complete chain of certificates leading from the sender of the message up to the root of the certification tree.

The message integrity code, as described above, follows. Next, if the message is encrypted, there appears one or more per-message keys. There will be one of these for each recipient of the mail message; each one is a copy of the same per-message key, encrypted with the public key of one of the recipients. Finally, the message itself appears, either encrypted, encoded for safe transit through mail gateways, or in the clear.

As it turns out, PEM has seen only moderate deployment, and the main reason for this seems to be its reliance on a full-fledged certification hierarchy before it can be useful. To understand this problem, consider the case of two people (*A* and *B*) in different organizations who wish to exchange email. Before they can exchange mail securely, the following steps must take place:

■ *A* must find a CA to issue a certificate for him; let's assume this is issued by the organization for whom *A* works.

■ *B* must similarly find a CA to issue a certificate for him; in all probability, this is a different CA than the one who certified *A*.

■ These two CAs must be certified by a suitable PCA; let's assume that each CA chooses a different PCA.

■ The two PCAs must be certified by the IPRA.

If one of the participants happens to work for an organization that isn't willing to establish a CA and get it certified by a PCA, that participant may just be out of luck as far as key distribution is concerned.

8.3.2 Pretty Good Privacy (PGP)

Pretty Good Privacy (PGP) is another approach to providing encryption and authentication capabilities for electronic mail. It differs from PEM in quite a few detailed ways (e.g., message formats and cryptographic algorithms), but the most significant and interesting difference is in the way PGP handles certificates. Whereas PEM enforces a strict hierarchy of certificates, PGP allows certificates to be arbitrarily meshed. This has had a significant positive impact on the deployment of PGP.

Recall that the basic problem of distribution of public keys is the establishment of a chain of trust. PGP acknowledges that each user will have his own set of criteria by which he wants to trust keys certified by someone else. For example, if *A*, a person I know well, gives me his public key in person, then I'll be quite confident that it really is his public key. But if *A* gives me a certificate for *B*, signed by *A*, I might have to wonder whether *A* is the type of guy who would falsely sign a certificate in exchange for money, or whether he was a bit sloppy in checking that it really was *B* and not someone else who asked him to sign the certificate. I might trust *A* to sign certificates for some people (e.g., his co-workers) but not others (e.g., politicians). Matters clearly get worse as the chain of "trust" (or mistrust) gets longer.

Rather than forcing a rigid hierarchy of certification, PGP allows certification relationships to form an arbitrary mesh. Furthermore, it allows each user to decide for themselves how much trust they wish to place in a given certificate. For example, suppose I have a certificate for *B* provided by *A*; I can assign a moderate level of trust to that certificate. However, if I have additional certificates for *B* that were provided to me by *C* and *D*, each of whom are also moderately trustworthy, that might considerably increase my level of confidence that the public key I have for *B* is valid. In short, PGP recognizes that the problem of establishing trust is quite a personal matter and gives users the raw material to make their own decisions, rather than assuming that they are all willing to trust in a single hierarchal structure of CAs. To quote Phil Zimmerman, the developer of PGP, "PGP is for people who prefer to pack their own parachutes."

PGP has become quite popular in the networking community. PGP key-signing parties are a regular feature of IETF meetings. At these gatherings, an individual can

- collect public keys from others whose identity he knows

- provide his public key to others

- get his public key signed by others, thus collecting certificates that will be persuasive to an increasingly large set of people

- sign the public key of other individuals, thus helping them build up their set of certificates that they can use to distribute their public keys

- collect certificates from other individuals whom he trusts enough to sign keys

Thus over time a user will collect a set of certificates with varying degrees of trust. PGP stores these in a file called a key ring.

Now suppose user A wants to send a message to user B and prove to B that it truly came from A. PGP tackles this problem in much the same way as PEM. First, the message body itself may either be encoded in a way that protects it against modification by mail gateways, or it may be sent in the clear. A then creates a cryptographic checksum over the message body (e.g., using MD5) and then encrypts the checksum using A's private key. (PGP allows a variety of different cryptographic algorithms to be used and specifies which one is used in the message.)

On receipt of the message, B uses PGP's key management software to search his key ring for A's public key. If it is not found, B is of course unable to verify the authenticity of the message. If the key is found, the checksum of the received message is calculated, the received encrypted checksum is decrypted using A's public key, and the two checksums are compared. If they agree, B knows that A sent the message and that it was not modified after A signed it. In addition to providing the result of the signature verification, PGP tells B the level of trust that he had previously assigned to this public key, based on the number of certificates he has for A and the trustworthiness of the individuals who signed the certificates.

Encryption of a message is again similar to PEM. A randomly picks a per-message key that is used to encrypt the message using a symmetric algorithm such as DES. The per-message key is encrypted using the public key of the recipient. PGP obtains this key from A's key ring and notifies A of the level of trust he has assigned to this key. The message is encoded to prevent damage by mail gateways and sent to B. On receipt,

B uses his private key to decrypt the per-message key, and then uses the appropriate algorithm to decrypt the message.

PGP allows a wide variety of different cryptographic algorithms to be used for the various functions. The actual algorithms used in a message are specified in header fields. The idea of making a security system protocol-independent is a very good one, because you never know when your favorite cryptographic algorithm might be proved to be insufficiently strong for your purposes. It would be nice if you could quickly change to a new algorithm without having to change the protocol specification or implementation. In addition to putting this information in a mail message, PGP allows a user to list his preferred algorithms in the file that contains his public key. Thus, anyone who has his public key will know which algorithms can be safely used when sending to that person.

8.3.3 Transport Layer Security (TLS, SSL, HTTPS)

To understand the design goals and requirements for the Transport Layer Security (TLS) standard that is being developed in the IETF, it is helpful to consider one of the main problems that it was intended to solve. As the World Wide Web became popular and commercial enterprises began to take an interest in it, it became clear that some level of security would be necessary for transactions on the Web. The canonical example of this is making purchases by credit card. There are several issues of concern when sending your credit card information to a computer on the Web. First, you might worry that the information would be intercepted in transit and subsequently used to make unauthorized purchases. You might also worry about the details of a transaction being modified, for example, to change the purchase amount. And you would certainly like to know that the computer to which you are sending your credit card information is in fact one belonging to the vendor in question and not some other party. Thus, we immediately see a need for privacy, integrity, and authentication in Web transactions. The first widely used solution to this problem was known as the Secure Socket Layer (SSL), which formed the basis for the IETF's TLS standard.

The designers of SSL and TLS recognized that these problems were not specific to Web transactions (i.e., those using HTTP) and instead built a general-purpose protocol that sits between the application protocol (e.g., HTTP) and the transport protocol (e.g., TCP). The reason for calling this "transport layer security" is that, from the application's perspective, this protocol layer looks just like a normal transport protocol, except for the fact that it is secure. That is, the sender can open connections and deliver bytes for transmission, and the secure transport layer will get them to the receiver with the necessary privacy, integrity, and authentication. By running the secure

| Application (e.g., HTTP) |
| Secure transport layer |
| TCP |
| IP |
| Subnet |

Figure 8.16   Secure transport layer inserted between application and TCP layers.

transport layer on top of TCP, all of the normal features of TCP (reliability, flow control, congestion control, etc.) are also provided to the application. This arrangement of protocol layers is depicted in Figure 8.16.

When HTTP is used in this way, it is known as HTTPS (Secure HTTP). In fact, HTTP itself is unchanged. It simply delivers data to and accepts data from the TLS layer rather than TCP. For convenience, a default TCP port has been assigned to "HTTPS" (443). That is, if I try to connect to a server on TCP port 443, it's likely that I will find myself talking to the TLS protocol, which will pass my data through to HTTP provided all goes well with authentication and decryption.

One of the interesting differences between a transport layer security protocol and one designed for email is that there is the possibility for real-time negotiation. As noted above, there are many different cryptographic algorithms that you might want to use for various operations, and you can't safely assume that the party with whom you want to communicate implements all of them. Thus you might need to negotiate until you find something that you can both agree on. You might even want to change algorithms in the middle of a connection if, for example, you had some very important data that warranted more computationally expensive encryption. For this reason, TLS is broken into two parts:

■ a handshake protocol, used to negotiate parameters of the communication

■ a "record" protocol, used for actual data transfer

The handshake protocol can be thought of as the means to get enough shared state to both ends of a connection to enable secure communication to proceed. The components of this shared state are the set of agreed-upon cryptographic algorithms, and parameters for these algorithms such as session keys, initialization vectors, and so on. This shared state is represented by a session ID that is stored by both client and server for purposes discussed below. Interestingly, the handshake protocol may also negotiate the use of a compression algorithm, not because this offers any security benefits, but because it's easy to do when you're negotiating all this other stuff and you've already decided to do some expensive per-byte operations on the data. The set

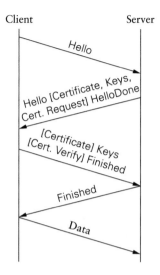

Figure 8.17 Handshake protocol to establish TLS session.

of messages used in the handshake is shown in Figure 8.17. Some messages are sent in certain situations only; these are shown in brackets. Note that the handshake takes at least two RTTs and up to a dozen messages.

The handshake protocol is also responsible for exchange of certificates among the participants, if required. For example, in making a credit card purchase, the client needs to know that it's talking to the real server, but the client need not necessarily be authenticated. In this case, the server would provide the client with a certificate, or a chain of certificates if necessary, as part of the initial handshake, thus furnishing the client with a reliable copy of its public key. The server is then able to authenticate subsequent messages by signing them with its private key. The client is now able to encrypt messages with the public key of the server, and one of the first things it will do with this key is encrypt and send a "pre-master secret" to the server. Subsequent secrets such as session keys, initialization vectors, and so on, are derived from this pre-master secret.

The record protocol defines a set of formats and procedures by which messages handed down from the application layer are

■ fragmented or coalesced into blocks of a convenient size for the following steps

■ optionally compressed

- integrity-protected using a hash such as MD5

- encrypted

- passed to the lower layer (e.g., TCP) for transmission

The ability to negotiate cryptographic algorithms, while useful, does open this approach up to a certain form of attack that is in the general category of "man-in-the-middle" attacks. This class of attack involves an intermediary who modifies messages in transit between the two legitimate participants. Because the initial negotiation of algorithms must take place without cryptographic protection, an intermediary could change the choice of algorithms to something that is weaker than the participants are in fact capable of supporting (and that the man-in-the-middle might be capable of breaking). A poorly designed application might just accept whatever algorithm the TLS protocol picks rather than verifying that it is in fact sufficiently strong for its needs. A well-designed application would abort the transaction, effectively turning this into a denial-of-service attack, which a man-in-the-middle can do in any case by simply discarding packets in transit.

Another interesting feature of the TLS protocol, which is quite a useful feature for Web transactions, is the ability to "resume" a session. To understand the motivation for this, it is helpful to understand how HTTP version 1 makes use of TCP connections. (The details of HTTP are presented in Section 9.2.2.) Each HTTP operation, such as getting a page of text or an image from a server, requires a new TCP connection to be opened. Retrieving a single page with a number of embedded graphical objects might take many TCP connections. Recall from Section 5.2 that opening a TCP connection requires a three-way handshake before data transmission can start. Once the TCP connection is ready to accept data, the client would then need to start the TLS handshake protocol, taking at least another two RTTs (and consuming some amount of processing resources and network bandwidth) before actual application data could be sent. The resumption capability of TLS alleviates this problem.

Session resumption is an optimization of the handshake that can be used in those cases where the client and the server have already established some shared state in the past. The client simply includes the session ID from a previously established session in its initial handshake message. If the server finds that it still has state for that session, and the resumption option was negotiated when that session was originally created, then the server can reply to the client with an indication of success, and data transmission can begin using the algorithms and parameters previously negotiated. If the session ID does not match any session state cached at the server, or if resumption was not allowed for the session, then the server will fall back to the normal handshake process.

Unlike PEM and PGP, TLS does not specify any particular key infrastructure. In practice, TLS has been very successful in enabling Web commerce through the use of a single certification authority. The CA's public key is included with the most popular Web browsers, and companies who want to accept credit card payment on their Web sites obtain certificates from that CA. This makes server authentication rather straightforward and enables the server to make its public key reliably known to any client that trusts the CA. As noted above, the server's public key is all that the client needs to establish any secrets necessary for encryption of data to or from the server.

8.3.4 IP Security (IPSEC)

Easily the most ambitious of all the efforts to integrate security into the Internet happens at the lowest level—IP. IPSEC, as the architecture is called, is really a framework (as opposed to a single protocol or system) for providing all the security services discussed throughout this chapter. As an architecture, IPSEC provides three degrees of freedom. First, it is highly modular, allowing users (or more likely, system administrators) to select from a variety of encryption algorithms and specialized security protocols. Second, IPSEC allows users to select from a large menu of security services, including access control, integrity, authentication, protection against replay, and confidentiality (privacy). Third, IPSEC allows users to control the granularity with which the security services are applied. For example, IPSEC can be used to protect both "narrow" streams (e.g., packets belonging to a particular TCP connection being sent between a pair of hosts) or "wide" streams (e.g., all packets flowing between a pair of gateways).

When viewed from a high level, IPSEC consists of two pieces. The first piece is a pair of protocols that implement the available security services. They are the Authentication Header (AH), which provides access control, connectionless message integrity, authentication, and antireplay protection, and the Encapsulating Security Payload (ESP), which supports these same services, plus confidentiality. These two protocols can be used by themselves or together to provide exactly the mix of services that the user wants. The second piece is support for key management, which fits under an umbrella protocol known as ISAKMP: Internet Security Association and Key Management Protocol.

The abstraction that binds these two pieces together is the *security association* (SA). An SA is a simplex (one-way) "connection" that is protected by one or more of the available security services. Security associations may be established between a pair of hosts, between a host and a security gateway (a router that supports IPSEC), or between a pair of security gateways. For example, an SA might be established to ensure the integrity of every packet sent from one security gateway to another; these

NextHdr	PayloadLength	Reserved
SPI		
SeqNum		
AuthenticationData		

Figure 8.18 IPSEC's Authentication Header.

packets are in effect tunneled between the security gateways. Securing a bidirectional communication between a pair of hosts—corresponding to a TCP connection, for example—requires two security associations, one in each direction.

From the local host's perspective, a given SA contains all the information required to execute the security services of AH and ESP. When created, an SA is assigned a *security parameters index* (SPI) by the receiving machine. A combination of this SPI and the destination IP addresses uniquely identifies a security association. Both AH and ESP put the SPI in their header. The receiving host then uses this information to determine which SA an incoming packet belongs to, and hence, what algorithms to apply to the packet.

ISAKMP's role is to define procedures and packet formats to establish, negotiate, modify, and delete security associations. It defines packet formats for exchanging key generation and authentication data. These formats aren't terribly interesting because they provide a framework only—the exact form of the keys and authentication data depend on the key generation technique, the encryption algorithm, and the authentication mechanism that is used. Moreover, ISAKMP does not specify a particular key exchange protocol, although it does suggest the Internet Key Exchange (IKE) as one possibility.

Authentication Header (AH)

The Authentication Header provides connectionless integrity and data origin authentication for IP datagrams. It also optionally provides protection against replays. The AH header is shown in Figure 8.18. It either follows the IPv4 header or is an IPv6 extension header, depending on which version of IP it is used with.

The NextHdr field identifies the type of the next payload after the Authentication Header. The PayloadLength field specifies the length of the AH in 32-bit words (4-byte units) minus 2.[5] The Reserved field is reserved for future use; it is set to 0 for now.

---

[5] All IPv6 extension headers encode the "Hdr Ext Len" field by first subtracting 1 (64-bit word) from the header length (measured in 64-bit words). AH is an IPv6 extension header, but since its length is measured in 32-bit words, the payload length is calculated by subtracting 2 (32-bit words).

The SPI field is an arbitrary 32-bit value that, in combination with the destination IP address, uniquely identifies the security association for this datagram.

The SeqNum field contains a monotonically increasing counter, or sequence number. This field is used to protect against replay, but it is present even if the receiver does not elect to enable the antireplay service for a specific SA. The sender's counter and the receiver's counter are initialized to 0 when an SA is established. If antireplay is enabled, which is the default, the transmitted sequence number must never be allowed to cycle. Thus, the sender's counter and the receiver's counter must be reset by establishing a new SA—and thus a new key—prior to transmitting the 2^{32}nd packet on an SA.

Finally, AuthenticationData is a variable-length field that contains the message integrity code for this packet. The field must be an integral multiple of 32 bits in length. AH does not prescribe a specific message digest algorithm. DES and MD5, among others, can be used. The only requirement is that the algorithm must specify the length of the MIC and the comparison rules and processing steps for validation.

Encapsulating Security Payload (ESP)

The Encapsulating Security Payload header is designed to provide a mix of security services in IPv4 and IPv6. ESP may be applied alone, or in combination with the AH. The ESP header is inserted after the IP header and before the upper-layer protocol header (when used between a pair of hosts), or before an encapsulated IP header when used to tunnel between a pair of security gateways.

ESP provides confidentiality, data origin authentication, connectionless integrity, and an antireplay service. The set of services provided depends on options selected at the time the SA is established. Confidentiality may be selected independent of all other services, but it is expected that confidentiality is supported in conjunction with integrity/authentication, either in ESP or separately in AH. Data origin authentication and connectionless integrity are joint services and are offered as an option in conjunction with (optional) confidentiality. The antireplay service may be selected only if data origin authentication is selected, and its election is solely at the discretion of the receiver. Note that although both confidentiality and authentication are optional, at least one of them must be selected.

Like AH, the ESP header either follows the IPv4 header or is an IPv6 extension header. Its format is shown in Figure 8.19. The SPI field has the same function as in the AH: It helps the receiving host identify the security association to which the packet belongs. Similarly, the SeqNum field protects against replay attacks. The packet's PayloadData contains the data described by the NextHdr field. If confidentiality is selected, then the data is encrypted by whatever encryption algorithm was associated with the SA. Padding is sometimes necessary, for example, because the encryption

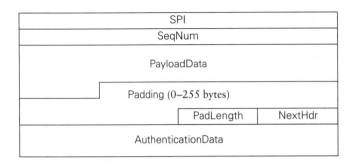

Figure 8.19   IPSEC's ESP header.

algorithm requires the plaintext to be a multiple of some number of bytes, or to ensure that the resulting ciphertext terminates on a 4-byte boundary. The PadLength field records how much padding was added to the data. Finally, the AuthenticationData carries the MIC, just as in AH. This field is present because ESP is general enough to support message integrity and authentication, in addition to privacy.

One of the most popular ways to use the ESP is to build an "IPSEC tunnel" between two routers. For example, a corporation wanting to link two sites using the Internet could configure a tunnel from a router at one site to a router at the other site, just as we discussed in Section 4.1.8. This tunnel may also be configured to use the ESP with confidentiality and authentication, thus preventing unauthorized access to the data that traverses this virtual link and ensuring that no spurious data is received at the far end of the tunnel.

8.4   Firewalls

We conclude our discussion of network security by discussing a mechanism that most security purists consider to be an abomination: *firewalls*. A firewall is a specially programmed router that sits between a site and the rest of the network, as illustrated in Figure 8.20. It is a router in the sense that it is connected to two or more physical networks and it forwards packets from one network to another, but it also filters the packets that flow through it. For example, it might throw away (rather than forward) all incoming packets addressed to a particular IP address or to a certain TCP port number. This is useful if you do not want external users to access a particular host or service within your site. The firewall might also filter packets based on the source's IP address. This is useful if you want to protect hosts within the site from an unwanted flood of packets from an external host. Such a flood of packets is sometimes called a *denial-of-service* attack.

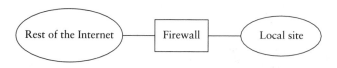

Figure 8.20 A firewall filters packets flowing between a site and the rest of the Internet.

If all the security mechanisms described throughout this chapter were in wide use, there would be no need for firewalls. When you tried to establish a connection to a node using, say, IPSEC, you would have to authenticate yourself as a valid peer. This being the case, why are firewalls so common? There are two reasons. The first is that the security mechanisms described in this chapter are not widely deployed. Getting security algorithms and protocols right is a very difficult task, and so firewalls have been devised as a stopgap measure while we wait for IPSEC. Even in the long term, unless every single system runs IPSEC or some similar end-to-end security mechanism, it seems likely that we will continue to depend on firewalls. The second reason is more fundamental. A firewall allows the system administrator to implement a security policy in one centralized place. End-to-end security mechanisms, in contrast, require the policy to be distributed, with a potentially different security configuration running on each node.

That said, firewalls are conceptually very simple devices that can be classified in one of two broad categories: *filter-based* and *proxy-based*. We now briefly describe each. To simplify our discussion, we limit ourselves to Internet firewalls.

8.4.1 Filter-Based Firewalls

Filter-based firewalls are the simplest and most widely deployed type of firewall. They are configured with a table of addresses that characterize the packets they will, and will not, forward. By addresses, we mean more than just the destination's IP address, although this is one possibility. Generally, each entry in the table is a 4-tuple: It gives the IP address and TCP (or UDP) port number for both the source and destination.

For example, a firewall might be configured to filter (not forward) all packets that match the following description:

⟨ 192.12.13.14, 1234, 128.7.6.5, 80 ⟩

This pattern says to filter all packets from port 1234 on host 192.12.13.14 addressed to port 80 on host 128.7.6.5. (Port 80 is the well-known TCP port for HTTP.) Of course it's often not practical to name every source host whose packets you want to filter, so the patterns can include wildcards. For example,

⟨ *, *, 128.7.6.5, 80 ⟩

says to filter all packets addressed to port 80 on 128.7.6.5, regardless of what source host or port sent the packet. Notice that address patterns like these require the firewall to make forwarding/filtering decisions based on level 4 port numbers, in addition to level 3 host addresses. It is for this reason that filter-based firewalls are sometimes called *level 4 switches*.

There are two important variations to the simple idea presented so far. First, there is the issue of whether the firewall forwards everything unless specifically instructed to filter certain kinds of packets (this is the assumption in the preceding example), or if the firewall filters everything unless explicitly instructed to forward it. This is a fundamental question in the design of any secure system: Do you explicitly identify what is allowed or what is disallowed? For example, instead of blocking access to port 80 on host 128.7.6.5, the firewall might be instructed to only allow access to port 25 (the SMTP mail port) on a particular mail server, for example,

⟨ *, *, 128.19.20.21, 25 ⟩

but to block all other traffic.

The second issue is whether the filters must be specified when the system is booted, or if new filters can be installed as the firewall is running. The examples given so far can all be known in advance. The reason you might need the latter is that you are running a "drop by default" firewall and don't know what port a particular valid connection is going to use until the last moment. This happens with FTP, for example, which establishes a new TCP connection for each file it transfers. The two ports used at either end of such a connection are not known until the transfer is going to take place, so the set of allowed patterns must be dynamically, and temporarily, extended to include these ports. A firewall that supports this capability is said to provide *dynamic port selection*.

8.4.2 Proxy-Based Firewalls

A proxy is a general networking technique that shows up in a number of situations, including firewalls. Generally speaking, a proxy is a process that sits between a client process and a server process. To the client, the proxy appears to be the server; in a sense, the proxy is standing in for the server. To the server, the proxy appears to be the client. Because a proxy imitates both the client and the server, it necessarily has application knowledge built into it. One thing a proxy might do is implement a cache. This allows the proxy to respond to a client request without having to pass the request along to the server. It passes the request on to the server only if it doesn't have the

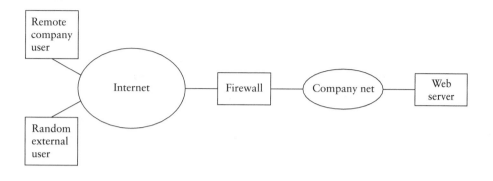

Figure 8.21 Firewall protecting a company Web server from some external accesses.

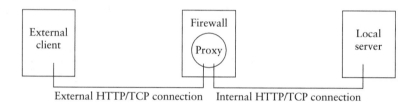

Figure 8.22 HTTP proxy mediating access to a corporate Web server.

requested item in its cache. Proxies also provide an opportunity to implement a security policy. It is this security role that we now consider.

To understand how a proxy-based firewall works—and why you would want one—consider a corporate Web server, where the company wants to make some of the server's pages accessible to all external users (i.e., it won't work to simply program the firewall to block all external access to HTTP's well-known port 80), but it wants to restrict certain of the pages to corporate users at one or more remote sites. This situation is illustrated in Figure 8.21. There is no way to express this policy as a filter since it depends on the URL contained in each HTTP request.[6]

The solution is to put an *HTTP proxy* on the firewall. Remote users establish an HTTP/TCP connection to the proxy, which looks at the URL contained in the request message. If the requested page is allowed for the source host, the proxy establishes a second HTTP/TCP connection to the server, and forwards the request on to the server. The proxy then forwards the response in the reverse direction between the two TCP

---

[6] If you are unfamiliar with how the Web works, you might want to first read Section 9.2.2.

Figure 8.23 Simple internet, with source S sending message to receiver R through proxy P.

connections. This situation is depicted in Figure 8.22. If the request is not allowed, the proxy does not create this second connection, but instead returns an error to the source. In a sense, the firewall dynamically decides what packets to forward and what packets to drop, with the policy embodied in the application-specific proxy.

There are several things to notice about this example. First, the proxy has to understand the HTTP protocol in order to respond to the client. Second, once an HTTP proxy is in place for security reasons, it might be extended to decide which of many local Web servers to forward a given request to, perhaps in an effort to balance the load among the servers. It might also cache hot Web pages, as suggested above. Third, proxies can be defined for applications other than HTTP; for example, FTP and Telnet proxies are quite common.

Finally, proxy-based firewalls can be characterized as being either *transparent* or *classical*. A transparent proxy, as the name implies, is not explicitly visible to either the sender or the receiver; it just happens to intercept messages that flow through it. In contrast, the source purposely addresses messages to a classical proxy, which then forwards the message to the ultimate destination. Consider the simple network shown in Figure 8.23, in which source S sends a message to receiver R through proxy P. If P is transparent, then S addresses the message to R, and the message just happens to pass through P en route to R. P either forwards the message to R, or not. With a classical firewall, S does not know about R, but instead addresses the message to P. In other words, P acts as an addressable front door to the site. When the message arrives at P, it selects a node "behind it" to which it forwards the message.

8.4.3 Limitations

We conclude this discussion by observing that while a traditional firewall protects internal users from external users, it does nothing to protect or isolate internal users from each other. While social and legal pressures may keep users from violating local security policies, these pressures are ineffective against mobile code imported by these users into the local site. Specifically, traditional firewalls cannot keep mobile code out of the local network—for example, programs might arrive in otherwise innocent-looking email messages—and once running locally, such programs have virtually unlimited access to all local hosts.

Mobile code is not the only concern. For example, large companies often want to isolate portions of the company's computing infrastructure. This might happen if the company has an external partner working on one project—thus having access to some subset of machines—but it wants to keep the partner from having access to the entire infrastructure. As another example, mobile computers make it easy for users to anonymously attach their machines to the network at arbitrary points.

Another vulnerability of firewalls is gaining attention as wireless communication becomes more ubiquitous. Consider a telecommuter that connects to a corporate site through a firewall. The firewall has to be programmed to allow the user's computer to send packets to the site, since the user is legitimate. Now suppose that the telecommuter has a wireless network that connects multiple machines in his or her house. There is nothing to prevent a neighbor, or a competitor parked across the street, from becoming part of this "home network," and hence gaining access to the corporate network through the firewall.

In general, it is impossible for existing firewalls to know who is accessing the network and, therefore, who has the ability to connect to other machines on the network. What is needed is the ability to move access protection inward from the periphery of the network and closer to the hosts that initiate the access. Ultimately, security mechanisms like IPSEC are probably required to support such a level of security.

8.5 Summary

Encryption algorithms are the backbone of network security. Public key algorithms like RSA are often used by authentication protocols to establish the identity of two communicating processes. Once authenticated, the two participants can establish a shared key that is used by a secret key algorithm like DES to encrypt any messages they exchange, thereby ensuring the privacy of their communication. Alternatively, a message digest algorithm like MD5 can be used to protect the integrity of messages. The whole system is held together by a key distribution mechanism that is used to obtain the public key needed by RSA in the first place.

Several recent systems use these algorithms and protocols to offer security services on the Internet. At the application level, PEM and PGP can be used to protect email messages. At the transport level, TLS can be used to protect commercial transactions on the World Wide Web. At the network level, the IPSEC architecture can be used to secure communication among any set of hosts or gateways on the Internet. At the same time these systems are becoming more widely available, system administrators continue to use firewalls to protect their site from external threats.

OPEN ISSUE

Denial-of-Service Attacks

Systems like IPSEC and TLS have the potential to give the Internet the level of security required by many emerging business and government applications. The key to the success of these systems rests with the success of the key distribution process. Without trusted access to public keys, the entire scheme breaks down.

Key distribution is only one of the security-related challenges facing computer networks, though. An equally daunting problem is finding ways to protect computers connected to wide area networks from *denial-of-service* attacks. Unlike a privacy attack, where an adversary is trying to gain access to information it is not allowed to see, a denial-of-service attack involves an adversary trying to keep you from accessing information or resources you have every right to access.

One well-known denial-of-service attack is called a SYN attack, named after the TCP's connection setup packet. In a SYN attack, a remote attacker floods your machine with SYN packets, causing it to spend all its cycles setting up bogus TCP connections. The key to this attack is that, unlike simply flooding a machine with bogus data packets, each SYN packet requires nontrivial processing to determine that it's OK to just throw the packet away. Firewalls offer some level of protection, in that they can be programmed to drop all packets from a known attacking host, but it's easy for the attacker to simply put a different source IP address in each SYN packet.

A less well-known example illustrates how subtle a denial-of-service attack can be. An attacker flooded an ISP's router with IP packets carrying a serial sequence of IP addresses. The sequence blew the router's first-level route cache, which ultimately caused the router's processor to spend all its time building new forwarding tables. This happened at the expense of the router responding to its neighbors' routing probes, which caused the neighbors to believe the router was down.

Protecting against denial-of-service attacks involves three steps. The first is to account for all resources consumed by every user (or flow). The second is to detect when the resources consumed by a given user exceed those allowed by some system policy. Once an attack is detected, the final step is to reclaim the consumed resources using as few additional resources as possible; otherwise, removal of an offending user becomes a denial-of-service attack in its own right. Unfortunately, few of today's systems—including both hosts and routers—accurately account for all resources used in the system, let alone define a policy as to what constitutes a denial-of-service attack.

FURTHER READING

The first two security-related papers, taken together, give a good overview of the topic. The article by Lampson et al. contains a formal treatment of security, while the Satyanarayanan paper gives a nice description of how a secure system is designed in practice. The third paper gives an overview of the IPSEC security architecture and is the right place to start to fully understand the state of security in the Internet today.

- ■ Lampson, B., et al. Authentication in distributed systems: Theory and practice. *ACM Transactions on Computer Systems* 10(4):265–310, November 1992.

- ■ Satyanarayanan, M. Integrating security in a large distributed system. *ACM Transactions on Computer Systems* 7(3):247–280, August 1989.

- ■ Kent, S., and R. Atkinson. Security architecture for the Internet Protocol. *Request for Comments* 2401, November 1998.

There are several good books covering the full gamut of network security. We recommend Schneier [Sch94] and Kaufman et al. [KPS95]. The former gives a comprehensive treatment of the topic, including sample code, while the latter gives a very readable overview of the subject. The full IPSEC architecture is defined in a series of RFCs: [KA98a, MG98a, MG98b, MD98, KA98b, Pip98, MSST98, HC98]. A discussion of the problem of denial-of-service attacks, and how to defend against them, can be found in a paper by Spatscheck and Peterson [SP99].

Finally, we recommend the following live reference:

- ■ ftp://cert.org/pub: a collection of security-related notices posted by the Computer Emergency Response Team (CERT)

EXERCISES

1 Find an encryption utility (e.g., the Unix **des** command or **pgp**) on your system. Read its documentation and experiment with it. Measure how fast it is able to encrypt and decrypt data. Are these two rates the same? Try to compare these timing results using different key sizes; for example, compare single-DES with triple-DES.

2 Section 8.1.2 gives the DES encryption transformation from $\langle L_{i-1}, R_{i-1} \rangle$ at round $i-1$ to $\langle L_i, R_i \rangle$ at round i. Give the reverse, that is, express $\langle L_{i-1}, R_{i-1} \rangle$ in terms of $\langle L_i, R_i \rangle$.

3 Suppose that at round i in DES, L_{i-1} is all 0s, R_{i-1} is (in hex) deadbeef, and K_i is a5bd96 860841. Give R_i, assuming that we use a simplified S box that reduces each 6-bit chunk to 4 bits by dropping the first and last bits.

4 Again suppose DES used the simplified S box of the previous exercise, and also assume we perform only a single round of encryption.

   (a) Suppose an attacker has both the plaintext $\langle L_0, R_0 \rangle$ and the ciphertext $\langle L_1, R_1 \rangle$. How much does this tell the attacker about the key K_1? How about K? (This is not intended to suggest a weakness in the real DES, but rather as a justification for the S box DES actually uses.)

   (b) Being able to recover the key given a plaintext and ciphertext would be bad enough for any encryption mechanism; explain why it would be particularly fatal for public key cryptosystems.

5 Suppose you are doing RSA encryption with $p = 101$, $q = 113$, and $e = 3$.

   (a) Find the decryption exponent d. (Hint: Although there are methodical ways to do this, trial and error is efficient for $e = 3$.)

   (b) Encrypt the message $m = 9876$. Note that evaluating m^3 with 32-bit arithmetic results in overflow.

6 Prove that the RSA decryption algorithm recovers the original message; that is, $m^{ed} \equiv m \bmod pq$. Hint: You may assume that, because p and q are relatively prime, it suffices to prove the congruence mod p and mod q.

7 If n is a prime number and $b < n$, then $b^{n-1} \equiv 1 \bmod n$. There are a few composite n (e.g., 561) for which this congruence also holds for all $b < n$, but by adding a little extra bookkeeping to the calculation we get *Miller's test*, which if n is prime succeeds for all $b < n$ and if n is composite always fails for (here we need the extra bookkeeping) at least three-quarters of all $b < n$. If we try the test with a large number of $b < n$ chosen at random, and it does not fail for any of them, then n is "probably" prime.

   (a) Show that calculating $b^{n-1} \bmod n$ can be done with $O(\log n)$ multiplications. Hint: $b^{13} = b^8 b^4 b$.

   (b) Show, using this method, that $n = 50{,}621$ is composite. Use $b = 2$. You will not need the "extra bookkeeping"; just show $b^{n-1} \not\equiv 1 \bmod n$.

   (c) Show $2^{280} \equiv 1 \bmod 561$ (and hence automatically $2^{560} \equiv (2^{280})^2 \equiv 1$), but that $2^{140} \not\equiv \pm 1 \bmod 561$. This last fact makes the full Miller's test fail, showing

$561 (= 3 \times 11 \times 17)$ is composite, even though the simpler $b^{n-1} \equiv 1 \bmod n$ test succeeds.

8 In the three-way authentication handshake of Figure 8.9, why is the server unsure of the client's identity until it receives the third message? To what attack might a server be exposed if it trusted the client's identity before the third message was received?

9 Suppose the values x and y used in the three-way handshake of Figure 8.9 were clock-driven rather than random; for example, x and y were incremented once per second or per connection.

(a) Show that the technique used in the IP spoofing attack outlined in Exercise 17 of Chapter 5 fails.

(b) Suppose in addition an attacker could eavesdrop on the connection and knows past transmissions from the client. Would this help the attacker?

(c) Suppose that furthermore the attacker could reset the clock on the server host, perhaps using the Network Time Protocol. Show how an attacker could now authenticate itself to the server without knowing CHK (although it could not decrypt SK).

10 Figure 8.7 shows CBC encryption. Give the corresponding diagram for decryption.

11 Figure 8.11 shows one-way authentication using RSA. Show how RSA can be used for two-way authentication.

12 Learn about a key escrow encryption scheme (for example, Clipper). What are the pros and cons of key escrow?

13 One mechanism for resisting "replay" attacks in password authentication is to use *one-time passwords*: a list of passwords is prepared, and once *password*[N] has been accepted, the server decrements N and prompts for *password*[$N - 1$] next time. At $N = 0$ a new list is needed. Outline a mechanism by which the user and server need only remember one master password mp and have available locally a way to compute *password*[N] $= f(mp, N)$. Hint: Let g be an appropriate one-way function (e.g., MD5) and let *password*[N] $= g^N(mp) = g$ applied N times to mp. Explain why knowing *password*[N] doesn't help reveal *password*[$N - 1$].

14 Suppose a user employs one-time passwords as above (or, for that matter, reusable passwords), but that the password is transmitted "sufficiently slowly."

(a) Show that an eavesdropper can gain access to the remote server with a relatively modest number of guesses. Hint: The eavesdropper starts guessing after the original user has typed all but one character of the password.

(b) To what other attacks might a user of one-time passwords be subject?

15 Suppose that RSA is used to send a message m to three recipients, who have relatively prime encryption moduli n_1, n_2, and n_3. All three recipients use the same encryption exponent $e = 3$, a once-popular choice as it makes encryption very fast. Show that someone who intercepts all three encrypted messages $c_1 = m^3 \bmod n_1$, $c_2 = m^3 \bmod n_2$, and $c_3 = m^3 \bmod n_1$ can efficiently decipher m. Hint: The *Chinese remainder theorem* implies that you can efficiently find a c such that $c = c_1 \bmod n_1$, $c = c_2 \bmod n_2$, and $c = c_3 \bmod n_3$. Assume this, and show that it implies $c = m^3 \bmod n_1 n_2 n_3$. Then note $m^3 < n_1 n_2 n_3$.

16 Suppose we have a very short secret s (e.g., a single bit or even a Social Security number), and we wish to send someone else a message m now that will not reveal s but that can be used later to verify that we did know s. Explain why $m = \mathrm{MD5}(s)$ or $m = \mathrm{E}(s)$ with RSA encryption would not be secure choices, and suggest a better choice.

17 Suppose two people want to play poker over the network. To "deal" the cards they need a mechanism for fairly choosing a random number x between them; each party stands to lose if the other party can unfairly influence the choice of x. Describe such a mechanism. Hint: You may assume that if either of two bit strings x_1 and x_2 are random, then the exclusive-OR $x = x_1 \oplus x_2$ is random.

18 Estimate the probabilities of finding two messages with the same MD5 checksum, given total numbers of messages of 2^{63}, 2^{64}, and 2^{65}. Hint: This is the birthday problem again, as in Exercise 41 of Chapter 2, and again the probability that the $k + 1$th message has a different checksum from each of the preceding k is $1 - k/2^{128}$. However, the approximation in the hint there for simplifying the product fails rather badly now. So, instead, take the log of each side and use the approximation $\log(1 - k/2^{128}) \approx -k/2^{128}$.

19 Suppose we wanted to encrypt a Telnet session with, say, DES. Telnet sends lots of 1-byte messages, while DES encrypts in blocks of 8 bytes at a time. Explain how DES might be used securely in this setting.

20 Consider the following simple UDP protocol (based loosely on TFTP, *Request for Comments* 1350) for downloading files:

- Client sends a file request.
- Server replies with first data packet.
- Client sends ACK, and the two proceed using stop-and-wait.

Suppose client and server each possess keys K_C and K_S, respectively, and that these keys are known to each other.

(a) Extend the file downloading protocol, using these keys and MD5, to provide sender authentication and message integrity. Your protocol should also be resistant to replay attacks.

(b) How does the extra information in your revised protocol protect against arrival of late packets from prior connection incarnations, and sequence number wraparound?

21 Using the browser of your choice, find out what certification authorities for HTTPS your browser is configured by default to trust. Do you trust these agencies? Find out what happens when you disable trust of some or all of these certification authorities.

22 Suppose you want your filter-based firewall to block all incoming Telnet connections, but to allow outbound Telnet connections. One approach would be to block all inbound packets to the designated Telnet port (23).

(a) We might want to block inbound packets to other ports as well, but what inbound TCP connections *must* be permitted in order not to interfere with outbound Telnet?

(b) Now suppose your firewall is allowed to use the TCP header Flags bits in addition to the port numbers. Explain how you can achieve the desired Telnet effect here while at the same time allowing no inbound TCP connections.

23 Suppose a firewall is configured to allow outbound TCP connections but inbound connections only to specified ports. The FTP protocol now presents a problem: When an inside client contacts an outside server, the outbound TCP control connection can be opened normally but the TCP data connection traditionally is inbound.

(a) Look up the FTP protocol in, for example, *Request for Comments 959*. Find out how the PORT command works. Discuss how the client might be written

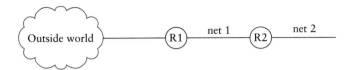

Figure 8.24   Diagram for Exercise 24.

so as to limit the number of ports to which the firewall must grant inbound access. Can the number of such ports be limited to one?

(b) Find out how the FTP PASV command can be used to solve this firewall problem.

24 Suppose filtering routers are arranged as in Figure 8.24; the primary firewall is R1. Explain how to configure R1 and R2 so that outsiders can Telnet to net 2 but not to hosts on net 1. To avoid "leapfrogging" break-ins to net 1, also disallow Telnet connections from net 2 to net 1.

25 Why might an Internet service provider want to block certain *outbound* traffic?

26 Compare a filtering firewall to a proxy firewall in terms of protection against spoofing attacks, as in Exercise 17 of Chapter 5. Assume a configuration as in Figure 8.21, where the internal host under attack trusts the remote company user.

We started this book by talking about application programs—everything from Web browsers to videoconferencing tools—that people want to run over computer networks. In the intervening chapters, we have developed, one layer at a time, the networking infrastructure needed to make such applications possible. We have now come full circle, back to network applications. These applications are part network protocol (in the sense that they exchange messages with their peers on other machines) and part traditional application program (in the sense that they interact with the windowing system, the file system, and ultimately, the user). This chapter explores some of the most popular network applications available today, with a focus on their protocols. What you will quickly recognize is that a protocol is a protocol, no matter what layer it runs at. Said another way, the best way to prepare yourself to write network applications is to first understand how to design good network protocols.

The first example we look at—a distributed name service—also happens to be the first application implemented on a network. Although it technically qualifies as a network application—it is, in effect, a distributed database built on top of the underlying transport protocols—it is not an application that users normally invoke explicitly. Nevertheless, it is an application that all other applications depend upon. This is because the name server is used to translate host names into host addresses; the existence of such an application allows the users of other applications to refer to remote hosts by name rather than by address. In other words, a name server is usually used by other applications, rather than by humans.

We then turn our attention to describing a variety of familiar, and not so familiar, network applications. These range from exchanging email and surfing the Web, to managing a set of network elements, to emerging audio

PROBLEM

Applications Need Their Own Protocols

Now this is not the end. It is not even the beginning of the end. But it is, perhaps, the end of the beginning.

—Winston Churchill

and video applications like vic and vat. This list is by no means exhaustive, but it does serve to illustrate the trick in designing application-level protocols, which is to augment the underlying transport services of TCP and UDP so as to provide the precise communication service required by the application.

9

Applications

9.1 Name Service (DNS)

Up to this point, we have been using addresses to identify hosts. While perfectly suited for processing by routers, addresses are not exactly user friendly. It is for this reason that a unique *name* is also typically assigned to each host in a network. This section describes how a naming service can be developed to map user-friendly names into router-friendly addresses. Such a service is often the first application program implemented in a network since it frees other applications to identify hosts by name rather than by address. Name services are sometimes called *middleware* because they fill a gap between applications and the underlying network.

Host names differ from host addresses in two important ways. First, they are usually of variable length and mnemonic, thereby making them easier for humans to remember. (In contrast, fixed-length numeric addresses are easier for routers to process.) Second, names typically contain no information that helps the network locate (route packets toward) the host. Addresses, in contrast, sometimes have routing information embedded in them; *flat* addresses (those not divisible into component parts) are the exception.

Before getting into the details of how hosts are named in a network, we first introduce some basic terminology. First, a *name space* defines the set of possible names. A name space can be either *flat* (names are not divisible into components), or it can be *hierarchical* (Unix file names are the obvious example). Second, the naming system maintains a collection of *bindings* of names to values. The value can be anything we want the naming system to return when presented with a name; in many cases it is an address. Finally, a *resolution mechanism* is a procedure that, when invoked with a name, returns the corresponding value. A *name server* is a specific implementation of a resolution mechanism that is available on a network and that can be queried by sending it a message.

Because of its large size, the Internet has a particularly well-developed naming system in place—the *domain name system* (DNS). We therefore use DNS as a framework for discussing the problem of naming hosts. Note that the Internet did not always use DNS. Early in its history, when there were only a few hundred hosts on the Internet, a central authority called the Network Information Center (NIC) maintained a flat table of name-to-address bindings; this table was called hosts.txt. Whenever a site wanted to add a new host to the Internet, the site administrator sent email to the NIC giving the new host's name/address pair. This information was manually entered into the table, the modified table was mailed out to the various sites every few days, and the system administrator at each site installed the table on every host at the site. Name resolution was then simply implemented by a procedure that looked up a host's name in the local copy of the table and returned the corresponding address.

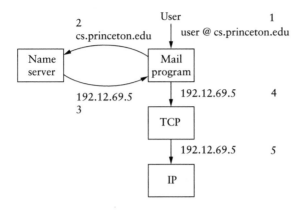

Figure 9.1 Names translated into addresses, where the numbers 1–5 show the sequence of steps in the process.

It should come as no surprise that the hosts.txt approach to naming did not work well as the number of hosts in the Internet started to grow. Therefore, in the mid-1980s, the domain naming system was put into place. DNS employs a hierarchical name space rather than a flat name space, and the "table" of bindings that implements this name space is partitioned into disjoint pieces and distributed throughout the Internet. These subtables are made available in name servers that can be queried over the network.

What happens in the Internet is that a user presents a host name to an application program (possibly embedded in a compound name such as an email address or URL), and this program engages the naming system to translate this name into a host address. The application then opens a connection to this host by presenting some transport protocol (e.g., TCP) with the host's IP address. This situation is illustrated (in the case of sending email) in Figure 9.1.

9.1.1 Domain Hierarchy

DNS implements a hierarchical name space for Internet objects. Unlike Unix file names, which are processed from left to right with the naming components separated with slashes, DNS names are processed from right to left and use periods as the separator. (Although they are "processed" from right to left, humans still "read" domain names from left to right.) An example domain name for a host is cicada.cs.princeton.edu. Notice that we said domain names are used to name Internet "objects." What we mean by this is that DNS is not strictly used to map host names

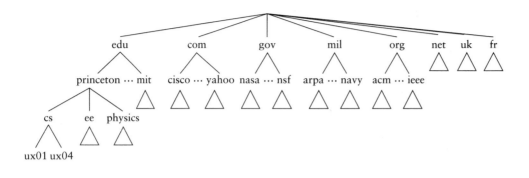

Figure 9.2 Example of a domain hierarchy.

into host addresses. It is more accurate to say that DNS maps domain names into values. For the time being, we assume that these values are IP addresses; we will come back to this issue later in this section.

Like the Unix file hierarchy, the DNS hierarchy can be visualized as a tree, where each node in the tree corresponds to a domain, and the leaves in the tree correspond to the hosts being named. Figure 9.2 gives an example of a domain hierarchy. Note that we should not assign any semantics to the term "domain" other than that it is simply a context in which additional names can be defined.

There was actually a substantial amount of discussion that took place when the domain name hierarchy was first being developed as to what conventions would govern the names that were to be handed out near the top of the hierarchy. Without going into that discussion in any detail, notice that the hierarchy is not very wide at the first level. There are domains for each country, plus the "big six" domains: edu, com, gov, mil, org, and net. These six domains are all based in the United States; the only domain names that don't explicitly specify a country are those in the United States. Aside from this U.S. bias, you might notice a military bias in the hierarchy. This is easy to explain, since the development of DNS was originally funded by ARPA, the major research arm of the U.S. Department of Defense.

9.1.2 Name Servers

The complete domain name hierarchy exists only in the abstract. We now turn our attention to the question of how this hierarchy is actually implemented. The first step is to partition the hierarchy into subtrees called *zones*. For example, Figure 9.3 shows how the hierarchy given in Figure 9.2 might be divided into zones. Each zone can be thought of as corresponding to some administrative authority that is responsible for that portion of the hierarchy. For example, the top level of the hierarchy forms a

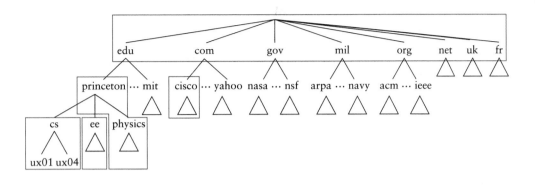

Figure 9.3   Domain hierarchy partitioned into zones.

zone that is managed by the NIC. Below this is a zone that corresponds to Princeton University. Within this zone, some departments do not want the responsibility of managing the hierarchy (and so they remain in the university-level zone), while others, like the Department of Computer Science, manage their own department-level zone.

The relevance of a zone is that it corresponds to the fundamental unit of implementation in DNS—the name server. Specifically, the information contained in each zone is implemented in two or more name servers. Each name server, in turn, is a program that can be accessed over the Internet. Clients send queries to name servers, and name servers respond with the requested information. Sometimes the response contains the final answer that the client wants, and sometimes the response contains a pointer to another server that the client should query next. Thus, from an implementation perspective, it is more accurate to think of DNS as being represented by a hierarchy of name servers rather than by a hierarchy of domains, as illustrated in Figure 9.4.

Note that each zone is implemented in two or more name servers for the sake of redundancy; that is, the information is still available even if one name server fails. On the flip side, a given name server is free to implement more than one zone.

Each name server implements the zone information as a collection of *resource records*. In essence, a resource record is a name-to-value binding, or more specifically, a 5-tuple that contains the following fields:

⟨ Name, Value, Type, Class, TTL ⟩

The Name and Value fields are exactly what you would expect, while the Type field specifies how the Value should be interpreted. For example, Type = A indicates that

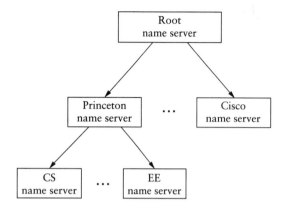

Figure 9.4 Hierarchy of name servers.

the Value is an IP address. Thus, A records implement the name-to-address mapping we have been assuming. Other record types include

- **NS:** The Value field gives the domain name for a host that is running a name server that knows how to resolve names within the specified domain.

- **CNAME:** The Value field gives the canonical name for a particular host; it is used to define aliases.

- **MX:** The Value field gives the domain name for a host that is running a mail server that accepts messages for the specified domain.

The Class field was included to allow entities other than the NIC to define useful record types. To date, the only widely used Class is the one used by the Internet; it is denoted IN. Finally, the TTL field shows how long this resource record is valid. It is used by servers that cache resource records from other servers; when the TTL expires, the server must evict the record from its cache.

To better understand how resource records represent the information in the domain hierarchy, consider the following examples drawn from the domain hierarchy given in Figure 9.2. To simplify the examples, we ignore the TTL field and we give the relevant information for only one of the name servers that implement each zone.

First, the root name server contains an NS record for each second-level server. It also has an A record that translates this name into the corresponding IP address. Taken together, these two records effectively implement a pointer from the root name server to each of the second-level servers.

⟨ princeton.edu, cit.princeton.edu, NS, IN ⟩

⟨ cit.princeton.edu, 128.196.128.233, A, IN ⟩

⟨ cisco.com, ns.cisco.com, NS, IN ⟩

⟨ ns.cisco.com, 128.96.32.20, A, IN ⟩

⋮

Next, the domain princeton.edu has a name server available on host cit.princeton .edu that contains the following records. Note that some of these records give the final answer (e.g., the address for host saturn.physics.princeton.edu), while others point to third-level name servers.

⟨ cs.princeton.edu, gnat.cs.princeton.edu, NS, IN ⟩

⟨ gnat.cs.princeton.edu, 192.12.69.5, A, IN ⟩

⟨ ee.princeton.edu, helios.ee.princeton.edu, NS, IN ⟩

⟨ helios.ee.princeton.edu, 128.196.28.166, A, IN ⟩

⟨ jupiter.physics.princeton.edu, 128.196.4.1, A, IN ⟩

⟨ saturn.physics.princeton.edu, 128.196.4.2, A, IN ⟩

⟨ mars.physics.princeton.edu, 128.196.4.3, A, IN ⟩

⟨ venus.physics.princeton.edu, 128.196.4.4, A, IN ⟩

⋮

Finally, a third-level name server, such as the one managed by domain cs.princeton.edu, contains A records for all of its hosts. It might also define a set of aliases (CNAME records) for each of those hosts. Aliases are sometimes just convenient (e.g., shorter) names for machines, but they can also be used to provide a level of indirection. For example, www.cs.princeton.edu is an alias for the host named cicada.cs.princeton.edu. This allows the site's Web server to move to another machine without affecting remote users; they simply continue to use the alias without regard for what machine currently runs the domain's Web server. The mail exchange (MX) records serve the same purpose for the email application—it allows an administrator to change which host receives mail on behalf of the domain without having to change everyone's email address.

⟨ cs.princeton.edu, gnat.cs.princeton.edu, MX, IN ⟩

⟨ cicada.cs.princeton.edu, 192.12.69.60, A, IN ⟩

⟨ cic.cs.princeton.edu, cicada.cs.princeton.edu, CNAME, IN ⟩

⟨ gnat.cs.princeton.edu, 192.12.69.5, A, IN ⟩

⟨ gna.cs.princeton.edu, gnat.cs.princeton.edu, CNAME, IN ⟩

⟨ www.cs.princeton.edu, 192.12.69.35, A, IN ⟩

⟨ cicada.cs.princeton.edu,

    roach.cs.princeton.edu, CNAME, IN ⟩

⋮

Note that although resource records can be defined for virtually any type of object, DNS is typically used to name hosts (including servers) and sites. It is not used to name individual people, or other objects like files or directories; other naming systems are typically used to identify such objects. For example, X.500 is an ISO naming system designed to make it easier to identify people. It allows you to name a person by giving a set of attributes: name, title, phone number, postal address, and so on. X.500 proved too cumbersome—and in some sense, was usurped by powerful search engines now available on the Web—but it did eventually evolve into LDAP (Lightweight Directory Access Protocol). LDAP is a subset of X.500 originally designed as a PC front end to X.500. Today it is gaining in popularity, mostly at the enterprise level, as a system for learning information about users.

9.1.3 Name Resolution

Given a hierarchy of name servers, we now consider the issue of how a client engages

Naming Conventions

Our description of DNS focuses on the underlying *mechanisms*, that is, how the hierarchy is partitioned over multiple servers and how the resolution process works. There is an equally interesting, but much less technical, issue of the *conventions* that are used to decide the names to use in the mechanism. For example, it is by convention that all U.S. universities are under the edu domain, while English universities are under the ac (academic) subdomain of the uk (United Kingdom) domain. In fact, the very existence of the uk domain, rather than a gb (Great Britain) domain, was a source of great controversy in the early days of DNS, since the latter does not include Northern Ireland.

The thing to understand about conventions is that they are sometimes defined without anyone making an explicit decision. For example, by convention a site hides the exact host that serves as its mail

these servers to resolve a domain name. To illustrate the basic idea, suppose the client wants to resolve the name cicada.cs.princeton.edu relative to the set of servers given in the previous subsection. The client first sends a query containing this name to the root server. The root server, unable to match the entire name, returns the best match it has—the NS record for princeton.edu. The server also returns all records that are related to this record, in this case, the A record for cit.princeton.edu. The client, having not received the answer it was after, next sends the same query to the name server at IP host 128.196.128.233. This server also cannot match the whole name, and so returns the NS and corresponding A records for the cs.princeton.edu domain. Finally, the client sends the same query as before to the server at IP host 192.12.69.5, and this time gets back the A record for cicada.cs.princeton.edu.

This example still leaves a couple of questions about the resolution process unanswered. The first question is, How did the client locate the root server in the first place, or said another way, How do you resolve the name of the server that knows how to resolve names? This is a fundamental problem in any naming system, and the answer is that the system has to be bootstrapped in some way. In this case, the name-to-address mapping for one or more root servers is well known, that is, published through some means outside the naming system itself.

In practice, however, not all clients know about the root servers. Instead, the client program running on each Internet host is initialized with the address of a *local* name server. For example, all the hosts in the Department of Computer Science at Princeton know about the server on gnat.cs.princeton.edu. This local name server, in turn, has resource records for one or more of the root servers, for example:

exchange behind the MX record. An alternative would have been to adopt the convention of sending mail to user@mail.cs.princeton.edu, much as we expect to find a site's public FTP directory at ftp.cs.princeton.edu and its WWW server at www.cs.princeton.edu.

Conventions also exist at the local level, where an organization names its machines according to some consistent set of rules. Given that the host names venus, saturn, and mars are among the most popular in the Internet, it's not too hard to figure out one common naming convention. Some host naming conventions are more imaginative, however. For example, one site named its machines up, down, crashed, rebooting, and so on, resulting in confusing statements like "rebooting has crashed" and "up is down." Of course, there are also less imaginative names, such as those who name their machines after the integers.

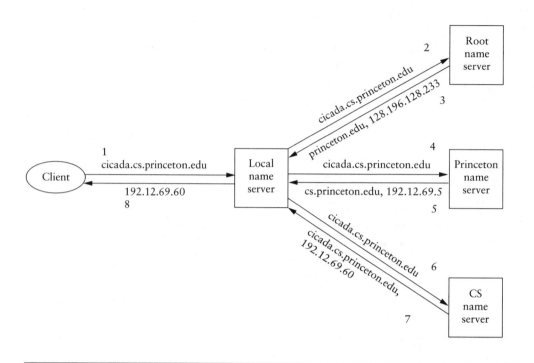

Figure 9.5   Name resolution in practice, where the numbers 1–8 show the sequence of steps in the process.

⟨ 'root', venera.isi.edu, NS, IN ⟩

⟨ venera.isi.edu, 128.9.0.32, A, IN ⟩

Thus, resolving a name actually involves a client querying the local server, which in turn acts as a client that queries the remote servers on the original client's behalf. This results in the client/server interactions illustrated in Figure 9.5. One advantage of this model is that all the hosts in the Internet do not have to be kept up-to-date on where the current root servers are located; only the servers have to know about the root. A second advantage is that the local server gets to see the answers that come back from queries that are posted by all the local clients. The local server caches these responses and is sometimes able to resolve future queries without having to go out over the network. The TTL field in the resource records returned by remote servers indicates how long each record can be safely cached.

The second question is how the system works when a user submits a partial name (e.g., cicada) rather than a complete domain name (e.g., cicada.cs.princeton.edu). The answer is that the client program is configured with the local domain in which the host resides (e.g., cs.princeton.edu) and it appends this string to any simple names before sending out a query.

▶ Just to make sure we are clear, we have now seen three different levels of identifiers—domain names, IP addresses, and physical network addresses—and the mapping of identifiers at one level into identifiers at another level happens at different points in the network architecture. First, users specify domain names when interacting with the application. Second, the application engages DNS to translate this name into an IP address; it is the IP address that is placed in each datagram, not the domain name. (As an aside, this translation process involves IP datagrams being sent over the Internet, but these datagrams are addressed to a host that runs a name server, not to the ultimate destination.) Third, IP does forwarding at each router, which often means that it maps one IP address into another; that is, it maps the ultimate destination's address into the address for the next hop router. Finally, IP engages ARP to translate the next hop IP address into the physical address for that machine; the next hop might be the ultimate destination or it might be an intermediate router. Frames sent over the physical network have these physical addresses in their headers.

9.2 Traditional Applications

The domain name system may be an essential Internet application, but it's one that users only indirectly interact with. We now turn our attention to those applications that are directly invoked by users, focusing on two of the most popular—the World Wide Web and email. We also look at network management, which although not so familiar to the average user, is the application of choice for system administrators. Like DNS, all three applications employ the request/reply paradigm—users send requests to servers, which then respond accordingly. We refer to these as "traditional" applications because they typify the sort of applications that have existed since the early days of computer networks. By contrast, the next section looks at a class of applications that have become feasible only relatively recently: streaming applications, that is, multimedia applications like video and audio.

Before taking a close look at each of these applications, there are three general points that we need to make. The first is that it is important to distinguish between application *programs* and application *protocols*. For example, the HyperText Transport Protocol (HTTP) is an application protocol that is used to retrieve Web pages from remote servers. There can be many different application programs—that is, Web clients like Internet Explorer, Mosaic, and Netscape—that provide users with a different look and feel, but all of them use the same HTTP protocol to communicate with Web servers over the Internet. This section focuses on three application protocols:

- SMTP: Simple Mail Transfer Protocol is used to exchange electronic mail.

- HTTP: HyperText Transport Protocol is used to communicate between Web browsers and Web servers.

- SNMP: Simple Network Management Protocol is used to query (and sometimes modify) the state of remote network nodes.

The second point is that since all of the application protocols described in this section follow the same request/reply communication pattern, we would expect that they are all built on top of an RPC transport protocol. This is not the case, however, as they are all implemented on top of either TCP or UDP. In effect, each protocol reinvents a simple RPC-like mechanism on top of one of the existing transport protocols. We say "simple" because each protocol is not designed to support arbitrary remote procedure calls, but is instead designed to send and respond to a specific set of request messages. In fact, it is no coincidence that two of the protocols have the word "Simple" in their name.

All three protocols have a companion protocol that specifies the format of the data that can be exchanged. This is one reason these protocols are relatively simple: Much of the complexity is managed in this companion document. For example, SMTP is a protocol for exchanging electronic mail messages, but RFC 822 (this specification has no other name) and MIME (Multipurpose Internet Mail Extensions) define the format of email messages. Similarly, HTTP is a protocol for fetching Web pages, but HTML (HyperText Markup Language) is a companion specification that defines the form of those pages. Finally, SNMP is a protocol for querying a network node, but MIB (management information base) defines the variables that can be queried.

9.2.1 Electronic Mail (SMTP, MIME)

Email is one of the oldest network applications. After all, what could be more natural than wanting to send a message to the user at the other end of a crosscountry link you just managed to get running? In fact, the pioneers of the ARPANET had not really envisioned email as a key application when the network was created—remote access to computing resources was the main design goal—but it turned out to be a surprisingly successful application. Out of this work evolved the Internet's email system, which is now used by millions of people every day.

As with all the applications described in this section, the place to start in understanding how email works is to (1) distinguish the user interface (i.e., your mail reader) from the underlying message transfer protocol (in this case, SMTP), and (2) to distinguish between this transfer protocol and a companion protocol (RFC 822 and MIME) that defines the format of the messages being exchanged. We start by looking at the message format.

Message Format

RFC 822 defines messages to have two parts: a *header* and a *body*. Both parts are represented in ASCII text. Originally, the body was assumed to be simple text. This is still the case, although RFC 822 has been augmented by MIME to allow the message body to carry all sorts of data. This data is still represented as ASCII text, but because it may be an encoded version of, say, a JPEG image, it's not necessarily readable by human users. More on MIME in a moment.

The message header is a series of <CRLF>-terminated lines. (<CRLF> stands for carriage-return + line-feed, which are a pair of ASCII control characters often used to indicate the end of a line of text.) The header is separated from the message body by a blank line. Each header line contains a type and value separated by a colon. Many of these header lines are familiar to users since they are asked to fill them out when they compose an email message. For example, the To: header identifies the message recipient, and the Subject: header says something about the purpose of the message. Other headers are filled in by the underlying mail delivery system. Examples include Date: (when the message was transmitted), From: (what user sent the message), and Received: (each mail server that handled this message). There are, of course, many other header lines; the interested reader is referred to RFC 822.

RFC 822 was extended in 1993 (and updated again in 1996) to allow email messages to carry many different types of data: audio, video, images, Word documents, and so on. MIME consists of three basic pieces. The first piece is a collection of header lines that augment the original set defined by RFC 822. These header lines describe, in various ways, the data being carried in the message body. They include MIME-Version: (the version of MIME being used), Content-Description: (a human-readable description of what's in the message, analogous to the Subject: line), Content-Type: (the type of data contained in the message), and Content-Transfer-Encoding (how the data in the message body is encoded).

The second piece is definitions for a set of content types (and subtypes). For example, MIME defines two different still image types, denoted image/gif and image/jpeg, each with the obvious meaning. As another example, text/plain refers to simple text you might find in a vanilla 822-style message, while text/richtext denotes a message that contains "marked up" text (e.g., text using special fonts, italics, etc.). As a third example, MIME defines an application type, where the subtypes correspond to the output of different application programs (e.g., application/postscript and application/msword).

MIME also defines a multipart type that says how a message carrying more than one data type is structured. This is like a programming language that defines both base types (e.g., integers and floats) and compound types (e.g., structures and arrays). One possible multipart subtype is mixed, which says that the message contains a set of independent data pieces in a specified order. Each piece then has its own header line that describes the type of that piece.

The third piece is a way to encode the various data types so they can be shipped in an ASCII email message. The problem is that for some data types (a JPEG image, for example), any given 8-bit byte in the image might contain one of 256 different values. Only a subset of these values are valid ASCII characters. It is important that email messages contain only ASCII, because they might pass through a number of intermediate systems (gateways, as described below) that assume all email is ASCII and would corrupt the message if it contained non-ASCII characters. To address this issue, MIME uses a straightforward encoding of binary data into the ASCII character set. The encoding is called base64. The idea is to map every three bytes of the original binary data into four ASCII characters. This is done by grouping the binary data into 24-bit units, and breaking each such unit into four 6-bit pieces. Each 6-bit piece maps onto one of 64 valid ASCII characters; for example, 0 maps onto *A*, 1 maps onto *B*, and so on. If you look at a message that has been encoded using the base64 encoding scheme, you'll notice only the 52 upper- and lowercase letters, the 10 digits 0 through 9, and the special characters + and /. These are the first 64 values in the ASCII character set.

As one aside, so as to make reading mail as painless as possible for those of us that insist on using text-only mail readers, a MIME message that consists of regular text only can be encoded using 7-bit ASCII. There's also a readable encoding for mostly ASCII data.

Putting this all together, a message that contains some plain text, a JPEG image, and a PostScript file would look something like this:

```
MIME-Version: 1.0
Content-Type: multipart/mixed; boundary="-------417CA6E2DE4ABCAFBC5"
From: Alice Smith <Alice@cisco.com>
To: Bob@cs.Princeton.edu
Subject: promised material
Date: Mon, 07 Sep 1998 19:45:19 -0400

---------417CA6E2DE4ABCAFBC5
Content-Type: text/plain; charset=us-ascii
```

```
Content-Transfer-Encoding: 7bit

Bob,

Here's the jpeg image and draft report I promised.

--Alice

---------417CA6E2DE4ABCAFBC5
Content-Type: image/jpeg
Content-Transfer-Encoding: base64
```
   unreadable encoding of a jpeg figure

```
---------417CA6E2DE4ABCAFBC5
Content-Type: application/postscript; name="draft.ps"
Content-Transfer-Encoding: 7bit
```
   readable encoding of a PostScript document

In this example, the Content-Type line in the message header says that this message contains various pieces, each denoted by a character string that does not appear in the data itself. Each piece then has its own Content-Type and Content-Transfer-Encoding lines.

Message Transfer

Finally, we get to SMTP—the protocol used to transfer messages from one host to another. To place SMTP in the right context, we need to identify the key players. First, users interact with a *mail reader* when they compose, file, search, and read their email. There are countless mail readers available, just like there are many Web browsers to choose from. In fact, most Web browsers now include a mail reader. Second, there is a *mail daemon* (or process) running on each host. You can think of this process as playing the role of a post office: Mail readers give the daemon messages they want to send to other users, the daemon uses SMTP running over TCP to transmit the message to a daemon running on another machine, and the daemon puts incoming messages into the user's mailbox (where that user's mail reader can later find it). Since SMTP is a protocol that anyone could implement, in theory there could be many different

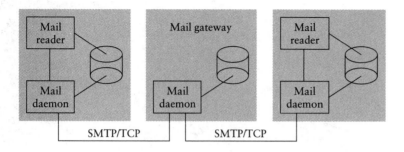

Figure 9.6 Sequence of mail gateways store and forward email messages.

implementations of the mail daemon. It turns out, though, that the mail daemon running on most hosts is derived from the **sendmail** program originally implemented on Berkeley Unix.

While it is certainly possible that the **sendmail** program on a sender's machine establishes an SMTP/TCP connection to the **sendmail** program on the recipient's machine, in many cases the mail traverses one or more *mail gateways* on its route from the sender's host to the receiver's host. Like the end hosts, these gateways also run a **sendmail** process. It's not an accident that these intermediate nodes are called "gateways" since their job is to store and forward email messages, much like an "IP gateway" (which we have referred to as a router) stores and forwards IP datagrams. The only difference is that a mail gateway typically buffers messages on disk and is willing to try retransmitting them to the next machine for several days, while an IP router buffers datagrams in memory and is only willing to retry transmitting them for a fraction of a second. Figure 9.6 illustrates a two-hop path from the sender to the receiver.

Why, you might ask, are mail gateways necessary? Why can't the sender's host send the message to the receiver's host? One reason is that the recipient does not want to include the specific host on which he or she reads email in his or her address. For example, mail delivered to **Bob@cs.princeton.edu** is first sent to a mail gateway in the CS Department at Princeton (that is, to the host named **cs.princeton.edu**), and then forwarded—involving a second SMTP/TCP connection—to the specific machine on which **Bob** happens to be reading his email today. The forwarding gateway maintains a database that maps users into the machine on which they currently want to receive their mail; the sender need not be aware of this specific name. (The list of **Received:** header lines in the message will help you trace the mail gateways that a given message traversed.) Another reason is that the recipient's machine may not always be up, in which case the mail gateway holds the message until it can be delivered. In this case, it is possible that the recipient would use a mail fetching protocol, such as the Post Office Protocol (POP3), instead of SMTP to retrieve any messages that have arrived, but SMTP would still be used to get the message from the sender's to the recipient's gateway.

Independent of how many mail gateways are in the path, an independent SMTP connection is used between each host to move the message closer to the recipient. Each SMTP session involves a dialog between the two mail daemons, with one acting as the client and the other acting as the server. Multiple messages might be transferred between the two hosts during a single session. Since RFC 822 defines messages using ASCII as the base representation, it should come as no surprise to learn that SMTP is also ASCII based. This means it is possible for a human at a keyboard to pretend to be an SMTP client program.

SMTP is best understood by a simple example. The following is an exchange between sending host cs.princeton.edu and receiving host cisco.com. In this case, user Bob at Princeton is trying to send mail to users Alice and Tom at Cicso. The lines sent by cs.princeton.edu are shown in black and the lines sent by cisco.com are shown in green. Extra blank lines have been added to make the dialog more readable.

```
HELO cs.princeton.edu
250 Hello daemon@mail.cs.princeton.edu [128.12.169.24]

MAIL FROM:<Bob@cs.princeton.edu>
250 OK

RCPT TO:<Alice@cisco.com>
250 OK

RCPT TO:<Tom@cisco.com>
550 No such user here

DATA
354 Start mail input; end with <CRLF>.<CRLF>
Blah blah blah...
...etc. etc. etc.
<CRLF>.<CRLF>
250 OK

QUIT
221 Closing connection
```

As you can see, SMTP involves a sequence of exchanges between the client and the server. In each exchange, the client posts a command (e.g., HELO, MAIL, RCPT, DATA, QUIT) and the server responds with a code (e.g., 250, 550, 354, 221). The server also returns a human-readable explanation for the code (e.g., No such user here). In this particular example, the client first identifies itself to the server with the HELO command. It gives its domain name as an argument. The server verifies that this name corresponds to the IP address being used by the TCP connection; you'll notice the server states this IP address back to the client. The client then asks the server if it is willing to accept mail for two different users; the server responds by saying "yes" to one and "no" to the other. Then the client sends the message, which is terminated by a line with a single period (".") on it. Finally, the client terminates the connection.

There are, of course, many other commands and return codes. For example, the server can respond to a client's RCPT command with a 251 code, which indicates that the user does not have a mailbox on this host, but that the server promises to forward the message onto another mail daemon. In other words, the host is functioning as a mail gateway. As another example, the client can issue a VRFY operation to verify a user's email address, but without actually sending a message to the user.

The only other point of interest is the arguments to the MAIL and RCPT operations; for example, FROM:<Bob@cs.princeton.edu> and TO:<Alice@cisco.com>, respectively. These look a lot like 822 header fields, and in some sense, they are. What actually happens is that the mail daemon parses the message to extract the information it needs to run SMTP. The information it extracts is said to form an *envelope* for the message. The SMTP client uses this envelope to parameterize its exchange with the SMTP server. One historical note: The reason sendmail became so popular is that no one wanted to reimplement this message parsing function. While today's email addresses look pretty tame (e.g., Bob@cs.princeton.edu), this was not always the case. In the days before everyone was connected to the Internet, it was not uncommon to see email addresses of the form user%host@site!neighbor.

9.2.2 World Wide Web (HTTP)

The World Wide Web has been so successful and has made the Internet accessible to so many people that sometimes it seems to be synonymous with the Internet. One helpful way to think of the Web is as a set of cooperating clients and servers, all of whom speak the same language: HTTP. Most people are exposed to the Web through a graphical client program, or Web browser, like Netscape or Explorer. Figure 9.7 shows the Netscape browser in use, displaying a page of information from Princeton University.

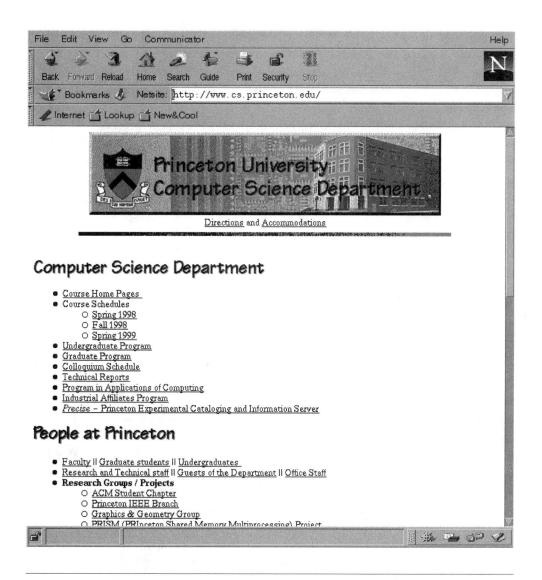

Figure 9.7 The Netscape Web browser.

Any Web browser has a function that allows the user to "open a URL." URLs (uniform resource locators) provide information about the location of objects on the Web; they look like the following:

http://www.cs.princeton.edu/index.html

If you opened that particular URL, your Web browser would open a TCP connection to the Web server at a machine called **www.cs.princeton.edu** and immediately retrieve and display the file called **index.html**. Most files on the Web contain images and text, and some have audio and video clips. They also include URLs that point to other files, and your Web browser will have some way in which you can recognize URLs and ask the browser to open them. These embedded URLs are called hypertext links. When you ask your Web browser to open one of these embedded URLs (e.g., by pointing and clicking on it with a mouse), it will open a new connection and retrieve and display a new file. This is called "following a link." It thus becomes very easy to hop from one machine to another around the network, following links to all sorts of information.

When you select to view a page, your browser (the client) fetches the page from the server using HTTP running over TCP. Like SMTP, HTTP is a text-oriented protocol. At its core, each HTTP message has the general form

```
START_LINE <CRLF>
MESSAGE_HEADER <CRLF>
<CRLF>
MESSAGE_BODY <CRLF>
```

where as before, <CRLF> stands for carriage-return-line-feed. The first line (START_LINE) indicates whether this is a request message or a response message. In effect, it identifies the "remote procedure" to be executed (in the case of a request message), or the "status" of the request (in the case of a response message). The next set of lines specify a collection of options and parameters that qualify the request or response. There are zero or more of these MESSAGE_HEADER lines—the set is terminated by a blank line—each of which looks like a header line in an email message. HTTP defines many possible header types, some of which pertain to request messages, some to response messages, and some to the data carried in the message body. Instead of giving the full set of possible header types, though, we just give a handful of representative examples. Finally, after the blank line comes the contents of the requested message (MESSAGE_BODY); this part of the message is typically empty for request messages.

Request Messages

The first line of an HTTP request message specifies three things: the operation to be performed, the Web page the operation should be performed on, and the version of HTTP being used. Although HTTP defines a wide assortment of possible request operations—including "write" operations that allow a Web page to be posted on a server—the two most common operations are GET (fetch the specified Web page) and HEAD (fetch status information about the specified Web page). The former is obviously

Operation	Description
OPTIONS	request information about available options
GET	retrieve document identified in URL
HEAD	retrieve metainformation about document identified in URL
POST	give information (e.g., annotation) to server
PUT	store document under specified URL
DELETE	delete specified URL
TRACE	loopback request message
CONNECT	for use by proxies

Table 9.1 HTTP request operations.

used when your browser wants to retrieve and display a Web page. The latter is used to test the validity of a hypertext link or to see if a particular page has been modified since the browser last fetched it. The full set of operations is summarized in Table 9.1.

For example, the START_LINE

```
GET http:www.cs.princeton.edu/index.html HTTP/1.1
```

says that the client wants the server on host www.cs.princeton.edu to return the page named index.html. This particular example uses an *absolute* URL. It is also possible to use a *relative* identifier and specify the host name in one of the MESSAGE_HEADER lines; for example,

```
GET index.html HTTP/1.1
Host: www.cs.princeton.edu
```

Here, Host is one of the possible MESSAGE_HEADER fields. One of the more interesting of these is If-Modified-Since, which gives the client a way to conditionally request a Web page—the server returns the page only if it has been modified since the time specified in that header line.

Response Messages

Like request messages, response messages begin with a single START_LINE. In this case, the line specifies the version of HTTP being used, a three-digit code indicating whether

Code	Type	Example Reasons
1xx	Informational	request received, continuing process
2xx	Success	action successfully received, understood, and accepted
3xx	Redirection	further action must be taken to complete the request
4xx	Client Error	request contains bad syntax or cannot be fulfilled
5xx	Server Error	server failed to fulfill an apparently valid request

Table 9.2   Five types of HTTP result codes.

or not the request was successful, and a text string giving the reason for the response. For example, the START_LINE

```
HTTP/1.1 202 Accepted
```

indicates that the server was able to satisfy the request, while

```
HTTP/1.1 404 Not Found
```

indicates that it was not able to satisfy the request because the page was not found. There are five general types of response codes, with the first digit of the code indicating its type. Table 9.2 summarizes the five types of codes.

Also similar to request messages, response messages can contain one or more MESSAGE_HEADER lines. These lines relay additional information back to the client. For example, the Location header line specifies that the requested URL is available at another location. Thus, if the Princeton CS Department Web page had moved from http://www.cs.princeton.edu/index.html to http://www.princeton.edu/cs/index.html, for example, then the server at the original address might respond with

```
HTTP/1.1 301 Moved Permanently
Location: http://www.princeton.edu/cs/index.html
```

In the common case, the response message will also carry the requested page. This page is an HTML document, but since it may carry nontextual data (e.g., a GIF image), it is encoded using MIME (see Section 9.2.1). Certain of the MESSAGE_HEADER lines give attributes of the page contents, including Content-Length (number of bytes in the contents), Expires (time at which the contents are considered stale), and Last-Modified (time at which the contents were last modified at the server).

TCP Connections

The original version of HTTP (1.0) established a separate TCP connection for each data item retrieved from the server. It's not too hard to see how this was a very inefficient mechanism: connection setup and teardown messages had to be exchanged between the client and server even if all the client wanted to do was verify that it had the most recent copy of a page. Thus, retrieving a page that included some text and a dozen icons or other small graphics would result in 13 separate TCP connections being established and closed.

The most important improvement in the latest version of HTTP (1.1) is to allow *persistent connections*—the client and server can exchange multiple request/response messages over the same TCP connection. Persistent connections have two advantages. First, they obviously eliminate the connection setup overhead, thereby reducing the load on the server, the load on the network caused by the additional TCP packets, and the delay perceived by the user. Second, because a client can send multiple request messages down a single TCP connection, TCP's congestion window mechanism is able to operate more efficiently. This is because it's not necessary to go through the slow start phase for each page.

Persistent connections do not come without a price, however. The problem is that neither the client nor server necessarily knows how long to keep a particular TCP connection open. This is especially critical on the server, which might be asked to keep connections opened on behalf of thousands of clients. The solution is that the server must time out and close a connection if it has received no requests on the connection for a period of time. Also, both the client and server must watch to see if the other side has elected to close the connection, and they must use that information as a signal that they should close their side of the connection as well. (Recall that both sides must close a TCP connection before it is fully terminated.)

Caching

One of the most active areas of research (and entrepreneurship) in the Internet today is how to effectively cache Web pages. Caching has many benefits. From the client's perspective, a page that can be retrieved from a nearby cache can be displayed much more quickly than if it has to be fetched from across the world. From the server's perspective, having a cache intercept and satisfy a request reduces the load on the server.

Caching can be implemented in many different places. For example, a user's browser can cache recently accessed pages, and simply display the cached copy if the user visits the same page again. As another example, a site can support a single sitewide cache. This allows users to take advantage of pages previously downloaded by other users. Closer to the middle of the Internet, ISPs can cache pages. Note that in the second case, the users within the site most likely know what machine is caching pages on behalf of the site, and they configure their browsers to connect directly to the caching host. This node is sometimes called a *proxy*. In contrast, the sites that connect to the ISP are probably not aware that the ISP is caching pages. It simply happens to be the case that HTTP requests coming out of the various sites pass through a common ISP router. This router can peek inside the request message and look at the URL for the requested page. If it has the page in its cache, it returns it. If not, it forwards the request to the server, and watches for the response to fly by in the other direction. When it does, the router saves a copy in the hope that it can use it to satisfy a future request.

No matter where pages are cached, the ability to cache Web pages is important enough that HTTP has been designed to make the job easier. The trick is that the cache needs to make sure it is not responding with an out-of-date version of the page. For example, the server assigns an expiration date (the Expires header field) to each page it sends back to the client (or to a cache between the server and client). The cache remembers this date and knows that it need not reverify the page each time it is requested until after that expiration date has passed. After that time (or if that header field is not set) the cache can use the HEAD or conditional GET operation (GET with If-Modified-Since header line) to verify that it has the most recent copy of the page. More generally, there are a set of "cache directives" that must be obeyed by all caching mechanisms along the request/response chain. These directives specify whether or not a document can be cached, how long it can be cached, how fresh a document must be, and so on.

9.2.3 Network Management (SNMP)

A network is a complex system, both in terms of the number of nodes that are involved and in terms of the suite of protocols that can be running on any one node. Even if you restrict yourself to worrying about the nodes within a single administrative domain, such as a campus, there might be dozens of routers and hundreds—or even thousands—of hosts to keep track of. If you think about all the state that is maintained and manipulated on any one of those nodes—for example, address translation tables, routing tables, TCP connection state, and so on—then it is easy to become depressed about the prospect of having to manage all of this information.

It is easy to imagine wanting to know about the state of various protocols on different nodes. For example, you might want to monitor the number of IP datagram reassemblies that have been aborted, so as to determine if the timeout that garbage collects partially assembled datagrams needs to be adjusted. As another example, you might want to keep track of the load on various nodes (i.e., the number of packets sent or received) so as to determine if new routers or links need to be added to the network. Of course, you also have to be on the watch for evidence of faulty hardware and misbehaving software.

What we have just described is the problem of network management, an issue that pervades the entire network architecture. Since the nodes we want to keep track of are distributed, our only real option is to use the network to manage the network. This means we need a protocol that allows us to read, and possibly write, various pieces of state information on different network nodes. The most widely used protocol for this purpose is the Simple Network Management Protocol (SNMP).

SNMP is essentially a specialized request/reply protocol that supports two kinds of request messages: GET and SET. The former is used to retrieve a piece of state from some node, and the latter is used to store a new piece of state in some node. (SNMP also supports a third operation—GET-NEXT—which we explain below.) The following discussion focuses on the GET operation, since it is the one most frequently used.

SNMP is used in the obvious way. A system administrator interacts with a client program that displays information about the network. This client program usually has a graphical interface. You can think of this interface as playing the same role as a Web browser. Whenever the administrator selects a certain piece of information that he or she wants to see, the client program uses SNMP to request that information from the node in question. (SNMP runs on top of UDP.) An SNMP server running on that node receives the request, locates the appropriate piece of information, and returns it to the client program, which then displays it to the user.

There is only one complication to this otherwise simple scenario: Exactly how does the client indicate which piece of information it wants to retrieve, and likewise, how does the server know which variable in memory to read to satisfy the request? The answer is that SNMP depends on a companion specification called the management information base (MIB). The MIB defines the specific pieces of information—the MIB *variables*—that you can retrieve from a network node.

The current version of MIB, called MIB-II, organizes variables into 10 different *groups*. You will recognize that most of the groups correspond to one of the protocols described in this book, and nearly all of the variables defined for each group should look familiar. For example:

■ System: general parameters of the system (node) as a whole, including where the node is located, how long it has been up, and the system's name.

■ Interfaces: information about all the network interfaces (adaptors) attached to this node, such as the physical address of each interface, how many packets have been sent and received on each interface.

- Address translation: information about the Address Resolution Protocol (ARP), and in particular, the contents of its address translation table.

- IP: variables related to IP, including its routing table, how many datagrams it has successfully forwarded, and statistics about datagram reassembly. Includes counts of how many times IP drops a datagram for one reason or another.

- TCP: information about TCP connections, such as the number of passive and active opens, the number of resets, the number of timeouts, default timeout settings, and so on. Per-connection information persists only as long as the connection exists.

- UDP: information about UDP traffic, including the total number of UDP datagrams that have been sent and received.

There are also groups for ICMP, EGP, and SNMP itself. The 10th group is used by different media.

Returning to the issue of the client stating exactly what information it wants to retrieve from a node, having a list of MIB variables is only half the battle. Two problems remain. First, we need a precise syntax for the client to use to state which of the MIB variables it wants to fetch. Second, we need a precise representation for the values returned by the server. Both problems are addressed using ASN.1.

Consider the second problem first. As we already saw in Chapter 7, ASN.1/BER defines a representation for different data types, such as integers. The MIB defines the type of each variable, and then it uses ASN.1/BER to encode the value contained in this variable as it is transmitted over the network. As far as the first problem is concerned, ASN.1 also defines an object identification scheme; this identification system is not described in Chapter 7. The MIB uses this identification system to assign a globally unique identifier to each MIB variable. These identifiers are given in a "dot" notation, not unlike domain names. For example, 1.3.6.1.2.1.4.3 is the unique ASN.1 identifier for the IP-related MIB variable ipInReceives; this variable counts the number of IP datagrams that have been received by this node. In this example, the 1.3.6.1.2.1 prefix identifies the MIB database (remember, ASN.1 object IDs are for all possible objects in the world), the 4 corresponds to the IP group, and the final 3 denotes the third variable in this group.

Thus, network management works as follows. The SNMP client puts the ASN.1 identifier for the MIB variable it wants to get into the request message, and it sends this message to the server. The server then maps this identifier into a local variable (i.e., into a memory location where the value for this variable is stored), retrieves the current value held in this variable, and uses ASN.1/BER to encode the value it sends back to the client.

There is one final detail. Many of the MIB variables are either tables or structures. Such compound variables explain the reason for the SNMP GET-NEXT operation. This operation, when applied to a particular variable ID, returns the value of that variable plus the ID of the next variable, for example, the next item in the table or the next field in the structure. This aids the client in "walking through" the elements of a table or structure.

9.3 Multimedia Applications

Just like the traditional applications of the previous section, multimedia applications such as audio- and videoconferencing applications need application-layer protocols. Much of the initial experience in designing protocols for multimedia applications came from the "MBone tools"—applications such as vat and vic that were developed for use on the MBone, using IP multicast to enable multiparty conferencing. Initially, each application had its own protocol, but it became apparent that many multimedia applications have common requirements. This ultimately led to the development of a general-purpose protocol for use by multimedia applications called the Real-time Transport Protocol (RTP).

You might wonder why a protocol whose name identifies it as a "transport protocol" appears in a chapter on application-layer issues. The reason for this is that RTP contains a considerable amount of functionality that is specific to multimedia applications. Furthermore, it typically runs on top of one of the transport-layer protocols described in Chapter 5—UDP—which provides some of the application-independent functions you usually associate with a transport protocol. RTP is nevertheless called a transport protocol because it provides common end-to-end functions to a number of applications. (Most application-layer protocols, like HTTP and SMTP, for example, are specific to a single application.) A point to note here is the difficulty of fitting real-world protocols into a strict layerist model.

Before we look at RTP in detail, it will help to consider some of the applications that might use it. Multimedia applications are sometimes divided into two classes—*conferencing* applications and *streaming* applications. A popular example of the former class is vat, the audioconferencing tool that is often used over networks supporting IP multicast. The control panel for a typical vat conference is shown in Figure 9.8. Another conferencing application is vic, the videoconferencing tool discussed in Chapter 1 and illustrated in Figure 1.7.

Streaming applications typically deliver audio or video streams from a server to a client, and are typified by such commercial products as Real Audio. Because of the lack

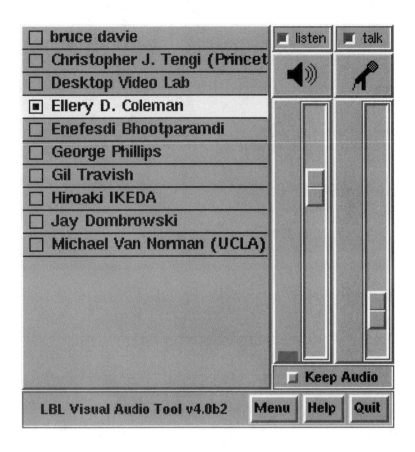

Figure 9.8   User interface of a vat audioconference.

of human interaction, such applications place somewhat different requirements on the underlying protocols. It should by now be apparent that designers of a transport protocol for multimedia applications face a real challenge in defining the requirements broadly enough to meet the needs of very different applications. They must also pay attention to the interactions among different applications, for example, the synchronization of audio and video streams. We will see how these concerns affected the design of RTP below.

Much of RTP actually derives from the application protocol that was originally embedded in vat. Newer versions of vat (and many other applications) run over RTP. RTP can run over many lower-layer protocols, but commonly runs over UDP. That leads to the protocol stack shown in Figure 9.9.

Application
RTP
UDP
IP
Subnet

Figure 9.9 Protocol stack for multimedia applications using RTP.

9.3.1 Requirements

The most basic requirement for a general-purpose multimedia protocol is that it allow similar applications to interoperate with each other. For example, it should be possible for two independently implemented audioconferencing applications to talk to each other. This immediately suggests that the applications had better use the same method of encoding and compressing voice; otherwise, the data sent by one party will be incomprehensible to the receiving party. Since there are quite a few different coding schemes for voice, each with its own trade-offs between quality, bandwidth requirements, and computational cost, it would probably be a bad idea to decree that only one such scheme can be used. Instead, our protocol should provide a way that a sender can tell a receiver which coding scheme it wants to use, and possibly negotiate until a scheme that is available to both parties is identified.

Just as with audio, there are many different video coding schemes. Thus, we see that the first common function that RTP can provide is the ability to communicate that choice of coding scheme. Note that this also serves to identify the type of application (e.g., audio or video); once we know what coding algorithm is being used, we know what type of data is being encoded as well.

Another important requirement for RTP is to enable the recipient of a data stream to determine the timing relationship among the received data. Recall from Section 6.5 that real-time applications need to place received data into a *playback buffer* to smooth out the jitter that may have been introduced into the data stream during transmission across the network. Thus, some sort of timestamping of the data will be necessary to enable the receiver to play it back at the appropriate time.

Related to the timing of a single media stream is the issue of synchronization of multiple media in a conference. The obvious example of this would be to synchronize an audio and video stream that are originating from the same sender. As we will see below, this is a slightly more complex problem than playback time determination for a single stream.

Another important function to be provided is an indication of packet loss. Note that an application with tight latency bounds generally cannot use a reliable transport like TCP because retransmission of data to correct for loss would probably cause the packet to arrive too late to be useful. Thus, the application must be able to deal with missing packets, and the first step in dealing with them is noticing that they are in fact missing. As an example, a video application using MPEG encoding will need to take different actions when a packet is lost, depending on whether the packet came from an I frame, a B frame, or a P frame.

Since multimedia applications generally do not run over TCP, they also miss out on the congestion avoidance features of TCP (as described in Section 6.3). Yet many multimedia applications are capable of responding to congestion, for example, by changing the parameters of the coding algorithm to reduce the bandwidth consumed. Clearly, to make this work, the receiver needs to notify the sender that losses are occurring so that the sender can adjust its coding parameters.

Another common function across multimedia applications is the concept of frame boundary indication. A frame in this context is application-specific. For example, it may be helpful to notify a video application that a certain set of packets correspond to a single frame. In an audio application it is helpful to mark the beginning of a "talkspurt," which is a collection of sounds or words followed by silence. The receiver can then identify the silences between talkspurts and use them as opportunities to move the playback point. This follows the observation that slight shortening or lengthening of the spaces between words are not perceptible to users, whereas shortening or lengthening the words themselves is both perceptible and annoying.

A final function that we might want to put into the protocol is some way of identifying senders that is more user-friendly than an IP address. Tools such as vat and vic can display strings such as Joe User (user@domain.com) on their control panels, and thus the application protocol should support the association of such a string with a data stream.

In addition to the functionality that is required from our protocol, we note an additional requirement: It should make reasonably efficient use of bandwidth. Put another way, we don't want to introduce a lot of extra bits that need to be sent with every packet in the form of a long header. The reason for this is that audio packets, which are one of the most common types of multimedia data, tend to be small, so as to reduce the time it takes to fill them with samples. Long audio packets would mean high latency due to packetization, which has a negative effect on the perceived quality of conversations. (Recall that this was one of the factors in choosing the length of ATM cells.) Since the data packets themselves are short, a large header would mean that a relatively large amount of link bandwidth would be used by headers, thus reducing the available capacity for "useful" data. We will see several aspects of the design of RTP that have been influenced by the necessity of keeping the header short.

9.3.2 Real-time Transport Protocol (RTP)

Now that we have seen the rather long list of requirements for our application-layer protocol for multimedia, we turn to the details of the protocol that has been specified to meet those requirements. This protocol, RTP, was developed in the IETF and is in widespread use. The RTP standard actually defines a pair of protocols, RTP and the Real-time Transport Control Protocol (RTCP). The former is used for the exchange of multimedia data, while the latter is used to periodically send control information associated with a certain data flow. When running over UDP, the RTP data stream and the associated RTCP control stream use consecutive transport-layer ports. The RTP data uses an even port number and the RTCP control information uses the next higher (odd) port number.

Because RTP is designed to support a wide variety of applications, it provides a flexible mechanism by which new applications can be developed without repeatedly revising the RTP protocol itself. For each class of application (e.g., audio), RTP defines a *profile* and one or more *formats*. The profile provides a range of information that ensures a common understanding of the fields in the RTP header for that application class, as will be apparent when we examine the header in detail. The format specification explains how the data that follows the RTP header is to be interpreted. For example, the RTP header might just be followed by a sequence of bytes, each of which represents a single audio sample taken a defined interval after the previous one. Alternatively, the format of the data might be much more complex; an MPEG-encoded video stream, for example, would need to have a good deal of structure to represent all the different types of information.

The design of RTP embodies an architectural principle known as *Application Level Framing* (ALF). This principle was put forward by Clark and Tennenhouse in 1990 as a new way to design protocols for emerging multimedia applications. They recognized that these new applications were unlikely to be well served by existing protocols such as TCP, and that furthermore they might not be well served by any sort of "one-size-fits-all" protocol. At the heart of this principle is the belief that an application understands its own needs best. For example, an MPEG video application knows how best to recover from lost frames, and how to react differently if an I frame or a B frame is lost. The same application also understands best how to segment the data for transmission—for example, it's better to send the data from different frames in different datagrams, so that a lost packet only corrupts a single frame, not two. It is for this reason that RTP leaves so many of the protocol details to the profile and format documents that are specific to an application.

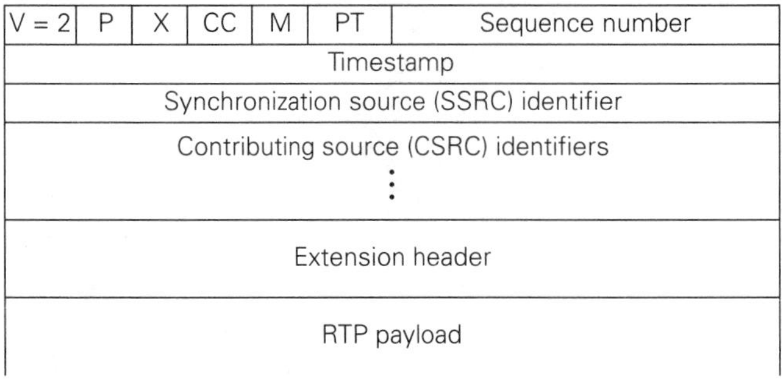

V = 2	P	X	CC	M	PT	Sequence number

Figure 9.10   RTP header format.

Header Format

Figure 9.10 shows the header format used by RTP. The first 12 bytes are always present, whereas the contributing source identifiers are only used in certain circumstances. After this header there may be optional header extensions, as described below. Finally, the header is followed by the RTP payload, the format of which is determined by the application. The intention of this header is that it contain only the fields that are likely to be used by many different applications, since anything that is very specific to a single application would be more efficiently carried in the RTP payload for that application only.

The first two bits are a version identifier, which contains the value 2 in the RTP version deployed at the time of writing. You might think that the designers of the protocol were rather bold to think that 2 bits would be enough to contain all future versions of RTP, but recall that bits are at a premium in the RTP header. Furthermore, the use of profiles for different applications makes it less likely that many revisions to the base RTP protocol would be needed. In any case, if it turns out that another version of RTP is needed beyond version 2, it would be possible to consider a change to the header format so that more than one future version would be possible. For example, a new RTP header with the value 3 in the version field could have a "subversion" field somewhere else in the header.

The next bit is the "padding" (P) bit, which is set in circumstances in which the RTP payload has been padded for some reason. RTP data might be padded to fill up a block of a certain size as required by an encryption algorithm, for example. In such a case, the complete length of the RTP header, data, and padding would be conveyed by the lower-layer protocol header (e.g., the UDP header) and the last byte of the padding would contain a count of how many bytes should be ignored. This is illustrated in Figure 9.11. Note that this approach to padding removes any need for a length field

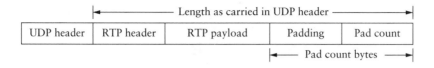

Figure 9.11 Padding of an RTP packet.

in the RTP header (thus serving the goal of keeping the header short); in the common case of no padding, the length is deduced from the lower-layer protocol.

The extension (X) bit is used to indicate the presence of an extension header, which would be defined for a specific application and follow the main header. Such headers are rarely used, since it is generally possible to define a payload-specific header as part of the payload format definition for a particular application.

The X bit is followed by a 4-bit field that counts the number of "contributing sources," if any are included in the header. Contributing sources are discussed below.

We noted above the frequent need for some sort of frame indication; this is provided by the marker bit, which could be set at the beginning of a talkspurt, for example. The 7-bit payload type field follows; it indicates what type of multimedia data is carried in this packet. One possible use of this field would be to enable an application to switch from one coding scheme to another based on information about resource availability in the network or feedback on application quality. The exact usage of the marker bit and the payload type is determined by the application profile.

Note that the payload type is generally not used as a demultiplexing key to direct data to different applications (or to different streams within a single application, for example, the audio and video stream for a videoconference). This is because such demultiplexing is typically provided at a lower layer (e.g., by UDP, as described in Section 5.1). Thus, two media streams using RTP would typically use different UDP port numbers.

The sequence number is used to enable the receiver of an RTP stream to detect missing and misordered packets. The sender simply increments the value by one for each transmitted packet. Note that RTP does not do anything when it detects a lost packet, in contrast to TCP, which both corrects for the loss (by retransmission) and interprets the loss as a congestion indication (which may cause it to reduce its window size). Rather, it is left to the application to decide what to do when a packet is lost because this decision is likely to be highly application-dependent. For example, a video application might decide that the best thing to do when a packet is lost is to replay the last frame that was correctly received. Some applications might also decide to modify their coding algorithms to reduce bandwidth needs in response to loss, but this is not a function of RTP. It would not be sensible for RTP to decide that the sending rate should be reduced, as this might make the application useless.

The function of the timestamp field is to enable the receiver to play back samples at the appropriate intervals and to enable different media streams to be synchronized. Because different applications may require different granularities of timing, RTP itself does not specify the units in which time is measured. Instead, the timestamp is just a counter of "ticks," where the time between ticks is dependent on the encoding in use. For example, an audio application that samples data once every 125 μs could use that value as its clock resolution. The clock granularity is one of the details that is specified in the RTP profile or payload format for an application.

The timestamp value in the packet is a number representing the time at which the *first* sample in the packet was generated. The timestamp is not a reflection of the time of day; only the differences between timestamps are relevant. For example, if the sampling interval is 125 μs and the first sample in packet $n + 1$ was generated 10 ms after the first sample in packet n, then the number of sampling instants between these two samples is

$$\text{TimeBetweenPackets} \div \text{TimePerSample} = (10 \times 10^{-3}) \div (125 \times 10^{-6})$$

$$= 80$$

Assuming the clock granularity is the same as the sampling interval, then the timestamp in packet $n + 1$ would be greater than that in packet n by 80. Note that fewer than 80 samples might have been sent due to compression techniques such as silence detection, and yet the timestamp allows the receiver to play back the samples with the correct temporal relationship.

The synchronization source (SSRC) is a 32-bit number that uniquely identifies a single source of an RTP stream. In a given multimedia conference, each sender picks a random SSRC and is expected to resolve conflicts in the unlikely event that two sources pick the same value. By making the source identifier something other than the network or transport address of the source, RTP ensures independence from the lower-layer protocol. It also enables a single node with multiple sources (e.g., several cameras) to distinguish those sources. When a single node generates different media streams (e.g., audio and video), it is not required to use the same SSRC in each stream, as there are mechanisms in RTCP (described below) to allow intermedia synchronization.

The contributing source (CSRC) is used only when a number of RTP streams pass through a "mixer." A mixer can be used to reduce the bandwidth requirements for a conference by receiving data from many sources and sending it as a single stream. For example, the audio streams from several concurrent speakers could be decoded and recoded as a single audio stream. In this case, the mixer lists itself as the synchronization source but also lists the contributing sources—the SSRC values of the speakers who contributed to the packet in question.

Control Protocol

RTCP provides a control stream that is associated with a data stream for a multimedia application. This control stream provides three main functions:

1 feedback on the performance of the application and the network

2 a way to correlate and synchronize different media streams that have come from the same sender

3 a way to convey the identity of a sender for display on a user interface (e.g., the vat interface shown in Figure 9.8)

The first function may be useful for rate-adaptive applications, which may use performance data to decide to use a more aggressive compression scheme to reduce congestion, or to send a higher-quality stream when there is little congestion. It can also be useful in diagnosing network problems.

You might think that the second function is already provided by the synchronization source ID of RTP, but in fact it is not. As already noted, multiple cameras from a single node might have different SSRC values. Furthermore, there is no requirement that an audio and video stream from the same node use the same SSRC. Because collisions of SSRC values may occur, it may be necessary to change the SSRC value of a stream. To deal with this problem, RTCP uses the concept of a "canonical name" (CNAME) that is assigned to a sender, which is then associated with the various SSRC values that might be used by that sender using RTCP mechanisms.

Simply correlating two streams is only part of the problem of intermedia synchronization. Because different streams may have completely different clocks (with different granularities and even different amounts of inaccuracy, or drift), there needs to be a way to accurately synchronize streams with each other. RTCP addresses this problem.

RTCP defines a number of different packet types, including

■ sender reports, which enable active senders to a session to report transmission and reception statistics

■ receiver reports, which receivers who are not senders use to report reception statistics

■ source descriptions, which carry CNAMEs and other sender description information

■ application-specific control packets

These different RTCP packet types are sent over the lower-layer protocol, which, as we have noted, is typically UDP. Several RTCP packets can be packed into a single PDU of the lower-level protocol. It is required that at least two RTCP packets are sent in every lower-level PDU: One of these is a report packet; the other is a source description packet. Other packets may be included up to the size limits imposed by the lower-layer protocols.

Before looking closely at the contents of an RTCP packet, we note that there is a potential problem with every member of a multicast group sending periodic control traffic. Unless we take some steps to limit it, this control traffic has the potential to be a significant consumer of bandwidth. For example, in an audioconference, no more than two or three senders are likely to send audio data at any instant, since there is no point in everyone talking at once. But there is no such social limit on everyone sending control traffic, and this could be a severe problem in a conference with thousands of participants. To deal with this problem, RTCP has a set of mechanisms by which the participants scale back their reporting frequency as the number of participants increases. These rules are somewhat complex, but the basic goal is this: Limit the total amount of RTCP traffic to a small percentage (typically 5%) of the RTP data traffic. To accomplish this goal, the participants should know how much data bandwidth is likely to be in use (e.g., the amount to send three audio streams) and the number of participants. They learn the former from means outside RTP (known as session management, discussed at the end of this section), and they learn the latter from the RTCP reports of other participants. Because RTCP reports might be sent at a very low rate, it might only be possible to get an approximate count of the current number of recipients, but that is typically sufficient. Also, it is recommended to allocate more RTCP bandwidth to active senders, on the assumption that most participants would like to see reports from them, for example, to find out who is speaking.

Once a participant has determined how much bandwidth it can consume with RTCP traffic, it sets about sending periodic reports at the appropriate rate. Sender reports and receiver reports differ only in that the former include some extra information about the sender. Both types of reports contain information about the data that was received from all sources in the most recent reporting period.

The extra information in a sender report consists of

- a timestamp containing the actual time of day when this report was generated

- the RTP timestamp corresponding to the time when the report was generated

- cumulative counts of the packets and bytes sent by this sender since it began transmission

Note that the first two quantities can be used to enable synchronization of different media streams from the same source, even if those streams use different clock granularities in their RTP data streams, since it gives the key to convert time of day to the RTP timestamps.

Both sender and receiver reports contain one block of data per source that has been heard from since the last report. Each block contains the following statistics for the source in question:

- its SSRC

- the fraction of data packets from this source that were lost since the last report was sent (calculated by comparing the number of packets received with the number of packets expected; this last value can be determined from the RTP sequence numbers)

- total number of packets lost from this source since the first time it was heard from

- highest sequence number received from this source (extended to 32 bits to account for wrapping of the sequence number)

- estimated interarrival jitter for the source (calculated by comparing the inter-arrival spacing of received packets with the expected spacing at transmission time)

- last actual timestamp received via RTCP for this source

- delay since last sender report received via RTCP for this source

As you might imagine, the recipients of this information can learn all sorts of things about the state of the session. In particular, they can see if other recipients are getting much better quality from some sender than they are, which might be an indication that a resource reservation needs to be made, or that there is a problem in the network that needs to be attended to. In addition, if a sender notices that many receivers are experiencing high loss of its packets, it might decide that it should reduce its sending rate or use a coding scheme that is more resilient to loss.

The final aspect of RTCP that we will consider is the source description packet. Such a packet contains, at a minimum, the SSRC of the sender and the sender's CNAME. The canonical name is derived in such a way that all applications that generate media streams that might need to be synchronized (e.g., separately generated audio and video streams from the same user) will choose the same CNAME even though they might choose different SSRC values. This enables a receiver to identify the media stream that came from the same sender. The most common format of the CNAME is user@host, where host is the fully qualified domain name of the sending machine. Thus, an application launched by the user whose user name is jdoe running on the machine cicada.cs.princeton.edu would use the string jdoe@cicada.cs.princeton.edu as its CNAME. The large and variable number of bytes used in this representation would make it a bad choice for the format of an SSRC, since the SSRC is sent with every data packet and must be processed in real time. Allowing CNAMEs to be bound to SSRC values in periodic RTCP messages enables a compact and efficient format for the SSRC.

Other items may be included in the source description packet, such as the real name and email address of the user. These are used in user interface displays and to contact participants, but are less essential to the operation of RTP than the CNAME.

9.3.3 Session Control and Call Control (H.323)

While RTP and RTCP provide a wide range of functionality to multimedia applications, there is an aspect of multimedia conferencing that they do not address, usually referred to as *session control*. To understand this issue, consider the following problem. Suppose you want to hold a videoconference at a certain time and make it available to a wide number of participants. Perhaps you have decided to encode the video stream using the MPEG-2 standard, to use the multicast IP address 224.1.1.1 for transmission of the data, and to send it using RTP over UDP port number 4000. How would you make all that information available to the intended participants? One way would be to put all that information in an email and send it out, but ideally there should be a standard format and protocol for disseminating this sort of information. The IETF has a working group (the Multiparty Multimedia Session Control group) that has defined protocols for just this purpose. The protocols that have been defined include

- SDP (Session Description Protocol)
- SAP (Session Announcement Protocol)
- SIP (Session Initiation Protocol)
- SCCP (Simple Conference Control Protocol)

You might think that this is a lot of protocols for a seemingly simple task, but there are many aspects of the problem and several different situations in which it must be addressed. For example, there is a difference between announcing the fact that a certain conference session is going to be made available on the MBone (which would be done using SDP and SAP) and trying to make an internet phone call to a certain user at a particular time (which could be done using SDP and SIP). In the former case, you could consider your job done once you have sent all the session information in a standard format to a well-known multicast address. In the latter, you would need to locate one or more users, get a message to them announcing your desire to talk (analogous to ringing their phone), and perhaps negotiate a suitable audio encoding among all parties.

The ITU has also been very active in this area, which is not surprising given its relevance to telephony, the traditional realm of that body. Fortunately, there has been considerable coordination between the IETF and the ITU in this instance, so that the various protocols are somewhat interoperable. The major ITU recommendation for multimedia communication over packet networks is known as H.323, which ties together many other recommendations, including H.245 for call control. The full set of recommendations covered by H.323 runs to many hundreds of pages, and the protocol is known for its complexity, so it is only possible to give a brief overview of it here.

H.323 is popular as a protocol for Internet telephony, and we consider that application here. A device that originates or terminates calls is known as an H.323 terminal; this might be a workstation running an Internet telephony application, or it might be a specially designed "appliance"—a telephonelike device with networking software and an Ethernet port, for example. H.323 terminals can talk to each other directly, but the calls are frequently mediated by a device known as a *gatekeeper*. Gatekeepers perform a number of functions such as translating among the various address formats used for phone calls, and controlling how many calls can be placed at a given time to limit the bandwidth used by the H.323 applications. H.323 also includes the concept of a *gateway*, which connects the H.323 network to other types of networks. The most common use of a gateway is to connect an H.323 network to the public switched telephone network (PSTN) as illustrated in Figure 9.12. This enables a user running an H.323 application on a computer to talk to a person using a conventional phone on the public telephone network. One useful function performed by the gatekeeper is to help a terminal find a gateway, perhaps choosing among several options to find one that is relatively close to the ultimate destination of the call. This is clearly useful in a world where conventional phones greatly outnumber PC-based phones. When an H.323 terminal makes a call to an endpoint that is a conventional phone, the gateway becomes the effective endpoint for the H.323 call and is responsible for performing the appropriate translation of both signalling information and the media stream that need to be carried over the telephone network.

An important part of H.323 is the H.245 call control protocol. When one H.323 terminal wants to call another, it uses H.245 to negotiate the properties of the call. It might list a number of different audio codec standards that it can support, and the far endpoint of the call would reply with a list of its own supported codecs, and the two ends could pick a coding standard that they can both live with. H.245 can also be used to signal the UDP port numbers that will be used by RTP and RTCP for the

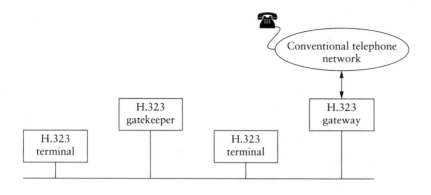

Figure 9.12 Devices in an H.323 network.

media stream (or streams—a call might include both audio and video, for example) in this call. Once this is accomplished, the call can proceed, with RTP being used to transport the media streams and RTCP carrying the relevant control information.

9.4 Summary

We have seen five different application-level protocols: the DNS protocol used by the domain naming system, SMTP used to exchange electronic mail, HTTP used to walk the World Wide Web, SNMP used to query remote nodes for the sake of network management, and RTP used by multimedia applications like vic and vat. While not by any means exhaustive, this discussion covers a number of different classes of applications. DNS, being rarely invoked directly by users, is more often thought of as a piece of infrastructure or middleware. SMTP and HTTP fall into the "traditional" application category, in contrast to real-time, multimedia applications that use RTP. And SNMP is the protocol most often relied upon by network managers, being rarely used by "average" users.

Application protocols are a curious lot. In many ways, they are like another layer of transport protocol. In other ways, they have application-specific knowledge that we would never want to pollute an application-independent transport protocol with. In effect, you could argue that all the protocols described in this chapter are just specialized transport protocols, and that transport protocols get layered on top of each other until producing the precise service needed by the application.

It's difficult to put a finger on a specific open issue in the realm of application protocols—the entire field is open as new applications are invented every day, and the networking needs of these applications are, well, application-dependent.

The real challenge to network designers is to recognize that what applications need from the network changes over time, and these changes drive the transport protocols we develop and the functionality we put into network routers.

Developing new transport protocols is a reasonably tractable problem. You may not be able to get the IETF to bless your transport protocol as an equal of TCP or UDP, but there's certainly nothing stopping you from designing the world's greatest multimedia application that comes bundled with a new end-to-end protocol that runs on top of UDP, much like happens with RTP.

On the other hand, pushing application-specific knowledge into the middle of the network—into the routers—is a much more difficult problem. This is because in order to effect a particular application, any new network service or functionality may need to be loaded into many, if not all, of the routers in the Internet. Web caching is an example of an advanced service you might want to load into network routers—cache-enhanced routers not only forward IP datagrams, but they also peek inside them and look at URLs—but Web caching works because you don't have to change all routers to gain a benefit. Just changing the router(s) you control is good enough.

In general, though, there are countless services you might want to load into the network—services that cannot be effectively provided only at the end hosts. For example, imagine a data dissemination service in which multiple sources are publishing a diverse collection of data items, and multiple clients are subscribing to some subset of those items. The items might be stock quotes, event notifications, or news articles, for example. Each source could use a traditional IP multicast group to disseminate the items to the clients, except this would be wasteful since a given client might be interested in only a small subset of items published by a given source. An alternative would be for the source to send the data items "downstream" and the clients to send their subscriptions (requests for specific item types) "upstream." The intermediate router could be programmed to *prune* the items it sends downstream based on the subscriptions it had received on a given link.

How can applications hope to place functionality like this into the network itself? One possibility is that an emerging idea called *active networking* will eventually replace the relatively static model provided by today's routers. The idea of active networks is that packets will not only carry data, but they will also carry code (or possibly pointers to code) that tell the router how it should process the packet. Active networks raise many challenging problems—not the least of which is how to enforce security in a world where arbitrary applications can effectively program routers—but researchers are now starting to bring solutions together to build an *active backbone*, or ABone. Will today's vision of active networking succeed? It is hard to say, and there are voices on both sides of the argument in the networking community. What does seem certain is that there will continue to be demands for rapidly modifiable functionality in network devices.

FURTHER READING

The seminal paper on application-layer protocols is that by Clark and Tennenhouse, which is cited by the designers of RTP as their guiding vision. Rose's book on SNMP is an authoritative reference on the subject and explains many of the design decisions behind SNMP. The development of DNS is well described by Mockapetris and Dunlap.

- ■ Clark, D., and D. Tennenhouse. Architectural considerations for a new generation of protocols. *Proceedings of the SIGCOMM '90 Symposium*, pages 200–208, September 1990.

- ■ Rose, M. *The Simple Book. An Introduction to Internet Management*. Prentice Hall, Englewood Cliffs, NJ, 1994.

- ■ Mockapetris, P., and K. Dunlap. Development of the domain name system. *Proceedings of the SIGCOMM '88 Symposium*, pages 123–133, August 1988.

There are a wealth of papers on naming, as well as on the related issue of resource discovery (finding out what resources exist in the first place). General studies of naming can be found in Terry [Ter86], Comer and Peterson [CP89], Birrell et al. [BLNS82], Saltzer [Sal78], Shoch [Sho78], and Watson [Wat81]; attribute-based (descriptive) naming systems are described in Peterson [Pet88] and Bowman et al. [BPY90]; and resource discovery is the subject of Bowman et al. [BDMS94].

SMTP is originally defined in RFC 821 [Pos82], and of course, RFC 822 is RFC 822 [Cro82]. MIME is defined in a series of RFCs; the original specification was in RFC 1521 [BF93] and the most recent version is defined in RFC 2045 [FB96].

Version 1.0 of HTTP is specified in RFC 1945 [BLFF96], and the latest version (1.1) is defined in RFC 2068 [FGMBL97]. There are a wealth of papers written about Web performance, especially Web caching. A good example is a paper by Danzig on Web traffic and its implications on the effectiveness of caching [Dan98].

Certificate of Authenticity

This Certificate of Authenticity is your assurance that the software that you have purchased with your computer system is legally licensed from Microsoft Corporation.

If you have any concerns about the legitimacy of this Certificate of Authenticity or the software you have received, call the Microsoft Piracy Hotline at 1-800-RU-LEGIT (in the U.S. or Canada), or contact your local Microsoft subsidiary. **For product support, contact the manufacturer of the PC accompanying your operating system software.**

Microsoft

Ægthedsgaranti- Denne ægthedsgaranti er Deres garanti for, at den software, som De har erhvervet sammen med Deres computersystem, er et softwareprodukt, der lovligt er givet i licens fra Microsoft Corporation. Hvis De måtte have spørgsmål angående gyldigheden af denne ægthedsgaranti eller den software, som De har erhvervet, skal De kontakte Deres lokale Microsoft-afdeling (45) 44 89 01 00. **Hvis De har brug for produktstøtte, bedes De kontakte fabrikanten af den PC, men med hvilken De købte Deres operativsystemsoftware.** Sikkerhedsmærkaterne angiver, at dette er et originalt Microsoft-softwareprodukt. Reproduktion af denne ægthedsgaranti er ulovlig.

Bewijs van Echtheid - Dit Bewijs van Echtheid garandeert u dat de software die u hebt gekocht bij uw computer, officieel door Microsoft Corporation in licentie is gegeven. Als u vragen hebt over de rechtsgeldigheid van dit Bewijs van Echtheid of over de authenticiteit van de ontvangen software, kunt u contact opnemen met de Microsoft-vestiging in uw land of met de Microsoft Piracy Hotline op telefoonnummer 1-800-RU-LEGIT (in de US or Canada). **Voor productondersteuning dient u contact op te nemen met de computerfabrikant die uw operating system-programmatuur heeft meegeleverd.** Door middel van de waarborgsticker(s) wordt aangegeven dat dit product authentieke Microsoft-software bevat. Namaak van dit Bewijs van Echtheid is verboden en strafbaar.

Aitoustodistus - Tämä aitoustodistus on takeena siitä että tietokonejärjestelmän mukana ostamallanne ohjelmalla on voimassa oleva Microsoft Corporationin laillinen käyttöoikeussopimus. Jos Teillä on kysyttävää tämän aitoustodistuksen tai hankkimanne ohjelman laillisuudesta, soittakaa Microsoft Piracy Hotlinen numeroon 1-800-RU-LEGIT (USA:ssa tai Kanadassa) tai ottakaa yhteys Microsoftin paikalliseen tytäryhtiöön. **Tuotetuen osalta ottakaa yhteys PC-tietokoneenne valmistajaan.** Oheisena toimitetut tarrat ovat osoituksena siitä että tämä tuote on aito Microsoft-ohjelma. Tämän aitoustodistuksen kopioiminen on lain vastaista.

Certificat d'Authenticité - Ce Certificat d'Authenticité est la garantie que le logiciel dont vous avez fait l'acquisition lors de l'achat de votre ordinateur est valablement commercialisé sous licence Microsoft. Si vous avez des doutes quant à l'authenticité de ce Certificat ou du logiciel que vous venez d'acquérir, contactez la filiale Microsoft la plus proche (ou composez le 1-800-RU-LEGIT si vous résidez aux Etats-Unis ou au Canada). **Pour l'assistance produit, adressez-vous au fabricant de l'ordinateur individuel accompagnant votre logiciel système d'exploitation.** Le(s) autocollant(s) de sécurité figurant sur la couverture du manuel garantissent que ce produit est un logiciel Microsoft authentique. Toute reproduction de ce Certificat d'Authenticité est strictement interdite par la loi.

Echtheitsbescheinigung - Diese Echtheitsbescheinigung versichert Ihnen, daß es sich bei dem mit Ihrem Computersystem erworbenen Software-Produkt um ein rechtmäßig lizenziertes Produkt von Microsoft handelt. Falls Sie Fragen bezüglich der Rechtmäßigkeit der Echtheitsbescheinigung oder der erhaltenen Software (deleted word "fragen") haben, setzen Sie sich bitte mit der Microsoft- Niederlassung in Ihrer Nähe in Verbindung. **Für Produktunterstützung wenden Sie sich bitte an den Hersteller des PC, mit dem zusammen Sie die Betriebssystemsoftware erhalten haben.** Der (die) Sicherheitsaufkleber bedeutet (n), dass dieses Produkt ein Original-Microsoft-Produkt ist. Die Vervielfältigung dieser Echtheitsbescheinigung ist rechtswidrig und gesetzlich streng verboten.

Certificato di autenticità - Il presente certificato è a garanzia che il software acquistato con il proprio computer è legalmente concesso in licenza dalla Microsoft Corporation. Chiunque desideri porre domande in ordine a questo certificato, o abbia dubbi sull'autenticità del software, può scrivere a: Microsoft SpA, Via Cassanese, 224, 20090 SEGRATE (MI). **Per l'assistenza relativa al prodotto, si prega di contattare il fabbricante del PC annesso al software di sistema operativo.** Gli adesivi di sicurezza sono a garanzia dell'autenticità del prodotto acquistato. Ogni riproduzione di questo Certificato di autenticità, sarà perseguibile civilmente e penalmente.

Gyldighhetsbevis - Dette gyldighetsbeviset din garati for at programvaren som du har kjøpt med datamaskinen din er lisensiert fra Microsoft Corporation. Hvis du tviler på ekthetan av dette gyldighetsbeviset eller programvaren du har mottatt, kontakt Microsoft Norge AS på telefon 22 95 06 65. Hvis du er i USA eller Canada, kan du ringe Microsoft Piracy Hotline på 1-800-RU-LEGIT. eller om du er på et annet sted kan du ringe et av Microsofts underkontor. **Dersom du har spørsmål vedrørende programvaren som sådan, skal du kontakte leverandøren av den PC som inneholder ditt operativsystem.** Hologram-klistremerket/ -klistremerkene er din indikasjon på at dette produktet er en originalpakke med Microsoft-programvare. Reproduksjon av dette gyldighetsbeviset er strengt forbudt ved lov.

Certificado de Autenticidade - Este Certificado de Autenticidade é a garantia de que o software que você adquiriu com o sistema de computador está legalmente licenciado pela Microsoft Corporation. No caso de dúvidas sobre a legitimidade deste Certificado de Autenticidade ou sobre o software incluído, ligue para a sua o representante local da Microsoft. **Para assistencia a produtos, contacte o fabricante do PC que acompanha o seu software de sistema operativo.** O(s) adesivo(s) de segurança certificam que este produto é um software genuíno da Microsoft. A reprodução deste Certificado de Autenticidade é ilegal e profbida por lei.

Certificado de autenticidad - Este Certificado de autenticidad es su garantía de que el software que ha adquirido con su PC cuenta con una licencia legal de Microsoft Corporation. Si tuviese la más mínima duda acerca de la legitimidad de este Certificado de autenticidad o acerca del software que ha recibido, póngase en contacto con la línea gratuita Contra Piratería Informática de Microsoft, marcando el número de teléfono 1-800-RU-LEGIT (si reside en Canadá o en EE.UU.), o con la subsidiaria de Microsoft más próxima. **Para soporte del producto, póngase en contacto con el fabricante del PC que acompaña al software de su sistema operativo.** Ls reproducción de esta Certificado de autenticidad es illegal y está rigurosamente penalizada por la ley.

Äkthetsbevis - Detta äkthetsbevis är en garanti för att programvaran som inköpts tillsammans med datorsystemet är licensierad från Microsoft Corporation. Om Ni har frågor rörande giltigheten av detta äkthetsbevis eller programvaran är Ni välkommen att kontakta Microsoft Piracy Hotline på telefon 0091-800-RU-LEGIT (i USA och Canada) eller Microsoft AB på telefon 08-752 56 00. **Beträffande produktsupport, kontakta tillverkaren av den dator som inköpts tillsammans med Er programvara.** Säkerhetsetiketten är ett bevis på att detta är en äkta Microsoft-produkt. Kopiering av detta äkthetsbevis är olagligt och förbjudet enligt lag.

Network management is a sufficiently large and important field that the IETF devotes an entire area to it. There are well over 100 RFCs describing various aspects of SNMP and MIBs. The two key references, however, are Case et al. [CMRW93], which defines version 2 of SNMP (SNMPv2), and McCloghrie and Rose [MR91], which defines the second version of the mandatory MIB variables (MIB-II). Many of the other SNMP/MIB-related RFCs define extensions to the core set of MIB variables— for example, variables that are specific to a particular network technology or to a particular vendor's product.

RTP is described in RFC 1889 [SCFJ96], although much of the interesting detail is in Internet drafts that are yet to be published. McCanne and Jacobson [MJ95] describe vic, one of the applications to use RTP.

Several research papers report results in the emerging area of active networking. Wetherall et al. [WGT99], Alexander et al. [ASNS97], and Hartman et al. [HPB+99] describe early active network prototypes. Smith et al. [SCM+99] reports on a consensus architecture coming out of the active networks research community.

Finally, we recommend the following live reference to help keep tabs on the rapid evolution of the Web:

■ http://www.w3.org: World Wide Web Consortium

EXERCISES

1 ARP and DNS both depend on caches; ARP cache entry lifetimes are typically 10 minutes, while DNS cache is on the order of days. Justify this difference. What undesirable consequences might there be in having too long a DNS cache entry lifetime?

2 IPv6 simplifies ARP out of existence by allowing hardware addresses to be part of the IPv6 address. How does this complicate the job of DNS? How does this affect the problem of finding your local DNS server?

3 DNS servers also allow reverse lookup; given an IP address 128.112.169.4, it is reversed into a text string 4.169.112.128.in-addr.arpa and looked up using DNS PTR records (which form a hierarchy of domains analogous to that for the address domain hierarchy). Suppose you want to authenticate the sender of a packet based on its host name and are confident that the source IP *address* is genuine. Explain the insecurity in converting the source address to a name as above and then comparing this name to a given list of trusted hosts. Hint: Whose DNS servers would you be trusting?

4 What is the relationship between a domain name (e.g., cs.princeton.edu) and an IP subnet number (e.g., 192.12.69.0)? Do all hosts on the subnet have to be identified by the same name server? What about reverse lookup, as in the previous exercise?

5 Suppose a host elects to use a name server not within its organization for address resolution. When would this result in no more total traffic, for queries not found in any DNS cache, than with a local name server? When might this result in a better DNS cache hit rate and possibly less total traffic?

6 Figure 9.4 shows the hierarchy of name servers. How would you represent this hierarchy if one name server served multiple zones? In that setting, how does the name server hierarchy relate to the zone hierarchy? How do you deal with the fact that each zone may have multiple name servers?

7 Use the whois utility/service to find out who is in charge of your site, at least as far as the InterNIC is concerned. Look up your site both by DNS name and by IP network number; for the latter you may have to try an alternative whois server (e.g., whois -h whois.arin.net . . .). Try princeton.edu and cisco.com as well.

8 Many smaller organizations have their Web sites maintained by a third party. How could you use whois to find if this is the case, and, if so, the identity of the third party?

9 One feature of the existing DNS .com hierarchy is that it is extremely "wide."

   (a) Propose a more hierarchical reorganization of the .com hierarchy. What objections might you foresee to your proposal's adoption?

   (b) What might be some of the consequences of having most DNS domain names contain four or more levels, versus the two of many existing names?

10 Suppose, in the other direction, we abandon any pretense at all of DNS hierarchy, and simply move all the .com entries to the root name server: www.cisco.com would become www.cisco, or perhaps just cisco. How would this affect root name server traffic in general? How would this affect such traffic for the specific case of resolving a name like cisco into a Web server address?

11 What DNS cache issues are involved in changing the IP address of, say, a Web server host name? How might these be minimized?

12 Take a suitable DNS-lookup utility (e.g., nslookup) and disable the recursive lookup feature (e.g., with set norecurse), so that when your utility sends a query to a DNS server, and that server is unable to fully answer the request from its own records, the server sends back the next DNS server in the lookup sequence rather than automatically forwarding the query to that next server. Then carry out manually a name lookup such as that in Figure 9.5; try the host name www.cs.princeton.edu. List each intermediate name server contacted. You may also need to specify that queries are for NS records rather than the usual A records.

13 Discuss how you might rewrite SMTP or HTTP to make use of a hypothetical general-purpose request/reply protocol (perhaps something like CHAN RPC). Could an appropriate analog of persistent connections be moved from the application layer into such a transport protocol? What other application tasks might be moved into this protocol?

14 Most Telnet clients can be used to connect to port 25, the SMTP port, instead of to the Telnet port. Using such a tool, connect to an SMTP server and send yourself (or someone else, with permission) some forged email. Then examine the headers for evidence the message isn't genuine.

15 What features might be used by (or added to) SMTP and/or a mail daemon such as sendmail to provide some resistance to email forgeries as in the previous exercise?

16 Find out how SMTP hosts deal with unknown commands from the other side, and how in particular this mechanism allows for the evolution of the protocol (e.g., to "extended SMTP"). You can either read the RFC, or contact an SMTP server as in Exercise 14 and test its responses to nonexistent commands.

17 As presented in the text, SMTP involves the exchange of several small messages. In most cases, the server responses do not affect what the client sends subsequently. The client might thus implement *command pipelining*: sending multiple commands in a single message.

  (a) For what SMTP commands *does* the client need to pay attention to the server's responses?

  (b) Assume the server reads each client message with gets() or the equivalent, which reads in a string up to a <LF>. What would it have to do even to detect that a client had used command pipelining?

(c) Pipelining is nonetheless known to break with some servers; find out how a client can negotiate its use.

18 Find out what other features DNS MX records provide in addition to supplying an alias for a mail server; the latter could, after all, be provided by a DNS CNAME record. MX records are provided to support email; would an analogous WEB record be of use in supporting HTTP?

19 One of the central problems faced by a protocol such as MIME is the vast number of data formats available. Consult the MIME RFC to find out how MIME deals with new or system-specific image and text formats.

20 MIME supports multiple representations of the same content using the multipart/alternative syntax; for example, text could be sent as text/plain, text/richtext, and application/postscript. Why do you think plaintext is supposed to be the *first* format, even though implementations might find it easier to place plaintext after their native format?

21 Consult the MIME RFC to find out how base64 encoding handles binary data of a length not evenly divisible by three bytes.

22 In HTTP version 1.0, a server marked the end of a transfer by closing the connection. Explain why, in terms of the TCP layer, this was a problem for servers. Find out how HTTP version 1.1 avoids this. How might a general-purpose request/reply protocol address this?

23 Find out how to configure an HTTP server so as to eliminate the 404 not found message, and have a default (and hopefully friendlier) message returned instead. Decide if such a feature is part of the protocol or part of an implementation, or is technically even permitted by the protocol. (Documentation for the apache HTTP server can be found at www.apache.org.)

24 Why does the HTTP GET command on page 643,

```
GET http:www.cs.princeton.edu/index.html HTTP/1.1
```

contain the name of the server being contacted? Wouldn't the server already know its name? Use Telnet, as in Exercise 14, to connect to port 80 of an HTTP server and find out what happens if you leave the host name out.

25 When an HTTP server initiates a close() at its end of a connection, it must then wait in TCP state FIN_WAIT_2 for the client to close the other end. What mechanism within the TCP protocol could help an HTTP server deal with noncooperative or poorly implemented clients that don't close from their end? If possible, find out about the programming interface for this mechanism, and indicate how an HTTP server might apply it.

26 The POP3 Post Office Protocol only allows a client to retrieve email, using a password for authentication. Traditionally, to *send* email a client would simply send it to its server and expect that it be relayed.

   (a) Explain why email servers often no longer permit such relaying from arbitrary clients.

   (b) Propose an SMTP option for remote client authentication.

   (c) Find out what existing methods are available for addressing this issue.

27 Suppose a very large Web site wants a mechanism by which clients access whichever of multiple HTTP servers is "closest" by some suitable measure.

   (a) Discuss developing a mechanism within HTTP for doing this.

   (b) Discuss developing a mechanism within DNS for doing this.

   Compare the two. Can either approach be made to work without upgrading the browser?

28 Find out if there is available to you an SNMP node that will answer queries you send it. If so, locate some SNMP utilities (e.g., the ucd-snmp suite) and try the following:

   (a) Fetch the entire system group, using something like

```
snmpwalk nodename public system
```

   Also try the above with 1 in place of system.

   (b) Manually walk through the system group, using multiple SNMP GET-NEXT operations (e.g., using snmpgetnext or equivalent), retrieving one entry at a time.

29 Using the SNMP device and utilities of the previous exercise, fetch the tcp group (numerically group 6), or some other group. Then do something to make some of the group's counters change, and fetch the group again to show the change. Try to do this in such a way that you can be sure your actions were the cause of the change recorded.

30 What information provided by SNMP might be useful to someone planning the IP spoofing attack of Exercise 17 in Chapter 5? What other SNMP information might be considered sensitive?

31 Try to find situations where an RTP application might reasonably do the following:

- Send multiple packets at essentially the same time that need different timestamps.
- Send packets at different times that need the same timestamp.

Argue, in consequence, that RTP timestamps must, in at least some cases, be provided (at least indirectly) by the application. Hint: Think of cases where the sending rate and playback rate might not match.

32 Having the timestamp clock count time in units of one frame time or one voice sample time would be the minimum resolution to ensure accurate playback. But the time unit is usually considerably smaller; what is the purpose of this?

33 Suppose we want returning RTCP reports from receivers to amount to no more than 5% of the outgoing primary RTP stream. If each report is 84 bytes, and the RTP traffic is 20KBps, and there are 1000 recipients, how often do individual receivers get to report? What if there are 10,000 recipients?

34 RFC 1889 specifies that the time interval between receiver RTCP reports include a randomization factor to avoid having all the receivers send at the same time. If all the receivers sent in the same 5% subinterval of their reply time interval, the arriving upstream RTCP traffic would rival the downstream RTP traffic.

(a) Video receivers might reasonably wait to send their reports until the higher-priority task of processing and displaying one frame is completed; this might mean their RTCP transmissions were synchronized on frame boundaries. Is this likely to be a serious concern?

(b) With 10 receivers, what is the probability of their all sending in one particular 5% subinterval?

(c) With 10 receivers, what is the probability half will send in one particular 5% subinterval? Multiply this by 20 for an estimate of the probability half will all send in the same arbitrary 5% subinterval. Hint: How many ways can we choose 5 receivers out of 10?

35 What might a server actually do with the packet-loss-rate data and jitter data in receiver reports?

36 Suppose some receivers in a large conference can receive data at a significantly higher bandwidth than others. What sorts of things might be implemented to address this? Hint: Consider both the session announcement protocol (SAP) and the possibility of utilizing third-party "mixers."

37 Propose a mechanism for deciding when to report an RTP packet as lost. How does your mechanism compare with the TCP adaptive retransmission mechanisms of Section 5.2.5?

38 How might you encode audio (or video) data in two packets so that if one packet is lost, then the resolution is simply reduced to what would be expected with half the bandwidth? Explain why this is much more difficult if a JPEG-type encoding is used.

4B/5B: A type of bit encoding scheme used in FDDI, in which every 4 bits of data are transmitted as a 5-bit sequence.

802.3: IEEE Ethernet standard.

802.5: IEEE token ring standard.

802.11: IEEE wireless network standard.

822: Refers to RFC 822, which defines the format of Internet email messages. See *SMTP*.

AAL: ATM Adaptation Layer. A protocol layer, configured over ATM. Two AALs are defined for data communications, AAL3/4 and AAL5. Each protocol layer provides a mechanism to segment large packets into cells at the sender and to reassemble the cells back together at the receiver.

ABR: (1) Available bit rate. A rate-based congestion-control scheme being developed for use on ATM networks. ABR is intended to allow a source to increase or decrease its allotted rate, based on feedback from switches within the network. Contrast with *CBR, UBR,* and *VBR.* (2) Area border router. Router at the edge of an *area* in a link-state protocol.

ACK: An abbreviation for *acknowledgment*. An acknowledgment is sent by a receiver of data to indicate to the sender that the data transmission was successful.

additive increase/multiplicative decrease: Congestion window strategy used by TCP. TCP opens the congestion window at a linear rate, but halves it when losses are experienced due to congestion. It has been shown that additive increase/multiplicative decrease is a necessary condition for a congestion-control mechanism to be stable.

AF: Assured forwarding. One of the per-hop behaviors proposed for Differentiated Services.

ALF: Application Level Framing. A protocol design principle that says that application programs better understand their communication needs than do general-purpose transport protocols.

AMPS: Advanced Mobile Phone System. Analog-based cell phone system. Currently being replaced by digital system, known as PCS.

ANSI: American National Standards Institute. Private U.S. standardization body that commonly participates in the ISO standardization process. Responsible for SONET.

API: Application programming interface. Interface that application programs use to access the network subsystem (usually the transport protocol). Usually OS-specific. The socket API from Berkeley Unix is a widely used example.

area: In the context of link-state routing, a collection of adjacent routers that share full routing information with each other. A routing domain is divided into areas to improve scalability.

ARP: Address Resolution Protocol. Protocol of the Internet architecture, used to translate high-level protocol addresses into physical hardware addresses. Commonly used on the Internet to map IP addresses into Ethernet addresses.

ARPA: Advanced Research Projects Agency. One of the research and development organizations within the Department of Defense. Responsible for funding the ARPANET as well as the research that led to the development of the TCP/IP Internet. Also known as DARPA, the *D* standing for Defense.

ARPANET: An experimental wide area packet-switched network funded by ARPA and begun in the late 1960s, which became the backbone of the developing Internet.

ARQ: Automatic repeat request. General strategy for reliably sending packets over an unreliable link. If the sender does not receive an ACK for a packet after a certain time period, it assumes that the packet did not arrive (or was delivered with bit errors) and retransmits it. Stop-and-wait and sliding window are two example ARQ protocols. Contrast with *FEC*.

ASN.1: Abstract Syntax Notation One. In conjunction with BER, a presentation-formatting standard devised by the ISO as part of the OSI architecture.

ATM: Asynchronous transfer mode. A connection-oriented network technology that uses small, fixed-size packets (called *cells*) to carry data.

ATMARP: Address Resolution Protocol as enhanced for ATM networks.

ATM Forum: A key ATM standards-setting body.

authentication: Security protocol by which two suspicious parties prove to each other that they are who they claim to be.

autonomous system (AS): A group of networks and routers, subject to a common authority and using the same intradomain routing protocol.

bandwidth: A measure of the capacity of a link or connection, usually given in units of bits per second.

Bellman-Ford: A name for the distance-vector routing algorithm, from the names of the inventors.

BER: Basic Encoding Rules. Rules for encoding data types defined by ASN.1.

best-effort delivery: The service model of the current Internet architecture. Delivery of a message is attempted but is not guaranteed.

BGP: Border Gateway Protocol. An interdomain routing protocol by which autonomous systems exchange reachability information. The most recent version is BGP-4.

BISYNC: Binary Synchronous Communication. A byte-oriented link-level protocol developed in the late 1960s by IBM.

bit stuffing: A technique used to distinguish control sequences and data on the bit level. Used by the HDLC protocol.

BLAST: A protocol that performs fragmentation and reassembly of large messages, used to build an RPC protocol.

block: An OS term used to describe a situation in which a process suspends execution while awaiting some event, such as a change in the state of a *semaphore*.

bridge: A device that forwards link-level frames from one physical network to another, sometimes called a LAN switch. Contrast with *repeater* and *router*.

broadcast: A method of delivering a packet to every host on a particular network or internet. May be implemented in hardware (e.g., Ethernet) or software (e.g., IP broadcast).

BUS: Broadcast and unknown server. A device used in LAN emulation (LANE).

CA: Certification authority (also known as certificate authority). An entity that signs security certificates, thereby promising that the public key contained in the certificate belongs to the entity named in the certificate.

CBR: Constant bit rate. A class of service in ATM that guarantees transmission of data at a constant bit rate, thus emulating a dedicated transmission link. Contrast with *ABR, UBR,* and *VBR.*

CCITT: The now defunct *Comité Consultif International de Telegraphique et Telephonique*, a unit of the International Telecommunications Union (ITU) of the United Nations. Now replaced by ITU-T.

cell: A 53-byte ATM packet, capable of carrying up to 48 bytes of data.

certificate: A document digitally signed by one entity that contains the name and public key of another entity. Used to distribute public keys. Also see *CA*.

CHAN: A protocol that implements request/reply channels.

channel: A generic communication term used in this book to denote a logical process-to-process connection.

checksum: Typically a ones complement sum over some or all of the bytes of a packet, computed and appended to the packet by the sender. The receiver recomputes the checksum and compares it to the one carried in the message. Checksums are used to detect errors in a packet and may also be used to verify that the packet has been delivered to the correct host. The term *checksum* is also sometimes (imprecisely) used to refer generically to error-detecting codes.

chipping code: Random sequence of bits that is XORed with the data stream to implement the direct sequence technique of spread spectrum.

CIDR: Classless interdomain routing. A method of aggregating routes that treats a block of contiguous Class C IP addresses as a single network.

circuit switching: A general strategy for switching data through a network. It involves establishing a dedicated path (circuit) between the source and destination. Contrast with *packet switching*.

client: The requester of a service in a distributed system.

CLNP: Connectionless Network Protocol. The ISO counterpart to the Internet's IP.

clock recovery: The process of deriving a valid clock from a serially transmitted digital signal.

concurrent logical channels: Multiplexing several stop-and-wait logical channels onto a single point-to-point link. No delivery order is enforced. This mechanism was used by the IMP-IMP protocol of the ARPANET.

congestion: A state resulting from too many packets contending for limited resources (e.g., link bandwidth and buffer space on routers or switches), which may force the router (switch) to discard packets.

congestion control: Any network resource management strategy that has, as its goal, the alleviation or avoidance of congestion. A congestion-control mechanism may be implemented on the routers (switches) inside the network, by the hosts at the edges of the network, or by a combination of both.

connection: In general, a channel that must be established prior to use (e.g., by the transmission of some setup information). For example, TCP provides a connection abstraction that offers reliable, ordered delivery of a byte stream. Connection-oriented networks, such as ATM, are often said to provide a *virtual circuit* abstraction.

connectionless protocol: A protocol in which data may be sent without any advance setup. IP is an example of such a protocol.

context switch: An operation in which an operating system suspends the execution of one process and begins the execution of another. A context switch involves saving the state of the former process (e.g., the contents of all registers) and loading the state of the latter process.

controlled load: One of the service classes available in the Internet's Integrated Services architecture.

CRC: Cyclic redundancy check. An error-detecting code computed over the bytes composing a packet and then appended to the packet by the network hardware (e.g., Ethernet adaptor). CRC provides stronger error detection than a simple checksum.

crossbar switch: A simple switch design in which every input is directly connected to every output and the output port is responsible for resolving contention.

CSMA/CD: Carrier Sense Multiple Access with Collision Detect. CSMA/CD is a functionality of network hardware. "Carrier sense multiple access" means that multiple stations can listen to the link and detect when it is in use or idle; "collision detect" indicates that if two or more stations are transmitting on the link simultaneously, they will detect the collision of their signals. Ethernet is the best-known technology that uses CSMA/CD.

cut-through: A form of switching or forwarding in which a packet starts to be transferred to an output before it has been completely received by the switching node, thus reducing latency through the node.

datagram: The basic transmission unit in the Internet architecture. A datagram contains all of the information needed to deliver it to its destination, analogous to a letter in the U.S. postal system. Datagram networks are connectionless.

DCE: Distributed Computing Environment. An RPC-based suite of protocols and standards that support distributed computing. Defined by OSF.

DDCMP: Digital Data Communication Message Protocol. A byte-oriented link-level protocol used in Digital Equipment Corporation's DECNET.

DECbit: A congestion-control scheme in which routers notify the endpoints of imminent congestion by setting a bit in the header of routed packets. The endpoints decrease their sending rates when a certain percentage of received packets have the bit set.

decryption: The act of reversing an *encryption* process to recover the data from an encrypted message.

delay bandwidth product: The product of a network's RTT and bandwidth. Gives a measure of how much data can be in transit on the network.

demultiplexing: Using information contained in a packet header to direct it upward through a protocol stack. For example, IP uses the ProtNum field in the IP header to decide which higher protocol (i.e., TCP, UDP) a packet belongs to, and TCP uses the port number to demultiplex a TCP packet to the correct application process. Contrast with *multiplexing*.

demultiplexing key: A field in a packet header that enables demultiplexing to take place (e.g., the ProtNum field of IP).

dense mode multicast: PIM mode used when most routers or hosts need to receive multicast packets.

DES: Data Encryption Standard. An algorithm for data encryption based on a 64-bit secret key.

DHCP: Dynamic Host Configuration Protocol. A protocol used by a host, as it boots, to learn various network information, such as its IP address.

Differentiated Services: A new architecture for providing better than best-effort service on the Internet. It has been proposed as an alternative to Integrated Services.

direct sequence: A spread spectrum technique that involves XORing the data stream with a random bit sequence known as a chipping code.

distance vector: A lowest-cost-path algorithm used in routing. Each node advertises reachability information and associated costs to its immediate neighbors, and uses the updates it receives to construct its forwarding table. The routing protocol RIP uses a distance-vector algorithm. Contrast with *link state*.

DMA: Direct memory access. An approach to connecting hosts to I/O devices, in which the device directly reads data from and writes data to the host's memory. Also see *PIO*.

DNA/DECNET: Digital Network Architecture. An OSI-based architecture that supports a connectionless network model and a connection-oriented transport protocol.

DNS: Domain name system. The distributed naming system of the Internet, used to resolve host names (e.g., cicada.cs.princeton.edu) into IP addresses (e.g., 192.12.69.35). The DNS is implemented by a hierarchy of name servers.

domain: Can refer either to a context in the hierarchical DNS name space (e.g., the "edu" domain) or to a region of the Internet that is treated as a single entity for the purpose of hierarchical routing. The latter is equivalent to *autonomous system*.

DS3: A 44.7-Mbps transmission link service offered by the phone company. Also called T3.

DSL: Digital subscriber line. A family of standards for transmitting data over twisted pair telephone lines at multimegabit-per-second speeds.

duplicate ACK: A retransmission of a TCP acknowledgment. The duplicate ACK does not acknowledge any new data. The receipt of multiple duplicate ACKs triggers the TCP *fast retransmit* mechanism.

DVMRP: Distance Vector Multicast Routing Protocol. Multicast routing protocol used by the majority of the routers in the MBone.

EF: Expedited forwarding. One of the per-hop behaviors proposed for Differentiated Services.

EGP: Exterior Gateway Protocol. An early interdomain routing protocol of the Internet, which was used by exterior gateways (routers) of autonomous systems to exchange routing information with other ASs. Replaced by BGP.

encapsulation: The operation, performed by a lower-level protocol, of attaching a protocol-specific header and/or trailer to a message passed down by a higher-level protocol. As a message travels down the protocol stack, it gathers a sequence of headers, of which the outermost corresponds to the protocol at the bottom of the stack.

encryption: The act of applying a transforming function to data, with the intention that only the receiver of the data will be able to read it (after applying the inverse function, *decryption*). Encryption generally depends on either a secret shared by the sender and receiver or on a public/private key pair.

Ethernet: A popular local area network technology that uses CSMA/CD and has a bandwidth of 10 Mbps. An Ethernet itself is just a passive wire; all aspects of Ethernet transmission are completely implemented by the host adaptors.

exponential backoff: A retransmission strategy that doubles the timeout value each time a packet is retransmitted.

exposed node problem: Situation that occurs on a wireless network where two nodes receive signals from a common source, but each is able to reach other nodes that do not receive this signal.

extended LAN: A collection of LANs connected by bridges.

fabric: The part of a switch that actually does the switching, that is, moves packets from input to output. Contrast with *port*.

fair queuing (FQ): A round-robin-based queuing algorithm that prevents a badly behaved process from capturing an arbitrarily large portion of the network capacity.

fast retransmit: A strategy used by TCP that attempts to avoid timeouts in the presence of lost packets. TCP retransmits a segment after receiving three consecutive duplicate ACKs, acknowledging the data up to (but not including) that segment.

FDDI: Fiber Distributed Data Interface. A high-speed token ring networking technology designed to run over optical fiber.

FEC: Forward error correction. A general strategy for recovering from bit errors introduced into data packets without having to retransmit the packet. Redundant information is included with each packet that can be used by the receiver to determine which bits in a packet are incorrect. Contrast with *ARQ*.

Fiber Channel: A bidirectional link protocol commonly used to connect computers (usually supercomputers) to peripherals. Fiber Channel has a bandwidth of 100 MBps and can span up to 30 m. Used in the same way as HiPPI.

firewall: A router that has been configured to filter (not forward) packets from certain sources. Used to enforce a security policy.

flow control: A mechanism by which the receiver of data throttles the transmission rate of the sender, so that data will not arrive too quickly to be processed. Contrast with *congestion control*.

flowspec: Specification of a flow's bandwidth and delay requirements presented to the network to establish a reservation. Used with RSVP.

forwarding: The operation performed by a router on every packet: receiving it on an input, deciding what output to send it to, and sending it there.

forwarding table: The table maintained in a router that lets it make decisions on how to forward packets. The process of building up the forwarding table is called routing, and thus the forwarding table is sometimes called a *routing table*. In some implementations, the routing and forwarding tables are separate data structures.

fragmentation/reassembly: A method for transmission of messages larger than the network's MTU. Messages are fragmented into small pieces by the sender and reassembled by the receiver.

frame: Another name for a packet, typically used in reference to packets sent over a single link rather than a whole network. An important problem is how the receiver detects the beginning and ending of a frame, a problem known as framing.

Frame Relay: A connection-oriented public packet-switched service offered by the phone company.

frequency hopping: A spread spectrum technique that involves transmitting data over a random sequence of frequencies.

FTP: File Transfer Protocol. The standard protocol of the Internet architecture for transferring files between hosts. Built on top of TCP.

GMS: Global Mobile System. Digital cellular phone system being deployed throughout the world (except the United States and Canada). Similar to PCS, which is being deployed throughout the United States and Canada.

gopher: An Internet information service.

H.323: Session control protocol often used for Internet telephony.

handle: In programming, an identifer or pointer that is used to access an object.

hardware address: The link-level address used to identify the host adaptor on the local network.

HDLC: High-Level Data Link Control protocol. An ISO-standard link-level protocol. It uses bit stuffing to solve the framing problem.

hidden node problem: Situation that occurs on a wireless network where two nodes are sending to a common destination, but are unaware that the other exists.

hierarchical routing: A multilevel routing scheme that uses the hierarchical structure of the address space as the basis for making forwarding decisions. For example, packets might first be routed to a destination network and then to a specific host on that network.

HiPPI: High Performance Parallel Interface. An ANSI-standard network technology capable of Gbps transmission rates, typically used to connect supercomputers to peripheral devices. Used in same way as *Fiber Channel*.

host: A computer attached to one or more networks that supports users and runs application programs.

HTML: HyperText Markup Language. A language used to construct World Wide Web pages.

HTTP: HyperText Transport Protocol. An application-level protocol based on a request/reply paradigm and used in the World Wide Web. HTTP uses TCP connections to transfer data.

IAB: Internet Activities Board. The main body that oversees the development and standardization of protocols of the Internet architecture. The IRTF and IETF are task forces of the IAB.

IBGP: Interior BGP, the protocol used to exchange interdomain routing information among routers in the same domain.

ICMP: Internet Control Message Protocol. This protocol is an integral part of IP. It allows a router or destination host to communicate with the source, typically to report an error in IP datagram processing.

IEEE: Institute for Electrical and Electronics Engineers. A professional society for engineers that also defines network standards, including the 802 series of LAN standards.

IETF: Internet Engineering Task Force. A task force of the IAB, responsible for providing short-term engineering solutions for the Internet.

IMP-IMP: A byte-oriented link-level protocol used in the original ARPANET.

Integrated Services: Usually taken to mean a packet-switched network that can effectively support both conventional computer data and real-time audio and video. Also, a name given to a proposed Internet service model that is being designed to replace the current best-effort service model.

integrity: In the context of network security, a service that ensures that a received message is the same one that was sent.

interdomain routing: The process of exchanging routing among different routing domains. BGP is an example of an interdomain protocol.

internet: A collection of (possibly heterogeneous) packet-switching networks interconnected by routers. Also called an internetwork.

Internet: The global internet based on the Internet (TCP/IP) architecture, connecting millions of hosts worldwide.

interoperability: The ability of heterogeneous hardware and multivendor software to communicate by correctly exchanging messages.

interrupt: An event (typically generated by a hardware device) that tells the operating system to stop its current activity and take some action. For example, an interrupt is used to notify the OS that a packet has arrived from the network.

intradomain routing: The exchange of routing information within a single domain or autonomous system. RIP and OSPF are example intradomain protocols.

IP: Internet Protocol (also known as IPv4). A protocol that provides a connectionless, best-effort delivery service of datagrams across the Internet.

IPng: Internet Protocol—Next Generation (also known as IPv6). Proposed version of IP that provides a larger, more hierarchical address space and other new features.

IPSEC: IP Security. An architecture for authentication, privacy, and message integrity, among other security services to the Internet architecture.

IRTF: Internet Research Task Force. A task force of the IAB, responsible for charting direction in research and development for the Internet.

IS-IS: A link-state routing protocol, similar to OSPF.

ISDN: Integrated Services Digital Network. A digital communication service offered by telephone carriers and standardized by ITU-T. ISDN combines voice connection and digital data services in a single physical medium.

ISO: International Standards Organization. The international body that drafted the seven-layer OSI architecture, and a suite of protocols that has not enjoyed commercial success.

ITU-T: A subcommittee of the International Telecommunications Union, a global body that drafts technical standards for all areas of international analog and digital communication. ITU-T deals with standards for telecommunications, notably ATM.

jitter: Variation in network latency. Large jitter has a negative impact on the quality of video and audio applications.

JPEG: Joint Photographic Experts Group. Typically used to refer to a widely used algorithm for compressing still images that was developed by the JPEG.

Kerberos: A TCP/IP-based authentication system developed at MIT, in which two hosts use a trusted third party to authenticate each other.

key distribution: Mechanism by which users learn each others' public keys through the exchange of digitally signed certificates.

LAN: Local area network. A network based on any physical network technology that is designed to span distances of up to a few thousand meters (e.g., Ethernet or FDDI). Contrast with *SAN, MAN,* and *WAN.*

LANE: Local area network emulation. Adding functionality to ATM to make it behave like a shared-media (i.e., Ethernet-like) LAN.

LAN switch: Another term for a *bridge*, usually applied to a bridge with many ports. Also called an Ethernet switch if the link technology it supports is Ethernet.

latency: A measure of how long it takes a single bit to propagate from one end of a link or channel to the other. Latency is measured strictly in terms of time.

LDAP: Lightweight Directory Access Protocol. A subset of the X.500 directory service that has recently become a popular directory service for information about users.

LES: LAN emulation (LANE) server.

link: A physical connection between two nodes of a network. It may be implemented over copper or fiberoptic cable or it may be a wireless link (e.g., a satellite).

link-level protocol: A protocol that is responsible for delivering frames over a directly connected network (e.g., an Ethernet, token ring, or point-to-point link). (Also called link-layer protocol.)

link state: A lowest-cost-path algorithm used in routing. Information on directly connected neighbors and current link costs are flooded to all routers; each router uses this information to build a view of the network on which to base forwarding decisions. The OSPF routing protocol uses a link-state algorithm. Contrast with *distance vector*.

MAC: Media access control. Algorithms used to control access to shared-media networks like Ethernet and FDDI.

MACA: Multiple Access with Collision Avoidance. Distributed algorithm used to mediate access to a shared media.

MACAW: Multiple Access with Collision Avoidance for Wireless. Enhancement of the general MACA algorithm to better support wireless networks. Used by 802.11.

MAN: Metropolitan area network. A network based on any of several new network technologies that operate at high speeds (up to several Gbps) and across distances wide enough to span a metropolitan area. Contrast with *SAN*, *LAN*, and *WAN*.

Manchester: A bit encoding scheme that transmits the exclusive-OR of the clock and the NRZ-encoded data. Used on the Ethernet.

MBone: Multicast Backbone. A logical network imposed over the top of the Internet, in which multicast-enhanced routers use tunneling to forward multicast datagrams across the Internet.

MD5: Message Digest version 5. An efficient cryptographic checksum algorithm commonly used to verify that the contents of a message are unaltered.

MIB: Management information base. Defines the set of network-related variables that may be read or written on a network node. The MIB is used in conjunction with SNMP.

MIME: Multipurpose Internet Mail Extensions. Specifications for converting binary data (such as image files) to ASCII text, which allows it to be sent via email.

Mosaic: A popular and free graphical World Wide Web browser developed at the National Center for Supercomputing Applications at the University of Illinois.

MP3: MPEG Layer 3. Audio compression standard used with MPEG.

MPEG: Moving Picture Experts Group. Typically used to refer to an algorithm for compressing video streams developed by the MPEG.

MPLS: Multiprotocol Label Switching. A collection of techniques used to effectively implement IP routers on top of level 2 (e.g., ATM) switches.

MSAU: Multistation access unit. A device used in token ring networks to connect several stations to the ring and remove them in the event of failure.

MTU: Maximum transmission unit. The size of the largest packet that can be sent over a physical network.

multicast: A special form of broadcast in which packets are delivered to a specified subgroup of network hosts.

multiplexing: Combining distinct channels into a single, lower-level channel. For example, separate TCP and UDP channels are multiplexed into a single host-to-host IP channel. The inverse operation, *demultiplexing*, takes place on the receiving host.

name resolution: The action of resolving host names (which are easy for humans to read) into their corresponding addresses (which machines can read). See *DNS*.

NAT: Network address translation. A technique for extending the IP address space that involves translating between globally understood IP addresses and local-only addresses at the edge of a network or site.

NDR: Network Data Representation. The data-encoding standard used in the Distributed Computing Environment (DCE), as defined by the Open Software Foundation. NDR uses a receiver-makes-right strategy and inserts an architecture tag at the front of each message.

Netscape: A popular graphical WWW browser.

network-level protocol: A protocol that runs over switched networks, directly above the link level.

NFS: Network File System. A popular distributed file system developed by Sun Microsystems. NFS is based on SunRPC, an RPC protocol developed by Sun.

NIST: National Institute for Standards and Technology. The official U.S. standardization body.

node: A generic term used for individual computers that make up a network. Nodes include general-purpose computers, switches, and routers.

NRZ: Non-return to zero. A bit encoding scheme that encodes a 1 as the high signal and a 0 as the low signal.

NRZI: Non-return to zero inverted. A bit encoding scheme that makes a transition from the current signal to encode a 1 and stays at the current signal to encode a 0.

NSF: National Science Foundation. An agency of the U.S. government that funds scientific research in the United States, including research on networks and on the Internet infrastructure.

NV: Network Video. A videoconferencing application that runs over the MBone.

OC: Optical Carrier. The prefix for various rates of SONET optical transmission. For example, OC-1 refers to the SONET standard for 51.84-Mbps transmission over fiber. An OC-n signal differs from an STS-n signal only in that the OC-n signal is scrambled for optical transmission.

ONC: Open Network Computing. A version of SunRPC that is being standardized for the Internet.

OSF: Open Software Foundation. A consortium of computer vendors that have defined standards for distributed computing, including the NDR presentation format.

OSI: Open Systems Interconnection. The seven-layer network reference model developed by the ISO. Guides the design of ISO and ITU-T protocol standards.

OSPF: Open Shortest Path First. A routing protocol developed by the IETF for the Internet architecture. OSPF is based on a *link-state* algorithm, in which every node constructs a topography of the Internet and uses it to make forwarding decisions. Today known as Open Group.

packet: A data unit sent over a packet-switched network. Also see *frame* and *segment*.

packet switching: A general strategy for switching data through a network. Packet switching uses store-and-forward switching of discrete data units called packets, and implies *statistical multiplexing*.

participants: A generic term used to denote the processes, protocols, or hosts that are sending messages to each other.

PAWS: Protection against wrapped sequence numbers. Engineering transport protocol with a large enough sequence number space to protect against the numbers wrapping around on a network where packets can be delayed for a long period of time.

PCS: Personal Communication Services. New digital cellular phone system being deployed throughout the United States and Canada. Similar to GMS, which is being deployed throughout the rest of the world.

PDU: Protocol data unit. Another name for a packet or frame.

peer: A counterpart on another machine that a protocol module interoperates with to implement some communication service.

PEM: Privacy Enhanced Mail. Extensions to Internet email that support privacy and integrity protection. See also *PGP*.

PGP: Pretty Good Privacy. A collection of public domain software that provides privacy and authentication capabilities using RSA and that uses a mesh of trust for public key distribution.

PHB: Per-hop behavior. Behavior of individual routers in the Differentiated Services architecture. AF and EF are two proposed PHBs.

physical-level protocol: The lowest layer of the OSI protocol stack. Its main function is to encode bits onto the signals that are propagated across the physical transmission media.

piconet: Wireless network spanning short distances (e.g., 10 m). Used to connect office computers (laptops, printers, PDAs, workstations, etc.) without cables.

PIM: Protocol Independent Multicast. A multicast routing protocol that can be built on top of different unicast routing protocols.

Ping: A Unix utility used to test the RTT to various hosts over the Internet. Ping sends an ICMP ECHO_REQUEST message, and the remote host sends an ECHO_RESPONSE message back.

PIO: Programmed Input/Ouput. An approach to connecting hosts to I/O devices, in which the CPU reads data from and writes data to the I/O device. Also see *DMA*.

poison reverse: Used in conjunction with *split horizon*. A heuristic technique to avoid routing loops in distance-vector routing protocols.

port: A generic term usually used to mean the point at which a network user attaches to the network. On a switch, a port denotes the input or output on which packets are received and sent.

POTS: Plain old telephone service. Used to specify the existing phone service, in contrast to ISDN, ATM, or other technologies that the telephone companies offer now or may offer in the future.

PPP: Point-to-Point Protocol. Data link protocol typically used to connect computers over a dial-up line.

process: An abstraction provided by an operating system to enable different operations to take place concurrently. For example, each user application usually runs inside its own process, while various operating system functions take place in other processes.

promiscuous mode: A mode of operation for a network adaptor in which it receives all frames transmitted on the network, not just those addressed to it.

protocol: A specification of an interface between modules running on different machines, as well as the communication service that those modules implement. The term is also used to refer to an implementation of the module that meets this specification. To distinguish between these two uses, the interface is often called a *protocol specification*.

pseudoheader: A subset of fields from the IP header that are passed up to transport protocols TCP and UDP for use in their checksum calculation. The pseudoheader contains source and destination IP addresses and IP datagram length, thus enabling detection of corruption of these fields or delivery of a packet to an incorrect address.

public key encryption: Any of several encryption algorithms (e.g., RSA), in which each participant has a private key (shared with no one else) and a public key (available to everyone). A secure message is sent to a user by encrypting the data with that user's public key; possession of the private key is required to decrypt the message, and so only the receiver can read it.

QoS: Quality of service. Packet delivery guarantees provided by a network architecture. Usually related to performance guarantees, such as bandwidth and delay. The Internet offers a best-effort delivery service, meaning that every effort is made to deliver a packet but delivery is not guaranteed.

RED: Random early detection. A queuing discipline for routers in which, when congestion is anticipated, packets are randomly dropped to alert the senders to slow down.

rendezvous point: A router used by PIM to allow receivers to learn about senders.

repeater: A device that propagates electrical signals from one Ethernet cable to another. There can be a maximum of two repeaters between any two hosts in an Ethernet. Repeaters forward signals, whereas *bridges* forward *frames*, and *routers* and *switches* forward *packets*.

reverse-path broadcast (RPB): A technique used to eliminate duplicate broadcast packets.

RFC: Request for Comments. Internet reports that contain, among other things, specifications for protocols like TCP and IP.

RIO: RED with In and Out. A packet drop policy based on RED, but involving two drop curves: one for packets that have been marked as being "in" profile and one for packets that have been marked "out" of profile. Designed to be used to implement differentiated services.

RIP: Routing Information Protocol. An intradomain routing protocol supplied with Berkeley Unix. Each router running RIP dynamically builds its forwarding table based on a *distance-vector* algorithm.

router: A network node connected to two or more networks that forwards packets from one network to another. Contrast with *bridge*, *repeater*, and *switch*.

routing: The process by which nodes exchange topological information to build correct forwarding tables. See *forwarding*, *link state*, and *distance vector*.

routing table: See *forwarding table*.

RPC: Remote Procedure Call. Synchronous request/reply transport protocol used in many client/server interactions.

RSA: A public key encryption algorithm named after its inventors: Rivest, Shamir, and Adleman.

RSVP: Resource Reservation Protocol. A protocol for reserving resources in the network. RSVP uses the concept of *soft state* in routers and puts responsibility for making reservations on receivers instead of on senders.

RTCP: Real-time Transport Control Protocol. Control protocol associated with RTP.

RTP: Real-time Transport Protocol. An end-to-end protocol used by multimedia applications that have real-time constraints.

RTT: Round-trip time. The time it takes for a bit of information to propagate from one end of a link or channel to the other and back again; in other words, double the latency of the channel.

SAN: System area network. A network that spans the components of a computer system (e.g., display, camera, disk). Sometimes stands for storage area network and includes interfaces like HiPPI and Fiber Channel. Contrast with *LAN, MAN,* and *WAN.*

scrambling: The process of XORing a signal with a pseudorandom bit stream before transmission to cause enough signal transitions to allow clock recovery. Scrambling is used in SONET.

segment: A TCP packet. A segment contains a portion of the byte stream that is being sent by means of TCP.

SELECT: A synchronous demultiplexing protocol used to build an RPC protocol.

semaphore: A variable used to support synchronization between processes. Typically a process *blocks* on a semaphore while it waits for some other process to signal the semaphore.

server: The provider of a service in a client/server distributed system.

signalling: At the physical level, denotes the transmission of a signal over some physical medium. In ATM, signalling refers to the process of establishing a virtual circuit.

silly window syndrome: A condition occurring in TCP that may arise if each time the receiver opens its receive window a small amount, the sender sends a small segment to fill the window. The result is many small segments and an inefficient use of bandwidth.

sliding window: An algorithm that allows the sender to transmit multiple packets (up to the size of the window) before receiving an acknowledgment. As acknowledgments are returned for those packets in the window that were sent first, the window "slides" and more packets may be sent. The sliding window algorithm combines reliable delivery with a high throughput. See *ARQ*.

slow start: A congestion-avoidance algorithm for TCP that attempts to pace outgoing segments. For each ACK that is returned, two additional packets are sent, resulting in an exponential increase in the number of outstanding segments.

SMDS: Switched Multimegabit Data Service. A service supporting LAN-to-WAN connectivity, offered by some telephone companies.

SMTP: Simple Mail Transfer Protocol. The electronic mail protocol of the Internet. See *822*.

SNA: System Network Architecture. The proprietary network architecture of IBM.

SNMP: Simple Network Management Protocol. An Internet protocol that allows the monitoring of hosts, networks, and routers.

socket: The abstraction provided by Unix that provides the application programming interface (API) to TCP/IP.

soft state: Connection-related information contained in a router that is cached for a limited period of time rather than being explicitly established (and requiring explicit teardown) through a connection setup.

SONET: Synchronous Optical Network. A clock-based framing standard for digital transmission over optical fiber. It defines how telephone companies transmit data over optical networks.

source routing: Routing decisions performed at the source before the packet is sent. The route consists of the list of nodes that the packet should traverse on the way to the destination.

sparse mode multicast: A mode used in PIM when relatively few hosts or routers need to receive multicast data for a certain group.

split horizon: A method of breaking routing loops in a distance-vector routing algorithm. When a node sends a routing update to its neighbors, it does not send those routes it learned from each neighbor back to that neighbor. Split horizon is used with *poison reverse*.

spread spectrum: Encoding technique that involves spreading a signal over a wider frequency than necessary, so as to minimize the impact of interference.

SSL: Secure Socket Layer. A protocol layer that runs over TCP to provide authentication and encryption of connections. Also known as Transport Layer Security (TLS).

statistical multiplexing: Demand-based multiplexing of multiple data sources over a shared link or channel.

stop-and-wait: A reliable transmission algorithm in which the sender transmits a packet and waits for an acknowledgment before sending the next packet. Compare with *sliding window* and *concurrent logical channels*. See also *ARQ*.

STS: Synchronous Transport Signal. The prefix for various rates of SONET transmission. For example, STS-1 refers to the SONET standard for 51.84-Mbps transmission.

subnetting: The use of a single IP network address to denote multiple physical networks. Routers within the subnetwork use a subnet mask to discover the physical network to which a packet should be forwarded. Subnetting effectively introduces a third level to the two-level hierarchical IP address.

SunRPC: Remote procedure call protocol developed by Sun Microsystems. SunRPC is used to support NFS. See also *ONC*.

switch: A network node that forwards packets from inputs to outputs based on header information in each packet. Differs from a *router* mainly in that it typically does not interconnect networks of different types.

switching fabric: The component of a switch that directs packets from their inputs to the correct outputs.

T1: A standard telephone carrier service equal to 24 ISDN circuits, or 1.544 Mbps. Also called DS1.

T3: A standard telephone carrier service equal to 24 T1 circuits, or 44.736 Mbps. Also called DS3.

TCP: Transmission Control Protocol. Connection-oriented transport protocol of the Internet architecture. TCP provides a reliable, byte-stream delivery service.

Telnet: Remote terminal protocol of the Internet architecture. Telnet allows you to interact with a remote system as if your terminal is directly connected to that machine.

throughput: The observed rate at which data is sent through a channel. The term is often used interchangeably with *bandwidth*.

TLS: Transport Layer Security. Security services that can be layered on top of a transport protocol like TCP. It is often used by HTTP to perform secure transactions on the World Wide Web. Derived from *SSL*.

token bucket: A way to characterize or police the bandwidth used by a flow. Conceptually, processes accumulate tokens over time, and they must spend a token to transmit a byte of data and then must stop sending when they have no tokens left. Thus, overall bandwidth is limited, with the accommodation of some burstiness.

token ring: A physical network technology in which hosts are connected in a ring. A token (bit pattern) circulates around the ring. A given node must possess the token before it is allowed to transmit. 802.5 and FDDI are examples of token ring networks.

TP4: OSI Transport Protocol Class 4. The most powerful OSI transport protocol. TP4 is the ISO equivalent of TCP.

transport protocol: An end-to-end protocol that enables processes on different hosts to communicate. TCP is the canonical example.

TTL: Time to live: Usually a measure of the number of hops (routers) an IP datagram can visit before it is discarded.

tunneling: Encapsulating a packet using a protocol that operates at the same layer as the packet. For example, multicast IP packets are encapsulated inside unicast IP packets to tunnel across the Internet to implement the MBone. Tunneling will also be used during the transition from IPv4 to IPv6.

two-dimensional parity: A parity scheme in which bytes are conceptually stacked as a matrix, and parity is calculated for both rows and columns.

Tymnet: An early network in which a *virtual circuit* abstraction was maintained across a set of routers.

UBR: Unspecified bit rate. The "no frills" service class in ATM, offering best-effort cell delivery. Contrast with *ABR, CBR*, and *VBR*.

UDP: User Datagram Protocol. Transport protocol of the Internet architecture that provides a connectionless datagram service to application-level processes.

unicast: Sending a packet to a single destination host. Contrast with *broadcast* and *multicast*.

URL: Uniform resource locator. A text string used to identify the location of Internet resources. A typical URL looks like http://www.bellcore.com. In this URL, http is the protocol to use to access the resource located on host www.bellcore.com.

vat: Audioconferencing tool used on the Internet that runs over RTP.

VBR: Variable bit rate. One of the classes of service in ATM, intended for applications with bandwidth requirements that vary with time, such as compressed video. Contrast with *ABR, CBR,* and *UBR.*

VCI: Virtual circuit identifier. An identifier in the header of a packet that is used for virtual circuit switching. In the case of ATM, the VPI and VCI together identify the end-to-end connection.

vic: Unix-based videoconferencing tool that uses RTP.

virtual circuit: The abstraction provided by connection-oriented networks such as ATM. Messages must usually be exchanged between participants to establish a virtual circuit (and perhaps to allocate resources to the circuit) before data can be sent. Contrast with *datagram.*

virtual clock: A service model that allows the source to reserve resources on routers using a rate-based description of its needs. Virtual clock goes beyond the best-effort delivery service of the current Internet.

VPI: Virtual path identifier. An 8-bit or 12-bit field in the ATM header. VPI can be used to hide multiple virtual connections across a network inside a single virtual "path," thus decreasing the amount of connection state that the switches must maintain. See also *VCI.*

VPN: Virtual private network. A logical network overlaid on top of some existing network. For example, a company with sites around the world may build a virtual network on top of the Internet rather than lease lines between each site.

WAN: Wide area network. Any physical network technology that is capable of spanning long distances (e.g., crosscountry). Compare with *SAN, LAN,* and *WAN.*

weighted fair queuing (WFQ): A variation of *fair queuing* in which each flow can be given a different proportion of the network capacity.

well-known port: A port number that is, by convention, dedicated for use by a particular server. For instance, the Domain Name Server receives messages at well-known UDP and TCP port 53 on every host.

WWW: World Wide Web. A hypermedia information service on the Internet.

X.25: The ITU packet-switching protocol standard.

X.400: The ITU electronic mail standard. The counterpart to SMTP in the Internet architecture.

X.500: The ITU directory services standard, which defines an attribute-based naming service.

X.509: An ITU standard for digital certificates.

XDR: External Data Representation. Sun Microsystems' standard for machine-independent data structures. Contrast with *ASN.1* and *NDR*.

x-kernel: An object-oriented framework for implementing network protocols developed at the University of Arizona.

zone: A partition of the domain name hierarchy, corresponding to an administrative authority that is responsible for that portion of the hierarchy. Each zone must have at least two name servers to field DNS requests for the zone.

REFERENCES

[ASNS97]   Alexander, D., M. Shaw, S. Nettles, and J. Smith. Active bridging. *Proceedings of the SIGCOMM '97 Symposium*, pages 101–111, October 1997.

[Bat68]   Batcher, K. E. Sorting networks and their applications. *Proc. 1968 Spring AFIPS Joint Computer Conference*, 32:307–314, 1968.

[BBC+98]   Blake, S., D. Black, M. Carlson, E. Davies, Z. Wang, and W. Weiss. An architecture for differentiated services. *Request for Comments* 2475, December 1998.

[BCDB95]   Borden, M., E. Crawley, B. Davie, and S. Batsell. Integration of real-time services in an IP-ATM network architecture. *Request for Comments* 1821, August 1995.

[BCS94]   Braden, R., D. Clark, and S. Shenker. Integrated services in the internet architecture: An overview. *Request for Comments* 1633, September 1994.

[BDMS94]   Bowman, C. M., P. B. Danzig, U. Manber, and M. F. Schwartz. Scalable internet resource discovery: Research problems and approaches. *Communications of the ACM* 37(8):98–107, August 1994.

[BF93]   Borenstein, N., and N. Freed. MIME (multipurpose internet mail extensions) part one: Mechanisms for specifying and describing the format of internet message bodies. *Request for Comments* 1521, September 1993.

[BG92]   Bertsekas, D., and R. Gallager. *Data Networks*. Prentice Hall, Englewood Cliffs, NJ, second edition, 1992.

[BG93]   Bjorkman, M., and P. Gunningberg. Locking effects in multiprocessor implementations of protocols. *Proceedings of the SIGCOMM '93 Symposium*, pages 74–83, September 1993.

[Bla87]   Blahut, R. E. *Principles and Practice of Information Theory*. Addison-Wesley, Reading, MA, 1987.

[BLFF96]   Berners-Lee, T., R. Fielding, and H. Frystyk. Hypertext transfer protocol—HTTP/1.0. *Request for Comments* 1945, May 1996.

[BLNS82]   Birrell, A., R. Levin, R. Needham, and M. Schroeder. Grapevine: An exercise in distributed computing. *Communications of the ACM* 25:250–273, April 1982.

[BM95]   Bradner, S., and A. Mankin, editors. *IPng: Internet Protocol Next Generation*. Addison-Wesley, Reading, MA, 1995.

[BMK88]   Boggs, D., J. Mogul, and C. Kent. Measured capacity of an Ethernet. *Proceedings of the SIGCOMM '88 Symposium*, pages 222–234, August 1988.

[BN84]   Birrell, A., and B. Nelson. Implementing remote procedure calls. *ACM Transactions on Computer Systems* 2(1):39–59, February 1984.

[Boo95]   Boorsook, P. How anarchy works. *Wired* 3(10):110–118, October 1995.

[BP95]   Brakmo, L. S., and L. L. Peterson. TCP Vegas: End-to-end congestion avoidance on a global internet. *IEEE Journal of Selected Areas in Communication (JSAC)* 13(8):1465–1480, October 1995.

[BPY90]   Bowman, M., L. L. Peterson, and A. Yeatts. Univers: An attribute-based name server. *Software—Practice and Experience* 20(4):403–424, April 1990.

[BS88]   Bic, L., and A. C. Shaw. *The Logical Design of Operating Systems*. Prentice Hall, Englewood Cliffs, NJ, 1988.

[Buf94]   Buford, J. F. K. *Multimedia Systems*. ACM Press/Addison-Wesley, Reading, MA, 1994.

[BZ96]   Bennett, T., and H. Zhang. Hierarchical packet fair queueing algorithms. *Proceedings of the SIGCOMM '96 Symposium*, pages 143–156, August 1996.

[CCITT92a]   Comité Consultif International de Telegraphique et Telephonique. Open systems interconnection: Specification of abstract syntax notation one (ASN.1). CCITT Recommendation X.208, 1992.

[CCITT92b]   Comité Consultif International de Telegraphique et Telephonique. Open systems interconnection: Specification of Basic Encoding Rules for abstract syntax notation one (ASN.1). CCITT Recommendation X.209, 1992.

[CF98]   Clark, D., and W. Fang. Explicit allocation of best-effort packet delivery service. *IEEE/ACM Transactions on Networking* 6(4):362–373, August 1998.

[CFFD93]   Cohen, D., G. Finn, R. Felderman, and A. DeSchon. ATOMIC: A low-cost, very-high-speed, local communications architecture. *Proceedings of the 1993 Conference on Parallel Processing*, August 1993.

[Cha93]   Chapin, A. L. The billion node Internet. In D. C. Lynch and M. T. Rose, editors, *Internet System Handbook*, chapter 17, pages 707–716. Addison-Wesley, Reading, MA, 1993.

[CJRS89]   Clark, D. D., V. Jacobson, J. Romkey, and H. Salwen. An analysis of TCP processing overhead. *IEEE Communications* 27(6):23–29, June 1989.

[CK74]   Cerf, V., and R. Kahn. A protocol for packet network intercommunication. *IEEE Transactions on Communications* COM-22(5):637–648, May 1974.

[Cla82]   Clark, D. D. Modularity and efficiency in protocol implementation. *Request for Comments* 817, July 1982.

[Cla85]   Clark, D. D. The structuring of systems using upcalls. *Proceedings of the Tenth ACM Symposium on Operating Systems Principles*, pages 171–180, December 1985.

[Cla88]   Clark, D. The design philosophy of the DARPA Internet protocols. *Proceedings of the SIGCOMM '88 Symposium*, pages 106–114, August 1988.

[Cla97]   Clark, D. Internet cost allocation and pricing. In L. Knight and J. Bailey, editors, *Internet Economics*, pages 215–253. MIT Press, Cambridge, MA, 1997.

[CLNZ89]   Chen, S. K., E. D. Lazowska, D. Notkin, and J. Zahorjan. Performance implications of design alternatives for remote procedure call stubs. *Proceedings of the Ninth International Conference on Distributed Computing Systems*, pages 36–41, June 1989.

[CMRW93]   Case, J., K. McCloghrie, M. Rose, and S. Waldbusser. Structure of management information for version 2 of the Simple Network Management Protocol (SNMPv2). *Request for Comments* 1442, April 1993.

[Com95]   Comer, D. E. *Internetworking with TCP/IP. Volume I: Principles, Protocols, and Architecture.* Prentice Hall, Englewood Cliffs, NJ, third edition, 1995.

[CP89]   Comer, D. E., and L. L. Peterson. Understanding naming in distributed systems. *Distributed Computing* 3(2):51–60, May 1989.

[Cro82]   Crocker, D. Standard for the format of ARPA Internet text message. *Request for Comments* 822, August 1982.

[CS93]   Comer, D. E., and D. L. Stevens. *Internetworking with TCP/IP. Volume III: Client-Server Programming and Applications, BSD Socket Version.* Prentice Hall, Englewood Cliffs, NJ, 1993.

[CS94]   Comer, D. E., and D. L. Stevens. *Internetworking with TCP/IP. Volume III: Client-Server Programming and Applications, AT&T TLI Version.* Prentice Hall, Englewood Cliffs, NJ, 1994.

[CSZ92]   Clark, D., S. Shenker, and L. Zhang. Supporting real-time applications in an integrated services packet network: Architecture and mechanism. *Proceedings of the SIGCOMM '92 Symposium*, pages 14–26, August 1992.

[CT90]   Clark, D., and D. Tennenhouse. Architectural considerations for a new generation of protocols. *Proceedings of the SIGCOMM '91 Symposium*, pages 200–208, September 1990.

[CZ85]   Cheriton, D. R., and W. Zwaenepoel. Distributed process groups in the V kernel. *ACM Transactions on Computer Systems* 3(2):77–107, May 1985.

[Dan98]   Danzig, P. NetCache architecture and deployment. *Third International WWW Caching Workshop*, June 1998.

[DBCP98]   Degermark, M., A. Brodnik, S. Carlsson, and S. Pink. Small forwarding tables for fast routing lookups. *Proceedings of the SIGCOMM '97 Symposium*, pages 3–14, October 1998.

[DC90]   Deering, S., and D. Cheriton. Multicast routing in datagram internetworks and extended LANs. *ACM Transactions on Computer Systems* 8(2):85–110, May 1990.

[DDR98]   Davie, B., P. Doolan, and Y. Rekhter. *Switching in IP Networks*. Morgan Kaufmann Publishers, San Francisco, CA, 1998.

[DEF+96]   Deering, S., D. Estrin, D. Farinacci, V. Jacobson, C. Liu, and L. Wei. The PIM architecture for wide-area multicast routing. *ACM/IEEE Transactions on Networking* 4(2):153–162, April 1996.

[DeP95]   De Prycker, M. *Asynchronous Transfer Mode: Solution for Broadband ISDN*. Prentice Hall, Englewood Cliffs, NJ, 1995.

[DH98]   Deering, S., and R. Hinden. Internet Protocol, version 6 (IPv6) specification. *Request for Comments* 2460, December 1998.

[DKS89]   Demers, A., S. Keshav, and S. Shenker. Analysis and simulation of a fair queuing algorithm. *Proceedings of the SIGCOMM '89 Symposium*, pages 1–12, September 1989.

[DP93]   Druschel, P., and L. L. Peterson. Fbufs: A high-bandwidth cross-
              domain transfer facility. *Proceedings of the 14th ACM Symposium
              on Operating Systems Principles*, pages 189–202, December 1993.

[DPD94]   Druschel, P., L. L. Peterson, and B. S. Davie. Experience with a high-
              speed network adaptor: A software perspective. *Proceedings of the
              SIGCOMM '94 Symposium*, pages 2–13, August 1994.

[DY75]   Drysdale, R. L., and F. H. Young. Improved divide/sort/merge sorting
              networks. *SIAM Journal on Computing* 4(3):264–270, September
              1975.

[EWL+94]   Edwards, A., G. Watson, J. Lumley, D. Banks, C. Calamvokis,
              and C. Dalton. User-space protocols deliver high performance to
              applications on a low-cost Gb/s LAN. *Proceedings of the SIGCOMM
              '94 Symposium*, pages 14–23, August 1994.

[FB96]   Freed, N., and N. Borenstein. Multipurpose Internet mail extensions
              (MIME) part one: Format of Internet message bodies. *Request for
              Comments* 2045, November 1996.

[FGMBL97]   Fielding, R., J. Gettys, J. Mogul, and T. Berners-Lee. HyperText
              Transfer Protocol—HTTP/1.1. *Request for Comments* 2068, January
              1997.

[Fin88]   Finkel, R. A. *An Operating Systems Vade Mecum*. Prentice Hall,
              Englewood Cliffs, NJ, 1988.

[FJ93]   Floyd, S., and V. Jacobson. Random early detection gateways for
              congestion avoidance. *IEEE/ACM Transactions on Networking*
              1(4):397–413, August 1993.

[FLYV93]   Fuller, V., T. Li, J. Yu, and K. Varadhan. Classless interdomain
              routing (CIDR): An address assignment and aggregation strategy.
              Request for Comments 1519, September 1993.

[GG94]   Gopal, I., and R. Guerin. Network transparency: The plaNET
              approach. *IEEE/ACM Transactions on Networking* 2(3):226–239,
              June 1994.

[GHMS91]   Giacopelli, J. N., J. J. Hickey, W. S. Marcus, and W. D. Sincoskie. Sunshine: A high performance self-routing broadband packet switch architecture. *IEEE Journal of Selected Areas in Communication (JSAC)* 9(8):1289–1298, October 1991.

[Gin96]   Ginsburg, D. *ATM: Solutions for Enterprise Internetworking.* Addison-Wesley, Reading, MA, 1996.

[GK80]   Gerla, M., and L. Kleinrock. Flow control: A comparative survey. *IEEE Transactions on Communications* COM-28(4):553–573, April 1980.

[GVC96]   Goyal, P., H. Vin, and H. Chen. Start-time fair queueing: A scheduling algorithm for integrated services packet switching networks. *Proceedings of the SIGCOMM '96 Symposium*, pages 157–168, August 1996.

[HC98]   Harkins, D., and D. Carrel. The Internet Key Exchange (IKE). *Request for Comments* 2409, November 1998.

[Hed88]   Hedrick, C. Routing information protocol. *Request for Comments* 1058, June 1988.

[Hei93]   Heinanen, J. Multiprotocol encapsulation over ATM Adaptation Layer 5. *Request for Comments* 1483, July 1993.

[HMPT89]   Hutchinson, N., S. Mishra, L. Peterson, and V. Thomas. Tools for implementing network protocols. *Software—Practice and Experience* 19(9):895–916, September 1989.

[HP91]   Hutchinson, N., and L. Peterson. The *x*-kernel: An architecture for implementing network protocols. *IEEE Transactions on Software Engineering* 17(1):64–76, January 1991.

[HP95]   Holzmann, G. J., and B. Pehrson. *The Early History of Data Networks.* IEEE Computer Society Press, Los Alamitos, CA, 1995.

[HP96]   Hennessy, J. L., and D. A. Patterson. *Computer Architecture: A Quantitative Approach.* Morgan Kaufmann, San Francisco, CA, second edition, 1996.

[HPB⁺99]   Hartman, J., L. Peterson, A. Bavier, P. Bigot, P. Bridges, B. Montz, R. Piltz, T. Proebsting, and O. Spatscheck. Joust: A platform for liquid software. *IEEE Computer* 32(4):50–56, April 1999.

[Huf52]   Huffman, D. A. A method for the construction of minimal-redundancy codes. *Proceedings of the IRE* 40(9):1098–1101, September 1952.

[Jac88]   Jacobson, V. Congestion avoidance and control. *Proceedings of the SIGCOMM '88 Symposium*, pages 314–329, August 1988.

[Jaf81]   Jaffe, J. M. Flow control power is nondecentralizable. *IEEE Transactions on Communications* COM-29(9):1301–1306, September 1981.

[Jai89]   Jain, R. A delay-based approach for congestion avoidance in interconnected heterogeneous computer networks. *ACM Computer Communication Review* 19(5):56–71, October 1989.

[Jai91]   Jain, R. *The Art of Computer Systems Performance Analysis: Techniques for Experimental Design, Measurement, Simulation, and Modeling.* John Wiley & Sons, New York, 1991.

[Jai94]   Jain, R. *FDDI Handbook: High-Speed Networking Using Fiber and Other Media.* Addison-Wesley, Reading, MA, 1994.

[JBB92]   Jacobson, V., R. Braden, and D. Borman. TCP extensions for high performance. *Request for Comments* 1323, May 1992.

[KA98a]   Kent, S., and R. Atkinson. IP authentication header. *Request for Comments* 2402, November 1998.

[KA98b]   Kent, S., and R. Atkinson. IP encapsulating security payload (ESP). *Request for Comments* 2406, November 1998.

[KA98c]   Kent, S., and R. Atkinson. Security architecture for the Internet protocol. *Request for Comments* 2401, November 1998.

[KC88]   Kanakia, H., and D. R. Cheriton. The VMP network adaptor board (NAB): High-performance network communication for multiprocessors. *Proceedings of the SIGCOMM '88 Symposium*, pages 175–187, August 1988.

[Kes91]   Keshav, S. A control-theoretic approach to flow control. *Proceedings of the SIGCOMM '91 Symposium*, pages 3–15, September 1991.

[Kle75]   Kleinrock, L. *Queuing Systems. Volume 1: Theory*. John Wiley & Sons, New York, 1975.

[Kle79]   Kleinrock, L. Power and deterministic rules of thumb for probabilistic problems in computer communications. *Proceedings of the International Conference on Communications*, pages 43.1.1–43.1.10, June 1979.

[KM87]   Kent, C., and J. Mogul. Fragmentation considered harmful. *Proceedings of the SIGCOMM '87 Symposium*, pages 390–401, August 1987.

[KP91]   Karn, P., and C. Partridge. Improving round-trip time estimates in reliable transport protocols. *ACM Transactions on Computer Systems* 9(4):364–373, November 1991.

[KPS95]   Kaufman, C., R. Perlman, and M. Speciner. *Network Security: Private Communication in a Public World*. Prentice Hall, Englewood Cliffs, NJ, 1995.

[LABW92]   Lampson, B., M. Abadi, M. Burrows, and E. Wobber. Authentication in distributed systems: Theory and practice. *ACM Transactions on Computer Systems* 10(4):265–310, November 1992.

[Lau94]   Laubach, M. Classical IP and ARP over ATM. *Request for Comments* 1577, January 1994.

[LeG91]   Le Gall, D. MPEG: A video compression standard for multimedia applications. *Communications of the ACM* 34(1):46–58, April 1991.

[Lei94]   Leiner, B. Issue on Internet technology. *Communications of the ACM* 37(8):32–33, August 1994.

[Lin93]   Lin, H. A. Estimation of the optimal performance of ASN.1/BER transfer syntax. *Computer Communications Review* 23(3):45–58, July 1993.

[LMKQ89]   Leffler, S. J., M. K. McKusick, M. J. Karels, and J. S. Quarterman. *The Design and Implementation of the 4.3BSD UNIX Operating System*. Addison-Wesley, Reading, MA, 1989.

[LS92]   Lyles, J., and D. Swinehart. The emerging gigabit environment and the role of local ATM. *IEEE Communications* 30(4):52–58, April 1992.

[LS98]   Lakshman, T. V., and D. Stiliadis. High speed policy-based packet forwarding using efficient multi-dimensional range matching. *Proceedings of the SIGCOMM '98 Symposium*, pages 203–214, September 1998.

[LTWW94]   Leland, W., M. Taqqu, W. Willinger, and D. Wilson. On the self-similar nature of Ethernet traffic. *IEEE/ACM Transactions on Networking* 2:1–15, February 1994.

[Mal93]   Malkin, G. RIP version 2 carrying additional information. *Request for Comments* 1388, January 1993.

[Mas86]   Mashey, J. RISC, MIPS, and the motion of complexity. *UniForum 1986 Conference Proceedings*, pages 116–124, 1986.

[MB76]   Metcalf, R., and D. Boggs. Ethernet: Distributed packet switching for local computer networks. *Communications of the ACM* 19(7):395–403, July 1976.

[MD88]   Mockapetris, P., and K. Dunlap. Development of the domain name system. *Proceedings of the SIGCOMM '88 Symposium*, pages 123–133, August 1988.

[MD90]   Mogul, J., and S. Deering. Path MTU discovery. *Request for Comments* 1191, November 1990.

[MD93]   McKenney, P. E., and K. F. Dove. Efficient demultiplexing of incoming
              TCP packets. *Proceedings of the SIGCOMM '92 Symposium*, pages
              269–280, August 1993.

[MD98]   Madson, C., and N. Doraswamy. The ESP DES-CBC cipher algorithm
              with explicit IV. *Request for Comments* 2405, November 1998.

[MG98a]   Madson, C., and R. Glenn. The use of HMAC-MD5-96 within ESP
              and AH. *Request for Comments* 2403, November 1998.

[MG98b]   Madson, C., and R. Glenn. The use of HMAC-SHA-1-96 within ESP
              and AH. *Request for Comments* 2404, November 1998.

[Min93]   Minoli, D. *Enterprise Networking: Fractional T1 to SONET, Frame
              Relay to BISDN*. Artech House, Norwood, MA, 1993.

[MJ95]   McCanne, S., and V. Jacobson. vic: A flexible framework for packet
              video. *ACM Multimedia '95*, pages 511–522, 1995.

[MJV96]   McCanne, S., V. Jacobson, and M. Vetterli. Receiver-driven layered
              multicast. *Proceedings of the SIGCOMM '96 Symposium*, pages
              117–130, September 1996.

[Mor68]   Morrison, D. PATRICIA—A practical algorithm to retrieve
              information coded in alphanumeric. *Journal of the ACM* 15(4):514–
              534, October 1968.

[Moy98]   Moy, J. OSPF version 2. *Request for Comments* 2328, April 1998.

[MP85]   Mogul, J., and J. Postel. Internet standard subnetting procedure.
              Request for Comments 950, August 1985.

[MPBO96]   Mosberger, D., L. Peterson, P. Bridges, and S. O'Malley. Analysis
              of techniques to improve protocol latency. *Proceedings of the
              SIGCOMM '96 Symposium*, pages 73–84, August 1996.

[MPFL96]   Mitchell, J. L., W. B. Pennebaker, C. E. Fogg, and D. J. LeGall.
              MPEG Video: Compression Standard. Chapman Hall, New York,
              1996.

[MR91]   McCloghrie, K., and M. Rose. Management information base for network management of TCP/IP-based internets: MIB-II. *Request for Comments* 1213, March 1991.

[MSST98]   Maughan, D., M. Schertler, M. Schneider, and J. Turner. Internet security association and key management protocol (ISAKMP). *Request for Comments* 2408, November 1998.

[Mul90]   Mullender, S. Amoeba: A distributed operating system for the 1990s. *IEEE Computer* 23(5):44–53, May 1990.

[Nel92]   Nelson, M. *The Data Compression Book*. M&T Books, San Mateo, CA, 1992.

[Nol97]   Noll, P. MPEG digital audio coding. *IEEE Signal Processing Magazine*, pages 59–81, September 1997.

[NRC94]   National Research Council, Computer Science and Telecommunications Board. *Realizing the Information Future: The Internet and Beyond*. National Academy Press, Washington, DC, 1994.

[NYKT94]   Nahum, E. M., D. J. Yates, J. F. Kurose, and D. Towsley. Performance issues in parallelized network protocols. *Proceedings of the First USENIX Symposium on Operating System Design and Implementation (OSDI)*, pages 125–137, November 1994.

[OCD$^+$88] Ousterhout, J. K., A. R. Cherenson, F. Douglis, M. N. Nelson, and B. B. Welch. The Sprite network operating system. *IEEE Computer* 21(2):23–36, February 1988.

[OP91]   O'Malley, S., and L. Peterson. TCP extensions considered harmful. *Request for Comments* 1263, October 1991.

[OP92]   O'Malley, S., and L. Peterson. A dynamic network architecture. *ACM Transactions on Computer Systems* 10(2):110–143, May 1992.

[OPM94]   O'Malley, S. W., T. A. Proebsting, and A. B. Montz. Universal stub compiler. *Proceedings of the SIGCOMM '94 Symposium*, pages 295–306, August 1994.

[OSF94] Open Software Foundation. *OSF DCE Application Environment Specification*. Prentice Hall, Englewood Cliffs, NJ, 1994.

[Pad85] Padlipsky, M. A. *The Elements of Networking Style and Other Essays and Animadversions on the Art of Intercomputer Networking*. Prentice Hall, Englewood Cliffs, NJ, 1985.

[Par94] Partridge, C. *Gigabit Networking*. Addison-Wesley, Reading, MA, 1994.

[Par98] Partridge, C., et al. A 50 Gb/s IP router. *IEEE/ACM Transactions on Networking* 6(3):237–247, June 1998.

[Pax96] Paxson, V. End-to-end routing behavior in the Internet. *Proceedings of the SIGCOMM '96 Symposium*, pages 25–38, August 1996.

[PB61] Peterson, W. W., and D. T. Brown. Cyclic codes for error detection. *Proceedings of the IRE* 49:228–235, January 1961.

[Per85] Perlman, R. An algorithm for distributed computation of spanning trees in an extended LAN. *Proceedings of the Ninth Data Communications Symposium*, pages 44–53, September 1985.

[Per92] Perlman, R. *Interconnections: Bridges and Routers*. Addison-Wesley, Reading, MA, 1992.

[Pet88] Peterson, L. L. The Profile naming service. *ACM Transactions on Computer Systems* 6(4):341–364, November 1988.

[PF94] Paxson, V., and S. Floyd. Wide-area traffic: The failure of Poisson modeling. *Proceedings of the SIGCOMM '94 Symposium*, pages 257–268, London, UK, August 1994.

[Pie84] Pierce, J. Telephony—a personal view. *IEEE Communications* 22(5):116–120, May 1984.

[Pip98] Piper, D. The Internet IP security domain of interpretation for ISAKMP. *Request for Comments* 2407, November 1998.

[Pos81]   Postel, J. Internet Protocol. *Request for Comments* 791, September 1981.

[Pos82]   Postel, J. Simple Mail Transfer Protocol. *Request for Comments* 821, August 1982.

[Ram93]   Ramakrishnan, K. K. Performance considerations in designing network interfaces. *IEEE Journal of Selected Areas in Communication (JSAC)* 11(2):203–219, February 1993.

[RDR+97]   Rekhter, Y., B. Davie, E. Rosen, G. Swallow, D. Farinacci, and D. Katz. Tag switching architecture overview. *Proceeedings of the IEEE* 82(12):1973–1983, December 1997.

[RF89]   Rao, T. R. N., and E. Fujiwara. *Error-Control Coding for Computer Systems*. Prentice Hall, Englewood Cliffs, NJ, 1989.

[RF94]   Romanow, A., and S. Floyd. Dynamics of TCP traffic over ATM networks. *Proceedings of the SIGCOMM '94 Symposium*, pages 79–88, October 1994.

[Rit84]   Ritchie, D. A stream input-output system. *AT&T Bell Laboratories Technical Journal* 63(8):311–324, October 1984.

[RJ90]   Ramakrishnan, K. K., and R. Jain. A binary feedback scheme for congestion avoidance in computer networks with a connectionless network layer. *ACM Transactions on Computer Systems* 8(2):158–181, May 1990.

[RL95]   Rekhter, Y., and T. Li. A Border Gateway Protocol 4 (BGP-4). *Request for Comments* 1771, March 1995.

[Rob93]   Robertazzi, T. G., editor. *Performance Evaluation of High Speed Switching Fabrics and Networks: ATM, Broadband ISDN, and MAN Technology*. IEEE Press, Piscataway, NJ, 1993.

[Ros86]   Ross, F. E. FDDI—A tutorial. *IEEE Communications* 24(5):10–17, May 1986.

[Ros94]   Rose, M. *The Simple Book: An Introduction to Internet Management.* Prentice Hall, Englewood Cliffs, NJ, second edition, 1994.

[Sal78]   Saltzer, J. Naming and binding of objects. *Lecture Notes on Computer Science* 60:99–208, 1978.

[Sat89]   Satyanarayanan, M. Integrating security in a large distributed system. *ACM Transactions on Computer Systems* 7(3):247–280, August 1989.

[SB89]   Schroeder, M. D., and M. Burrows. Performance of Firefly RPC. *Proceedings of the 12th ACM Symposium on Operating Systems Principles*, pages 83–90, December 1989.

[SCFJ96]   Schulzrinne, H., S. Casner, R. Frederick, and V. Jacobson. RTP: A transport protocol for real-time applications. *Request for Comments* 1889, January 1996.

[Sch94]   Schneier, B. *Applied Cryptography: Protocols, Algorithms, and Source Code in C.* John Wiley & Sons, New York, 1994.

[SCM+99]   Smith, J. M., K. L. Calvert, S. L. Murphy, H. K. Orman, and L. L. Peterson. Activating networks: A progress report. *IEEE Computer* 32(4):32–41, April 1999.

[Sha48]   Shannon, C. A mathematical theory of communication. *Bell Systems Technical Journal* 27:379–423, 623–656, 1948.

[Sho78]   Shoch, J. Inter-network naming, addressing, and routing. *Seventeenth IEEE Computer Society International Conference (COMPCON)*, pages 72–79, September 1978.

[SHP91]   Spragins, J., J. Hammond, and K. Pawlikowski. *Telecommunications: Protocols and Design.* Addison-Wesley, Reading, MA, 1991.

[Sit92]   Sites, R. L. *Alpha Architecture Reference Manual.* Digital Press, Maynard, MA, 1992.

[SP99]   Spatscheck, O., and L. Peterson. Defending against denial of service attacks in Scout. *Proceedings of OSDI '99*, pages 59–72, February 1999.

[SRC84]   Saltzer, J., D. Reed, and D. Clark. End-to-end arguments in system design. *ACM Transactions on Computer Systems* 2(4):277–288, November 1984.

[Sri95a]   Srinivasan, R. RPC: Remote procedure call protocol specification version 2. *Request for Comments* 1831, August 1995.

[Sri95b]   Srinivasan, R. XDR: External data representation standard. *Request for Comments* 1832, August 1995.

[Sta90]   Stallings, W. *Local Networks*. Macmillan, New York, third edition, 1990.

[Sta96]   Stallings, W. *Data and Computer Communications*. Macmillan, New York, fifth edition, 1996.

[Ste94a]   Steenkiste, P. A. A systematic approach to host interface design for high speed networks. *IEEE Computer* 27(3):47–57, March 1994.

[Ste94b]   Stevens, W. R. *TCP/IP Illustrated. Volume 1: The Protocols*. Addison-Wesley, Reading, MA, 1994.

[SVSW98]   Srinivasan, V., G. Varghese, S. Suri, and M. Waldvogel. Fast scalable level four switching. *Proceedings of the SIGCOMM '98 Symposium*, pages 191–202, September 1998.

[SW95]   Stevens, W. R., and G. R. Wright. *TCP/IP Illustrated. Volume 2: The Implementation*. Addison-Wesley, Reading, MA, 1995.

[Swe95]   Swerdlow, J. L. Information revolution. *National Geographic* 188(4):5–37, October 1995.

[SZ97]   Stoica, I., and H. Zhang. A hierarchical fair service curve algorithm for link-sharing and priority services. *Proceedings of the SIGCOMM '97 Symposium*, pages 29–262, October 1997.

[Tan92]   Tanenbaum, A. S. *Modern Operating Systems*. Prentice Hall, Englewood Cliffs, NJ, 1992.

[Tan96]   Tanenbaum, A. S. *Computer Networks*. Prentice Hall, Englewood Cliffs, NJ, third edition, 1996.

[Ter86]   Terry, D. Structure-free name management for evolving distributed environments. *Sixth International Conference on Distributed Computing Systems*, pages 502–508, May 1986.

[TL93]   Thekkath, C. A., and H. M. Levy. Limits to low-latency communication on high-speed networks. *ACM Transactions on Computer Systems* 11(2):179–203, May 1993.

[TS93]   Traw, C. B. S., and J. M. Smith. Hardware/software organization of a high-performance ATM host interface. *IEEE Journal of Selected Areas in Communications (JSAC)* 11(2):240–253, February 1993.

[USC81]   USC-ISI. Transmission Control Protocol. *Request for Comments* 793, September 1981.

[VL87]   Varghese, G., and T. Lauck. Hashed and hierarchical timing wheels: Data structures for the efficient implementation of a timer facility. *Proceedings of the 11th ACM Symposium on Operating Systems Principles*, pages 25–38, November 1987.

[Wal91]   Wallace, G. K. The JPEG still picture compression standard. *Communications of the ACM* 34(1):30–44, April 1991.

[Wat81]   Watson, R. Identifiers (naming) in distributed systems. In B. Lampson, M. Paul, and H. Siegert, editors, *Distributed System—Architecture and Implementation*, pages 191–210. Springer-Verlag, New York, 1981.

[WC91]   Wang, Z., and J. Crowcroft. A new congestion control scheme: Slow start and search (Tri-S). *ACM Computer Communication Review* 21(1):32–43, January 1991.

[WC92]   Wang, Z., and J. Crowcroft. Eliminating periodic packet losses in 4.3-Tahoe BSD TCP congestion control algorithm. *ACM Computer Communication Review* 22(2):9–16, April 1992.

[Wel84]   Welch, T. A technique for high-performance data compression. *IEEE Computer* 17(6):8–19, June 1984.

[WGT99]   Wetherall, D., J. Guttag, and D. Tennenhouse. ANTS: Network services without the red tape. *IEEE Computer* 32(4):42–48, April 1999.

[WM87]   Watson, R. W., and S. A. Mamrak. Gaining efficiency in transport services by appropriate design and implementation choices. *ACM Transactions on Computer Systems* 5(2):97–120, May 1987.

[WMB94]   Witten, I. H., A. Moffat, and T. C. Bell. *Managing Gigabytes*. Van Nostrand Reinhold, New York, 1994.

[WVTP97]   Waldvogel, M., G. Varghese, J. Turner, and B. Plattner. Scalable high speed routing lookups. *Proceedings of the SIGCOMM '97 Symposium*, pages 25–36, October 1997.

[YHA87]   Yeh, Y.-S., M. B. Hluchyj, and A. S. Acampora. The knockout switch: A simple, modular architecture for high-performance packet switching. *IEEE Journal of Selected Areas in Communication (JSAC)* 5(8):1274–1283, October 1987.

[ZDE⁺93]   Zhang, L., S. Deering, D. Estrin, S. Schenker, and D. Zappala. RSVP: A new Resource Reservation Protocol. *IEEE Network* 7(9):8–18, September 1993.

[Zim80]   Zimmerman, H. OSI reference model—The ISO model of architecture for open systems interconnection. *IEEE Transactions on Communications* COM-28(4):425–432, April 1980.

[ZL77]   Ziv, J., and A. Lempel. A universal algorithm for sequential data compression. *IEEE Transactions on Information Theory* 23(3):337–343, May 1977.

[ZL78]   Ziv, J., and A. Lempel. Compression of individual sequences via variable-rate coding. *IEEE Transactions on Information Theory* 24(5):530–536, September 1978.

INDEX

ABOUT THE AUTHORS

Larry L. Peterson is a professor of computer science at Princeton University. He has been involved in the design and evaluation of several network protocols, as well as the *x*-kernel and Scout operating systems. He is editor-in-chief of *ACM Transactions on Computer Systems* and is a member of the Internet's End-to-End Research Group.

Bruce S. Davie joined Cisco Systems in 1995, where he is a Cisco Fellow. He works on the development of quality of service features and is actively involved in the Internet Engineering Task Force. Prior to joining Cisco, he was chief scientist at Bellcore and conducted research on gigabit networks. He is the author of *Switching in IP Networks: IP Switching, Tag Switching, and Related Technologies* (Morgan Kaufmann Publishers, 1998).